HARDPRESS.NET
HOME OF HARD-TO-FIND BOOKS

The Hague Court Reports 1St- Series
by Permanent Court of Arbitration

Address:
HardPress
8345 NW 66TH ST #2561
MIAMI FL 33166-2626
USA
Email: info@hardpress.net

Carnegie Endowment for International Peace
DIVISION OF INTERNATIONAL LAW

THE

HAGUE COURT REPORTS

COMPRISING THE AWARDS, ACCOMPANIED BY SYLLABI,
THE AGREEMENTS FOR ARBITRATION, AND OTHER
DOCUMENTS IN EACH CASE SUBMITTED TO THE PER-
MANENT COURT OF ARBITRATION AND TO COMMISSIONS
OF INQUIRY UNDER THE PROVISIONS OF THE CONVEN-
TIONS OF 1899 AND 1907 FOR THE PACIFIC SETTLEMENT
OF INTERNATIONAL DISPUTES

EDITED WITH AN INTRODUCTION
BY
JAMES BROWN SCOTT
DIRECTOR

NEW YORK
OXFORD UNIVERSITY PRESS
AMERICAN BRANCH : 35 WEST 32ND STREET
London, Toronto, Melbourne and Bombay
HUMPHREY MILFORD
1916

6

BYRON S. ADAMS, PRINTER
WASHINGTON, D. C.

PREFACE

This publication, as indicated on the title-page, comprises "awards, accompanied by syllabi, the agreements for arbitration, and other documents in each case submitted to the Permanent Court of Arbitration and to Commissions of Inquiry under the provisions of the Conventions of 1899 and 1907 for the pacific settlement of international disputes." It was the purpose in preparing and publishing this volume to meet the numerous requests received by the Division of International Law of the Endowment for accurate information respecting the various cases which have come before tribunals of the Permanent Court or before commissions of inquiry under the provisions of the above-named Conventions.

In pursuance of this purpose, a syllabus was prepared on each case giving in as brief form as possible the essential facts and holdings of the tribunal or commission of inquiry. The awards or findings, together with the agreements for arbitration or inquiry and other essential documents, have been obtained in translated form from the most reliable sources available, appropriate references to which appear in footnotes to the respective documents. Where translations have been obtained from official sources, they have been reproduced in their official form, except that a few obvious misprints and an occasional mistranslation have been corrected. Where translations have been obtained from unofficial sources, they have been edited to such a degree as seemed necessary, but they are essentially reproductions of the original translations. In some cases, however, where there were no official or other sources from which to obtain them, the translations were made by the Endowment. It will be observed that in some instances translations of quotations are not verbally identical with the translations of the original passages quoted. This is due to the fact that different persons made the translations. Since the sense is unaffected by these variations, it was not deemed advisable to harmonize the wording in such cases.

There are also maps and charts accompanying certain of the cases, namely: *Grisbadarna Case, North Atlantic Coast Fisheries Case, Island of Timor Case*, and *Tavignano, Camouna and Gaulois Cases.* These maps and charts are reproductions of the originals accompanying the official reports of the different cases, and therefore necessarily have

the legend and the names of the countries, places, rivers, etc., in
the language used on the original maps or charts.

In view of the fact that the accuracy of the translations might be
questioned, especially with respect to the more important documents,
an Appendix has been added which contains the original official texts
of the translated documents. While this adds very materially to the
size of the volume, yet the Director felt that this disadvantage was
more than counterbalanced by the usefulness of such a collection of
original texts.

The original texts and translations of the Hague Conventions of
1899 and 1907 for the pacific settlement of international disputes have
been printed as an annex to the Introduction, in order that the reader
may be informed of the method of procedure under which the various
arbitral tribunals and commissions of inquiry were instituted and
regulated.

While considerable difficulty has been met with in securing certain
original texts and authoritative translations, it is believed that the
volume as now issued will be found of much service, not only to the
casual reader, but to any one desiring to study the various cases from
documents of unquestioned accuracy and authority, and that nothing
has been omitted which is essential to that purpose.

JAMES BROWN SCOTT,
Director of the Division of International Law.

WASHINGTON, D. C.,
February 28, 1916.

CONTENTS

INTRODUCTION

Arbitration, the gift of the Grecian world, was frequently resorted to in the Middle Ages, but was passing out of the minds of men and the practice of nations in the eighteenth century, when it was brought again to honor by the Republic of the New World. The statesman to whom the renascence of arbitration is due was John Jay, who was Secretary of State for Foreign Affairs during the Confederation from 1784 to the institution of the Government under the Constitution, and who continued to act as Secretary of State in Washington's administration until Jefferson's assumption of the office on March 22, 1790, upon his return from France, in which country he had represented the United States as its Minister. It is important to bear this in mind, because it was John Jay who, as Secretary of State under the Confederation proposed the arbitration of the outstanding difficulties with Great Britain and sent a report to Congress advocating this form of settlement. The report was sent to Congress on April 21, 1785, recommending that "effectual measures should be immediately taken to settle all disputes with the Crown of Great Britain" with respect to the northeastern boundary of the United States, and Secretary Jay suggested that the papers in the case "should be transmitted to the Minister Plenipotentiary of the United States at that Court, with instructions to make a proper representation of the case, and to propose that commissioners be appointed to hear and finally decide those disputes."[1]

It was likewise John Jay, as Acting Secretary of State in Washington's Cabinet, who urged President Washington to secure by arbitration the settlement of the outstanding difficulties which unfortunately had not been settled as Jay had proposed. Washington, acting upon Jay's suggestion, sent a copy of Jay's original report to the first Congress under the Constitution, stating in his letter of transmission, dated February 9, 1790, that "it is desirable that all questions between this and other nations be speedily and amicably settled."[2]

Congress took no action, and the disputes between Great Britain and the United States remained unsettled, a constant source of irritation and a pretext for war if either country should be disposed to resort to force. The outbreak of the French Revolution and the war

[1] *American State Papers*, vol. i, p. 94.
[2] *Ibid.*, p. 90.

between Great Britain and France in 1793 further embittered the relations of Great Britain and the United States, because France claimed and exercised the right, over the protest alike of Great Britain and the United States, to fit out and to arm privateers within the jurisdiction of the United States; to cruise upon British commerce, taking the prizes when captured either within or without our territorial waters into American ports, and to condemn them in prize courts organized within our jurisdiction. The actions of Great Britain were not wholly beyond criticism, and the two nations found themselves slowly drifting into war, when Washington proposed to Great Britain to negotiate directly in order to settle all of their outstanding difficulties, and selected John Jay, then Chief Justice of the Supreme Court of the United States, to repair to England as the representative of the United States in such negotiations.

It was in a way poetic justice that Jay, who had originally proposed, in the days of the Confederation, to settle the outstanding disputes with Great Britain by arbitration, and who had influenced Washington to espouse that method of settling controversies with the mother country, should have been chosen to carry into effect his own recommendations. Some of the outstanding difficulties he was able to settle by direct negotiation; others, particularly the claims which he had previously proposed to arbitrate and the difficulties which had arisen since the outbreak of the wars of the French Revolution, he was unable to settle by direct negotiation, but he succeeded in prevailing upon Great Britain to submit these disputes to arbitration. He preserved the peace of his country, and by the treaty which bears his name, he introduced to the favorable notice of the modern world arbitration for the settlement of disputes which diplomacy had failed to adjust. But in so doing, he sacrificed every hope he might have cherished for political preferment, for his treaty, which was very unpopular with the partisans of a stiff foreign policy, was advised and consented to by a narrow margin in the Senate; the appropriations for carrying it into effect were passed in the House by yeas 51, nays 48,[1] and Jay himself shared the unpopularity of his treaty. He had had, however, no illusion as to the outcome of his mission, saying, "If Washington shall think fit to call me to perform this service, I will go and perform it to the best of my abilities, foreseeing as I do the consequences to my personal popularity. The good of my country I believe demands the sacrifice, and I am ready to make it." To

---

[1]*Annals of Congress*, vol. 5, 4th Cong., 1st sess., p. 1291.

Mrs. Jay he confided his views without reserve. "This is not of my seeking," he said in a letter to her; "on the contrary I regard it as a measure not to be desired, but to be submitted to." And in another letter, a little later, after Jay had been appointed special envoy to Great Britain he wrote: "No appointment ever operated more unpleasantly upon me; but the public considerations which were urged, and the manner in which it was pressed, strongly impressed me with a conviction that to refuse it would be to desert my duty for the sake of my ease and domestic concerns and comforts."[1]

Jay's treaty provided in its 5th, 6th and 7th articles for the arbitration of the boundary disputes between the two countries; the settlement of disputes concerning debts claimed by British merchants, to be due and unpaid, but which could not be collected because of legal impediments interposed by the States of the Union; and, finally, the complaints of citizens of the United States, on the one hand, and of British subjects, on the other, for losses since the outbreak of the war between Great Britain and France, due to the alleged illegal conduct of Great Britain and the United States. The success of the commission organized under the 7th article to settle this last category of claims, and the admirable opinions of the commission showing that model judgments could be rendered between nations, as well as within nations, convinced the world that arbitration could safely be resorted to. The result was that during the nineteenth century arbitration became the favorite method of settling disputes between nations after the breakdown of diplomacy, and the submission by Great Britain and the United States of the so-called *Alabama* claims to the arbitration of the Geneva tribunal in 1872, showed the nations that arbitration had no limits which good-will and mutual desire might not overcome. It thus happened that in the course of the nineteenth century the nations generally had had sufficient experience in arbitration to suggest that the new remedy had come to stay; that it was in their interest to devise machinery in order to facilitate a recourse to arbitration and a method of procedure in order to bring the issue to a decision.

The Institute of International Law, founded in 1873, upon the initiative of the American publicist, Francis Lieber, and through the efforts of the Belgian publicist, Rolin-Jaequemyns, foresaw the need and the advantages of a code of arbitral procedure, and within a year after its organization drafted a code which served as the basis of discussion at the First Hague Conference, and which with sundry

---

[1] Pellow's *John Jay*, pp. 267–8.

amendments, not always for the better, was adopted by that august assembly. It was not only the jurists who foresaw the necessity of facilitating a recourse to arbitration and provided the means therefor; men in public life felt the need and took appropriate steps to meet it. Thus through the happy coöperation of Mr. William Randel Cremer, a labor Member of Parliament, and Frédéric Passy, then a Member of the French Chamber of Deputies, the Interparliamentary Union was formed in 1888, and held its first meeting in Paris the next year, on the centenary of the French Revolution. At the meeting of the Union at The Hague in 1894, five years before the great and fertile idea of the Czar took visible form and shape in the capital of the Netherlands, the following resolution was voted:

1. National sovereignty remains inalienable and inviolate;
2. Adherence by any government to the creation of a permanent international court must be entirely voluntary;
3. All adhering States must be on a footing of perfect equality before the permanent international court;
4. The decision of the permanent court must have the force of decisions, subject to execution.[1]

These enlightened and practical men of affairs foresaw that arbitration should have its machinery just as the jurists of the Institute of International Law foresaw the need and provided a code of procedure for international tribunals. A year later, that is to say, in 1895, at the Brussels session, a project based upon these resolutions was adopted by the Interparliamentary Union, and this draft of a Permanent Court of Arbitration,[2] like the draft of arbitral procedure of the Institute of International Law, served as the basis of discussion at the Czar's Conference held at The Hague in 1899, where it was accepted in principle, adopted with many modifications and put into effect.

On the twelfth day of August, 1898,[3] the staid and sedate diplomats accredited to the Court of St. Petersburg were astonished to receive from the hands of Count Mourawieff, Russian Minister for Foreign Affairs, a circular note proposing a conference to consider the question of the limitation of armaments, and the burdens which they had imposed, which, in the opinion of the Czar, were unendurable in themselves and fatal to economic and social progress. On December 30, 1898,[4] a second circular modifying the first and elaborating it in certain

[1]Lange, *Union Interparlementaire. Résolutions des Conférences et Décisions principales du Conseil,* 2d ed., 1911. p. 50.
[2]*Ibid.,* p. 53.
[3]August 24. 1898. new style.
[4]January 11, 1899, new style.

respects, was handed to the same staid and sedate but now somewhat expectant diplomats accredited to The Hague, proposing not only definitely the Conference, but outlining its program, of which the following article alone is important for present purposes:

> Acceptance, in principle, of the use of good offices, mediation, and voluntary arbitration, in cases where they are available, with the purpose of preventing armed conflicts between nations; understanding in relation to their mode of application and establishment of a uniform practice in employing them.[1]

This assembly, known in history as the First Hague Peace Conference, which it is devoutly to be hoped will be only the first of an endless series of conferences meeting at The Hague, basing its action upon the proposal of the Interparliamentary Union, created the so-called Permanent Court of Arbitration, in reality, machinery by which a temporary tribunal can be created; and, basing its action upon the code of procedure of the Institute of International Law, drafted a code of arbitral procedure for adoption by the nations. It has generally been supposed that the proposal to establish a Court of Arbitration was due to American initiative, and it appears to be the fact that the American delegation was the only one sent to The Hague with specific instructions on this point and a definite plan for an International Court of Arbitration. It is, of course, well known to all persons interested in the subject that the proposal to establish a Court of Arbitration was made in the First Conference[2] by the first British delegate, Lord, then Sir Julian Pauncefote, and the reason for such a proposal and the agreement to make it were stated only recently at the dinner of the American Society for the Judicial Settlement of International Disputes, held at Washington on December 6, 1913, by a person who was in a position to know whereof he spoke. The Honorable David Jayne Hill, at that time Assistant Secretary of State, later our distinguished Ambassador to Berlin, lifted the curtain and showed the setting of the stage. Mr. Hill said:

> One day [in the month of November, 1898] the door of my office opened, and the genial face of John Hay appeared. He walked into my room saying, "I have brought you a visitor"; and Lord Pauncefote, following, as the door was swung open, entered the room. Mr. Hay said, "Lord Pauncefote has brought to the department a little pamphlet about international justice.

---

[1] Scott, *The Hague Conventions and Declarations of 1899 and 1907*, 2d ed., p. xviii.
[2] *Procès-verbaux*, pt. i, p. 134; pt. iv, p. 3.

He has come to talk with regard to the answer to be given to the
Czar's rescript calling the Conference at The Hague. I think
you have thought a little about that subject, and I believe you
have written something upon it. Won't you sit down with Lord
Pauncefote and discuss it?" And so that venerable diplomat and
jurist sat down with me and for half an hour we discussed this
subject. "It is quite impossible," he said very calmly, "that anything should be done at that Conference in the direction of disarmament or of arresting armament; but isn't it possible that
there should be a movement in the direction of a court of
arbitration?"[1]

After relating this very interesting incident, Mr. Hill proceeded:

I will not detain you very long upon that. The instructions of
our department to our delegation sent to The Hague contained a
brief history of the peace movement in America and a plan for
an international court. The British Government also instructed
Lord Pauncefote to propose, at the opportune moment, if an
opportune moment ever came, in the Hague Conference, a tribunal
of arbitration; and that was done by him. Afterward, a similar
proposal was made by the Russian Government, but no proposal
of that kind had been contained in the original rescript of the
Czar.
The result . . . was that the First Hague Conference
produced important conventions, the chief of which was the
Convention for the pacific settlement of international disputes;
but almost as nugatory as the idea of disarmament, was the idea
that a merely diplomatic court, such as this arbitral tribunal was
designed to be, would ever settle the differences between nations
in any judicial way.[2]

Mr. Hill's modesty did not permit him to say that the pamphlet
which Lord Pauncefote held in his hand, to which Mr. Hay so gently
and smilingly referred, was none other than the pamphlet entitled
"International Justice,"[3] which Mr. Hill had written upon the subject
and which Mr. Hay had himself given to Sir Julian. Mr. Hill's
modesty likewise prevented him from saying that it was his own hand
that drafted the instructions which Mr. Hay approved and signed,
containing "a brief history of the peace movement in America, and a
plan for an international court." The pamphlet on international justice, which figured so prominently when the fate of the Hague Conference hung in the balance, thus ends in language which is as timely
to-day as when it was written in 1896:

[1] *Proceedings of Fourth National Conference of the American Society for
Judicial Settlement of International Disputes, 1913*, pp. 383-4.
[2] *Ibid.*, p. 384.
[3] Printed in the *Yale Law Journal*, October, 1896, p. 1.

All that has yet been said or written upon this great problem probably constitutes little more than the rude scaffolding of that great temple of international justice whose dome will yet shelter the nations of the earth from the wrongs of oppression and the horrors of battle. But its foundations are laid in the moral nature of humanity; and, although—like a vast cathedral grown old with passing centuries—it is still uncompleted, we may bring our unhewn stones to lay upon its rising walls, in the faith that its invisible Builder and Maker will shape them to a place in the permanent structure.

Reserving for later consideration the service which can be expected of a diplomatic court, to use Mr. Hill's language, it is advisable to consider somewhat in detail the court which he termed diplomatic, but which the Conference preferred to call the "Permanent Court of Arbitration of The Hague."

The Conference stated, in Article 15 of the Convention for the pacific settlement of international disputes, the object of international arbitration to be "the settlement of differences between States by judges of their own choice, and on the basis of respect for law," and in the 16th article it recognizes arbitration as the most effective and most equitable method of settling disputes of a legal nature which diplomacy has failed to settle, especially in the interpretation and application of international conventions. For the purpose of facilitating an immediate recourse to arbitration in such cases the signatory Powers agreed in Article 20 of this Convention "to organize a Permanent Court of Arbitration, accessible at all times and operating, unless otherwise stipulated by the parties, in accordance with the rules of procedure inserted in the present Convention." That is to say, the Conference declaring arbitration to be effective and equitable especially in questions of a legal nature, or, as we would say, in questions of a justiciable nature, proposed to facilitate the recourse to arbitration by creating the necessary machinery to carry into effect the recommendation of the Interparliamentary Union, and inserted in the Convention rules of procedure to give effect to the recommendation of the Institute of International Law.

Now the Permanent Court was, according to Article 21, to receive and to decide all cases of arbitration, unless the parties agreed to institute a special tribunal without reference to the pacific settlement Convention. The Court must have judges; therefore the Conference provided in Article 23 that within three months after the ratification of the Convention "each signatory Power shall select four persons at the most, of known competency in questions of international law, of the highest moral reputation, and disposed to accept the duties of arbitrators." These persons were to be appointed for a period of six years; they were to be eligible for reappointment, and their names were to be inscribed in a list to be placed in the International Bureau created by Article 22 of the Convention, to serve as a clerk to the Court.

The next step to be taken was the creation of a temporary tribunal from the list of the judges inscribed in the Bureau, and notified to the signatory Powers, and according to Article 24, the procedure to be observed was as follows:

> When the signatory Powers desire to have recourse to the Permanent Court for the settlement of a difference that has arisen between them, the arbitrators called upon to form the competent tribunal to decide this difference must be chosen from the general list of members of the Court.
>
> Failing the direct agreement of the parties on the composition of the arbitration tribunal, the following course shall be pursued:
>
> Each party appoints two arbitrators, and these together choose an umpire.

The seat of the tribunal was to be at The Hague, and its place of session was only to be altered with the assent of the parties (Article 25). A body called the "Permanent Administrative Council," composed of the diplomatic representatives of the signatory Powers accredited to The Hague, was to organize the International Bureau which when organized was to be placed under its direction and control, to notify to the Powers the constitution of the Court, to provide for its installation, and in general to supervise the Court and the Bureau, whose expenses were to be borne by the signatory Powers in the proportion fixed for the International Bureau of the Universal Postal Union.

Such were the provisions concerning the Court adopted by the Conference, recommended to the twenty-six Powers participating therein, and ratified by them without exception, and to which all the Powers invited to the Second Hague Conference, some forty-four in number, have since adhered.

The provisions of the Convention of 1899 have been modified in only one essential point, which it is necessary to consider in this place. It will be observed that under Article 24, as quoted, each of the Powers in dispute could select two arbitrators both of whom could be its subjects or citizens. This meant that in all probability four of the five judges would be interested in the outcome of the proceedings, with the result that the dispute either would or could be decided by the umpire, who was likely to be the only disinterested and therefore impartial person. The second Hague Conference of 1907 modified this procedure by providing in Article 45 of the revised Convention that "Each party appoints two arbitrators, of whom one only can be its national or chosen from among the persons selected by it as members of the Permanent Court." That is to say, three persons constituting a majority of the Court were to be disinterested parties, so that the decision of the case would rest in their impartial hands.

Now what was the nature of the institution created by the First Conference? Its framers considered that they had established not merely a Court, but a Permanent Court, for they so said. But it is difficult to call a Court "Permanent," which does not exist, and which only comes into being when it is created for the trial of a particular case, and goes out of existence as soon as the case is tried. It is difficult to consider as a court, a temporary tribunal, which is not composed of judges, because by Article 24 of the Convention of 1899 the tribunal does not exist, but is to be created. It is therefore difficult to see how the Court is "accessible at all times," when, as a matter of fact, it does not exist, and only becomes accessible when it has been created by the parties in litigation and is then only accessible to them. The Conference did not call the creature of their hands a court of justice. It was to be one of arbitration, and in Article 15 they defined what they meant by arbitration, stating that it is "the settlement of differences between States by judges of their own choice, and on the basis of respect for law." That is to say, differing from courts of justice, the judges are to be of the choice of the parties in controversy; whereas judges of the parties in litigation are rigorously excluded from national courts of justice. Again, the decision is to be on the basis of respect for law, which does not mean necessarily that the decision is to be reached by the impartial and passionless application of principles of law, as in the case of municipal courts, but the decision is to be reached "on the basis of respect for law," which may be a very different matter.

Three delegates to the Second Hague Conference, two of whom had attended the First Conference and had taken an active part in the creation of the so-called Permanent Court, spoke their minds freely on the nature of the Court. The late Mr. Asser said:

Instead of a Permanent Court, the Convention of 1899 only created the phantom of a court, an impalpable ghost, or, to speak more plainly, it created a clerk's office with a list.[1]

The late Mr. de Martens, whose interest in arbitration has been so keen and his success as an arbitrator so marked that he has been called the Chief Justice of Christendom, said:

What, then, is this court whose judges do not even know each other? The Court of 1899 is only an idea which sometimes takes the form of body and soul and then disappears again.[2]

Finally, an American delegate to the Second Conference stated:

In a word, the Permanent Court is not permanent, because it is not composed of permanent judges; it is not accessible because it has to be formed for each individual case; finally, it is not a court, because it is not composed of judges.[3]

It is not disrespectful to point out the real nature of an institution, even though the result may be to show that it is not what its name would seem to imply, and that instead of being a Permanent Court, it is merely a list of the names of persons kept in a Bureau at The Hague, from which nations in controversy can select five persons to form a temporary tribunal. This right of selection of arbitrators nations have always possessed, and doubtless in many cases they would have chosen the very persons inscribed in the list at The Hague. But it is only fair to say that the machinery, however imperfect, devised by the First Hague Conference has nevertheless rendered inestimable services to the cause of arbitration by putting the stamp of approval of an international conference upon arbitration as a means of settling difficulties, and by turning the minds and the thoughts of nations in controversy to The Hague, where this temporary tribunal of a very special kind can be called into being for the settlement of their disputes which diplomacy has failed to adjust.

A proposition had been made at the First Conference to conclude a treaty of arbitration, pledging the Powers to submit certain categories of disputes to arbitration without reservation of any kind. The proposition was rejected, owing to the unyielding opposition of Germany and Article 19, the material portion of which has been quoted, seemed to register defeat instead of a triumph. And yet a triumph it was,

[1] *Actes et documents*, vol. ii, p. 315.
[2] *Ibid.*, p. 322.
[3] *Ibid.*, p. 315.

because the great series of treaties beginning with the Treaty of October 14, 1903, between Great Britain and France, and including the twenty-six treaties which Mr. Root negotiated during his Secretaryship of State, are based upon the reserved right contained in this article. We are, therefore, not justified in belittling the Permanent Court of The Hague, which is in reality a permanent list of judges, although it is both proper and necessary that the exact nature of this institution be pointed out. Faulty as it is, it has advanced the cause of arbitration more perhaps than any single act of recent times.

But it is not enough to have a court or machinery by which a temporary tribunal can be devised; there should, in the interest of disputants, be uniform procedure to be applied in the conduct of a case. This is what the First Conference provided, adopting as the basis of its discussion the code of arbitral procedure drafted by the Institute of International Law.

Article 30 of the Convention is thus worded:

> With a view to encourage the development of arbitration, the signatory Powers have agreed on the following rules which shall be applicable to arbitral procedure, unless other rules have been agreed on by the parties.

It will be observed, however, that the code of procedure is drafted to encourage the development of arbitration, and that the Powers agree upon the rules laid down as applicable to arbitral procedure. It is also to be noted that they do not bind themselves to accept the rules, reserving to themselves the right to agree upon other rules if they so desire. This is a familiar device of diplomacy to adopt in fact, although leaving the parties free in form not to adopt if they so desire. If the parties in dispute agree to submit the difference to arbitration, they sign, according to Article 31, a "special act (*compromis*), in which the subject of the difference is clearly defined, as well as the extent of the arbitrators' powers." In the revision of this article by the Second Conference a number of important changes and additions are made. Thus, "the *compromis* likewise defines, if there is occasion, the manner of appointing arbitrators, any special powers which may eventually belong to the tribunal, where it shall meet, the language it shall use, and the languages the employment of which shall be authorized before it, and, generally speaking, all the conditions on which the parties are agreed" (Article 52).

This is a very necessary proceeding because without defining the dispute and determining the extent of the arbitrators' powers, there is nothing definite for submission to the arbitrators, and the duty of the arbitrators in the premises is not stated.

"The parties have the right," according to Article 37, "to appoint delegates or special agents to attend the tribunal," constituted in the manner already described, to serve as intermediaries between the Powers and the tribunal, and the parties in dispute have likewise the right to appoint counsel or advocates to appear before the tribunal and to present the views of the governments in conflict. The agent here mentioned is appointed by the government in controversy to prepare and to present its case to the tribunal, and to represent the government in its political capacity before the tribunal. The agent may or may not argue the case ; but it is only he, not the counsel, who can bind the government, as the counsel is merely authorized to argue the case as a lawyer or barrister argues the case of his client.

The question arose at the Second Conference whether the members of the Permanent Court might act as agents or counsel, and although the American delegation urged that the members of the Permanent Court should not be permitted to act as agents or counsel as it was grossly improper for members of a court to appear before it, either in a political or professional capacity, the Conference rejected the contention of the American delegation on the theory that the members of the Court were not really judges ; but acceded to it in part by providing that the members of the Permanent Court could only appear as agent or counsel on behalf of the Power which had appointed them members of the Court (Article 62).

The Conventions divide arbitral procedure into two distinct phases called "pleadings and oral discussions" (Article 39, Convention of 1899 ; Article 63, Convention of 1907). The pleadings are the cases made by the contending governments, delivered to each other and laid before the Court for the information and consideration of the judges. In other words, they are the written documents which the nations consider necessary or advisable to submit to the tribunal. The oral discussions are the arguments of the contending nations made by their agents, counsel, or advocates, and the agents and counsel are authorized by Article 45 to "present orally to the tribunal all the arguments they may think expedient in defense of their case," and by Article 46 "they have the right to raise objections and points," upon which, however, "the decisions of the tribunal" are "final, and can not form the subject of any subsequent discussion."

The discussions or oral pleadings are under the direction of the president (Article 41). The tribunal takes into consideration the documents presented to it; by Article 43 it "is free to take into consideration fresh acts or documents to which its attention may be drawn by the agents or counsel of the parties;" by Article 44 it can, in addition, "require from the agents of the parties the production of all acts, and can demand all necessary explanations;" and, "in case of refusal, the tribunal takes note of it."

The discussions, as previously stated, are under the direction of the President, but the members of the tribunal have, according to Article 47, "the right to put questions to the agents and counsel of the parties, and to demand explanations from them on doubtful points." But neither the questions put nor remarks made by the members are to be regarded as expressions of opinion. The tribunal is specifically authorized by Article 48 to "declare its competence in interpreting the *compromis* as well as the other treaties which may be invoked in the case, and in applying the principles of international law." A tribunal is universally regarded as competent to interpret a *compromis*, and it was therefore not necessary to state it, but it was perhaps well to do so in order to avoid doubt or discussion.

It is also competent to interpret the other treaties invoked in the case, or as the revision of 1907 says, in Article 73, "the other papers and documents." It is of course authorized to apply the principles of international law, for in the absence of an agreement of the contending countries excluding the law of nations and laying down specifically the law to be applied, international law is the law of an international tribunal.

After the agents and counsel have submitted the case or cases, the oral proceedings are closed and the judges withdraw to consider the case and to reach their conclusion, which may be the opinion of all or of a majority. The award "given," as Article 52 says, "by a majority of votes, is accompanied by a statement of reasons. It is drawn up in writing and signed by each member of the tribunal." The revision of this article prescribes that "the award must give the reasons on which it is based. It contains the names of the arbitrators; it is signed by the president and registrar or by the secretary acting as registrar" (Article 79 of the Convention of 1907). The meaning of this is that the opinions of the judges are not to be made known, for Article 78 of the revised Convention provides that "the proceedings remain secret." According to the revision it is signed by the president and an officer of the court, not as indicating the opinion of the president, but as certifying that the opinion thus signed is in very truth the opinion of a majority of the tribunal.

The award when drafted is read at a public meeting of the tribunal in the presence of the agents and counsel, or in their absence if they have been duly summoned (Article 53). The award according to Article 54 puts an end to the dispute definitively and without appeal, and, according to expressed provisions of the Convention, the agreement to arbitrate implies an agreement to abide by and to execute the provisions of the award (Article 18 of 1899; Article 37 of 1907).

The question as to whether the award was subject to revision was much debated at the First Conference, and it was sought to reopen it at the Second. It was strenuously maintained by the American delegation to the First Conference that the award was subject to reconsideration, and the homely statement of President Lincoln was quoted, "that nothing is settled until it is settled right." On the other hand, it was insisted that the award was final, that it could not be, and, even if it could, that it should not be reopened. The late Mr. de Martens was especially insistent that the purpose of the award was really to settle the dispute, whereas the American delegation insisted, and with better reason it would seem, that the purpose was not merely to settle the dispute, but to settle it right. The result was the following compromise, due to Mr. Asser's deft hand, forming Article 55 of the Convention of 1899 and Article 83 of the revised Convention:

> The parties can reserve in the *compromis* the right to demand the revision of the award.
>
> In this case and unless there be a stipulation to the contrary, the demand must be addressed to the tribunal which pronounced the award. It can only be made on the ground of the discovery of some new fact calculated to exercise a decisive influence upon the award and which was unknown to the tribunal and to the party which demanded the revision at the time the discussion was closed.
>
> Proceedings for revision can only be instituted by a decision of the tribunal expressly recording the existence of the new fact, recognizing in it the character described in the preceding paragraph, and declaring the demand admissible on this ground.
>
> The *compromis* fixes the period within which the demand for revision must be made.

It does not seem to be necessary to comment upon the provisions of this article, as they are reasonably clear and definite, other than to say that it is the undoubted right of sovereign nations to reserve the right to demand the revision of an award, and it seems strange that if it be the right of sovereign nations to agree on matters of the most vital importance, it should be necessary to reserve the right to revise an award.

What is the effect of the award? As between the parties it is final, unless the right to revision has been reserved. It affects only the parties to it. This is familiar doctrine, and is to be found in Article 56 of the original Convention and Article 84 of the Second Convention. The article in question, however, allows a third party to intervene in a case affecting it, in which event the award naturally binds it, otherwise not. It may be, however, that a dispute arises as to the interpretation and execution of the award, admitting that it is final. The Second Conference considered this question and provided the following means of settling disputes of this kind in Article 82:

> Any dispute arising between the parties as to the interpretation and execution of the award shall, in the absence of an agreement to the contrary, be submitted to the tribunal which pronounced it.

The Second Peace Conference, held at The Hague in 1907, revised the pacific settlement Convention in the light of experience but did not change it in essentials. It may be considered, as it doubtless is, a better document, but the Permanent Court of Arbitration is the Court of 1899, the arbitral procedure is the procedure slightly modified of 1899, although it must be admitted that the temporary tribunal composed of three disinterested arbitrators makes a nearer approach to a judicial tribunal than its prototype of 1899. The one important addition of the Second Conference, distinguished from sundry amendments, is due to the French delegation. It is the creation of summary procedure (Articles 86–90) by means of a smaller tribunal composed of three judges, one appointed by each of the two litigating parties with a disinterested umpire chosen by the arbitrators. Each party is represented by an agent serving as an intermediary between his government and the tribunal, not by counsel or advocates; the proceedings are in writing, with the right reserved to each party to ask that witnesses and experts be called, and with the right reserved to the tribunal to demand oral explanations from the agents as well as from the experts and witnesses. It is, of course, within the province of the countries to modify these provisions and to appoint counsel for them, should they desire; but the purpose of the innovation is that the delays incident to arbitration be avoided and that the procedure be summary in fact, as well as in theory.

The First Hague Peace Conference has another institution to its credit: the so-called international commission of inquiry, which has already justified its existence and shown that it is capable of rendering great services in ascertaining facts in dispute, if only the nations are willing to pledge themselves to resort to it and actually do so resort to it. Article 9 of the Convention creates the new institution, and for this reason it is quoted:

> In differences of an international nature involving neither honor nor vital interests, and arising from a difference of opinion on points of fact, the signatory Powers recommend that the parties, who have not been able to come to an agreement by means of diplomacy, should, as far as circumstances allow, institute an international commission of inquiry, to facilitate a solution of these differences by elucidating the facts by means of an impartial and conscientious investigation.

It will be observed that the purpose of the commission is to find the facts involved in the dispute "by means of an impartial and conscientious investigation" in the expectation and, indeed, in the belief that, the facts being found, the dispute will either be settled by their determination, or that the parties themselves will apply the principles of law to the facts, or refer the legal questions to a tribunal of arbitration for its award. It is also to be noted the careful, not to say timid, way in which the nations created a moral rather than a legal obligation. The Powers do not agree, they recommend (in the revision of 1907 the contracting Powers deem it expedient and desirable), and the recommendation is not unqualified for it is "as far as circumstances allow"; and finally, lest they should, through inadvertence, bind themselves upon questions involving honor or vital interests, such questions are excluded from the scope of the recommendation. However, it is better to grope in the dark, if dark it be, than to make a leap in the dark, and it is just by such uncertain and questioning steps that permanent progress is made in matters international.

Supposing that the Powers comply with the recommendation, constitute the commission and submit the facts in dispute to its determination, the result is a report limited, as Article 14 says, to a "statement" which has not, in any way, the character of an arbitral award. "It leaves the conflicting Powers entire freedom as to the effect to be given to this statement." It was the earnest desire of the Russian delegation at the First Conference to create a legal obligation instead of a recommendation to submit disputed facts to a commission of inquiry. And it was also the hope of the Russian delegation at the Second Conference to add a clause to the 14th article, by which the parties bind themselves to settle the dispute on the facts thus found, or to submit the dispute to arbitration, thus removing it definitely from the field of controversy.[1]

It was thought best, however, to treat the commission of inquiry as a jury finding facts without imposing upon it the functions of a court, or without binding the nations to take further and definite action. The opposition to this change of the Russian Government was very general, although in the Dogger Bank Case,[2] the very first case submitted to a commission of inquiry, the parties in dispute, namely, Great Britain and Russia, invested the commission, not merely with the duty of determining the facts in dispute, but of finding liability as well. The opposition to the original proposition of an agreement to submit facts in dispute to an international commission instead of a recommendation to find the facts gave rise to a protracted and heated discussion, due to the unwillingness of the Balkan States to accept the commission on the ground that its creation menaced the rights of small Sates.[3]

It is not necessary to discuss the details of procedure devised by the First Conference and modified by the Second other than to say that the original Convention was to be constituted, unless the Powers should decide otherwise, in the same manner as the temporary tribunal of the Permanent Court, and that the Powers in dispute agreed to supply the commission "as fully as they may think possible, with all means and facilities necessary to enable it to be completely acquainted with and to accurately understand the facts in question" (Article 12). The revised Convention of 1907 has very much enlarged the provisions of the articles relating to the commission of inquiry by setting out, at length, the details of the procedure to be followed. This is, no doubt, both helpful and wise, as parties in controversy are not in a frame of mind to devise a method of procedure, but for present purposes it is not necessary to consider those details as they are to be found in the Conventions annexed to this introduction.[4]

It will be recalled, that, in the passage quoted from Mr. Hill, he suggested that the Permanent Court of The Hague was merely diplomatic and that it was almost futile to believe that such a diplomatic body "would ever settle the differences between nations in any judicial way." The reasons for his belief he stated in the following passage

---

[1] *Actes et documents,* vol i, p. 415.
[2] For the North Sea or Dogger Bank Case, see *post,* p. 403.
[3] Scott, *The Hague Peace Conferences of 1899 and 1907,* vol. i, pp. 77, 78, 307.
[4] *Post,* p. xxxiv.

taken from his address before the meeting of the Judicial Settlement Society held in 1913:

> That Conference was made up almost entirely of diplomatists, was conducted almost exclusively in the diplomatic spirit, and its results were of a purely diplomatic nature. There was nothing binding. There was nothing that looked strongly in the direction of judicial decisions, in the proper sense. The idea was that judges selected by the different Powers were to be convoked whenever there was a case to be tried, and they would try to compose the difficulty; and, as one of the most eminent jurists in that Conference said, "The object is not to render justice, but to settle and to end the dispute." That is to say, the object was not to do what was intrinsically right, but to do that which the loser would feel obliged, in the circumstances, to accept.[1]

The purpose of the present introduction is not to be unduly critical, but to show exactly what was done by the first Conference in the matter of establishing an international court of justice. And it is abundantly clear by the analysis of the provisions of the Convention creating the court and from the statements of Messrs. Asser, de Martens and Hill that the idea of a court was proposed rather than devised at the Conference.

At the Second Hague Conference, held in 1907, the American delegation was instructed by the then Secretary of State, Mr. Elihu Root, to advocate a truly permanent international court, to be formed of judges acting under a sense of judicial responsibility. A joint project of Germany, Great Britain and the United States, with the warm-hearted and outspoken support of France, was proposed, and after weeks of discussion a draft convention of thirty-five articles, dealing with the composition, jurisdiction and procedure of a permanent international court, composed of judges, as distinct from arbitrators, was adopted. Owing to the inability to hit upon a method of appointing the judges acceptable to the States generally, the Conference contented itself with the draft convention adopted by the Conference and the recommendation that it should be put into effect as soon as an agreement could be reached through diplomatic channels upon the method of appointing the judges and the constitution of the court. The Court of Arbitral Justice, for this was the name of the new institution, although it should have been called more simply and accurately the International Court of Justice, was thus agreed to in prin-

---

[1] *Proceedings of Fourth National Conference of the American Society for Judicial Settlement of International Disputes, 1913*, p. 384.

ciple and requires only the coöperation of a limited number of Powers, for no number is specified in the recommendation, to establish it in fact. When this is done there will be in existence a permanent international court of justice, composed of trained judges, permanently in session through a committee thereof at The Hague, ready to receive and capable of deciding all justiciable questions. which may be submitted to it by the countries composing the society of nations.

There will always be a field for the so-called Permanent Court of Arbitration and a truly permanent Court of Justice because nations may well prefer, in acute disputes where their policy is involved, to refer the controversy to arbitrators of their own choice in order to adjust conflicting interests rather than to submit differences of a political nature to a court of justice to be decided according to principles of law. And, on the other hand, there are nations that, no doubt, would prefer to submit their justiciable disputes when and as they arise, to an international court of justice to be decided according to principles of law, so that those disputes, insignificant in their beginning, may not assume political importance, embitter the relations of nations and render it easier for them to drift unconsciously, it may be, into war. That wise and shrewd man of affairs, the venerable Dr. Franklin, said: "It is in human nature that injuries as well as benefits received in times of weakness and distress, national as well as personal, make deep and lasting impressions; and those ministers are wise who look into futurity and quench the first sparks of misunderstanding between two nations which, neglected, may in time grow into a flame, all the consequences whereof no human prudence can foresee, which may produce much mischief to both, and can not possibly produce any good to either."[1]

The service which the Permanent Court of Arbitration and which the International Court of Justice would render and the reasons which would justify the retention of the former and the creation of the latter were thus admirably stated by Mr. Léon Bourgeois at the Second Hague Conference:

> As Mr. Asser has said: "There must be judges at The Hague."
> If there are at present no judges at The Hague, it is because the Conference of 1899, taking into consideration the whole field open to arbitration, intended to leave to the parties the duty of choosing their judges, which choice is essential in all cases of peculiar gravity. We should not like to see the court created in

---

[1]Letter of Benjamin Franklin, dated December 22, 1779, to R. Bernstorf, Minister of Foreign Affairs in Denmark. Wharton, *Diplomatic Correspondence of the American Revolution*, vol. iii, p. 435.

1899 lose its essentially arbitral character, and we intend to preserve this freedom in the choice of judges in all cases where no other rule is provided.

In controversies of a political nature, especially, we think that this will always be the real rule of arbitration, and that no nation, large or small, will consent to go before a court of arbitration unless it takes an active part in the appointment of the members composing it.

But is the case the same in questions of a purely legal nature? Can the same uneasiness and distrust appear here? And does not every one realize that a real court composed of real jurists may be considered as the most competent organ for deciding controversies of this character and for rendering decisions on pure questions of law?

In our opinion, therefore, either the old system of 1899 or the new system of a truly permanent court may be preferred, according to the nature of the case. At all events there is no intention whatever of making the new system compulsory. The choice between the tribunal of 1899 and the court of 1907 will be optional; and, as Sir Edward Fry has so well said, experience will show the advantages or disadvantages of the two systems.[1]

The following resolution was unanimously adopted by the Institute of International Law at its session in Christiania in 1913:

While recognizing the great value of the Court of Arbitration, instituted by the Peace Conference of 1899, to international justice and the maintenance of peace;

The Institute of International Law:

In order to facilitate and to hasten recourse to arbitration; to assure the settlement of differences of a legal nature by arbiters representing the different systems of legislation and of jurisprudence;

In order to reinforce the authority of the tribunals in the eyes of the representatives of the parties in controversy by having the members of the tribunal known to them in advance, and likewise to increase the moral force of the decision by having it rendered by a larger number and by the authority of arbiters recognized by the totality of the States;

In order to resolve, in case of a treaty of compulsory arbitration containing a clause to this effect, the doubts which might arise as to whether or not a particular controversy belongs to the category of questions subject to compulsory arbitration under the treaty;

In order to create a court of appeals for decisions rendered by tribunals constituted otherwise than in conformity with the rules of the Hague Convention, in case the special *compromis* should provide for the possibility of such a revision;

---

[1] *Actes et documents*, vol ii, pp. 347-8.

Considers it highly desirable that satisfaction be given to the first *vœu* adopted by the Second Peace Conference in favor of the establishment of a Court of Arbitral Justice.[1]

It will be observed that there is no provision in the original or revised Convention for the pacific settlement of international disputes for the use of force either to compel nations to submit their disputes to the so-called Permanent Court at The Hague or to an international commission of inquiry, and there is likewise no provision for the use of force to secure compliance with the decision of the temporary tribunal of the so-called Permanent Court or to compel the nations to take further action upon the report of the international commission. The Conventions for the pacific settlement of international disputes state simply that the agreement to arbitrate implies the engagement to submit loyally to the award (Article 18 of the Convention of 1899; Article 37 of the revised Convention of 1907).

Experience had with arbitration justifies the action of both Conferences in this respect, for the awards of arbitral tribunals have invariably been complied with, although there may have been grumbling and delay and, in some cases, a modification of the award itself. If such is the result of experience it would seem wise to allow experience to decide whether, in the future, a sanction be necessary in the matter of awards, and it is also better to allow experience to decide whether some form of sanction be necessary in order to compel nations to submit their disputes to the so-called Permanent Court, and their justiciable disputes to a permanent international court, when they shall have specifically agreed to do so. The American delegation to the Second Hague Conference drafted several articles which provided that nations might resort freely to the permanent court to be created, and that the defendant nation might, upon the application of the plaintiff nation, be invited by the court to attend and to litigate the question, not summoned or hailed before the court.

The Articles referred to, which have had the good fortune to meet with the approval of eminent publicists,[2] are:

ARTICLE 12. The Permanent Court of Arbitration shall not be competent to receive or consider any petition, application or communication whatever from any person natural or artificial except a sovereign State, nor shall it be competent to receive any appli-

[1]*Annuaire de l'Institut de droit international*, 1912, pp. 603-4.
[2]See an article by the distinguished Belgian publicist, Professor Nys, entitled "The Development and Formation of International Law," in the *American Journal of International Law*, vol. 6, pp. 308-10.

cation or petition from any sovereign State unless it relates exclusively to a difference of an international character with another State which diplomacy has failed to settle and which is not political in character and does not affect the honor, independence or vital interests of any State.

ARTICLE 13. The Permanent Court of Arbitration shall not take any action on any petition or application which it is competent to receive unless it shall be of the opinion that a justiciable case, and one which it is competent to entertain and decide and worthy of its consideration, has been brought before it, in which case it may in not less than thirty or more than ninety days after presentation of the petition invite the other sovereign State to appear and submit the matter to judicial determination by the Court.

In the latter event the State so invited may (a) refuse to submit the matter; (b) refrain from submitting the matter by failing for ————— days to make any response to the invitation, in which event it shall be deemed to have refused to submit the matter; (c) submit the matter in whole, or (d) offer to submit the matter in part or in different form from that stated in the petition, in which event the petitioning State shall be free either to accept the qualified submission or to withdraw its petition or application, and shall signify its election within a time to be determined by the Court; (e) appear for the sole purpose of denying the right of the petitioning State to any redress or relief on the petition or application presented—that is to say, it may except for demur; in case the court does not sustain this, it shall renew the invitation to appear and submit the matter.

ARTICLE 14. In case, however, the States in controversy can not agree upon the form and scope of the submission of the difference referred to in the petition, the Court of Arbitration may appoint, upon the request by either party, a committee of three from the members of the Administrative Council, none of whom shall represent the States involved, without suggestion from either party, and the committee thus constituted shall frame the questions to be submitted and the scope of the inquiry, and thereafter if either party shall withdraw it shall be deemed to have refused to submit the matter involved to judicial or arbitral determination.

ARTICLE 15. The Administrative Council shall transmit to every signatory power a copy of every petition which may be submitted to the Permanent Court of Arbitration, and any power affected thereby shall have the right to present through the Administrative Council any matter bearing on the question involved which it sees fit to do, and any matter so presented shall be transmitted by the Administrative Council to every signatory Power.

The Permanent Court of Arbitration was installed in 1902, ready for cases that might be submitted to the temporary tribunal, formed from the list of judges inscribed in the International Bureau at The

Hague. Two republics of the Western Hemisphere were the first to avail themselves of the institution and to confess their faith in this method of settling their disputes. Porfirio Diaz, President of Mexico, and Theodore Roosevelt, President of the United States of America, submitted the so-called Pious Fund Case[1] in 1902 to the first temporary tribunal, formed from the list of judges composing the Permanent Court of Arbitration, thus starting this institution upon what is hoped will be a great and a beneficent career.

Whether the awards of the various temporary tribunals which have since been formed justify the expectations of the diplomats and jurists who founded it at the First Conference and confessed their faith anew in its efficacy at the Second Conference at The Hague, is left to the judgment of the intelligent reader. But the undersigned is unwilling to close this introduction without stating his opinion that the institution has unquestionably succeeded, although he is of the equally firm opinion that it can only be regarded as a first step, albeit a very long one, toward the creation of a truly permanent international court of justice, which, to use the happy phrase of Elihu Root, will be composed of judges acting under a sense of judicial responsibility. That the day may not be far distant when this consummation shall take place should be the hope and prayer of every partisan of justice and of every lover of his kind. We must have agencies which will settle the disputes between nations without jeopardizing civilization, for we dare not forget that although "there are many nations there is only one civilization."

JAMES BROWN SCOTT,
Director of the Division of International Law.

WASHINGTON, D. C.,
February 28, 1916.

---

[1]*Post,* p. 1.

THE HAGUE CONVENTIONS OF 1899 AND 1907 FOR THE

[ORIGINAL TEXTS¹]

1899

Convention pour le Règlement Pacifique des Conflits Internationaux.

Sa Majesté l'Empereur d'Allemagne, Roi de Prusse; [etc.:]

Animés de la ferme volonté de concourir au maintien de la paix générale;

Résolus à favoriser de tous leurs efforts le règlement amiable des conflits internationaux;

Reconnaissant la solidarité qui unit les membres de la société des nations civilisées;

Voulant étendre l'empire du droit et fortifier le sentiment de la justice internationale;

Convaincus que l'institution permanente d'une juridiction arbitrale, accessible à tous, au sein des Puissances indépendantes, peut contribuer efficacement à ce résultat;

Considérant les avantages d'une organisation générale et régulière de la procédure arbitrale;

Estimant, avec l'Auguste Initiateur de la Conférence Internationale de la Paix, qu'il importe de consacrer dans un accord international les principes d'équité et de droit sur lesquels reposent la sécurité des États et le bien-être des peuples;

1907

Convention pour le Règlement Pacifique des Conflits Internationaux.

Sa Majesté l'Empereur d'Allemagne, Roi de Prusse; [etc.:]

Animés de la ferme volonté de concourir au maintien de la paix générale;

Résolus à favoriser de tous leurs efforts le règlement amiable des conflits internationaux;

Reconnaissant la solidarité qui unit les membres de la société des nations civilisées;

Voulant étendre l'empire du droit et fortifier le sentiment de la justice internationale;

Convaincus que l'institution permanente d'une juridiction arbitrale, accessible à tous, au sein des Puissances indépendantes, peut contribuer efficacement à ce résultat;

Considérant les avantages d'une organisation générale et régulière de la procédure arbitrale;

Estimant avec l'Auguste Initiateur de la Conférence Internationale de la Paix qu'il importe de consacrer dans un accord international les principes d'équité et de droit sur lesquels reposent la sécurité des États et le bien-être des peuples;

¹*U. S. Statutes at Large*, vol. 32, p. 1779; vol. 36, p. 2199. Italics indicate differences between the Conventions of 1899 and 1907.

PACIFIC SETTLEMENT OF INTERNATIONAL DISPUTES
[OFFICIAL TRANSLATIONS[1]]

1899	1907
Convention for the pacific settlement of international disputes.	*Convention for the pacific settlement of international disputes.*

His Majesty the German Emperor, King of Prussia; [etc.]:

Animated by a strong desire to concert for the maintenance of the general peace;

Resolved to second by their best efforts the friendly settlement of international disputes;

Recognizing the solidarity which unites the members of the society of civilized nations;

Desirous of extending the empire of law and of strengthening the appreciation of international justice;

Convinced that the permanent institution of a Court of Arbitration, accessible to all, in the midst of the independent Powers, will contribute effectively to this result;

Having regard to the advantages attending the general and regular organization of arbitral procedure;

Sharing the opinion of the august initiator of the International Peace Conference that it is expedient to record in an international agreement the principles of equity and right on which are based the security of States and the welfare of peoples;

His Majesty the German Emperor, King of Prussia; [etc.]:

Animated by the sincere desire to work for the maintenance of general peace;

Resolved to promote by all the efforts in their power the friendly settlement of international disputes;

Recognizing the solidarity uniting the members of the society of civilized nations;

Desirous of extending the empire of law and of strengthening the appreciation of international justice;

Convinced that the permanent institution of a tribunal of arbitration, accessible to all, in the midst of independent Powers, will contribute effectively to this result;

Having regard to the advantages attending the general and regular organization of the procedure of arbitration;

Sharing the opinion of the august initiator of the International Peace Conference that it is expedient to record in an international agreement the principles of equity and right on which are based the security of States and the welfare of peoples;

[1]These translations are the official translations of the Department of State of the United States (*Ibid.*), slightly revised in order to indicate by italics in the English texts also the differences between the two Conventions so indicated in the French texts.

1899

Désirant conclure une Convention à cet effet, ont nommé pour Leurs Plénipotentiaires, savoir :

[Dénomination des Plénipotentiaires.]

Lesquels, après s'être communiqué leurs pleins pouvoirs, trouvés en bonne et due forme, sont convenus des dispositions suivantes :

Titre I.—Du Maintien de la Paix Générale

Article 1

En vue de prévenir autant que possible le recours à la force dans les rapports entre les États, les Puissances signataires conviennent d'employer tous leurs efforts pour assurer le règlement pacifique des différends internationaux.

Titre II.—Des Bons Offices et de la Médiation

Article 2

En cas de dissentiment grave ou de conflit, avant d'en appeler aux armes, les Puissances signa-

1907

Désireux, dans ce but, de mieux assurer le fonctionnement pratique des Commissions d'enquête et des tribunaux d'arbitrage et de faciliter le recours à la justice arbitrale lorsqu'il s'agit de litiges de nature à comporter une procédure sommaire;

Ont jugé nécessaire de reviser sur certains points et de compléter l'œuvre de la Première Conférence de la Paix pour le règlement pacifique des conflits internationaux;

Les Hautes Parties contractantes ont résolu de conclure une *nouvelle* Convention à cet effet *et* ont nommé pour Leurs Plénipotentiaires, savoir : [Dénomination des Plénipotentiaires.]

Lesquels, après *avoir déposé* leurs pleins pouvoirs, trouvés en bonne et due forme, sont convenus de ce qui suit :

Titre I.—Du Maintien de la Paix Générale

Article 1

En vue de prévenir autant que possible le recours à la force dans les rapports entre les États, les Puissances *contractantes* conviennent d'employer tous leurs efforts pour assurer le règlement pacifique des différends internationaux.

Titre II.—Des Bons Offices et de la Médiation

Article 2

En cas de dissentiment grave ou de conflit, avant d'en appeler aux armes, les Puissances *con-*

1899	1907
	Being desirous, with this object, of insuring the better working in practice of commissions of inquiry and tribunals of arbitration, and of facilitating recourse to arbitration in cases which allow of a summary procedure;
	Have deemed it necessary to revise in certain particulars and to complete the work of the First Peace Conference for the pacific settlement of international disputes;
Being desirous of concluding a Convention to this effect, have appointed as their plenipotentiaries, to wit:	*The high contracting Parties have resolved* to conclude a *new* Convention for this purpose, *and* have appointed the following as their plenipotentiaries:
[Here follow the names of plenipotentiaries.]	[Here follow the names of plenipotentiaries.]
Who, after communication of their full powers, found in good and due form, have agreed on the following provisions:	Who, after *having deposited* their full powers, found in good and due form, have agreed upon the following:

TITLE I.—ON THE MAINTENANCE OF THE GENERAL PEACE	PART I.—THE MAINTENANCE OF GENERAL PEACE
ARTICLE 1	ARTICLE 1
With a view to obviating, as far as possible, recourse to force in the relations between States, the signatory Powers agree to use their best efforts to insure the pacific settlement of international differences.	With a view to obviating as far as possible recourse to force in the relations between States, the *contracting* Powers agree to use their best efforts to insure the pacific settlement of international differences.

TITLE II.—ON GOOD OFFICES AND MEDIATION	PART II.—GOOD OFFICES AND MEDIATION
ARTICLE 2	ARTICLE 2
In case of serious disagreement or conflict, before an appeal to arms, the signatory Powers agree	In case of serious disagreement or dispute, before an appeal to arms, the *contracting* Powers

1899

ARTICLE 3

taires conviennent d'avoir recours, en tant que les circonstances le permettront, aux bons offices ou à la médiation d'une ou de plusieurs Puissances amies.

Indépendamment de ce recours, les Puissances signataires jugent utile qu'une ou plusieurs Puissances étrangères au conflit, offrent de leur propre initiative. en tant que les circonstances s'y prêtent, leurs bons offices ou leur médiation aux États en conflit.

Le droit d'offrir les bons offices ou la médiation appartient aux Puissances étrangères au conflit, même pendant le cours des hostilités.

L'exercice de ce droit ne peut jamais être considéré par l'une ou l'autre des Parties en litige comme un acte peu amical.

ARTICLE 4

Le rôle de médiateur consiste à concilier les prétentions opposées et à apaiser les ressentiments qui peuvent s'être produits entre les États en conflit.

ARTICLE 5

Les fonctions de médiateur cessent du moment où il est constaté, soit par l'une des Parties en litige, soit par le médiateur lui-même, que les moyens de conciliation proposés par lui ne sont pas acceptés.

ARTICLE 6

Les bons offices et la médiation, soit sur le recours des Parties en conflit, soit sur l'initiative des Puissances étrangères au con-

1907

ARTICLE 3

tractantes conviennent d'avoir recours, en tant que les circonstances le permettront, aux bons offices ou à la médiation d'une ou de plusieurs Puissances amies.

Indépendamment de ce recours, les Puissances *contractantes* jugent utile *et désirable* qu'une ou plusieurs Puissances étrangères au conflit offrent de leur propre initiative, en tant que les circonstances s'y prêtent, leurs bons offices ou leur médiation aux États en conflit.

Le droit d'offrir les bons offices ou la médiation appartient aux Puissances étrangères au conflit même pendant le cours des hostilités.

L'exercice de ce droit ne peut jamais être considéré par l'une ou l'autre des Parties en litige comme un acte peu amical.

ARTICLE 4

Le rôle du médiateur consiste à concilier les prétentions opposées et à apaiser les ressentiments qui peuvent s'être produits entre les États en conflit.

ARTICLE 5

Les fonctions du médiateur cessent du moment où il est constaté, soit par l'une des Parties en litige, soit par le médiateur lui-même, que les moyens de conciliation proposés par lui ne sont pas acceptés.

ARTICLE 6

Les bons offices et la médiation, soit sur le recours des Parties en conflit, soit sur l'initiative des Puissances étrangères au con-

1899

ARTICLE 3

to have recourse, as far as circumstances allow, to the good offices or mediation of one or more friendly Powers.

Independently of this recourse, the signatory Powers recommend that one or more Powers, strangers to the dispute, should, on their own initiative, and as far as circumstances may allow, offer their good offices or mediation to the States at variance.

Powers, strangers to the dispute, have the right to offer good offices or mediation, even during the course of hostilities.

The exercise of this right can never be regarded by one or the other of the parties in conflict as an unfriendly act.

ARTICLE 4

The part of the mediator consists in reconciling the opposing claims and appeasing the feelings of resentment which may have arisen between the States at variance.

ARTICLE 5

The functions of the mediator are at an end when once it is declared, either by one of the parties to the dispute, or by the mediator himself, that the means of reconciliation proposed by him are not accepted.

ARTICLE 6

Good offices and mediation, either at the request of the parties at variance, or on the initiative of Powers strangers to the

1907

ARTICLE 3

agree to have recourse, as far as circumstances allow, to the good offices or mediation of one or more friendly Powers.

Independently of this recourse, the *contracting* Powers deem it expedient *and desirable* that one or more Powers, strangers to the dispute, should, on their own initiative and as far as circumstances may allow, offer their good offices or mediation to the States at variance.

Powers strangers to the dispute have the right to offer good offices or mediation even during the course of hostilities.

The exercise of this right can never be regarded by either of the parties in dispute as an unfriendly act.

ARTICLE 4

The part of the mediator consists in reconciling the opposing claims and appeasing the feelings of resentment which may have arisen between the States at variance.

ARTICLE 5

The functions of the mediator are at an end when once it is declared, either by one of the parties to the dispute or by the mediator himself, that the means of reconciliation proposed by him are not accepted.

ARTICLE 6

Good offices and mediation undertaken either at the request of the parties in dispute or on the initiative of Powers strangers to the

1899

flit, ont exclusivement le caractère de conseil et n'ont jamais
force obligatoire.

ARTICLE 7

L'acceptation de la médiation
ne peut avoir pour effet, sauf convention contraire, d'interrompre,
de retarder ou d'entraver la
mobilisation et autres mesures
préparatoires à la guerre.

Si elle intervient après l'ouverture des hostilités, elle n'inter-
rompt pas, sauf convention contraire, les opérations militaires
en cours.

ARTICLE 8

Les Puissances signataires sont
d'accord pour recommander l'application, dans les circonstances
qui le permettent, d'une médiation spéciale sous la forme suivante:

En cas de différend grave com-
promettant la paix, les États en
conflit choisissent respectivement
une Puissance à laquelle ils con-
fient la mission d'entrer en rapport direct avec la Puissance
choisie d'autre part, à l'effet de
prévenir la rupture des relations
pacifiques.

Pendant la durée de ce mandat
dont le terme, sauf stipulation
contraire, ne peut excéder trente
jours, les États en litige cessent
tout rapport direct au sujet du
conflit, lequel est considéré
comme déféré exclusivement aux
Puissances médiatrices. Celles-ci
doivent appliquer tous leurs
efforts à régler le différend.

En cas de rupture effective des
relations pacifiques, ces Puissances demeurent chargées de la

1907

flit, ont exclusivement le caractère de conseil et n'ont jamais
force obligatoire.

ARTICLE 7

L'acceptation de la médiation
ne peut avoir pour effet, sauf convention contraire, d'interrompre,
de retarder ou d'entraver la
mobilisation et autres mesures
préparatoires à la guerre.

Si elle intervient après l'ouverture des hostilités, elle n'inter-
rompt pas, sauf convention contraire, les opérations militaires
en cours.

ARTICLE 8

Les Puissances *contractantes*
sont d'accord pour recommander
l'application, dans les circonstances qui le permettent, d'une
médiation spéciale sous la forme
suivante:

En cas de différend grave com-
promettant la paix, les États en
conflit choisissent respectivement
une Puissance à laquelle ils con-
fient la mission d'entrer en rapport direct avec la Puissance
choisie d'autre part, à l'effet de
prévenir la rupture des relations
pacifiques.

Pendant la durée de ce mandat
dont le terme, sauf stipulation
contraire, ne peut excéder trente
jours, les États en litige cessent
tout rapport direct au sujet du
conflit, lequel est considéré
comme déféré exclusivement aux
Puissances médiatrices. Celles-ci
doivent appliquer tous leurs
efforts à régler le différend.

En cas de rupture effective des
relations pacifiques, ces Puissances demeurent chargées de la

1899

dispute, have exclusively the character of advice and never have binding force.

ARTICLE 7

The acceptance of mediation can not, unless there be an agreement to the contrary, have the effect of interrupting, delaying, or hindering mobilization or other measures of preparation for war.

If mediation occurs after the commencement of hostilities it causes no interruption to the military operations in progress, unless there be an agreement to the contrary.

ARTICLE 8

The signatory Powers are agreed in recommending the application, when circumstances allow, of special mediation in the following form:

In case of a serious difference endangering the peace, the States at variance choose respectively a Power, to whom they intrust the mission of entering into direct communication with the Power chosen on the other side, with the object of preventing the rupture of pacific relations.

For the period of this mandate, the term of which, unless otherwise stipulated, can not exceed thirty days, the States in conflict cease from all direct communication on the subject of the dispute, which is regarded as referred exclusively to the mediating Powers, who must use their best efforts to settle it.

In case of a definite rupture of pacific relations, these Powers are charged with the joint task of

1907

dispute have exclusively the character of advice, and never have binding force.

ARTICLE 7

The acceptance of mediation can not, unless there be an agreement to the contrary, have the effect of interrupting, delaying, or hindering mobilization or other measures of preparation for war.

If it takes place after the commencement of hostilities, the military operations in progress are not interrupted in the absence of an agreement to the contrary.

ARTICLE 8

The *contracting* Powers are agreed in recommending the application, when circumstances allow, of special mediation in the following form:

In case of a serious difference endangering peace, the States at variance choose respectively a Power, to which they intrust the mission of entering into direct communication with the Power chosen on the other side, with the object of preventing the rupture of pacific relations.

For the period of this mandate, the term of which, unless otherwise stipulated, can not exceed thirty days, the States in dispute cease from all direct communication on the subject of the dispute, which is regarded as referred exclusively to the mediating Powers, which must use their best efforts to settle it.

In case of a definite rupture of pacific relations, these Powers are charged with the joint task of tak-

1899

mission commune de profiter de toute occasion pour rétablir la paix.

TITRE III.—DES COMMISSIONS INTERNATIONALES D'ENQUÊTE

ARTICLE 9

Dans les litiges d'ordre international n'engageant ni l'honneur ni des intérêts essentiels et provenant d'une divergence d'appréciation sur des points de fait, les Puissances signataires jugent utile que les Parties qui n'auraient pu se mettre d'accord par les voies diplomatiques instituent, en tant que les circonstances le permettront, une Commission internationale d'enquête chargée de faciliter la solution de ces litiges en éclaircissant, par un examen impartial et consciencieux, les questions de fait.

ARTICLE 10

Les Commissions internationales d'enquête sont constituées par convention spéciale entre les Parties en litige.

La convention d'enquête précise les faits à examiner et l'étendue des pouvoirs des Commissaires.

Elle règle la procédure.

L'enquête a lieu contradictoirement.[1]

La forme et les délais à observer, en tant qu'ils ne sont pas fixés par la Convention d'enquête, sont déterminés par la Commission elle-même.

---

[1] See footnote on opposite page.

1907

mission commune de profiter de toute occasion pour rétablir la paix.

TITRE III.—DES COMMISSIONS INTERNATIONALES D'ENQUÊTE

ARTICLE 9

Dans les litiges d'ordre international n'engageant ni l'honneur ni des intérêts essentiels et provenant d'une divergence d'appréciation sur des points de fait, les Puissances *contractantes* jugent utile *et désirable* que les Parties qui n'auraient pu se mettre d'accord par les voies diplomatiques instituent, en tant que les circonstances le permettront, une Commission internationale d'enquête chargée de faciliter la solution de ces litiges en éclaircissant, par un examen impartial et consciencieux, les questions de fait.

ARTICLE 10

Les Commissions internationales d'enquête sont constituées par convention spéciale entre les Parties en litige.

La convention d'enquête précise les faits à examiner; *elle détermine le mode et le délai de formation de la Commission et l'étendue des pouvoirs des commissaires.*

Elle détermine également, s'il y a lieu, le siège de la Commission et la faculté de se déplacer, la langue dont la C. . . . . . . fera usage et celles d. . . . . . .i sera autorisé devant . . . . ainsi que la date à laqu. . . . .

1899	1907

taking advantage of any opportunity to restore peace.

ing advantage of any opportunity to restore peace.

TITLE III.—ON INTERNATIONAL COMMISSIONS OF INQUIRY

PART III.—INTERNATIONAL COMMISSIONS OF INQUIRY

ARTICLE 9

In differences of an intertional nature involving neither honor nor vital interests, and arising from a difference of opinion on points of fact, the signatory Powers recommend that the parties, who have not been able to come to an agreement by means of diplomacy, should as far as circumstances allow, institute an international commission of inquiry, to facilitate a solution of these differences by elucidating the facts by means of an impartial and conscientious investigation.

ARTICLE 9

In disputes of an international nature involving neither honor nor vital interests, and arising from a difference of opinion on points of *fact*, the *contracting* Powers deem it expedient *and desirable* that the parties who have not been able to come to an agreement by means of diplomacy, should, as far as circumstances allow, institute an international commission of inquiry, to facilitate a solution of these disputes by elucidating the facts by means of an impartial and conscientious investigation.

ARTICLE 10

The international commissions of inquiry are constituted by special agreement between the parties in conflict.

The convention for an inquiry defines the facts to be examined and the extent of the commissioners' powers.

It settles the procedure.

On the inquiry both sides must be heard.[1]

The form and the periods to be observed, if not stated in the inquiry convention, are decided by the commission itself.

ARTICLE 10

International commissions of inquiry are constituted by special agreement between the parties in dispute.

The inquiry convention defines the facts to be examined; *it determines the mode and time in which the commission is to be formed* and the extent of the powers of the commissioners.

It also determines, if there is need, where the commission is to sit, and whether it may remove to another place, the language the commission shall use and the languages the use of which shall be authorized before it, as well as the

---

[1] This provision appears in Article 19 of the 1907 Convention.

1899

1907

Partie devra déposer son exposé des faits, et généralement toutes les conditions dont les Parties sont convenues.

Si les Parties jugent nécessaire de nommer des assesseurs, la convention d'enquête détermine le mode de leur désignation et l'étendue de leurs pouvoirs.

ARTICLE 11

Si la convention d'enquête n'a pas désigné le siège de la Commission, celle-ci siégera à La Haye.
Le siège une fois fixé ne`peut être changé par la Commission qu'avec l'assentiment des Parties.

Si la convention d'enquête n'a pas déterminé les langues à employer, il en est décidé par la Commission.

ARTICLE 11

Les Commissions internationales d'enquête sont formées, sauf stipulation contraire, de la manière déterminée par l'article 32 de la présente Convention.

ARTICLE 12

Sauf stipulation contraire, les Commissions d'enquête sont formées de la manière déterminée par *les Articles 45 et 57* de la présente Convention.

ARTICLE 13

En cas de décès, de démission ou d'empêchement, pour quelque cause que ce soit, de l'un des commissaires, ou éventuellement de l'un des assesseurs, il est pourvu à son remplacement selon le mode fixé pour sa nomination.

ARTICLE 14

Les Parties ont le droit de nommer auprès de la Commission

1899

1907

date on which each party must deposit its statement of facts, and, generally speaking, all the conditions upon which the parties have agreed.

If the parties consider it necessary to appoint assessors, the convention of inquiry shall determine the mode of their selection and the extent of their powers.

ARTICLE 11

If the inquiry convention has not determined where the commission is to sit, it will sit at The Hague.

The place of meeting, once fixed, can not be altered by the commission except with the assent of the parties.

If the inquiry convention has not determined what languages are to be employed, the question shall be decided by the commission.

ARTICLE 11

The international commissions of inquiry are formed, unless otherwise stipulated, in the manner fixed by Article 32 of the present convention.

ARTICLE 12

Unless an undertaking is made to the contrary, commissions of inquiry shall be formed in the manner determined by *Articles 45 and 57* of the present Convention.

ARTICLE 13

Should one of the commissioners or one of the assessors, should there be any, either die, or resign, or be unable for any reason whatever to discharge his functions, the same procedure is followed for filling the vacancy as was followed for appointing him.

ARTICLE 14

The parties are entitled to appoint special agents to attend the

1899   **1907**

d'enquête des agents spéciaux
avec la mission de Les représenter
et de servir d'intermédiaires entre
Elles et la Commission.

Elles sont, en outre, autorisées
à charger des conseils ou avocats
nommés par Elles, d'exposer et de
soutenir Leurs intérêts devant la
Commission.

ARTICLE 15

Le Bureau International de la
Cour permanente d'arbitrage sert
de greffe aux Commissions qui
siègent à La Haye, et mettra ses
locaux et son organisation à la
disposition des Puissances contractantes pour le fonctionnement de la Commission d'enquête.

ARTICLE 16

Si la Commission siège ailleurs
qu'à La Haye, elle nomme un
Secrétaire-Général dont le bureau
lui sert de greffe.

Le greffe est chargé, sous l'autorité du Président, de l'organisation matérielle des séances de la
Commission, de la rédaction des
procès-verbaux et, pendant le
temps de l'enquête, de la garde
des archives qui seront ensuite
versées au Bureau International
de La Haye.

ARTICLE 17

En vue de faciliter l'institution et le fonctionnement des
Commissions d'enquête, les
Puissances contractantes recom-
mandent les règles suivantes qui
seront applicables à la procédure
d'enquête en tant que les Parties
n'adopteront pas d'autres règles.

1899	1907

commission of inquiry, whose duty it is to represent them and to act as intermediaries between them and the commission.

They are further authorized to engage counsel or advocates, appointed by themselves, to state their case and uphold their interests before the commission.

ARTICLE 15

The International Bureau of the Permanent Court of Arbitration acts as registry for the commissions which sit at The Hague, and shall place its offices and staff at the disposal of the contracting Powers for the use of the commission of inquiry.

ARTICLE 16

If the commission meets elsewhere than at The Hague, it appoints a secretary general, whose office serves as registry.

It is the function of the registry, under the control of the president, to make the necessary arrangements for the sittings of the commission, the preparation of the minutes, and, while the inquiry lasts, for the charge of the archives, which shall subsequently be transferred to the International Bureau at The Hague.

ARTICLE 17

In order to facilitate the constitution and working of commissions of inquiry, the contracting Powers recommend the following rules, which shall be applicable to the inquiry procedure in so far as the parties do not adopt other rules.

1899

1907

ARTICLE 18

La Commission règlera les détails de la procédure non prévus dans la convention spéciale d'enquête ou dans la présente Convention, et procèdera à toutes les formalités que comporte l'administration des preuves.

ARTICLE 19

L'enquête a lieu contradictoirement.[1]

Aux dates prévues, chaque Partie communique à la Commission et à l'autre Partie les exposés des faits, s'il y a lieu, et, dans tous les cas, les actes, pièces et documents qu'Elle juge utiles à la découverte de la vérité, ainsi que la liste des témoins et des experts qu'elle désire faire entendre.

ARTICLE 20

La Commission a la faculté, avec l'assentiment des Parties, de se transporter momentanément sur les lieux où elle juge utile de recourir à ce moyen d'information ou d'y déléguer un ou plusieurs de ses membres. L'autorisation de l'État sur le territoire duquel il doit être procédé à cette information devra être obtenue.

ARTICLE 21

Toutes constatations matérielles, et toutes visites des lieux doivent être faites en présence des agents et conseils des Parties ou eux dûment appelés.

ARTICLE 22

La Commission a le droit de solliciter de l'une ou l'autre

---

[1]See footnote on opposite page.

1899

1907

ARTICLE 18

The commission shall settle the details of the procedure not covered by the special inquiry convention or the present Convention, and shall arrange all the formalities required for dealing with the evidence.

ARTICLE 19

On the inquiry both sides must be heard.[1]

At the dates fixed, each party communicates to the commission and to the other party the statements of facts, if any, and, in all cases, the instruments, papers, and documents which it considers useful for ascertaining the truth, as well as the list of witnesses and experts whose evidence it wishes to be heard.

ARTICLE 20

The commission is entitled, with the assent of the Powers, to move temporarily to any place where it considers it may be useful to have recourse to this means of inquiry or to send one or more of its members. Permission must be obtained from the State on whose territory it is proposed to hold the inquiry.

ARTICLE 21

Every investigation, and every examination of a locality, must be made in the presence of the agents and counsel of the parties or after they have been duly summoned.

ARTICLE 22

The commission is entitled to ask from either party for such ex-

---

[1] See Article 10 of the 1899 Convention.

1899

1907

Partie telles explications ou informations qu'elle juge utiles.

ARTICLE 12

Les Puissances en litige s'engagent à fournir à la Commission internationale d'enquête, dans la plus large mesure qu'Elles jugeront possible, tous les moyens et toutes les facilités nécessaires pour la connaissance complète et l'appréciation exacte des faits en question.

ARTICLE 23

Les *Parties* s'engagent à fournir à la Commission d'enquête, dans la plus large mesure qu'Elles jugeront possible, tous les moyens et toutes les facilités nécessaires pour la connaissance complète et l'appréciation exacte des faits en question.

Elles s'engagent à user des moyens dont Elles disposent d'après leur législation intérieure, pour assurer la comparution des témoins ou des experts se trouvant sur leur territoire et cités devant la Commission.

Si ceux-ci ne peuvent comparaître devant la Commission, Elles feront procéder à leur audition devant leurs autorités compétentes.

ARTICLE 24

Pour toutes les notifications que la Commission aurait à faire sur le territoire d'une tierce Puissance contractante, la Commission s'adressera directement au Gouvernement de cette Puissance. Il en sera de même s'il s'agit de faire procéder sur place à l'établissement de tous moyens de preuve.

Les requêtes adressées à cet effet seront exécutées suivant les moyens dont la Puissance requise dispose d'après sa législation intérieure. Elles ne peuvent être refusées que si cette Puissance les juge de nature à porter atteinte à Sa souveraineté ou à Sa sécurité.

1899	1907

planations and information as it considers necessary.

ARTICLE 12

The Powers in dispute engage to supply the international commission of inquiry, as fully as they may think possible, with all means and facilities necessary to enable it to be completely acquainted with and to accurately understand the facts in question.

ARTICLE 23

The *parties* undertake to supply the commission of inquiry, as fully as they may think possible, with all means and facilities necessary to enable it to become completely acquainted with, and to accurately understand, the facts in question.

They undertake to make use of the means at their disposal, under their municipal law, to insure the appearance of the witnesses or experts who are in their territory and have been summoned before the commission.

If the witnesses or experts are unable to appear before the commission, the parties will arrange for their evidence to be taken before the qualified officials of their own country.

ARTICLE 24

For all notices to be served by the commission in the territory of a third contracting Power, the commission shall apply direct to the Government of the said Power. The same rule applies in the case of steps being taken on the spot to procure evidence.

The requests for this purpose are to be executed so far as the means at the disposal of the Power applied to under its municipal law allow. They can not be rejected unless the Power in question considers they are calculated to impair its sovereign rights or its safety.

1899	1907

La Commission aura aussi toujours la faculté de recourir à l'intermédiaire de la Puissance sur le territoire de laquelle elle a son siège.

ARTICLE 25

Les témoins et les experts sont appelés à la requête des Parties ou d'office par la Commission, et, dans tous les cas, par l'intermédiaire du Gouvernement de l'État sur le territoire duquel ils se trouvent.

Les témoins sont entendus, successivement et séparément, en présence des agents et des conseils et dans un ordre à fixer par la Commission.

ARTICLE 26

L'interrogatoire des témoins est conduit par le Président.

Les membres de la Commission peuvent néanmoins poser à chaque témoin les questions qu'ils croient convenables pour éclaircir ou compléter sa déposition, ou pour se renseigner sur tout ce qui concerne le témoin dans les limites nécessaires à la manifestation de la vérité.

Les agents et les conseils des Parties ne peuvent interrompre le témoin dans sa déposition, ni lui faire aucune interpellation directe, mais peuvent demander au Président de poser au témoin telles questions complémentaires qu'ils jugent utiles.

ARTICLE 27

Le témoin doit déposer sans qu'il lui soit permis de lire aucun projet écrit. Toutefois, il peut être autorisé par le Président à s'aider de notes ou documents si

1899   **1907**

The commission will equally be always entitled to act through the Power on whose territory it sits.

ARTICLE 25

The witnesses and experts are summoned on the request of the parties or by the commission of its own motion, and, in every case, through the Government of the State in whose territory they are.

The witnesses are heard in succession and separately, in the presence of the agents and counsel, and in the order fixed by the commission.

ARTICLE 26

The examination of witnesses is conducted by the president.

The members of the commission may however put to each witness questions which they consider likely to throw light on and complete his evidence, or get information on any point concerning the witness within the limits of what is necessary in order to get at the truth.

The agents and counsel of the parties may not interrupt the witness when he is making his statement, nor put any direct question to him, but they may ask the president to put such additional questions to the witness as they think expedient.

ARTICLE 27

The witness must give his evidence without being allowed to read any written draft. He may, however, be permitted by the president to consult notes or

1899	1907
	la nature des faits rapportés en nécessite l'emploi.

ARTICLE 28

Procès-verbal de la déposition du témoin est dressé séance tenante et lecture en est donnée au témoin. Le témoin peut y faire tels changements et additions que bon lui semble et qui seront consignés à la suite de sa déposition.

Lecture faite au témoin de l'ensemble de sa déposition, le témoin est requis de signer.

ARTICLE 29

Les agents sont autorisés, au cours ou à la fin de l'enquête, à présenter par écrit à la Commission et à l'autre Partie tels dires, réquisitions ou résumés de fait, qu'ils jugent utiles à la découverte de la vérité.

ARTICLE 30

Les délibérations de la Commission ont lieu à huis clos et restent secrètes.

Toute décision est prise à la majorité des membres de la Commission.

Le refus d'un membre de prendre part au vote doit être constaté dans le procès-verbal.

ARTICLE 31

Les séances de la Commission ne sont publiques et les procès-verbaux et documents de l'enquête ne sont rendus publics qu'en vertu d'une décision de la Commission, prise avec l'assentiment des Parties.

1899	1907

documents if the nature of the facts referred to necessitates their employment.

ARTICLE 28

A minute of the evidence of the witness is drawn up forthwith and read to the witness. The latter may make such alterations and additions as he thinks necessary, which will be recorded at the end of his statement.

When the whole of his statement has been read to the witness, he is asked to sign it.

ARTICLE 29

The agents are authorized, in the course of or at the close of the inquiry, to present in writing to the commission and to the other party such statements, requisitions, or summaries of the facts as they consider useful for ascertaining the truth.

ARTICLE 30

The commission considers its decisions in private and the proceedings are secret.

All questions are decided by a majority of the members of the commission.

If a member declines to vote, the fact must be recorded in the minutes.

ARTICLE 31

The sittings of the commission are not public, nor the minutes and documents connected with the inquiry published except in virtue of a decision of the commission taken with the consent of the parties.

1899

1907

ARTICLE 32

Les Parties ayant présenté tous les éclaircissements et preuves, tous les témoins ayant été entendus, le Président prononce la clôture de l'enquête et la Commission s'ajourne pour délibérer et rédiger son rapport.

ARTICLE 13

La Commission internationale d'enquête présente aux Puissances en litige son rapport signé par tous les membres de la Commission.

ARTICLE 33

Le rapport *est* signé par tous les membres de la Commission.
Si un des membres refuse de signer, mention en est faite; le rapport reste néanmoins valable.

ARTICLE 34

Le rapport de la Commission est lu en séance publique, les agents et les conseils des Parties présents ou dûment appelés.
Un exemplaire du rapport est remis à chaque Partie.

ARTICLE 14

Le rapport de la Commission internationale d'enquête, limité à la constatation des faits, n'a nullement le caractère d'une Sentence arbitrale. Il laisse aux Puissances en litige une entière liberté pour la suite à donner à cette constatation.

ARTICLE 35

Le rapport de la Commission, limité à la constatation des faits, n'a nullement le caractère d'une sentence arbitrale. Il laisse aux *Parties* une entière liberté pour la suite à donner à cette constatation.

ARTICLE 36

Chaque Partie supporte ses propres frais et une part égale des frais de la Commission.

TITRE IV.—DE L'ARBITRAGE INTERNATIONAL

CHAPITRE I.—*De la Justice arbitrale*

ARTICLE 15

L'arbitrage international a pour objet le règlement de litiges entre

TITRE IV.—DE L'ARBITRAGE INTERNATIONAL

CHAPITRE I.—*De la Justice arbitrale*

ARTICLE 37

L'arbitrage international a pour objet le règlement de litiges entre

1899

1907

ARTICLE 32

After the parties have presented all the explanations and evidence, and the witnesses have all been heard, the president declares the inquiry terminated, and the commission adjourns to deliberate and to draw up its report.

ARTICLE 13

The international commission of inquiry communicates its report to the conflicting Powers, signed by all the members of the commission.

ARTICLE 33

The report *is* signed by all the members of the commission.

If one of the members refuses to sign, the fact is mentioned; but the validity of the report is not affected.

ARTICLE 34

The report of the commission is read at a public sitting, the agents and counsel of the parties being present or duly summoned.

A copy of the report is given to each party.

ARTICLE 14

The report of the international commission of inquiry is limited to a statement of facts, and has in no way the character of an arbitral award. It leaves the conflicting Powers entire freedom as to the effect to be given to this statement.

ARTICLE 35

The report of the commission is limited to a statement of facts, and has in no way the character of an award. It leaves to the *parties* entire freedom as to the effect to be given to the statement.

ARTICLE 36

Each party pays its own expenses and an equal share of the expenses incurred by the commission.

TITLE IV.—ON INTERNATIONAL ARBITRATION

CHAPTER I.—*On the System of Arbitration*

ARTICLE 15

International arbitration has for its object the settlement of

PART IV.—INTERNATIONAL ARBITRATION

CHAPTER I.—*The System of Arbitration*

ARTICLE 37

International arbitration has for its object the settlement of dis-

1899

les États par des juges de leur choix et sur la base du respect du droit.

ARTICLE 16

Dans les questions d'ordre juridique, et en premier lieu dans les questions d'interprétation ou d'application des Conventions internationales, l'arbitrage est reconnu par les Puissances signataires comme le moyen le plus efficace et en même temps le plus équitable de régler les litiges qui n'ont pas été résolus par les voies diplomatiques.

ARTICLE 17

La Convention d'arbitrage est conclue pour des contestations déjà nées ou pour des contestations éventuelles.

Elle peut concerner tout litige ou seulement les litiges d'une catégorie déterminée.

ARTICLE 18

La Convention d'arbitrage implique l'engagement de se soumettre de bonne foi à la Sentence arbitrale.[2]

1907

les États par des juges de leur choix et sur la base du respect du droit.

Le recours à l'arbitrage implique l'engagement de se soumettre de bonne foi à la sentence.[1]

ARTICLE 38

Dans les questions d'ordre juridique, et en premier lieu, dans les questions d'interprétation ou d'application des Conventions internationales, l'arbitrage est reconnu par les Puissances *contractantes* comme le moyen le plus efficace et en même temps le plus équitable de régler les litiges qui n'ont pas été résolus par les voies diplomatiques.

En conséquence, il serait désirable que, dans les litiges sur les questions susmentionnées, les Puissances contractantes eussent, le cas échéant, recours à l'arbitrage, en tant que les circonstances le permettraient.

ARTICLE 39

La Convention d'arbitrage est conclue pour des contestations déjà nées ou pour des contestations éventuelles.

Elle peut concerner tout litige ou seulement les litiges d'une catégorie déterminée.

---

[1] See footnote 1, opposite page.
[2] See footnote 4, opposite page.

1899	1907

1899

differences between States by judges of their own choice, and on the basis of respect for law.

1907

putes between States by judges of their own choice and on the basis of respect for law.

Recourse to arbitration implies an engagement to submit in good faith to the award.[1]

Article 16[2]

In questions of a legal nature, and especially in the interpretation or application of international conventions, arbitration is recognized by the signatory Powers as the most effective, and at the same time the most equitable, means of settling disputes which diplomacy has failed to settle.

Article 38[2]

In questions of a legal nature, and especially in the interpretation or application of international conventions, arbitration is recognized by the *contracting* Powers as the most effective, and, at the same time, the most equitable means of settling disputes which diplomacy has failed to settle.

Consequently, it would be desirable that, in disputes about the above-mentioned questions, the contracting Powers should, if the case arose, have recourse to arbitration, in so far as circumstances permit.

Article 17[2]

The arbitration convention is concluded for questions already existing or for questions which may arise eventually.

It may embrace any dispute or only disputes of a certain category.

Article 39[2]

The arbitration convention is concluded for questions already existing or for questions which may arise eventually.

It may embrace any dispute or only disputes of a certain category.[3]

Article 18

The arbitration convention implies the engagement to submit loyally to the award.[4]

---

[1]Cf. Articles 18 and 31 of the 1899 Convention.
[2]See the reservations of Roumania respecting Articles 16, 17 and 19 of the 1899 Convention and the corresponding articles of the 1907 Convention, *post*, pp. ciii, cvi.
[3]Chile also made a reservation respecting Article 39.
[4]Cf. Article 37, paragraph 2, of the 1907 Convention.

1899
ARTICLE 19

Indépendamment des Traités généraux ou particuliers qui stipulent actuellement l'obligation du recours à l'arbitrage pour les Puissances signataires, ces Puissances se réservent de conclure, soit avant la ratification du présent Acte, soit postérieurement, des accords nouveaux, généraux ou particuliers, en vue d'étendre l'arbitrage obligatoire à tous les cas qu'Elles jugeront possible de lui soumettre.

CHAPITRE II.—*De la Cour permanente d'arbitrage*
ARTICLE 20

Dans le but de faciliter le recours immédiat à l'arbitrage pour les différends internationaux qui n'ont pu être réglés par la voie diplomatique, les Puissances signataires s'engagent à organiser une Cour permanente d'arbitrage, accessible en tout temps et fonctionnant, sauf stipulation contraire des Parties, conformément aux Règles de procédure insérées dans la présente Convention.

ARTICLE 21

La Cour permanente sera compétente pour tous les cas d'arbitrage, à moins qu'il n'y ait entente entre les Parties pour l'établissement d'une juridiction spéciale.

ARTICLE 22

Un Bureau international éta-

1907
ARTICLE 40

Indépendamment des Traités généraux ou particuliers qui stipulent actuellement l'obligation du recours à l'arbitrage pour les Puissances *contractantes,* ces Puissances se réservent de conclure des accords nouveaux, généraux ou particuliers, en vue d'étendre l'arbitrage obligatoire à tous les cas qu'Elles jugeront possible de lui soumettre.

CHAPITRE II.—*De la Cour permanente d'arbitrage*
ARTICLE 41

Dans le but de faciliter le recours immédiat à l'arbitrage pour les différends internationaux qui n'ont pu être réglés par la voie diplomatique, les Puissances *contractantes* s'engagent à *maintenir, telle qu'elle a été établie par la Première Conférence de la Paix, la* Cour permanente d'arbitrage, accessible en tout temps et fonctionnant, sauf stipulation contraire des Parties, conformément aux Règles de procédure insérées dans la présente Convention.

ARTICLE 42

La Cour permanente est compétente pour tous les cas d'arbitrage, à moins qu'il n'y ait entente entre les Parties pour l'établissement d'une juridiction spéciale.

ARTICLE 43

La Cour permanente a son siège à La Haye.[1]
Un Bureau International sert

---

[1]See footnote 2, opposite page.

1899
ARTICLE 19[1]

Independently of general or private treaties expressly stipulating recourse to arbitration as obligatory on the signatory Powers, these Powers reserve to themselves the right of concluding, either before the ratification of the present Act or later, new agreements, general or private, with a view to extending obligatory arbitration to all cases which they may consider it possible to submit to it.

CHAPTER II.—*On the Permanent Court of Arbitration*
ARTICLE 20

With the object of facilitating an immediate recourse to arbitration for international differences, which it has not been possible to settle by diplomacy, the signatory Powers undertake to organize a Permanent Court of Arbitration, accessible at all times and operating, unless otherwise stipulated by the parties, in accordance with the rules of procedure inserted in the present Convention.

ARTICLE 21

The Permanent Court shall be competent for all arbitration cases, unless the parties agree to institute a special tribunal.

ARTICLE 22

An International Bureau, estab-

1907
ARTICLE 40[1]

Independently of general or private treaties expressly stipulating recourse to arbitration as obligatory on the *contracting* Powers, the said Powers reserve to themselves the right of concluding new agreements, general or particular, with a view to extending compulsory arbitration to all cases which they may consider it possible to submit to it.

CHAPTER II.—*The Permanent Court of Arbitration*
ARTICLE 41

With the object of facilitating an immediate recourse to arbitration for international differences, which it has not been possible to settle by diplomacy, the *contracting* Powers undertake to *maintain the* Permanent Court of Arbitration, *as established by the First Peace Conference*, accessible at all times, and operating, unless otherwise stipulated by the parties, in accordance with the rules of procedure inserted in the present Convention.

ARTICLE 42

The Permanent Court *is* competent for all arbitration cases, unless the parties agree to institute a special tribunal.

ARTICLE 43

The Permanent Court sits at The Hague.[2]
An International Bureau serves

---

[1] See footnote 2, *ante*, p. lvii.
[2] Cf. Article 25, paragraph 1, of the 1899 Convention.

1899

bli à La Haye sert de greffe à la Cour.

Ce Bureau est l'intermédiaire des communications relatives aux réunions de celle-ci.

Il a la garde des archives et la gestion de toutes les affaires administratives.

Les Puissances signataires s'engagent à communiquer au Bureau international de La Haye, une copie certifiée conforme de toute stipulation d'arbitrage intervenue entre elles et de toute sentence arbitrale les concernant et rendue par des juridictions spéciales.

Elles s'engagent à communiquer de même au Bureau, les lois, règlements et documents constatant éventuellement l'exécution des sentences rendues par la Cour.

ARTICLE 23

Chaque Puissance signataire désignera, dans les trois mois qui suivront la ratification par elle du présent Acte, quatre personnes au plus, d'une compétence reconnue dans les questions de droit international, jouissant de la plus haute considération morale et disposées à accepter les fonctions d'arbitres.

Les personnes ainsi désignées seront inscrites, au titre de membres de la Cour, sur une liste qui sera notifiée à toutes les Puissances signataires par les soins du Bureau.

Toute modification à la liste des Arbitres est portée, par les soins du Bureau, à la connaissance des Puissances signataires.

Deux ou plusieurs Puissances peuvent s'entendre pour la désig-

1907

de greffe à la Cour; *il* est l'intermédiaire des communications relatives aux réunions de celle-ci; il a la garde des archives et la gestion de toutes les affaires administratives.

Les Puissances *contractantes* s'engagent à communiquer au Bureau, *aussitôt que possible,* une copie certifiée conforme de toute stipulation d'arbitrage intervenue entre Elles et de toute sentence arbitrale Les concernant et rendue par des juridictions spéciales.

Elles s'engagent à communiquer de même au Bureau les lois, règlements et documents constatant éventuellement l'exécution des sentences rendues par la Cour.

ARTICLE 44

Chaque Puissance *contractante désigne* quatre personnes au plus, d'une compétence reconnue dans les questions de droit international, jouissant de la plus haute considération morale et disposées à accepter les fonctions d'arbitres.

Les personnes ainsi désignées *sont* inscrites, au titre de Membres de la Cour, sur une liste qui sera notifiée à toutes les Puissances *contractantes* par les soins du Bureau.

Toute modification à la liste des arbitres est portée, par les soins du Bureau, à la connaissance des Puissances *contractantes*.

Deux ou plusieurs Puissances peuvent s'entendre pour la dé-

1899	1907
lished at The Hague, serves as record office for the Court.	as registry for the Court. *It* is the channel for communications relative to the meetings of the Court; it has charge of the archives and conducts all the administrative business.
This Bureau is the channel for communications relative to the meetings of the Court.	
It has the custody of the archives and conducts all the administrative business.	
The signatory Powers undertake to communicate to the International Bureau at The Hague a duly certified copy of any conditions of arbitration arrived at between them, and of any award concerning them delivered by special tribunals.	The *contracting* Powers undertake to communicate to the Bureau, *as soon as possible,* a certified copy of any conditions of arbitration arrived at between them and of any award concerning them delivered by a special tribunal.
They undertake also to communicate to the Bureau the laws, regulations, and documents eventually showing the execution of the awards given by the Court.	They likewise undertake to communicate to the Bureau the laws, regulations, and documents eventually showing the execution of the awards given by the Court.

ARTICLE 23	ARTICLE 44
Within the three months following its ratification of the present Act, each signatory Power shall select four persons at the most, of known competency in questions of international law, cf the highest moral reputation, and disposed to accept the duties of arbitrators.	Each *contracting* Power *selects* four persons at the most, of known competency in questions of international law, of the highest moral reputation, and disposed to accept the duties of arbitrator.
The persons thus selected shall be inscribed, as members of the Court, in a list which shall be notified by the Bureau to all the signatory Powers.	The persons thus selected *are* inscribed, as members of the Court, in a list which shall be notified to all the *contracting* Powers by the Bureau.
Any alteration in the list of arbitrators is brought by the Bureau to the knowledge of the signatory Powers.	Any alteration in the list of arbitrators is brought by the Bureau to the knowledge of the *contracting* Powers.
Two or more Powers may agree on the selection in common of one	Two or more Powers may agree on the selection in common of one

1899

nation en commun d'un ou de plusieurs membres.

La même personne peut être désignée par des Puissances différentes.

Les membres de la Cour sont nommés pour un terme de six ans. Leur mandat peut être renouvelé.

En cas de décès ou de retraite d'un membre de la Cour, il est pourvu à son remplacement selon le mode fixé pour sa nomination.

ARTICLE 24

Lorsque les Puissances signataires veulent s'adresser à la Cour permanente pour le règlement d'un différend survenu entre elles, le choix des Arbitres appelés à former le Tribunal compétent pour statuer sur ce différend, doit être fait dans la liste générale des Membres de la Cour.

A défaut de constitution du Tribunal arbitral par l'accord immédiat des Parties, il est procédé de la manière suivante:

Chaque Partie nomme deux Arbitres et ceux-ci choisissent ensemble un Surarbitre.

En cas de partage des voix, le choix de Surarbitre est confié à une Puissance tierce, désignée de commun accord par les Parties.

Si l'accord ne s'établit pas à ce sujet, chaque Partie désigne une Puissance différente et le choix

1907

signation en commun d'un ou de plusieurs Membres.

La même personne peut être désignée par des Puissances différentes.

Les Membres de la Cour sont nommés pour un terme de six ans. Leur mandat peut être renouvelé.

En cas de décès ou de retraite d'un Membre de la Cour, il est pourvu à son remplacement selon le mode fixé pour sa nomination, *et pour une nouvelle période de six ans.*

ARTICLE 45

Lorsque les Puissances *contractantes* veulent s'adresser à la Cour permanente pour le règlement d'un différend survenu entre Elles, le choix des arbitres appelés à former le Tribunal compétent pour statuer sur ce différend, doit être fait dans la liste générale des Membres de la Cour.

A défaut de constitution du Tribunal arbitral par l'accord 'es Parties, il est procédé de ¿a manière suivante:

Chaque Partie nomme deux arbitres, *dont un seulement peut être son national ou choisi parmi ceux qui ont été désignés par Elle comme Membres de la Cour permanente.* Ces arbitres choisissent ensemble un surarbitre.

En cas de partage des voix, le choix du surarbitre est confié à une Puissance tierce, désignée de commun accord par les Parties.

Si l'accord ne s'établit pas à ce sujet, chaque Partie désigne une Puissance différente et le choix

1899	1907

or more members.

The same person can be selected by different Powers.

The members of the Court are appointed for a term of six years. Their appointments can be renewed.

In case of the death or retirement of a member of the Court, his place shall be filled in accordance with the method of his appointment.

or more members.

The same person can be selected by different Powers.

The members of the Court are appointed for a term of six years. These appointments are renewable.

Should a member of the Court die or resign, the same procedure is followed for filling the vacancy as was followed for appointing him. *In this case the appointment is made for a fresh period of six years.*

ARTICLE 24

When the signatory Powers desire to have recourse to the Permanent Court for the settlement of a difference that has arisen between them, the arbitrators called upon to form the competent tribunal to decide this difference must be chosen from the general list of members of the Court.

Failing the direct agreement of the parties on the composition of the arbitration tribunal, the following course shall be pursued:

Each party appoints two arbitrators, and these together choose an umpire.

If the votes are equal, the choice of the umpire is intrusted to a third Power, selected by the parties by common accord.

If an agreement is not arrived at on this subject, each party selects a different Power, and the

ARTICLE 45

When the *contracting* Powers wish to have recourse to the Permanent Court for the settlement of a difference which has arisen between them, the arbitrators called upon to form the tribunal with jurisdiction to decide this difference must be chosen from the general list of members of the Court.

Failing the direct agreement of the parties on the composition of the arbitration tribunal, the following course shall be pursued:

Each party appoints two arbitrators, *of whom one only can be its national or chosen from among the persons selected by it as members of the Permanent Court.* These arbitrators together choose an umpire.

If the votes are equally divided, the choice of the umpire is intrusted to a third Power, selected by the parties by common accord.

If an agreement is not arrived at on this subject each party selects a different Power, and the

1899

du Surarbitre est fait de concert par les Puissances ainsi désignées.

Le Tribunal étant ainsi composé, les Parties notifient au Bureau leur décision de s'adresser à la Cour et les noms des arbitres.

Le Tribunal arbitral se réunit à la date fixée par les Parties.

Les Membres de la Cour, dans l'exercice de leurs fonctions et en dehors de leur Pays, jouissent des privilèges et immunités diplomatiques.

ARTICLE 25

Le Tribunal arbitral siège d'ordinaire à La Haye.[1]

Le siège ne peut, sauf le cas de force majeure, être changé par le Tribunal que de l'assentiment des Parties.

ARTICLE 26

Le Bureau international de La

1907

du surarbitre est fait de concert par les Puissances ainsi désignées.

Si, dans un délai de deux mois, ces deux Puissances n'ont pu tomber d'accord, chacune d'Elles présente deux candidats pris sur la liste des Membres de la Cour permanente, en dehors des Membres désignés par les Parties et n'étant les nationaux d'aucune d'Elles. Le sort détermine lequel des candidats ainsi présentés sera le surarbitre.

ARTICLE 46

Dès que le Tribunal *est* composé, les Parties notifient au Bureau leur décision de s'adresser à la Cour, *le texte de leur compromis,* et les noms des arbitres.

Le Bureau communique sans délai à chaque arbitre le compromis et les noms des autres Membres du Tribunal.

Le Tribunal se réunit à la date fixée par les Parties. *Le Bureau pourvoit à son installation.*

Les Membres *du Tribunal,* dans l'exercice de leurs fonctions et en dehors de leur pays, jouissent des privilèges et immunités diplomatiques.

ARTICLE 47

Le Bureau est autorisé à

---

[1] See footnote on opposite page.

1899

choice of the umpire is made in concert by the Powers thus selected.

The tribunal being thus composed, the parties notify to the Bureau their determination to have recourse to the Court and the names of the arbitrators.

The tribunal of arbitration assembles on the date fixed by the parties.

The members of the Court, in the discharge of their duties and out of their own country, enjoy diplomatic privileges and immunities.

ARTICLE 25

The tribunal of arbitration has its ordinary seat at The Hague.[1]

Except in cases of necessity, the place of session can only be altered by the tribunal with the assent of the parties.

ARTICLE 26

The International Bureau at

1907

choice of the umpire is made in concert by the Powers thus selected.

If, within two months' time, these two Powers can not come to an agreement, each of them presents two candidates taken from the list of members of the Permanent Court, exclusive of the members selected by the parties and not being nationals of either of them. Drawing lots determines which of the candidates thus presented shall be umpire.

ARTICLE 46

As soon as the tribunal *is* composed, the parties notify to the Bureau their determination to have recourse to the Court, *the text of their compromis,* and the names of the arbitrators.

The Bureau communicates without delay to each arbitrator the compromis, and the names of the other members of the tribunal.

The tribunal assembles at the date fixed by the parties. *The Bureau makes the necessary arrangements for the meeting.*

The members of the *tribunal,* in the exercise of their duties and out of their own country, enjoy diplomatic privileges and immunities.

ARTICLE 47

The Bureau is authorized to

---

[1]Cf. Article 43, paragraph 1, of the 1907 Convention.

1899

Haye est autorisé à mettre ses locaux et son organisation à la disposition des Puissances signataires pour le fonctionnement de toute juridiction spéciale d'arbitrage.

La juridiction de la Cour permanente peut être étendue, dans les conditions prescrites par les Règlements, aux litiges existant entre des Puissances non signataires ou entre des Puissances signataires et des Puissances non signataires, si les Parties sont convenues de recourir à cette juridiction.

ARTICLE 27

Les Puissances signataires considèrent comme un devoir, dans le cas où un conflit aigu menacerait d'éclater entre deux ou plusieurs d'entre Elles, de rappeler à celles-ci que la Cour permanente leur est ouverte.

En conséquence, Elles déclarent que le fait de rappeler aux Parties en conflit les dispositions de la présente Convention, et le conseil donné, dans l'intérêt supérieur de la paix, de s'adresser à la Cour permanente, ne peuvent être considérés que comme actes de Bons Offices.

1907

mettre ses locaux et son organisation à la disposition des Puissances *contractantes* pour le fonctionnement de toute juridiction spéciale d'arbitrage.

La juridiction de la Cour permanente peut être étendue, dans les conditions prescrites par les règlements, aux litiges existant entre des Puissances non *contractantes* ou entre des Puissances *contractantes* et des Puissances non *contractantes,* si les Parties sont convenues de recourir à cette juridiction.

ARTICLE 48

Les Puissances *contractantes* considèrent comme un devoir, dans les cas où un conflit aigu menacerait d'éclater entre deux ou plusieurs d'entre Elles, de rappeler à celles-ci que la Cour permanente leur est ouverte.

En conséquence, Elles déclarent que le fait de rappeler aux Parties en conflit les dispositions de la présente Convention, et le conseil donné, dans l'intérêt supérieur de la paix, de s'adresser à la Cour permanente, ne peuvent être considérés que comme actes de bons offices.

En cas de conflit entre deux Puissances, l'une d'Elles pourra toujours adresser au Bureau International une note contenant sa déclaration qu'Elle serait disposée à soumettre le différend à un arbitrage.

Le Bureau devra porter aussitôt la déclaration à la connaissance de l'autre Puissance.

1899

The Hague is authorized to place its premises and its staff at the disposal of the signatory Powers for the operations of any special board of arbitration.

The jurisdiction of the Permanent Court, may, within the conditions laid down in the regulations, be extended to disputes between non-signatory Powers, or between signatory Powers and non-signatory Powers, if the parties are agreed on recourse to this tribunal.

ARTICLE 27

The signatory Powers consider it their duty, if a serious dispute threatens to break out between two or more of them, to remind these latter that the Permanent Court is open to them.

Consequently, they declare that the fact of reminding the conflicting parties of the provisions of the present Convention, and the advice given to them, in the highest interests of peace, to have recourse to the Permanent Court, can only be regarded as friendly actions.

1907

place its offices and staff at the disposal of the *contracting* Powers for the use of any special board of arbitration.

The jurisdiction of the Permanent Court may, within the conditions laid down in the regulations, be extended to disputes between *non-contracting* Powers or between *contracting* Powers and *non-contracting* Powers, if the parties are agreed on recourse to this tribunal.

ARTICLE 48[1]

The *contracting* Powers consider it their duty, if a serious dispute threatens to break out between two or more of them, to remind these latter that the Permanent Court is open to them.

Consequently, they declare that the fact of reminding the parties at variance of the provisions of the present Convention, and the advice given to them, in the highest interests of peace, to have recourse to the Permanent Court, can only be regarded as friendly actions.

In case of dispute between two Powers, one of them can always address to the International Bureau a note containing a declaration that it would be ready to submit the dispute to arbitration.

The Bureau must at once inform the other Power of the declaration.

---

[1]See the reservation of the United States on the subject of this article, *post,* p. cvi.

1899

ARTICLE 28

Un Conseil administratif permanent, composé des représentants diplomatiques des Puissances signataires accrédités à La Haye et du Ministre des Affaires Étrangères des Pays-Bas qui remplira les fonctions de Président, sera constitué dans cette ville le plus tôt possible après la ratification du présent Acte par neuf Puissances au moins.

Ce Conseil sera chargé d'établir et d'organiser le Bureau international, lequel demeurera sous sa direction et sous son contrôle.

Il notifiera aux Puissances la constitution de la Cour et pourvoira à l'installation de celle-ci.

Il arrêtera son règlement d'ordre ainsi que tous autres règlements nécessaires.

Il décidera toutes les questions administratives qui pourraient surgir touchant le fonctionnement de la Cour.

Il aura tout pouvoir quant à la nomination, la suspension ou la révocation des fonctionnaires et employés du Bureau.

Il fixera les traitements et salaires et contrôlera la dépense générale.

La présence de cinq membres dans les réunions dûment convoquées suffit pour permettre au Conseil de délibérer valablement. Les décisions sont prises à la majorité des voix.

Le Conseil communique sans délai aux Puissances signataires les règlements adoptés par lui. Il leur adresse chaque année un rapport sur les travaux de la Cour, sur le fonctionnement des

1907

ARTICLE 49

Le Conseil administratif permanent, composé des Représentants diplomatiques des Puissances contractantes accrédités à La Haye et du Ministre des Affaires Étrangères des Pays-Bas, qui remplit les fonctions de Président, a la direction et le contrôle du Bureau International.

Le Conseil arrête son règlement d'ordre ainsi que tous autres règlements nécessaires.

Il décide toutes les questions administratives qui pourraient surgir touchant le fonctionnement de la Cour.

Il a tout pouvoir quant à la nomination, la suspension ou la révocation des fonctionnaires et employés du Bureau.

Il fixe les traitements et salaires, et contrôle la dépense générale.

La présence de neuf membres dans les réunions dûment convoquées suffit pour permettre au Conseil de délibérer valablement. Les décisions sont prises à la majorité des voix.

Le Conseil communique sans délai aux Puissances contractantes les règlements adoptés par lui. Il Leur présente chaque année un rapport sur les travaux de la Cour, sur le fonctionnement

1899

ARTICLE 28

A Permanent Administrative Council, composed of the diplomatic representatives of the signatory Powers accredited to The Hague and of the Netherland Minister for Foreign Affairs, who will act as president, shall be instituted in this town as soon as possible after the ratification of the present Act by at least nine Powers.

This Council will be charged with the establishment and organization of the International Bureau, which will be under its direction and control.

It will notify to the Powers the constitution of the Court and will provide for its installation.

It will settle its rules of procedure and all other necessary regulations.

It will decide all questions of administration which may arise with regard to the operations of the Court.

It will have entire control over the appointment, suspension or dismissal of the officials and employes of the Bureau.

It will fix the payments and salaries, and control the general expenditure.

At meetings duly summoned the presence of five members is sufficient to render valid the discussions of the Council. The decisions are taken by a majority of votes.

The Council communicates to the signatory Powers without delay the regulations adopted by it. It addresses to them an annual report on the labors of the Court, the working of the

1907

ARTICLE 49

The Permanent Administrative Council, composed of the diplomatic representatives of the *contracting* Powers accredited to The Hague and of the Netherland Minister for Foreign Affairs, who *acts* as president, is charged with the direction and control of the International Bureau.

The Council settles its rules of procedure and all other necessary regulations.

It *decides* all questions of administration which may arise with regard to the operations of the Court.

It *has* entire control over the appointment, suspension, or dismissal of the officials and employes of the Bureau.

It *fixes* the payments and salaries, and *controls* the general expenditure.

At meetings duly summoned the presence of *nine* members is sufficient to render valid the discussions of the Council. The decisions are taken by a majority of votes.

The Council communicates to the *contracting* Powers without delay the regulations adopted by it. It presents to them an annual report on the labors of the Court, the working of the admin-

1899

services administratifs et sur les dépenses.

ARTICLE 29

Les frais du Bureau seront supportés par les Puissances signataires dans la proportion établie pour le Bureau international de l'Union postale universelle.

CHAPITRE III.—*De la Procédure arbitrale*

ARTICLE 30

En vue de favoriser le développement de l'arbitrage, les Puissances signataires ont arrêté les règles suivantes qui seront applicables à la procédure arbitrale, en tant que les Parties ne sont pas convenues d'autres règles.

ARTICLE 31

Les Puissances qui recourent à l'arbitrage signent un Acte spécial (compromis) dans lequel sont nettement déterminés l'objet du litige ainsi que l'étendue des pouvoirs des arbitres. Cet Acte implique l'engagement des Parties de se soumettre de bonne foi à la sentence arbitrale.[1]

---

[1] See footnote on opposite page.

1907

des services administratifs et sur les dépenses. *Le rapport contient également un résumé du contenu essentiel des documents communiqués au Bureau par les Puissances en vertu de l'article 43 alinéas 3 et 4.*

ARTICLE 50

Les frais du Bureau seront supportés par les Puissances *contractantes* dans la proportion établie pour le Bureau international de l'Union postale universelle.

Les frais à la charge des Puissances adhérentes seront comptés à partir du jour où leur adhésion produit ses effets.

CHAPITRE III.—*De la Procédure arbitrale*

ARTICLE 51

En vue de favoriser le développement de l'arbitrage, les Puissances *contractantes* ont arrêté les règles suivantes qui sont applicables à la procédure arbitrale, en tant que les Parties ne sont pas convenues d'autres règles.

ARTICLE 52

Les Puissances qui recourent à l'arbitrage signent un compromis dans lequel sont déterminés l'objet du litige, *le délai de nomination des arbitres, la forme, l'ordre et les délais dans lesquels la communication visée par l'article 63 devra être faite, et le montant de la somme que chaque Partie aura à déposer à titre d'avance pour les frais.*

Le compromis détermine égale-

1899

administration, and the expenditure.

ARTICLE 29

The expenses of the Bureau shall be borne by the signatory Powers in the proportion fixed for the International Bureau of the Universal Postal Union.

CHAPTER III.—*On Arbitral Procedure*

ARTICLE 30

With a view to encourage the development of arbitration, the signatory Powers have agreed on the following rules which shall be applicable to arbitral procedure, unless other rules have been agreed on by the parties.

ARTICLE 31

The Powers who have recourse to arbitration sign a special act (compromis), in which the subject of the difference is clearly defined, as well as the extent of the arbitrators' powers. This act implies the undertaking of the parties to submit loyally to the award.[1]

1907

istration, and the expenditure. *The report likewise contains a résumé of what is important in the documents communicated to the Bureau by the Powers in virtue of Article 43, paragraphs 3 and 4.*

ARTICLE 50

The expenses of the Bureau shall be borne by the *contracting* Powers in the proportion fixed for the International Bureau of the Universal Postal Union.

The expenses to be charged to the adhering Powers shall be reckoned from the date on which their adhesion comes into force.

CHAPTER III.—*Arbitration Procedure*

ARTICLE 51

With a view to encouraging the development of arbitration, the *contracting* Powers have agreed on the following rules, which are applicable to arbitration procedure, unless other rules have been agreed on by the parties.

ARTICLE 52

The Powers which have recourse to arbitration sign a compromis, in which the subject of the dispute is clearly defined, *the time allowed for appointing arbitrators, the form, order, and time in which the communication referred to in Article 63 must be made, and the amount of the sum which each party must deposit in advance to defray the expenses. The compromis likewise de-*

---

[1] Cf. Article 37, paragraph 2, of the 1907 Convention.

1899   **1907**

*ment, s'il y a lieu, le mode de
nomination des arbitres, tous
pouvoirs spéciaux éventuels du
Tribunal, son siège, la langue
dont il fera usage et celles dont
l'emploi sera autorisé devant lui,
et généralement toutes les conditions dont les Parties sont convenues.*

ARTICLE 53

*La Cour permanente est com-
pétente pour l'établissement du
compromis, si les Parties sont
d'accord pour s'en remettre à
elle.*

*Elle est également compétente,
même si la demande est faite
seulement par l'une des Parties,
après qu'un accord par la voie
diplomatique a été vainement
essayé, quand il s'agit:*

*1°. d'un différend rentrant dans
un Traité d'arbitrage général conclu ou renouvelé après la mise en
vigueur de cette Convention et qui
prévoit pour chaque différend
un compromis et n'exclut pour
l'établissement de ce dernier ni
explicitement ni implicitement la
compétence de la Cour. Toutefois, le recours à la Cour n'a pas
lieu si l'autre Partie déclare qu'à
son avis le différend n'appartient
pas à la catégorie des différends
à soumettre à un arbitrage obligatoire, à moins que le Traité
d'arbitrage ne confère au Tribunal arbitral le pouvoir de
décider cette question préalable;*

*2°. d'un différend provenant de
dettes contractuelles réclamées à
une Puissance par une autre
Puissance comme dues à ses
nationaux, et pour la solution
duquel l'offre d'arbitrage a été*

1899	1907

fines, if there is occasion, the manner of appointing arbitrators, any special powers which may eventually belong to the tribunal, where it shall meet, the language it shall use, and the languages the employment of which shall be authorised before it, and, generally speaking, all the conditions on which the parties are agreed.

ARTICLE 53[1]

The Permanent Court is competent to settle the compromis, if the parties are agreed to have recourse to it for the purpose.

It is similarly competent, even if the request is only made by one of the parties, when all attempts to reach an understanding through the diplomatic channel have failed, in the case of—

1. A dispute covered by a general treaty of arbitration concluded or renewed after the present Convention has come into force, and providing for a compromis in all disputes and not either explicitly or implicitly excluding the settlement of the compromis from the competence of the Court. Recourse can not, however, be had to the Court if the other party declares that in its opinion the dispute does not belong to the category of disputes which can be submitted to compulsory arbitration, unless the treaty of arbitration confers upon the arbitration tribunal the power of deciding this preliminary question.

2. A dispute arising from contract debts claimed from one Power by another Power as due to its nationals, and for the settlement of which the offer of arbi-

---

[1]See the reservations of this article, *post*, pp. cv. *et seq.*

1899

1907

acceptée. Cette disposition n'est pas applicable si l'acceptation a été subordonnée à la condition que le compromis soit établi selon un autre mode.

ARTICLE 54

Dans les cas prévus par l'article précédent, le compromis sera établi par une commission composée de cinq membres désignés de la manière prévue à l'article 45 alinéas 3 à 6.

Le cinquième membre est de droit Président de la commission.

ARTICLE 32

Les fonctions arbitrales peuvent être conférées à un arbitre unique ou à plusieurs arbitres désignés par les Parties à leur gré, ou choisis par Elles parmi les membres de la Cour permanente d'arbitrage établie par le présent Acte.

A défaut de constitution du Tribunal par l'accord immédiat des Parties, il est procédé de la manière suivante :

Chaque Partie nomme deux arbitres et ceux-ci choisissent ensemble un surarbitre.

En cas de partage des voix, le choix de surarbitre est confié à une Puissance tierce, désignée de commun accord par les Parties.

Si l'accord ne s'établit pas à ce sujet, chaque Partie désigne une Puissance différente et le choix du surarbitre est fait de concert par les Puissances ainsi désignées.

ARTICLE 55

Les fonctions arbitrales peuvent être conférées à un arbitre unique ou à plusieurs arbitres désignés par les Parties à leur gré, ou choisis par Elles parmi les Membres de la Cour permanente d'arbitrage établie par la présente *Convention*.

A défaut de constitution du Tribunal par l'accord des Parties, il est procédé de la manière *indiquée à l'article 45 alinéas 3 à 6.*

1899	1907

1907 (right column):

tration has been accepted. This arrangement is not applicable if acceptance is subject to the condition that the compromis should be settled in some other way.

ARTICLE 54[1]

In the cases contemplated in the preceding article, the compromis shall be settled by a commission consisting of five members selected in the manner arranged for in Article 45, paragraphs 3 to 6.

The fifth member is president of the commission ex officio.

ARTICLE 32

The duties of arbitrator may be conferred on one arbitrator alone or on several arbitrators selected by the parties as they please, or chosen by them from the members of the Permanent Court of Arbitration established by the present Act.

Failing the constitution of the tribunal by direct agreement between the parties, the following course is pursued:

Each party appoints two arbitrators, and these latter together choose an umpire.

In case of equal voting, the choice of the umpire is intrusted to a third Power, selected by the parties by common accord.

If no agreement is arrived at on this subject, each party selects a different Power, and the choice of the umpire is made in concert by the Powers thus selected.

ARTICLE 55

The duties of arbitrator may be conferred on one arbitrator alone or on several arbitrators selected by the parties as they please, or chosen by them from the members of the Permanent Court of Arbitration established by the present *Convention*.

Failing the constitution of the tribunal by direct agreement between the parties, the course *referred to in Article 45, paragraphs 3 to 6* is pursued.

---

[1]Japan made reservation of Article 54.

1899

ARTICLE 33

Lorsqu'un Souverain ou un Chef d'État est choisi pour arbitre, la procédure arbitrale est réglée par Lui.

ARTICLE 34

Le surarbitre est de droit Président du Tribunal.

Lorsque le Tribunal ne comprend pas de surarbitre, il nomme lui-même son président.

ARTICLE 35

En cas de décès, de démission ou d'empêchement, pour quelque cause que ce soit, de l'un des arbitres, il est pourvu à son remplacement selon le mode fixé pour sa nomination.

ARTICLE 36

Le siège du Tribunal est désigné par les Parties. A défaut de cette désignation, le Tribunal siège à La Haye.

Le siège ainsi fixé ne peut, sauf le cas de force majeure, être changé par le Tribunal que de l'assentiment des Parties.

1907

ARTICLE 56

Lorsqu'un Souverain ou un Chef d'État est choisi pour arbitre, la procédure arbitrale est réglée par Lui.

ARTICLE 57

Le surarbitre est de droit Président du Tribunal.

Lorsque le Tribunal ne comprend pas de surarbitre, il nomme lui-même son Président.

ARTICLE 58

En cas d'établissement du compromis par une commission, telle qu'elle est visée à l'article 54, et sauf stipulation contraire, la commission elle même formera le Tribunal d'arbitrage.

ARTICLE 59

En cas de décès, de démission ou d'empêchement, pour quelque cause que ce soit, de l'un des arbitres, il est pourvu à son remplacement selon le mode fixé pour sa nomination.

ARTICLE 60

A défaut de désignation par les Parties, le Tribunal siège à La Haye.

Le Tribunal ne peut siéger sur le territoire d'une tierce Puissance qu'avec l'assentiment de celle-ci.

Le siège *une fois* fixé ne peut être changé par le Tribunal qu'*avec* l'assentiment des Parties.

ARTICLE 61

Si le compromis n'a pas déter-

1899

ARTICLE 33

When a sovereign or the chief of a State is chosen as arbitrator, the arbitral procedure is settled by him.

ARTICLE 34

The umpire is by right president of the tribunal.

When the tribunal does not include an umpire, it appoints its own president.

ARTICLE 35

In case of the death, retirement, or disability from any cause of one of the arbitrators, his place shall be filled in accordance with the method of his appointment.

ARTICLE 36

The tribunal's place of session is selected by the parties. Failing this selection the tribunal sits at The Hague.

The place thus fixed can not, except in case of necessity, be changed by the tribunal without the assent of the parties.

1907

ARTICLE 56

When a sovereign or the chief of a State is chosen as arbitrator, the arbitration procedure is settled by him.

ARTICLE 57

The umpire is president of the tribunal ex officio.

When the tribunal does not include an umpire, it appoints its own president.

ARTICLE 58

When the compromis is settled by a commission, as contemplated in Article 54, and in the absence of an agreement to the contrary, the commission itself shall form the arbitration tribunal.

ARTICLE 59

Should one of the arbitrators either die, retire, or be unable for any reason whatever to discharge his functions, the same procedure is followed for filling the vacancy as was followed for appointing him.

ARTICLE 60

The tribunal sits at The Hague unless some other place is selected by the parties.

The tribunal can only sit in the territory of a third Power with the latter's consent.

The place of meeting *once* fixed can not be altered by the tribunal, except *with* the consent of the parties.

ARTICLE 61

If the question as to what lan-

1899

1907

miné les langues à employer, il en est décidé par le Tribunal.[1]

ARTICLE 37

Les Parties ont le droit de nommer auprès du Tribunal des Délégués ou agents spéciaux, avec la mission de servir d'intermédiaires entre Elles et le Tribunal.

Elles sont en outre autorisées à charger de la défense de leurs droits et intérêts devant le Tribunal, des conseils ou avocats nommés par Elles à cet effet.

ARTICLE 62

Les Parties ont le droit de nommer auprès du Tribunal des agents spéciaux, avec la mission de servir d'intermédiaires entre Elles et le Tribunal.

Elles sont en outre autorisées à charger de la défense de leurs droits et intérêts devant le Tribunal, des conseils ou avocats nommés par Elles à cet effet.

Les Membres de la Cour permanente ne peuvent exercer les fonctions d'agents, conseils ou avocats, qu'en faveur de la Puissance qui les a nommés Membres de la Cour.

ARTICLE 38

Le Tribunal décide du choix des langues dont il fera usage et dont l'emploi sera autorisé devant lui.[2]

ARTICLE 39

La procédure arbitrale comprend en règle générale deux phases distinctes: l'instruction et les débats.

L'instruction consiste dans la communication faite par les Agents respectifs, aux membres du Tribunal et à la Partie adverse, de tous actes imprimés ou écrits et de tous documents contenant les moyens invoqués dans la cause. Cette communication aura lieu dans la forme

ARTICLE 63

La procédure arbitrale comprend en règle générale deux phases distinctes: l'instruction *écrite* et les débats.

L'instruction *écrite* consiste dans la communication faite par les agents respectifs, aux membres du Tribunal et à la Partie adverse, *des mémoires, des contre-mémoires, et, au besoin, des répliques; les Parties y joignent toutes pièces et* documents invoqués dans la cause. Cette

---

[1] See footnote 1, opposite page.
[2] See footnote 2, opposite page.

1899

1907

guages are to be used has not been settled by the compromis, it shall be decided by the tribunal.[1]

ARTICLE 37

The parties have the right to appoint delegates or special agents to attend the tribunal, for the purpose of serving as intermediaries between them and the tribunal.

They are further authorized to retain, for the defense of their rights and interests before the tribunal, counsel or advocates appointed by them for this purpose.

ARTICLE 62

The parties are entitled to appoint special agents to attend the tribunal to act as intermediaries between themselves and the tribunal.

They are further authorized to retain for the defence of their rights and interests before the tribunal counsel or advocates appointed by themselves for this purpose.

The members of the Permanent Court may not act as agents, counsel, or advocates except on behalf of the Power which appointed them members of the Court.

ARTICLE 38

The tribunal decides on the choice of languages to be used by itself, and to be authorized for use before it.[2]

ARTICLE 39

As a general rule the arbitral procedure comprises two distinct phases: pleadings and oral discussions.

Preliminary examination consists in the communication by the respective agents to the members of the tribunal and to the opposite party of all printed or written acts and of all documents containing the arguments invoked in the case. This communication shall be made in the form and within

ARTICLE 63

As a general rule, arbitration procedure comprises two distinct phases: *written* pleadings and oral discussions.

The pleadings consist in the communication by the respective agents to the members of the tribunal and the opposite party of *cases, counter-cases, and, if necessary, of replies; the parties annex thereto all papers* and documents called for in the case. This communication shall be made

---

[1]Cf. Article 38 of the 1899 Convention.
[2]Cf. Article 61 of the 1907 Convention.

1899

et dans les délais déterminés par le Tribunal en vertu de l'article 49.

Les débats consistent dans le développement oral des moyens des Parties devant le Tribunal.

ARTICLE 40

Toute pièce produite par l'une des Parties doit être communiquée à l'autre Partie.

ARTICLE 41

Les débats sont dirigés par [le] Président.

Ils ne sont publics qu'en vertu d'une décision du Tribunal, prise avec l'assentiment des Parties.

Ils sont consignés dans les procès-verbaux rédigés par des Secrétaires que nomme le Président. Ces procès-verbaux ont seuls caractère authentique.

ARTICLE 42

L'instruction étant close, le Tribunal a le droit d'écarter du débat tous actes ou documents nouveaux qu'une des Parties

1907

communication aura lieu, *directement ou par l'intermédiaire du Bureau International, dans l'ordre et* dans les délais déterminés par le *compromis.*

Les délais fixés par le compromis pourront être prolongés de commun accord par les Parties, ou par le Tribunal quand il le juge nécessaire pour arriver à une décision juste.

Les débats consistent dans le développement oral des moyens des Parties devant le Tribunal.

ARTICLE 64

Toute pièce produite par l'une des Parties doit être communiquée, *en copie certifiée conforme,* à l'autre Partie.

ARTICLE 65

A moins de circonstances spéciales, le Tribunal ne se réunit qu'après la clôture de l'instruction.

ARTICLE 66

Les débats sont dirigés par le Président.

Ils ne sont publics qu'en vertu d'une décision du Tribunal, prise avec l'assentiment des Parties.

Ils sont consignés dans les procès-verbaux rédigés par des secrétaires que nomme le Président. Ces procès-verbaux *sont signés par le Président et par un des secrétaires; ils* ont seuls caractère authentique.

ARTICLE 67

L'instruction étant close, le Tribunal a le droit d'écarter du débat tous actes ou documents nouveaux qu'une des Parties

1899

the periods fixed by the tribunal in accordance with Article 49.

Discussion consists in the oral development before the tribunal of the arguments of the parties.

ARTICLE 40.

Every document produced by one party must be communicated to the other party.

ARTICLE 41

The discussions are under the direction of the president.

They are only public if it be so decided by the tribunal, with the assent of the parties.

They are recorded in the procès-verbaux drawn up by the secretaries appointed by the president. These procès-verbaux alone have an authentic character.

ARTICLE 42

When the preliminary examination is concluded, the tribunal has the right to refuse discussion of all fresh acts or documents

1907

either directly or through the intermediary of the International Bureau, in the *order* and within the time fixed by the *compromis.*

The time fixed by the compromis may be extended by mutual agreement by the parties, or by the tribunal when the latter considers it necessary for the purpose of reaching a just decision.

The discussions consist in the oral development before the tribunal of the arguments of the parties.

ARTICLE 64

A *certified copy* of every document produced by one party must be communicated to the other party.

ARTICLE 65

Unless special circumstances arise, the tribunal does not meet until the pleadings are closed.

ARTICLE 66

The discussions are under the control of the president.

They are only public if it be so decided by the tribunal, with the assent of the parties.

They are recorded in minutes drawn up by the secretaries appointed by the president. These minutes *are signed by the president and by one of the secretaries and* alone have an authentic character.

ARTICLE 67

After the close of the pleadings, the tribunal is entitled to refuse discussion of all new papers or documents which one of the par-

1899

voudrait lui soumettre sans le consentement de l'autre.

ARTICLE 43

Le Tribunal demeure libre de prendre en considération les actes ou documents nouveaux sur lesquels les agents ou conseils des Parties appelleraient son attention.

En ce cas, le Tribunal a le droit de requérir la production de ces actes ou documents, sauf l'obligation d'en donner connaissance à la Partie adverse.

ARTICLE 44

Le Tribunal peut, en outre, requérir des agents des Parties la production de tous actes et demander toutes explications nécessaires. En cas de refus, le Tribunal en prend acte.

ARTICLE 45

Les agents et les conseils des Parties sont autorisés à présenter oralement au Tribunal tous les moyens qu'ils jugent utiles à la défense de leur cause.

ARTICLE 46

Ils ont le droit de soulever des exceptions et incidents. Les décisions du Tribunal sur ces points sont définitives et ne peuvent donner lieu à aucune discussion ultérieure.

ARTICLE 47

Les Membres du Tribunal ont le droit de poser des questions aux agents et aux conseils des

1907

voudrait lui soumettre sans le consentement de l'autre.

ARTICLE 68

Le Tribunal demeure libre de prendre en considération les actes ou documents nouveaux sur lesquels les agents ou conseils des Parties appelleraient son attention.

En ce cas, le Tribunal a le droit de requérir la production de ces actes ou documents, sauf l'obligation d'en donner connaissance à la Partie adverse.

ARTICLE 69

Le Tribunal peut, en outre, requérir des agents des Parties la production de tous actes et demander toutes explications nécessaires. En cas de refus, le Tribunal en prend acte.

ARTICLE 70

Les agents et les conseils des Parties sont autorisés à présenter oralement au Tribunal tous les moyens qu'ils jugent utiles à la défense de leur cause.

ARTICLE 71

Ils ont le droit de soulever des exceptions et des incidents. Les décisions du Tribunal sur ces points sont définitives et ne peuvent donner lieu à aucune discussion ultérieure.

ARTICLE 72

Les Membres du Tribunal ont le droit de poser des questions aux agents et aux conseils des

1899

which one party may desire to submit to it without the consent of the other party.

ARTICLE 43

The tribunal is free to take into consideration fresh acts or documents to which its attention may be drawn by the agents or counsel of the parties.

In this case, the tribunal has the right to require the production of these acts or documents, but is obliged to make them known to the opposite party.

ARTICLE 44

The tribunal can, besides, require from the agents of the parties the production of all acts, and can demand all necessary explanations. In case of refusal, the tribunal takes note of it.

ARTICLE 45

The agents and counsel of the parties are authorized to present orally to the tribunal all the arguments they may think expedient in defense of their case.

ARTICLE 46

They have the right to raise objections and points. The decisions of the tribunal on those points are final, and can not form the subject of any subsequent discussion.

ARTICLE 47

The members of the tribunal have the right to put questions to the agents and counsel of the par-

1907

ties may wish to submit to it without the consent of the other party.

ARTICLE 68

The tribunal is free to take into consideration new papers or documents to which its attention may be drawn by the agents or counsel of the parties.

In this case, the tribunal has the right to require the production of these papers or documents, but is obliged to make them known to the opposite party.

ARTICLE 69

The tribunal can, besides, require from the agents of the parties the production of all papers, and can demand all necessary explanations. In case of refusal the tribunal takes note of it.

ARTICLE 70

The agents and the counsel of the parties are authorized to present orally to the tribunal all the arguments they may consider expedient in defense of their case.

ARTICLE 71

They are entitled to raise objections and points. The decisions of the tribunal on these points are final and can not form the subject of any subsequent discussion.

ARTICLE 72

The members of the tribunal are entitled to put questions to the agents and counsel of the par-

1899

Parties et de leur demander des éclaircissements sur les points douteux.

Ni les questions posées, ni les observations faites par les Membres du Tribunal pendant le cours des débats ne peuvent être regardées comme l'expression des opinions du Tribunal en général ou de ses membres en particulier.

ARTICLE 48

Le Tribunal est autorisé à déterminer sa compétence en interprétant le compromis ainsi que les autres traités qui peuvent être invoqués dans la matière, et en appliquant les principes du droit international.

ARTICLE 49

Le Tribunal a le droit de rendre des ordonnances de procédure pour la direction du procès, de déterminer les formes et délais dans lesquels chaque Partie devra prendre ses conclusions et de procéder à toutes les formalités que comporte l'administration des preuves.

1907

Parties et de leur demander des éclaircissements sur les points douteux.

Ni les questions posées, ni les observations faites par les membres du Tribunal pendant le cours des débats ne peuvent être regardées comme l'expression des opinions du Tribunal en général ou de ses membres en particulier.

ARTICLE 73

Le Tribunal est autorisé à déterminer sa compétence en interprétant le compromis ainsi que les autres *actes et documents* qui peuvent être invoqués dans la matière, et en appliquant les principes du droit.

ARTICLE 74

Le Tribunal a le droit de rendre des ordonnances de procédure pour la direction du procès, de déterminer les formes, *l'ordre* et les délais dans lesquels chaque Partie devra prendre ses conclusions *finales*, et de procéder à toutes les formalités que comporte l'administration des preuves.

ARTICLE 75

Les Parties s'engagent à fournir au Tribunal, dans la plus large mesure qu'Elles jugeront possible, tous les moyens nécessaires pour la décision du litige.

ARTICLE 76

Pour toutes les notifications que le Tribunal aurait à faire sur le territoire d'un tierce Puissance contractante, le Tribunal s'adressera directement au Gouvernement de cette Puissance. Il en

1899

ties, and to demand explanations from them on doubtful points.

Neither the questions put nor the remarks made by members of the tribunal during the discussions can be regarded as an expression of opinion by the tribunal in general, or by its members in particular.

ARTICLE 48

The tribunal is authorized to declare its competence in interpreting the compromis as well as the other treaties which may be invoked in the case, and in applying the principles of international law.

ARTICLE 49

The tribunal has the right to issue rules of procedure for the conduct of the case, to decide the forms and periods within which each party must conclude its arguments, and to arrange all the formalities required for dealing with the evidence.

1907

ties, and to ask them for explanations on doubtful points.

Neither the questions put, nor the remarks made by members of the tribunal in the course of the discussions, can be regarded as an expression of opinion by the tribunal in general or by its members in particular.

ARTICLE 73

The tribunal is authorized to declare its competence in interpreting the compromis, as well as the other *papers and documents* which may be invoked, and in applying the principles of law.

ARTICLE 74

The tribunal is entitled to issue rules of procedure for the conduct of the case, to decide the forms, *order,* and time in which each party must conclude its *final* arguments, and to arrange all the formalities required for dealing with the evidence.

ARTICLE 75

The parties undertake to supply the tribunal, as fully as they consider possible, with all the information required for deciding the case.

ARTICLE 76

For all notices which the tribunal has to serve in the territory of a third contracting Power, the tribunal shall apply direct to the Government of that Power. The same rule applies in the case of

1899

1907

sera de même s'il s'agit de faire procéder sur place à l'établissement de tous moyens de preuve.

Les requêtes adressées à cet effet seront exécutées suivant les moyens dont la Puissance requise dispose d'après sa législation intérieure. Elles ne peuvent être refusées que si cette Puissance les juge de nature à porter atteinte à sa souveraineté ou à sa sécurité.

Le Tribunal aura aussi toujours la faculté de recourir à l'intermédiaire de la Puissance sur le territoire de laquelle il a son siège.

ARTICLE 50

Les agents et les conseils des Parties ayant présenté tous les éclaircissements et preuves à l'appui de leur cause, le Président prononce la clôture des débats.

ARTICLE 77

Les agents et les conseils des Parties ayant présenté tous les éclaircissements et preuves à l'appui de leur cause, le Président prononce la clôture des débats.

ARTICLE 51

Les délibérations du Tribunal ont lieu à huis clos. Toute décision est prise à la majorité des Membres du Tribunal.

Le refus d'un Membre de prendre part au vote doit être constaté dans le procès-verbal.

ARTICLE 78

Les délibérations du Tribunal ont lieu à huis clos *et restent secrètes.*

Toute décision est prise à la majorité *de ses* membres.

ARTICLE 52

La sentence arbitrale, votée à la majorité des voix, est motivée. Elle est rédigée par écrit et signée par chacun des membres du Tribunal.

Ceux des membres qui sont restés en minorité peuvent constater, en signant, leur dissentiment.

ARTICLE 79

La sentence arbitrale est motivée. *Elle mentionne les noms des arbitres;* elle est signée par *le Président et par le greffier ou le secrétaire faisant fonctions de greffier.*

1899

1907

steps being taken to procure evidence on the spot.

The requests for this purpose are to be executed as far as the means at the disposal of the Power applied to under its municipal law allow. They can not be rejected unless the Power in question considers them calculated to impair its own sovereign rights or its safety.
The Court will equally be always entitled to act through the Power on whose territory it sits.

ARTICLE 50

When the agents and counsel of the parties have submitted all explanations and evidence in support of their case, the president pronounces the discussion closed.

ARTICLE 51

The deliberations of the tribunal take place in private. Every decision is taken by a majority of members of the tribunal.

The refusal of a member to vote must be recorded in the procès-verbal.

ARTICLE 52

The award, given by a majority of votes, is accompanied by a statement of reasons. It is drawn up in writing and signed by each member of the tribunal.

Those members who are in the minority may record their dissent when signing.

ARTICLE 77

When the agents and counsel of the parties have submitted all the explanations and evidence in support of their case the president shall declare the discussion closed.

ARTICLE 78

The tribunal considers its decisions in private and *the proceedings remain secret.*

All questions are decided by a majority of *its* members.

ARTICLE 79

The award must give the reasons on which it is based. *It contains the names of the arbitrators; it is signed by the president and registrar or by the secretary acting as registrar.*

1899

ARTICLE 53

La sentence arbitrale est lue en séance publique du Tribunal, les agents et les conseils des Parties présents ou dûment appelés.

ARTICLE 54

La sentence arbitrale, dûment prononcée et notifiée aux agents des Parties en litige, décide définitivement et sans appel la contestation.

ARTICLE 55

Les Parties peuvent se réserver dans le compromis de demander la revision de la sentence arbitrale.

Dans ce cas, et sauf convention contraire, la demande doit être adressée au Tribunal qui a rendu la sentence. Elle ne peut être motivée que par la découverte d'un fait nouveau qui eût été de nature à exercer une influence décisive sur la sentence et qui, lors de la clôture des débats, était inconnu du Tribunal lui-même et de la Partie qui a demandé la revision.

La procédure de revision ne peut être ouverte que par une décision du Tribunal constatant expressément l'existence du fait nouveau, lui reconnaissant les caractères prévus par le para-

1907

ARTICLE 80

La sentence est lue en séance publique, les agents et les conseils des Parties présents ou dûment appelés.

ARTICLE 81

La sentence, dûment prononcée et notifiée aux agents des Parties, décide définitivement et sans appel la contestation.

ARTICLE 82

Tout différend qui pourrait surgir entre les Parties, concernant l'interprétation et l'exécution de la sentence, sera, sauf stipulation contraire, soumis au jugement du Tribunal qui l'a rendue.

ARTICLE 83

Les Parties peuvent se réserver dans le compromis de demander la révision de la sentence arbitrale.

Dans ce cas, et sauf *stipulation* contraire, la demande doit être adressée au Tribunal qui a rendu la sentence. Elle ne peut être motivée que par la découverte d'un fait nouveau qui eût été de nature à exercer une influence décisive sur la sentence et qui, lors de la clôture des débats, était inconnu du Tribunal lui-même et de la Partie qui a demandé la révision.

La procédure de révision ne peut être ouverte que par une décision du Tribunal constatant expressément l'existence du fait nouveau, lui reconnaissant les caractères prévus par le para-

1899

ARTICLE 53

The award is read out at a public meeting of the tribunal, the agents and counsel of the parties being present, or duly summoned to attend.

ARTICLE 54

The award, duly pronounced and notified to the agents of the parties at variance, puts an end to the dispute definitively and without appeal.

ARTICLE 55

The parties can reserve in the compromis the right to demand the revision of the award.

In this case, and unless there be an agreement to the contrary, the demand must be addressed to the tribunal which pronounced the award. It can only be made on the ground of the discovery of some new fact calculated to exercise a decisive influence on the award, and which, at the time the discussion was closed, was unknown to the tribunal and to the party demanding the revision.

Proceedings for revision can only be instituted by a decision of the tribunal expressly recording the existence of the new fact, recognizing in it the character described in the foregoing para-

1907

ARTICLE 80

The award is read out in public sitting, the agents and counsel of the parties being present or duly summoned to attend.

ARTICLE 81

The award, duly pronounced and notified to the agents of the parties, settles the dispute definitively and without appeal.

ARTICLE 82

Any dispute arising between the parties as to the interpretation and execution of the award shall, in the absence of an agreement to the contrary, be submitted to the tribunal which pronounced it.

ARTICLE 83

The parties can reserve in the compromis the right to demand the revision of the award.

In this case and unless there be a *stipulation* to the contrary, the demand must be addressed to the tribunal which pronounced the award. It can only be made on the ground of the discovery of some new fact calculated to exercise a decisive influence upon the award and which was unknown to the tribunal and to the party which demanded the revision at the time the discussion was closed.

Proceedings for revision can only be instituted by a decision of the tribunal expressly recording the existence of the new fact, recognizing in it the character described in the preceding para-

1899

graphe précédent et déclarant à ce titre la demande recevable.

Le compromis détermine le délai dans lequel la demande de revision doit être formée.

ARTICLE 56

La sentence arbitrale n'est obligatoire que pour les Parties qui ont conclu le compromis.

Lorsqu'il s'agit de l'interprétation d'une convention à laquelle ont participé d'autres Puissances que les Parties en litige, celles-ci notifient aux premières le compromis qu'elles ont conclu. Chacune de ces Puissances a le droit d'intervenir au procès. Si une ou plusieurs d'entre Elles ont profité de cette faculté, l'interprétation contenue dans la sentence est également obligatoire à leur égard.

ARTICLE 57

Chaque Partie supporte ses propres frais et une part égale des frais du Tribunal.

1907

graphe précédent et déclarant à ce titre la demande recevable.

Le compromis détermine le délai dans lequel la demande de révision doit être formée.

ARTICLE 84

La sentence arbitrale n'est obligatoire que pour les Parties *en litige*.

Lorsqu'il s'agit de l'interprétation d'une convention à laquelle ont participé d'autres Puissances que les Parties en litige, celles-ci *avertissent en temps utile toutes les Puissances signataires.* Chacune de ces Puissances a le droit d'intervenir au procès. Si une ou plusieurs d'entre Elles ont profité de cette faculté, l'interprétation contenue dans la sentence est également obligatoire à leur égard.

ARTICLE 85

Chaque Partie supporte ses propres frais et une part égale des frais du Tribunal.

CHAPITRE IV.—*De la procédure sommaire d'arbitrage*

ARTICLE 86

En vue de faciliter le fonctionnement de la justice arbitrale, lorsqu'il s'agit de litiges de nature à comporter une procédure sommaire, les Puissances contractantes arrêtent les règles ci-après qui seront suivies en l'absence de stipulations différentes, et sous réserve, le cas échéant, de l'application des dispositions du chapitre III qui ne seraient pas contraires.

1899

graph, and declaring the demand admissible on this ground.

The compromis fixes the period within which the demand for revision must be made.

ARTICLE 56

The award is only binding on the parties who concluded the compromis.

When there is a question of interpreting a Convention to which Powers other than those concerned in the dispute are parties, the latter notify to the former the compromis they have concluded. Each of these Powers has the right to intervene in the case. If one or more of them avail themselves of this right, the interpretation contained in the award is equally binding on them.

ARTICLE 57

Each party pays its own expenses and an equal share of those of the tribunal.

1907

graph, and declaring the demand admissible on this ground.

The compromis fixes the period within which the demand for revision must be made.

ARTICLE 84

The award is not binding except on the parties *in dispute.*

When it concerns the interpretation of a Convention to which Powers other than those in dispute are parties, they *shall inform all the signatory Powers in good time.* Each of these Powers is entitled to intervene in the case. If one or more avail themselves of this right, the interpretation contained in the award is equally binding on them.

ARTICLE 85

Each party pays its own expenses and an equal share of the expenses of the tribunal.

CHAPTER IV.—*Arbitration by Summary Procedure*

ARTICLE 86

With a view to facilitating the working of the system of arbitration in disputes admitting of a summary procedure, the contracting Powers adopt the following rules, which shall be observed in the absence of other arrangements and subject to the reservation that the provisions of Chapter III apply so far as may be.

1899

1907

ARTICLE 87

Chacune des Parties en litige nomme un arbitre. Les deux arbitres ainsi désignés choisissent un surarbitre. S'ils ne tombent pas d'accord à ce sujet, chacun présente deux candidats pris sur la liste générale des Membres de la Cour permanente en dehors des Membres indiqués par chacune des Parties Elles-mêmes et n'étant les nationaux d'aucune d'Elles; le sort détermine lequel des candidats ainsi présentés sera le surarbitre.

Le surarbitre préside le Tribunal, qui rend ses décisions à la majorité des voix.

ARTICLE 88

A défaut d'accord préalable, le Tribunal fixe, dès qu'il est constitué, le délai dans lequel les deux Parties devront lui soumettre leurs mémoires respectifs.

ARTICLE 89

Chaque Partie est représentée devant le Tribunal par un agent qui sert d'intermédiaire entre le Tribunal et le Gouvernement qui l'a désigné.

ARTICLE 90

La procédure a lieu exclusivement par écrit. Toutefois, chaque Partie a le droit de demander la comparution de témoins et d'experts. Le Tribunal a, de son côté, la faculté de demander des explications orales aux agents des deux Parties, ainsi qu'aux experts et aux témoins dont il juge la comparution utile.

1899

1907

ARTICLE 87

Each of the parties in dispute appoints an arbitrator. The two arbitrators thus selected choose an umpire. If they do not agree on this point, each of them proposes two candidates taken from the general list of the members of the Permanent Court exclusive of the members appointed by either of the parties and not being nationals of either of them; which of the candidates thus proposed shall be the umpire is determined by lot.

The umpire presides over the tribunal, which gives its decisions by a majority of votes.

ARTICLE 88

In the absence of any previous agreement the tribunal, as soon as it is formed, settles the time within which the two parties must submit their respective cases to it.

ARTICLE 89

Each party is represented before the tribunal by an agent, who serves as intermediary between the tribunal and the Government who appointed him.

ARTICLE 90

The proceedings are conducted exclusively in writing. Each party, however, is entitled to ask that witnesses and experts should be called. The tribunal has, for its part, the right to demand oral explanations from the agents of the two parties, as well as from the experts and witnesses whose appearance in Court it may consider useful.

1899

DISPOSITIONS GÉNÉRALES

1907

TITRE V.—DISPOSITIONS *Finales*

ARTICLE 91

La présente Convention dûment ratifiée remplacera, dans les rapports entre les Puissances contractantes, la Convention pour le règlement pacifique des conflits internationaux du 29 juillet 1899.

ARTICLE 58

La présente Convention sera ratifiée dans le plus bref délai possible.

Les ratifications seront déposées à La Haye.

Il sera dressé du dépôt de chaque ratification un procès-verbal, dont une copie, certifiée conforme, sera remise par la voie diplomatique à toutes les Puissances qui ont été représentées à la Conférence Internationale de la Paix de La Haye.

ARTICLE 92

La présente Convention sera ratifiée *aussitôt que* possible.

Les ratifications seront déposées à La Haye.

Le premier dépôt de ratifications sera constaté par un procès-verbal signé par les représentants des Puissances qui y prennent part et par le Ministre des Affaires Étrangères des Pays-Bas.

Les dépôts ultérieurs de ratifications se feront au moyen d'une notification écrite, adressée au Gouvernement des Pays-Bas et accompagnée de l'instrument de ratification.

Copie certifiée conforme du procès-verbal relatif au premier dépôt de ratifications, des notifications mentionnées à l'alinéa précédent, ainsi que des instruments de ratification, sera immédiatement remise, par les soins du Gouvernement des Pays-Bas et par la voie diplomatique, aux Puissances conviées à la Deuxième Conférence de la Paix, ainsi qu'aux autres Puissances qui auront adhéré à la Convention. Dans les cas visés par l'alinéa précédent, ledit Gouvernement Leur fera connaître

1899

GENERAL PROVISIONS

1907

PART V.—*Final* PROVISIONS

ARTICLE 91

The present Convention, duly ratified, shall replace, as between the contracting Powers, the Convention for the pacific settlement of international disputes of the 29th July, 1899.

ARTICLE 58

The present Convention shall be ratified as speedily as possible.

The ratifications shall be deposited at The Hague.

A procès-verbal shall be drawn up recording the receipt of each ratification, and a copy duly certified shall be sent, through the diplomatic channel, to all the Powers who were represented at the International Peace Conference at The Hague.

ARTICLE 92

The present Convention shall be ratified as *soon* as possible.

The ratifications shall be deposited at The Hague.
The first deposit of ratifications shall be recorded in a procès-verbal signed by the representatives of the Powers which take part therein and by the Netherland Minister for Foreign Affairs.

The subsequent deposits of ratifications shall be made by means of a written notification, addressed to the Netherland Government and accompanied by the instrument of ratification.
A duly certified copy of the procès-verbal relative to the first deposit of ratifications, of the notifications mentioned in the preceding paragraph, and of the instruments of ratification, shall be immediately sent by the Netherland Government, through the diplomatic channel, to the Powers invited to the Second Peace Conference, as well as to those Powers which have adhered to the Convention. In the cases contemplated in the preceding paragraph, the said Government shall at the same time inform the Powers of

1899

ARTICLE 59

Les Puissances non signataires qui ont été représentées à la Conférence Internationale de la Paix pourront adhérer à la présente Convention. Elles auront à cet effet à faire connaître leur adhésion aux Puissances contractantes, au moyen d'une notification écrite, adressée au Gouvernement des Pays-Bas et communiquée par celui-ci à toutes les autres Puissances contractantes.

ARTICLE 60

Les conditions auxquelles les Puissances qui n'ont pas été représentées à la Conférence Internationale de la Paix pourront adhérer à la présente Convention formeront l'objet d'une entente ultérieure entre les Puissances contractantes.

1907

en même temps la date à laquelle il a reçu la notification.

ARTICLE 93

Les Puissances non signataires qui ont été *conviées* à la *Deuxième* Conférence de la Paix pourront adhérer à la présente Convention.

La Puissance qui désire adhérer notifie par écrit son intention au Gouvernement des Pays-Bas en lui transmettant l'acte d'adhésion qui sera déposé dans les archives dudit Gouvernement.

Ce Gouvernement transmettra immédiatement à toutes les autres Puissances conviées à la Deuxième Conférence de la Paix copie certifiée conforme de la notification ainsi que de l'acte d'adhésion, en indiquant la date à laquelle il a reçu la notification.

ARTICLE 94

Les conditions auxquelles les Puissances qui n'ont pas été *conviées* à la *Deuxième* Conférence de la Paix, pourront adhérer à la présente Convention, formeront l'objet d'une entente ultérieure entre les Puissances contractantes.

ARTICLE 95

La présente Convention produira effet, pour les Puissances qui auront participé au premier dépôt de ratifications, soixante jours après la date du procès-

1899

1907

the date on which it received the notification.

ARTICLE 59

The non-signatory Powers who were represented at the International Peace Conference can adhere to the present Convention. For this purpose they must make known their adhesion to the contracting Powers by a written notification addressed to the Netherland Government, and communicated by it to all the other contracting Powers.

ARTICLE 93

Non-signatory Powers which have been *invited to* the *Second* Peace Conference may adhere to the present Convention.

The Power which desires to adhere notifies its intention in writing to the Netherland Government, forwarding to it the act of adhesion, which shall be deposited in the archives of the said Government.

This Government shall immediately forward to all the other Powers invited to the Second Peace Conference a duly certified copy of the notification as well as of the act of adhesion, mentioning the date on which it received the notification.

ARTICLE 60[1]

The conditions on which the Powers who were not represented at the International Peace Conference can adhere to the present Convention shall form the subject of a subsequent agreement among the contracting Powers.

ARTICLE 94

The conditions on which the Powers which have not been *invited to* the *Second* Peace Conference may adhere to the present Convention shall form the subject of a subsequent agreement between the contracting Powers.

ARTICLE 95

The present Convention shall take effect, in the case of the Powers which were not a party to the first deposit of ratifications, sixty days after the date of the

---

[1] A protocol establishing, as regards the Powers unrepresented at the First Conference, the mode of adhesion to this Convention, was signed at The Hague, June 14, 1907, by representatives of all the Powers represented at the 1899 Conference.

1899

1907

verbal de ce dépôt et, pour les Puissances qui ratifieront ultérieurement ou qui adhèreront, soixante jours après que la notification de leur ratification ou de leur adhésion aura été reçue par le Gouvernement des Pays-Bas.

ARTICLE 61

S'il arrivait qu'une des Hautes Parties contractantes dénonçât la présente Convention, cette dénonciation ne produirait ses effets qu'un un après la notification faite par écrit au Gouvernement des Pays-Bas et communiquée immédiatement par celui-ci à toutes les autres Puissances contractantes.

Cette dénonciation ne produira ses effets qu'à l'égard de la Puissance qui l'aura notifiée.

ARTICLE 96

S'il arrivait qu'une des *Puissances* contractantes *voulût dénoncer* la présente Convention, *la* dénonciation *sera notifiée* par écrit au Gouvernement des Pays-Bas *qui communiquera* immédiatement *copie certifiée conforme de* la notification à toutes les autres Puissances *en leur faisant savoir la date à laquelle il l'a reçue.*
La dénonciation ne produira ses effets qu'à l'égard de la Puissance qui l'aura notifiée *et un an après que la notification en sera parvenue au Gouvernement des Pays-Bas.*

ARTICLE 97

Un registre tenu par le Ministère des Affaires Étrangères des Pays-Bas indiquera la date du dépôt de ratifications effectué en vertu de l'article 92 alinéas 3 et 4, ainsi que la date à laquelle auront été reçues les notifications d'adhésion (article 93 alinéa 2) ou de dénonciation (article 96 alinéa 1).
Chaque Puissance contractante est admise à prendre connaissance de ce registre et à en demander des extraits certifiés conformes.

En foi de quoi, les Plénipotentiaires ont signé la présente Convention et l'ont revêtue de leurs sceaux.

En foi de quoi, les Plénipotentiaires ont *revêtu* la présente Convention *de leurs signatures.*

1899	1907

procès-verbal of this deposit, and, in the case of the Powers which ratify subsequently or which adhere, sixty days after the notification of their ratification or of their adhesion has been received by the Netherland Government.

ARTICLE 61

In the event of one of the high contracting Parties denouncing the present Convention, this denunciation would not take effect until a year after its notification made in writing to the Netherland Government, and by it communicated at once to all the other contracting Powers.

This denunciation shall only affect the notifying Power.

ARTICLE 96

In the event of one of the contracting *Powers wishing to denounce* the present Convention, *the* denunciation *shall be notified* in writing to the Netherland Government, *which shall* immediately *communicate a duly certified copy of* the notification to all the other Powers *informing them of the date on which it was received.*

The denunciation shall only have effect in regard to the notifying Power, *and one year after the notification has reached the Netherland Government.*

ARTICLE 97

A register kept by the Netherland Minister for Foreign Affairs shall give the date of the deposit of ratifications effected in virtue of Article 92, paragraphs 3 and 4, as well as the date on which the notifications of adhesion (Article 93, paragraph 2) or of denunciation (Article 96, paragraph 1) have been received.
    Each contracting Power is entitled to have access to this register and to be supplied with duly certified extracts from it.

In faith of which the plenipotentiaries have signed the present Convention and affixed their seals to it.

In faith whereof the plenipotentiaries have *appended their signatures to* the present Convention.

1899

Fait à La Haye, le vingt neuf juillet, mille huit cents quatre vingt dix-neuf, en un seul exemplaire qui restera déposé dans les archives du Gouvernement des Pays-Bas, et dont des copies, certifiées conformes, seront remises par la voie diplomatique aux Puissances contractantes.

1907

Fait à La Haye, *le dix-huit octobre mil neuf cent sept,* en un seul exemplaire qui restera déposé dans les archives du Gouvernement des Pays-Bas et dont des copies certifiées conformes, seront remises par la voie diplomatique aux Puissances contractantes.

1899

Done at The Hague, the 29th July, 1899, in a single copy, which shall remain in the archives of the Netherland Government, and copies of it, duly certified, be sent through the diplomatic channel to the contracting Powers.

[Here follow signatures.]

1907

Done at The Hague, the *18th October, 1907,* in a single copy, which shall remain deposited in the archives of the Netherland Government, and duly certified copies of which shall be sent, through the diplomatic channel, to the contracting Powers.

[Here follow signatures.]

RATIFICATIONS, ADHESIONS AND RESERVATIONS

The 1899 Convention was *ratified* by all the signatory Powers on the dates indicated:

Austria-Hungary ....September 4, 1900
Belgium ....September 4, 1900
Bulgaria ....September 4, 1900
China ....November 21, 1904
Denmark ....September 4, 1900
France ....September 4, 1900
Germany ....September 4, 1900
Great Britain ....September 4, 1900
Greece ....April 4, 1901
Italy ....September 4, 1900
Japan ....October 6, 1900
Luxemburg ....July 12, 1901
Mexico ....April 17, 1901
Montenegro ....October 16, 1900
Netherlands ....September 4, 1900
Norway.................................(See Sweden and Norway.)
Persia ....September 4, 1900
Portugal ....September 4, 1900
Roumania ....September 4, 1900
Russia ....September 4, 1900
Serbia ....May 11, 1901
Siam ....September 4, 1900
Spain ....September 4, 1900
Sweden and Norway ....September 4, 1900
Switzerland ....December 29, 1900
Turkey ....June 12, 1907
United States ....September 4, 1900

Adhesions:

Argentine Republic ....June 15, 1907
Bolivia ....June 15, 1907
Brazil ....June 15, 1907
Chile ....June 15, 1907
Colombia ....June 15, 1907
Cuba ....June 15, 1907
Dominican Republic ....June 15, 1907
Ecuador ....July 3, 1907
Guatemala ....June 15, 1907
Haiti ....June 15, 1907
Nicaragua ....June 15, 1907
Panama ....June 15, 1907
Paraguay ....June 15, 1907
Peru ....June 15, 1907
Salvador ....June 20, 1907
Uruguay ....June 17, 1907
Venezuela ....June 15, 1907

Reservations:[1]

Roumania

Under the reservations formulated with respect to Articles 16, 17 and 19 of the present Convention (15, 16 and 18 of the project presented by the committee on examination), and recorded in the *procès-verbal* of the sitting of the Third Commission of July 20, 1899.[2]

Extract from the procès-verbal:
The Royal Government of Roumania being completely in favor of the principle of *facultative* arbitration, of which it appreciates the great importance in international relations, nevertheless does not intend to undertake, by Article 15, an engagement to accept arbitration in every case there provided for, and it believes it ought to form express reservations in that respect.

It can not therefore vote for this article, except under that reservation.

The Royal Government of Roumania declares that it can not adhere to Article 16 except with the express reservation, entered in the *procès-verbal,* that it has decided not to accept, in any case, an international arbitration for disagreements or disputes previous to the conclusion of the present Convention.

The Royal Government of Roumania declares that in adhering to Article 18 of the Convention, it makes no engagement in regard to obligatory arbitration.[3]

Serbia

Under the reservations recorded in the *procès-verbal* of the Third Commission of July 20, 1899.[3]

Extract from the procès-verbal:
In the name of the Royal Government of Serbia, we have the honor to declare that our adoption of the principle of good offices and mediation does not imply a recognition of the right of third States to use these means except with the extreme reserve which proceedings of this delicate nature require.

We do not admit good offices and mediation except on condition that their character of purely friendly counsel is maintained fully and completely, and we never could accept them in forms and circumstances such as to impress upon them the character of intervention.[4]

Turkey

Under reservation of the declaration made in the plenary sitting of the Conference of July 25, 1899.

Extract from the procès-verbal:
The Turkish delegation, considering that the work of this Conference has been a work of high loyalty and humanity, destined solely to assure general peace by safeguarding the interests and the rights of each one, declares, in the name of its Government, that it adheres to the project just adopted, on the following conditions:

---

[1] All these reservations were made at signature.
[2] Reservations maintained at ratification.
[3] Declaration of Mr. Beldiman. *Procès-verbaux*, pt. iv, pp. 48, 49.
[4] Declaration of Mr. Miyatovitch, *Ibid.*, p. 47.

1. It is formally understood that recourse to good offices and mediation, to commissions of inquiry and arbitration is purely facultative and could not in any case assume an obligatory character or degenerate into interventions;
2. The Imperial Government itself will be the judge of the cases where its interests would permit it to admit these methods without its abstention or refusal to have recourse to them being considered by the signatory States as an unfriendly act.
It goes without saying that in no case could the means in question be applied to questions concerning interior regulation.[1]

United States
Under reservation of the declaration made at the plenary sitting of the Conference on the 25th of July, 1899.[2]
Extract from the procès-verbal:
The delegation of the United States of America on signing the Convention for the pacific settlement of international disputes, as proposed by the International Peace Conference, makes the following declaration:
Nothing contained in this Convention shall be so construed as to require the United States of America to depart from its traditional policy of not intruding upon, interfering with, or entangling itself in the political questions or policy or internal administration of any foreign State; nor shall anything contained in the said Convention be construed to imply a relinquishment by the United States of America of its traditional attitude toward purely American questions.[3]

The 1907 Convention was *ratified* by the following signatory Powers on the dates indicated:

Austria-Hungary ....November 27, 1909
Belgium ....August 8, 1910
Bolivia ....November 27, 1909
Brazil ....January 5, 1914
China ....November 27, 1909
Cuba ....February 22, 1912
Denmark ....November 27, 1909
France ....October 7, 1910
Germany ....November 27, 1909
Guatemala ....March 15, 1911
Haiti ....February 2, 1910
Japan ....December 13, 1911
Luxemburg ....September 5, 1912
Mexico ....November 27, 1909
Netherlands ....November 27, 1909
Norway ....September 19, 1910
Panama ....September 11, 1911

---

[1] Declaration of Turkhan Pasha. *Procès-verbaux*, pt. i, p. 70. This reservation does not appear in the instrument of ratification.
[2] Reservation maintained at ratification.
[3] *Ibid.*, p. 69. Compare the reservation of the United States to the 1907 Convention.

Portugal ....April 13, 1911
Roumania ....March 1, 1912
Russia ....November 27, 1909
Salvador ....November 27, 1909
Siam ....March 12, 1910
Spain ....March 18, 1913
Sweden ....November 27, 1909
Switzerland ....May 12, 1910
United States ....November 27, 1909

Adhesion:

Nicaragua ....December 16, 1909

The following Powers signed the Convention but have not yet ratified :

Argentine Republic	Montenegro
Bulgaria	Paraguay
Chile	Persia
Colombia	Peru
Dominican Republic	Serbia
Ecuador	Turkey
Great Britain	Uruguay
Greece	Venezuela
Italy	

Reservations:[1]

Brazil
　　With reservation as to Article 53, paragraphs 2, 3, and 4.[2]

Chile
　　Under reservation of the declaration formulated with regard to Article 39 in the seventh meeting of the First Commission on October 7.

　　　Extract from the procès-verbal:
　　　　The delegation of Chile desires to make the following declaration in the name of its Government with respect to this article. Our delegation at the time of signing the Convention of 1899 for the pacific settlement of international disputes did so with the reservation that the adhesion of its Government as regards Article 17 would not include controversies or questions prior to the celebration of the Convention.
　　　　The delegation of Chile believes it to be its duty to-day to renew, with respect to the same provision, the reservation that it has previously made, although it may not be strictly necessary in view of the similar character of the provision.[3]

---

[1] All these reservations were made at signature except the second reservation of the United States.
[2] Reservation maintained at ratification.
[3] Statement of Mr. Domingo Gana. *Actes et documents*, vol. ii, p. 121.

Greece
>With the reservation of paragraph 2 of Article 53.

Japan
>With reservation of paragraphs 3 and 4 of Article 48, of paragraph 2 of Article 53 and of Article 54.[1]

Roumania
>With the same reservations formulated by the Roumanian plenipotentiaries on signing the Convention for the pacific settlement of international disputes of July 29, 1899.[1]

Switzerland
>Under reservation of Article 53, number 2.[1]

Turkey
>Under reservation of the declarations recorded in the *procès-verbal* of the ninth plenary session of the Conference held on October 16, 1907.
>
>>*Extract from the procès-verbal:*
>>The Ottoman delegation declares, in the name of its Government, that while it is not unmindful of the beneficent influence which good offices, mediation, commissions of inquiry and arbitration are able to exercise on the maintenance of the pacific relations between States, in giving its adhesion to the whole of the draft, it does so on the understanding that such methods remain, as before, purely optional; it could in no case recognize them as having an obligatory character rendering them susceptible of leading directly or indirectly to an intervention.
>>The Imperial Government proposes to remain the sole judge of the occasions when it shall be necessary to have recourse to the different proceedings or to accept them without its determination on the point being liable to be viewed by the signatory States as an unfriendly act.
>>It is unnecessary to add that such methods should never be applied in cases of internal order.[2]

United States
>Under reservation of the declaration made in the plenary session of the Conference held on October 16, 1907.[1]
>
>>*Extract from the procès-verbal:*
>>The delegation of the United States renews the reservation made in 1899 on the subject of Article 48 of the Convention for the pacific settlement of international disputes in the form of the following declaration:
>>Nothing contained in this Convention shall be so construed as to require the United States of America to depart from its traditional policy of not intruding upon, interfering with, or entangling itself in the political questions of policy or internal administration of any foreign State; nor shall anything contained in the said Convention be construed to imply a relinquishment by the United States of America of its traditional attitude toward purely American questions.[3]

---

[1] Reservation maintained at ratification.
[2] Statements of Turkhan Pasha. *Actes et documents,* vol. i. p. 336.
[3] Statement of Mr. David Jayne Hill. *Ibid.,* vol. i, p. 335.

The act of ratification contains the following reservation:

That the United States approves this Convention with the understanding that recourse to the Permanent Court for the settlement of differences can be had only by agreement thereto through general or special treaties of arbitration heretofore or hereafter concluded between the parties in dispute; and the United States now exercises the option contained in Article 53 of said Convention, to exclude the formulation of the *compromis* by the Permanent Court, and hereby excludes from the competence of the Permanent Court the power to frame the *compromis* required by general or special treaties of arbitration concluded or hereafter to be concluded by the United States, and further expressly declares that the *compromis* required by any treaty of arbitration to which the United States may be a party shall be settled only by agreement between the contracting parties, unless such treaty shall expressly provide otherwise.

LIST OF AUTHORITIES

OFFICIAL PUBLICATIONS OF THE
INTERNATIONAL BUREAU OF THE PERMANENT COURT OF ARBITRATION

Canevaro Case: *Protocoles des Séances et Sentence du Tribunal d'arbitrage constitué en exécution du Compromis signé entre l'Italie et le Pérou le 20 avril 1910. Différend au sujet de la réclamation des Frères Canevaro.* The Hague, Van Langenhuysen Brothers, 1912.

Carthage and *Manouba* Cases: *Compromis, Protocoles des Séances et Sentences du Tribunal d'arbitrage Franco-Italien. I. Affaire du "Carthage." II. Affaire du "Manouba."* The Hague, Van Langenhuysen Brothers, 1913.

Casablanca Case: *Protocoles des Séances du Tribunal arbitral, constitué en exécution du Protocole signé à Berlin le 10 novembre 1908 et du Compromis du 24 novembre 1908.*

Grisbadarna Case: *Recueil des Comptes rendus de la visite des lieux et des Protocoles des Séances du Tribunal arbitral, constitué en vertu de la Convention du 14 mars 1908, pour juger la question de la délimitation d'une certaine partie de la frontière maritime entre la Norvège et la Suède.* The Hague, Van Langenhuysen Brothers, 1909.

Island of Timor Case: *Sentence arbitrale rendue en exécution du Compromis signé à La Haye le 3 avril 1913 entre les Pays-Bas et le Portugal au sujet de la délimitation d'une partie de leurs possessions dans l'Ile de Timor.* Neuchâtel, Attinger Brothers, 1914.

Japanese House Tax Case: *Recueil des Actes et Protocoles concernant le Litige entre l'Allemagne, la France et la Grande Bretagne d'une part et le Japon d'autre part. Tribunal d'arbitrage constitué en vertu de Protocoles signés à Tokyo le 28 août 1902 entre les Puissances susmentionnées.* The Hague, Van Langenhuysen Brothers, 1905.

Manouba Case: See *Carthage* and *Manouba* Cases.

Muscat Dhows Case: *Recueil des Actes et Protocoles concernant le Différend entre la France et la Grande Bretagne à propos des boutres de Mascate, soumis au Tribunal d'arbitrage constitué en vertu du Compromis arbitral conclu à Londres le 13 octobre 1904 entre les Puissances susmentionnées.* The Hague, Van Langenhuysen Brothers, 1905.

North Atlantic Coast Fisheries Case: *North Atlantic Coast Fisheries Tribunal of Arbitration constituted under a Special Agreement signed at Washington, January 27, 1909, between the United States of America and Great Britain.* The Hague, Van Langenhuysen Brothers, 1910.

Orinoco Steamship Company Case: *Protocoles des Séances du Tribunal d'arbitrage constitué en exécution du Compromis signé entre les Etats-Unis d'Amérique et les Etats-Unis du Vénézuela le 13 février 1909. Différend au sujet d'une réclamation de la Compagnie des bateaux à vapeur "Orinoco."* The Hague, Van Langenhuysen Brothers, 1910.

Pious Fund Case: *Recueil des Actes et Protocoles concernant le Litige du "Fonds Pieux des Californies" soumis au Tribunal d'arbitrage constitué en vertu du Traité conclu à Washington le 22 mai 1902 entre les Etats-Unis d'Amérique et les Etats-Unis Mexicains.* The Hague, Van Langenhuysen Brothers, 1902.

Rapport du Conseil Administratif de la Cour Permanente d'Arbitrage sur les travaux de la Cour, sur le fonctionnement des services administratifs et sur les depénses pendant l'année 1914. The Hague, Van Langenhuysen Brothers.

Russian Indemnity Case: *Protocoles des Séances et Sentence du Tribunal d'arbitrage constitué en vertu du Compromis d'arbitrage signé à Constantinople entre la Russie et la Turquie le 22 juillet/4 août 1910. Litige Russo-Turc relatif aux dommages-intérêts réclamés par la Russie pour le retard apporté dans le payement des indemnités dues aux particuliers russes lésés par la guerre de 1877–1878.* The Hague, Van Langenhuysen Brothers, 1912.

Savarkar Case: *Protocoles des Séances et Sentence du Tribunal d'arbitrage constitué en exécution du Compromis signé entre la France et la Grande-Bretagne le 25 octobre 1910. Différend au sujet de l'arrestation et de la réintégration à bord du paquebot "Morea" le 8 juillet 1910, à Marseille du sujet britannique (British Indian) Savarkar.* The Hague, Van Langenhuysen Brothers, 1911.

Tavignano, Camouna and *Gaulois* Cases: *(1) Commission Internationale d'Enquête constitué à Malte en vertu de la convention d'enquête signée à Rome entre la France et l'Italie, le 20 mai 1912. Incidents du vapeur Français "Tavignano" et des Mahonnes "Camouna" et "Gaulois" arrêtés et visités par les contre-torpilleurs "Fulmine" et "Canopo" de la marine royale Italienne. Documents et procès-verbaux. (2) Affaire de la Capture et de la Saisie momentanée du Vapeur postal français "Tavignano" et des coups de canon tirés sur les Mahonnes tunisiennes "Kamouna" et "Gaulois" par les Forces navales italiennes. Mémoire présenté au nom du Gouvernement de la République français.*

Venezuelan Preferential Case: *Recueil des Actes et Protocoles concernant le Litige entre l'Allemagne, l'Angleterre et l'Italie d'une part et le Vénézuela d'autre part. Tribunal d'arbitrage constitué en vertu des protocoles signés à Washington, le 7 mai 1903 entre les Puissances susmentionnées.* The Hague, Van Langenhuysen Brothers, 1904.

MISCELLANEOUS

American Journal of International Law. New York, Baker, Voorhis and Company.

American State Papers, Foreign Relations. Documents, Legislative and Executive, of the Congress of the United States [1789–1833]. 6 vols.

Annals of the Congress of the United States. First to Eighteenth Congress. 47 vols., Washington, D. C.

Annuaire de l'Institut de droit international, vol. 25, 1912.

Boletín del Ministerio de Relaciones Exteriores (Peru) No. xxxv.

British and Foreign State Papers.

Conférence international de la paix. La Haye, 18 mai–29 juillet 1899. Ministère des affaires etrangères. New ed. The Hague, Martinus Nijhoff, 1907. (Cited *Procès-verbaux.*)

Deuxième conférence international de la paix. La Haye, 15 juin–18 octobre 1907. Actes et documents. Ministère des affaires etrangères. The Hague, National print, 1907. (Cited *Actes et documents.*)

Foreign Relations of the United States. Washington, Government Printing Office.

Hague Conventions and Declarations of 1899 and 1907 accompanied by Tables of Signatures, Ratifications and Adhesions of the Various Powers and Texts of Reservations. Edited by James Brown Scott, New York, Oxford University Press, American Branch, 2d ed., 1915.

Lange, Chr.-L. *Union Interparlementaire. Résolutions des Conférences et Décisions principales du Conseil.* 2d. ed., 1911.

Mémorial Diplomatique, Le. Paris.

Malloy, William M. *Treaties, Conventions, International Acts, Protocols and Agreements between the United States of America and Other Powers, 1776–1909.* 2 vols. Washington, Government Printing Office, 1910.

Martens, G. Fr. de. *Nouveau Recueil Général de Traités et Autres Actes relatives aux Rapports de Droit International.* Leipsic.

Official records of the Imperial German Embassy at Washington, D. C.

Pellew, George. *John Jay.*

Proceedings of Fourth National Conference of the American Society for Judicial Settlement of International Disputes, 1913. Baltimore, Williams and Wilkins Company, 1914.

Report of Jackson H. Ralston, Agent of the United States and of Counsel, in the Matter of the Case of the Pious Fund of the Californias, Heard before a Tribunal of the Permanent Court of Arbitration under the Hague Convention of 1899, Sitting at The Hague, September 15, 1902, to October 14, 1902, with Pleadings, Appendix, Briefs, and Record of the Entire Proceedings. Washington, Government Printing Office, 1902.

Statutes at Large of the United States of America.

Sweden. *Royal Resolution, No. 70, 1904.*

United States and Mexican Claims Commission, Opinions. (MS. Department of State.)

United States and Venezuela Arbitration at The Hague, Appendix to the Case of the United States. 2 vols. Washington, Government Printing Office, 1910.

United States Treaty Series.

Wharton, Francis. *Diplomatic Correspondence of the American Revolution,* Washington, Government Printing Office.

Yale Law Journal, New Haven, Conn.

ARBITRATIONS

BEFORE THE

HAGUE TRIBUNALS

THE PIOUS FUND CASE

between

MEXICO *and* THE UNITED STATES

Decided October 14, 1902

Syllabus

The case on trial was known as the "Pious Fund of the Californias." It originated in donations made by Spanish subjects during the latter part of the seventeenth and the first half of the eighteenth centuries for the spread of the Roman Catholic faith in the Californias. These gifts, amounting approximately to $1,700,000, were made in trust to the Society of Jesus for the execution of the pious wish of the founders. The Jesuits accepted the trust and discharged its duties until they were disabled from its further administration by their expulsion in 1767 from the Spanish dominions by the King of Spain and by the suppression of the order by the Pope in 1773. The Crown of Spain took possession of and administered the trust for the uses declared by the donors until Mexico, after her independence was achieved, succeeded to the administration of the trust. Finally, in 1842, President Santa Anna ordered the properties to be sold, that the proceeds thereof be incorporated into the national treasury, and that six per cent annual interest on the capitalization of the property should be paid and devoted to the carrying out of the intention of the donors in the conversion and civilization of the savages.

Upper California having been ceded to the United States in 1848 by the treaty of Guadalupe Hidalgo, the Mexican Government refused to pay to the prelates of the Church in Upper California any share of the interest which accrued after the ratification of the treaty. The latter presented their claims therefor to the Department of State and requested the interposition of the Government. A mixed commission for the settlement of the cross claims between the two Governments was formed under the Convention of July 4, 1868.[1] On the presentation and hearing of the claim the United States and Mexican commissioners divided in opinion. The case was accordingly referred to the umpire, Sir Edward Thornton, who rendered an award[2] in favor of the United States for twenty-one annuities of $43,050.99 each, as the equitable proportion to which the prelates of Upper California were entitled of the interest accrued on the entire fund from the making of the treaty of peace down to February 2, 1869. The Mexican Government paid the award, but, asserting that the claim was extinguished, refused to make any further payments of interest for the benefit of the Church in Upper California. Again the prelates appealed to the

---

[1]*Post*, p. 12.   [2]*Post*, p. 48.

Department of State for support, and in 1898 active diplomatic discussions between the two Governments as to the merits of the claim
were begun and carried forward until they culminated, on May 22,
1902, in a formal agreement[1] to refer the case to the determination of
the Hague tribunal, to be composed of five members, none of whom
were to be natives or citizens of the contracting Parties. Only two
issues were presented by the protocol, namely: 1. Is the case, as a
consequence of the decision of Sir Edward Thornton, within the governing principle of *res judicata?* 2. If not, is the claim just? The
tribunal was authorized to render whatever judgment might be found
just and equitable.

As judges the United States selected Professor Martens of Russia
and Sir Edward Fry of Great Britain; Mexico chose Dr. Asser and
Jonkheer de Savornin Lohman of Holland; and these judges selected
as president of the tribunal, Dr. Matzen of Denmark. All were members of the Permanent Court of Arbitration. The sessions of the
tribunal began September 15, 1902, and ended October 1, 1902.

The material part of the unanimous award of the tribunal in favor
of the United States, rendered on October 14, 1902, was as follows:

1. That the said claim of the United States of America for the
benefit of the Archbishop of San Francisco and of the Bishop of
Monterey is governed by the principle of *res judicata* by virtue of the
arbitral sentence of Sir Edward Thornton, of November 11, 1875;
amended by him, October 24, 1876.

2. That conformably to this arbitral sentence the Government of
the Republic of the United Mexican States must pay to the Government of the United States of America the sum of $1,420,682.67 Mexi-
can, in money having legal currency in Mexico, within the period
fixed by Article 10 of the protocol of Washington of May 22, 1902.

This sum of $1,420,682.67 will totally extinguish the annuities ac-
crued and not paid by the Government of the Mexican Republic—
that is to say, the annuity of $43,050.99 Mexican from February 2,
1869, to February 2, 1902.

3. The Government of the Republic of the United Mexican States
shall pay to the Government of the United States of America on
February 2, 1903, and each following year on the same date of February 2, perpetually, the annuity of $43,050.99 Mexican, in money
having legal currency in Mexico.[2]

---

[1]*Post*, p. 7.   [2]*Post*, p. 6.

AWARD OF THE TRIBUNAL

Award of the tribunal of arbitration constituted in virtue of the protocol signed at Washington, May 22, 1902, between the United States and Mexico for the adjustment of certain contentions arising under what is known as the "Pious Fund of the Californias."—The Hague, October 14, 1902.[1]

The tribunal of arbitration constituted by virtue of the treaty concluded at Washington, May 22, 1902,[2] between the United States of America and the United Mexican States:

Whereas, by a *compromis* (agreement of arbitration) prepared under the form of protocol between the United States of America and the United Mexican States, signed at Washington, May 22, 1902, it was agreed and determined that the differences which existed between the United States of America and the United Mexican States, relative to the subject of the "Pious Fund of the Californias," the annuities of which were claimed by the United States of America for the benefit of the Archbishop of San Francisco and the Bishop of Monterey, from the Government of the Mexican Republic, should be submitted to a tribunal of arbitration, constituted upon the basis of the Convention for the pacific settlement of international disputes, signed at The Hague, July 29, 1899, which should be composed in the following manner, that is to say:

The President of the United States of America should designate two arbitrators (non-nationals), and the President of the United Mexican States equally two arbitrators (non-nationals); these four arbitrators should meet, September 1, 1902, at The Hague, for the purpose of nominating the umpire, who at the same time should be of right the president of the tribunal of arbitration.

Whereas the President of the United States of America named as arbitrators:

The Right Hon. Sir Edward Fry, LL.D., former member of the Court of Appeals, member of the Privy Council of His Britannic Majesty, member of the Permanent Court of Arbitration; and

His Excellency Mr. de Martens, LL.D., Privy Councilor, member of the Council of the Imperial Ministry of Foreign Affairs of Rus-

[1] *Report of Jackson H. Ralston, Agent of the United States and of Counsel, in the matter of the Case of the Pious Fund of the Californias*, etc., pt. 1, p. 13. For the original French text, see Appendix, p. 429.
[2] *Post*, p. 7.

sia, member of the Institute of France, member of the Permanent Court of Arbitration.

Whereas the President of the United Mexican States named as arbitrators:

Mr. T. M. C. Asser, LL.D., member of the Council of State of the Netherlands, former professor at the University of Amsterdam, member of the Permanent Court of Arbitration; and

Jonkheer A. F. de Savornin Lohman, LL.D., former Minister of the Interior of the Netherlands, former professor at the Free University at Amsterdam, member of the second chamber of the States-General, member of the Permanent Court of Arbitration; which arbitrators at their meeting, September 1, 1902, elected, conformably to Articles 32-34 of the Convention of The Hague of July 29, 1899, as umpire and president of right of the tribunal of arbitration;

Mr. Henning Matzen, LL.D., professor at the University of Copenhagen, Counselor Extraordinary to the Supreme Court, President of the Landsthing, member of the Permanent Court of Arbitration; and

Whereas, by virtue of the protocol of Washington of May 22, 1902, the above-named arbitrators, united in tribunal of arbitration, were required to decide:

1. If the said claim of the United States of America for the benefit of the Archbishop of San Francisco and the Bishop of Monterey was within the governing principle of *res judicata* by virtue of the arbitral sentence of November 11, 1875, pronounced by Sir Edward Thornton, as umpire[1];

2. If not, whether the said claim was just, with power to render such judgment as would seem to them just and equitable.

Whereas, the above-named arbitrators having examined with impartiality and care all the documents and papers presented to the tribunal of arbitration by the agents of the United States of America and of the United Mexican States, and having heard with the greatest attention the oral arguments presented before the tribunal by the agents and the counsel of the two parties in litigation;

---

[1] *Post*, p. 48.

Considering that the litigation submitted to the decision of the tribunal of arbitration consists in a conflict between the United States of America and the United Mexican States which can only be decided upon the basis of international treaties and the principles of international law;

Considering that the international treaties concluded from the year 1848 to the *compromis* of May 22, 1902, between the two Powers in litigation manifest the eminently international character of this conflict;

Considering that all the parts of the judgment or the decree concerning the points debated in the litigation enlighten and mutually supplement each other, and that they all serve to render precise the meaning and the bearing of the *dispositif* (decisory part of the judgment) and to determine the points upon which there is *res judicata* and which thereafter can not be put in question;

Considering that this rule applies not only to the judgments of tribunals created by the State, but equally to arbitral sentences rendered within the limits of the jurisdiction fixed by the *compromis;*

Considering that this same principle should for a still stronger reason be applied to international arbitration;

Considering that the Convention of July 4, 1868,[1] concluded between the two States in litigation, had accorded to the mixed commission named by these States, as well as to the umpire to be eventually designated, the right to pass upon their own jurisdiction;

Considering that in the litigation submitted to the decision of the tribunal of arbitration, by virtue of the *compromis* of May 22, 1902, there is not only identity of parties to the suit, but also identity of subject-matter, compared with the arbitral sentence of Sir Edward Thornton, as umpire, in 1875, and amended by him, October 24, 1876[2];

Considering that the Government of the United Mexican States conscientiously executed the arbitral sentence of 1875 and 1876 by paying the annuities adjudged by the umpire;

Considering that since 1869 thirty-three annuities have not been paid by the Government of the United Mexican States to the Government of the United States of America, and that the rules of prescription, belonging exclusively to the domain of civil law, can

---

[1] *Post,* p. 12.   [2] *Post,* p. 53.

not be applied to the present dispute between the two States in litigation;

Considering, so far as the money is concerned in which the annual payment should take place, that the silver dollar having legal currency in Mexico, payment in gold can not be exacted except by virtue of an express stipulation;

Considering that in the present instance such stipulation not existing, the party defendant has the right to free itself by paying in silver; that with relation to this point the sentence of Sir Edward Thornton has not the force of *res judicata*, except for the twenty-one annuities with regard to which the umpire decided that the payment should take place in Mexican gold dollars, because question of the mode of payment does not relate to the basis of the right in litigation, but only to the execution of the sentence;

Considering that according to Article 10 of the protocol of Washington of May 22, 1902, the present tribunal of arbitration must determine, in case of an award against the Republic of Mexico, in what money payment must take place;

For these reasons the tribunal of arbitration decides and unanimously pronounces as follows:

1. That the said claim of the United States of America for the benefit of the Archbishop of San Francisco and of the Bishop of Monterey is governed by the principle of *res judicata* by virtue of the arbitral sentence of Sir Edward Thornton, of November 11, 1875; amended by him, October 24, 1876.

2. That conformably to this arbitral sentence the Government of the Republic of the United Mexican States must pay to the Government of the United States of America the sum of $1,420,682.67 Mexican, in money having legal currency in Mexico, within the period fixed by Article 10 of the protocol of Washington of May 22, 1902.

This sum of $1,420,682.67 will totally extinguish the annuities accrued and not paid by the Government of the Mexican Republic— that is to say, the annuity of $43,050.99 Mexican from February 2, 1869, to February 2, 1902.

3. The Government of the Republic of the United Mexican States shall pay to the Government of the United States of America on February 2, 1903, and each following year on the same date of

February 2, perpetually, the annuity of $43,050.99 Mexican, in money having legal currency in Mexico.

Done at The Hague in the hotel of the Permanent Court of Arbitration in triplicate original, October 14, 1902.

> HENNING MATZEN
> EDW. FRY
> MARTENS
> T. M. C. ASSER
> A. F. DE SAVORNIN LOHMAN

AGREEMENT FOR ARBITRATION

Protocol of an Agreement between the United States of America and the Republic of Mexico for the adjustment of certain contentions arising under what is known as the "Pious Fund of the Californias."—Signed at Washington, May 22, 1902.[1]

Whereas, under and by virtue of the provisions of a convention entered into between the high contracting Parties above-named, of date July 4, 1868,[2] and subsequent conventions supplementary thereto,[3] there was submitted to the mixed commission provided for by said convention a certain claim advanced by and on behalf of the prelates of the Roman Catholic Church of California against the Republic of Mexico for an annual interest upon a certain fund known as "The Pious Fund of the Californias," which interest was said to have accrued between February 2, 1848, the date of the signature of the treaty of Guadalupe Hidalgo, and February 1, 1869, the date of the exchange of the ratifications of said convention above referred to; and

Whereas, said mixed commission, after considering said claim, the same being designated as No. 493 upon its docket, and entitled Thaddeus Amat, Roman Catholic Bishop of Monterey, a corporation sole, and Joseph S. Alemany, Roman Catholic Bishop of San Francisco, a corporation sole, against the Republic of Mexico, adjudged the same adversely to the Republic of Mexico and in favor of said claimants, and made an award thereon of nine hundred and four thousand, seven hundred and 99/100 (904,700.99) dollars; the same, as expressed in the findings of said court, being for twenty-one years' interest of the

---

[1] *U. S. Statutes at Large*, vol. 32, p. 1916. For the Spanish text, see Appendix, p. 432.

[2] *Post*, p. 12.

[3] Supplementary conventions not printed as they have no bearing on the Pious Fund Case.

annual amount of forty-three thousand and eighty and 99/100 (43,080.99) dollars upon seven hundred and eighteen thousand and sixteen and 50/100 (718,016.50) dollars, said award being in Mexican gold dollars, and the said amount of nine hundred and four thousand, seven hundred and 99/100 (904,700.99) dollars having been fully paid and discharged in accordance with the terms of said conventions; and

Whereas, the United States of America on behalf of said Roman Catholic Bishops, above-named, and their successors in title and interest, have since such award claimed from Mexico further instalments of said interest, and háve insisted that the said claim was conclusively established, and its amount fixed as against Mexico and in favor of said original claimants and their successors in title and interest under the said first-mentioned convention of 1868 by force of the said award as *res judicata;* and have further contended that apart from such former award their claim against Mexico was just, both of which propositions are controverted and denied by the Republic of Mexico, and the high contracting Parties hereto, animated by a strong desire that the dispute so arising may be amicably, satisfactorily and justly settled, have agreed to submit said controversy to the determination of arbitrators, who shall, unless otherwise herein expressed, be controlled by the provisions of the international Convention for the pacific settlement of international disputes, commonly known as the Hague Convention, and which arbitration shall have power to determine:

1. If said claim, as a consequence of the former decision, is within the governing principle of *res judicata;* and

2. If not, whether the same be just.

And to render such judgment or award as may be meet and proper under all the circumstances of the case.

It is therefore agreed by and between the United States of America, through their representative, John Hay, Secretary of State of the United States of America, and the Republic of Mexico, through its representative, Manuel de Azpiroz, Ambassador Extraordinary and Plenipotentiary to the United States of America for the Republic of Mexico as follows:

1

That the said contentions be referred to the special tribunal hereinafter provided, for examination, determination and award.

2

The special tribunal hereby constituted shall consist of four arbitrators (two to be named by each of the high contracting Parties) and an umpire to be selected in accordance with the provisions of the Hague Convention. The arbitrators to be named hereunder shall be signified by each of the high contracting Parties to the other within sixty days after the date of this protocol. None of those so named shall be a native or citizen of the parties hereto. Judgment may be rendered by a majority of said court.

All vacancies occurring among the members of said court because of death, retirement or disability from any cause before a decision shall be reached, shall be filled in accordance with the method of appointment of the member affected as provided by said Hague Convention, and if occurring after said court shall have first assembled, will authorize in the judgment of the court an extension of time for hearing or judgment, as the case may be, not exceeding thirty days.

3

All pleadings, testimony, proofs, arguments of counsel and findings or awards of commissioners or umpire, filed before or arrived at by the mixed commission above referred to, are to be placed in evidence before the court hereinbefore provided for, together with all correspondence between the two countries relating to the subject-matter involved in this arbitration; originals or copies thereof duly certified by the Departments of State of the high contracting Parties being presented to said new tribunal. Where printed books are referred to in evidence by either party, the party offering the same shall specify volume, edition and page of the portion desired to be read, and shall furnish the court in print the extracts relied upon; their accuracy being attested by affidavit. If the original work is not already on file as a portion of the record of the former mixed commission, the book itself shall be placed at the disposal of the opposite party in the respective offices of the Secretary of State or of the Mexican Ambassador in Washington, as the case may be, thirty days before the meeting of the tribunal herein provided for.

4

Either party may demand from the other the discovery of any fact or of any document deemed to be or to contain material evidence for the party asking it; the document desired to be described with sufficient accuracy for identification, and the demanded discovery shall be made by delivering a statement of the fact or by depositing a copy of such document (certified by its lawful custodian, if it be a public document, and verified as such by the possessor, if a private one), and the opposite party shall be given the opportunity to examine the original in the City of Washington at the Department of State, or at the office of the Mexican Ambassador, as the case may be. If notice of the desired discovery be given too late to be answered ten days before the tribunal herein provided for shall sit for hearing, then the answer desired thereto shall be filed with or documents produced before the court herein provided for as speedily as possible.

5

Any oral testimony additional to that in the record of the former arbitration may be taken by either party before any judge, or clerk of court of record, or any notary public, in the manner and with the precautions and conditions prescribed for that purpose in the rules of the joint commission of the United States of America, and the Republic of Mexico, as ordered and adopted by that tribunal August 10, 1869, and so far as the same may be applicable. The testimony when reduced to writing, signed by the witness, and authenticated by the officer before whom the same is taken, shall be sealed up, addressed to the court constituted hereby, and deposited so sealed up in the Department of State of the United States, or in the Department of Foreign Relations of Mexico to be delivered to the court herein provided for when the same shall convene.

6

Within sixty days from the date hereof the United States of America, through their agent or counsel, shall prepare and furnish to the Department of State aforesaid, a memorial in print of the origin and amount of their claim, accompanied by references to printed books, and to such portions of the proofs or parts of the record of the former arbitration, as they rely on in support of their claim, delivering copies of the same to the Embassy of the Republic of Mexico in Washington, for the use of the agent or counsel of Mexico.

7

Within forty days after the delivery thereof to the Mexican Embassy the agent or counsel for the Republic of Mexico shall deliver to the Department of State of the United States of America in the same manner and with like references a statement of its allegations and grounds of opposition to said claim.

8

The provisions of paragraphs 6 and 7 shall not operate to prevent the agents or counsel for the parties hereto from relying at the hearing or submission upon any documentary or other evidence which may have become open to their investigation and examination at a period subsequent to the times provided for service of memorial and answer.

9

The first meeting of the arbitral court hereinbefore provided for shall take place for the selection of an umpire on September 1, 1902, at The Hague in the quarters which may be provided for such purpose by the International Bureau at The Hague, constituted by virtue of the Hague Convention hereinbefore referred to, and for the commencement of its hearings September 15, 1902, is designated, or, if an umpire may not be selected by said date, then as soon as possible thereafter, and not later than October 15, 1902, at which time and place and at such other times as the court may set (and at Brussels if the court should determine not to sit at The Hague) explanations and arguments shall be heard or presented as the court may determine, and the cause be submitted. The submission of all arguments, statements of facts, and documents shall be concluded within thirty days after the time provided for the meeting of the court for hearing (unless the court shall order an extension of not to exceed thirty days) and its decision and award announced within thirty days after such conclusion, and certified copies thereof delivered to the agents or counsel of the respective parties and forwarded to the Secretary of State of the United States and the Mexican Ambassador at Washington, as well as filed with the Netherland Minister for Foreign Affairs.

10

Should the decision and award of the tribunal be against the Republic of Mexico, the findings shall state the amount and in what currency the same shall be payable, and shall be for such amount as under the contentions and evidence may be just. Such final award, if any, shall be paid to the Secretary of State of the United States of America within eight months from the date of its making.

11

The agents and counsel for the respective parties may stipulate for the admission of any facts, and such stipulation, duly signed, shall be accepted as proof thereof.

12

Each of the parties hereto shall pay its own expenses, and one-half of the expenses of the arbitration, including the pay of the arbitrators; but such costs shall not constitute any part of the judgment.

13

Revision shall be permitted as provided in Article 55 of the Hague Convention, demand for revision being made within eight days after announcement of the award. Proofs upon such demand shall be submitted within ten days after revision be allowed (revision only being granted, if at all, within five days after demand therefor) and counter-proofs within the following ten days, unless further time be granted by the court. Arguments shall be submitted within ten days after the presentation of all proofs, and a judgment or award given within ten days thereafter. All provisions applicable to the original judgment or award shall apply as far as possible to the judgment or award on revision. Provided, that all proceedings on revision shall be in the French language.

14

The award ultimately given hereunder shall be final and conclusive as to the matters presented for consideration.

Done in duplicate in English and Spanish at Washington, this 22d day of May, A. D. 1902.

JOHN HAY   [SEAL]
M. DE AZPIROZ [SEAL]

ADDITIONAL DOCUMENTS

Convention between the United States of America and the Republic of Mexico for the Adjustment of Claims.—Concluded July 4, 1868.[1]

Whereas it is desirable to maintain and increase the friendly feelings between the United States and the Mexican Republic, and so to

---

[1] *U. S. Statutes at Large*, vol. 15, p. 679.

strengthen the system and principles of Republican Government on the American Continent; and whereas since the signature of the Treaty of Guadalupe Hidalgo of the 2d of February, 1848, claims and complaints have been made by citizens of the United States, on account of injuries to their persons and their property by authorities of that Republic, and similar claims and complaints have been made on account of injuries to the persons and property of Mexican citizens by authorities of the United States, the President of the United States of America and the President of the Mexican Republic have resolved to conclude a Convention for the adjustment of the said claims and complaints and have named as their plenipotentiaries:

The President of the United States, William H. Seward, Secretary of State;

And the President of the Mexican Republic, Matias Romero, accredited as Envoy Extraordinary and Minister Plenipotentiary of the Mexican Republic to the United States; who, after having communicated to each other their respective full powers, found in good and due form, have agreed to the following articles:

ARTICLE 1

All claims on the part of corporations, companies or private individuals, citizens of the United States, upon the government of the Mexican Republic, arising from injuries to their persons or property by authorities of the Mexican Republic, and all claims on the part of corporations, companies or private individuals, citizens of the Mexican Republic, upon the government of the United States, arising from injuries to their persons or property by authorities of the United States, which may have been presented to either government for its interposition with the other since the signature of the Treaty of Guadalupe Hidalgo between the United States and the Mexican Republic of the 2d of February, 1848, and which yet remain unsettled, as well as any other such claims which may be presented within the time hereinafter specified, shall be referred to two commissioners, one to be appointed by the President of the United States by and with the advice and consent of the Senate, and one by the President of the Mexican Republic. In case of the death, absence or incapacity of either commissioner, or in the event of either commissioner omitting or ceasing to act as such, the President of the United States or the President of the Mexican Republic respectively shall forthwith name another person to act as commissioner in the place or stead of the commissioner originally named.

The commissioners so named, shall meet at Washington within six months after the exchange of the ratifications of this Convention, and shall, before proceeding to business, make and subscribe a solemn declaration that they will impartially and carefully examine and decide, to the best of their judgment, and according to public law, justice and equity, without fear, favor or affection to their own country, upon all such claims above specified as shall be laid before them on the part of the Governments of the United States and of the Mexican Republic respectively; and such declaration shall be entered on the record of their proceedings.

The commissioners shall then name some third person to act as an umpire in any case or cases on which they may themselves differ in opinion. If they should not be able to agree upon the name of such third person, they shall each name a person, and in each and every case in which the commissioners may differ in opinion as to the decision which they ought to give, it shall be determined by lot which of the two persons so named shall be umpire in that particular case. The person or persons so to be chosen to be umpire shall, before proceeding to act as such in any case, make and subscribe a solemn declaration in a form similar to that which shall already have been made and subscribed by the commissioners, which shall be entered on the record of their proceedings. In the event of the death, absence, or incapacity of such person or persons, or of his or their omitting, or declining, or ceasing to act as such umpire, another and different person shall be named, as aforesaid, to act as such umpire, in the place of the person so originally named, as aforesaid, and shall make and subscribe such declaration, as aforesaid.

ARTICLE 2

The commissioners shall then conjointly proceed to the investigation and decision of the claims which shall be presented to their notice, in such order and in such manner as they may conjointly think proper, but upon such evidence or information only as shall be furnished by or on behalf of their respective governments. They shall be bound to receive and peruse all written documents or statements which may be presented to them by or on behalf of their respective governments in support of or in answer to any claim, and to hear, if required, one person on each side on behalf of each government on each and every separate claim. Should they fail to agree in opinion upon any individual claim, they shall call to their assistance the umpire whom they may have agreed to name, or who may be determined by lot, as the case may be; and such umpire, after having examined the evidence adduced for and against the claim, and after having heard, if required, one person on each side as aforesaid, and consulted with the commissioners, shall decide thereupon finally and without appeal. The decision of the commissioners and of the umpire shall be given upon each claim in writing, shall designate whether any sum which may be allowed shall be payable in gold or in the currency of the United States, and shall be signed by them respectively. It shall be competent for each government to name one person to attend the commissioners as agent on its behalf, to present and support claims on its behalf, and to answer claims made upon it, and to represent it generally in all matters connected with the investigation and decision thereof.

The President of the United States of America and the President of the Mexican Republic hereby solemnly and sincerely engage to consider the decision of the commissioners conjointly or of the umpire, as the case may be, as absolutely final and conclusive upon each claim decided upon by them or him respectively, and to give full effect to such decisions without any objection, evasion, or delay whatsoever.

It is agreed that no claim arising out of a transaction of a date prior to the 2d of February, 1848, shall be admissible under this convention.

ARTICLE 3

Every claim shall be presented to the commissioners within eight months from the day of their first meeting, unless in any case where reasons for delay shall be established to the satisfaction of the commissioners, or of the umpire in the event of the commissioners differing in opinion thereupon, and then and in any such case the period for presenting the claim may be extended to any time not exceeding three months longer.

The commissioners shall be bound to examine and decide upon every claim within two years and six months from the day of their first meeting. It shall be competent for the commissioners conjointly, or for the umpire if they differ, to decide in each case whether any claim has or has not been duly made, preferred and laid before them, either wholly or to any and what extent, according to the true intent and meaning of this Convention.

ARTICLE 4

When decisions shall have been made by the commissioners and the arbiter in every case which shall have been laid before them, the total amount awarded in all the cases decided in favor of the citizens of the one party shall be deducted from the total amount awarded to the citizens of the other party, and the balance, to the amount of three hundred thousand dollars, shall be paid at the city of Mexico or at the city of Washington. in gold or its equivalent, within twelve months from the close of the commission, to the government in favor of whose citizens the greater amount may have been awarded, without interest or any other deduction than that specified in Article 6 of this Convention. The residue of the said balance shall be paid in annual installments to an amount not exceeding three hundred thousand dollars, in gold or its equivalent, in any one year until the whole shall have been paid.

ARTICLE 5

The high contracting Parties agree to consider the result of the proceedings of this commission as a full, perfect, and final settlement of every claim upon either government arising out of any transaction of a date prior to the exchange of the ratifications of the present Convention; and further engage that every such claim, whether or not the same may have been presented to the notice of, made, preferred, or laid before the said commission, shall, from and after the conclusion of the proceedings of the said commission, be considered and treated as finally settled, barred, and thenceforth inadmissible.

ARTICLE 6

The commissioners and the umpire shall keep an accurate record and correct minutes of their proceedings, with the dates. For that purpose they shall appoint two secretaries versed in the language of both countries to assist them in the transaction of the business of the commission. Each government shall pay to its commissioner an amount of salary not exceeding forty-five hundred dollars a year in the currency of the United States, which amount shall be the same for both governments. The amount of compensation to be paid to the umpire shall be determined by mutual consent at the close of the commission, but necessary and reasonable advances may be made by each government upon the joint recommendation of the commission. The salary of the secretaries shall not exceed the sum of twenty-five hundred dollars a year in the currency of the United States. The whole expenses of the commission, including contingent expenses, shall be defrayed by a ratable deduction on the amount of the sums awarded by the commission, provided always, that such deduction shall not exceed five per cent on the sums so awarded. The deficiency, if any, shall be defrayed in moieties by the two governments.

ARTICLE 7

The present Convention shall be ratified by the President of the United States, by and with the advice and consent of the Senate thereof, and by the President of the Mexican Republic with the approbation of the Congress of that Republic, and the ratifications shall be exchanged at Washington within nine months from the date hereof, or sooner if possible.

In witness whereof the respective plenipotentiaries have signed the same and have affixed thereto the seals of their arms.

Done at Washington, the fourth day of July, in the year of our Lord one thousand eight hundred and sixty-eight.

WILLIAM H. SEWARD [L. S.]

M. ROMERO   [L. S.]

Opinion of Mr. Wadsworth, in the original Pious Fund Case before the United States and Mexican Claims Commission of 1868.[1]

The commissioners having differed in opinion in this case, Mr. Commissioner Wadsworth delivered the following opinion:

The "Pious Fund of the Californias," was founded by a private charity, in aid of Christian missions in the Californias, Lower and Upper, for the purpose of spreading amongst their savage inhabitants the gospel according to the tenets of the Roman Catholic Church. The objects sought and pointed out by the founders, were exclusively charitable and religious, and not political.

They devoted their gifts to the conversion of the heathen in those territories for the glory of God, as they supposed, and not for the aggrandizement of the State. The latter was to be incidentally benefited by these missionary labors, but this, certainly, did not enter into the thoughts of the zealous men and women who disinherited their own heirs, for the sake of the savages of the Californias.

The fund never did, and does not now belong to the State, and the latter, be it said to its credit, never at any time claimed it, or avowed a purpose to divert it from the direction given it by its founders.

---

[1] *United States and Mexican Claims Commission, Opinions* (MS. Dep't of State), vol. v, p. 84.

Plainly enough, in the beginning, it was to be devoted in aid of a Roman Catholic Missionary Church in the Californias, under the exclusive control of the Jesuit fathers, for the spread of the Catholic faith amongst the inhabitants of these lands. Accordingly, the fund was continuously controlled and administered by the Jesuits, as its appointed trustees, until their expulsion from New Spain. When this took place, there was no longer any trustee to administer the fund. But equity never suffers a trust to fail for the want of a trustee, and under these circumstances, the sovereign, who by one of those useful fictions is held to be a fountain of justice and a sort of inner sanctuary of equity, took the place of the trustees whom he had extinguished, until he again provided for the more appropriate administration of the fund by the hands of the head of the Missionary Church of the Californias, who was at once president of the mission and Bishop of the Diocese, and when finally, the Mexican Government again took possession of the fund, under the decree of October 24, 1842, it took and held it as a trustee, as the decree of February 8, 1842, declared, "to fulfil the purpose proposed by the donor in the civilization and conversion of the savages," of the Californias. And the decree of October 24, 1842, declared that the action of the Government in resuming the administration was "intended to fulfil most faithfully the objects designed by the founders." This act calls it the "Pious Fund of the Californias," and with no propriety can it be called in any sense a political fund, unless it is intended thereby to affirm that the State at the time considered the spread of the Christian religion, under the direction of the Church, a national or political affair.

I think it therefore plain that by the decree of October 1842, the fund was still to be devoted to the aid of the missionary labors of the same Church in the Californias, and that its annual income was to be expended by that Church for missionary purposes in the Californias; that is, for the conversion of the heathen. This is what the decrees of the Government mean, if we are to give them any reading consistent with honesty and good faith; and we are not at liberty to give them any other. The State then became a mere trustee of funds, provided by private charity, to be expended for missionary purposes in a particular field of labor, under the direction of a particular religious organization: it should punctually pay the annual income to this religious organization, to be expended in the work of converting the heathen of the two Californias, for I think it is evident that the Californias are still full of heathen, and that the number has increased on the whole, since in addition to the autochthones and the Europeans dwelling there, Asia has contributed the "Heathen Chinese."

If a private individual held the fund the courts would compel him to pay the interest to the Church, which, although its missions have been abolished as organized by its priests, the Jesuits, still labors in that missionary field for the conversion of the savages. Nothing else can be done with the fund to carry out the object of the founders, and this is so near, and indeed so nearly identical with the ancient charity, that it is not necessary to frame a scheme for its administration.

The question then is how shall the income of the fund be apportioned between the two Californias, and what does it amount to in the aggregate,

It is claimed in the argument of the agent of Mexico, indeed, that the Upper California lost all interest in the fund by reason of the cession to the United States of that territory, but I can not perceive how this fact can change the direction given to the fund by the founders. If both the Californias had been ceded to the United States, would the beneficiaries have lost all interest in the fund provided by private zeal for their conversion? This was not claimed when *Spain* lost the Californias, or when the Philippine Islands claimed a share in the fund, and I do not see how it can affect the fund at all. The cession did not affect civil rights, or the interests of private property. Whether the estate was legal or equitable, an inhabitant of Upper California, having an estate or interest in property situated in Mexico, or a fund located there, had the same estate or interest after cession as before. It is also an error to hold that the cession dissolved corporations before created by the laws of the territory, whether these were sole or aggregate, public or private, lay or ecclesiastical.

I am clearly of opinion, that whatever right or interest in the fund pertained to the Church in Upper California in aid of its missionary work before, remained to it after the cession, unaffected and unimpaired.

The Californias were entitled to the benefits of the whole fund to be expended by the Church laboring in that field, first under the Jesuits and after their expulsion, under such other priests or officers of the same faith as the Church might authorize, and the State tolerate.

When it becomes necessary to divide the income, and to set apart the proportion to be expended in each of the Californias, how shall this income be divided? In my opinion it must be *divided;* that is, each of the Californias, must take a moiety. I do not know how else to apportion it, and do not see any fact calling for a different division. If we look at the population of each territory at the time of the cession, we discover no great disparity. Besides, I do not conceive that because a charitable fund is to be devoted to missionary work in two districts of country, that this gives an interest to each in proportion to population. On the contrary, when it became necessary to divide the bequest made by Doña Juefa Paula de Argüelles to the missions in China and New Spain, the courts divided it equally between the Philippine Islands and New Spain, the population being ignored.

I take the report of Pedro Ramirez, of February 28, 1842, upon the condition of the fund made to Ignacio de Cubas (Exhibit A to the deposition of José Maria de Romo Jesus) as a sufficiently accurate and satisfactory account.

According to this, the Government at that date owed the fund the sum of

		$1,082,078.00
But deduct a bad debt		7,000.00
Leaves in the Treasury balance.............		$1,075.078.00
Individuals owed the fund......$118,739.00		
Bad debts off	46,617.00	
		72,122.00
Rent of the estate of Ibarra.....	$2,000.00	
Rent of Nos. 11 & 12 Tergara St.	2,625.00	
Three estates rented to Señor		
Belauzaran for	12,705.00	
Total rents	$17,330.00	
Equal at six per cent to a capital of........		288,833.00
Total of the fund....................		$1,436,033.00

It will be seen, that I take no account of the Estate of Cienega del Pastor, because it was attached and held by Señor Jauregui for a large debt, and there is no evidence in this record, that the Government ever obtained the property, or derived any benefit from it.

By the decree of October 24, 1842, the public treasury acknowledged an indebtedness to the "Pious Fund of the Californias," of six per cent per annum, on the total proceeds of the sales, and pledged the revenues from the tobacco for the payment of the income. This pledge was never kept, but the revenue from the tobacco was otherwise appropriated by the Government. Nevertheless, there is an acknowledged indebtedness of six per cent on the capital of the fund payable annually. This amounts to the sum of $86,161.98 and the first instalment was due October 24, 1848, for which, according to my views, claimants can have any award here, and the last instalment fell due October 24, 1868, because the next falling due after February, 1869, can not be awarded by this commission.

This gives for twenty-one years, a grand total of $1,809,401.58, one moiety of which belongs to claimants to be used in aid of the missionary labors of the Church in Upper California, for the conversion of the heathen.

The beneficiaries of this moiety of the fund are in Upper California, citizens of the United States by the treaty of cession. They can not receive the benefit of the fund according to the will of the founders, except through the ministry of the Roman Catholic Church in Upper California, empowered by the Church at Rome to preach, convert and baptize the heathen of that land. But as the Roman Catholic ecclesiastical corporations sole and the beneficiaries of the fund are there, and all [are] citizens of the United States by the treaty of cession and the law of the place, and as the United States appears before this commission claiming redress for and on behalf of "the Roman Catholic Church of the State of California and of its clergy, laity and all persons actually or potentially within its fold and entitled to its ministration, and all others beneficially interested in the trust estate," we have before us undoubtedly all persons interested in the fund; and as the award is made to the United States, that Power will be responsible for the proper disbursement of the sum received; and its courts of justice will not ask our leave to settle and adjust the rights of all parties claiming, or to claim the same.

I see therefore no difficulty in the way of awarding to the United States whatever sum may be justly due from the Government of Mexico since the date of the treaty of cession. Certainly justice and equity call loudly on the Mexican Government to pay according to its pledged faith.

The annual income of the "Pious Fund of the Californias," to the Ministers responsible for its faithful disbursement in the Californias, for the conversion of their inhabitants, according to the will of the pious founders. The fund does not belong to the Government of Mexico, not a dollar of it. It is private property sacredly devoted, by the piety of a past age, to Christian charity, and fortified against political spoliation by all the sanctions of religion and all the obligations of good faith.

But the magnitude of the labors of this commission will not allow me time to go into the further discussion of this interesting and important case. I must content myself with the declaration of my purpose to respect the wishes of the pious people of the olden times, with reference to their own property, devoted according to the laws then in force, to objects of their own selection.

It is my decision, that the Government of Mexico pay to that of the United States, in the gold coin of the latter, with interest at the rate of six per cent per annum, from the 24th of October, 1868, to the close of the labors of this commission, for and on behalf of the claimants, the sum of nine hundred and four thousand and seven hundred dollars, and seventy-nine cents ($904,700.79) and $100 for printing and proofs.

Opinion of Mr. Zamacona, in the original Pious Fund Case before the United States and Mexican Claims Commission of 1868.[1]

The commissioners having differed in opinion in this case, Mr. Commissioner Zamacona delivered the following opinion:

The question raised by these claimants has a certain aspect of historical investigation, for it is impossible that persons versed in the history of the conquest of Mexico who know the system and means employed by the Government of Spain to carry that great undertaking to its completion, should be unacquainted with the national and strictly Mexican character of the resources which the Bishops of Upper California claim as if they were an appendage of that province, transmissible by virtue of the treaty by which it was ceded to the United States. At times an incorrect denomination is the cause of transcendental errors. That is the case with the phrase employed to designate the elements with which the Spaniards carried out the conquest of certain territories situated on the northwest of Mexico. With an impropriety, of which the spirit of the epoch is the explanation, those resources were called "The Pious Fund of California" (*el fondo piadoso de California*) and this must have been one of the principal causes of the errors which the present claim involves, and which consists [*sic*] in the claimants, believing that the constituent elements of that fund, so-called, belongs, notwithstanding its national character, its many transformations and its dilution, so to say, in the treasury of Mexico, to the Catholic Church of Upper California.

---

[1]*United States and Mexican Claims Commission, Opinions* (MS. Dep't of State), vol. v, p. 90.

The conquest of that country and of the Peninsula which is still retained by Mexico under the name of Lower California was undertaken by the Spanish Government with the same means by which the extension of its conquest in America was accomplished. The first acts of occupation and possession performed by the delegates of the monarch used to have the form of material acts supported by arms; but at a later time, there irradiated from that nucleus in which the Spanish flag had been planted, expeditions, apparently of a religious character, which were nothing more than a complement of conquest of little cost in money or blood. It passes for a proverb among those who have profitably studied the conquest of New Spain, that the history of that important event can only be found in the chronicles of the convents, and mention is made even of the various religious orders which respectively and successively conquered the provinces of Mexico. To the end of carrying the authority of the Spanish Government to the northwestern end of the country, the same method was applied, with this difference, that a more marked and prominent part was assigned to the priests charged with making the *reduction* (*la reducción*). The use of this term suggests an observation which ought not to be omitted, namely, that the aspect, in a certain way political, of the labors of the missionaries in Mexico is reflected upon even the locutions used to express their work, and that the tendency of this work was not less to conquer souls for the Catholic faith than subjects for the monarchs of Spain.

The Jesuits took this undertaking under their charge in regard to the Californias; their order had acquired a great development in the Spanish Colonies of America and represented not only a great and religious power, but a great monetary power. At a certain time, corporations of that kind, not only in Mexico, but even in Spain, united to the functions of agents of the political power those of institutions of credit, and they were soon to distribute the capital they had accumulated, thanks to their great influence over the consciences, not only in the sphere of industry but in that of Government.

The Government of Spain had little means when the conquest of the Californias was planned. Some attempts had been made in that direction by means of naval expeditions, but without result, and the viceroys of New Spain decided to avail themselves of the opportunity offered them by the Jesuits who were willing to take upon themselves continuation of the work and the raising of the means required by it. The acceptance of this offer is the starting point of the missions of

Lower California and the explanatory key with which their true character can be disclosed.

Here we meet with another term which may mislead such as are only acquainted with what is generally designated with the name of missions, and especially the missions organized in this country by some religious or benevolent societies. Reflecting upon the same history which the claimants give us of the missions of California, it must be recognized that they were institutions of an anomalous and equivocal character, and that in them civil, military and political aspect predominated over the religious. Further on we shall have occasion to demonstrate this; for the moment it suffices to say that the solicitude of the Jesuits and their arrangements calculated to extend the influence and labors of their order to California were all with the Government of Mexico, that they implied the mission of making a conquest for the Spanish metropolis, and that the acts and practical means being required to conform to this point of departure, the said Jesuits presented themselves in Lower California less as apostles than as delegates of the Government, invested with political and military powers and with such prerogatives in the matter of administration and war as were far from complying with the simple character of missionaries.

In furtherance of that arrangement the Jesuits obtained important donations for the enterprise which the Government of the Viceroy had intrusted to them, *and with the consent* of the latter they administered and invested the means thus obtained.

That was the condition of things until the Society of Jesus was expulsed from the Spanish dominions and at a later time extinguished, there being marked, as we shall see further on, during all this initial period of the missions, two circumstances which are very important for the decision of this case.

1st. The military, political and administrative functions performed by the missionaries.

2d. Their dependency on the Spanish Government and of its delegates sent to Mexico and known by the name of viceroys.

The Jesuits once expulsed and extinguished and their temporal concerns occupied, everything relating to the missions of California came into the hands of the Government, not only by virtue of its rights but because the circumstances did not permit to act otherwise.

The Government was the only one who could substitute those priests in the administration of the institutions which had been founded in California and of the means intended for their maintenance. The claimants who, casting a retrospective glance on the acts of the civil power in regard to the missions in question, censure very ancient transactions which neither they nor we are called upon to qualify, do not take notice that independently of the right, the interest of civilization and order required that the Government of Mexico should substitute itself in the place of the extinguished Jesuits in regard to the establishment to which the case refers.

So it happened, and the Colonial Government of Mexico, without contradiction, without claim on the part of the ecclesiastical authority, took entire control of the missions of California, so-called, and put them in charge of other religious orders.

The latter assumed the management of them, and acknowledged by many acts the mandate and the delegation on the part of the civil power. It is to be observed that in the keeping of the missions, after they were founded, the private donations were confounded, although not in equal proportions with the subsidies of the Government, and that the expenses required by them were considered as a burden of the public treasury.

When Mexico conquered her independence things continued on the same footing, and the executive and legislative power of the Republic continued without contradiction to arrange everything relating to the establishment founded in California. The position in which the Government of Mexico was in regard to that power, received even the sanction of some judicial decisions given in cases relative to some of the most important legacies made in favor of the missions. In said decisions not only the interest belonging to the mission was determined, but it was also declared that that interest remained at the disposal of the Government (see document 36, page 6[1]).

The administration of the fund in dispute sustained many changes since the end of the war of independence in Mexico, until the treaty of peace with the United States was concluded in 1848. Religious corporations, officers appointed by the authorities, boards of a lay character also appointed by the Government, and, finally, the Episcopal prelate of the Californias converted into a bishopric, had in succession the administration of said fund, but in all the phases of that administration the supremacy and superior authority of the Government was recognized.

The reference just made to the bishopric established in California in 1836, brings to the memory of the undersigned a circumstance very

---

[1] Not printed.

important for the decision of this case. As will be seen further on, since the conquest of the Californias was undertaken, when the fund of the missions was consolidated, when its administration was, in some cases, modified, when the bishopric was erected, and especially when the latter occurrence took place, it was given to understand by the missionaries, by the donors, by the Government, and even by the Bishop, when he made some complaints in regard to the Pious Fund, that the missions, their dotation, their arrangement, their administration, had among other objects that of protecting the possession of the Californias, first for the Crown of Spain and then for the Republic of Mexico, against the progressive danger arising from the vicinity of the United States. It is proper to observe here by the way, without prejudice to a more ample elucidation of this point, that it would be an absurdity to pretend, as these claimants do, that the elements which the Mexican Government employed to avoid the loss of Upper California should now be transferred to a society subsequently organized in the country by which that province was conquered.

It would be almost the same as if Russia [*sic*.] should keep France perpetually bound to pay the expenses of the fortifications which the latter nation vainly erected in Alsace and Lorraine for the defense of those provinces. Now again to the history of the fund. After the Government of Mexico placed it for its administration in the hands of the bishop who had been created by it, it withdrew from him such a commission, and, finally, the incorporation of the fund in the national treasury was decreed. At the same time it was ordered that a sum amounting to six per cent of the incorporated property should be annually applied to the objects for which the said fund had been established. Some of the estates in which the fund consisted were alienated, by virtue of said order, in favor of individuals. Subsequently, when, in consequence of one of the changes so frequent at that time in the Mexican politics, the spirit of the Government changed, it was decreed that the sale of said property should be stopped, and that that which still remained unsold should be delivered back to the Bishop of California.

This property must have been very small, because, as will be seen in the course of this opinion, the so-called Pious Fund of California had for a long time, and especially during the war for independence, sustained great and progressive detriments. The war with the United States came soon after the last-mentioned measures were taken. A portion of the Californias was occupied by the American Government even before the treaty of Guadalupe was concluded. By this treaty

Mexico ceded the territory of which she had already been dispossessed. The Mexican Bishopric of the two Californias ceased to exist, as also the local interests which the Government, seconded by the Church, had promoted in that part of the Republic, and things continued in the same condition after the peace with the United States was concluded. Now an ecclesiastical corporation newly organized in Upper California, in the bosom of the American nationality, in conformity with the laws of one of its States, in short, the Catholic Association of Upper California represented by its bishops (some of whom are of recent creation) pretend that Mexico should pay to them the interests of the so-called "Pious Fund," estimating them at their pleasure, and deducting only an insignificant fraction for the sake of the rights recognized in the Catholics of Lower California; in order to establish such a claim before us, the facts, or to say better, their character has been adulterated in the memorial. This adulteration may not be intentional, but can not fail to be noticed by any one who has read the documents in this case. The fund whose interests are claimed is described in the memorial as a foundation made for the precise and exclusive purpose of supporting the Catholic Church of the Californias, and everything is omitted which refers to the civil and political objects which presided over the first mission sent and the collection of the resources necessary for their sustenance.

In treating of the part which the Mexican Government took in the administration of those resources the real condition of things is inverted, because that Government is represented as possessor and administrator in the name of the Church, when the opposite is a truth which reflects on every part of the transaction, above all after the expulsion of the Jesuits. It was not the Mexican Government who received the funds in question from the Fernandinos and Dominicans and from the Bishop Garcia Diego to attend to their keeping and administration; on the contrary, those religious orders and that prelate took under their charge said administration as delegates of the Government of Mexico, who at certain times placed it in the hands of corporations and functionaries strictly civil. Upon the basis of this false precedent, the incorporation in the national treasury as ordered and carried into effect in the year '42 is described as a wrongful act by which the Government substituted itself, authoritatively and arbitrarily, in the place of the Bishop of California, and all is disregarded that relates to the antecedents showing the civil and political interest connected with the missions and their fund and with the views of the Government, of the donors and even of the Church; views which were not confined to definite localities, but referred, as will be seen further on, to the conquest of provinces distant from California.

It is, then, easy to see what ratification the incorrect history made of this affair in the memorial requires. It is necessary to repeat that the undertaking of the first missionaries in California was more of the Government than of the Church; that the persons of whom donations were obtained made them for establishments already founded for the principal and known purpose of continuing and consolidating the Spanish conquests in the northwestern part of Mexico, that the funds donated were originally placed in charge of the Jesuits, who had ample freedom of administration and were exempt from giving accounts; and that after the expulsion and extinction of that order, the Spanish Government first, and that of Mexico afterwards, substituted themselves in the place of the Jesuits. The fact that they had, during a certain period, their functions delegated in the monks of San Fernando and Santo Domingo and in the Bishop of California, does not take from the institutions or the interests connected with them what they have of national and civil [sic]; nor was that fact ever regarded by the religious orders and the Bishop in Mexico as a proof that they possessed and administered in their own right.

We also notice in the claimants' memorial a certain tendency to appreciate, to censure and to claim, in regard to former acts of the Spanish and Mexican Governments, without knowing that whatever the character and importance of those acts may have been, they can not constitute a proper subject for reclamation, as their date is anterior to the treaty of Guadalupe, by which Mexico and the United States agreed to consider all their national claims as settled. [Sic.] Whatever may be the measures by which in [sic] the position to which its original intervention in the organization of the missions and its substitution in the place of the Jesuits entitled it, this is not a proper subject to be submitted to discussion before us. The logical and legal starting-point from which to appreciate the rights alleged by these claimants is the condition of things at the time when the treaty of Guadalupe was concluded.

That situation implied a supreme power greater, as to the administration and investment of funds, than that which the Jesuits had exercised. The Mexican Government always showed great respect towards the will of those who bequeathed property for the reduction of the natives in the western part of Mexico. And there is no reason why the said Government, placed as it is in the same place which the first missionaries occupied, could not claim, with the same right, that it is exempt, in conformity with the will of the donors, from the obligation of giving account in regard to the administration and investment of the fund to which the present case refers.

The question raised by the claimants is not a question of facts. They really agree with the advocate of Mexico in the history of the affair and apply to the same sources to establish the precedents of the case. They only differ in regard to certain secondary points and as to the flattering calculations about the importance of the funds the interests of which are claimed by these prelates. The question, therefore, consists in the appreciation of facts in which the two interested parties agree, or to say better, in the philosophy of the history related by both.

In that history Mexico sees the antecedents of an affair in which the civil and political character prevails, whereas the present Bishops of California do not see in all that relates to the missions maintained there by the Spanish and Mexican Governments anything else than a work essentially and exclusively religious and an interest of a local character connected, by an indissoluble and perpetual bond, with the dignitaries of the Catholic Church in those regions.

After a little reflection we can see how incorrect that judgment of the claimants is, and that in the foundation, organization of resources and administration in question there is much more of a temporal than of a spiritual and religious character; much more of national and Mexican than of a philanthropic or local interest.

Two circumstances have led the claimants into error, which ought to be taken in consideration by him does not want to make, as they do, false appreciations.

One of them which has been already pointed out refers to the religious means used by the Spanish Government to colonize and extend its dominions. Without bearing in mind this undeniable fact we run the risk of regarding the conquest and colonization of the Spanish America, but as a spiritual work in which the political power of the monarchs of Spain becomes eclipsed before the activity and apostolical zeal of the missionaries. It is not necessary to repeat that at the time, and especially in the countries treated of here, the preaching and propagation of the faith was *inter instrumenta regni* with this circumstance is connected the one of which we spoke before, and which refers to that kind of solidarity between Church and State which existed in Mexico under the Colonial Government, and a long time after that country became independent.

This can not be easily understood by those who profess and practice the religious theory which recognizes Christ only as the head of the Church; but in some Catholic and monarchial countries in the eighteenth century there was, besides the visible head represented by the pope, a certain ecclesiastical and spiritual authority invested in the temporal sovereigns, and to the exercise of this authority correspond the prerogatives which the Spanish King defended with so great a zeal and which the Government of Mexico inherited and enjoyed for some time under the name of royalty. From the two facts just mentioned two consequences are derived which are very material in this case.

1st. That it was very easy at that time, owing to the duality of functions which the civil power performed, to take as acts and work of a religious character much that was done in the exercise of the political and temporal power.

2d. That the Spanish as well as the Mexican Catholic Church were of a national character, from which it follows that even if it be proved that the missions of California, their dotation and administration were within the sphere of the Church, it could not be claimed, as these claimants do, that the present American Catholic Church of Upper California is the heiress and continuator of the Mexican Catholic Church.

This idea will be developed further on, when we shall demonstrate that in the institution and in the resources to which this case refers not only the *temporal* interest prevailed, but the material also. It will, however, be well to state now in corroboration of what has just been said, that when Mexico was mutilated by the separation of Upper California, the system was still in force there according to which the first magistrate of the nation was a functionary of the religious order who intervened in the appointment of bishops, who exercised a kind of veto in regard to the ecclesiastical laws, and who, in short, was in a thousand ways incorporated in the administration of the Catholic Society. The latter having been essentially Mexican in Mexico, it must be recognized that when the political power of that country sustained the loss imposed by the treaty of Guadalupe, a similar loss was suffered by the Catholic Church of Mexico, and that as the Government withdrew from California, New Mexico and Texas, so the Catholic Church of the Republic also withdrew carrying with it its own elements of life and development.

This, which is natural, is proved by some facts brought to our knowledge by the claimants themselves, such as the reconstruction which the Catholic Church has been obliged to undergo in Upper California by being organized in conformity with the laws of the United States in the matter of corporations. The one which now exists there with the name of Catholic Church is not the one which the Viceroy of Mexico founded with the assistance of the Society of Jesus. So that even if we see in the interests claimed in this case a thing belonging to the Church, the claim could not be established by the American Catholics of Upper California. But this is doubly true because, as we said before, from a historical and philosophical point of view the political and temporal character predominated in the missions in question.

When they were planned and began to be founded the Spanish Government did not appear even in the mere character of propagator of the faith which in certain cases is assumed. At that time it had not been recognized yet that the political machine is not a good instrument for the propagation of religious truth. Indeed the rights of Spain in the American continent, based upon the bull of Alexander the Sixth were conditioned on the propagation of the catholic religion. The acts of the Spanish monarch and of his delegates in America, then, seemed at times to have a tendency towards that end only, but in this matter things went on in a different way, and the viceroys declared without the least hesitation that they accepted the coöperation of the Jesuits to extend the dominions of the Crown. Not only in the principle, but in the execution, the characteristic traits of the undertaking are revealed, as is also the transformation, so to say, to which the missionaries were subjected by being converted into civil magistrates and military chiefs to carry out the work which the Colonial Government had authorized them to do. It was when this work was in the course of execution, when there existed in California some establishments whose relations [were] much closer with the Viceroy and the King of Spain than with the Archbishop of Mexico, and could not escape notice, that several donations were made for the purpose of maintaining those establishments and others of the same kind; and in some instances the donor explained in an equivocal manner, that it was one of his desires to contribute to the enlargement of the dominions of his sovereign. It can be demonstrated in a thousand ways that the missions to which this case refers did not constitute an ecclesiastical and local corporation; but that they were derived from the Government of Mexico, their objects being in relation with the general interests and with the customs of the country. Certain it is that one of those objects was the conversion of the natives to Christianity; but this is not the end, nor the predominant or exclusive interest which appears in the historical monuments. It was pointed out before that the Jesuits made application for the license to found the missions not to their superiors in the ecclesiastical order but to the civil authority, and that the latter granted the permission in the form of an arrangement, in which the purpose of extending and consolidating the dominions of Spain appears.

If the present Catholics of California think that they are entitled to the means organized for that purpose they might in the same way claim the revenues of which the Spanish and the Mexican Governments made certain expenses to plant, develop and maintain the power of the Government, and the civil administration in the Californias (Exhibits Nos. 3, 4 and 5 of defensive evidence).

There was in the original acts stated and alleged by these claimants an undertaking of the temporal power in which the latter took the Jesuit missionary as an instrument. See the preamble in the authorizations and orders given to them (Exhibit No. 21) and it will be noticed that the conquest of the Californias had been already undertaken without result by means exclusively political and military, and that the arrangement between the Viceroy of Mexico and the Society of Jesus was the continuation of the same attempt with different means, to the power exclusively physical which had failed, they sought to add the moral ascendancy of the missionaries and the pecuniary means with whose collections the Jesuits had been entrusted, with a view to profit by their peculiar skill in the matter. The documents which had been cited, in which the preparatory steps, provisions and regulations favoring the development of the new plan are seen, plainly show that the minds of those who contributed to its conception and execution took less interest in the philanthropic and abstract object of converting and civilizing heathen barbarians, than in the result, much more positive and politic, of reducing the natives of California, and of incorporating them with the other subjects of Spain. All the authorizations given to the Jesuits, refer to points of authority and government.

In examining this point, the document marked No. 21 in the defensive evidence, must be read in all its parts. It contains the authorization or arrangement between the Viceroy of Mexico and the Society of Jesus, to prosecute the conquest of the Californias, which had been attempted and suspended. The Viceroy states that the necessity of making extraordinary expenses on account of an insurrection in the colony, prevented the drawing of resources from the royal treasury for an enterprise in which $225,000 had been already expended without fruit, and in consideration of that he accepts the proposition that the expenses of the new attempt to submit the natives of California should be met through the assistance which several persons had offered. But further down and indeed in every line of the document, it is given to be understood that the work proposed was nothing else than the continuation of the conquest attempted before. The license reads: "to go into the interior to make the *conquest* and reduction of the infidels."

The services rendered by the auxiliaries of the missionaries were considered as services done in war, and of the same character as those rendered in the conquests already achieved. The document contains the express clause that all the *conquests* should be made in the name of *His Majesty*.

The question being conquests and operations of war, the power of organizing and taking soldiers, of appointing and removing officers, and of issuing the necessary orders "in the service of His Majesty" was included in the authorization. After making provisions in regard to the objects of conquests, the document provides for the organization of the new colony, and the monks are empowered to appoint, "in the name of His Majesty," authorities who should administer justice, and to whom the newly conquered subjects should yield obedience. All this is done without prejudice to the approval of the sovereign and with the incentive of his gratitude, which is a most eloquent indication that it was the question of his services.

All the acts of the missionaries, after they arrived in the territories where the new plan of conquest was to be developed, have the character of a civil, political and military undertaking. Before they planted the cross in the territory of California, the flag of the King of Spain was hoisted, and all subsequent steps were directed less to establish the pulpit and the preaching, than to organize, according to the instruction of the viceroys, the military and civil power of which the Jesuits were the delegates, to take possession of the land in the name of the monarch, to fortify the places occupied, to attract there subjects rather than neophytes, and to appoint and establish judges, and other functionaries of the civil and political order.

In regard to this are also historical monuments which can be seen in the defensive evidence. One of them is the letter copied in document No. 22. In it we see the narrative of a true conquest and the proper terms used, the missionaries giving to themselves the name of *conquerors*. Relating their success, they state (page 17) that "all that land had been conquered, *not converted* by a few Spaniards."

It is useless to dwell upon the demonstration that the undertaking instructed to the missionaries of the Society of Jesus and carried on by them, was nothing else than an extension of the Spanish possessions in America. Although it was stipulated at the beginning that the expenses of the work should be met by private donations and that the conqueror could not draw against the royal treasury without previous consent of the sovereign, some expenses were made by the public treasury, and even the viceroys sometimes gave assistance out of their own money. Thus it is that we see in everything the religious and temporal ends and means confounded, the latter prevailing in most of the cases. The undertaking did not lose its original character in the course of time. It being attempted in 1697, twenty years later, the missionaries and their armed auxiliaries were "very especially recommended to attend to the advancement of that conquest" (document No. 27, page 13[1]). For that purpose it was called to mind (page 2) that the former arrangements had for their object *"the discovery of the provinces of the Californias* and the conversion of the Indians." Here we see again the political object fraternizing with the religious zeal, if not palliated by it. The latter is also spoken of in other documents, and it certainly exercises a great influence at the time that conquest was undertaken, because the habits and the feelings, sincere or affected, of the Spanish monarchs so required.

Boasting of being delegates of God, they had to show their zeal by sending him the souls of their subjects. It suited those times to mix in everything religion with politics. This alliance, which was very close in the Spanish colonies of America, is also observed in those of a different origin. Even in the original colonies which gave birth to the United States, we can point out works and objects of a religious character in the bosom of establishments which had nothing to do with the Church, and which were no more than a derivation of the civil power. Some of the first enactments in those colonies had a tendency to defray the expenses of public worship; in others the political capacity of those who did not belong to any Church, was declared as a fundamental measure.

In the charter of James the First to the Colony of Virginia, it was explicitly ordained that religion should be established according to the doctrines and rights of the English Church, and that the emigrants should owe fidelity to the King and to his creed. And certainly it would not occur to anybody, if in consequence of some human

---

[1] Not printed.

necessitude a part of the United States would pass to another nation, to pretend that the territory so lost should carry with itself as a dotation, the resources which had served at a remote time to lay the foundation of the political and the religious institutions. All the ancient documents which have been accumulated in this case proclaimed that the Government of the viceroy first, and afterwards the Republican Government of Mexico were the supreme authority in regard to the missions of the Californias. Notwithstanding that the said missions were entrusted to monks and ecclesiastical functionaries, the character of civil delegates which the latter had from the beginning was continued afterwards, and we see the Government regulating and controlling everything.

The sovereign, the viceroy, the president of the Republic, the interests of nationality and politics, always predominate as influence, as purpose, as principal end. In all the stages through which the missions passed, we see the Government act, in regard to them, as a superior authority by virtue of one of his rights, which was recognized by the Jesuits, the Fernandinos, the Dominicans and even by the Bishop of California, created, in a certain way, by the Government of the Republic. What can lead one into error is that in the first days of the conquest, and for many years afterwards, the Government had not in California any other delegates than the missionaries. It is not before the 24th of May, 1832, that we meet with a law enacted to send civil commissioners to California to put the local administration in harmony with the new forms which the Government and the general administration of the country had adopted. This, however, did not produce a divorce between the two orders of administration, and the civil Government retained the superior and exclusive authority which [it] had exercised in regard to the fund of the missions. Simultaneous with the above cited law, was the one issued on the 25th of May, and published on the 1st of June of the same year, in which provisions were made in relation to the lease of the estates in which the said fund consisted, and a commission of three persons appointed for the management of said fund.

On November 29th of the same year, we see the Government ordering the alienation of the houses situated in Vegara Street, and in Belemitas Alley. Soon afterwards (January 23, 1833) the same Government thought it proper to revoke the order relative to the alienation. On the 24th of the same month and year, it approved the regulations for the administrative board it had created. On March 16, 1833, it issued new orders in relation to the lease of the estates; and in all those laws, and especially in that which organized the administrative board, and in the said regulations, it appears that the Government acted as the superior authority in the matter, and that [*which*] was called the fund of California was no longer but an especial fund which the same Government had created, in the bosom of the public treasury, to serve to certain objects.

And there is no reason to regard those acts and measures as usurpations. Especially after the expulsion and extinction of the Society of Jesus, the Government of Mexico had to substitute itself in the place of that society and to continue to act in the matter with such fulness of authority as the missionaries could never have. The Government not only withdrew the faculty which the Jesuits had received from the principal contributions to the fund of California to administer and invest funds without giving account; but it added to that faculty of private origin those which were inherent in the public power, either by virtue of the eminent domain, by the character of the institution, or by the part which in regard to the latter the temporal government had always exercised.

Exhibit No. 25 throws much light on the character of the fund after the extinction of the Jesuits, as it contains a report made to the King of Spain upon the matter. In that report we find the confirmation of the fact, that to a certain degree, the civil administration and the temporal interest were interwoven with the missions, that the missionaries had been the chiefs of the conquering forces, and that their commission had for its principal object to further the conquest of America *"without leaving behind any Indians unreduced."* (*Sin dejar Indiis por reducir á la espalda.*)

All the antecedents above referred to serve to illustrate this subject, but they could not in any case, taking their date into consideration, be a proper matter for reclamation on the part of the present Catholics of California. The claim put forward by them through their bishops derived from the orders dictated by the public powers in Mexico in the year 1842 definitively incorporating the fund in question in the public treasury and constituting on one of the revenues. [*Sic.*]

Keeping in mind all the history of the fund, we see that its characteristic nature did not change after the new aspect which the said orders gave it. Nothing has been more common in Mexico, as well as in other countries, than to assign certain funds and especial guarantees for the supports of institutions and other proper matters of civil administration. Colleges, hospitals, and other like establishments have been founded and sustained in that way. At the present time there exists in Mexico an especial fund inlaid in the revenues of the federation and intended to pay interests for capitals invested in the Vera Cruz railroad. So that the legislative acts which the claimants regard as their fundamental argument and the basis of their allegations, do not in the least deprive the fund of its character of temporal and national interest, which could not be transmitted to the American Church of California when this province became a possession of the United States.

There are in the history of this affair two very marked periods which are, to a certain extent, different. The first is when the Jesuits administered the fund of the missions, which they did with a certain degree of independency and freedom, limited by the interference of the Government. But after the Jesuits were expulsed and extinguished, the Government is all in the matter. If some ecclesiastical functionaries have to interfere in it, that interference is altogether the work of delegation.

At the time of the establishment of the bishopric in California, the bishop received the said fund from the hands of the Government, and that, not by a virtue of a bilateral contract, but in consequence of a decree which could be, and was revoked by the same power which issued it. The resistance made by the bishop of California against the revocation of said decree, and which is now alleged as an argument by the American bishops of that country, was very natural on the part of a functionary who considered the fund of the missions as the principal support of his office, and who not making a right application of those resources applied them in part to the especial objects of the local Church and worship. But that resistance was without reason or precedents.

It did not occur to any prelate of the Mexican Church to protest against the action of the Spanish Government when the latter received the fund of California from the hands of the expulsed Jesuits and commenced to manage it through the officers of the crown. The delegation made in favor of the Dominicans and Fernandinos was accepted by them as a gracious act. Neither did the Republican Government of Mexico hear any censure or protest when it established some of the civil forms in which the fund was administered.

Nobody said a word against the law of May 25, 1832, for instance, which created the administrative board. All those acts of the civil power not only passed without contradiction on the part of the ecclesiastical authority, but were assented to and approved by documents and facts. It could not be otherwise, for, as was pointed out above, the judges who decided certain cases instituted by the successors of the contributors to the fund of California declared that the latter remained at the disposal of the Government; and this is the reason why we see its products collected as the other national revenues and the expenses of the missions confounded with those of the civil administration of California in the budget of the Republic. This case not only promises data to maintain that the interest to which the claim refers was a temporal concern, not depending upon the Church, but it also contains abundant proof that that interest was a national and Mexican one, incapable of being transmitted to another nationality as an appendage of a territory ceded. The decrees of the 8th of February and 24th of October, 1842, declared the objects of the fund national and "subject to the administration of the Government as they had been before." The author of this opinion does not think it necessary to discuss the point so unseasonably raised by these claimants and relative to the declarations of nationalization made by some administrations and to the censure the latter have incurred thereby, because what is important in this case is to ascertain the fact, not the right. If the declarations made by the Government of Mexico in 1842 were unjust and injurious, no complaint can be made on that account in the United States after the treaty of Guadalupe, still less before this commission the chronological starting point of whose powers is the 2d of February, 1843. What it is important to know under the circumstances of the case is that those declarations existed, and that in fact and according to the Mexican law the interest represented by what was called the "Pious Fund of California" was incorporated and identified with the nationality of Mexico.

Studying the history of this affair with impartiality it can be perceived that in the means to which the claimants refer there was not only a national character proper of interest and rights, so to say, Mexican, but a general character which was not confined to the locality of California. The document marked with No. 8 in the defensive evidence and with No. 28 in the list of papers of the case, besides showing (page 7) as above said, that the erogations of the public treasury and the contingents of individuals mingled together in the conquest and the civilization of the Californias, also proves (pages 24 and 25) that the missions by which the first civil administration of those provinces was really established, were not considered as an institution strictly local. That they were regarded as an instrument eventually applicable in the conquest of Sonora and which implied the purpose of consolidating the Spanish rule in those regions, "not leaving behind any Indian nation unreduced or not subject to the royal dominion."

In the report cited above, which can be seen in document No. 25, the views of nationality and of precaution against the dismemberment which Mexico sustained at a later time, views which were closely connected with the missions of the Californias, take the most energetic expression. Speaking of the origin and object of the Pious Fund the said report reads as follows: "After deploring that the patriotism and charity of those who contributed to the formation of the said fund have no imitators, there is no one to devote himself to solicit other benefactors like the Marquis de Villa Puente, his wife Doná Gertrudis de la Peña, the Marchioness de Forres de Rada, Don Juan Caballero, Don Nicolas de Aniage, his Excellency Don Luis de Velasco, the Jesuit Juan Maria de Luyando and her Excellency Doná Maria de Borja, who founded the fund with their large alms, they being, therefore, the true agents of the propagation of the faith in the Peninsula of California, and of the extension of the royal dominions of His Majesty, as they prevent the latter from being occupied by foreign Powers, as is intended in regard to our ancient Spanish possessions."

After the establishment of the Republican Government in Mexico, the views of the parties contending for power differed sometimes after the alienation of the property which constituted the oft-repeated fund; but they united in the conviction that the work of the missions, or more properly speaking, of the conquest of California by means of the missionaries, tended as the principal of its ends, towards the consolidation of the Mexican nationality in the Western States. These claimants have alluded to the memoir of the Minister of Justice published in Mexico in the year 1843. We see there, in fact, that the administration which succeeded that of General Santa Anna, deposed by a popular rising, censured the measures taken by that President in regard to the fund of California; but in the same document the national and autonomical objects of that fund, which made it to be regarded as sacred, are again asserted. The Minister of Justice deplored that the instrument with which the Spanish Government had been able to build a wall against the barbarism of the Indians and the cupidity of some enlightened neighbors, was, so to say, broken in his hands. That functionary recording the fact that there were no longer any missionaries who could continue the work of the ancient religious orders, wrote these words: "It is a matter of regret to the Government not to find in our cloisters the apostolical enthusiasm of their former founders; but, unfortunately, it is a palpable fact that for want of missionaries the missions have been diminishing in number; according to last year's memoir there are in the Republic six colleges for the propagation of the faith, seven colleges with but 87 priests who have under their charge 36 missions and their respective convents, for which reason it is clear that not even two priests can be assigned to each place. The Californias which have been considered as *a gem of inestimable value,* suffered much for want of ministers; it was thought that a bishop placed in those territories would provide with simple remedies which the distance from Mexico prevents from dictating *and would be a new support of the nationality of the Republic against the political speculations of cabinets who propose to prosper at the expense of our negligence and blunders.*

Here are revealed in a few lines the views which were entertained in treating of the missions of California and in collecting and employing the means with which they were maintained. When the Government of Mexico ordered the alienation of the property in which that fund consisted and whose value and products were diminishing year after year; when it incorporated the fund in the national treasury, when it assigned an interest guaranteed by a public revenue, it did not intend to serve, nor did it serve in fact, but to national and political objects, with which were combined in a second degree the civilization and conversion of the natives.

The loss which Mexico sustained at a later time when she was mutilated of a province which has become in a few years one of the most flourishing States of the American Union and which has just saved the United States from a terrible financial crisis, had been long foreseen, and the creation of a bishopric there and the organization of the means which were put in the hands of the Bishop, had no other object than to make tighter the bonds between the Californias and Mexico, which the sword of a neighboring nation was to sever soon afterwards. It would be very strange that those means created, organized and administered, well or badly, to save the integrity of the Mexican Republic, should pass into the hands of the people who succeeded at last in snatching some of her most covetable districts. To pretend this, after Mexico has been deprived of Upper California, is tantamount to ask that a quarter of a century after that loss she should surrender, also, to the victor one of the arms with which she defended her integrity.

And that national and patriotic spirit which notoriously animated the Mexican Government in the arrangements alluded to was participated in by the individuals whose donations contributed to the formation of the fund of California. It has been said above that those contingents came after the missions had been organized under the license of the viceroy with views the political character of which can not be denied without giving the lie to history. Taking into account the spirit of the times and of the nation to which the donors belonged, reflecting upon the position they occupied, studying the words in which they speak of the missions founded in this kingdom and allude *to the service of the sovereign and to the extension of his dominions,* it must be acknowledged that it could not be in the minds of those who promoted with their liberality the first missions in California, to found resources to be profited by an ecclesiastical corporation within the nationality of the United States. Certainly, neither the Marquis de Villa Puente, the Marchioness de Torres de Rada, nor the Viceroy Velasco, ever thought of a foundation which was not national in its character, like that, for instance, which exists in the United States under the name of Board of Foreign Missions. It has been said before and it is proper to repeat here that the claimants and the society which they represent are not the continuators of the Mexican Church originally established in California. To the foundation of that Mexican Church both the ecclesiastical and the civil power contributed. These are the facts as shown in the historical monuments, and this is, on the other hand, what answered the relations at that time existing between the Catholic Church and the Mexican Government. They did not revolve, as at present, in spheres without contact; there was something of reciprocal intercourse between the two Powers; the one served the views of the other; and the Church paid for the exclusive protection of the Catholic religion by causing, in many cases, the religious institution to serve the objects of the temporal power, as we have seen in the case of the first missionaries of California in whom the characters of priest and magistrate were confounded. The same Bishop sent to California in 1836 had something of this double character, not only on account of the part which the Government took in his appointment and institution, but because he went there, as the above-cited memoir shows, with the tacit mission of strengthening the Mexican nationality in that part of the Republic, and even of endeavoring to better a local administration which the arm of federation could not reach from Mexico. The Mexican Church of California is of an ancient date. The Catholic Church which now exists there dates from 1850, as the same claimants state in order to prove the American nationality of the corporation.

Many other considerations could be added to those which precede; but they might perhaps weaken the evidence of the fact, which is as clear as daylight in the mind of the author of this opinion, that the claimants in this case come to ask that Mexico should surrender to them a thing which is properly and exclusively national and which the Mexican Government ought to have carried with it when it withdrew from Upper California.

The claimants have endeavored to pick up the arms which a vanquished faction abandoned a long time ago in Mexico, and they use them against the Government of the Republic, complaining of some measures dictated and carried into effect by it in regard to the fund of California. In the indirect complaints about this matter we perceive the echo of the imputation which the reactionary party in Mexico has made to the liberal reformers on account of certain laws relative to the property which was formerly administered by the clergy of that country. They forget that the progressive steps taken by Mexico in the direction of rendering the immense mass of property possessed by the clergy alienable, have been taken following the example set by many other nations in their efforts towards emancipation from theocratical despotism. They forget that the reforms in regard to the property kept by some Mexican corporations have produced the fruit of consolidating the constitution of the country by putting an end to the revolutions which used to have their arsenal in the barracks and their banker in the ecclesiastical administration. But they forget above all that it was not even the Republican Government of Mexico who initiated the acts from which the situation which the bishops of California assume to subvert, arose; that it was the Spanish Government who expulsed the Jesuits, who occupied their temporalities including the fund of California which they administered, and who commenced to make use of the free administration which, for all the reasons already explained, the Government of the Republic continued to exercise afterwards.

All these antecedents gave origin to the condition of things existing at the time when Upper California passed into the hands of the United States by virtue of the treaty of Guadalupe. The two nations which made war first and then peace agreed not to turn their eyes to the past, forgetting all causes of complaint. The situation against which this claim is directed is the same which existed at the time of the signature of the treaty of Guadalupe. This act was preceded by long and profound debates between the negotiators in regard to the manner in which the painful amputation which Mexico then suffered

—

should be performed; in regard to which muscles and nerves should be cut and which should be left in the mutilated body. If the transfer of any revenues or property in favor of the new territories annexed to the American Union was contemplated at the time of the conclusion of said treaty, clauses in reference to that matter would have been introduced; but nothing, absolutely, was said; neither was there any agreement as to the funds which the religious corporations established in California had administered and which had served as dotation of the bishopric. The state of things in 1848, was, therefore, definitively consecrated, and no complaint can be made against Mexico on the part of the American Government or of its citizens with a view to reconstruct the situation in which, for instance, the Jesuits were when they managed the fund in question, or that in which the Fernandinos, the Dominicans and the Bishop Garcia Diego were when the Government of Mexico delivered to them the products of the property. When Mexico and the United States liquidated, so to say, their accounts in 1843, binding themselves not to look in the past for any cause of complaint and reclamation, the fund of California was already diluted in the national revenues of the Republic, and the Government of Mexico had only decreed some subsidies in favor of the ecclesiastical functionaries who served it as auxiliaries in that part of the federation.

This situation the claimants want to alter now, and they want also to oblige Mexico to pay the perpetual tribute of a rent to certain American corporations. Such a thing could only be exact if it had been included in the treaty which put an end to all questions which might arise between Mexico and the United States up to the peace of Guadalupe. After that peace the obligation which the claimants want to impose upon Mexico could only exist by common consent of the two Governments; but far from such a consent having ever been given, the Government of Mexico does not recognize such an obligation and protests against the demand tending to impose the same upon it.

What that Government has done in another case as a free and voluntary act, the Bishops of California want now to exact by compulsion. When the Mexican Government made with that of Spain the agreement relative to the fund of the Philippine Islands the onerous part of said agreement was counterbalanced by some useful stipulations in regard to claims which were settled by said agreement. What is there common between this and that which the claimants pretend? What do they give Mexico? What do they offer her in exchange for that kind of perpetual annuity which they want to secure in favor of their Churches? When they advance this pretension accompanied by deferences and renunciations like those which the Spanish Government made at the time of the arrangement which was called afterwards the Convention of Father Moran, then they will [have] a right to cite this act as a precedent, and that, if precedents can be alleged in regard to a subject which depends only upon the judgment and free will of a Government.

Many are the differential traits between the two affairs which the claimants attempt to compare. But in a certain point of view the argument rebounds on them, because the same fact of the matter relative to the fund of the Philippine Islands having been settled by means of a convention shows that the consent of the Government of Mexico was required, and that the claimants have mistaken the way, because instead of presenting this demand they should ask their Government to initiate near that of Mexico a convention similar to that which Spain negotiated in the case above alluded to. The Government of the United States would judge if it was agreeable to it to take such a step, and Mexico making use of her most free sovereignty would say if she was disposed to admit such a pretension.

If the demand in this case is exorbitant as to the philosophical principle on which it is founded, it is no less so in regard to the calculations made by the claimants in order to ascertain the interest claimed. As to this point the original memorial was vague and indecisive; those who signed it really own that they did not know what they ought to claim and indirectly gave the commission the charge, not little difficult, of finding it out. In the course of the case, and as new data and documents have been accumulated, the claimants have fixed their ideas, and these appear at last translated into ciphers on page 31 of the printed argument. The point of departure taken therein is the absorption of the fund of California in the Mexican treasury on February 3, 1842, and the memorandum which the Bishop Garcia Diego formed on that occasion regarding the importance of said fund.

Notwithstanding that that news contains conjectures rather than facts, and that let to perceive the inclination to increase the charge of the Government, the claimants ascribe to that document a mathematical exactness, calculating the rent that the funds already appropriated by the Mexican treasury are to produce, and capitalizing it at the rate of six per cent, make an amount of $577,583.37. [Sic.]

To this they add the old debts in favor of the said fund, as if it was a question of easy matter to convert into money at any time; and in this way they raise the capital to one million, six hundred and ninety-eight thousand, seven hundred and forty-five dollars. Upon this sum they charge interest since the year 1849, and by virtue of this operation they fix the responsibility of the Mexican Government at two millions, one hundred and forty thousand, one hundred and four dollars.

They have behind this the moderation to cede one-tenth of the sum for the missions of the Lower California, and in this manner the demand is condensed to a determined cipher.

In this calculation, as it has been said, the ground itself is meager, and fluctuating. If is read the instruction of the Attorney Ramirez, to whom the claimants ascribe as much infallibility as to the Pope, it will be found at every step, that the author of that work wanted documental facts in regard to some very important items, but when so much faith is given to the informations of that source, the bishops claiming ought not to have forgotten what the same Ramirez informed to the Government of Mexico, three days before the issue of the law which incorporated the said fund in the public treasury, and then, they will not make such whimful [*sic.*] and erroneous accounts.   This information reads at the foot of the page   .   .   .   among the last documents which, copied anew, the claimants have brought to the commission.   It reads so:

EXCELLENT SIR:
   The Pious Fund of Californias consists of three-quarter parts of the hacienda of "Cienega del Pastor" and other three-quarter parts of seventy thousand dollars in which were sold in emphyteusis some houses of Vergara Street, to build the new theater.
   The hacienda of "San Agustin de Amoles" and the annexed in the districts of San Luis and Tamaulipas and the other of Ibarra in the district of Guanajuato.   [*Sic.*]   A capital of forty thousand dollars imposed in the hacienda of "Arroga Zareo," and forty-two thousand dollars in the hacienda of "Santa Lugarda," and annexed farm, in the San Juan de los Llams.   A deed of one hundred and sixty-two thousand, six hundred and eighteen dollars, three reals and three grains, invested at interest at the rate of five per cent per annum in the *old Consulado* and of which nothing has been collected till now, and in other sums which in several occasions *has* [*sic.*] *been taken for the public treasury with the clause of devolution.*
   The three-quarter parts of the hacienda of the Cienega are embargoed and ordered to be sold pursuant a judicial demand prosecuted by Mr. José Ma. Jauregui vs. the Fund, and if the sentence is carried into effect in the manner it has been pronounced, the embargoed estate will not be sufficient to cover it. The fund is responsible to other credits, which could not be covered on account of loan which, with its mortgage, the supreme

Government raised, as almost all its income was applied to pay
the interest of said loan, and which is paying now at great sacrifice.   With the above stated I believe I answer to the note of
your Excellency, which I have just received, and I avail of this
opportunity to assure you of my considerations and respects.
God and Liberty, Mexico, February 5, 1842.
PEDRO RAMIREZ, to His Excellency
    the MINISTER OF JUSTICE AND PUBLIC INSTRUCTION.

It will be seen by the foregoing information report the bad condition in which was the fund of Californias at the time that the Mexican
treasury received it, that a great part of it consisted in old credits,
represented in Mexico by a paper which had almost no quotation in
the market, and that the author of the report declares that all the
fund was at the point of being absorbed by a judicial sentence pronounced in favor of one of the creditors.
It is not strange that the news hereabove copied should be so discouraging, as seventeen years before it was written, the Secretary of
the Treasury of Mexico gave the same discouraging facts about the
same matter, in his report presented to the Congress in the year 1825,
viz. :

CALIFORNIAS

The missions of the same established with the purpose of bringing to the faith the Indians who did not possess it, were in charge
of the Jesuits.   When these yet subsisted, the Marquis of Villa
Puente de la Pena, left in September, 1726, under the protection
of the Government, six haciendas with the object of sustaining
said missions.   When the Jesuits were suppressed, the haciendas
were managed by the administrator and auditor of the temporalities; afterwards the clergy of San Fernando and Santo Domingo,
and, in 1782, one of the Secretaries of the Mexican Treasury.
They are now under the responsibility of one administrator.
The hacienda called "Zarra," the one of "San Augustin de los
Amoles," the one of the "Buez," the "Valla," a part of the one
of "Ciénega," and another in the houses in Vergara St. of Mexico,
comprise the total estates, in the county and in the city, of the
fund of missions of Californias.
Their proceeds are very small, the insurrection of 1810 caused
to the five first named, such great damages that [they] were almost ruined.   The want of cattle and repairs keep them very low :
their proceeds may be in 1825, 12,150 dollars and 5 reals.
These missions have besides 631,056 dollars, 7 reals and 9
grains of capital imposed in consolidated, national treasury,
consulado, and others, of which no interest are collected.
The salaries of its employees amount to 3,300 dollars, 4 reals.

The *sinodes, viaticums,* and the other indispensable expenses of the missionaries, clergymen are calculated at present to be 19,250 dollars [*sic.*] ; the deficit will be a passive credit which will take its place when it has to be paid.

Here is the place to insist upon the point that not only the claimants exaggerate much the importance of the fund, to which interest they believe to be share-holders, but they want to divide it as the lion of the fable, when they only leave one-tenth for the Church of the Lower California.

If it is to be given to the documents which constitute the history of this matter the literal and strict interpretation that the Bishops of Upper California pretends [*sic.*] the fund in question had as single and exclusive object the sustain [*sustenance*] of the missions.

The greatest number of them were since the beginning founded in the Lower California, so that making an equitable division and adopting the same law, and the same history used by the claimants, it will only belong to them the smallest part of the interest they claim. (See the number of the missions respectively founded in the two Californias, detailed in the statement which appears in the page 15 of Exhibit No. 25.)

As it has been already said the Mexican Government was sustaining these foundations with resources derived of private donation as well as of the public revenues. The confirmation of this can be seen by the successive budgets of the federal administration.

Whether after the peace of Guadalupe the same thing has been done or not, or whether it has been or not erogations for the civilization of the indigenes in Lower California or in the other Western States is a matter that the undersigned does not believe himself under the necessity of demonstrating here, nor the Mexican Government has not thought itself undoubtedly under the obligation of proving it, because those who now move question about the matter have no right to do it. [*Sic.*]

So must have been the views of the Government of the United States, when, in 1859, it abstained from presenting this claim, when it was stimulated to do so by those who now present the said claim.

The Government of Washington must have opposed the exigency, to which they tried to push it, and this is the reason why it did not wish, as it was pretended, to ask for a dotation in money for the Catholic Church of Upper California, after depriving Mexico of that rich State.

Sometimes a daughter is taken by force or seduction from the paternal house, and the act is repaired by a forced marriage. The husband applies afterwards to demand a dower from the offended and abandoned father.

The Bishops interested in this matter tried to induce the American Government to act in a similar way.

As they did not succeed, they now reproduce before us the same pretension, and it must be dismissed without hesitation.

Such is the opinion of the undersigned.

Award of Sir Edward Thornton, umpire in the original Pious Fund Case before the United States and Mexican Claims Commission of 1868.—Washington, November 11, 1875.[1]

This case having been referred to the umpire for his decision upon a difference in opinion between the commissioners, the umpire rendered the following decision:

In the case of "Thaddeus Amat, Bishop of Monterey, and Joseph S. Alemany, Archbishop of San Francisco *vs.* Mexico" No. 493, it will be impossible for the umpire to discuss the various arguments which have been put forward on each side.

He will be able only to state the conclusions which he has arrived at after a careful and lengthened study of all. the documents which have been submitted to him.

He is about to give his decision with a profound sense of the importance of the case in accordance with what he considers to be just and equitable as far as he can rely upon his own judgment and conscience.

The first question to be considered is the citizenship of the claimants.

On this point the umpire is of opinion that the Roman Catholic Church of Upper California became a corporation of citizens of the United States on the 30th of May, 1848, the day of the exchange of ratifications of the Treaty of Guadalupe Hidalgo.

By the VIII Article of the treaty it was agreed that those Mexicans residing in the territories ceded by Mexico to the United States, who wished to retain the title and rights of Mexican citizens should be under the obligation to make their election within one year from the date of the exchange of the ratifications of the treaty; and that those who should remain in the said territories after the expiration of that year, without having declared their intention to retain the char-

---

[1] *United States and Mexican Claims Commission, Opinions* (MS. Dep't of State), vol. vii, p. 459.

acter of Mexicans, should be considered to have elected to have become citizens of the United States. It has not been shown that the Roman Catholic Church in Upper California had declared any intention of retaining its Mexican citizenship and it can not but be concluded that it had elected to assume the citizenship of the United States as soon as it was possible for it to do so, which in the opinion of the umpire was when Upper California was actually incorporated into the United States on the exchange of the ratifications of the Treaty of Guadalupe Hidalgo.

With regard to any claim which may have originated before that date the claimants could not have been entitled to appear before the mixed commission established by the Convention of July 4, 1868; but a claim arising after that date would come under the cognizance of the commission.

The claim now put forward is for interest upon the so-called "Pious Fund of the Californias." If this interest should have been paid to the Right Reverend Francisco Garcia Diego, the Bishop of California, before the separation of Upper California from the Republic of Mexico, it seems to the umpire that a fair proportion of it ought now and since the 30th of May, 1848, to be paid to the claimants, who in his opinion are the direct successors of that Bishop, as far as Upper California is concerned.

The "Pious Fund of the Californias" was the results of donations made by various private persons for the purpose of establishing, supporting and maintaining Roman Catholic missions in California, and for converting to the Roman Catholic faith the heathens of that region. The disbursements of the proceeds of these donations was entrusted by the donors to the Society of Jesus. The object of the donors was without doubt principally the advancement of the Roman Catholic religion. The donations were made by private persons for particular and expressed objects and had nothing public, political or national in their character. Once permission was granted to the Jesuit fathers Salvatierra and Kühu to establish missions in California, to take charge of the conversion to Christianity of the heathens, and to solicit alms for that purpose, it does not seem that the Spanish Government assisted them with any considerable sums, if any at all, and certainly with not so much as almost any Government would have considered itself bound to furnish for the benefit of a region over which it claimed dominion.

It can be easily understood that the Spanish Government was very glad to avail itself of the religious feelings of its subjects, and saw with great satisfaction that their donations would powerfully contribute to the political conquest of the Californias; but the object of the donors was the religious conquest alone, though they too might have felt some pride in the consciousness that they were at the same time contributing to the extension of the possessions of Spain.

The alms, however, solicited in the first instance by the Jesuit fathers, and the donations subsequently made by piously disposed persons were neither political nor national; they were directed to the religious conquest of the Californias, and were the gifts of private persons for that particular object.

On the expulsion of the Jesuits from the Spanish Dominions, and the abolition of the Order, occurrences which the donors to the Pious Fund could not have foreseen, the Spanish Government naturally became the trustee and caretaker of that fund, but it took charge of it avowedly with all the duties and obligations attached to it. The missions were confided to the Franciscan Order, and subsequently they were divided between this Order and the Dominicans, but although the Pious Fund was administered by the Spanish Government, its proceeds were applied to the maintenance of the missions belonging to both Orders.

When Mexico became independent she succeeded to the trust which had been held by the Spanish Government, and continued to apply the proceeds of the fund to the maintenance of the missions. In 1836 it was considered desirable to establish a Bishopric which was to comprise the two Californias.

An Act of Congress was passed for this purpose, and the same act entrusted to the Bishop, who was to be appointed, the administration and application of the Pious Fund in accordance with the wishes of its founders.

On the 8th of February, 1842, President Santa Anna repealed the latter part of the Act of 1836 and assigned the administration and application of the fund to the Mexican Government, but the decree which he signed for this purpose also declared that the object of the donor was to be carried out by the civilization and conversion of the savages. On the 24th of October of the same year another decree was issued by the above-mentioned President to the effect that the real estate and other property of the Pious Fund were to be incorporated into the national treasury and were to be sold at a certain price, the treasury recognizing the total proceeds of these sales at an interest of six per cent and the preamble of this decree declaring that the assumption by the Government of the care and the administration of the Pious Fund was for the express purpose of scrupulously carrying out the objects proposed by the founders.

Neither by the Spanish nor by the Mexican Government was it ever pretended that the proceeds of the fund were not finally to find their way into the hands of the ecclesiastical authorities in the Californias, or that they were to be applied to any other objects than those pointed out by the donors. Subsequently to the decree of October 24, 1842, the Mexican Government admitted its indebtedness and the obligation it was under to remit the proceeds of the fund to the Bishop of California by issuing orders in his favor on the custom house at Guaymas.

This obligation is still further acknowledged by the Act of Congress of April 3, 1845, which restored to the Bishop of the Californias and to his successors all credits and other properties belonging to the Pious Fund which were still unsold, for the objects mentioned in the law of September 29, 1836, without prejudice to what Congress might decide with regard to those properties which had already been alienated.

The above-mentioned credits must surely have included the indebtedness of the Government with regard to the unpaid interest upon the property sold, the proceeds of which had been incorporated into the national treasury. The umpire does not find that any further legislation has been effected upon the subject since the Decree of April 3, 1845.

Such then was the state of the Mexican laws with regard to the Pious Fund at the time of the cession of Upper California to the United States, and the umpire is clearly of opinion that both the acts of the Mexican Government and its decrees above mentioned as well as the Act of Congress of 1845 are so many admissions that the Mexican Government was under the obligation to remit to the Bishop of California and his successors the interest on the proceeds of the property belonging to the Pious Fund which were held in trust by the Mexican Treasury, in order that the Bishop and his successors might carry out the wishes of the founders of that fund.

The umpire has already stated that he considers that as far as Upper California is concerned, the claimants are the direct successors of the Bishop of California, whose Diocese before the Treaty of Guadalupe Hidalgo, comprised both Upper and Lower California; and they ought therefore to receive a fair share of the interest upon the proceeds of the Pious Fund, in order to devote it to the purposes for which it was founded, and which are of so decidedly a religious nature, that the ecclesiastical authorities must be the most proper persons to be employed in its application.

The beneficiaries of this share of the fund are the Roman Catholic Church in Upper California, and the heathens who are to be converted to Christianity; and indirectly all the inhabitants of the State of California, and even the whole population of the United States, are interested in the proper application of the portion which should be entrusted to the claimants, upon whom, considering the purposes to which the founders assigned their donations, the employment of the fund would most suitably devolve.

With regard to the proportion of the interest which should be paid to the claimants, the umpire is of opinion that nothing can be fairer than that the whole of the interest for twenty-one years should be divided into two equal parts, of which one should be paid to the claimants.

It has been argued that the award should be made in proportion to the populations respectively of Upper and Lower California.

The umpire is not of that opinion; for it seems to him that as the population and civilization increase, the number of conversions to be made diminish and there can be little doubt that Lower California needs the beneficial assistance of the Pious Fund as much and even more in proportion to its population than Upper California now does. The equal division of the interest seems to be the fairest award.

After a careful examination of the data furnished with regard to the yearly amount of the interest, the umpire is constrained to adopt the views of the commissioner of the United States. A larger sum is claimed on the part of the claimants; but even with regard to this larger sum the defense has not shown, except indirectly, that its amount was exaggerated.

There is no doubt that the Mexican Government must have in its possession all the accounts and documents relative to the sale of the real property belonging to the Pious Fund and the proceeds thereof : yet these have not been produced; and the only inference that can be drawn from silence upon this subject is that the amount of the proceeds actually received into the treasury was at least not less than it is claimed to be.

The annual amount of interest therefore which should fall to the share of the Roman Catholic Church of Upper California is $43,080.99 and the aggregate sum for twenty-one years will be $904,700.79.

It has been urged that interest should be paid upon each annual amount from the respective date at which it became due. The umpire is not of this opinion. It is true that the Archbishop of San Francisco states in his deposition that when in the City of Mexico in 1852, he demanded payment of the amounts, or property of the Pious Fund, and that receiving no answer to his demands he reiterated the same, and only after a long time was officially informed that the Government could not accede to them.

From a man of the position and character of the Archbishop there can be no doubt of the truth of this statement; but yet there is no documentary evidence of these facts, and the umpire therefore supposes that the demand and the refusal were both verbal. Upon a matter of such serious importance the umpire does not think that a verbal refusal by a Government to make a certain payment can be taken as its final determination upon the subject. The refusal may even have been qualified by the inability of the Government to provide the necessary funds at the time of the demand. Of this in the absence of any writing upon the subject, no judgment can be found. The umpire further thinks that considering the troubles and difficulties to which Mexico and her Government have been subject for several years past it would not be generous nor even fair to punish them for their failure to pay interest upon a capital of the nature of the Pious Fund, so far as to insist upon the payment of interest upon that interest. As a matter therefore both of justice and equity the umpire thinks that this second interest ought not to be demanded.

The umpire consequently awards that there be paid by the Mexican Government on account of the above-mentioned claim the sum of nine hundred and four thousand, seven hundred Mexican gold dollars and seventy-nine cents ($904,700.79) without interest.

Washington, November 11, 1875.

Decision of Sir Edward Thornton, amending the award of the original Pious Fund Case before the United States and Mexican Claims Commission of 1868.—Washington, October 24, 1876.[1]

Upon consideration of the agent of Mexico to amend the award made herein, the umpire rendered the following decision:

With reference to the case of "Thaddeus Amat et al. *vs.* Mexico"

----

[1] *United States and Mexican Claims Commission, Opinions* (MS. Dep't of State), vol vi, p. 544.

No. 493, the agent is quite right in stating that there is an error of $1,000 in the addition of the sums which are considered as bad debts, and which should be deducted from the total of the "Pious Fund."

Instead of being $46,617, these bad debts are $47,617. The total of the fund will therefore be $1,435,033. The half of the interest upon this sum at six per cent will be $43,050.99 the amount of which for twenty-one years will be $904,070.79.

The umpire therefore finally awards that there be paid by the Mexican Government on account of the above-mentioned claim the sum of nine hundred and four thousand and seventy Mexican gold dollars and seventy-nine cents ($904,070.79) without interest.

Washington, October 24, 1876.

THE VENEZUELAN PREFERENTIAL CASE

between

GERMANY, GREAT BRITAIN, ITALY *and* VENEZUELA ET AL

Decided February 22, 1904

Syllabus

The arbitration had its origin in a controversy which arose over certain pecuniary claims of the subjects of Great Britain, Germany and Italy against the Republic of Venezuela. A solution not having been reached by the diplomatic negotiations, the controversy culminated on December 11, 1902, in the ordering by Great Britain of a blockade of the ports of Venezuela. Two days afterward Venezuela offered to submit the controversy to arbitration. This offer was ignored and seven days later the blockade of the Venezuelan ports was declared by the British, German and Italian Governments.

At the same time the United States, Mexico, Spain, France, Belgium, the Netherlands, and Sweden and Norway also held claims against Venezuela, which had been the subject of diplomatic negotiations, but no forcible measures had been employed by these Governments to secure the adjustment of their claims.

After the blockade had been put into effect, Venezuela sent a representative to Washington with full powers to negotiate with the representatives of the creditor Powers a settlement of all the matters in controversy. The negotiations took place during the winter and spring of 1903. In the course of the negotiations the Venezuelan representative proposed that the claims of all the countries above-mentioned against Venezuela be paid out of the customs receipts of the ports of La Guaira and Puerto Cabello, thirty per cent of the receipts of which would be set aside each month for that purpose. The proposal was accepted by the claimant nations and an assignment of the revenues mentioned was made in their favor; but Great Britain, Germany and Italy, the blockading Powers, took the position that their claims should not rank with the claims of the other Powers for compensation, but should be given priority of payment. Venezuela declined to accept this view and the question was submitted by agreements signed May 7, 1903,[1] for determination by the Hague tribunal. The other creditor Powers were joined as parties to the arbitration.[2]

---

[1] *Post*, p. 62.

[2] The respective claims of all the creditor Powers were submitted to mixed commissions consisting of one national each of Venezuela and the claimant nation, with a neutral as umpire, which met at Carácas and subsequently reported their awards.

Pursuant to the provisions of the protocols, the Czar of Russia named three members of the panel of the Permanent Court of Arbitration as arbitrators, no one of whom was a citizen or subject of any of the signatory or creditor Powers, as follows: Nicolas V. Mourawieff and Fr. Martens of Russia, and Heinrich Lammasch of Austria-Hungary. The sessions of the tribunal began October 1, 1903, and ended November 13, 1903. The decision, which was rendered on February 22, 1904, held that:

1. Germany, Great Britain and Italy have a right to preferential treatment for the payment of their claims against Venezuela;

2. Venezuela having consented to put aside thirty per cent of the revenues of the customs of La Guaira and Puerto Cabello for the payment of the claims of all nations against Venezuela, the three above-named Powers have a right to preference in the payment of their claims by means of these thirty per cent of the receipts of the two Venezuelan ports above mentioned;

3. Each party to the litigation shall bear its own costs and an equal share of the costs of the tribunal.[1]

AWARD OF THE TRIBUNAL

Award of the tribunal of arbitration constituted in virtue of the protocols signed at Washington on May 7, 1903, between Great Britain, Germany and Italy, on the one hand, and Venezuela on the other.—The Hague, February 22, 1904.[2]

The tribunal of arbitration, constituted in virtue of the protocols signed at Washington on May 7, 1903,[3] between Germany, Great Britain and Italy on the one hand and Venezuela on the other hand;

Whereas other protocols were signed to the same effect by Belgium, France, Mexico, the Netherlands, Spain, Sweden and Norway and the United States of America on the one hand and Venezuela on the other hand[4];

Whereas all these protocols declare the agreement of all the contracting parties with reference to the settlement of the claims against the Venezuelan Government;

Whereas certain further questions, arising out of the action of the Governments of Germany, Great Britain and Italy concerning the settlement of their claims, were not susceptible of solution by the ordinary diplomatic methods;

[1]*Post*, p. 61.
[2]Official report, p. 123.   For the French text, see Appendix, p. 441.
[3]*Post*, p. 62.   [4]*Post*, p. 74.

Whereas the Powers interested decided to solve these questions by submitting them to arbitration, in conformity with the dispositions of the Convention, signed at The Hague on July 29th, 1899, for the pacific settlement of international disputes;

Whereas in virtue of Article 3 of the protocols of Washington of May 7th, 1903, His Majesty the Emperor of Russia was requested by all the interested Powers to name and appoint from among the members of the Permanent Court of Arbitration of The Hague three arbitrators who shall form the tribunal of arbitration charged with the solution and settlement of the questions which shall be submitted to it in virtue of the above-named protocols;

Whereas none of the arbitrators thus named could be a citizen or subject of any one of the signatory or creditor Powers and whereas the tribunal was to meet at The Hague on September 1st, 1903, and render its award within a term of six months;

His Majesty the Emperor of Russia, conforming to the request of all the signatory Powers of the above-named protocols of Washington of May 7th, 1903, graciously named as arbitrators the following members of the Permanent Court of Arbitration:

His Excellency Mr. N. V. Mourawieff, Secretary of State of His Majesty the Emperor of Russia, Actual Privy Councilor, Minister of Justice and Procurator of the Russian Empire,

Mr. H. Lammasch, Professor of Criminal and of International Law at the University of Vienna, member of the Upper House of the Austrian Parliament, and

His Excellency Mr. F. de Martens, Doctor of Law, Privy Councilor, permanent member of the Council of the Russian Ministry of Foreign Affairs, member of the *Institut de France;*

Whereas by unforeseen circumstances the tribunal of arbitration could not be definitely constituted till October 1st, 1903, the arbitrators, at their first meeting on that day proceeding in conformity with Article 34 of the Convention of July 29th, 1899, to the nomination of the president of the tribunal, elected as such his Excellency Mr. Mourawieff, Minister of Justice;

And whereas in virtue of the protocols of Washington of May 7th, 1903, the above-named arbitrators, forming the legally constituted tribunal of arbitration, had to decide, in conformity with Article 1 of the protocols of Washington of May 7th, 1903, the following points:

The question as to whether or not Germany, Great Britain, and Italy are entitled to preferential or separate treatment in the payment of their claims against Venezuela, and its decision shall be final.

Venezuela having agreed to set aside thirty per cent of the customs revenues of La Guaira and Puerto Cabello for the payment of the claims of all nations against Venezuela, the tribunal at The Hague shall decide how the said revenues shall be divided between the blockading Powers on the one hand and the other creditor Powers on the other hand, and its decision shall be final.

If preferential or separate treatment is not given to the blockading Powers, the tribunal shall decide how the said revenue shall be distributed among all the creditor Powers, and the parties hereto agree that the tribunal, in that case, shall consider, in connection with the payment of the claims out of the thirty per cent, any preference or pledges of revenues enjoyed by any of the creditor Powers, and shall accordingly decide the question of distribution so that no Power shall obtain preferential treatment, and its decision shall be final.[1]

Whereas the above-named arbitrators, having examined with impartiality and care all the documents and acts presented to the tribunal of arbitration by the agents of the Powers interested in this litigation, and having listened with the greatest attention to the oral pleadings delivered before the tribunal by the agents and counsel of the parties to the litigation;

Whereas the tribunal, in its examination of the present litigation, had to be guided by the principles of international law and the maxims of justice;

Whereas the various protocols signed at Washington since February 13th, 1903, and particularly the protocols of May 7th, 1903, the obligatory force of which is beyond all doubt, form the legal basis for the arbitral award;

Whereas the tribunal has no competence at all either to contest the jurisdiction of the mixed commissions of arbitration established at Carácas, nor to judge their action;

Whereas the tribunal considers itself absolutely incompetent to give a decision as to the character or the nature of the military operations undertaken by Germany, Great Britain and Italy against Venezuela;

---

[1]*Post*, p. 62.

Whereas also the tribunal of arbitration was not called upon to decide whether the three blockading Powers had exhausted all pacific methods in their dispute with Venezuela in order to prevent the employment of force;

And it can only state the fact that since 1901 the Government of Venezuela categorically refused to submit its dispute with Germany and Great Britain to arbitration which was proposed several times and especially by the note of the German Government of July 16th, 1901;

Whereas after the war between Germany, Great Britain and Italy on the one hand and Venezuela on the other hand no formal treaty of peace was concluded between the belligerent Powers;

Whereas the protocols, signed at Washington on February 13th, 1903[1], had not settled all the questions in dispute between the beligerent parties. leaving open in particular the question of the distribution of the receipts of the customs of La Guaira and Puerto Cabello;

Whereas the belligerent Powers in submitting the question of preferential treatment in the matter of these receipts to the judgment of the tribunal of arbitration, agreed that the arbitral award should serve to fill up this void and to ensure the definite reestablishment of peace between them;

Whereas on the other hand the warlike operations of the three great European Powers against Venezuela ceased before they had received satisfaction on all their claims, and on the other hand the question of preferential treatment was submitted to arbitration, the tribunal must recognize in these facts precious evidence in favor of the great principle of arbitration in all phases of international disputes;

Whereas the blockading Powers, in admitting the adhesion to the stipulations of the protocols of February 13th, 1903, of the other Powers which had claims against Venezuela, could evidently not have the intention of renouncing either their acquired rights or their actual privileged position;

Whereas the Government of Venezuela in the protocols of February 13th, 1903 (Article 1), itself recognizes *"in principle the justice of the claims"* presented to it by the Governments of Germany, Great Britain and Italy;

---

[1]*Post*, pp. 65, 67, 70.

While in the protocol signed between Venezuela and the so-called neutral or pacific Powers the justice of the claims of these latter was not recognized in principle;

Whereas the Government of Venezuela until the end of January 1903 in no way protested against the pretension of the blockading Powers to insist on special securities for the settlement of their claims;

Whereas Venezuela itself during the diplomatic negotiations always made a formal distinction between *"the allied Powers"* and *"the neutral Powers"*;

Whereas the neutral Powers, who now claim before the tribunal of arbitration equality in the distribution of the thirty per cent of the customs receipts of La Guaira and Puerto Cabello, did not protest against the pretensions of the blockading Powers to a preferential treatment either at the moment of the cessation of the war against Venezuela or immediately after the signature of the protocols of February 13th, 1903;

Whereas it appears from the negotiations which resulted in the signature of the protocols of February 13th and May 7th, 1903, that the German and British Governments constantly insisted on their being given guaranties for *"a sufficient and punctual discharge of the obligations"* (British memorandum of December 23d, 1902, communicated to the Government of the United States of America[1]);

Whereas the plenipotentiary of the Government of Venezuela accepted this reservation on the part of the allied Powers without the least protest;

Whereas the Government of Venezuela engaged, with respect to the allied Powers alone, to offer special guaranties for the accomplishment of its engagements;

Whereas the good faith which ought to govern international relations imposes the duty of stating that the words *"all claims"* used by the representative of the Government of Venezuela in his conferences with the representatives of the allied Powers (statement left in the hands of Sir Michael Herbert by Mr. H. Bowen of

---

[1]Not printed.

January 23rd, 1903[1]) could only mean the claims of these latter and could only refer to them;

Whereas the neutral Powers, having taken no part in the warlike operations against Venezuela, could in some respects profit by the circumstances created by those operations, but without acquiring any new rights;

Whereas the rights acquired by the neutral or pacific Powers with regard to Venezuela remain in the future absolutely intact and guaranteed by respective international arrangements;

Whereas in virtue of Article 5 of the protocols of May 7th, 1903, signed at Washington, the tribunal "shall also decide, subject to the general provisions laid down in Article 57 of the international Convention of July 29th, 1899, how, when and by whom the costs of this arbitration shall be paid";

For these reasons, the tribunal of arbitration decides and pronounces unanimously that:

1. Germany, Great Britain and Italy have a right to preferential treatment for the payment of their claims against Venezuela;

2. Venezuela having consented to put aside thirty per cent of the revenues of the customs of La Guaira and Puerto Cabello for the payment of the claims of all nations against Venezuela, the three above-named Powers have a right to preference in the payment of their claims by means of these thirty per cent of the receipts of the two Venezuelan ports above mentioned.

3. Each party to the litigation shall bear its own costs and an equal share of the costs of the tribunal.

The Government of the United States of America is charged with seeing to the execution of this latter clause within a term of three months.

Done at The Hague, in the Permanent Court of Arbitration, February 22nd, 1904.

(Signed)   N. MOURAWIEFF
(Signed)   H. LAMMASCH
(Signed)   MARTENS

---

[1] MR. BOWEN'S STATEMENT: Mr. Bowen proposes that all claims against Venezuela shall be paid out of the customs receipts of the two ports of La Guaira and Puerto Cabello, the percentage to be 30 per cent each month of the receipts. In case of failure on the part of Venezuela to pay the said 30 per cent, the creditor nations will be authorized to put, with the consent and without any opposition on the part of Venezuela, Belgian custom officials in charge of the said two custom houses, and to administer them until the entire foreign debt is paid. Official report, p. 159.

AGREEMENT FOR ARBITRATION

*Protocol of Agreement between Germany and Venezuela respecting
the reference of the question of the preferential treatment of claims
to the tribunal at The Hague.—Signed at Washington, May 7, 1903.*[1]

Whereas protocols have been signed between Germany, Great
Britain, Italy, the United States of America, France, Spain, Belgium,
the Netherlands, Sweden and Norway, and Mexico on the one hand,
and Venezuela on the other hand, containing certain conditions agreed
upon for the settlement of claims against the Venezuelan Government[2];

And whereas certain further questions arising out of the action taken
by the Governments of Germany, Great Britain and Italy, in connection with the settlement of their claims, have not proved to be susceptible of settlement by ordinary diplomatic methods;

And whereas the Powers interested are resolved to determine these
questions by reference to arbitration in accordance with the provisions
of the Convention for the pacific settlement of international disputes,
signed at The Hague on the 29th July, 1899;

Venezuela and Germany have, with a view to carry out that resolution, authorized their representatives, that is to say:

Mr. Herbert W. Bowen as plenipotentiary of the Government of
Venezuela, and

The Imperial German Minister, Baron Speck von Sternburg, as representative of the Imperial German Government to conclude the following agreement:

ARTICLE 1

The question as to whether or not Germany, Great Britain, and Italy
are entitled to preferential or separate treatment in the payment of their
claims against Venezuela shall be submitted for final decision to the
tribunal at The Hague.

Venezuela having agreed to set aside thirty per cent of the customs
revenues of La Guaira and Puerto Cabello for the payment of the
claims of all nations against Venezuela, the tribunal at The Hague shall
decide how the said revenues shall be divided between the blockading

---

[1]Official report, p. 17. For the German text, see Appendix, p. 445. Identical
protocols were signed on the same date by Venezuela with Great Britain and Italy
respectively, both of which were done in the English language. Belgium, Mexico,
the Netherlands, Sweden and Norway, and the United States signed as ad-
herents (*post,* p. 64). Spain, though not a signatory, also adhered and was
represented by counsel before the tribunal.
[2]*Post,* pp. 65, 67, 70, 74.

Powers, on the one hand, and the other creditor Powers, on the other hand, and its decision shall be final.

If preferential or separate treatment is not given to the blockading Powers, the tribunal shall decide how the said revenues shall be distributed among all the creditor Powers, and the parties hereto agree that the tribunal, in that case, shall consider, in connection with the payment of the claims out of the thirty per cent, any preference or pledges of revenue enjoyed by any of the creditor Powers, and shall accordingly decide the question of distribution so that no Power shall obtain preferential treatment, and its decision shall be final.

ARTICLE 2

The facts on which shall depend the decision of the questions stated in Article 1 shall be ascertained in such manner as the tribunal may determine.

ARTICLE 3

The Emperor of Russia shall be invited to name and appoint from the members of the Permanent Court of The Hague three arbitrators to constitute the tribunal which is to determine and settle the questions submitted to it under and by virtue of this agreement.

None of the arbitrators so appointed shall be a subject or citizen of any of the signatory or creditor Powers.

This tribunal shall meet on the first day of September 1903, and shall render its decision within six months thereafter.

ARTICLE 4

The proceedings shall be carried on in the English language but arguments may, with the permission of the tribunal, be made in any other language also.

Except as herein otherwise stipulated, the procedure shall be regulated by the Convention of The Hague of July 29th, 1899.

ARTICLE 5

The tribunal shall, subject to the general provision laid down in Article 57 of the international Convention of July 29th, 1899, also decide how, when and by whom the costs of this arbitration shall be paid.

ARTICLE 6

Any nation having claims against Venezuela may join as a party in the arbitration provided for by this agreement.

Done in duplicate at Washington this seventh day of May, one thousand nine hundred and three.

(Signed) HERBERT W. BOWEN
(Signed) STERNBURG

The undersigned nations having claims against Venezuela hereby join with her as parties in the arbitration provided for in the foregoing protocol.[1]

For the United States of America,

JOHN HAY

For the Republic of Mexico,
[SEAL]   M. DE AZPIROZ

For Sweden and Norway,
[SEAL]   May 27, 1903.   A. GRIP

L'Ambassadeur de France, dûment autorisé et agissant au nom de son Gouvernement, adhère au protocole ci-dessus, sous réserve qu'il est bien entendu que l'article 4 du dit protocole ne fera pas obstacle à l'application de la disposition de l'article 38 de l'acte de La Haye, aux termes de laquelle c'est le tribunal arbitral qui décide du choix des langues dont il fera usage et dont l'emploi sera autorisé devant lui.

1er Juin 1903.
[SEAL]   JUSSERAND

Le Ministre de Belgique, dûment autorisé et agissant au nom de son Gouvernement adhère au protocole ci-dessus.

12 Juin 1903.
[SEAL]   BN. MONCHEUR

Le Ministre des Pays-Bas, dûment autorisé et agissant au nom de son Gouvernement adhère au protocole ci-dessus.

Washington, le 13 Juin 1903.
[SEAL]   GEVERS

[1]Malloy, *Treaties, Conventions*, etc., *between the United States and Other Powers*, vol. 2, p. 1876.

ADDITIONAL DOCUMENTS

Protocol of Agreement between the Governments of Germany and Venezuela for the settlement of German claims.—Signed at Washington, February 13, 1903.[1]

Whereas certain differences have arisen between Germany and the United States of Venezuela in connection with the claims of German subjects against the Venezuelan Government, the undersigned, Baron Speck von Sternburg, His Imperial German Majesty's Envoy Extraordinary and Minister Plenipotentiary, duly authorized by the Imperial German Government, and Mr. Herbert W. Bowen, duly authorized by the Government of Venezuela, have agreed as follows:

ARTICLE 1

The Venezuela Government recognize in principle the justice of the claims of German subjects presented by the Imperial German Government.

ARTICLE 2

The German claims originating from the Venezuelan civil wars of 1898 to 1900 amount to 1,718,815.67 *bolívares.* The Venezuelan Government undertake to pay of said amount immediately in cash the sum of £5,500=137,500 *bolívares* (five thousand five hundred pounds=one hundred thirty-seven thousand five hundred *bolívares*) and for the payment of the rest to redeem five bills of exchange for the corresponding installments payable on the 15th of March, the 15th of April, the 15th of May, the 15th of June, and the 15th of July, 1903, to the Imperial German diplomatic agent in Carácas. These bills shall be drawn immediately by Mr. Bowen and handed over to Baron Sternburg.

Should the Venezuelan Government fail to redeem one of these bills, the payment shall be made from the customs receipts of La Guaira and Puerto Cabello, and the administration of both ports shall be put in charge of Belgian custom-house officials until the complete extinction of the said debts.

ARTICLE 3

The German claims not mentioned in Articles 2 and 6, in particular the claims resulting from the present Venezuelan civil war, the

---

[1]Official report, p. 5. For the German text, see Appendix, p. 447.

claims of the Great Venezuelan Railroad Company against the Venezuelan Government for passages and freight, the claims of the engineer Carl Henkel in Hamburg and of the Beton and Monierbau Company (Limited) in Berlin for the construction of a slaughterhouse at Carácas, are to be submitted to a mixed commission.

Said commission shall decide both whether the different claims are materially well founded and also upon their amount. The Venezuelan Government admit their liability in cases where the claim is for injury to, or wrongful seizure of, property and consequently the commission will not have to decide the question of liability, but only whether the injury to or the seizure of property were wrongful acts and what amount of compensation is due.

ARTICLE 4

The mixed commission mentioned in Article 3 shall have its seat in Carácas. It shall consist of two members, one of which is to be appointed by the Imperial German Government, the other by the Government of Venezuela. The appointments are to be made before May 1, 1903. In each case where the two members come to an agreement on the claims, their decision shall be considered as final; in cases of disagreement, the claims shall be submitted to the decision of an umpire to be nominated by the President of the United States of America.

ARTICLE 5

For the purpose of paying the claims specified in Article 3 as well as similar claims preferred by other Powers the Venezuelan Government shall remit to the representative of the Bank of England in Carácas in monthly instalments, beginning from March 1, 1903, 30 per cent of the customs revenues of La Guaira and Puerto Cabello, which shall not be alienated to any other purpose. Should the Venezuelan Government fail to carry out this obligation Belgian customs officials shall be placed in charge of the customs of the two ports and shall administer them until the liabilities of the Venezuelan Government in respect to the above-mentioned claims shall have been discharged.

Any questions as to the distribution of the customs revenues specified in the foregoing paragraph, as well as to the rights of Germany, Great Britain and Italy to a separate payment of their claims, shall be determined in default of another agreement, by the permanent tribunal of arbitration at The Hague. All other Powers interested may join as parties in the arbitration proceedings against the above-mentioned three Powers.

ARTICLE 6

The Venezuelan Goverment undertake to make a new satisfactory arrangement to settle simultaneously the five per cent Venezuelan loan of 1896 which is chiefly in German hands, and the entire exterior debt. In this arrangement the State revenues to be employed for the service of the debt are to be determined without prejudice to the obligations already existing.

ARTICLE 7

The Venezuelan men-of-war and merchant vessels captured by the German naval forces shall be returned to the Venezuelan Government in their actual condition. No claims for indemnity can be based on the capture and on the holding of these vessels, neither will an indemnity be granted for injury to or destruction of the same.

ARTICLE 8

Immediately upon the signature of this protocol the blockade of the Venezuelan ports shall be raised by the Imperial German Government in concert with the Governments of Great Britain and Italy. Also the diplomatic relations between the Imperial German and the Venezuelan Government will be resumed.

Done in duplicate in German and English texts at Washington this thirteenth day of February, one thousand nine hundred and three.

(Signed) STERNBURG
(Signed) HERBERT W. BOWEN

Protocol between Great Britain and the United States of Venezuela relating to the settlement of the British claims and other matters. —Signed at Washington, February 13, 1903.[1]

Whereas certain differences have arisen between Great Britain and the United States of Venezuela in connection with the claims of British subjects against the Venezuelan Government, the undersigned, his Excellency the Right Honorable Sir Michael H. Herbert, K. C.

---

[1]Official Report, p. 9.

M. G., C. B., His Britannic Majesty's Ambassador Extraordinary and Plenipotentiary to the United States of America, and Mr. Herbert W. Bowen, duly authorized thereto by the Government of Venezuela, have agreed as follows:

ARTICLE 1

The Venezuelan Government declare that they recognize in principle the justice of the claims which have been preferred by His Majesty's Government on behalf of British subjects.

ARTICLE 2

The Venezuelan Government will satisfy at once, by payment in cash or its equivalent, the claims of British subjects, which amount to about £5,500, arising out of the seizure and plundering of British vessels and the outrages on their crews, and the maltreatment and false imprisonment of British subjects.

ARTICLE 3

The British and Venezuelan Governments agree that the other British claims, including claims by British subjects other than those dealt with in Article 6 hereof, and including those preferred by the railway companies, shall, unless otherwise satisfied, be referred to a mixed commission constituted in the manner defined in Article 4 of this protocol, and which shall examine the claims and decide upon the amount to be awarded in satisfaction of each claim.

The Venezuelan Government admit their liability in cases where the claim is for injury to, or wrongful seizure of property, and consequently the questions which the mixed commission will have to decide in such cases will only be—

(a) Whether the injury took place, and whether the seizure was wrongful and

(b) If so, what amount of compensation is due.

In other cases the claims shall be referred to the mixed commission without reservation.

ARTICLE 4.

The mixed commission shall consist of one British member and one Venezuelan member. In each case where they come to an agreement, their decision shall be final. In cases of disagreement, the claims shall be referred to the decision of an umpire nominated by the President of the United States of America.

ARTICLE 5

The Venezuelan Government being willing to provide a sum sufficient for the payment within a reasonable time of the claims specified in Article 3 and similar claims preferred by other Governments, undertake to assign to the British Government, commencing the 1st day of March, 1903, for this purpose, and to alienate to no other purpose, thirty per cent in monthly payments of the customs revenues of La Guaira and Puerto Cabello. In the case of failure to carry out this undertaking, Belgian officials shall be placed in charge of the customs of the two ports, and shall administer them until the liabilities of the Venezuelan Government, in respect of the abovementioned claims, shall have been discharged.

Any question as to the distribution of the customs revenues so to be assigned and as to the rights of Great Britain, Germany, and Italy to a separate settlement of their claims, shall be determined, in default of arrangement, by the tribunal at The Hague, to which any other Power interested may appeal.

Pending the decision of the Hague tribunal, the said thirty per cent of the receipts of the customs of the ports of La Guaira and Puerto Cabello are to be paid over to the representatives of the Bank of England at Carácas.

ARTICLE 6

The Venezuelan Government further undertake to enter into a fresh arrangement respecting the external debt of Venezuela, with a view to the satisfaction of the claims of the bondholders. This arrangement shall include a definition of the sources from which the necessary payments are to be provided.

ARTICLE 7

The British and Venezuelan Governments agree that, inasmuch as it may be contended that the establishment of a blockade of Venezuelan ports by the British naval forces has, *ipso facto,* created a state of war between Great Britain and Venezuela, and that any treaty existing between the two countries has been thereby abrogated, it shall be recorded in an exchange of notes between the undersigned that the convention between Great Britain and Venezuela of October 29, 1834, which adopted and confirmed, *mutatis mutandis,* the treaty of April 18, 1825, between Great Britain and the State of Colombia, shall be deemed to be renewed and confirmed, or provisionally renewed and confirmed, pending conclusion of a new treaty of amity and commerce.

ARTICLE 8

Immediately upon the signature of this protocol arrangements will be made by His Majesty's Government, in concert with the Governments of Germany and Italy, to raise the blockade of the Venezuelan ports.

His Majesty's Government will be prepared to restore the vessels of the Venezuelan navy which have been seized, and further to release any other vessels captured under the Venezuelan flag, on the receipt of a guarantee from the Venezuelan Government that they will hold His Majesty's Government indemnified in respect of any proceedings which might be taken against them by the owners of such ships or of goods on board them.

ARTICLE 9

The treaty of amity and commerce of October 29, 1834, having been confirmed in accordance with the terms of Article 7 of this protocol, His Majesty's Government will be happy to renew diplomatic relations with the Government of Venezuela.

Done in duplicate at Washington, this 13th day of February, 1903.

(Signed) MICHAEL H. HERBERT
(Signed) HERBERT W. BOWEN

Protocol of Agreement between Italy and Venezuela relative to the settlement of Italian claims.—Signed at Washington, February 13, 1903.[1]

Whereas certain differences have arisen between Italy and the United States of Venezuela in connection with the Italian claims against the Venezuelan Government, the undersigned, his Excellency Nobile Edmondo Mayor des Planches, Commander of the Orders of SS. Maurice and Lazarus and the Crown of Italy, Ambassador Extraordinary and Plenipotentiary of His Majesty the King of Italy to the United States of America, and Mr. Herbert W. Bowen duly authorized thereto by the Government of Venezuela, have agreed as follows:

---

[1] Official Report, p. 13.

ARTICLE 1

The Venezuelan Government declare that they recognize in principle the justice of claims which have been preferred by His Majesty's Government on behalf of Italian subjects.

ARTICLE 2

The Venezuelan Government agree to pay to the Italian Government, as a satisfaction of the point of honor, the sum of £5,500, (five thousand five hundred pounds sterling), in cash or its equivalent, which sum is to be paid within sixty days.

ARTICLE 3

The Venezuelan Government recognize, accept and will pay the amount of the Italian claims of the first rank derived from the revolutions [of] 1898-1900, in the sum of 2,810,255 (two million eight hundred and ten thousand, two hundred and fifty-five) *bolívares*.

It is expressly agreed that the payment of the above Italian claims of the first rank will be made without being the same claims or the same sum submitted to the mixed commission and without any revision or objection.

ARTICLE 4

The Italian and Venezuelan Governments agree that all the remaining Italian claims, without exception, other than those dealt within Article 7 hereof, shall, unless otherwise satisfied, be referred to a mixed commission to be constituted, as soon as possible, in the manner defined in Article 6 of the protocol, and which shall examine the claims and decide upon the amount to be awarded in satisfaction of each.

The Venezuelan Government admit their liability in cases where the claim is for injury to persons and property and for wrongful seizure of the latter, and consequently the questions which the mixed commission will have to decide in such cases will only be:

(*a*) Whether the injury took place or whether the seizure was wrongful and

(*b*) If so, what amount of compensation is due.

In other cases the claims will be referred to the mixed commission without reservation.

ARTICLE 5

The Venezuelan Government being willing to provide a sum sufficient for the payment, within a reasonable time, of the claims specified in Articles 3 and 4 and similar claims preferred by other Governments, undertake and obligate themselves to assign to the Italian Government, commencing the first day of March 1903, for this purpose, and to alienate to no other purpose, thirty per cent of the customs revenues of La Guaira and Puerto Cabello. In the case of failure to carry out this undertaking and obligation, Belgian officials shall be placed in charge of the two ports, and shall administer them until the liabilities of the Venezuelan Government, in respect of the abovementioned claims, shall have been discharged.

Any question as to the distribution of the customs revenues so to be assigned, and as to the rights of Italy, Great Britain, and Germany to a separate settlement of their claims, shall be determined, in default of arrangement, by the tribunal at The Hague, to which any other Power interested may appeal.

Pending the decision of The Hague tribunal the said thirty per cent of the receipts of the customs of the ports of La Guaira and Puerto Cabello are to be paid over to the representatives of the Bank of England at Carácas.

ARTICLE 6

The mixed commission shall consist of one Italian member and one Venezuelan member.

In each case, where they come to an agreement, their decision shall be final. In case of disagreement, the claims shall be referred to the decision of an umpire nominated by the President of the United States of America.

ARTICLE 7

The Venezuelan Government further undertake to enter into a fresh arrangement respecting the external debt of Venezuela with a view to the satisfaction of the claims of the bondholders. This arrangement shall include a definition of the sources from which the necessary payments are to be provided.

ARTICLE 8

The treaty of amity, commerce, and navigation between Italy and Venezuela of June 19, 1861, is renewed and confirmed. It is however expressly agreed between the two Governments that the interpretation to be given to the Articles 4 and 26 is the following:

According to the Article 4, Italians in Venezuela and Venezuelans in Italy can not in any case receive a treatment less favorable than the natives, and, according to Article 26, Italians in Venezuela and Venezuelans in Italy are entitled to receive, in every matter and especially in the matter of claims, the treatment of the most favored nation, as it is established in the same Article 26.

If there is doubt or conflict between the two articles, the Article 26 will be followed.

It is further specifically agreed that the above treaty shall never be invoked, in any case, against the provisions of the present protocol.

ARTICLE 9

At once upon the signing of this protocol, arrangements shall be made by His Majesty's Government, in concert with the Governments of Germany and Great Britain, to raise the blockade of the Venezuelan ports.

His Majesty's Government will be prepared to restore the vessels of the Venezuelan navy which may have been seized, and further to release any other vessel captured under the Venezuelan flag during the blockade.

ARTICLE 10

The treaty of amity, commerce, and navigation of June 19th, 1861, having been renewed and confirmed in accordance with the terms of Article 8 of this protocol, His Majesty's Government declare that they will be happy to re-establish regular diplomatic relations with the Government of Venezuela.

Washington, D. C., February 13, 1903.

(Signed)   E. MAYOR DES PLANCHES
(Signed)   HERBERT W. BOWEN

We interpret our three protocols to mean that the thirty per cent referred to therein, of the total income of the custom-houses of La Guaira and Puerto Cabello, shall be delivered to the representative of the Bank of England at Carácas, and that the said thirty per cent is not assigned to any one Power but it is to be retained by the said representative of the Bank of England in Carácas and paid out by him in conformity with the decision rendered by the tribunal at The Hague.

Washington, February 14th, 1903.

Protocol of an Agreement between the United States of America and the Republic of Venezuela for submission to arbitration of all unsettled claims against Venezuela.—Signed at Washington, February 17, 1903.[1]

The United States of America and the Republic of Venezuela, through their representatives, John Hay, Secretary of State of the United States of America, and Herbert W. Bowen, the plenipotentiary of the Republic of Venezuela, have agreed upon and signed the following protocol.

ARTICLE 1

All claims owned by citizens of the United States of America against the Republic of Venezuela which have not been settled by diplomatic agreement or by arbitration between the two Governments, and which shall have been presented to the commission hereinafter named by the Department of State of the United States or its Legation at Carácas, shall be examined and decided by a mixed commission, which shall sit at Carácas, and which shall consist of two members, one of whom is to be appointed by the President of the United States and the other by the President of Venezuela.

It is agreed that an umpire may be named by the Queen of the Netherlands. If either of said commissioners or the umpire should fail or cease to act, his successor shall be appointed forthwith in the same manner as his predecessor. Said commissioners and umpire are to be appointed before the first day of May, 1903.

The commissioners and the umpire shall meet in the city of Carácas on the first day of June, 1903. The umpire shall preside over their deliberations, and shall be competent to decide any question on which the commissioners disagree. Before assuming the functions of their office the commissioners and the umpire shall take solemn oath carefully to examine and impartially decide, according to justice and the provisions of this convention, all claims submitted to them, and such oaths shall be entered on the record of their proceedings. The commissioners, or in case of their disagreement, the umpire, shall decide all claims upon a basis of absolute equity, without regard to objections of a technical nature, or of the provisions of local legislation.

---

[1]Malloy, *Treaties, Conventions,* etc., *between the United States and Other Powers,* vol. 2, p. 1870. For the Spanish text, see Appendix, p. 449. Similar protocols were signed by Venezuela with the following countries: Belgium (March 7, 1903), France (February 27, 1903), Mexico (February 26, 1903), Netherlands (February 28, 1903), Spain (April 2, 1903), Sweden and Norway (March 10, 1903).

The decisions of the commission, and in the event of their disagreement, those of the umpire, shall be final and conclusive. They shall be in writing. All awards shall be made payable in United States gold, or its equivalent in silver.

ARTICLE 2

The commissioners, or umpire, as the case may be, shall investigate and decide said claims upon such evidence or information only as shall be furnished by or on behalf of the respective Governments. They shall be bound to receive and consider all written documents or statements which may be presented to them by or on behalf of the respective Governments in support of or in answer to any claim, and to hear oral or written arguments made by the agent of each Government on every claim. In case of their failure to agree in opinion upon any individual claim, the umpire shall decide.

Every claim shall be formally presented to the commissioners within thirty days from the day of their first meeting, unless the commissioners or the umpire in any case extend the period for presenting the claim not exceeding three months longer. The commissioners shall be bound to examine and decide upon every claim within six months from the day of its first formal presentation, and in case of their disagreement, the umpire shall examine and decide within a corresponding period from the date of such disagreement.

ARTICLE 3

The commissioners and the umpire shall keep an accurate record of their proceedings. For that purpose, each commissioner shall appoint a secretary versed in the language of both countries, to assist them in the transaction of the business of the commission. Except as herein stipulated, all questions of procedure shall be left to the determination of the c mmission, or in case of their disagreement, to the umpire.

ARTICLE 4

Reasonable compensation to the commissioners and to the umpire for their services and expenses, and the other expenses of said arbitration, are to be paid in equal moities by the contracting parties.

ARTICLE 5

In order to pay the total amount of the claims to be adjudicated as aforesaid, and other claims of citizens or subjects of other nations, the Government of Venezuela shall set apart for this purpose, and alienate to no other purpose, beginning with the month of March, 1903, thirty per cent in monthly payments of the customs revenues of La Guaira and Puerto Cabello, and the payments thus set aside shall be divided and distributed in conformity with the decision of The Hague tribunal.

In case of the failure to carry out the above agreement, Belgian officials shall be placed in charge of the customs of the two ports, and shall administer them until the liabilities of the Venezuelan Government in respect to the above claims shall have been discharged. The reference of the question above stated to the Hague tribunal will be the subject of a separate protocol.

ARTICLE 6

All existing and unsatisfied awards in favor of citizens of the United States shall be promptly paid, according to the terms of the respective awards.

Washington, D. C., February 17, 1903.

JOHN HAY   [SEAL]

HERBERT W. BOWEN   [SEAL]

THE JAPANESE HOUSE TAX CASE

between

FRANCE, GERMANY, GREAT BRITAIN *and* JAPAN

Decided May 22, 1905

Syllabus

This case had its origin in the extraterritorial jurisdiction which was maintained respecting the citizens of foreign nations resident in Japan prior to 1894. By treaties with Great Britain, Germany and France, dated respectively, July 16, 1894,[1] April 4, 1896,[2] and August 4, 1896,[3] this practice was abandoned, Japan agreeing to set aside for perpetual lease to citizens or subjects of foreign nations certain tracts of land at various treaty ports. It was provided that no conditions other than those contained in the leases would be imposed in respect to such property. Accordingly, no taxes or charges, except those named in the leases, were paid for municipal or other purposes for a number of years subsequent to the signature of the treaties. Finally, however, the Japanese assumed the position that the leases had reference only to unimproved land, and that the houses or other improvements were not included. The interested Governments declined to accede to Japan's view and the question was referred, by a *compromis* dated August 28, 1902,[4] to a tribunal selected from the panel of the Permanent Court of Arbitration at The Hague as follows: Gregers Gram of Norway, Louis Renault of France, and Itchiro Motono of Japan. The sessions began November 21, 1904, and ended May 15, 1905, and the decision was rendered May 22, 1905. By a majority opinion, signed by the French and Norwegian members, the tribunal held that:

The provisions of the treaties and other engagements mentioned in the arbitration protocols not only exempt the lands held by virtue of the perpetual leases granted by the Japanese Government or in its name, but they exempt the lands and the buildings of every nature constructed or which may be constructed on these lands from all imposts, taxes, charges, contributions, or conditions whatsoever other than those expressly stipulated in the leases in question.

The Japanese member dissented from this decision and upheld the contentions of his Government.

---

[1]*Post*, p. 89.   [2]*Post*, p. 91.   [3]*Post*, p. 92.   [4]*Post*, p. 85.

AWARD OF THE TRIBUNAL

Award of the tribunal of arbitration constituted in virtue of the protocols signed at Tokio, August 28, 1902, between Japan, on the one hand, and Germany, France and Great Britain on the other hand.—The Hague, May 22, 1905.[1]

Whereas, according to the protocols signed at Tokio on August 28, 1902,[2] a disagreement has arisen between the Government of Japan on the one hand and the Governments of Germany, France, and Great Britain on the other regarding the real meaning and scope of the following provisions of the respective treaties and other agreements existing between them, namely:

Paragraph 4, Article 18, of the treaty of commerce and navigation of April 4, 1896, between Japan and Germany: "When such incorporation takes place [that is to say, when the several foreign settlements in Japan shall have been incorporated with the respective Japanese communes], the existing leases in perpetuity under which property is now held in the said settlements shall be confirmed, and no conditions whatsoever other than those contained in such existing leases shall be imposed in respect of such property"; and paragraph 3 of the complementary communication of the same date from the German Secretary for Foreign Affairs to the Japanese Minister at Berlin: "3. That, as the proprietary rights in the settlements mentioned in Article 18 of the treaty continue to belong to the Japanese State, the owners or their legal successors shall not have to pay duties or taxes of any kind for their land except the contract ground rent"; and the clause in the reply of the Japanese Minister of the same date, to the foregoing communication: "That he entirely indorses the explanatory statements set forth therein, in Nos. 1 to 4, concerning the acquisition of real rights in landed property, the construction of warehouses, the freedom from taxation in the foreign settlements, and the preservation of duly-acquired rights after the expiration of the treaty";

Paragraph 4, Article 21, of the revised treaty of August 4, 1896, between Japan and France: "When the changes above-indicated shall have taken place [that is to say, when the several foreign set-

---

[1]*American Journal of International Law*, vol. 2, p. 915. For the original French text, see Appendix, p. 452.
[2]*Post*, p. 85.

tlements in Japan shall have been incorporated with the respective Japanese communes and made a part of the municipal system of Japan; and when the competent Japanese authorities shall have assumed all municipal obligations and duties, and the municipal funds and property belonging to such settlements shall have been transferred to said Japanese authorities], the leases in perpetuity, in virtue of which foreigners now possess property in the settlements, shall be confirmed, and property of that character shall not be subject to any duties, taxes, charges, contributions or conditions whatsoever, other than those expressly stipulated in the leases in question";

Paragraph 4 of Article 18 of the revised treaty of July 16, 1894, between Japan and Great Britain: "When such incorporation takes place" [that is, when the various foreign quarters existing in Japan shall have been incorporated into the respective communes of Japan], "existing leases in perpetuity under which property is now held in the said settlements shall be confirmed, and no conditions whatsoever other than those contained in such existing leases shall be imposed in respect of such property."

Whereas the Powers at variance have agreed to submit their differences to the decision of a tribunal of arbitration;

And whereas in virtue of the above-mentioned protocols the Governments of Germany, France, and Great Britain have designated as arbitrator Mr. Louis Renault, Minister Plenipotentiary, member of the Institute of France, professor in the Faculty of Law at Paris, Jurisconsult of the Department of Foreign Affairs, and the Government of Japan has designated as arbitrator his Excellency Mr. Itchiro Motono, Envoy Extraordinary and Minister Plenipotentiary of His Majesty the Emperor of Japan at Paris, Doctor of Laws;

And whereas the two above-mentioned arbitrators have chosen as umpire Mr. Gregers Gram, former Minister of State of Norway, Provincial Governor;

And whereas the tribunal thus composed has as its mission to decide, in the last resort, on the following question:

Do the provisions of the treaties and other engagements hereinabove mentioned exempt only the lands held by virtue of the perpetual leases granted by the Japanese Government or in its name, or do they exempt the lands and the buildings of every nature constructed or which may be constructed on these lands, from all imposts, taxes, charges, contributions, or conditions whatsoever other than those especially stipulated in the leases in question?

Whereas the Japanese Government maintains that the lands alone are exempt from the payment of imposts and other charges to the extent which has just been indicated;

And whereas the Governments of Germany, France, and Great Britain claim, on the contrary, that the buildings constructed on these lands enjoy the same exemption;

And whereas, in order to understand the nature and the scope of the engagements contracted on both sides through the perpetual leases it is necessary to examine several arrangements and agreements concluded, under the old treaties, between the Japanese authorities and the representatives of several Powers;

And whereas from these acts and stipulations inserted in the leases it is shown:

That the Japanese Government had consented to lend its assistance for the creation of foreign quarters in certain cities and ports of Japan, open to the citizens of other nations;

That on the lands designated for the use of the foreigners in the various localities the Japanese Government has executed, at its own expense, works for the purpose of facilitating their urban occupation;

That as foreigners are not allowed to acquire ownership of lands situated in the country according to the principles of Japanese law, the Government has given them a perpetual lease on the lands;

That the leases determine the extent of the lots leased and stipulate a fixed annual rent, calculated in proportion to the area leased;

That it was agreed that in principle the foreign quarters should remain outside the municipal system of Japan, but that they were not subjected to a uniform organization;

That it was decided, by means of regulations, how the various administrative functions should be provided for, and that it was prescribed that the holders of the lands should be obliged to contribute partially toward the expenses of the municipality by means of dues the amount and mode of collection of which were determined;

And whereas it would be easy to explain the care taken in wording these documents in order to define the obligations of every nature incumbent on foreigners toward the Japanese Government, if it were understood that the annual rent represented not only the price of the lease but also the counterpart of the imposts which the lessees would have been owing by reason of the situation created in their favor by the leases, and that, consequently, they would not, in this capacity, have to bear any imposts and charges but those expressly mentioned in the said leases;

And whereas, moreover, it is not denied that this is the real meaning of this document, as far as lands are concerned, but the Japanese Government alleges that the leases referred only to the bare lands and does not admit that the buildings erected on the lands shall be comprised in the stipulations on which the exemption from taxes would be based;

And whereas it alleged that the lands alone belonged to the Government, the buildings being, on the contrary, the property of the lessees and that in consequence the immunity in question can only extend to the real estate which had never been separated from the Government domain; and whereas, nevertheless, the question to be decided is whether, from the Government's point of view, the buildings erected on the leased lands were, by mutual consent, considered as accessories of these lands or not, and the solution of this question does not depend on distinctions drawn from a pretended difference with regard to the ownership of the real estate;

And whereas the tribunal can therefore not stop to take up the discussion begun on this subject and based on the principles of civil law;

And whereas the lands were leased for the purpose of building houses on them, as is shown at once by the situation of the lands and the nature of the improvements made thereon by the Japanese Government;

And whereas the obligation to erect buildings was imposed in some localities under penalty of forfeiture, and the leases often contained a clause according to which the buildings situated on the lands should become the property of the Japanese Government in case the lessee failed to fulfil his engagements;

And whereas it must be admitted that the circumstances just related offer arguments in refutation of the claim that the soil and the buildings constitute entirely different objects from the Government's standpoint in the relations between the parties;

And whereas in concluding these acts the Japanese Government acted not only as owner of the lands leased but also in its capacity as the sovereign Power of the country;

And whereas the will of the parties was consequently the law in the matter, and, in order to determine how the acts were really interpreted we must examine the treatment to which the holders of the lands have actually been subjected in the various localities as far as the taxes are concerned;

And whereas, in this regard, it is known that, according to a practice which has never varied and has been in existence for a long number of years, not only the lands in question but also the buildings erected thereon have been exempt from all taxes, imposts, charges, contributions, or conditions other than those expressly stipulated in the perpetual leases;

And whereas the Government of Japan maintains, to be sure, that this state of affairs, as well as the fiscal immunity which was enjoyed by foreigners in general in that country, was due only to the circumstance that the consular tribunals refused to give the necessary sanction to the fiscal laws of the country;

Whereas, however, this claim is unsustained by evidence and it is not even alleged that the Japanese Government ever made any reservations with respect to the German, French, and British Governments for the purpose of maintaining the rights which it says were violated;

And whereas, although it has been alleged that the immunity enjoyed by foreigners with respect to taxes under the old treaties was general and extended to foreigners residing outside the concession in question, it is nevertheless shown from information furnished on the subject of the holders of real estate (lands and houses) at Hiogo that the said rule was not universally applied;

And whereas, at all events, the actual situation is not doubtful, however it is explained;

And whereas, from the standpoint of the interpretation of the provisions of the new treaties with regard to which there is a dispute among the parties:

The drafting of Article 18 of the treaty between Great Britain and Japan (which treaty was previous to the two others), had been preceded by propositions to place foreigners holding lands on the same footing as Japanese subjects, both from the standpoint of the ownership of real estate which had been granted them on lease and in regard to the payment of taxes and imposts, but it was afterwards agreed upon to continue the system which had prevailed until then;

And the Japanese Government claims, to be sure, that the question of maintaining the *status quo* referred only to the lands, but this claim is not substantiated by the expressions employed during the course of negotiations;

And, on the contrary, the representative of the Japanese Government who took the initiative in order to reach an agreement along these lines confined himself to proposing the maintenance of the *status quo* in the foreign settlements;

And it is not to be presumed that the delegate of Great Britain, in presenting a project worked out on the basis of said proposition, intended to make a restriction with regard to the buildings, which is neither shown by the words inserted in the record nor by the purport of the article proposed by him;

And, in order to maintain the *status quo* integrally, it would not be sufficient to admit that the fiscal immunity, which up to that time had extended to both lands and buildings in the foreign settlement, should be maintained with regard to the soil only and that it should cease to exist as far as the houses are concerned;

And this must especially be the case if we consider that, in order to conform to what had been agreed upon, the parties did not confine themselves to drawing up a provision with regard to the confirmation of the leases, but added that no conditions whatsoever other than those contained in such existing leases shall be imposed with respect to such property;

And this latter clause is worded still more explicitly in the treaty with France;

And whereas, moreover, the Powers did not speak of lands in the clauses in question as they must necessarily have done if the immunity, contrary to what had been practiced up to that time, ought to have been confined to the lands;

And whereas, on the contrary, they employed expressions which were broad enough to comprise the entire situation created by the leases for the lessees;

And whereas the tribunal can not, either, admit that the notes exchanged between the German and Japanese Governments at the time of conclusion of the new treaty contained explanations of such a nature as to place Germany in any less favorable situation than the other two Powers;

And whereas the Japanese Government has desired above all to derive an argument from the fact that the German Government based fiscal immunity on the fact that foreigners are prohibited from acquiring ownership to lands situated in Japan, but it is necessary in this regard to consider that the buildings had really always had the character of appurtenances of the lands from the standpoint of taxes, and it can not be presumed that the German Government intended to renounce the advantages allowed in favor of Great Britain by the new treaty, which would moreover be in contradiction with the clause assuring to Germany the treatment of the most-favored nation;

Therefore, the tribunal of arbitration, by majority of votes, decides and declares:

The provisions of the treaties and other engagements mentioned in the arbitration protocols not only exempt the lands held by virtue of the perpetual leases granted by the Japanese Government or in its name, but they exempt the lands and the buildings of every nature constructed or which may be constructed on these lands from all imposts, taxes, charges, contributions, or conditions whatsoever other than those expressly stipulated in the leases in question.

Done at The Hague, in the building of the Permanent Court of Arbitration, on May 22, 1905.

(Signed)   G. GRAM
            L. RENAULT

At the time of the proceeding to the signature of the present award, availing myself of the privilege conferred by Article 52, paragraph 2, of the Convention for the pacific settlement of international disputes, concluded at The Hague on July 29, 1899, I wish to state my absolute disagreement with the majority of the tribunal with regard to both the grounds and the decision of the award.

(Signed)   I. MOTONO

AGREEMENT FOR ARBITRATION

Protocol between Great Britain and Japan for submitting to arbitration certain questions as to the interpretation of treaties with Japan with regard to leases held in perpetuity.—Signed at Tokio, August 28, 1902.[1]

Whereas, a dispute has arisen between the Government of Japan on the one side and the Governments of Great Britain, France and Germany on the other, respecting the true intent and meaning of the following provisions of the treaties and other engagements respectively existing between them, that is to say:

Paragraph 4, Article 18, of the treaty of commerce and navigation of April 4, 1896, between Japan and Germany: "Sobald diese Einverleibung erfolgt," [that is to say: when the several foreign settlements in Japan shall have been incorporated with the respective Japanese communes], "sollen die bestehenden, zietlich unbegrenzten Ueberlassungsverträge, unter welchen jetzt in den gedachten Niederlassungen Grundstücke besessen werden, bestätigt und hinsichtlich dieser Grundstücke sollen keine Bedingungen irgend einer anderen Art auferlegt werden, als sie in den bestehenden Ueberlassungsverträgen enthalten sind"[2]; and § 3 of the complementary communication of the same date from the German Secretary for Foreign Affairs to the Japanese Minister at Berlin: "3, dass, da das Eigenthum an den im Artikel XVIII des Vertrages erwähnten Niederlassungsgrundstücken dem Japanischen Staate verbleibt, die Besitzer oder deren Rechtsnachfolger für ihre Grundstücke ausser dem kontraktmässigen Grundzins Abgaben oder Steuern irgend welcher Art nicht zu entrichten haben werden"[3]; and

---

[1] Official report, p. 13. Similar protocols between France and Japan and between Germany and Japan were also signed on August 28, 1902. For the original German and French texts, see Appendix, pp. 457, 461.

[2] TRANSLATION: When such incorporation takes place [..........], the existing leases in perpetuity under which property is now held in the said settlements shall be confirmed, and no conditions whatsoever other than those contained in such existing leases shall be imposed in respect of such property.

[3] TRANSLATION: 3. That, as the proprietary rights in the settlements mentioned in Article 18 of the treaty continue to belong to the Japanese State, the owners or their legal successors shall not have to pay duties or taxes of any kind for their land except the contract ground rent.

the clause in the reply of the Japanese Minister of the same date, to the foregoing communication: "dass die darin unter Nummer 1 bis 4 zum Ausdruck gebrachten Voraussetzungen, welche den Erwerb dinglicher Rechte an Grundstücken, die Errichtung von Waarenhäusern, die Steuerfreiheit der Grundstücke in den Fremdenniederlassungen und die Erhaltung wohlerworbener Rechte nach Ablauf des Vertrages zum Gegenstande haben, in allen Punkten zutreffend sind"[1];

Paragraph 4, Article 21, of the revised treaty of August 4, 1896, between Japan and France: "Lorsque les changements ci-dessus indiqués auront été effectués," [that is to say: when the several foreign settlements in Japan shall have been incorporated with the respective Japanese communes and made a part of the municipal system of Japan; and when the competent Japanese authorities shall have assumed all municipal obligations and duties, and the municipal funds and property belonging to such settlements shall have been transferred to said Japanese authorities], "les baux à perpétuité en vertu desquels les étrangers possèdent actuellement des propriétés dans les quartiers seront confirmés, et les propriétés de cette nature ne donneront lieu à aucuns impôts, taxes, charges, contributions ou conditions quelconques autres que ceux expressément stipulés dans les baux en question"[2]; and

Paragraph 4, Article 18, of the revised treaty of July 16, 1894, between Japan and Great Britain: "When such incorporation takes place [that is to say, when the several foreign settlements in Japan shall have been incorporated with the respective Japanese communes], existing leases in perpetuity under which property is now held in the said settlements shall be confirmed, and no conditions whatsoever other than those contained in such existing leases shall be imposed in respect of such property"; and

Whereas, the controversy is not amenable to ordinary diplomatic methods; and

Whereas, the Powers at variance, co-signatories of the Convention of The Hague for the peaceful adjustment of international differences,

---

[1]TRANSLATION: That he entirely indorses the explanatory statements set forth therein, in Nos. 1 to 4, concerning the acquisition of real rights in landed property, the construction of warehouses, the freedom from taxation in the foreign settlements, and the preservation of duly-acquired rights after the expiration of the treaty.

[2]TRANSLATION: When the changes above indicated shall have taken place [................], the leases in perpetuity, in virtue of which foreigners now possess property in the settlements, shall be confirmed, and property of that character shall not be subject to any duties, taxes, charges, contributions or conditions whatsoever, other than those expressly stipulated in the leases in question.

have resolved to terminate the controversy by referring the question at issue to impartial arbitration in accordance with the provisions of said convention;

The said Powers have, with a view to carry out that resolution, authorized the following representatives, that is to say:

The Government of Great Britain: Sir Claude Maxwell MacDonald, G. C. M. G., K. C. B., His Britannic Majesty's Envoy Extraordinary and Minister Plenipotentiary;

The Government of France: Monsieur G. Dubail, Minister Plenipotentiary, Chargé d'Affaires of France;

The Government of Germany: Count von Arco Valley, Envoy Extraordinary and Minister Plenipotentiary of His Majesty the German Emperor, King of Prussia;

The Government of Japan: Baron Komura Jutaro, His Imperial Japanese Majesty's Minister of State for Foreign Affairs; to conclude the following protocol:

1

The Powers in difference agree that the arbitral tribunal, to which the question at issue is to be submitted for final decision, shall be composed of three members who are members of the Permanent Court of Arbitration of The Hague, to be selected in the following manner:

Each party, as soon as possible and not later than two months after the date of this protocol, to name one arbitrator, and the two arbitrators so named together to choose an umpire. In case the two arbitrators fail for the period of two months after their appointment to choose an umpire, His Majesty the King of Sweden and Norway shall be requested to name an umpire.

2

The question at issue upon which the parties to this arbitration request the arbitral tribunal to pronounce a final decision, is as follows:

Whether or not the provisions of the treaties and other engagements above quoted exempt only land held under leases in perpetuity granted by or on behalf of the Japanese Government, or land and buildings of whatever description constructed or which may hereafter be constructed on such land, from any imposts, taxes, charges, contributions, or conditions whatsoever, other than those expressly stipulated in the leases in question.

3

Within eight months after the date of this protocol, each party shall deliver to the several members of the arbitral tribunal and to the other party complete written or printed copies of the case, evidence and arguments upon which it relies in the present arbitration. And not later than six months thereafter a similar delivery shall be made of written or printed copies of the counter-cases, additional evidence, and final arguments of the two parties; it being understood that such counter-cases, additional evidence and final arguments, shall be limited to answering the principal cases, evidence, and arguments previously delivered.

4

Each party shall have the right to submit to the arbitral tribunal as evidence in the case all such documents, records, official correspondence, and other official or public statements or acts bearing on the subject of this arbitration as it may consider necessary. But if in its case, counter-case, or arguments submitted to the tribunal either party shall have specified or alluded to any document or paper in its own exclusive possession without annexing a copy, such party shall be bound, if the other party thinks proper to apply for it, to furnish that party with a copy thereof within thirty days after such application is made.

5

Either party may, if it thinks fit, but subject to the right of reply on the part of the other party within such time as may be fixed by the arbitral tribunal, present to the tribunal for such action as the tribunal may deem proper a statement of objections to the counter-case, additional evidence, and final arguments of the other party if it is of opinion that those documents or any of them are irrelevant, erroneous, or not strictly limited to answering its principal case, evidence, and arguments.

6

No papers or communications other than those contemplated by sections 3 and 5 of this protocol, either written or oral, shall be admitted or considered in the present arbitration unless the arbitral tribunal shall request from either party additional or supplementary explanation or information to be given in writing. If the explanation or information is given, the other party shall have the right to present a written reply within such time as may be fixed by the arbitral tribunal.

7

The tribunal shall meet at a place to be designated later by the parties as soon as practicable, but not earlier than two months nor later than three months after the delivery of the counter-cases as provided in section 3 of this protocol, and shall proceed impartially and carefully to examine and decide the question at issue. The decision of the tribunal shall, if possible, be pronounced within one month after the president thereof shall have declared the arbitral hearing closed.

8

For the purposes of this arbitration, the Government of Japan shall be regarded as one party and the Governments of Great Britain, France, and Germany, jointly, shall be regarded as the other party.

9

So far as is not otherwise provided in this protocol, the provisions of the Convention of The Hague for the peaceful adjustment of international differences shall apply to this arbitration.

Done at Tokio, this 28th day of August, 1902, corresponding to the 28th day of the 8th month of the 35th year of Meiji.

(Signed) CLAUDE M. MACDONALD
(Signed) JUTARO KOMURA

ADDITIONAL DOCUMENTS

Extract from the Treaty of Commerce and Navigation between Great Britain and Japan, signed at London, July 16, 1894[1]

18. Her Britannic Majesty's Government, so far as they are concerned, give their consent to the following arrangement:

The several foreign settlements in Japan shall be incorporated with the respective Japanese communes, and shall thenceforth form part of the general municipal system of Japan.

The competent Japanese authorities shall thereupon assume all municipal obligations and duties in respect thereof, and the common funds and property, if any, belonging to such settlements, shall at the same time be transferred to the said Japanese authorities.

When such incorporation takes place the existing leases in perpetuity under which property is now held in the said settlements shall be confirmed, and no conditions whatsoever other than those contained in

---

[1]*British and Foreign State Papers*, vol. 86, p. 46.

such existing leases shall be imposed in respect of such property.   It is, however, understood that the consular authorities mentioned in the same are in all cases to be replaced by the Japanese authorities.

All lands which may previously have been granted by the Japanese Government free of rent for the public purposes of the said settlements shall, subject to the right of eminent domain, be permanently reserved free of all taxes and charges for the public purposes for which they were originally set apart.

19. The stipulations of the present treaty shall be applicable, so far as the laws permit, to all the colonies and foreign possessions of Her Britannic Majesty, excepting to those hereinafter-named, that is to say, except to—

India   Victoria
The Dominion of Canada   Queensland
Newfoundland   Tasmania
The Cape   South Australia
Natal   Western Australia
New South Wales   New Zealand

Provided always that the stipulations of the present treaty shall be made applicable to any of the above-named colonies or foreign possessions on whose behalf notice to that effect shall have been given to the Japanese Government by Her Britannic Majesty's representative at Tokio within two years from the date of the exchange of ratifications of the present treaty.

20. The present treaty shall, from the date it comes into force, be substituted in place of the conventions respectively of the 23d day of the 8th month of the 7th year of Kayei, corresponding to the 14th day of October, 1854, and of the 13th day of the 5th month of the 2nd year of Keiou, corresponding to the 25th day of June, 1866, the treaty of the 18th day of the 7th month of the 5th year of Ansei, corresponding to the 26th day of August, 1858, and all arrangements and agreements subsidiary thereto concluded or existing between the high contracting Parties; and from the same date such conventions, treaty, arrangements, and agreements shall cease to be binding, and, in consequence, the jurisdiction then exercised by British courts in Japan, and all the exceptional privileges, exemptions, and immunities then enjoyed by British subjects as a part of or appurtenant to such jurisdiction, shall absolutely and without notice cease and determine, and thereafter all such jurisdiction shall be assumed and exercised by Japanese courts.

Extract from the Treaty of Commerce and Navigation between Germany and Japan, signed at Berlin, April 4, 1896 [1]

18. The contracting Parties have agreed upon the following arrangement :

The several foreign settlements in Japan shall be incorporated with the respective Japanese communes, and shall thenceforth form integral parts of the Japanese communes.

The competent Japanese authorities shall thereupon assume all municipal obligations and duties in respect thereof, and the common funds and property, if any, belonging to such settlements, shall at the same time be transferred to the said Japanese authorities.

When such incorporation takes place the existing leases in perpetuity under which property is now held in the said settlements shall be confirmed, and no conditions whatsoever other than those contained in such existing leases shall be imposed in respect of such property.

The proprietary rights in the lands belonging to these settlements may in the future be granted to natives or foreigners by their proprietors free of charge and without the consent of the consular or Japanese authorities, as has hitherto been required in certain cases.

The functions, however, attached according to the original leases to the consular authorities, shall devolve upon the Japanese authorities.

All lands which may previously have been granted by the Japanese Government free of rent for the public purposes of the said settlements shall, subject to the right of eminent domain, be permanently reserved free of all taxes and charges for the public purposes for which they were originally set apart.

19. The stipulations of the present treaty shall be applicable to the territories which now, or shall in future, form a customs union with one or other of the contracting Parties.

20. The present treaty shall, from the date it comes into force, be substituted in place of the treaty of the 20th February, 1869, and all arrangements and agreements subsidiary thereto concluded or existing between the high contracting Parties. From the same date these earlier conventions shall cease to be binding, and, in consequence, the jurisdiction till then exercised by German courts in Japan, and all the exceptional privileges, exemptions, and immunities then enjoyed by German subjects as a part of or appurtenant to such jurisdiction, shall absolutely and without notice cease and determine. Thereafter all such jurisdiction shall be assumed and exercised by Japanese courts.

---

[1] *British and Foreign State Papers*, vol. 88, p. 588. For the original German text, see Appendix, p. 464.

Extract from the Treaty of Commerce and Navigation between France and Japan, signed at Paris, August 4, 1896[1]

21. The Government of the French Republic, so far as it is concerned, gives its consent to the following arrangement:

The several foreign settlements existing in Japan shall be incorporated in the respective Japanese communes and shall thenceforth form a part of the municipal system of Japan.

The competent Japanese authorities shall thereupon assume all municipal obligations and powers resulting from this new state of affairs, and the municipal funds and property belonging to such settlements shall, at the same time, be transferred to the said Japanese authorities.

When the changes above indicated shall have taken place, the leases in perpetuity, in virtue of which foreigners now possess property in the settlements, shall be confirmed, and property of that character shall not be subject to any duties, taxes, charges, contributions, or conditions whatsoever, other than those expressly stipulated in the leases in question. It is understood, however, that the consular authorities mentioned in the same shall be replaced by Japanese authorities.

Those lands which the Japanese Government may have previously exempted from the payment of rent, in view of the fact that they were used for public purposes, shall, subject to the right of eminent domain, be permanently reserved free of all duties, taxes, and charges; and they shall never be diverted to other uses than those for which they were originally intended.

22. The provisions of the present treaty shall be applicable to Algeria. It is understood that they shall also be applicable to all French colonies for which the French Government shall claim the privilege. The representative of the French Republic at Tokio shall, to this end, notify the Japanese Government of such colonies within a period of ten days, dating from the day of the exchange of ratifications of the present treaty.

23. From the date that the present treaty becomes operative, the treaty of October 9, 1858, the convention of June 25, 1866, and, in general, all the agreements concluded between the high contracting Parties prior to this date shall be abrogated. In consequence, French jurisdiction in Japan, and all privileges, exemptions or immunities enjoyed by French subjects resulting therefrom, shall cease absolutely and without notice from the day that the present treaty becomes operative; and thereafter French subjects shall submit to the jurisdiction of the Japanese tribunals.

---

[1] Translation. For the original French text, see Appendix, p. 465.

THE MUSCAT DHOWS CASE

between

FRANCE *and* GREAT BRITAIN

Decided August 8, 1905

Syllabus

In an adjustment of conflicting interests, Great Britain and France, on March 10, 1862,[1] signed a declaration in which they engaged reciprocally to respect the independence of the Sultan of Muscat. Subsequently, France, acting under the treaty of November 17, 1844,[2] with the Sultan, adopted the practice of issuing to certain of his subjects papers authorizing them to fly the French flag upon dhows or vessels carrying on the coastwise trade in the Indian Ocean, the Red Sea, and the Persian Gulf and also commonly employed in the slave trade from the east coast of Africa. After the signature, on July 2, 1890, of the General Act of Brussels[3] for the repression of the African slave trade, Great Britain protested that the issuance of such authorizations to natives and the privileges and immunities claimed by them thereunder affected the jurisdiction of the Sultan over his subjects in derogation of the engagements entered into by France and Great Britain in the declaration of 1862. Failing a settlement through diplomatic channels, the question was referred by a *compromis* signed October 13, 1904,[4] to a tribunal consisting of Heinrich Lammasch of Austria, A. F. de Savornin Lohman of Holland, and Chief Justice Melville W. Fuller of the United States. The sessions began July 25, 1905, and ended August 2, 1905, the decision being rendered on August 8, 1905.

The tribunal decided that:

(1) Every sovereign may decide to whom it will accord the right to fly its flag and to prescribe the rules governing its use, and the granting of the right to subjects of another sovereign constitutes no attack upon the latter's independence.

(2) This right of France was, however, limited by Article 32 of the General Act of Brussels, which went into effect on January 2, 1892, under which both France and Great Britain as signatories agreed to grant authority to fly their flags only to native vessels owned or fitted out by their subjects or *protégés*. The latter term was defined to mean the subjects of a protectorate of the Power in question; the individuals enumerated in the Ottoman law of 1863, which was accepted by the Powers who enjoy the capitulations, and in the treaty between France and Morocco of the same year, acceded to by other Powers

---

[1]*Post*, p. 103.   [2]*Post*, p. 103.
[3]For Articles 30 *et seq.* of this Act, see *post*, p. 104.
[4]*Post*, p. 101.

and confirmed by the convention of Madrid, of 1880; persons recognized as *protégés* by special treaties; and individuals who were considered and treated as *protégés* by the Power in question before the creation of new *protégés* was regulated and limited in 1863.

(3) The restriction on the creation of *protégés* in Turkey and Morocco applies by analogy to other Oriental States, but, owing to the difference in racial conditions in Turkey and Muscat, the right of inheritance of the status of *protégé* conceded by Turkey can not be extended by analogy to Muscat.

(4) The French-Muscat treaty of 1844, specially recognizing certain persons as French *protégés*, applies only to persons *bona fide* in the service of French subjects, and not to persons who ask for ship's papers simply for the purpose of carrying on commerce under the French flag; but the granting of such papers prior to the ratification of the Act of Brussels was not in violation of any international obligation of France.

Held: That before January 2, 1892, France was entitled to authorize vessels belonging to the subjects of Muscat to fly the French flag, and that such grantees are entitled to retain their authorizations as long as France renews them; but, after the above-mentioned date, France was not entitled to grant such authorizations except when the owners or fitters-out of the vessels had established or could establish the fact that they were considered and treated as French *protégés* before 1863.

Concerning the privileges and immunities of natives in possession of such papers, the tribunal decided that the treaty between France and Muscat of 1844 prohibiting without the authorization of the French consul the entry or search of houses, warehouses and other property possessed or occupied by French citizens or persons in their employ, was comprehensive enough to include the prohibition of the entry of vessels, but Articles 31–41 of the General Act of Brussels limits the grant of the right to fly the national flag to that particular vessel and its owner, and the right is not transferrable to any other person or vessel.

The provision of the treaty of 1844, which accords French protection to persons in the employ of French citizens, does not include the owners, masters and crews of dhows authorized to fly the French flag or the members of their families, and the withdrawal of these persons from the sovereignty and jurisdiction of the Sultan would be a violation of the declaration of 1862.

Held: That dhows of Muscat authorized, as aforesaid, to fly the French flag are entitled in the territorial waters of Muscat to the inviolability provided by the French-Muscat treaty of 1844, but the right can not be transmitted to any other person or dhow, and the owners, masters, and crews of such dhows or members of their families do not enjoy any right of extraterritoriality which exempts them from the jurisdiction of the Sultan of Muscat.

AWARD OF THE TRIBUNAL

Award of the arbitration tribunal appointed to decide on the question of the grant of the French flag to Muscat dhows.—The Hague, August 8, 1905.[1]

The tribunal of arbitration constituted in virtue of the *compromis* concluded at London on October 13, 1904,[2] between Great Britain and France;

Whereas the Government of His Britannic Majesty and that of the French Republic have thought it right by the declaration of March 10, 1862,[3] "to engage reciprocally to respect the independence"[3] of His Highness the Sultan of Muscat;

Whereas difficulties as to the scope of that declaration have arisen in relation to the issue, by the French Republic, to certain subjects of His Highness the Sultan of Muscat of papers authorizing them to fly the French flag, and also as to the nature of the privileges and immunities claimed by subjects of His Highness who are owners or masters of dhows and in possession of such papers or are members of the crew of such dhows and their families, especially as to the manner in which such privileges and immunities affect the jurisdiction of His Highness the Sultan over his said subjects;

Whereas the two Governments have agreed by the *compromis* of October 13, 1904, that these questions shall be determined by reference to arbitration, in accordance with the provisions of Article 1 of the convention concluded between the two Powers on the 14th of October, 1903;[4]

Whereas in virtue of that *compromis* were named as arbitrators,
by the Government of His Britannic Majesty:

Mr. Melville W. Fuller, Chief Justice of the United States of America, and

by the Government of the French Republic:

Jonkheer A. F. de Savornin Lohman, Doctor of Law, former Minister of the Interior of the Netherlands, former professor at the

---

[1] Official report, p. 69. For the original French text, see Appendix, p. 467.
[2] *Post*, p. 101.   [3] *Post*, p. 103.   [4] A treaty of general arbitration.

free University at Amsterdam, member of the Second Chamber of the States-General;

Whereas the two arbitrators not having agreed within one month from the date of their appointment in the choice of an umpire, and that choice having then been entrusted, in virtue of Article 1 of the *compromis,* to the King of Italy, His Majesty has named umpire:

Mr. H. Lammasch, Doctor of Law, professor at the University at Vienna, member of the Upper House of the Austrian Parliament;

Whereas the cases, counter-cases and arguments have been duly communicated to the tribunal and to the parties;

Whereas the tribunal has carefully examined these documents, and the supplementary observations which were delivered to it by the two parties;

As to the first question:

Whereas generally speaking it belongs to every sovereign to decide to whom he will accord the right to fly his flag and to prescribe the rules governing such grants, and whereas, therefore, the granting of the French flag to subjects of His Highness the Sultan of Muscat in itself constitutes no attack on the independence of the Sultan;

Whereas nevertheless a sovereign may be limited by treaties in the exercise of this right, and whereas the tribunal is authorized in virtue of Article 48 of the Convention for the pacific settlement of international disputes of July 29, 1899, and of Article 5 of the *compromis* of October 13, 1904, "to declare its competence in interpreting the *compromis* as well as the other treaties which may be invoked in the case, and in applying the principles of international law," and whereas therefore the question arises, under what conditions Powers which have acceded to the General Act of the Brussels Conference of July 2, 1890,[1] relative to the African slave trade, especially to Article 32 of this Act, are entitled to authorize native vessels to fly their flags;

Whereas by Article 32 of this Act the faculty of the signatory Powers to grant their flag to native vessels has been limited for the purpose of suppressing slave trading and in the general interests of humanity, irrespective of whether the applicant for the flag may

---

[1] For Articles 30 *et seq.* of this Act, see *post,* p. 104.

belong to a State signatory of this Act or not, and whereas at any rate France is in relation to Great Britain bound to grant her flag only under the conditions prescribed by this Act;

Whereas in order to attain the above-mentioned purpose, the signatory Powers of the Brussels Act have agreed in its Article 32 that the authority to fly the flag of one of the signatory Powers shall in future only be granted to such native vessels which shall satisfy all the three following conditions:

1. Their fitters-out or owners must be either subjects of or persons protected by the Power whose flag they claim to fly;

2. They must furnish proof that they possess real estate situated in the district of the authority to whom their application is addressed, or supply a solvent security as a guaranty for any fines to which they may eventually become liable;

3. Such fitters-out or owners, as well as the captain of the vessel, must furnish proof that they enjoy a good reputation, and especially that they have never been condemned for acts of slave trade;

Whereas in default of a definition of the term *protégé* in the General Act of the Brussels Conference this term must be understood in the sense which corresponds best as well to the elevated aims of the conference and its final Act as to the principles of the law of nations, as they have been expressed in treaties existing at that time, in internationally recognized legislation and in international practice;

Whereas the aim of the said Article 32 is to admit to navigation in the seas infested by slave trade only those native vessels which are under the strictest surveillance of the signatory Powers, a condition which can only be secured if the owners, fitters-out, and crews of such vessels are exclusively subjected to the sovereignty and jurisdiction of the State under whose flag they are sailing;

Whereas, since the restriction which the term *protégé* underwent in virtue of the legislation of the Ottoman Porte of 1863, 1865, and 1869, especially of the Ottoman law of 23 Sefer, 1280 (August, 1863), implicitly accepted by the Powers who enjoy the rights of capitulations, and since the treaty concluded between France and Morocco in 1863,[1] to which a great number of other Powers have

---

[1] An agreement of August 19, 1863, relative to the French right of protection in Morocco.

acceded and which received the sanction of the convention of Madrid of July 30, 1880,[1] the term *protégé* embraces in relation to states of capitulations only the following classes: first, persons being subjects of a country which is under the protectorate of the Power whose protection they claim; secondly, individuals corresponding to the classes enumerated in the treaties with Morocco of 1863 and 1880 and in the Ottoman law of 1863; thirdly, persons who under a special treaty have been recognized as *protégés* like those enumerated by Article 4 of the French-Muscat convention of 1844,[2] and, fourthly, those individuals who can establish that they had been considered and treated as *protégés* by the Power in question before the year in which the creation of new *protégés* was regulated and limited, that is to say, before the year 1863, these individuals not having lost the status they had once legitimately acquired.

Whereas that, although the Powers have *expressis verbis* resigned the exercise of the pretended right to create *protégés* in unlimited number only in relation to Turkey and Morocco, nevertheless the exercise of this pretended right has been abandoned also in relation to other Oriental States, analogy having always been recognized as a means to complete the very deficient written regulations of the capitulations as far as circumstances are analogous;

Whereas, on the other hand, the concession *de facto* made by Turkey, that the status of *protégés* be transmitted to the descendants of persons who in 1863 had enjoyed the protection of a Christian Power can not be extended by analogy to Muscat, where the circumstances are entirely dissimilar, the *protégés* of the Christian Powers in Turkey being of race, nationality, and religion different from their Ottoman rulers, whilst the inhabitants of Sur and other Muscat people who might apply for French flags are in all these respects entirely in the same condition as the other subjects of the Sultan of Muscat;

Whereas the dispositions of Article 4 of the French-Muscat treaty of 1844 apply only to persons who are *bona fide* in the service of French subjects, but not to persons who ask for ship's papers for the purpose of doing any commercial business;

---

[1]An agreement between France, Great Britain, Morocco *et al.* for the settlement of the right of protection in Morocco.
[2]*Post*, p. 103.

Whereas the fact of having granted before the ratification of the Brussels Act on January 2, 1892, authorizations to fly the French flag to native vessels not satisfying the conditions prescribed by Article 32 of this Act was not in contradiction with any international obligation to France:

For these reasons decides and pronounces as follows:

1. Before the 2d of January, 1892, France was entitled to authorize vessels belonging to subjects of His Highness the Sultan of Muscat to fly the French flag, only bound by her own legislation and administrative rules;

2. Owners of dhows, who before 1892 have been authorized by France to fly the French flag, retain this authorization as long as France renews it to the grantee;

3. After January 2, 1892, France was not entitled to authorize vessels belonging to subjects of His Highness the Sultan of Muscat to fly the French flag, except on condition that their owners or fitters-out had established or should establish that they had been considered and treated by France as her *protégés* before the year 1863.

As to the second question:

Whereas the legal situation of vessels flying foreign flags and of the owners of such vessels in the territorial waters of an oriental State is determined by the general principles of jurisdiction, by the capitulations or other treaties and by the practice resulting therefrom;

Whereas the terms of the treaty of friendship and commerce between France and the Iman of Muscat of November 17, 1844, are particularly in view of the language of Article 3, *"Nul ne pourra, sousaucun prétexte, pénétrer dans les maisons, magasins et autres propriétés, possédés ou occupés par des Français ou par des personnes au service des Français, ni les visiter sans le consentement de l'occupant à moins que ce ne soit avec l'intervention du Consul de France,"* comprehensive enough to embrace vessels as well as other property;

Whereas, although it can not be denied that by admitting the

---

[1]TRANSLATION: No person shall, under any pretext whatsoever, penetrate or search the houses, warehouses or other property possessed or occupied by French citizens or by persons in the employ of French citizens, without the consent of the occupant, unless authorized by the French Consul.

right of France to grant under certain circumstances her flag to native vessels and to have these vessels exempted from visitation by the authorities of the Sultan or in his name, slave trade is facilitated, because slave traders may easily abuse the French flag for the purpose of escaping from search, the possibility of this abuse, which can be entirely suppressed by the accession of all Powers to Article 42 of the Brussels convention, can not affect the decision of this case, which must only rest on juridical grounds;

Whereas, according to the Articles 31—41 of the Brussels Act, the grant of the flag to a native vessel is strictly limited to this vessel and its owner and [is] therefore not transmissible or transferable to any other person or to any other vessel, even if belonging to the same owner;

Whereas Article 4 of the French-Muscat treaty of 1844 grants to those subjects of His Highness the Sultan of Muscat *"qui seront au service des Français [who are in the employ of French citizens]"* the same protection as to the French themselves, but whereas the owners, masters, and crews of dhows authorized to fly the French flag do not belong to that class of persons and still less do the members of their families;

Whereas the withdrawal of these persons from the sovereignty, especially from the jurisdiction of His Highness the Sultan of Muscat, would be in contradiction with the declaration of March 10, 1862, by which France and Great Britain engaged themselves reciprocally to respect the independence of this Prince:

For these reasons decides and pronounces as follows:

1. Dhows of Muscat authorized as aforesaid to fly the French flag are entitled in the territorial waters of Muscat to the inviolability provided by the French-Muscat treaty of November 17, 1844;

2. The authorization to fly the French flag can not be transmitted or transferred to any other person or to any other dhow, even if belonging to the same owner;

3. Subjects of the Sultan of Muscat, who are owners or masters of dhows authorized to fly the French flag or who are members of the crews of such vessels or who belong to their families, do not enjoy in consequence of that fact any right of extraterritoriality, which could exempt them from the sovereignty, especially from the jurisdiction, of His Highness the Sultan of Muscat.

Done at The Hague, in the Permanent Court of Arbitration, August 8, 1905.

> (Signed)   H. LAMMASCH
> (Signed)   MELVILLE W. FULLER
> (Signed)   A. F. DE SAVORNIN LOHMAN

AGREEMENT FOR ARBITRATION

Agreement between Great Britain and France referring to arbitration the question of the grant of the French flag to Muscat dhows.— Signed at London, October 13, 1904.[1]

Whereas the Government of His Britannic Majesty and that of the French Republic have thought it right, by the declaration of the 10th March, 1862,[2] "to engage reciprocally to respect the independence" of His Highness the Sultan of Muscat;

And whereas difficulties as to the scope of that declaration have arisen in relation to the issue, by the French Republic, to certain subjects of His Highness the Sultan of Muscat of papers authorizing them to fly the French flag, and also as to the nature of the privileges and immunities claimed by subjects of His Highness who are owners or masters of dhows and in possession of such papers or are members of the crew of such dhows and their families, especially as to the manner in which such privileges and immunities affect the jurisdiction of His Highness the Sultan over his said subjects:

The undersigned, being duly authorized thereto by their respective Governments, hereby agree that these questions shall be determined by reference to arbitration, in accordance with the provisions of Article 1 of the convention concluded between the two countries on the 14th October last, and that the decision of the Hague tribunal shall be final.

It is also hereby agreed as follows:

ARTICLE 1

Each of the high contracting Parties shall nominate one arbitrator, and these two arbitrators shall together choose an umpire; if they can not agree within one month from the date of their appointment, the choice of an umpire shall be entrusted to His Majesty the King of

---

[1] Official report, p. 5.   For the French text, see Appendix, p. 471.
[2] *Post*, p. 103.

Italy. The arbitrators and the umpire shall not be subjects or citizens of either of the high contracting Parties, and shall be chosen from among the members of the Hague tribunal.

ARTICLE 2

Each of the high contracting Parties shall, within three months from the signature of this agreement, deliver to each member of the tribunal hereby constituted, and to the other party, a written or printed case setting forth and arguing its claims, and a written or printed file containing the documents or any other evidence in writing or print on which it relies.

Within three months after the delivery of the above-mentioned cases, each of the high contracting Parties shall deliver to each member of the tribunal, and to the other party, a written or printed counter-case, with the documents which support it.

Within one month after the delivery of the counter-cases, each party may deliver to each arbitrator and to the other party a written or printed argument in support of its contentions.

The time fixed by this agreement for the delivery of the case, counter-case, and argument may be extended by the mutual consent of the high contracting Parties.

ARTICLE 3

The tribunal will meet at The Hague within a fortnight of the delivery of the arguments.

Each party shall be represented by one agent.

The tribunal may, if they shall deem further elucidation with regard to any point necessary, require from either agent an oral or written statement, but in such case the other party shall have the right to reply.

ARTICLE 4

The decision of the tribunal shall be rendered within thirty days of its meeting at The Hague or of the delivery of the statements which may have been supplied at its request, unless, on the request of the tribunal, the contracting Parties shall agree to extend the period.

ARTICLE 5

On all points not covered by this agreement, the provisions of the Conventions of The Hague of the 29th July, 1899, shall apply.

Done in duplicate at London, the 13th day of October, 1904.

[L. S.] LANDSDOWNE
[L. S.] PAUL CAMBON

ADDITIONAL DOCUMENTS

Extract from the Treaty of Friendship and Commerce between France and the Iman of Muscat, concluded at Zanzibar, November 17, 1844[1]

3. French citizens shall have the right to buy, sell, or lease land, houses, and warehouses in the States of His Highness the Sultan of Muscat. No person shall, under any pretext whatsoever, penetrate or search the houses, warehouses, or other property possessed or occupied by French citizens, or by persons in the employ of French citizens, without the consent of the occupant, unless authorized by the French consul.

French citizens shall not, under any pretext whatsoever, be detained against their will in the States of the Sultan of Muscat.

4. The subjects of His Highness the Sultan of Muscat who are in the employ of French citizens shall enjoy the same protection as the French citizens themselves; but, if they commit any crime or misdemeanor punishable by law, they shall be discharged by the French employers and delivered up to the local authorities.

Declaration between Great Britain and France, engaging reciprocally to respect the Independence of the Sultans of Muscat and Zanzibar.—Signed at Paris, March 10, 1862.[2]

Her Majesty the Queen of the United Kingdom of Great Britain and Ireland and His Majesty the Emperor of the French, taking into consideration the importance of maintaining the independence of His Highness the Sultan of Muscat and His Highness the Sultan of Zanzibar, have thought it right to engage reciprocally to respect the independence of these sovereigns.

The undersigned, Her Britannic Majesty's Ambassador Extraordinary and Plenipotentiary at the Court of France, and the Minister Secretary of State for Foreign Affairs of His Majesty the Emperor of the French, being furnished with the necessary powers, hereby declare, in consequence, that their said Majesties take reciprocally that engagement.

In witness whereof, the undersigned have signed the present Declaration, and have affixed thereto the seals of their arms.

Done at Paris, the 10th March, 1862.

[L. S.] COWLEY
[L. S.] E. THOUVENEL

---

[1] Translation. For the original French text, see Appendix, p. 473.
[2] *British and Foreign State Papers*, vol. 57, p. 785. For the French text, see Appendix, p. 473.

Extract from the General Act of Brussels of July 2, 1890, for the Suppression of the African Slave Trade[1]

SECTION II.—REGULATION CONCERNING THE USE OF THE FLAG AND SUPERVISION BY CRUISERS

1. RULES FOR GRANTING THE FLAG TO NATIVE VESSELS, AND AS TO CREW LIST AND MANIFESTS OF BLACK PASSENGERS ON BOARD

ARTICLE 30

The signatory Powers engage to exercise a strict surveillance over native vessels authorized to carry their flag in the zone mentioned in Article 21, and over the commercial operations carried on by such vessels.

ARTICLE 31

The term "native vessel" applies to vessels fulfilling one of the following conditions:

1. It shall present the outward appearance of native build or rigging.

2. It shall be manned by a crew of whom the captain and a majority of the seamen belong by origin to one of the countries on the coast of the Indian Ocean, the Red Sea, or the Persian Gulf.

ARTICLE 32

The authorization to carry the flag of one of the said Powers shall in future be granted only to such native vessels as shall satisfy at the same time the three following conditions:

1. Fitters-out or owners of ships must be either subjects of or persons protected by the Power whose flag they ask to carry.

2. They shall be obliged to prove that they possess real estate situated in the district of the authority to whom their application is addressed, or to furnish *bona fide* security as a guaranty of the payment of such fines as may be incurred.

3. The above-named fitters-out or owners of ships, as well as the captain of the vessel, shall prove that they enjoy a good reputation, and that in particular they have never been sentenced to punishment for acts connected with the slave trade.

---

[1]Translation. For the original French text, see Appendix, p. 474.

ARTICLE 33

This authorization granted shall be renewed every year. It may at any time be suspended or withdrawn by the authorities of the Power whose colors the vessel carries.

ARTICLE 34

The act of authorization shall contain the statements necessary to establish the identity of the vessel. The captain shall have the keeping thereof. The name of the native vessel and the amount of its tonnage shall be cut and painted in Latin characters on the stern, and the initial or initials of the name of the port of registry, as well as the registration number in the series of the numbers of that port, shall be printed in black on the sails.

ARTICLE 35

A list of the crew shall be issued to the captain of the vessel at the port of departure by the authorities of the Power whose colors it carries. It shall be renewed at every fresh venture of the vessel, or, at the latest, at the end of a year, and in accordance with the following provisions:

1. The vessel shall be visaed at the departure of the vessel by the authority that has issued it.

2. No negro can be engaged as a seaman on a vessel without having previously been questioned by the authority of the Power whose colors it carries, or, in default thereof, by the territorial authority with a view to ascertaining the fact of his having contracted a free engagement.

3. This authority shall see that the proportion of seamen and boys is not out of proportion to the tonnage or rigging.

4. The authorities who shall have questioned the men before their departure shall enter them on the list of the crew in which they shall be mentioned with a summary description of each of them alongside his name.

5. In order the more effectively to prevent any substitution, the seamen may, moreover, be provided with a distinctive mark.

ARTICLE 36

When the captain of a vessel shall desire to take negro passengers on board, he shall make his declaration to that effect to the authority of the Power whose colors he carries, or in default thereof, to the territorial authority.   The passengers shall be questioned, and after it has been ascertained that they embarked of their own free will, they shall be entered in a special manifest, bearing the description of each of them alongside of his name, and specially sex and height.   Negro children shall not be taken as passengers unless they are accompanied by their relations, or by persons whose respectability is well known. At the departure, the passenger roll shall be visaed by the aforesaid authority after it has been called.   If there are no passengers on board, this shall be specially mentioned in the crew-list.

ARTICLE 37

At the arrival at any port of call or of destination, the captain of the vessel shall show to the authority of the Power whose flag he carries, or, in default thereof, to the territorial authority, the crew-list, and, if need be, the passenger-roll previously delivered.   The authority shall check the passengers who have reached their destination or who are stopping in a port of call, and shall mention their landing in the roll.   At the departure of the vessel, the same authority shall affix a fresh visa to the list and roll, and call the roll of the passengers.

ARTICLE 38

On the African coast and on the adjacent islands, no negro passengers shall be taken on board of a native vessel, except in localities where there is a resident authority belonging to one of the signatory Powers.

Throughout the extent of the zone mentioned in Article 21, no negro passenger shall be landed from a native vessel except at a place in which there is a resident officer belonging to one of the high contracting Powers, and unless such officer is present at the landing.

Cases of *force majeure* that may have caused an infraction of these provisions shall be examined by the authority of the Power whose colors the vessel carries, or, in default thereof, by the territorial authority of the port at which the vessel in question calls.

ARTICLE 39

The provisions of Articles 35, 36, 37, and 38 are not applicable to vessels only partially decked, having a crew not exceeding ten men, and fulfilling one of the two following conditions:

1. That it be exclusively used for fishing within the territorial waters.

2. That it be occupied in the petty coasting trade between the different ports of the same territorial Power, without going further than five miles from the coast.

These different boats shall receive, as the case may be, a special license from the territorial or consular authority, which shall be renewed every year, and subject to revocation as provided in Article 40, the uniform model of which license is annexed to the present General Act and shall be communicated to the international information office.

ARTICLE 40

Any act or attempted act connected with the slave trade that can be legally shown to have been committed by the captain, fitter-out, or owner of a ship authorized to carry the flag of one of the signatory Powers, or having procured the license provided for in Article 39, shall entail the immediate withdrawal of the said authorization or license. All violations of the provisions of section 2 of Chapter III shall render the person guilty thereof liable to the penalties provided by the special laws and ordinances of each of the contracting Parties.

ARTICLE 41

The signatory Powers engage to deposit at the international information office the specimen forms of the following documents:

1. License to carry the flag;
2. The crew-list;
3. The negro passenger list.

These documents, the tenor of which may vary according to the different regulations of each country, shall necessarily contain the following particulars, drawn up in one of the European languages:

1. As regards the authorization to carry the flag:

(a) The name, tonnage, rig, and the principal dimensions of the vessel;

(b) The register number and the signal letter of the port of registry;

(c) The date of obtaining the license, and the office held by the person who issued it.

2. As regards the list of the crew:

(a) The name of the vessel, of the captain and the fitter-out or owner;

(b) The tonnage of the vessel;

(c) The register number and the port of registry, its destination, as well as the particulars specified in Article 25.

3. As regards the list of negro passengers:

The name of the vessel which conveys them, and the particulars indicated in Article 36, for the proper identification of the passengers.

The signatory Powers shall take the necessary measures so that the territorial authorities or their consuls may send to the same office certified copies of all authorizations to carry their flag as soon as such authorizations shall have been granted, as well as notices of the withdrawal of any such authorization.

The provisions of the present article have reference only to papers intended for native vessels.

Agreement, supplementary to the agreement for arbitration, providing that the term for the delivery of the cases shall be extended to February 1, 1905.—Signed at London, January 13, 1905.[1]

The formation of the arbitral tribunal established by the agreement signed at London on the 13th October, 1904,[2] having been delayed for some days by circumstances beyond the control of the high contracting Parties, the Government of His Britannic Majesty and the Government of the French Republic have agreed that it is desirable to avail themselves of the power granted to them by paragraph 4 of Article 2 of the said agreement to extend the period fixed for the delivery of the case.

They therefore hereby agree to fix the 1st February as the date on which the case or documents shall be delivered by the parties to the members of the arbitral tribunal and the two Governments concerned.

It is also agreed that the successive periods fixed by Article 2 of the agreement for the several stages of the procedure in the arbitration shall date from the 1st February instead of from the 13th January, the date fixed by the terms of the agreement signed by Lord Lansdowne and M. Paul Cambon on the 13th October, 1904.

Done in duplicate, at London, the 13th day of January, 1905.

[L. S.] LANSDOWNE
[L. S.] PAUL CAMBON

---

[1]Official report, p. 9. For the French text, see Appendix, p. 477.
[2]*Ante*, p. 101.

Agreement supplementary to the agreement for arbitration, providing that the period fixed for the delivery of the argument shall be extended to a date to be fixed by the arbitral tribunal.—Signed at London, May 19, 1905.[1]

The constitution of the arbitral tribunal created by the agreement signed at London on October 13, 1904, having been delayed for some days owing to circumstances beyond the control of the high contracting Parties, the Government of His Britannic Majesty and the Government of the French Republic have, by mutual consent, deemed it expedient to avail themselves of the power granted to them by paragraph four of Article 2 of the said agreement to extend the period fixed for the delivery of the arguments.

They therefore hereby agree to leave to the arbitral tribunal the duty of fixing the date on which the members of the said tribunal and the two Governments concerned shall receive the arguments presented by the parties.

This additional agreement shall be communicated to the arbitral tribunal through the medium of the International Bureau of the Permanent Court of Arbitration.

Done in duplicate at London, the 19th day of May, 1905.

(L. S.) LANSDOWNE
(L. S.) PAUL CAMBON

---

[1] Official report, p. 11. For the French text, see Appendix, p. 477.

THE CASABLANCA CASE

between

FRANCE *and* GERMANY

Decided May 22, 1909

Syllabus

This arbitration arose from a conflict of jurisdiction between the French military authorities in occupation of Casablanca, Morocco, and the German consul, acting under the extraterritorial jurisdiction of his Government in Morocco.

In the fall of 1908 six soldiers belonging to the French Foreign Legion stationed at Casablanca, three of whom subsequently turned out to be of German nationality, deserted and applied to the German consul for protection and were granted by him safe conduct to their homes. Before they could be embarked, however, they were forcibly arrested by French soldiers and taken from the protection of the consul. France protested that Germany had no right to afford protection to persons in Morocco not of German nationality; that the territory in her military occupancy in Morocco was subject to her exclusive jurisdiction, and, therefore, that Germany had no right to attempt to protect the three deserters of German nationality. Germany claimed that the deserters of German nationality were, by virtue of the extraterritorial jurisdiction of Germany in Morocco, subject exclusively to the jurisdiction and protection of the German consul at Casablanca, that the forcible arrest of the deserters was a breach of the inviolability of her consular agents, and she demanded that the three Germans be delivered up.

Failing a diplomatic settlement, the case was referred by a *compromis* signed November 24, 1908,[1] to a tribunal selected from the Permanent Court as follows: K. Hj. L. Hammarskjöld of Sweden, Sir Edward Fry of England, Louis Renault of France, Guido Fusinato of Italy, and J. Kriege of Germany. The sessions began May 1, 1909, and ended May 17, 1909, the decision being rendered on May 22, 1909.

The tribunal decided that the conflict between the two jurisdictions could not be determined by any absolute and general rule, but that, under the circumstances of this case, the deserters of German nationality who belonged to the French military forces stationed at and in control of the fortified city of Casablanca were subject to the exclusive military jurisdiction of France while they remained within the territory occupied and controlled by her forces. Owing to the complexity of the question of the conflict of jurisdiction, however, the

---

[1] *Post*, p. 117.

tribunal held that no blame attached to the German consul for granting protection to such deserters, but the secretary of the consulate was held guilty of a grave violation of his duties for obtaining the protection of the consul for the deserters not of German nationality. The tribunal further held that the French military authorities should have respected the authority of the German consul by leaving the deserters in his possession until the question of jurisdiction could be decided, taking only such steps as were necessary to prevent their escape. The use of force by the French soldiers was declared to be unwarranted, but, in view of the tribunal's previous holding that the military jurisdiction of France took precedence over the extraterritorial jurisdiction of Germany, it declined to direct the surrender of the deserters.

AWARD OF THE TRIBUNAL

Award of the arbitration tribunal in the Casblanca case.—The Hague, May 22, 1909.[1]

Whereas, by a protocol of November 10, 1908,[2] and an agreement to arbitrate of the 24th of the same month,[3] the Government of the French Republic and the Imperial German Government agreed to refer to a tribunal of arbitration composed of five members the settlement of the questions of fact and law arising from the events which occurred at Casablanca on September 25, 1908, between agents of the two countries; and

Whereas, in accordance with said agreement to arbitrate, the two Governments have respectively appointed as arbitrators the following persons, namely:

The Government of the French Republic, the Right Honorable Sir Edward Fry, Doctor of Laws, former judge of the Court of Appeals, member of the Privy Council of the King, member of the Permanent Court of Arbitration, and Mr. Louis Renault, member of the Institute of France, Minister Plenipotentiary, professor in the Faculty of Law of Paris, Solicitor of the Ministry of Foreign Affairs, member of the Permanent Court of Arbitration; and

The Imperial German Government, Mr. Guido Fusinato, Doctor of Laws, former Minister of Public Instruction, former professor of international law at the University of Turin, deputy to the Italian

---

[1]*American Journal of International Law,* vol. 3, p. 755. For the original French text, see Appendix, p. 479.
[2]*Post,* p. 119.   [3]*Post,* p. 117.

Parliament, Counselor of State, member of the Permanent Court of Arbitration, and Mr. Kriege, Doctor of Laws, present Privy Counselor of Legation, reporting Counselor and Solicitor of the Department of Foreign Affairs, member of the Permanent Court of Arbitration; and

Whereas, the arbitrators thus appointed being instructed to name an umpire, chose as such Mr. K. Hj. L. Hammarskjöld, Doctor of Laws, former Minister of Justice, former Minister of Worship and Public Instruction, former Envoy Extraordinary and Minister Plenipotentiary to Copenhagen, former president of the Court of Appeals of Jönköping, former professor in the Faculty of Law of Upsal, Governor of the Province of Upsal, member of the Permanent Court of Arbitration; and

Whereas, in accordance with the provisions of the agreement to arbitrate of November 24, 1908, the cases and counter-cases were duly exchanged between the parties and communicated to the arbitrators; and

Whereas, the tribunal, constituted as above stated, convened at The Hague on May 1, 1909; and

Whereas, the two Governments respectively designated as their agents the following persons, namely:

The Government of the French Republic, Mr. André Weiss, professor in the Faculty of Law in Paris, assistant solicitor of the Ministry of Foreign Affairs; and

The Imperial German Government, Mr. Albrecht Lentze, Doctor of Laws, Privy Counselor of Legation, reporting Counselor of the Department of Foreign Affairs; and

Whereas, the agents of the parties have presented to the tribunal the following conclusions, namely:

The agent of the Government of the French Republic:

May it please the tribunal—

To say and decide that it was wrong for the consul and the officers of the Imperial German consulate at Casablanca to attempt to embark on a German ship deserters from the French Foreign Legion who were not German subjects;

To say and decide that it was wrong for said consul and consular officers, under the same circumstances, to grant, on the territory occupied by the French landing corps at Casablanca, their protection and material assistance to three other members of the Legion whom they thought or might have thought to be Germans, thus disregarding the exclusive right of jurisdiction belonging to the occupying nation in foreign territory, even in a country granting extraterritorial jurisdiction, with respect to the soldiers of the army of occupation and to acts likely to endanger its safety, whatever they be or wherever they may originate;

To say and decide that, in the persons of Mr. Just, chancellor of the Imperial consulate, Casablanca, and of the Moroccan soldier Abd-el-Kerim ben Mansour, no breach of the rules regarding consular inviolability was committed by the French officers, soldiers, and sailors, who arrested the deserters, and that in repelling the attacks and acts of violence directed against them the said officers, soldiers, and sailors, merely availed themselves of the right of self-defense.

The agent of the Imperial German Government:

May it please the tribunal—

1. As regards the points of fact, to declare that three individuals who had previously served in the French Foreign Legion, namely, Walter Bens, Heinrich Heinnemann, and Julius Meyer, all three Germans, were, on September 25, 1908, at the port of Casablanca, while accompanied by agents of Germany, violently wrested from the latter and arrested by agents of France, and that on this occasion agents of Germany were attacked, maltreated, outraged, and threatened by the agents of France;

2. As regards the points of law, to declare that the three individuals mentioned under No. 1 above were, on September 25, 1908, subject exclusively to the jurisdiction and protection of the Imperial German consulate at Casablanca, and that agents of France had no authority at that time to interfere with agents of Germany in granting German protection to these three individuals and to claim for themselves a right of jurisdiction over said individuals;

3. As regards the status of the individuals arrested on September 25, 1908, and concerning whom there is a dispute, to decide that the Government of the French Republic shall release the three Germans mentioned under No. 1 above as soon as possible and place them at the disposal of the German Government.

And whereas, the agent of the French Republic, in the hearing of

May 17, 1909, declared that in his conclusions the only measures referred to, either with respect to the deserters of German nationality, or the others, are those taken by the German agents after the desertion and with a view to embarking the deserters; and

Whereas, after the tribunal had heard the oral statements of the agents of the parties and the explanations which they furnished it at its request, the debates were declared closed at the hearing of May 17, 1909; and

Whereas, under the extraterritorial jurisdiction in force in Morocco the German consular authority as a rule exercises exclusive jurisdiction over all German subjects in that country; and

Whereas, on the other hand, a corps of occupation as a rule also exercises exclusive jurisdiction over all persons belonging to it; and

Whereas, this right of jurisdiction should be recognized as a rule even in countries granting extraterritorial jurisdiction; and

Whereas, in case the subjects of a Power enjoying the rights of territorial jurisdiction in Morocco belong to a corps of occupation sent to that country by another Power, there necessarily arises a conflict between the two jurisdictions mentioned; and

Whereas, the French Government did not make known the composition of the expeditionary corps and did not declare that the fact of the military occupation modified the exclusive consular jurisdiction arising from the extraterritorial rights, and that, on the other hand, the German Government made no protest regarding the employment in Morocco of the Foreign Legion, which is known to be composed in part of German subjects; and

Whereas, it is not within the province of this tribunal to express an opinion regarding the organization of the Foreign Legion or its employment in Morocco; and

Whereas, the conflict of jurisdictions mentioned above can not be decided by an absolute rule which would in a general manner accord the preference to either of the two concurrent jurisdictions; and

Whereas, in each particular case account must be taken of the actual circumstances which tend to determine the preference; and

Whereas, the jurisdiction of the corps of occupation should have the preference in case of a conflict when the persons belonging to this corps have not left the territory which is under the immediate, lasting, and effective control of the armed force; and

Whereas, at the period in question the fortified city of Casablanca was occupied and guarded by French military forces which constituted the garrison of that city and were stationed either in the city itself or in the surrounding camps; and

Whereas, under these circumstances the deserters of German nationality who belonged to the military forces of one of these camps and were within the inclosure of the city, remained subject to the exclusive military jurisdiction; and

Whereas, on the other hand, in a country granting extraterritorial jurisdiction the question of the respective competency of the consular and the military jurisdiction is very complicated and has never been settled in an express, distinct, and universally recognized manner, so that the German consular authority could not incur any blame for having granted his protection to the afore-mentioned deserters who had solicited it; and

Whereas, the German consul at Casablanca did not grant the protection of the consulate to the deserters of non-German nationality and the dragoman of the consulate also did not exceed the limits of his authority in this regard; and

Whereas, the fact that the consul, without reading it, signed the safe-conduct for six persons instead of three and omitted to state that they were of German nationality, as he had prescribed himself, can not be imputed against him except as an unintentional error; and

Whereas, the Moroccan soldier at the consulate, in aiding the deserters to embark, acted only in accordance with orders from his superiors and, by reason of his inferior position, could not have incurred any personal responsibility; and

Whereas, the secretary of the consulate intentionally sought to embark the deserters of non-German nationality as enjoying the protection of the consulate; and

Whereas, for this purpose he deliberately induced the consul to sign the above-mentioned safe-conduct and with the same intention took measures both to conduct the deserters to the port and to have them embarked; and

Whereas, in acting thus he exceeded the limits of his authority and committed a grave and manifest violation of his duties; and

Whereas, the deserters of German nationality were found at the

port under the actual protection of the German consular authority
and this protection was not manifestly illegal; and

Whereas, this actual situation should have been respected by the
French military authority as far as possible; and

Whereas, the deserters of German nationality were arrested by
said authority despite the protests made in the name of the consulate; and

Whereas, the military authority might and therefore ought to
have confined itself to preventing the embarkation and escape of
the deserters, and, before proceeding to their arrest and imprisonment, to offering to leave them in sequestration at the German consulate until the question of the competent jurisdiction had been decided; and

Whereas, this mode of procedure would also have tended to maintain the prestige of the consular authority, in conformity with the
common interests of all Europeans living in Morocco; and

Whereas, even if we admit the legality of the arrest the circumstances did not warrant, on the part of the French soldiers, either
the threats made with a revolver or the prolongation of the shots
fired at the Moroccan soldier of the consulate even after his resistance had been overcome; and

Whereas, as regards the other outrages or acts of violence alleged
on both sides, the order and the exact nature of the events can not
be determined; and

Whereas, in accordance with what was said above, the deserters
of German nationality should have been returned to the consulate
in order to restore the actual situation which was disturbed by their
arrest; and

Whereas, such restitution would also have been desirable with a
view to maintaining the consular prestige; however, inasmuch as, in
the present state of things, this tribunal being called upon to determine the final status of the deserters, there is no occasion for ordering their provisional and temporary surrender which should have
taken place;

Therefore:

The tribunal of arbitration declares and decides as follows:

It was wrong and a grave and manifest error for the secretary of
the Imperial German consulate at Casablanca to attempt to have em-

barked, on a German steamship, deserters from the French Foreign Legion who were not of German nationality.

The German consul and the other officers of the consulate are not responsible in this regard; however, in signing the safe-conduct which was presented to him, the consul committed an unintentional error.

The German consulate did not, under the circumstances of the case, have a right to grant its protection to the deserters of German nationality; however, the error of law committed on this point by the officers of the consulate can not be imputed against them either as an intentional or unintentional error.

It was wrong for the French military authorities not to respect, as far as possible, the actual protection being granted to these deserters in the name of the German consulate.

Even leaving out of consideration the duty to respect consular protection, the circumstances did not warrant, on the part of the French soldiers, either the threat made with a revolver or the prolongation of the shots fired at the Moroccan soldier of the consulate.

There is no occasion for passing on the other charges contained in the conclusions of the two parties.

Done at The Hague in the building of the Permanent Court of Arbitration, May 22, 1909.

HJ. L. HAMMARSKJÖLD, *President*
MICHIELS VAN VERDUYNEN, *Secretary General*

AGREEMENT FOR ARBITRATION

Compromis of arbitration relative to the questions raised by the events which occurred at Casablanca, September 25, 1908.—Signed at Berlin, November 24, 1908.[1]

The Imperial German Government and the Government of the French Republic, having agreed, November 10, 1908,[2] to submit to arbitration all the questions raised by the events which occurred at Casablanca September 25, last, the undersigned, duly authorized for that purpose, have agreed upon the following *compromis.*

ARTICLE 1

An arbitral tribunal, composed as hereinafter stipulated, is charged

---

[1]Translation. For the original French text, see Appendix, p. 484.
[2]*Post*, p. 119.

with the settlement of questions of fact and of law which brought about the events which occurred at Casablanca September 25, last, between the agents of the two countries.

ARTICLE 2

The arbitral tribunal shall be composed of five arbitrators, to be chosen from among the members of the Permanent Court of Arbitration at The Hague.

Each Government, as soon as possible and within a period not to exceed fifteen days from the date of the present *compromis*, shall choose two arbitrators, of which only one may be its national. The four arbitrators thus designated shall choose an umpire within a fortnight from the day on which they are notified of their own designation.

ARTICLE 3

On February 1, 1909, each party shall transmit to the Bureau of the Permanent Court eighteen copies of its memorial, with the certified copies of all papers and documents which it intends to present in the case. The Bureau shall guarantee their transmission without delay to the arbitrators and parties, to wit: two copies for each arbitrator, three copies for each party. Two copies shall remain in the archives of the Bureau.

On April 1, 1909, the parties shall in like manner deposit their counter-memorials, with the papers appertaining thereto, and their final conclusions.

ARTICLE 4

Each party shall deposit with the International Bureau, not later than the 15th of April, the advance sum of 3,000 Netherland florins for the expenses of the litigation.

ARTICLE 5

The tribunal shall meet at The Hague on May 1, 1909, and shall proceed immediately to the investigation of the dispute.

It shall have authority to move itself temporarily or to delegate one or more of its members to move to whatever place seems necessary in order to proceed with the securing of information under the conditions of Article 20 of the Convention for the pacific settlement of international disputes, of October 18, 1907.

ARTICLE 6

The parties may make use of either the German or the French language.

The members of the tribunal may, according to choice, use either the German or the French language.   The decisions of the tribunal shall be rendered in both languages.

ARTICLE 7

Each party shall be represented by a special agent whose duty it shall be to serve as intermediary between it and the tribunal.   These agents shall give the expositions demanded of them by the tribunal and may present any pleas which they may deem useful in the defense of their cause.

ARTICLE 8

On all points not set forth in the present *compromis,* the stipulations of the above-mentioned Convention of October 18, 1907, of which ratifications have not yet been exchanged but which has been signed alike by Germany and France, shall be applicable to the present arbitration.

ARTICLE 9

After the arbitral tribunal shall have solved the questions of fact and of law which have been submitted to it, it shall decide, in consequence, the case of the individuals arrested September 25, last, on which subject the present dispute rests.

Done, in duplicate, at Berlin, November 24, 1908.

[SEAL]   KIDERLEN
[SEAL]   JULES CAMBON

ADDITIONAL DOCUMENTS

Protocol between France and Germany containing a formula of regrets for events which occurred at Casablanca on the 25th September, 1908.—Signed at Berlin, November 10, 1908.[1]

The two Governments, regretting the events which occurred at Casablanca on September 25, last, and which led the sub-agents into violence and grievous assault, are resolved to submit all the questions raised on this subject to arbitration.

By mutual consent, each of the two Governments agrees to express its regrets for the acts of these agents, following the decisions which

[1]Translation.   For the original French text, see Appendix, p. 485.

the arbitrators shall render based upon the facts and the question of law.

Berlin, November 10, 1908.

JULES CAMBON
KIDERLEN

Procès-verbal by which the Governments of France and Germany mutually express their regrets for the acts occurring at Casablanca, which were charged against their respective agents by the Permanent Court of Arbitration on May 22, 1909.—Signed at Berlin, May 29, 1909.[1]

Whereas the Government of the Republic and the Imperial Government agreed, on November 10, last,[2] to lay before a tribunal of arbitration assembled for the purpose, all the questions arising out of the occurrences which took place at Casablanca on September 25, preceding, and whereas both Governments undertook to express mutually their regret at the action of their officials in accordance with the decision on the question of fact and of law which should be reached by the arbitrators;

And, whereas the tribunal of arbitration at The Hague, on May 22, 1909, recognized and announced the following:

[Here follow the findings of the Hague tribunal.]

The Government of the French Republic and the Imperial German Government declare therefore, each in so far as it is concerned, that they express their regret for the conduct for which their officials are blamed in the award of the tribunal of arbitration.

Done at Berlin in duplicate.

May 29, 1909.

---

[1]*American Journal of International Law,* vol. 3, p. 946. For the original French text, see Appendix, p. 485.
[2]*Ante,* p. 119.

THE GRISBADARNA CASE

between

NORWAY *and* SWEDEN

Decided October 23, 1909

Syllabus

By a *compromis* signed on March 14, 1908,[1] Norway and Sweden agreed to arbitrate the question of the maritime boundary between the two countries in so far as it had not been regulated by the Royal Resolution of March 15, 1904.[2] The arbitral tribunal was called upon to decide whether the boundary was fixed either in whole or in part by the boundary treaty of 1661, and, if not, to fix the boundary or parts thereof in accordance with the principles of international law. The tribunal consisted of a national from each of the two Governments and an umpire chosen from a neutral Power. As finally agreed upon, it was composed as follows: J. A. Loeff of Holland, F. V. N. Beichmann of Norway, and K. Hj. L. Hammarskjöld of Sweden. Only the last-named was a member of the Permanent Court of Arbitration at The Hague. The tribunal held sessions from August 28 to October 18, 1909, in the course of which it visited the disputed zone. The decision was rendered on October 23, 1909.

The tribunal found that the boundary line had not been fixed by the treaty of 1661 beyond a certain point, and that a portion of the line within that point was uncertain. The tribunal therefore fixed the boundary according to the principles in force and applied by Norway and Sweden when the original boundary treaty was made. The application of these principles resulted in a line which gave the Grisbadarna fishing banks to Sweden and the Skjöttegrunde to Norway. Such a division was also supported by the state of things which the tribunal found had actually existed for a long time, especially the use made of the banks by the fishermen of the two countries and the acts of possession and ownership exercised by the two Governments.

---

[1]*Post*, p. 133.   [2]*Post*, p. 136.

AWARD OF THE TRIBUNAL

Arbitral award in the question of the delimitation of a certain part of the maritime boundary between Norway and Sweden.—The Hague, October 23, 1909.[1]

Whereas, by convention dated March 14, 1908,[2] Norway and Sweden agreed to submit to the final decision of a tribunal of arbitration, comprised of a president who shall neither be a subject of either of the contracting parties nor domiciled in either of the two countries, and of two other members of whom one shall be a Norwegian and the other a Swede, the question of the maritime boundary between Norway and Sweden as far as this boundary has not been determined by the Royal Resolution of March 15, 1904;[3]

Whereas, in pursuance to said convention, the two Governments have appointed respectively as president and arbitrators:

Mr. J. A. Loeff, Doctor of Law and Political Sciences, former Minister of Justice, member of the Second Chamber of the States-General of the Netherlands;

Mr. F. V. N. Beichmann, President of the Court of Appeals of Trondhjem, and

Mr. K. Hj. L. Hammarskjöld, Doctor of Law, former Minister of Justice, former Minister of Public Worship and Public Construction, former Envoy Extraordinary and Minister Plenipotentiary to Copenhagen, former President of the Court of Appeals of Jönköping, former professor in the Faculty of Law of Upsal, Governor of the Province of Upsal, member of the Permanent Court of Arbitration;

Whereas, in accordance with the provisions of the convention, the memorials, counter-memorials, and replies have been duly exchanged between the parties and communicated to the arbitrators within the periods fixed by the president of the tribunal;

Whereas, the two Governments have respectively appointed as agents, to wit:

The Government of Norway, Mr. Kristen Johanssen, attorney at the Supreme Court of Norway; and the Government of Sweden, Mr. C. O. Montan, former member of the Court of Appeals of Svea, judge in the Mixed Court of Alexandria;

---

[1] *American Journal of International Law*, vol. 4, p. 226. For the original French text, see Appendix, p. 487.
[2] *Post*, p. 133.   [3] *Post*, p. 136.

Whereas, it has been agreed by Article 2 of the convention:

1. That the tribunal of arbitration shall determine the boundary line in the waters from point 18 on the chart[1] annexed to the proposal of the Norwegian and Swedish commissioners of August 18, 1897, into the sea up to the limit of the territorial waters;

2. That the lines limiting the zone which is the subject of litigation in consequence of the conclusions of the parties and within which the boundary-line shall consequently be established, must not be traced in such a way as to comprise either islands, islets, or reefs which are not constantly under water;

Whereas, it has likewise been agreed by Article 3 of the said convention:

1. That the tribunal of arbitration shall determine whether the boundary line is to be considered, either wholly or in part, as being fixed by the boundary treaty of 1661 together with the chart thereto annexed, and in what manner the line thus established should be traced.

2. That, as far as the boundary-line shall not be considered as established by said treaty and said chart, the tribunal shall determine this boundary-line, taking into account the circumstances of fact and the principles of international law;

Whereas, the agents of the parties have presented the following conclusions to the tribunal:

The agent of the Norwegian Government:

That the boundary between Norway and Sweden within the zone which constitutes the object of the arbitral decision, shall be determined in accordance with the line indicated on the chart annexed, under No. 35, to the memorial presented in behalf of the Norwegian Government.

And the agent of the Swedish Government:

I. As regards the preliminary questions:

May it please the tribunal of arbitration to declare that the boundary-line in dispute, as regards the space between point 18 as already fixed on the chart of the commissioners of 1897, and point A on the chart of the boundary treaty of 1661, is but incompletely established by the said treaty and the chart annexed thereto, for the reason that the exact situation of this point is not shown clearly therein, and, as regards the rest of the space, extending westward from the same

---

[1]*Post,* opposite p. 140.

point A to the territorial boundary, that the boundary-line was not established at all by these documents.

II. As regards these main questions:

1. May it please the tribunal to be guided by the treaty and chart of 1661, to take into account the circumstances of fact and the principles of the law of nations, and to determine the maritime boundary-line in dispute between Sweden and Norway from point 18 as already fixed, in such a manner that in the first place the boundary-line shall be traced in a straight line to a point which constitutes the middle point of a straight line, connecting the northernmost reef of the Röskären, belonging to the Koster Islands, that is to say, the reef indicated on table 5 of the report of 1906 as being surrounded with depths 9, 10 and 10 [*sic.*], and the southernmost reef of the Svatskjär, belonging to the Tisler Islands, and which is furnished with a beacon, which point is indicated on the same table 5 as the point 19.

2. May it please the tribunal further to take account of the circumstances of fact and the principles of the law of nations and establish the rest of the disputed boundary in such a manner that—

(*a*) Starting from the point fixed according to the conclusions of paragraph 1 and designated as point 19, the boundary-line shall be traced in a straight line to a point situated midway on a straight line connecting the northernmost of the reefs indicated under the name of Stora Drammen, on the Swedish side and the Hejeknub rock, situated to the southeast of Heja Island, on the Norwegian side, which point is indicated on the said table 5 as point 20; and

(*b*) Starting from the point last-mentioned, the boundary shall be traced in a straight line due west as far into the sea as the maritime territories of the two nations are supposed to extend;

Whereas, the line mentioned in the conclusions of the Norwegian agent is traced as follows:

From point 18 as indicated on the chart of the commissioners of 1897, in a straight line to point 19 situated midway on a line drawn between the southernmost reef of the Svartskjär (the reef which is furnished with a beacon) and the northernmost reef of the Röskären;

From this point 19 in a straight line to point 20, situated midway on a line drawn between the southernmost reef of the Heiefluer (söndre Heieflu) and the northernmost of the reefs comprised under the name of Stora Drammen;

From this point 20 to point 20a, following a perpendicular drawn from the middle of the last-mentioned line.

From this point 20a to point 20b, following a perpendicular drawn from the middle of the line connecting the said southernmost reef of the Heieflu with the southernmost of the reefs comprised under the name of Stora Drammen.

From this point 20b to point 20c, following a perpendicular drawn from the middle of a line connecting the Söndre Heiefluer with the small reef situated to the north of Klöfningen islet near Mörholmen.

From this point 20c to point 20d, following a perpendicular drawn from the middle of a line connecting the Midtre Heieflu with the said reef to the north of Klöfningen islet.

From this point 20d, following a perpendicular drawn from the middle of the line connecting the Midtre Heieflu with a small reef situated west of the said Klöfningen to point 21, where the circles cross which are drawn around said reefs with a radius of 4 nautical miles (60 to a degree).

Whereas, after the tribunal had visited the disputed zone, examined the documents and maps which had been presented to it, and heard the pleas and replies as well as the explanations furnished it at its request, the discussion was declared terminated at the session of October 18, 1909;

Whereas, as regards the interpretation of certain expressions used in the convention and regarding which the two parties expressed different opinions during the course of the discussion,

In the first place, the tribunal is of opinion that the clause in accordance with which it is to determine the boundary-line in the sea *as far as the limit of the territorial waters* has no other purpose than to exclude the possibility of an incomplete determination, which might give rise to a new boundary dispute in future; and

It was obviously not the intention of the parties to fix in advance the terminal point of the boundary, so that the tribunal would have only to determine the direction between two given points;

In the second place, the clause in accordance with which the lines bounding the zone which may be the subject of dispute in consequence of the conclusions of the parties *must not be traced in such a manner as to comprise either islands, islets, or reefs which are not constantly under water* can not be interpreted so as to imply that the islands, islets, and reefs aforementioned ought necessarily to be taken as points of departure in the determination of the boundary;

Whereas, therefore, in the two respects aforementioned, the tribunal preserves full freedom to pass on the boundary within the limits of the respective contentions;

Whereas, under the terms of the convention, the task of the tribunal consists in determining the boundary line in the water from the point indicated as 18 on the chart annexed to the project of the Norwegian and Swedish commissioners of August 18, 1897, in the sea as far as the limit of the territorial waters;

Whereas, as regards the question, "whether the boundary-line should be considered, either wholly or in part, as being fixed by the boundary treaty of 1661 and the map thereto annexed," the answer to this question should be negative, at least as regards the boundary-line beyond point A on the aforementioned map;

Whereas, the exact situation of point A on this chart can not be determined with absolute precision, but at all events it is a point situated between points 19 and 20, as these points will be determined hereinafter;

Whereas, the parties in litigation agree as regards the boundary-line from point 18 on the chart of August 18, 1897, to point 19 as indicated in the Swedish conclusions;

Whereas, as regards the boundary-line from the said point 19 to a point indicated by 20 on the charts annexed to the memorials, the parties likewise agree, except that they differ with regard to whether, in determining point 20, the Heiefluer or the Heieknub should be taken as a starting point from the Norwegian side;

Whereas, in this connection, the parties have adopted, at least in practice, the rule of making the division along the median line drawn between the islands, islets, and reefs situated on both sides and not constantly submerged, as having been in their opinion the rule which was applied on this side of point A by the treaty of 1661;

The adoption of a rule on such grounds should, without regard to the question whether the rule invoked was really applied by said treaty, have as a logical consequence, in applying it at the present time, that one should take into account at the same time the circumstances of fact which existed at the time of the treaty;

Whereas, the Heiefluer are reefs which, it may be asserted with sufficient certainty, did not immerge from the water at the time of the boundary treaty of 1661 and consequently they could not have served as a starting point in defining a boundary;

Whereas, therefore, from the above-mentioned standpoint the Heieknub should be preferred to the Heiefluer;

Whereas, point 20 being fixed, there remains to be determined the boundary from this point 20 to the limit of the territorial waters;

Whereas, point 20 is situated, without any doubt, beyond point A as indicated on the chart annexed to the boundary treaty of 1661;

Whereas, Norway has held the contention, which for that matter has not been rejected by Sweden, that from the sole fact of the Peace of Roskilde in 1658 the maritime territory in question was divided automatically between her and Sweden;

Whereas, the tribunal fully indorses this opinion;

Whereas, this opinion is in conformity with the fundamental principles of the law of nations, both ancient and modern, in accordance with which the maritime territory is an essential appurtenance of land territory, whence it follows that at the time when, in 1658, the land territory called the Bohuslan was ceded to Sweden, the radius of maritime territory constituting an inseparable appurtenance of this land territory must have automatically formed a part of this cession;

Whereas, it follows from this line of argument that in order to ascertain which may have been the automatic dividing line of 1658 we must have recourse to the principles of law in force at that time;

Whereas, Norway claims that, inside (on this side) of the Koster-Tisler line, the rule of the boundary documents of 1661 having been that the boundary ought to follow the median line between the islands, islets, and reefs on both sides, the same principle should be applied with regard to the boundary beyond this line;

Whereas, it is not demonstrated that the boundary-line fixed by the treaty and traced on the boundary chart was based on this rule.

and there are some details and peculiarities in the line traced which even give rise to serious doubts in this regard, and even if one admitted the existence of this rule in connection with the boundary-line fixed by the treaty, it would not necessarily follow that the same rule ought to have been applied in determining the boundary in the exterior territory;

Whereas, in this connection,

The boundary treaty of 1661 and the chart thereto annexed make the boundary-line *begin* between the Koster and Tisler Islands;

Whereas, in determining the boundary-line they went in a direction from the sea toward the coast and not from the coast toward the sea;

Whereas, it is out of the question to say that there might have been a continuation of this boundary-line in a seaward direction;

Whereas, consequently, the connecting link is lacking in order to enable us to presume, without decisive evidence, that the same rule was applied simultaneously to the territories situated this side and to those situated that side of the Koster-Tisler line;

Whereas, moreover, neither the boundary treaty nor the chart appertaining thereto mention any islands, islets, or reefs situated beyond the Koster-Tisler line, and therefore, in order to keep within the probable intent of these documents we must disregard such islands, islets, and reefs;

Whereas, again, the maritime territory belonging to a zone of a certain width presents numerous peculiarities which distinguish it from the land territory and from the maritime spaces more or less completely surrounded by these territories;

Whereas, furthermore, in the same connection, the rules regarding maritime territory can not serve as a guide in determining the boundary between two contiguous countries, especially as, in the present case, we have to determine a boundary which is said to have been automatically traced in 1658, whereas the rules invoked date from subsequent centuries;

And it is the same way with the rules of Norwegian municipal law concerning the definition of boundaries between private properties or between administrative districts;

Whereas, for all these reasons, one can not adopt the method by which Norway has proposed to define the boundary from point 20 to the territorial limit;

Whereas, the rule of drawing a median line midway between the inhabited lands does not find sufficient support in the law of nations in force in the seventeenth century;

Whereas, it is the same way with the rule of the *thalweg* or the most important channel, inasmuch as the documents invoked for the purpose do not demonstrate that this rule was followed in the present case. And,

Whereas, we shall be acting much more in accord with the ideas of the seventeenth century and with the notions of law prevailing at that time if we admit that the automatic division of the territory in question must have taken place according to the general direction of the land territory of which the maritime territory constituted an appurtenance, and if we consequently apply this same rule at the present time in order to arrive at a just and lawful determination of the boundary;

Whereas, consequently, the automatic dividing line of 1658 should be determined (or, what is exactly the same thing expressed in other words), the delimitation should be made to-day by tracing a line perpendicularly to the general direction of the coast, while taking into account the necessity of indicating the boundary in a clear and unmistakable manner, thus facilitating its observation by the interested parties as far as possible;

Whereas, in order to ascertain what is this direction we must take equally into account the direction of the coast situated on both sides of the boundary;

Whereas, the general direction of the coast, according to the expert and conscientious survey of the tribunal, swerves about 20 degrees westward from due north, and therefore the perpendicular line should run toward the west to about 20 degrees to the south;

Whereas, the parties agree in admitting the great unsuitability of tracing the boundary-line across important bars; and

A boundary-line drawn from point 20 in a westerly direction to 19 degrees to the south would completely obviate this inconvenience, since it would pass just to the north of the Grisbadarna and to the south of Skjöttegrunde and would also not cut through any other important bank; and

Consequently, the boundary-line ought to be traced from point 20 westward to 19 degrees south, so that it would pass midway between the Grisbadarna banks on the one side and Skjöttegrunde on the other;

Whereas, although the parties have not indicated any marks of alignment for a boundary-line thus traced there is reason to believe that it will not be impossible to find such marks;

Whereas, on the other hand, we could, if necessary, avail ourselves of other known methods of marking the boundary;

Whereas, a demarkation which would assign the Grisbadarna to Sweden is supported by all of several circumstances of fact which were pointed out during the discussion and of which the following are the principal ones:

(*a*) The circumstance that lobster fishing in the shoals of Grisbadarna has been carried on for a much longer time, to a much larger extent, and by a much larger number of fishermen by the subjects of Sweden than by the subjects of Norway.

(*b*) The circumstance that Sweden has performed various acts in the Grisbadarna region, especially of late, owing to her conviction that these regions were Swedish, as, for instance, the placing of beacons, the measurement of the sea, and the installation of a light-boat, being acts which involved considerable expense and in doing which she not only thought that she was exercising her right but even more that she was performing her duty; whereas Norway, according to her own admission, showed much less solicitude in this region in these various regards;

Whereas, as regards the circumstance of fact mentioned in paragraph *a* above, it is a settled principle of the law of nations that a state of things which actually exists and has existed for a long time should be changed as little as possible; and

This rule is specially applicable in a case of private interests which, if once neglected, can not be effectively safeguarded by any manner of sacrifice on the part of the Government of which the interested parties are subjects; and

Lobster fishing is much the most important fishing on the Grisbadarna banks, this fishing being the very thing that gives the banks their value as fisheries; and

Without doubt the Swedes were the first to fish lobsters by means of the tackle and craft necessary to engage in fishing as far out at sea as the banks in question are situated; and

Fishing is, generally speaking, of more importance to the inhabitants of Koster than to those of Hvaler, the latter having, at least until comparatively recent times, engaged rather in navigation than fishing; and

From these various circumstances it appears so probable as to be almost certain that the Swedes utilized the banks in question much earlier and much more effectively than the Norwegians; and

The depositions and declarations of the witnesses are, generally speaking, in perfect harmony with this conclusion; and

The arbitration convention is likewise in full accord with the same conclusion; and

According to this convention there is a certain connection between the enjoyment of the fisheries of the Grisbadarna and the keeping up of the light-boat, and, as Sweden will be obliged to keep up the light-boat as long as the present state of affairs continues, this shows that, according to the arguments of this clause, the principal enjoyment thereof is now due to Sweden;

Whereas, as regards the circumstances of fact as mentioned under *b*:

As regards the placing of beacons and of a light-boat—

The stationing of a light-boat, which is necessary to the safety of navigation in the regions of Grisbadarna, was done by Sweden without meeting any protest and even at the initiative of Norway, and likewise a large number of beacons were established there without giving rise to any protests; and

This light-boat and these beacons are always maintained by Sweden at her own expense; and

Norway has never taken any measures which are in any way equivalent except by placing a bell-buoy there at a time subsequent to the placing of the beacons and for a short period of time, it being impossible to even compare the expenses of setting out and keeping up this buoy with those connected with the beacons and the light-boat; and

It is shown by the foregoing that Sweden had no doubt as to her rights over the Grisbadarna and that she did not hesitate to incur the expenses incumbent on the owner and possessor of these banks even to the extent of a considerable sum of money.

As to the measurements of the sea—

Sweden took the first steps, about thirty years before the beginning of any dispute, toward making exact, laborious, and expensive measurements of the regions of Grisbadarna, while the measurements made some years later by Norway did not even attain the limits of the Swedish measurements.   And

Whereas, therefore, there is no doubt whatever that the assignment of the Grisbadarna banks to Sweden is in perfect accord with the most important circumstances of fact;

Whereas, a demarkation assigning the Skjöttegrunde (which are the least important parts of the disputed territory) to Norway is sufficiently warranted by the serious circumstance of fact that, although one must infer from the various documents and testimony that the Swedish fishermen, as was stated above, have carried on fishing in the regions in question for a longer period, to a greater extent, and in greater numbers, it is certain on the other hand that the Norwegian fishermen have never been excluded from fishing there;

Whereas, moreover, it is averred that the Norwegian fishermen have almost always participated in the lobster fishing on the Skjötte-grunde in a comparatively more effective manner than at the Grisbadarna:

Therefore

The tribunal decides and pronounces:

That the maritime boundary between Norway and Sweden, as far as it was not determined by the Royal Resolution of March 15, 1904, is fixed as follows:

From point 18 situated as indicated on the chart annexed to the project of the Norwegian and Swedish commissioners of August 18, 1897, a straight line is traced to point 19, constituting the middle point of a straight line drawn from the northernmost reef of the Röskären to the southernmost reef of the Svartskjär, the one which is provided with a beacon;

From point 19 thus fixed, a straight line is traced to point 20, which constitutes the middle point of a straight line drawn from the northernmost reef of the group of reefs called Stora Drammen to the Hejeknub situated to the southeast of Heja Islands; from point 20 a straight line is drawn in a direction of west 19 degrees south, which line passes midway between the Grisbadarna and the Skjöttegrunde south and extends in the same direction until it reaches the high sea.

Done at The Hague, October 23, 1909, in the Palace of the Permanent Court of Arbitration.

J. A. LOEFF, *President*

MICHIELS VAN VERDUYNEN, *Secretary General*

RÖELL, *Secretary*

AGREEMENT FOR ARBITRATION

Convention between Norway and Sweden for the reference to arbitration of the question of a certain portion of the sea-limit between the two countries in connection with the Grisbadarna rocks.—Signed at Stockholm, March 14, 1908.[1]

His Majesty the King of Sweden and His Majesty the King of Norway, having found it desirable that the question of the sea-limit between Sweden and Norway, in so far as it was not determined by the Resolution of the 15th March, 1904,[2] should be referred to arbitration, have for this purpose appointed as their representatives:

His Majesty the King of Sweden: His Minister for Foreign Affairs, Eric Birger Trolle;

His Majesty the King of Norway: His Envoy Extraordinary and Minister Plenipotentiary, Paul Benjamin Vogt;

Who, after exchanging full powers, have agreed to the following conditions:

ARTICLE 1

The parties pledge themselves to the extent stated below to leave the settling of the question of the sea-limit between Sweden and Norway to a tribunal of arbitration, consisting of a president who is neither a subject of nor domiciled in either of the two countries, and of two other members: one Swede and one Norwegian. The president shall be appointed by Her Majesty the Queen of the Netherlands, the other members one each by the parties concerned. The parties, however, retain the right, should they agree, to appoint by special arrangement either the president only or the collective members of the tribunal.

---

[1]*British and Foreign State Papers*, vol. 102, p. 731. For the original Swedish and Norwegian texts, see Appendix, p. 496.

[2]*Post*, p. 136.

Representation to Her Majesty the Queen of the Netherlands, or the arbitrator who may be appointed by agreement, shall be made by both parties together.

ARTICLE 2

The tribunal of arbitration shall, after having examined the case of each of the parties and their respective reasons and proofs, determine the boundary-line in the waters from point 18 on the chart[1] annexed to the Swede-Norwegian proposal of the 18th August, 1897, into the sea up to the limit of the territorial waters. It is agreed that the boundary-line of the zone which the parties maintain to be under discussion, and for which, consequently, the limit is to be defined, may not be so drawn as to include islands, islets, or reefs which are not perpetually covered with water.

ARTICLE 3

The tribunal of arbitration shall have power to determine how far the boundary-line shall be considered to be, either wholly or in part, determined by the boundary treaty of 1661, together with the chart appertaining to the same, and how such boundary-line is to be traced, and also, in so far as the boundary-line can not be considered as established by the treaty and chart in question, shall have power to determine the same, taking into account the circumstances of fact and the principles of international law.

ARTICLE 4

Until the expiry of the third calendar year after the announcement of the decision of the tribunal of arbitration, irrespective of the boundary line fixed by that decision, fishing may be carried on within the waters which, according to Article 2, are the subject of dispute by the subjects of both countries to the same extent as during the five-year period 1901–1905. In considering the extent to which fishing is carried on, regard shall be had to the number of fishermen, the kind of fish, and the manner of catching.

ARTICLE 5

It is agreed that that country on whose side of the eventual boundary-line the Grisbadarna fishing grounds are situated shall have no claim against the other country for contribution towards the expense of light-ships or other arrangements on or in the neighborhood of such grounds.

---

[1] *Post*, opposite p. 140.

Sweden undertakes to maintain the present light-ship situated outside the territorial limit until the expiration of the time mentioned in Article 4.

ARTICLE 6

The president of the tribunal of arbitration shall appoint the time and place for the first meeting of the tribunal and shall summon the other members to it.

Time and place for further meetings shall be decided by the tribunal of arbitration.

ARTICLE 7

The official language to be used by the tribunal shall be English, French, or German, as may be decided in consultation with the other members.

For petitions, evidence, and directions the parties may use the language of either country, the tribunal retaining the right to have translations made.

ARTICLE 8

With respect to procedure and expenses, there shall apply such portions of the regulations contained in Articles 62 to 85 of the revised Convention adopted at the Second Hague Conference of 1907 for the pacific settlement of international disputes as may be applicable.

Petitions, rejoiners, and evidence referred to in Article 63 paragraph 2, of the above-mentioned Convention, shall be filed within a period to be determined by the president of the tribunal of arbitration, but before the 1st March, 1909. No change is hereby entailed in the rules of procedure for the second part, especially as regards the regulations in Articles 68, 72, and 74 of the said Convention.

The tribunal of arbitration has the right, when it is found necessary for the elucidation of the case, to arrange for the hearing of witnesses or experts in the presence of both parties and to order the undertaking in common of a hydrographical survey of the waters under dispute.

ARTICLE 9

This Convention shall be ratified, and the ratifications exchanged as soon as possible in Stockholm.

In respect whereof the respective plenipotentiaries have signed this Convention and affixed thereto their seals.

Done in duplicate, in Swedish and Norwegian, at Stockholm, on the 14th March, 1908.

(L. S.)   ERIC TROLLE
(L. S.)   BENJAMIN VOGT

ADDITIONAL DOCUMENTS

*His Royal Majesty's gracious resolution of March 26, 1904, with ac-
companying Protocol of March 15, 1904, concerning the determination of the extent of a certain part of the maritime boundary between Sweden and Norway.*[1]

In reference to the accompanying protocol of the joint Norwegian
and Swedish Council of State of March 15, 1904, as well as the extract
from the protocol of the State Council regarding civil matters for this
day, His Royal Majesty herewith authorizes the Riksdag to propose
that the question of the extent of the maritime boundary between
Sweden and Norway, from point 18 mentioned in the said protocol,
and to the sea, as far as the territorial boundary extends, be referred
to the decision of a special arbitral tribunal, in accordance with the
text of the protocols.

The authorities of the Riksdag shall appoint a committee to conduct
the examination of the acts; and with all Royal grace and favor His
Royal Majesty remains ever well disposed to the Riksdag.

In the absence of His Majesty my Most gracious King and Lord,

GUSTAF

H<small>JALMAR</small> W<small>ESTRING</small>

PROTOCOL CONSIDERED IN THE JOINT NORWEGIAN AND SWEDISH STATE
COUNCIL BEFORE HIS ROYAL HIGHNESS THE CROWN PRINCE REGENT
AT THE CASTLE OF CHRISTIANIA, MARCH 15, 1904.

Present: His Excellency the Minister of State Hagerup, his Excellency the Minister of State Ibsen, his Excellency the Minister of
State Boström, his Excellency the Minister for Foreign Affairs Lagerheim, State Councilors: Kildal, Strugstad, Hauge, Schöning, Vogt,
Mathiesen, and the Swedish State Councilor, Westring.

The Chief of the Department of Commerce and Industry, State
Councilor Schöning submitted the following:

> The Department takes the liberty of presenting considerations
> concerning measures anent the more definite fixation of national
> boundaries in the waters between Norway and Sweden.
> Maritime boundaries between the two countries running from
> the interior of Idefjard and out to the sea were fixed in a boun-
> dary regulation of October 26, 1661, carried out in accord with the
> peace treaty of Roskilde of February 26/March 9, 1658, and of
> Copenhagen of March 27/June 6, 1660.

---

[1]Translation. For the original Swedish text, see Appendix, p. 500.

In the meantime much uncertainty has arisen regarding several points of this boundary line in view of the fact that during the long interval between 1661 and 1897 nothing was done in the matter by joint survey and investigation. In 1897 the Norwegian Department of the Interior and the Swedish Department for Civil Affairs took action whereby they might ascertain the exact course of that section of the boundary; and in the month of August of the same year two Norwegian and two Swedish commissioners met for the purpose of making a thorough search of the records and an investigation on the spot, etc., and of their presenting a proposition for the fixation and tracing upon charts of the boundary line between Norway and Sweden, from the interior of Idefjard and out into the sea.

Bureau Secretary Hroar Olsen and Commander A. Rieck were the Norwegian commissioners; Commander E. Oldberg and Judge H. Westring were the Swedish commissioners.

As the result of their labors and investigations, the commissioners presented on August 18, 1897, the "proposition of the Royal Swedish and Norwegian Commission for and description of the maritime boundary between Norway and Sweden from the interior of Idefjard to the sea."

From this it appears, as witnessed by all four commissioners, that they had reached a unanimous conclusion regarding the boundary line from the interior of Idefjard to a point between the Jyete buoy (Norwegian) and a small Island, northwest of Narro Hellsö (Swedish), which point is numbered 18 on a draft chart accompanying the proposition, so that Helleholmen is transferred to Sweden, and Knivsöarna to Norway.

Regarding the extent of the boundary line from the said point 18 even to the sea, no agreement was arrived at by the commission. The Norwegian and the Swedish members each submitted their respective proposition in reference to that part, and according to which Grisbadarna together with some shallows and ground to the north of Koster should go respectively to Norway or to Sweden.

The commissioners' propositions[1] together with two charts in reference thereto are subjoined.[2]

The Department is of opinion that the line proposed by the Norwegian and Swedish commission, from the interior of Idefjard to point 18, as indicated on the accompanying map, should be regarded as the correct boundary line.

Inasmuch as with regard to the more detailed description of this line, reference is made to the proposition of the commissioners, the Department permits itself to recommend that Your Majesty approve that line as the correct boundary between the two kingdoms.

Provided that Your Majesty be pleased to decide according to this recommendation, the Department assumes that subsequently

[1]Post, p. 138.   [2]Post, opposite p. 140.

the royal proclamation with regard to the boundary line agreed
upon, will be issued by the State Council of each of the two kingdoms.

It is furthermore to be observed that it would be of importance
to demarkate as soon as possible this part of the boundary line.
It seems most expedient that a commissioner of each kingdom be
appointed to undertake this demarkation, and the Department
recommends therefore that Your Majesty approve this proposal to
the effect that the State Council of each of the two kingdoms shall
designate respectively one Norwegian and one Swedish commissioner.

As hereinbefore stated, the Norwegian and Swedish commissioners have not been able to agree upon the matter regarding the
rectification of the extent of the boundary from the said point 18
to the sea.

The following is a more detailed presentation of the views held
by the Norwegian and Swedish parties with regard to the disputed
boundary line.

NORWEGIAN VIEW

From point 18, between the buoy Jyete and a small island
northwest of Narra Hellsö, the line should run straight to the
open sea through the center of a straight line from the southern
extremity of the southernmost Norwegian Tislarön, Klöveren,
to the northern extremity of the northern Koster island (Swedish), so that the boundary line run by Båtshake, and all islands
situated to the north of this line, including Grisbadarna, remain
Norwegian.

This line is traced in red color on the chart of the commissioners, and said point between Klöveren and Koster island is indicated as point 19.

SWEDISH VIEW

From point 18, the boundary line should be drawn in a straight
line to the open sea, through a point about 300 meters north of
Rödkärs Nordgrund and therefore about midway between Grisbadarna and Skättegrund, so that all islands to the south outside of this line, water and land, including Grisbadarna, remain
Swedish.

Upon the chart of the commissioners this line is traced in yellow
color, and the said point north of Rödkärs Nordgrund marked
point 19.

This Department permits itself respectfully to propose that the
question of the disputed boundary line to the arbitral decision of a
special tribunal, after the consent thereto shall have been given by
the representatives of both kingdoms, and that the following procedure be observed:

In each of the two kingdoms, the respective State Council shall
appoint two judges.

The judges thus designated shall mutually agree upon a fifth judge who shall at the same time act as president of the tribunal. In case of a tie, the designation of the fifth member shall be referred to such foreign chief of State as Your Majesty might request to that end.

The rules of procedure of the tribunal, the deliberations as well as the place where the tribunal shall sit to be adopted by the judges themselves.

The duly announced judicial decision regarding the disputed boundary line shall be binding upon both parties.

Each kingdom shall meet the expenses of its own representatives, and the expenses of the fifth member, etc., shall be met in equal shares by the two kingdoms.

In accordance with the foregoing, the Department takes the liberty of submitting most respectfully:

That Your Majesty may most graciously resolve:

(1) That the boundary line between Norway and Sweden as proposed by the joint Norwegian and Swedish commission of 1897, from the upper end of Idefjard to point 18 as shown on the two accompanying charts[1] be approved according to the proposal of the commissioners;

(2) That the demarkation of the said boundary line shall be undertaken by commissioners chosen for the purpose, one from each kingdom;

(3) That questions concerning boundary lines between Norway and Sweden, from the aforesaid point 18 to the sea, as far as the territorial boundary extends shall be referred to the decision of a special arbitral tribunal, in accordance with what is hereinbefore stated, provided the representatives of the two kingdoms consent thereto.

The Swedish members of the State Council have concurred in what the present reporter has hereinbefore submitted as to the approval of the boundary lines proposed by the Swedish and Norwegian commissioners, from the upper end of Idefjard to the said point 18, including the demarkation of the boundary line.

Regarding the section of the boundary line from point 18 to the sea as far as the territorial boundary, those members declare that in several statements that have been sent in regarding this matter, suggestions have been made regarding the boundary according to which this line would in part be moved still further north than proposed by the Swedish commissioners. Expressing in regard to this the opinion that the proposal to submit to a special arbitral tribunal the decision as to

---

[1]*Post*, opposite p. 140.

the question of the position of the boundary line in this part, that this implied that both parties should have the opportunity to submit to the tribunal the demands in regard thereto which they might find necessary, these members agree to the proposition of the reporter even as to this part of the question.

The Norwegian members had no objection to make to the foregoing statement, which corresponded to what had been already taken for granted by the Norwegian side.

In accordance with what the members of the Council of State thus advise, may it please Your Royal Majesty the Crown Prince Regent to approve the proposal set forth by the chief of the Norwegian Department of Commerce and Industry.

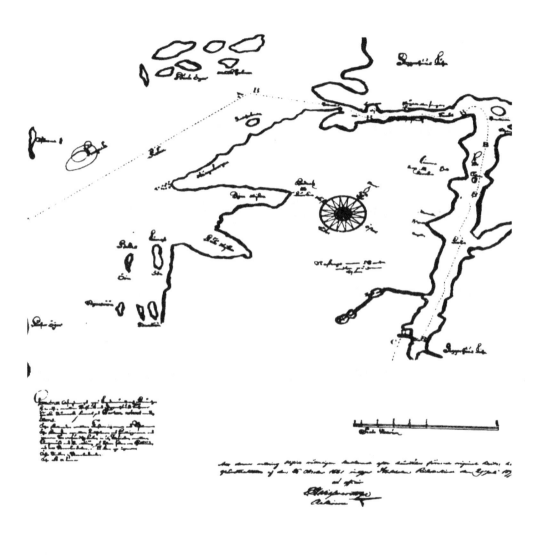

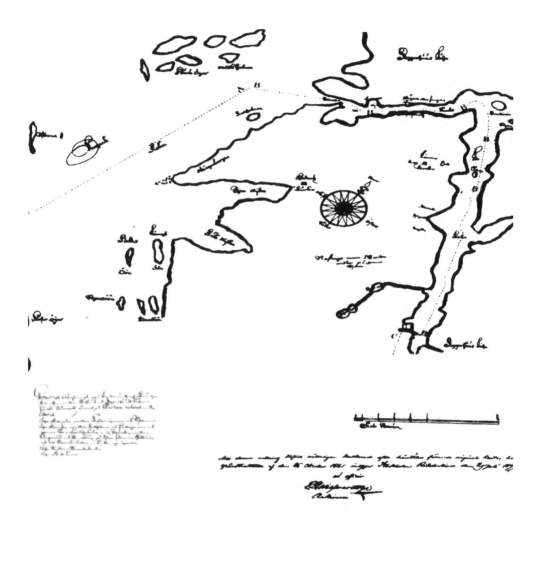

THE NORTH ATLANTIC COAST FISHERIES CASE

between

GREAT BRITAIN *and* THE UNITED STATES

Decided September 7, 1910

Syllabus

The treaty of peace of 1783 between Great Britain and the United States continued to inhabitants of the United States the privileges theretofore enjoyed in common with British subjects in the fisheries off Newfoundland, Labrador, and other parts of the North Atlantic Coast.

Great Britain regarded this treaty as abrogated by the war of 1812, whereas the United States considered it as only suspended by and during the war. However, on October 20, 1818, a new treaty was signed with a view of defining the rights of inhabitants of the United States to take fish in certain parts of British north Atlantic coast waters, and to enter bays and harbors for the purpose of repairs, etc. Article 1 reads as follows:

Whereas differences have arisen respecting the liberty claimed by the United States for the inhabitants thereof, to take, dry, and cure fish on certain coasts, bays, harbors, and creeks of His Britannic Majesty's dominions in America, it is agreed between the high contracting Parties, that the inhabitants of the said United States shall have forever, in common with the subjects of His Britannic Majesty, the liberty to take fish of every kind on that part of the southern coast of Newfoundland which extends from Cape Ray to the Rameau Islands, on the western and northern coast of Newfoundland, from the said Cape Ray to the Quirpon Islands on the shores of the Magdalen Islands, and also on the coasts, bays, harbors, and creeks from Mount Joly on the southern coast of Labrador, to and through the Straits of Belleisle and thence northwardly indefinitely along the coast, without prejudice, however, to any of the exclusive rights of the Hudson Bay Company: And that the American fishermen shall also have liberty forever, to dry and cure fish in any of the unsettled bays, harbors, and creeks of the southern part of the coast of Newfoundland hereabove described, and of the coast of Labrador; but so soon as the same, or any portion thereof, shall be settled, it shall not be lawful for the said fishermen to dry or cure fish at such portion so settled, with-

out previous agreement for such purpose with the inhabitants, proprietors, or possessors of the ground.   And the United States hereby
renounce forever, any liberty heretofore enjoyed or claimed by the
inhabitants thereof, to take, dry, or cure fish on, or within three marine
miles of any of the coasts, bays, creeks, or harbors of His Britannic
Majesty's dominions in America not included within the above-mentioned limits : Provided, however, that the American fishermen shall
be admitted to enter such bays or harbors for the purpose of shelter
and of repairing damages therein, of purchasing wood, and of obtaining water, and for no other purpose whatever.   But they shall be
under such restrictions as may be necessary to prevent their taking,
drying or curing fish therein, or in any other manner whatever abusing
the privileges hereby reserved to them.

Differences arose as to the scope and meaning of this article and of
the rights and liberties referred to in the article or claimed on behalf
of the inhabitants of the United States.   Beginning with the seizure of
American fishing vessels in 1821-2, the controversy over fishing rights
continued in more or less menacing form until 1905 when, on account
of the severe restrictive legislation by Newfoundland, affairs reached
a critical stage.   Negotiations were begun looking to a settlement, and
in 1906 a *modus vivendi*[1] covering the fishing season of 1906-7 was
agreed upon by the two Governments for the purpose of allaying friction until some definite adjustment could be reached.   The *modus* was
renewed for the fishing seasons of 1907-8,[2] 1908-9[3] and 1909-10,[4]
and on January 27, 1909, a *compromis*[5] was signed submitting the controversy to the Permanent Court of Arbitration at The Hague.   A
tribunal was created composed of the following members of the panel
of the court: Heinrich Lammasch, of Austria-Hungary ; A. F. de
Savornin Lohman, of Holland ; George Gray, of the United States ;
Luis M. Drago, of Argentine ; and Sir Charles Fitzpatrick, of Great
Britain.   The sessions of the tribunal began June 1, 1910, and ended
August 12, 1910 ; the decision was rendered September 7, 1910.
There were seven questions submitted to the tribunal.
First. Great Britain contended for the right, directly or indirectly
through Canada or Newfoundland, to make regulations applicable to
American fishermen in treaty waters without the consent of the
United States, "in respect of (1) the hours, days, or seasons when
fish may be taken on the treaty coasts ; (2) the method, means and implements to be used in the taking of fish or in the carrying on of fishing operations on such coasts ; (3) any other matters of a similar character ;" provided such regulations were "reasonable, as being, for instance, appropriate or necessary for the protection and preservation of
such fisheries ; desirable on grounds of public order and morals ;

[1]*Post*, p. 208.   [2]*Post*, p. 212.   [3]*Post*, p. 214.   [4]*Post*, p. 220.   [5]*Post*, p. 147.

equitable and fair as between local fishermen and the inhabitants of the United States."

The United States, on the other hand, denied the right of Great Britain to make such regulations "unless their appropriateness, necessity, reasonableness, and fairness be determined by the United States and Great Britain by common accord and the United States concurs in their enforcement."

The tribunal in its decision on this question affirmed the right of Great Britain "to make regulations without the consent of the United States" but held that "such regulations must be made *bona fide* and must not be in violation of the said treaty;" and that "regulations which are (1) appropriate or necessary for the preservation of such fisheries, or (2) desirable or necessary on grounds of public order and morals without unnecessarily interfering with the fishery itself, and in both cases equitable and fair as between local and American fishermen, and not so framed as to give an advantage to the former over the latter class, are not inconsistent with the obligation to execute the treaty in good faith, and are therefore not in violation of the treaty."

The award thus far is in favor of Great Britain, but the tribunal held further that, if the reasonableness of the regulation is contested by the United States, Great Britain is not to be the judge of what is or what is not reasonable, but that it must be decided not by either of the parties but by an impartial authority. To this end the tribunal recommended certain rules and methods of procedure in case any regulation was contested, the important feature being that any such contested regulation, before becoming effective, should be referred to a permanent mixed fishery commission, whose membership, procedure and authority the tribunal also defined. In proposing this recommendation, accepted by the parties in controversy, the tribunal relied upon Article 4 of the special agreement, which was considered both by the tribunal and by Great Britain and the United States, as in the nature of a permanent treaty of unlimited duration for the settlement of any disputes that might arise between the two countries under the convention of 1818. This article is as follows:

The tribunal shall recommend for the consideration of the high contracting Parties rules and a method of procedure under which all questions which may arise in the future regarding the exercise of the liberties above referred to may be determined in accordance with the principles laid down in the award. If the high contracting Parties shall not adopt the rules and method of procedure so recommended, or if they shall not, subsequently to the delivery of the award, agree upon such rules and method, then any differences which may arise in the future between the high contracting Parties relating to the interpretation of the treaty of 1818 or to the effect and application of the award of the tribunal shall be referred informally to the Permanent Court at The Hague for decision by the summary procedure provided in Chapter IV of the Hague Convention of the 18th October, 1907.[1]

----
[1] *Post*, p. 151.

Second. This was as to the right of the inhabitants of the United States, while exercising the liberties referred to, to employ as members of the fishing crews of their vessels persons not inhabitants of the United States.

The United States contended (1) that the liberty assured to their inhabitants by the treaty plainly includes the right to use all the means customary or appropriate for fishing upon the sea, not only ships and nets and boats, but crews to handle the ships, the nets and the boats; (2) that no right to control or limit the means which these inhabitants shall use in fishing can be admitted unless it is provided in the terms of the treaty and no right to question the nationality or inhabitancy of the crews employed is contained in the terms of the treaty.

Great Britain, on the other hand, contended (1) that the treaty confers the liberty to inhabitants of the United States exclusively; (2) that the Governments of Great Britain, Canada or Newfoundland may, without infraction of the treaty, prohibit persons from engaging as fishermen in American vessels.

The tribunal held in favor of the United States but expressed the view that non-inhabitants employed as members of crews of American fishing vessels derive no rights from the treaty, but only from their employer.

Third. The United States contended that its inhabitants were not, without its consent, to be subjected "to the requirements of entry or report at custom-houses or the payment of light or harbor dues, or to any other similar requirement or condition or exaction."

The United States stated in its case that American fishing vessels exercising their treaty rights might properly be called upon to make known their presence and exhibit their credentials by a report at customs, but on the other hand, the United States denied that such vessels could be subjected to the customs regulations imposed upon other vessels, or required to pay light, harbor or other dues not imposed upon local fishing vessels.

The tribunal held that the duty to report is not unreasonable, if the report may be made conveniently either in person or by telegraph; otherwise the vessel need not report. It was also held that "the exercise of the fishing liberty by the inhabitants of the United States should not be subjected to the purely commercial formalities of report, entry and clearance at a custom-house, nor to light, harbor or other dues not imposed upon Newfoundland fishermen."

Fourth. This question was as to the right to require payment of light and harbor dues by fishermen of the United States, or to report at custom-houses, and similar requirements when resorting to certain bays and harbors for shelter, wood, water, etc.

The treaty provided that American fishermen might enter bays or harbors on the non-treaty coast "for the purpose of shelter and of repairing damages therein, of purchasing wood and of obtaining water, and for no other purpose whatever."

Great Britain contended that vessels, seeking these non-treaty ports were to be treated as ordinary vessels, subject to local ordinances and regulations, whereas the United States maintained that the ports were to be treated as ports of refuge and that subjection of fishing vessels to the prerequisite of entering and reporting at custom-houses, or of paying light, harbor or other dues would unjustly impair and limit the privileges which the clause meant to concede.

The tribunal held that the treaty provision was an exercise, in large measure, of the "duties of hospitality and humanity which all civilized nations impose upon themselves," and was not dependent upon the payment of dues or other similar requirements, although the privilege should not be abused.

Fifth. By the convention of 1818 the United States renounced the right "to take, dry, or cure fish on, or within three marine miles of any of the coasts, bays, creeks or harbors of His Britannic Majesty's dominions in America" not included within the limits specified by the treaty. The fifth question asked "from where must be measured the 'three marine miles of any of the coasts, bays, creeks, or harbors' referred to in the said article?"

Great Britain contended that the United States had renounced the right to fish within *all* bays and within three miles thereof, that is, that the word "bays" in the treaty was used in both a geographical and territorial sense, thereby excluding American fishermen from all bodies of water on the non-treaty coast known as bays on the charts of the period. On the contrary the United States maintained that the word "bays" was used in the territorial sense, and therefore limited to small bays, and that it had renounced merely the right to fish within such bays as formed part of His Majesty's dominions, that is to say, territorial bays; that only such bays whose entrance was less than double the marine league were renounced, and that in such cases the three marine miles were to be measured from a line drawn across the bays where they were six miles or less in width.

The tribunal decided in favor of the British contention that the word "bays" must be interpreted as applying to geographical bays, and held that "in case of bays, the three marine miles are to be measured from a straight line drawn across the body of water at the place where it ceases to have the configuration and characteristics of a bay," but that "at all other places the three marine miles are to be measured following the sinuosities of the coast." That is, a body of water, *geographically* called a bay, may cease to have "the configuration and characteristic of a bay" and at this point the line is to be drawn.

The tribunal, however, in view of the difficulty in the practical application of the rule laid down, recommended a procedure to determine the limits of particular bays, which were specified, and provided also that as to bays not specified "the limits of exclusion should be three miles seaward from a straight line across the bay at the part nearest the entrance at the first point where the width does not exceed ten miles."

The decision was not unanimous, Dr. Drago submitting a dissenting opinion, in which he maintained that there was no certain rule laid down for the guidance of the parties, and that the recommendation of a special series of lines, however practical they might be supposed to be, was beyond the scope of the award and could not be adopted without a new treaty being entered into by the parties.

Sixth. The United States contended that the inhabitants of the United States have the liberty, under Article 1 of the treaty, of taking fish in the bays, harbors, and creeks on what was known as the treaty coast, that is, on that part of the southern coast of Newfoundland which extends from Cape Ray to Rameau Islands, or on the western and northern coasts of Newfoundland from Cape Ray to Quirpon Islands and on the Magdalen Islands. Great Britain contended that they had no such liberty, and endeavored to show that evidence could be found in the correspondence submitted to the tribunal indicating an intention to exclude Americans from Newfoundland bays on the treaty coast, and that no value would have been attached at that time by the United States Government to the liberty of fishing in such bays because there was no cod fishery there as there was in the bays of Labrador.

The tribunal decided in favor of the United States.

Seventh. This was whether vessels belonging to inhabitants of the United States resorting to the treaty coasts for the purposes of exercising the liberties referred to, were entitled to have the commercial privileges which were accorded by agreement or otherwise to trading vessels of the United States generally. The tribunal held that there was nothing in the treaty provisions to disentitle them, provided the treaty liberty of fishing and the commercial privileges were not exercised concurrently.

The tribunal decided in favor of the United States.

AWARD OF THE TRIBUNAL

Award of the tribunal of arbitration in the question relating to the north Atlantic coast fisheries.—The Hague, September 7, 1910.[1]

PREAMBLE

Whereas a special agreement between the United States of America and Great Britain, signed at Washington the 27th January, 1909,[2] and confirmed by interchange of notes dated the 4th March, 1909,[3] was concluded in conformity with the provisions of the general arbitration treaty between the United States of America and

---

[1]Official report, p. 104.   [2]*Post*, p. 147.   [3]*Post*, p. 215.

Great Britain, signed the 4th April, 1908, and ratified the 4th June, 1908;

And whereas the said special agreement for the submission of questions relating to fisheries on the North Atlantic coast under the general treaty of arbitration concluded between the United States and Great Britain on the 4th day of April, 1908, is as follows:[1]

ARTICLE 1

Whereas by Article 1 of the convention signed at London on the 20th day of October, 1818, between Great Britain and the United States, it was agreed as follows:

Whereas differences have arisen respecting the liberty claimed by the United States for the inhabitants thereof, to take, dry and cure fish on certain coasts, bays, harbors and creeks of His Britannic Majesty's dominions in America, it is agreed between the high contracting Parties, that the inhabitants of the said United States shall have forever, in common with the subjects of His Britannic Majesty, the liberty to take fish of every kind on that part of the southern coast of Newfoundland which extends from Cape Ray to the Rameau Islands, on the western and northern coast of Newfoundland, from the said Cape Ray to the Quirpon Islands, on the shores of Magdalen Islands, and also on the coasts, bays, harbors, and creeks from Mount Joly on the southern coast of Labrador, to and through the Straits of Belleisle and thence northwardly indefinitely along the coast, without prejudice, however, to any of the exclusive rights of the Hudson Bay Company; and that the American fishermen shall also have liberty forever, to dry and cure fish in any of the unsettled bays, harbors and creeks of the southern part of the coast of Newfoundland hereabove described, and of the coast of Labrador; but so soon as the same, or any portion thereof, shall be settled, it shall not be lawful for the said fishermen to dry or cure fish at such portion so settled, without previous agreement for such purpose with the inhabitants. proprietors, or possessors of the ground.—And the United States hereby renounce forever, any liberty heretofore enjoyed or claimed by the inhabitants thereof, to take, dry, or cure fish on, or within three marine miles of any of the coasts, bays, creeks, or harbors of His Britannic Majesty's dominions in America not included within the above-mentioned limits; provided, however, that the American fishermen

---

[1] As the full text of the agreement for arbitration is here given, it is not printed again under a special heading.

shall be admitted to enter such bays and harbors for the purpose of shelter and of repairing damages therein, of purchasing wood, and of obtaining water, and for no other purpose whatever. But they shall be under such restrictions as may be necessary to prevent their taking, drying or curing fish therein, or in any other manner whatever abusing the privileges hereby reserved to them.

And, whereas, differences have arisen as to the scope and meaning of the said article, and of the liberties therein referred to, and otherwise in respect of the rights and liberties which the inhabitants of the United States have or claim to have in the waters or on the shores therein referred to:

It is agreed that the following questions shall be submitted for decision to a tribunal of arbitration constituted as hereinafter provided:

Question 1. To what extent are the following contentions or either of them justified?

It is contended on the part of Great Britain that the exercise of the liberty to take fish referred to in the said article, which the inhabitants of the United States have forever in common with the subjects of His Britannic Majesty, is subject, without the consent of the United States, to reasonable regulation by Great Britain, Canada, or Newfoundland in the form of municipal laws, ordinances, or rules, as, for example, to regulations in respect of (1) the hours, days, or seasons when fish may be taken on the treaty coasts; (2) the method, means, and implements to be used in the taking of fish or in the carrying on of fishing operations on such coasts; (3) any other matters of a similar character relating to fishing; such regulations being reasonable, as being, for instance—

(*a*) Appropriate or necessary for the protection and preservation of such fisheries and the exercise of the rights of British subjects therein and of the liberty which by the said Article 1 the inhabitants of the United States have therein in common with British subjects;

(*b*) Desirable on grounds of public order and morals;

(*c*) Equitable and fair as between local fishermen and the inhabitants of the United States exercising the said treaty liberty and not so framed as to give unfairly an advantage to the former over the latter class.

It is contended on the part of the United States that the exercise of such liberty is not subject to limitations or restraints by Great Britain, Canada, or Newfoundland in the form of municipal laws, ordinances, or regulations in respect of (1) the hours, days, or seasons when the inhabitants of the United States may take fish on the treaty coasts, or (2) the method, means, and implements used by them in taking fish or in carrying on fishing operations on such coasts, or (3) any other limitations or restraints of similar character—

(*a*) Unless they are appropriate and necessary for the protection and preservation of the common rights in such fisheries and the exercise thereof; and

(*b*) Unless they are reasonable in themselves and fair as between local fishermen and fishermen coming from the United States, and not so framed as to give an advantage to the former over the latter class; and

(*c*) Unless their appropriateness, necessity, reasonableness, and fairness be determined by the United States and Great Britain by common accord and the United States concurs in their enforcement.

Question 2. Have the inhabitants of the United States, while exercising the liberties referred to in said article, a right to employ as members of the fishing crews of their vessels persons not inhabitants of the United States?

Question 3. Can the exercise by the inhabitants of the United States of the liberties referred to in the said article be subjected, without the consent of the United States, to the requirements of entry or report at custom-houses or the payment of light or harbor and other dues, or to any other similar requirement or condition or exaction?

Question 4. Under the provision of the said article that the American fishermen shall be admitted to enter certain bays or harbors for shelter, repairs, wood, or water, and for no other purpose whatever, but that they shall be under such restrictions as may be necessary to prevent their taking, drying, or curing fish therein or in any other manner whatever abusing the privileges thereby reserved to them, is it permissible to impose restrictions making the exercise of such privileges conditional upon the payment of light or harbor or other dues, or entering or reporting at custom-houses or any similar conditions?

Question 5. From where must be measured the "three marine miles of any of the coasts, bays, creeks, or harbors" referred to in the said article?

Question 6. Have the inhabitants of the United States the liberty under the said article or otherwise to take fish in the bays, harbors, and creeks on that part of the southern coast of Newfoundland which extends from Cape Ray to Rameau Islands, or on the western and northern coasts of Newfoundland from Cape Ray to Quirpon Islands, or on the Magdalen Islands?

Question 7. Are the inhabitants of the United States whose vessels resort to the treaty coasts for the purpose of exercising the liberties referred to in Article 1 of the treaty of 1818 entitled to have for those vessels, when duly authorized by the United States in that behalf, the commercial privileges on the treaty coasts accorded by agreement or otherwise to United States trading vessels generally?

ARTICLE 2

Either party may call the attention of the tribunal to any legislative or executive act of the other party, specified within three months of the exchange of notes enforcing this agreement, and which is claimed to be inconsistent with the true interpretation of the treaty of 1818; and may call upon the tribunal to express in its award its opinion upon such acts, and to point out in what respects, if any, they are inconsistent with the principles laid down in the award in reply to the preceding questions; and each party agrees to conform to such opinion.

ARTICLE 3

If any question arises in the arbitration regarding the reasonableness of any regulation or otherwise which requires an examination of the practical effect of any provisions in relation to the conditions surrounding the exercise of the liberty of fishery enjoyed by the inhabitants of the United States, or which requires expert information about the fisheries themselves, the tribunal may, in that case, refer such question to a commission of three expert specialists in such matters; one to be designated by each of the parties hereto, and the third, who shall not be a national of either party, to be designated by the tribunal. This commission shall examine into and report their conclusions on any question or questions so referred to it by the tribunal and such report shall be considered by the tribunal and shall, if incorporated by them in the award, be accepted as a part thereof.

Pending the report of the commission upon the question or questions so referred and without awaiting such report, the tribunal may make a separate award upon all or any other questions before it, and such separate award, if made, shall become immediately effective, provided that the report aforesaid shall not be incorporated in the award until it has been considered by the tribunal. The expenses of such commission shall be borne in equal moieties by the parties hereto.

ARTICLE 4

The tribunal shall recommend for the consideration of the high contracting Parties rules and a method of procedure under which all questions which may arise in future regarding the exercise of the liberties above referred to may be determined in accordance with the principles laid down in the award. If the high contracting Parties shall not adopt the rules and method of procedure so recommended, or if they shall not, subsequently to the delivery of the award, agree upon such rules and methods, then any differences which may arise in the future between the high contracting Parties relating to the interpretation of the treaty of 1818 or to the effect and application of the award of the tribunal shall be referred informally to the Permanent Court at The Hague for decision by the summary procedure provided in Chapter IV of the Hague Convention of the 18th October, 1907.

ARTICLE 5

The tribunal of arbitration provided for herein shall be chosen from the general list of members of the Permanent Court at The Hague, in accordance with the provisions of Article 45 of the Convention for the settlement of international disputes, concluded at the Second Peace Conference at The Hague on the 18th of October, 1907. The provisions of said Convention, so far as applicable and not inconsistent herewith, and excepting Articles 53 and 54, shall govern the proceedings under the submission herein provided for.

The time allowed for the direct agreement of His Britannic Majesty and the President of the United States on the composition of such tribunal shall be three months.

ARTICLE 6

The pleadings shall be communicated in the order and within the time following:

As soon as may be and within a period not exceeding seven months from the date of the exchange of notes making this agreement binding the printed case of each of the parties hereto, accompanied by printed copies of the documents, the official correspondence, and all other evidence on which each party relies, shall be delivered in duplicate (with such additional copies as may be agreed upon) to the agent of the other party. It shall be sufficient for this purpose if such case is delivered at the British Embassy at Washington or at the American Embassy at London, as the case may be, for transmission to the agent for its Government.

Within fifteen days thereafter such printed case and accompanying evidence of each of the parties shall be delivered in duplicate to each member of the tribunal, and such delivery may be made by depositing within the stated period the necessary number of copies with the International Bureau at The Hague for transmission to the arbitrators.

After the delivery on both sides of such printed case, either party may, in like manner, and within four months after the expiration of the period above fixed for the delivery to the agents of the case, deliver to the agent of the other party (with such additional copies as may be agreed upon), a printed counter-case accompanied by printed copies of additional documents, correspondence, and other evidence in reply to the case, documents, correspondence, and other evidence so presented by the other party, and within fifteen days thereafter such party shall, in like manner as above provided, deliver in duplicate such counter-case and accompanying evidence to each of the arbitrators.

The foregoing provisions shall not prevent the tribunal from permitting either party to rely at the hearing upon documentary or other evidence which is shown to have become open to its investigation or examination or available for use too late to be submitted within the period hereinabove fixed for the delivery of copies of evidence, but in case any such evidence is to be presented, printed copies of it, as soon as possible after it is secured, must be delivered, in like manner as provided for the delivery of copies of other evidence, to each of the arbitrators and to the agent of the other party. The admission of any such additional evidence, however, shall be subject to such conditions as the tribunal may impose, and the other party shall have a reasonable opportunity to offer additional evidence in rebuttal.

The tribunal shall take into consideration all evidence which is offered by either party.

<h2 style="text-align:center">ARTICLE 7</h2>

If in the case or counter-case (exclusive of the accompanying evidence) either party shall have specified or referred to any documents, correspondence, or other evidence in its own exclusive possession without annexing a copy, such party shall be bound, if the other party shall demand it within thirty days after the delivery of the case or counter-case respectively, to furnish to the party applying for it a copy thereof; and either party may, within the like time, demand that the other shall furnish certified copies or produce for inspection the originals of any documentary evidence adduced by the party upon whom the demand is made. It shall be the duty of the party upon whom any such demand is made to comply with it as soon as may be, and within a period not exceeding fifteen days after the demand has been received. · The production for inspection or the furnishing to the other party of official governmental publications, publishing, as authentic, copies of the documentary evidence referred to, shall be a sufficient compliance with such demand, if such governmental publications shall have been published prior to the 1st day of January, 1908. If the demand is not complied with, the reasons for the failure to comply must be stated to the tribunal.

<h2 style="text-align:center">ARTICLE 8</h2>

The tribunal shall meet within six months after the expiration of the period above fixed for the delivery to the agents of the case, and upon the assembling of the tribunal at its first session each party, through its agent or counsel, shall deliver in duplicate to

each of the arbitrators and to the agent and counsel of the other
party (with such additional copies as may be agreed upon) a printed
argument showing the points and referring to the evidence upon
which it relies.

The time fixed by this agreement for the delivery of the case,
counter-case, or argument, and for the meeting of the tribunal,
may be extended by mutual consent of the parties.

ARTICLE 9

The decision of the tribunal shall, if possible, be made within
two months from the close of the arguments on both sides, unless
on the request of the tribunal the parties shall agree to extend the
period.

It shall be made in writing, and dated and signed by each member of the tribunal, and shall be accompanied by a statement of
reasons.

A member who may dissent from the decision may record his
dissent when signing.

The language to be used throughout the proceedings shall be
English.

ARTICLE 10

Each party reserves to itself the right to demand a revision of
the award. Such demand shall contain a statement of the grounds
on which it is made and shall be made within five days of the promulgation of the award, and shall be heard by the tribunal within
ten days thereafter. The party making the demand shall serve a
copy of the same on the opposite party, and both parties shall be
heard in argument by the tribunal on said demand. The demand
can only be made on the discovery of some new fact or circumstance calculated to exercise a decisive influence upon the award
and which was unknown to the tribunal and to the party demanding the revision at the time the discussion was closed, or upon the
ground that the said award does not fully and sufficiently, within
the meaning of this agreement, determine any question or questions submitted. If the tribunal shall allow the demand for a revision, it shall afford such opportunity for further hearings and
arguments as it shall deem necessary.

ARTICLE 11

The present agreement shall be deemed to be binding only when confirmed by the two Governments by an exchange of notes.

In witness whereof this agreement has been signed and sealed by His Britannic Majesty's Ambassador at Washington, the Right Honorable James Bryce, O.M., on behalf of Great Britain, and by the Secretary of State of the United States, Elihu Root, on behalf of the United States.

Done at Washington on the 27th day of January, one thousand nine hundred and nine.

JAMES BRYCE   [SEAL]

ELIHU ROOT   [SEAL]

And whereas, the parties to the said agreement have by common accord, in accordance with Article 5, constituted as a tribunal of arbitration the following members of the Permanent Court at The Hague: Mr. H. Lammasch, Doctor of Law, professor of the University of Vienna, Aulic Councilor, member of the Upper House of the Austrian Parliament; his Excellency Jonkheer A. F. de Savornin Lohman, Doctor of Law, Minister of State, former Minister of the Interior, member of the Second Chamber of the Netherlands; the Honorable George Gray, Doctor of Laws, Judge of the United States Circuit Court of Appeals, former United States Senator; the Right Honorable Sir Charles Fitzpatrick, member of the Privy Council, Doctor of Laws, Chief Justice of Canada; the Honorable Luis Maria Drago, Doctor of Law, former Minister of Foreign Affairs of the Argentine Republic, member of the Law Academy of Buenos Aires;

And whereas, the agents of the parties to the said agreement have duly and in accordance with the terms of the agreement communicated to this tribunal their cases, counter-cases, printed arguments, and other documents;

And whereas, counsel for the parties have fully presented to this tribunal their oral arguments in the sittings held between the first assembling of the tribunal on 1st June, 1910, to the close of the hearings on 12th August, 1910;

Now, therefore, this tribunal having carefully considered the said agreement, cases, counter-cases, printed and oral arguments, and the documents presented by either side, after due deliberation makes the following decisions and awards:

QUESTION 1

To what extent are the following contentions or either of them justified?

It is contended on the part of Great Britain that the exercise of the liberty to take fish referred to in the said article, which the inhabitants of the United States have forever in common with the subjects of His Britannic Majesty, is subject, without the consent of the United States, to reasonable regulation by Great Britain, Canada, or Newfoundland in the form of municipal laws, ordinances, or rules, as, for example, to regulations in respect of (1) the hours, days, or seasons when fish may be taken on the treaty coasts; (2) the method, means, and implements to be used in the taking of fish or in the carrying on of fishing operations on such coasts; (3) any other matters of a similar character relating to fishing; such regulations being reasonable, as being, for instance—

(a) Appropriate or necessary for the protection and preservation of such fisheries and the exercise of the rights of British subjects therein and of the liberty which by the said Article 1 the inhabitants of the United States have therein in common with British subjects;

(b) Desirable on grounds of public order and morals;

(c) Equitable and fair as between local fishermen and the inhabitants of the United States exercising the said treaty liberty, and not so framed as to give unfairly an advantage to the former over the latter class.

It is contended on the part of the United States that the exercise of such liberty is not subject to limitations or restraints by Great Britain, Canada, or Newfoundland in the form of municipal laws, ordinances, or regulations in respect of (1) the hours, days, or seasons when the inhabitants of the United States may take fish on the treaty coasts, or (2) the method, means, and implements used by them in taking fish or in carrying on fishing operations on such coasts, or (3) any other limitations or restraints of similar character—

(a) Unless they are appropriate and necessary for the protection and preservation of the common rights in such fisheries and the exercise thereof; and (*b*) Unless they are reasonable in themselves and fair as between local fishermen and fishermen coming from the United States, and not so framed as to give an advantage to the former over the latter class; and

(*c*) Unless their appropriateness, necessity, reasonableness, and fairness be determined by the United States and Great Britain by common accord and the United States concurs in their enforcement.

Question I, thus submitted to the tribunal, resolves itself into two main contentions:

1st. Whether the right of regulating reasonably the liberties conferred by the treaty of 1818 resides in Great Britain;

2nd. And, if such right does so exist, whether such reasonable exercise of the right is permitted to Great Britain without the accord and concurrence of the United States.

The treaty of 1818 contains no explicit disposition in regard to the right of regulation, reasonable or otherwise; it neither reserves that right in express terms, nor refers to it in any way. It is therefore incumbent on this tribunal to answer the two questions above indicated by interpreting the general terms of Article 1 of the treaty, and more especially the words "the inhabitants of the United States shall have, for ever, in common with the subjects of His Britannic Majesty, the liberty to take fish of every kind." This interpretation must be conformable to the general import of the instrument, the general intention of the parties to it, the subject matter of the contract, the expressions actually used and the evidence submitted.

Now in regard to the preliminary question as to whether the right of reasonable regulation resides in Great Britain:

Considering that the right to regulate the liberties conferred by the treaty of 1818 is an attribute of sovereignty, and as such must be held to reside in the territorial sovereign, unless the contrary be provided; and considering that one of the essential elements of sovereignty is that it is to be exercised within territorial limits, and that, failing proof to the contrary, the territory is coterminous with the sovereignty, it follows that the burden of the assertion involved in the contention of the United States (viz., that the right to regulate does not reside independently in Great Britain, the territorial sovereign) must fall on the United States. And for the purpose of sustaining this burden, the United States have put forward the following series of propositions, each one of which must be singly considered.

It is contended by the United States:

(1) That the French right of fishery under the treaty of 1713 designated also as a liberty, was never subjected to regulation by Great Britain, and therefore the inference is warranted that the American liberties of fishery are similarly exempted.

The tribunal is unable to agree with this contention:

(a) Because although the French right designated in 1713 merely "an allowance," (a term of even less force than that used in regard to the American fishery) was nevertheless converted, in practice, into an exclusive right, this concession on the part of Great Britain was presumably made because France, before 1713, claimed to be the sovereign of Newfoundland, and, in ceding the island, had, as the American argument says, "reserved for the benefit of its subjects the right to fish and to use the strand";

(b) Because the distinction between the French and American right is indicated by the different wording of the statutes for the observance of treaty obligations towards France and the United States, and by the British Declaration of 1783;

(c) And, also, because this distinction is maintained in the treaty with France of 1904, concluded at a date when the American claim was approaching its present stage, and by which certain common rights of regulation are recognized to France.

For the further purpose of such proof it is contended by the United States:

(2) That the liberties of fishery, being accorded to the inhabitants of the United States "for ever," acquire, by being in perpetuity and unilateral, a character exempting them from local legislation.

The tribunal is unable to agree with this contention:

(a) Because there is no necessary connection between the duration of a grant and its essential status in its relation to local regulation; a right granted in perpetuity may yet be subject to regulation, or, granted temporarily, may yet be exempted therefrom; or being reciprocal may yet be unregulated, or being unilateral may yet be regulated : as is evidenced by the claim of the United States that the liberties of fishery accorded by the reciprocity treaty of 1854 and the treaty of 1871 were exempt from regulation, though they were neither permanent nor unilateral ;

(*b*) Because no peculiar character need be claimed for these liberties in order to secure their enjoyment in perpetuity, as is evidenced by the American negotiators in 1818 asking for the insertion of the words "for ever." International law in its modern development recognizes that a great number of treaty obligations are not annulled by war, but at most suspended by it ;

(*c*) Because the liberty to dry and cure is, pursuant to the terms of the treaty, provisional and not permanent, and is nevertheless, in respect of the liability to regulation, identical in its nature with, and never distinguished from, the liberty to fish.

For the further purpose of such proof, the United States allege :

(3) That the liberties of fishery granted to the United States constitute an international servitude in their favor over the territory of Great Britain, thereby involving a derogation from the sovereignty of Great Britain, the servient State, and that therefore Great Britain is deprived, by reason of the grant, of its independent right to regulate the fishery.

The tribunal is unable to agree with this contention :

(*a*) Because there is no evidence that the doctrine of international servitude was one with which either American or British statesmen were conversant in 1818, no English publicists employing the term before 1818, and the mention of it in Mr. Gallatin's report being insufficient ;

(*b*) Because a servitude in the French law, referred to by Mr. Gallatin, can, since the code, be only real and can not be personal (*Code Civil*, Art. 686) ;

(*c*) Because a servitude in international law predicates an express grant of a sovereign right and involves an analogy to the relation of a *praedium dominans* and a *praedium serviens;* whereas by the treaty of 1818 one State grants a liberty to fish, which is not a sovereign right, but a purely economic right, to the inhabitants of another State ;

(d) Because the doctrine of international servitude in the sense which is now sought to be attributed to it originated in the peculiar and now obsolete conditions prevailing in the Holy Roman Empire of which the *domini terrae* were not fully sovereigns; they holding territory under the Roman Empire, subject at least theoretically, and in some respects also practically, to the courts of that Empire; their right being, moreover, rather of a civil than of a public nature, partaking more of the character of *dominium* than of *imperium,* and therefore certainly not a complete sovereignty. And because in contradistinction to this quasi-sovereignty with its incoherent attributes acquired at various times, by various means, and not impaired in its character by being incomplete in any one respect or by being limited in favor of another territory and its possessor, the modern State, and particularly Great Britain, has never admitted partition of sovereignty, owing to the constitution of a modern State requiring essential sovereignty and independence;

(e) Because this doctrine being but little suited to the principle of sovereignty which prevails in States under a system of constitutional government such as great Britain and the United States, and to the present international relations of sovereign States, has found little, if any, support from modern publicists. It could therefore in the general interest of the community of nations, and of the parties to this treaty, be affirmed by this tribunal only on the express evidence of an international contract;

(f) Because even if these liberties of fishery constituted an international servitude, the servitude would derogate from the sovereignty of the servient State only in so far as the exercise of the rights of sovereignty by the servient State would be contrary to the exercise of the servitude right by the dominant State. Whereas it is evident that, though every regulation of the fishery is to some extent a limitation, as it puts limits to the exercise of the fishery at will, yet such regulations as are reasonable and made for the purpose of securing and preserving the fishery and its exercise for the common benefit, are clearly to be distinguished from those restrictions and "molestations," the annulment of which was the purpose of the American demands formulated by Mr. Adams in 1782, and such regulations consequently can not be held to be inconsistent with a servitude;

(*g*) Because the fishery to which the inhabitants of the United States were admitted in 1783, and again in 1818, was a regulated fishery, as is evidenced by the following regulations:

Act 15 Charles II, Cap. 16, s. 7 (1663) forbidding "to lay any seine or other net in or near any harbor in Newfoundland, whereby to take the spawn or young fry of the Poor-John, or for any other use or uses, except for the taking of bait only," which had not been superseded either by the order in council of March 10th, 1670, or by the statute 10 and 11 Wm. III, Cap. 25, 1699. The order in council provides expressly for the obligation "to submit unto and to observe all rules and orders as are now, or hereafter shall be established," an obligation which can not be read as referring only to the rules established by this very act, and having no reference to anteceding rules "as are now established." In a similar way, the statute of 1699 preserves in force prior legislation, conferring the freedom of fishery only "as fully and freely as at any time heretofore." The order in council, 1670, provides that the admirals, who always were fishermen, arriving from an English or Welsh port, "see that His Majesty's rules and orders concerning the regulation of the fisheries are duly put in execution" (sec. 13). Likewise the Act 10 and 11 Wm. III, Cap. 25 (1699) provides that the admirals do settle differences between the fishermen arising in respect of the places to be assigned to the different vessels. As to Nova Scotia, the proclamation of 1665 ordains that no one shall fish without license; that the licensed fishermen are obliged "to observe all laws and orders which now are made and published, or shall hereafter be made and published in this jurisdiction," and that they shall not fish on the Lord's day and shall not take fish at the time they come to spawn. The judgment of the Chief Justice of Newfoundland, October 26th, 1820, is not held by the tribunal sufficient to set aside the proclamations referred to. After 1783, the statute 26 Geo. III, Cap. 26, 1786, forbids "the use, on the shores of Newfoundland, of seines or nets for catching cod by hauling on shore or taking into boat, with meshes less than 4 inches"; a prohibition which can not be considered as limited to the bank fishery. The act for regulating the fisheries of New Brunswick, 1793, which forbids "the placing of nets or seines across any cove or creek in the province so as to obstruct the natural course of

fish" and which makes specific provision for fishing in the harbor
of St. John, as to the manner and time of fishing, can not be read
as being limited to fishing from the shore. The act for regulating
the fishing on the coast of Northumberland (1799) contains very
elaborate dispositions concerning the fisheries in the bay of Miramichi which were continued in 1823, 1829, and 1834. The statutes
of Lower Canada, 1788 and 1807, forbid the throwing overboard
of offal. The fact that these acts extend the prohibition over a
greater distance than the first marine league from the shore may
make them non-operative against foreigners without the territorial
limits of Great Britain, but is certainly no reason to deny their
obligatory character for foreigners within these limits;

(*h*) Because the fact that Great Britain rarely exercised the
right of regulation in the period immediately succeeding 1818 is to
be explained by various circumstances and is not evidence of the
non-existence of the right;

(*i*) Because the words "in common with British subjects" tend
to confirm the opinion that the inhabitants of the United States
were admitted to a regulated fishery;

(*j*) Because the statute of Great Britain, 1819, which gives legislative sanction to the treaty of 1818, provides for the making of
"regulations with relation to the taking, drying and curing fish by
inhabitants of the United States in 'common.' "

For the purpose of such proof, it is further contended by the
United States, in this latter connection:

(4) That the words "in common with British subjects" used in
the treaty should not be held as importing a common subjection to regulation, but as intending to negative a possible
pretension on the part of the inhabitants of the United States
to liberties of fishery exclusive of the right of British subjects to fish.

The tribunal is unable to agree with this contention:

(*a*) Because such an interpretation is inconsistent with the historical basis of the American fishing liberty. The ground on which
Mr. Adams founded the American right in 1782 was that the people
then constituting the United States had always, when still under

British rule, a part in these fisheries and that they must continue to enjoy their past right in the future. He proposed "that the subjects of His Britannic Majesty and the people of the United States shall continue to enjoy unmolested the right to take fish . . . where the inhabitants of both countries used, at any time heretofore, to fish." The theory of the partition of the fisheries, which by the American negotiators had been advanced with so much force, negatives the assumption that the United States could ever pretend to an exclusive right to fish on the British shores; and to insert a special disposition to that end would have been wholly superfluous;

(b) Because the words "in common" occur in the same connection in the treaty of 1818 as in the treaties of 1854 and 1871. It will certainly not be suggested that in these treaties of 1854 and 1871 the American negotiators meant by inserting the words "in common" to imply that without these words American citizens would be precluded from the right to fish on their own coasts and that, on American shores, British subjects should have an exclusive privilege. It would have been the very opposite of the concept of territorial waters to suppose that, without a special treaty provision, British subjects could be excluded from fishing in British waters. Therefore that can not have been the scope and the sense of the words "in common";

(c) Because the words "in common" exclude the supposition that American inhabitants were at liberty to act at will for the purpose of taking fish, without any regard to the coexisting rights of other persons entitled to do the same thing; and because these words admit them only as members of a social community, subject to the ordinary duties binding upon the citizens of that community, as to the regulations made for the common benefit; thus avoiding the *bellum omnium contra omnes* which would otherwise arise in the exercise of this industry;

(d) Because these words are such as would naturally suggest themselves to the negotiators of 1818 if their intention had been to express a common subjection to regulations as well as a common right.

In the course of the Argument it has also been alleged by the United States:

(5) That the treaty of 1818 should be held to have entailed a transfer or partition of sovereignty, in that it must in respect to the liberties of fishery be interpreted in its relation to the treaty of 1783; and that this latter treaty was an act of partition of sovereignty and of separation, and as such was not annulled by the war of 1812.

Although the tribunal is not called upon to decide the issue whether the treaty of 1783 was a treaty of partition or not, the questions involved therein having been set at rest by the subsequent treaty of 1818, nevertheless the tribunal could not forbear to consider the contention on account of the important bearing the controversy has upon the true interpretation of the treaty of 1818. In that respect the tribunal is of opinion:

(a) That the right to take fish was accorded as a condition of peace to a foreign people; wherefore the British negotiators refused to place the right of British subjects on the same footing with those of American inhabitants; and further, refused to insert the words also proposed by Mr. Adams ("continue to enjoy") in the second branch of Art. 3 of the treaty of 1783;

(b) That the treaty of 1818 was in different terms, and very different in extent, from that of 1783, and was made for different considerations. It was, in other words, a new grant.

For the purpose of such proof it is further contended by the United States:

(6) That as contemporary commercial treaties contain express provisions for submitting foreigners to local legislation, and the treaty of 1818 contains no such provision, it should be held, *a contrario,* that inhabitants of the United States exercising these liberties are exempt from regulation.

The tribunal is unable to agree with this contention:

(a) Because the commercial treaties contemplated did not admit foreigners to all and equal rights, seeing that local legislation excluded them from many rights of importance, *e. g.*, that of holding land; and the purport of the provisions in question consequently was to preserve these discriminations. But no such discriminations existing in the common enjoyment of the fishery by American and British fishermen, no such provision was required;

(*b*) Because no proof is furnished of similar exemptions of foreigners from local legislation in default of treaty stipulations subjecting them thereto;

(*c*) Because no such express provision for subjection of the nationals of either party to local law was made either in this treaty, in respect to their reciprocal admission to certain territories as agreed in Art. 3, or in Art. 3 of the treaty of 1794; although such subjection was clearly contemplated by the parties.

For the purpose of such proof it is further contended by the United States:

(7) That, as the liberty to dry and cure on the treaty coasts and to enter bays and harbors on the non-treaty coasts are both subjected to conditions, and the latter to specific restrictions, it should therefore be held that the liberty to fish should be subjected to no restrictions, as none are provided for in the treaty.

The tribunal is unable to apply the principle of *expressio unius exclusio alterius* to this case:

(*a*) Because the conditions and restrictions as to the liberty to dry and cure on the shore and to enter the harbors are limitations of the rights themselves, and not restrictions of their exercise. Thus the right to dry and cure is limited in duration, and the right to enter bays and harbors is limited to particular purposes;

(*b*) Because these restrictions of the right to enter bays and harbors applying solely to American fishermen must have been expressed in the treaty, whereas regulations of the fishery, applying equally to American and British, are made by right of territorial sovereignty.

For the purpose of such proof it has been contended by the United States:

(8) That Lord Bathurst in 1815 mentioned the American right under the treaty of 1783 as a right to be exercised "at the

discretion of the United States"; and that this should be held as to be derogatory to the claim of exclusive regulation by Great Britain.

But the tribunal is unable to agree with this contention:

(*a*) Because these words implied only the necessity of an express stipulation for any liberty to use foreign territory at the pleasure of the grantee, without touching any question as to regulation;

(*b*) Because in this same letter Lord Bathurst characterized this right as a policy "temporary and experimental, depending on the use that might be made of it, on the condition of the islands and places where it was to be exercised, and the more general conveniences or inconveniences from a military, naval, and commercial point of view"; so that it can not have been his intention to acknowledge the exclusion of British interference with this right;

(*c*) Because Lord Bathurst in his note to Governor Sir C. Hamilton in 1819 orders the Governor to take care that the American fishery on the coast of Labrador be carried on *in the same manner* as previous to the late war; showing that he did not interpret the treaty just signed as a grant conveying absolute immunity from interference with the American fishery right.

For the purpose of such proof it is further contended by the United States:

(9) That on various other occasions following the conclusion of the treaty, as evidenced by official correspondence, Great Britain made use of expressions inconsistent with the claim to a right of regulation.

The tribunal, unwilling to invest such expressions with an importance entitling them to affect the general question, considers that such conflicting or inconsistent expressions as have been exposed on either side are sufficiently explained by their relations to ephemeral phases of a controversy of almost secular duration, and should be held to be without direct effect on the principal and present issues.

Now with regard to the second contention involved in Question I, as to whether the right of regulation can be reasonably exercised by Great Britain without the consent of the United States:

Considering that the recognition of a concurrent right of consent in the United States would affect the independence of Great Britain, which would become dependent on the Government of the United States for the exercise of its sovereign right of regulation, and considering that such a co-dominium would be contrary to the constitution of both sovereign States; the burden of proof is imposed on the United States to show that the independence of Great Britain was thus impaired by international contract in 1818 and that a co-dominium was created.

For the purpose of such proof it is contended by the United States:

(10) That a concurrent right to coöperate in the making and enforcement of regulations is the only possible and proper security to their inhabitants for the enjoyment of their liberties of fishery, and that such a right must be held to be implied in the grant of those liberties by the treaty under interpretation.

The tribunal is unable to accede to this claim on the ground of a right so implied:

(a) Because every State has to execute the obligations incurred by treaty *bona fide,* and is urged thereto by the ordinary sanctions of international law in regard to observance of treaty obligations. Such sanctions are, for instance, appeal to public opinion, publication of correspondence, censure by parliamentary vote, demand for arbitration with the odium attendant on a refusal to arbitrate, rupture of relations, reprisal, etc. But no reason has been shown why this treaty, in this respect, should be considered as different from every other treaty under which the right of a State to regulate the action of foreigners admitted by it on its territory is recognized;

(b) Because the exercise of such a right of consent by the United States would predicate an abandonment of its independence in this respect by Great Britain, and the recognition by the latter of a concurrent right of regulation in the United States. But the treaty conveys only a liberty to take fish in common, and neither directly nor indirectly conveys a joint right of regulation;

(c) Because the treaty does not convey a common right of fishery, but a liberty to fish in common. This is evidenced by the attitude of the United States Government in 1823, with respect to the relations of Great Britain and France in regard to the fishery;

(d) Because if the consent of the United States were requisite for the fishery a general veto would be accorded them, the full exercise of which would be socially subversive and would lead to the consequence of an unregulatable fishery;

(e) Because the United States can not by assent give legal force and validity to British legislation;

(f) Because the liberties to take fish in British territorial waters and to dry and cure fish on land in British territory are in principle on the same footing; but in practice a right of coöperation in the elaboration and enforcement of regulations in regard to the latter liberty (drying and curing fish on land) is unrealizable.

In any event, Great Britain, as the local sovereign, has the duty of preserving and protecting the fisheries. In so far as it is necessary for that purpose, Great Britain is not only entitled, but obliged, to provide for the protection and preservation of fisheries; always remembering that the exercise of this right of legislation is limited by the obligation to execute the treaty in good faith. This has been admitted by counsel and recognized by Great Britain in limiting the right of regulation to that of reasonable regulation. The inherent defect of this limitation of reasonableness, without any sanction except in diplomatic remonstrance, has been supplied by the submission to arbitral award as to existing regulations in accordance with Arts. 2 and 3 of the special agreement, and as to further regulation by the obligation to submit their reasonableness to an arbitral test in accordance with Art. 4 of the agreement.

It is finally contended by the United States:

That the United States did not expressly agree that the liberty granted to them could be subjected to any restriction that the grantor might choose to impose on the ground that in her judgment such restriction was reasonable. And that while admitting that all laws of a general character, controlling the conduct of men within the territory of Great Britain, are effective, binding, and beyond objection by the United States, and competent to be made upon the sole determination of Great Britain or her colony, without accountability to anyone whomsoever; yet there is somewhere a line, beyond which it is not competent for Great Britain to go, or beyond which she can not rightfully go, because to go beyond it would be an invasion of the right granted to the United States in 1818. That the legal effect of the grant of 1818 was not to leave the determination as to where that line is to be drawn to the uncontrolled judgment of the grantor, either upon the grantor's consideration as to what would be a reasonable exercise of its sovereignty over the British Empire, or upon the grantor's consideration of what would be a reasonable exercise thereof towards the grantee.

But this contention is founded on assumptions, which this tribunal can not accept for the following reasons in addition to those already set forth:

(*a*) Because the line by which the respective rights of both parties accruing out of the treaty are to be circumscribed, can refer only to the right granted by the treaty; that is to say to the liberty of taking, drying, and curing fish by the American inhabitants in certain British waters in common with British subjects, and not to the exercise of rights of legislation by Great Britain not referred to in the treaty;

(*b*) Because a line which would limit the exercise of sovereignty of a State within the limits of its own territory, can be drawn only on the ground of express stipulation, and not by implication from stipulations concerning a different subject-matter;

(*c*) Because the line in question is drawn according to the principle of international law that treaty obligations are to be executed in perfect good faith, therefore excluding the right to legislate *at will* concerning the subject-matter of the treaty, and limiting the exercise of sovereignty of the States bound by a treaty with respect to that subject-matter to such acts as are consistent with the treaty;

(*d*) Because on a true construction of the treaty the question does not arise whether the United States agreed that Great Britain should retain her right to legislate with regard to the fisheries in her own territory; but whether the treaty contains an abdication by Great Britain of the right which Great Britain, as the sovereign power, undoubtedly possessed when the treaty was made, to regulate those fisheries;

(e) Because the right to make reasonable regulations, not inconsistent with the obligations of the treaty, which is all that is claimed by Great Britain, for a fishery which both parties admit requires regulation for its preservation, is not a restriction of or an invasion of the liberty granted to the inhabitants of the United States. This grant does not contain words to justify the assumption that the sovereignty of Great Britain upon its own territory was in any way affected; nor can words be found in the treaty transferring any part of that sovereignty to the United States. Great Britain assumed only duties with regard to the exercise of its sovereignty. The sovereignty of Great Britain over the coastal waters and territory of Newfoundland remains after the treaty as unimpaired as it was before. But from the treaty results an obligatory relation whereby the right of Great Britain to exercise its sovereignty by making regulations is limited to such regulations as are made in good faith, and are not in violation of the treaty;

(f) Finally, to hold that the United States, the grantee of the fishing right, has a voice in the preparation of fishery legislation involves the recognition of a right in that country to participate in the internal legislation of Great Britain and her colonies, and to that extent would reduce these countries to a state of dependence.

While therefore unable to concede the claim of the United States as based on the treaty, this tribunal considers that such claim has been and is to some extent, conceded in the relations now existing between the two parties. Whatever may have been the situation under the treaty of 1818 standing alone, the exercise of the right of regulation inherent in Great Britain has been, and is, limited by the repeated recognition of the obligations already referred to, by the limitations and liabilities accepted in the special agreement, by the unequivocal position assumed by Great Britain in the presentation of its case before this tribunal, and by the consequent view of this tribunal that it would be consistent with all the circumstances, as revealed by this record, as to the duty of Great Britain, that she should submit the reasonableness of any future regulation to such an impartial arbitral test, affording full opportunity therefor, as is hereafter recommended under the authority of Article 4 of the special agreement, whenever the reasonableness of any regulation is objected to or challenged by the United States in the manner, and within the time hereinafter specified in the said recommendation.

Now therefore this tribunal decides and awards as follows:

The right of Great Britain to make regulations without the consent of the United States, as to the exercise of the liberty to take fish referred to in Article 1 of the treaty of October 20th, 1818, in the form of municipal laws, ordinances, or rules of Great Britain, Canada, or Newfoundland is inherent to the sovereignty of Great Britain.

The exercise of that right by Great Britain is, however, limited by the said treaty in respect of the said liberties therein granted to the inhabitants of the United States in that such regulations must be made *bona fide* and must not be in violation of the said treaty.

Regulations which are (1) appropriate or necessary for the protection and preservation of such fisheries, or (2) desirable or necessary on grounds of public order and morals without unnecessarily interfering with the fishery itself, and in both cases equitable and fair as between local and American fishermen, and not so framed as to give unfairly an advantage to the former over the latter class, are not inconsistent with the obligation to execute the treaty in good faith, and are therefore reasonable and not in violation of the treaty.

For the decision of the question whether a regulation is or is not reasonable, as being or not in accordance with the dispositions of the treaty and not in violation thereof, the treaty of 1818 contains no special provision. The settlement of differences in this respect that might arise thereafter was left to the ordinary means of diplomatic intercourse. By reason, however, of the form in which Question I is put, and by further reason of the admission of Great Britain by her counsel before this tribunal that it is not now for either of the parties to the treaty to determine the reasonableness of any regulation made by Great Britain, Canada, or Newfoundland, the reasonableness of any such regulation, if contested, must be decided not by either of the parties, but by an impartial authority in accordance with the principles hereinabove laid down, and in the manner proposed in the recommendations made by the tribunal in virtue of Article 4 of the agreement.

The tribunal further decides that Article 4 of the agreement is, as stated by counsel of the respective parties at the argument, permanent in its effect, and not terminable by the expiration of the general arbitration treaty of 1908, between Great Britain and the United States.

In execution, therefore, of the responsibilities imposed upon this tribunal in regard to Articles 2, 3, and 4 of the special agreement, we hereby pronounce in their regard as follows:

As to Article 2

Pursuant to the provisions of this article, hereinbefore cited, either party has called the attention of this tribunal to acts of the other claimed to be inconsistent with the true interpretation of the treaty of 1818.

But in response to a request from the tribunal, recorded in Protocol No. XXVI of 19th July, for an exposition of the grounds of such objections, the parties replied as reported in Protocol No. XXX of 28th July to the following effect:

His Majesty's Government considered that it would be unnecessary to call upon the tribunal for an opinion under the second clause of Article 2, in regard to the executive act of the United States of America in sending war-ships to the territorial waters in question, in view of the recognized motives of the United States of America in taking this action and of the relations maintained by their representatives with the local authorities. And this being the sole act to which the attention of this tribunal has been called by His Majesty's Government, no further action in their behalf is required from this tribunal under Article 2.

The United States of America presented a statement in which their claim that specific provisions of certain legislative and executive acts of the Governments of Canada and Newfoundland were inconsistent with the true interpretation of the treaty of 1818 was based on the contention that these provisions were not "reasonable" within the meaning of Question 1.

After calling upon this tribunal to express an opinion on these acts, pursuant to the second clause of Article 2, the United States of America pointed out in that statement that under Article 3 any question regarding the reasonableness of any regulation might be referred by the tribunal to a commission of expert specialists, and expressed an intention of asking for such reference under certain circumstances.

The tribunal having carefully considered the counter-statement presented on behalf of Great Britain at the session of August 2nd, is of opinion that the decision on the reasonableness of these regulations requires expert information about the fisheries themselves and an examination of the practical effect of a great number of these provisions in relation to the conditions surrounding the exercise of the liberty of fishery enjoyed by the inhabitants of the United States, as contemplated by Article 3. No further action on behalf of the United States is therefore required from this tribunal under Article 2.

As to Article 3

As provided in Article 3, hereinbefore cited and above referred to, "any question regarding the reasonableness of any regulation, or otherwise, which requires an examination of the practical effect of any provisions surrounding the exercise of the liberty of fishery enjoyed by the inhabitants of the United States, or which requires expert information about the fisheries themselves, may be referred by this tribunal to a commission of expert specialists; one to be designated by each of the parties hereto and the third, who shall not be a national of either party, to be designated by the tribunal."

The tribunal now therefore calls upon the parties to designate within one month their national commissioners for the expert examination of the questions submitted.

As the third non-national commissioner this tribunal designates Doctor P. P. C. Hoek, scientific adviser for the fisheries of the Netherlands, and if any necessity arises therefor a substitute may be appointed by the president of this tribunal.

After a reasonable time, to be agreed on by the parties, for the expert commission to arrive at a conclusion, by conference, or, if necessary, by local inspection, the tribunal shall, if convoked by the president at the request of either party, thereupon at the earliest convenient date, reconvene to consider the report of the commission, and if it be on the whole unanimous shall incorporate it in the award. If not on the whole unanimous, *i. e.*, on all points which in the opinion of the tribunal are of essential importance, the tribunal shall make its award as to the regulations concerned after consideration of the conclusions of the expert commissioners and after hearing argument by counsel.

But while recognizing its responsibilities to meet the obligations imposed on it under Article 3 of the special agreement, the tribunal hereby recommends as an alternative to having recourse to a reconvention of this tribunal, that the parties should accept the unanimous opinion of the commission or the opinion of the non-national commissioner on any points in dispute as an arbitral award rendered under the provisions of Chapter IV of the Hague Convention of 1907.

As to Article 4

Pursuant to the provisions of this article, hereinbefore cited, this tribunal recommends for the consideration of the parties the following rules and method of procedure under which all questions which may arise in future regarding the exercise of the liberties above referred to may be determined in accordance with the principles laid down in this award.

1

All future municipal laws, ordinances, or rules for the regulation of the fishery by Great Britain in respect of (1) the hours, days or seasons when fish may be taken on the treaty coasts; (2) the method, means and implements used in the taking of fish or in carrying on fishing operations; (3) any other regulation of a similar character shall be published in the London *Gazette* two months before going into operation.

Similar regulations by Canada or Newfoundland shall be similarly published in the Canada *Gazette* and the Newfoundland *Gazette* respectively.

2

If the Government of the United States considers any such laws or regulations inconsistent with the treaty of 1818, it is entitled to so notify the Government of Great Britain within the two months referred to in Rule No. 1.

3

Any law or regulation so notified shall not come into effect with respect to inhabitants of the United States until the permanent mixed fishery commission has decided that the regulation is reasonable within the meaning of this award.

4

Permanent mixed fishery commissions for Canada and Newfoundland respectively shall be established for the decision of such questions as to the reasonableness of future regulations, as contemplated by Article 4 of the special agreement; these commissions shall consist of an expert national appointed by either party for five years. The third member shall not be a national of either party; he shall be nominated for five years by agreement of the parties, or failing such agreement within two months, he shall be nominated by Her Majesty the Queen of the Netherlands. The two national members shall be convoked by the Government of Great Britain within one month from the date of notification by the Government of the United States.

5

The two national members having failed to agree within one month, within another month the full commission, under the presidency of the umpire, is to be convoked by Great Britain. It must deliver its decision, if the two Governments do not agree otherwise, at the latest in three months. The umpire shall conduct the procedure in accordance with that provided in Chapter IV of the Convention for the pacific settlement of international disputes, except in so far as herein otherwise provided.

6

The form of convocation of the commission including the terms of reference of the question at issue shall be as follows: "The provision hereinafter fully set forth of an act dated ——————, published in the ——————, has been notified to the Government of Great Britain by the Government of the United States, under date of ——————————, as provided by the award of the Hague tribunal of September 7th, 1910.

Pursuant to the provisions of that award the Government of Great Britain hereby convokes the permanent mixed fishery commission for ——————(Canada)——————, composed of ——————————, (Newfoundland) commissioner for the United States of America, and of ——————————————, commissioner for ——————(Canada)——————, which shall (Newfoundland) meet at —————————— and render a decision within one month as to whether the provision so notified is reasonable and consistent with the treaty of 1818, as interpreted by the award of the Hague tribunal of September 7th, 1910, and if not, in what respect it is unreasonable and inconsistent therewith.

Failing an agreement on this question within one month the commission shall so notify the Government of Great Britain in order that the further action required by that award may be taken for the decision of the above question.

The provision is as follows: ——————————————————"

7

The unanimous decision of the two national commissioners, or the majority decision of the umpire and one commissioner, shall be final and binding.

QUESTION 2

Have the inhabitants of the United States, while exercising the liberties referred to in said article, a right to employ as members of the fishing crews of their vessels persons not inhabitants of the United States?

In regard to this question the United States claim in substance:

1. That the liberty assured to their inhabitants by the treaty plainly includes the right to use all the means customary or appropriate for fishing upon the sea, not only ships and nets and boats, but crews to handle the ships and the nets and the boats;
2. That no right to control or limit the means which these inhabitants shall use in fishing can be admitted unless it is pro-

vided in the terms of the treaty and no right to question the nationality or inhabitancy of the crews employed is contained in the terms of the treaty.

And Great Britain claims:

1. That the treaty confers the liberty to inhabitants of the United States exclusively;
2. That the Governments of Great Britain, Canada or Newfoundland may, without infraction of the treaty, prohibit persons from engaging as fishermen in American vessels.

Now considering (1) that the liberty to take fish is an economic right attributed by the treaty; (2) that it is attributed to inhabitants of the United States, without any mention of their nationality; (3) that the exercise of an economic right includes the right to employ servants; (4) that the right of employing servants has not been limited by the treaty to the employment of persons of a distinct nationality or inhabitancy; (5) that the liberty to take fish as an economic liberty refers not only to the individuals doing the manual act of fishing, but also to those for whose profit the fish are taken.

But considering, that the treaty does not intend to grant to individual persons or to a class of persons the liberty to take fish in certain waters "in common," that is to say in company, with individual British subjects, in the sense that no law could forbid British subjects to take service on American fishing ships; (2) that the treaty intends to secure to the United States a share of the fisheries designated therein, not only in the interest of a certain class of individuals, but also in the interest of both the United States and Great Britain, as appears from the evidence and notably from the correspondence between Mr. Adams and Lord Bathurst in 1815; (3) that the inhabitants of the United States do not derive the liberty to take fish directly from the treaty, but from the United States Government as party to the treaty with Great Britain and moreover exercising the right to regulate the conditions under which its inhabitants may enjoy the granted liberty; (4) that it is in the interest of the inhabitants of the United States that the fishing liberty granted to them be restricted to exercise by them and removed from the enjoyment of other aliens not entitled by this treaty to participate in the fisheries; (5) that such restrictions have been throughout enacted in the British Statute of June 15, 1819, and that of June 3, 1824, to this effect, that no alien or stranger whatsoever shall fish in the waters designated therein, except in so far as by treaty thereto entitled, and that this exception will, in virtue of the treaty of 1818, as hereinabove interpreted by this award, exempt from these statutes American fishermen fishing by the agency of non-inhabitant aliens employed in their service; (6) that the treaty does not affect the sovereign right of Great Britain as to aliens, non-inhabitants of the United States, nor the right of Great Britain to regulate the engagement of British subjects, while these aliens or British subjects are on British territory.

Now, therefore, in view of the preceding considerations this tribunal is of opinion that the inhabitants of the United States while exercising the liberties referred to in the said article have a right to employ, as members of the fishing crews of their vessels, persons not inhabitants of the United States.

But in view of the preceding considerations the tribunal, to prevent any misunderstanding as to the effect of its award, expresses the opinion that non-inhabitants employed as members of the fishing crews of United States vessels derive no benefit or immunity from the treaty and it is so decided and awarded.

QUESTION 3

Can the exercise by the inhabitants of the United States of the liberties referred to in the said article be subjected, without the consent of the United States, to the requirements of entry or report at custom-houses or the payment of light or harbor or other dues, or to any other similar requirement or condition or exaction?

The tribunal is of opinion as follows:

It is obvious that the liberties referred to in this question are those that relate to taking fish and to drying and curing fish on certain coasts as prescribed in the treaty of October 20, 1818. The exercise of these liberties by the inhabitants of the United States in the prescribed waters to which they relate, has no reference to any commercial privileges which may or may not attach to such vessels by reason of any supposed authority outside the treaty, which itself confers no commercial privileges whatever upon the inhabitants of the United States or the vessels in which they may exercise the fishing liberty. It follows, therefore, that when the inhabitants of the United States are not seeking to exercise the commercial privileges accorded to trading vessels for the vessels in which they are exercising the granted liberty of fishing, they ought not to be subjected to requirements as to report and entry at custom-houses that are only appropriate to the exercise of commercial privileges. The exercise of the fishing liberty is distinct from the exercise of commercial or trading privileges and it is not competent for Great Britain or her colonies to impose upon the former exactions only appropriate to the latter. The reasons for the requirements enumerated in the case of commercial vessels, have no relation to the case of fishing vessels.

We think, however, that the requirement that American fishing vessels should report, if proper conveniences and an opportunity for doing so are provided, is not unreasonable or inappropriate. Such a report, while serving the purpose of a notification of the presence of a fishing vessel in the treaty waters for the purpose of exercising the treaty liberty, while it gives an opportunity for a proper surveillance of such vessel by revenue officers, may also serve to afford to such fishing vessel protection from interference in the exercise of the fishing liberty. There should be no such requirement, however, unless reasonably convenient opportunity therefor be afforded in person or by telegraph, at a custom-house or to a customs official.

The tribunal is also of opinion that light and harbor dues, if not imposed on Newfoundland fishermen, should not be imposed on American fishermen while exercising the liberty granted by the treaty. To impose such dues on American fishermen only would constitute an unfair discrimination between them and Newfoundland fishermen and one inconsistent with the liberty granted to American fishermen to take fish, etc., "in common with the subjects of His Britannic Majesty."

Further, the tribunal considers that the fulfilment of the requirement as to report by fishing vessels on arrival at the fishery would be greatly facilitated in the interests of both parties by the adoption of a system of registration, and distinctive marking of the fishing boats of both parties, analogous to that established by Articles 5 to 13, inclusive, of the international convention signed at The Hague, 8 May, 1882, for the regulation of the North Sea fisheries.

The tribunal therefore decides and awards as follows:

The requirement that an American fishing vessel should report, if proper conveniences for doing so are at hand, is not unreasonable, for the reasons stated in the foregoing opinion. There should be no such requirement, however, unless there be reasonably convenient opportunity afforded to report in person or by telegraph, either at a custom-house or to a customs official.

But the exercise of the fishing liberty by the inhabitants of the United States should not be subjected to the purely commercial formalities of report, entry and clearance at a custom-house, nor to light, harbor or other dues not imposed upon Newfoundland fishermen.

QUESTION 4

Under the provision of the said article that the American fishermen shall be admitted to enter certain bays or harbors for shelter, repairs, wood, or water, and for no other purpose whatever, but that they shall be under such restrictions as may be necessary to prevent their taking, drying, or curing fish therein or in any other manner whatever abusing the privileges thereby reserved to them, is it permissible to impose restrictions making the exercise of such privileges conditional upon the payment of light or harbor or other dues, or entering or reporting at custom-houses or any similar conditions?

The tribunal is of opinion that the provision in the first article of the treaty of October 20th, 1818, admitting American fishermen to enter certain bays or harbors for shelter, repairs, wood and water, and for no other purpose whatever, is an exercise in large measure of those duties of hospitality and humanity which all civilized nations impose upon themselves and expect the performance of from others. The enumerated purposes for which entry is permitted all relate to the exigencies in which those who pursue their perilous calling on the sea may be involved. The proviso which appears in the first article of the said treaty immediately after the so-called renunciation clause, was doubtless due to a recognition by

Great Britain of what was expected from the humanity and civilization of the then leading commercial nation of the world. To impose restrictions making the exercise of such privileges conditional upon the payment of light, harbor or other dues, or entering and reporting at custom-houses, or any similar conditions would be inconsistent with the grounds upon which such privileges rest and therefore is not permissible.

And it is decided and awarded that such restrictions are not permissible.

It seems reasonable, however, in order that these privileges accorded by Great Britain on these grounds of hospitality and humanity should not be abused, that the American fishermen entering such bays for any of the four purposes aforesaid and remaining more than 48 hours therein, should be required, if thought necessary by Great Britain or the Colonial Government, to report, either in person or by telegraph, at a custom-house or to a customs official, if reasonably convenient opportunity therefor is afforded.

And it is so decided and awarded.

QUESTION 5

From where must be measured the "three marine miles of any of the coasts, bays, creeks, or harbors" referred to in the said article?

In regard to this question, Great Britain claims that the renunciation applies to all bays generally and

The United States contend that it applies to bays of a certain class or condition.

Now, considering that the treaty used the general term "bays" without qualification, the tribunal is of opinion that these words of the treaty must be interpreted in a general sense as applying to every bay on the coast in question that might be reasonably supposed to have been considered as a bay by the negotiators of the treaty under the general conditions then prevailing, unless the United States can adduce satisfactory proof that any restrictions or qualifications of the general use of the term were or should have been present to their minds.

And for the purpose of such proof the United States contend:

1st. That while a State may renounce the treaty right to fish in foreign territorial waters, it can not renounce the natural right to fish on the high seas.

But the tribunal is unable to agree with this contention. Because though a State can not grant rights on the high seas it certainly can abandon the exercise of its right to fish on the high seas within certain definite limits. Such an abandonment was made with respect to their fishing rights in the waters in question by France and Spain in 1763. By a convention between the United Kingdom and the United States in 1846, the two countries assumed ownership over waters in Fuca Straits at distances from the shore as great as 17 miles.

The United States contend moreover:

2d. That by the use of the term "liberty to fish" the United States manifested the intention to renounce the liberty in the waters referred to only in so far as that liberty was dependent upon or derived from a concession on the part of Great Britain, and not to renounce the right to fish in those waters where it was enjoyed by virtue of their natural right as an independent State.

But the tribunal is unable to agree with this contention:

(a) Because the term "liberty to fish" was used in the renunciatory clause of the treaty of 1818 because the same term had been previously used in the treaty of 1783 which gave the liberty; and it was proper to use in the renunciation clause the same term that was used in the grant with respect to the object of the grant; and, in view of the terms of the grant, it would have been improper to use the term "right" in the renunciation. Therefore the conclusion drawn from the use of the term "liberty" instead of the term "right" is not justified;

(b) Because the term "liberty" was a term properly applicable to the renunciation which referred not only to fishing in the territorial waters but also to drying and curing on the shore. This latter right was undoubtedly held under the provisions of the treaty and was not a right accruing to the United States by virtue of any principle of international law.

3d. The United States also contend that the term "bays of His Britannic Majesty's Dominions" in the renunciatory clause must be read as including only those bays which were under the territorial sovereignty of Great Britain.

But the tribunal is unable to accept this contention:

(a) Because the description of the coast on which the fishery is to be exercised by the inhabitants of the United States is expressed throughout the treaty of 1818 in geographical terms and not by reference to political control; the treaty describes the coast as contained between capes;

(b) Because to express the political concept of dominion as equivalent to sovereignty, the word "dominion" in the singular would have been an adequate term and not "dominions" in the plural; this latter term having a recognized and well-settled meaning as descriptive of those portions of the earth which owe political allegiance to His Majesty; e. g., "His Britannic Majesty's dominions beyond the seas."

4th. It has been further contended by the United States that the renunciation applies only to bays six miles or less in width *inter fauces terrae*, those bays only being territorial bays, because the three-mile rule is, as shown by this treaty, a principle of international law applicable to coasts and should be strictly and systematically applied to bays.

But the tribunal is unable to agree with this contention:

(a) Because admittedly the geographical character of a bay contains conditions which concern the interests of the territorial sovereign to a more intimate and important extent than do those connected with the open coast. Thus conditions of national and territorial integrity, of defense, of commerce and of industry are all vitally concerned with the control of the bays penetrating the national coast line. This interest varies, speaking generally in proportion to the penetration inland of the bay; but as no principle of international law recognizes any specified relation between the concavity of the bay and the requirements for control by the territorial sovereignty, this tribunal is unable to qualify by the application of any new principle its interpretation of the treaty of 1818 as excluding bays in general from the strict and systematic application of the three-mile rule; nor can this tribunal take cognizance in this connection of other principles concerning the territorial sovereignty over bays such as ten-mile or twelve-mile limits of exclusion based on international acts subsequent to the treaty of 1818 and relating to coasts of a different configuration and conditions of a different character;

(*b*) Because the opinion of jurists and publicists quoted in the proceedings conduce to the opinion that speaking generally the three-mile rule should not be strictly and systematically applied to bays;

(*c*) Because the treaties referring to these coasts, antedating the treaty of 1818, made special provisions as to bays, such as the treaties of 1686 and 1713 between Great Britain and France, and especially the treaty of 1778 between the United States and France. Likewise Jay's treaty of 1794 Art. 25, distinguished bays from the space "within cannon-shot of the coast" in regard to the right of seizure in times of war. If the proposed treaty of 1806 and the treaty of 1818 contained no disposition to that effect, the explanation may be found in the fact that the first extended the marginal belt to five miles, and also in the circumstance that the American proposition of 1818 in that respect was not limited to "bays," but extended to "chambers formed by headlands" and to "five marine miles from a right line from one headland to another," a proposition which in the times of the Napoleonic wars would have affected to a very large extent the operations of the British navy;

(*d*) Because it has not been shown by the documents and correspondence in evidence here that the application of the three-mile rule to bays was present to the minds of the negotiators in 1818 and they could not reasonably have been expected either to presume it or to provide against its presumption;

(*e*) Because it is difficult to explain the words in Art. 3 of the treaty under interpretation "country . . . together with its bays, harbors and creeks" otherwise than that all bays without distinction as to their width were, in the opinion of the negotiators, part of the territory;

(*f*) Because from the information before this tribunal it is evident that the three-mile rule is not applied to bays strictly or systematically either by the United States or by any other Power;

(*g*) It has been recognized by the United States that bays stand apart, and that in respect of them territorial jurisdiction may be exercised farther than the marginal belt in the case of Delaware Bay by the report of the United States Attorney General of May 19th, 1793; and the letter of Mr. Jefferson to Mr. Genet of November 8th, 1793, declares the bays of the United States generally to be, "as being landlocked, within the body of the United States."

5th. In this latter regard it is further contended by the United States, that such exceptions only should be made from the application of the three-mile rule to bays as are sanctioned by conventions and established usage; that all exceptions for which the United States of America were responsible are so sanctioned; and that His Majesty's Government are unable to provide evidence to show that the bays concerned by the treaty of 1818 could be claimed as exceptions on these grounds either generally, or except possibly in one or two cases, specifically.

But the tribunal while recognizing that conventions and established usage might be considered as the basis for claiming as territorial those bays which on this ground might be called historic bays, and that such claims should be held valid in the absence of any principle of international law on the subject; nevertheless is unable to apply this, *a contrario*, so as to subject the bays in question to the three-mile rule, as desired by the United States:

(*a*) Because Great Britain has during this controversy asserted a claim to these bays generally, and has enforced such claim specifically in statutes or otherwise, in regard to the more important bays such as Chaleurs, Conception and Miramichi;

(*b*) Because neither should such relaxations of this claim, as are in evidence, be construed as renunciations of it; nor should omissions to enforce the claim in regard to bays as to which no controversy arose, be so construed. Such a construction by this tribunal would not only be intrinsically inequitable, but internationally injurious; in that it would discourage conciliatory diplomatic transactions and encourage the assertion of extreme claims in their fullest extent;

(*c*) Because any such relaxations in the extreme claim of Great Britain in its international relations are compensated by recognitions of it in the same sphere by the United States; notably in relations with France for instance in 1823 when they applied to Great Britain for the protection of their fishery in the bays on the western coast of Newfoundland, whence they had been driven by French war vessels on the ground of the pretended exclusive right of the French. Though they never asserted that their fishermen had been disturbed within the three-mile zone, only alleging that the disturbance had taken place in the bays, they claimed to be protected by Great Britain for having been molested in waters which were, as Mr. Rush stated, "clearly within the jurisdiction and sovereignty of Great Britain."

6th. It has been contended by the United States that the words "coasts, bays, creeks or harbors" are here used only to express different parts of the coast and are intended to express and be equivalent to the word "coast," whereby the three marine miles would be measured from the sinuosities of the coast and the renunciation would apply only to the waters of bays within three miles.

But the tribunal is unable to agree with this contention:

(*a*) Because it is a principle of interpretation that words in a document ought not to be considered as being without any meaning if there is not specific evidence to that purpose and the interpretation referred to would lead to the consequence, practically, of reading the words "bays, coasts and harbors" out of the treaty; so that it would read "within three miles of any of the coasts" including therein the coasts of the bays and harbors;

(*b*) Because the word "therein" in the proviso—"restrictions necessary to prevent their taking, drying or curing fish therein" can refer only to "bays," and not to the belt of three miles along the coast; and can be explained only on the supposition that the words "bays, creeks and harbors" are to be understood in their usual ordinary sense and not in an artificially restricted sense of bays within the three-mile belt;

(c) Because the practical distinction for the purpose of this fishery between coasts and bays and the exceptional conditions pertaining to the latter has been shown from the correspondence and the documents in evidence, especially the treaty of 1783, to have been in all probability present to the minds of the negotiators of the treaty of 1818;

(d) Because the existence of this distinction is confirmed in the same article of the treaty by the proviso permitting the United States fishermen to enter bays for certain purposes;

(e) Because the word "coasts" is used in the plural form whereas the contention would require its use in the singular;

(f) Because the tribunal is unable to understand the term "bays" in the renunciatory clause in other than its geographical sense, by which a bay is to be considered as an indentation of the coast, bearing a configuration of a particular character easy to determine specifically, but difficult to describe generally.

The negotiators of the treaty of 1818 did probably not trouble themselves with subtle theories concerning the notion of "bays"; they most probably thought that everybody would know what was a bay. In this popular sense the term must be interpreted in the treaty. The interpretation must take into account all the individual circumstances which for any one of the different bays are to be appreciated, the relation of its width to the length of penetration inland, the possibility and the necessity of its being defended by the State in whose territory it is indented; the special value which it has for the industry of the inhabitants of its shores; the distance which it is secluded from the highways of nations on the open sea and other circumstances not possible to enumerate in general.

For these reasons the tribunal decides and awards:

In case of bays the three marine miles are to be measured from a straight line drawn across the body of water at the place where it ceases to have the configuration and characteristics of a bay. At all other places the three marine miles are to be measured following the sinuosities of the coast.

But considering the tribunal can not overlook that this answer to Question 5, although correct in principle and the only one possible in view of the want of a sufficient basis for a more concrete answer, is not entirely satisfactory as to its practical applicability, and that it leaves room for doubts and differences in practice. Therefore the tribunal considers it its duty to render the decision more practicable and to remove the danger of future differences by adjoining to it, a recommendation in virtue of the responsibilities imposed by Art. 4 of the special agreement.

Considering, moreover, that in treaties with France, with the North German Confederation and the German Empire and likewise in the North Sea convention, Great Britain has adopted for similar cases the rule that only bays of ten miles width should be considered as those wherein the fishing is reserved to nationals. And that in the course of the negotiations between Great Britain and the United States a similar rule has been on various occasions proposed and adopted by Great Britain in instructions to the naval officers stationed on these coasts. And that though these circumstances are not sufficient to constitute this a principle of international law, it seems reasonable to propose this rule with certain exceptions, all the more that this rule with such exceptions has already formed the basis of an agreement between the two Powers.

Now therefore this tribunal in pursuance of the provisions of Art. 4 hereby recommends for the consideration and acceptance of the high contracting Parties the following rules and method of procedure for determining the limits of the bays hereinbefore enumerated.

1

In every bay not hereinafter specifically provided for the limits of exclusion shall be drawn three miles seaward from a straight line across the bay in the part nearest the entrance at the first point where the width does not exceed ten miles.

—

2

In the following bays where the configuration of the coast and the local climatic conditions are such that foreign fishermen when within the geographic headlands might reasonably and *bona fide* believe themselves on the high seas, the limits of exclusion shall be drawn in each case between the headlands hereinafter specified as being those at and within which such fishermen might be reasonably expected to recognize the bay under average conditions.

For the Baie des Chaleurs the line from the light at Birch Point on Miscou Island to Macquereau Point light; for the Bay of Miramichi, the line from the light at Point Escuminac to the light on the eastern point of Tabisintac Gully; for Egmont Bay, in Prince Edward Island, the line from the light at Cape Egmont to the light at West Point; and off St. Ann's Bay, in the province of Nova Scotia, the line from the light at Point Anconi to the nearest point on the opposite shore of the mainland.

For Fortune Bay, in Newfoundland, the line from Connaigre Head to the light on the southeasterly end of Brunet Island, thence to Fortune Head.

For or near the following bays the limits of exclusion shall be three marine miles seawards from the following lines, namely:

For or near Barrington Bay, in Nova Scotia, the line from the light on Stoddart Island to the light on the south point of Cape Sable, thence to the light at Baccaro Point; at Chedabucto and St. Peter's Bays, the line from Cranberry Island light to Green Island light, thence to Point Rouge; for Mira Bay, the line from the light on the east point of Scatari Island to the northeasterly point of Cape Morien; and at Placentia Bay, in Newfoundland, the line from Latine Point, on the eastern mainland shore, to the most southerly point of Red Island, thence by the most southerly point of Merasheen Island to the mainland.

Long Island and Bryer Island, on St. Mary's Bay, in Nova Scotia, shall, for the purpose of delimitation, be taken as the coasts of such bays.

It is understood that nothing in these rules refers either to the Bay of Fundy considered as a whole apart from its bays and creeks or as to the innocent passage through the Gut of Canso, which were excluded by the agreement made by exchange of notes between Mr. Bacon and Mr. Bryce dated February 21st, 1909, and March 4th, 1909; or to Conception Bay, which was provided for by the decision of the Privy Council in the case of the Direct United States Cable Company *v.* The Anglo American Telegraph Company, in which decision the United States have acquiesced.

QUESTION 6

Have the inhabitants of the United States the liberty under the said article or otherwise, to take fish in the bays, harbors, and creeks on that part of the southern coast of Newfoundland which extends from Cape Ray to Rameau Islands, or on the western and northern coasts of Newfoundland from Cape Ray to Quirpon Islands, or on the Magdalen Islands?

In regard to this question, it is contended by the United States that the inhabitants of the United States have the liberty under Art. 1 of the treaty of taking fish in the bays, harbors and creeks on that part of the southern coast of Newfoundland which extends from Cape Ray to Rameau Islands or on the western and northern coasts of Newfoundland from Cape Ray to Quirpon Islands and on the Magdalen Islands. It is contended by Great Britain that they have no such liberty.

Now considering that the evidence seems to show that the intention of the parties to the treaty of 1818, as indicated by the records of the negotiations and by the subsequent attitude of the Governments was to admit the United States to such fishery, this tribunal is of opinion that it is incumbent on Great Britain to produce satisfactory proof that the United States are not so entitled under the treaty.

For this purpose Great Britain points to the fact that whereas the treaty grants to American fishermen liberty to take fish "on the coasts, bays, harbors, and creeks from Mount Joly on the southern coast of Labrador" the liberty is granted to the "coast" only of Newfoundland and to the "shore" only of the Magdalen Islands;

and argues that evidence can be found in the correspondence submitted indicating an intention to exclude Americans from Newfoundland bays on the treaty coast, and that no value would have
been attached at that time by the United States Government to the
liberty of fishing in such bays because there was no cod fishery
there as there was in the bays of Labrador.

But the tribunal is unable to agree with this contention:

(a) Because the words "part of the southern coast...from....
to" and the words "western and northern coast...from....to,"
clearly indicate one uninterrupted coast-line; and there is no reason
to read into the words "coasts" a contradistinction to bays, in order
to exclude bays. On the contrary, as already held in the answer to
Question 5, the words "liberty, forever, to dry and cure fish in any
of the unsettled bays, harbors and creeks of the southern part of the
coast of Newfoundland hereabove described," indicate that in the
meaning of the treaty, as in all the preceding treaties relating to
the same territories, the words coast, coasts, harbors, bays, etc., are
used, without attaching to the word "coast" the specific meaning of
excluding bays. Thus in the provision of the treaty of 1783 giving
liberty "to take fish on such part of the coast of Newfoundland as
British fishermen shall use;" the word "coast" necessarily includes
bays, because if the intention had been to prohibit the entering of
the bays for fishing the following words "but not to dry or cure
the same on that island," would have no meaning. The contention
that in the treaty of 1783 the word "bays" is inserted lest otherwise
Great Britain would have had the right to exclude the Americans
to the three-mile line, is inadmissible, because in that treaty that line
is not mentioned;

(b) Because the correspondence between Mr. Adams and Lord
Bathurst also shows that during the negotiations for the treaty the
United States demanded the former rights enjoyed under the treaty
of 1783, and that Lord Bathurst in the letter of 30th October, 1815,
made no objection to granting those "former rights" "placed under
some modifications," which latter did not relate to the right of fishing in bays, but only to the "preoccupation of British harbors and
creeks by the fishing vessels of the United States and the forcible
exclusion of British subjects where the fishery might be most ad-
vantageously conducted," and "to the clandestine introduction of

prohibited goods into the British colonies." It may be therefore assumed that the word "coast" is used in both treaties in the same sense, including bays;

(c) Because the treaty expressly allows the liberty to dry and cure in the unsettled bays, etc., of the southern part of the coast of Newfoundland, and this shows that, *a fortiori*, the taking of fish in those bays is also allowed; because the fishing liberty was a lesser burden than the grant to cure and dry, and the restrictive clauses never refer to fishing in contradistinction to drying, but always to drying in contradistinction to fishing. Fishing is granted without drying, never drying without fishing;

(d) Because there is not sufficient evidence to show that the enumeration of the component parts of the coast of Labrador was made in order to discriminate between the coast of Labrador and the coast of Newfoundland;

(e) Because the statement that there is no codfish in the bays of Newfoundland and that the Americans only took interest in the codfishery is not proved; and evidence to the contrary is to be found in Mr. John Adams' *Journal of Peace Negotiations of November 25, 1782;*

(f) Because the treaty grants the right to take fish of every kind, and not only codfish;

(g) Because the evidence shows that, in 1823, the Americans were fishing in Newfoundland bays and that Great Britain when summoned to protect them against expulsion therefrom by the French did not deny their right to enter such bays.

Therefore this tribunal is of opinion that American inhabitants are entitled to fish in the bays, creeks and harbors of the treaty coasts of Newfoundland and the Magdalen Islands and it is so decided and awarded.

QUESTION 7

Are the inhabitants of the United States whose vessels resort to the treaty coasts for the purpose of exercising the liberties referred to in Article 1 of the treaty of 1818 entitled to have for those vessels, when duly authorized by the United States in that behalf, the commercial privileges on the treaty coasts accorded by agreement or otherwise to United States trading vessels generally.

Now assuming that commercial privileges on the treaty coasts are accorded by agreement or otherwise to United States trading vessels generally, without any exception, the inhabitants of the United States, whose vessels resort to the same coasts for the purpose of exercising the liberties referred to in Article 1 of the treaty of 1818, are entitled to have for those vessels when duly authorized by the United States in that behalf, the above-mentioned commercial privileges, the treaty containing nothing to the contrary. But they can not at the same time and during the same voyage exercise their treaty rights and enjoy their commercial privileges, because treaty rights and commercial privileges are submitted to different rules, regulations and restraints.

For these reasons this tribunal is of opinion that the inhabitants of the United States are so entitled in so far as concerns this treaty, there being nothing in its provisions to disentitle them provided the treaty liberty of fishing and the commercial privileges are not exercised concurrently and it is so decided and awarded.

Done at The Hague, in the Permanent Court of Arbitration, in triplicate original, September 7th, 1910.

> H. LAMMASCH
> A. F. DE SAVORNIN LOHMAN
> GEORGE GRAY
> C. FITZPATRICK
> LUIS M. DRAGO

Signing the award, I state pursuant to Article 9, clause 2, of the special agreement my dissent from the majority of the tribunal in respect to the considerations and enacting part of the award as to Question 5.

Grounds for this dissent have been filed at the International Bureau of the Permanent Court of Arbitration.

> LUIS M. DRAGO

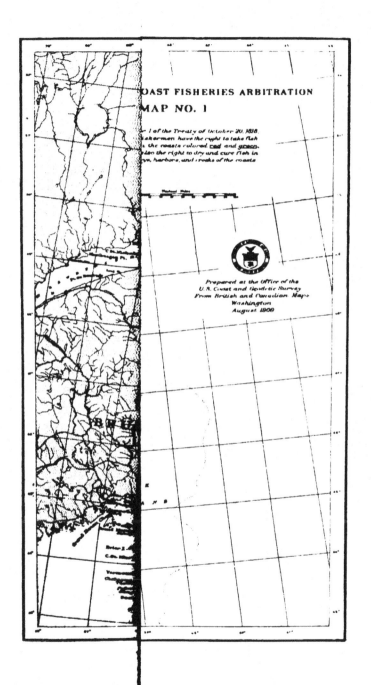

COAST FISHERIES ARBITRATION

MAP NO. 1

...l of the Treaty of October 20, 1818.
...fishermen have the right to take fish
...the coasts colored red and green.
...lso the right to dry and cure fish in
...ays, harbors, and creeks of the coasts

Prepared at the Office of the
U. S. Coast and Geodetic Survey
From British and Canadian Maps
Washington
August 1909

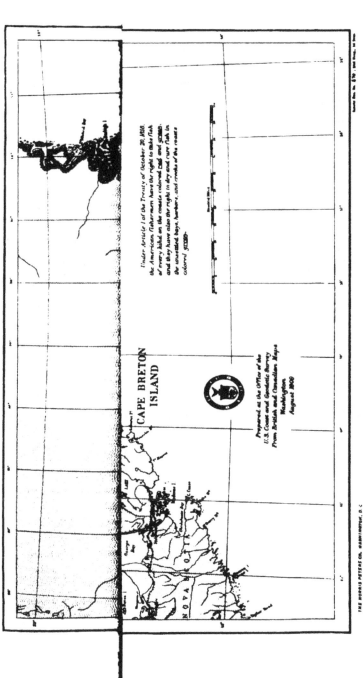

CAPE BRETON ISLAND

Under Article I of the Treaty of October 20, 1818, the American fishermen have the right to take fish of every kind on the coasts colored red and green, and they have also the right to dry and cure fish in the unsettled bays, harbors, and creeks of the coasts colored green.

Prepared at the Office of the
U.S. Coast and Geodetic Survey
From British and Canadian Maps
Washington
August 1909

NOVA SCOTIA

DISSENTING OPINION OF LUIS M. DRAGO
ON QUESTION 5[1]

Counsel for Great Britain have very clearly stated that according to their contention the territoriality of the bays referred to in the treaty of 1818 is immaterial because whether they are or are not territorial, the United States should be excluded from fishing in them by the terms of the renunciatory clause, which simply refers to "bays, creeks or harbors of His Britannic Majesty's dominions" without any other qualification or description. If that were so, the necessity might arise of discussing whether or not a nation has the right to exclude another by contract or otherwise from any portion or portions of the high seas. But in my opinion the tribunal need not concern itself with such general question, the wording of the treaty being clear enough to decide the point at issue.

Article 1 begins with the statement that differences have arisen respecting the liberty claimed by the United States for the inhabitants thereof to take, dry and cure fish on "certain coasts, bays, harbors and creeks of His Britannic Majesty's dominions in America," and then proceeds to locate the specific portions of the coast with its corresponding indentations, in which the liberty of taking, drying and curing fish should be exercised. The renunciatory clause, which the tribunal is called upon to construe, runs thus: "And the United States hereby renounce, forever, any liberty heretofore enjoyed or claimed by the inhabitants thereof, to take, dry or cure fish on, or within three marine miles of any of the coasts, bays, creeks or harbors of His Britannic Majesty's dominions in America not included within the above-mentioned limits." This language does not lend itself to different constructions. If the bays in which the liberty has been renounced are those "of His Britannic Majesty's dominions in America," they must necessarily be territorial bays, because in so far as they are not so considered they should belong to the high seas and consequently form no part of His Britannic Majesty's dominions, which, by definition, do not extend to the high seas. It can not be said, as has been suggested, that the use of the word "dominions," in the plural, implies a different meaning than would be conveyed by the same term as used in the singular, so that in the present case, "the British dominions in America" ought to be considered as a mere geographical expression, without reference

---

[1]Official report, p. 147.

to any right of sovereignty or *"dominion."*   It seems to me, on the contrary, that "dominions," or "possessions," or "estates," or such other equivalent terms, simply designate the places over which the "dominion" or property rights are exercised.   Where there is no possibility of appropriation or dominion, as on the high seas, we can not speak of dominions.   The "dominions" extend exactly to the point which the "dominion" reaches; they are simply the actual or physical thing over which the abstract power or authority, the *right*, as given to the proprietor or the ruler, applies.   The interpretation as to the territoriality of the bays as mentioned in the renunciatory clause of the treaty appears stronger when considering that the United States specifically renounced the "liberty," not the "right" to fish or to cure and dry fish.   "The United States renounce, forever, any *liberty* heretofore enjoyed or claimed, to take, cure or dry fish on, or within three marine miles of any of the coasts, bays, creeks or harbors of His Britannic Majesty's dominions in America."   It is well known that the negotiators of the treaty of 1783 gave a very different meaning to the terms *liberty* and *right*, as distinguished from each other.   In this connection Mr. Adams' *Journal* may be recited.   To this *Journal* the British counter-case refers in the following terms: "From an entry in Mr. Adams' *Journal* it appears that he drafted an article by which he distinguished the *right* to take fish (both on the high seas and on the shores) and the *liberty* to take and cure fish on the land.   But on the following day he presented to the British negotiators a draft in which he distinguishes between the *'right'* to take fish on the high seas, and the *'liberty'* to take fish on the *'coasts,'* and to dry and cure fish on the land . . .   The British commissioner called attention to the distinction thus suggested by Mr. Adams and proposed that the word *liberty* should be applied to the privileges both on the water and on the land.   Mr. Adams thereupon rose up and made a vehement protest, as is recorded in his diary, against the suggestion that the United States enjoyed the fishing on the banks of Newfoundland by any other title than that of *right*. . . . The application of the word *liberty* to the coast fishery was left as Mr. Adams proposed." "The incident," proceeds the British case, "is of importance, since it shows that the difference between the two phrases was intentional." (British counter-case, page 17.)   And the British argument emphasizes again the difference. "More cogent still is the distinction between the words *right* and *liberty*. The word *right* is applied to the sea fisheries, and the word *liberty* to the shore fisheries. The history of the negotiations shows that this distinction was advisedly adopted." If then a *liberty* is a grant and not the recognition of a *right;* if, as the British case, counter-case and argument recognize, the United States had the right to fish in the open sea in contradistinction with the *liberty* to fish near the shores or portions of the shores; and if what has been renounced in the words of the treaty is the *"liberty"* to fish on, or within three miles of the bays, creeks and harbors of His Britannic Majesty's dominions, it clearly follows that such *liberty* and the corresponding renunciation refers only to such portions of the bays which were under the sovereignty of Great Britain and not to such other portions, if any, as form part of the high seas.

And thus it appears that far from being immaterial the territoriality of bays is of the utmost importance. The treaty not containing any rule or indication upon the subject, the tribunal can not help a decision as to this point, which involves the second branch of the British contention that all so-called bays are not only geographical but wholly territorial as well, and subject to the jurisdiction of Great Britain. The situation was very accurately described on almost the same lines as above-stated by the British memorandum sent in 1870 by the Earl of Kimberley to Governor Sir John Young: "The right of Great Britain to exclude American fishermen from waters within three miles of the coasts is unambiguous, and, it is believed, uncontested. But there appears to be some doubt what are the waters described as within three miles of bays, creeks or harbors. When a bay is less than six miles broad its waters are within the three-mile limit, and therefore clearly within the meaning of the treaty; *but when it is more than that breadth, the question arises whether it is a bay of Her Britannic Majesty's dominions.* This is a question which has to be considered in each particular case with regard to international law and usage. When such a bay is not a bay of Her Majesty's dominions, the American fishermen shall be entitled to fish in it, except within three marine miles of the 'coast;' when it is a bay of Her Majesty's dominions they will not be entitled to fish within three miles of it, that is to say (it is presumed) within three miles of a line drawn from headland to headland." (American Case Appendix, page 629.)

Now, it must be stated in the first place that there does not seem to exist any general rule of international law which may be considered final, even in what refers to the marginal belt of territorial waters. The old rule of the cannon-shot, crystallized into the present three marine miles measured from low-water mark, may be modified at a later period inasmuch as certain nations claim a wider jurisdiction and an extension has already been recommended by the institute of International Law. There is an obvious reason for that. The marginal strip of territorial waters based originally on the cannon-shot, was founded on the necessity of the riparian State to protect itself from outward attack, by providing something in the nature of an insulating zone, which very reasonably should be extended with the accrued possibility of offense due to the wider range of modern ordnance. In what refers to bays, it has been proposed as a general rule (subject to certain important exceptions) that the marginal belt of territorial waters should follow the sinuosities of the coast more or less in the manner held by the United States in the present contention, so that the marginal belt being of three miles, as in the treaty under consideration, only such bays should be held as territorial as have an entrance not wider than six miles. (See Sir Thomas Barclay's Report to Institute of International Law, 1894, page 129, in which he also strongly recommends these limits.) This is the doctrine which Westlake, the eminent English writer on international law, has summed up in very few words: "As to bays," he says, "if the entrance to one of them is not more than twice the width of the littoral sea enjoyed by the country in question—that is, not more than six sea miles in the ordinary case, eight in that of Norway, and so forth,—there is no access from the open sea to the bay except through the territorial water of that country, and the inner part of the bay will belong to that country no matter how widely it may expand. The line drawn from shore to shore at the part where, in approaching from the open sea, the width first contracts to that mentioned, will take the place of the line of low water, and the littoral sea belonging to the State will be measured outwards from that line to the distance of three miles or more, proper to the State" (Westlake, vol. 1, page 187). But the learned author takes care to add: "But although this is the general rule it often meets with an exception in the case of bays which penetrate deep into the land and are called gulfs. Many of these are recognized by immemorial usage as territorial sea of the States into which they penetrate, notwithstanding that their entrance is wider than the general rule for bays would give as a limit for such appropriation." And he proceds to quote as examples of this kind the Bay of Conception in Newfoundland, which he considers as wholly British, Chesapeake and Delaware Bays, which belong to the United States, and others. (*Ibid*, page 188.) The Institute of International Law, in its annual meeting of 1894, recommended a marginal belt of six miles for the general line of the coast and as a consequence established that for bays the line should be drawn up across at the nearest portion of the entrance toward the sea where the distance between the two sides do not exceed twelve miles. But the learned association very wisely added a proviso to the effect, "that bays should be so considered and measured *unless a continuous and established usage* has sanctioned a greater breadth." Many great authorities are agreed as to that. Counsel for the United States proclaimed the right to the exclusive jurisdiction of certain bays, no matter what the width of their entrance should be, when the littoral nation has asserted its right to take it into their jurisdiction upon reasons which go always back to the doctrine of protection. Lord Blackburn, one of the most eminent of English judges, in delivering the opinion of the Privy Council about Conception Bay in Newfoundland, adhered to the same doctrine when he asserted the territoriality of that branch of the sea, giving as a reason for such finding "that the British Government for a long period had exercised dominion over this bay and its claim had been acquiesced in by other nations, so as to show that the bay had been for a long time occupied exclusively by-Great Britain, a circumstance which, in the tribunals of any country, would be very important." "And moreover," he added, "the British Legislature has, by Acts of Parliament, declared it to be part of the British territory, and part of the country made subject to the legislation of Newfoundland." (Direct U. S. Cable Co. *v*. The Anglo-American Telegraph Co., Law Reports, 2 Appeal Cases, 374.)

So it may be safely asserted that a certain class of bays, which might be properly called the historical bays such as Chesapeake Bay and Delaware Bay in North America and the great estuary of the River Plata in South America, form a class distinct and apart and undoubtedly belong to the littoral country, whatever be their depth of penetration and the width of their mouths, when such country has asserted its sovereignty over them, and particular circumstances such as geographical configuration, immemorial usage and above all, the requirements of self-defense, justify such a pretension. The right of Great Britain over the bays of Conception, Chaleur and Miramichi are of this description. In what refers to the other bays, as might be termed the common, ordinary bays, indenting the coasts, over which no special claim or assertion of sovereignty has been made, there does not seem to be any other general principle to be applied than the one resulting from the custom and usage of each individual nation as shown by their treaties and their general and time honored practice.

The well-known words of Bynkershoek might be very appropriately recalled in this connection when so many and divergent opinions and authorities have been recited: "The common law of nations," he says, "can only be learnt from reason and custom. I do not deny that authority may add weight to reason, but I prefer to seek it in a constant custom of concluding treaties in one sense or another and in examples that have occurred in one country or another." (*Questiones Jure Publici,* vol. 1, Cap. 3.)

It is to be borne in mind in this respect that the tribunal has been called upon to decide as the subject-matter of this controversy, the construction to be given to the fishery treaty of 1818 between Great Britain and the United States. And so it is that from the usage and the practice of Great Britain in this and other like fisheries and from treaties entered into by them with other nations as to fisheries, may be evolved the right interpretation to be given to the particular convention which has been submitted. In this connection the following treaties may be recited:

Treaty between Great Britain and France. 2nd August, 1839. It reads as follows:

Article 9. The subjects of Her Britannic Majesty shall enjoy the exclusive right of fishery within the distance of 3 miles from low water mark along the whole extent of the coasts of the British Islands.

It is agreed that the distance of three miles fixed as the general limit for the exclusive right of fishery upon the coasts of the two countries, shall, with respect to bays, the mouths of which do not exceed ten miles in width, be measured from a straight line drawn from headland to headland.

Article 10. It is agreed and understood, that the miles mentioned in the present convention are geographical miles, whereof 60 make a degree of latitude.

(Hertslett's *Treaties and Conventions,* vol. v, p. 89.)

Regulations between Great Britain and France. 24th May, 1843.

Art. 2. The limits, within which the general right of fishery is exclusively reserved to the subjects of the two kingdoms respectively, are fixed (with the exception of those in Granville Bay) at 3 miles distance from low water mark.

With respect to bays, the mouths of which do not exceed ten miles in width, the 3-mile distance is measured from a straight line drawn from headland to headland.

Art. 3. The miles mentioned in the present regulations are geographical miles, of which 60 make a degree of latitude.

(Hertslett, vol. vi, p. 416.)

Treaty between Great Britain and France. November 11, 1867.

Art. 1. British fishermen shall enjoy the exclusive right of fishery within the distance of 3 miles from low water mark, along the whole extent of the coasts of the British Islands.

The distance of 3 miles fixed as the general limit for the exclusive right of fishery upon the coasts of the two countries shall, with respect to bays, the mouths of which do not exceed ten miles in width be measured from a straight line drawn from headland to headland.

The miles mentioned in the present convention are geographical miles whereof 60 make a degree of latitude.

(Hertslett's *Treaties,* vol. xii, p. 1126, British Case App., p. 38.)

Great Britain and North German Confederation. British notice to fishermen by the Board of Trade. Board of Trade, November, 1868.

Her Majesty's Government and the North German Confederation having come to an agreement respecting the regulations to be observed by British fishermen fishing off the coasts of the North German Confederation, the following notice is issued for the guidance and warning of British fishermen:

1. The exclusive fishery limits of the German Empire are designated by the Imperial Government as follows: that tract of the sea which extends to a distance of 3 sea miles from the extremest limits which the ebb leaves dry of the German North Sea coast of the German islands or flats lying before it, as well as those bays and incurvations of the coast which are ten sea miles or less in breadth reckoned from the extremest points of the land and the flats, must be considered as under the territorial sovereignty of North Germany.

(Hertslett's *Treaties*, vol. xiv, p. 1055.)

Great Britain and German Empire.   British Board of Trade, December, 1874.

(Same recital referring to an arrangement entered into between Her Britannic Majesty and the German Government.)

Then the same articles follow with the alteration of the words "German Empire" for "North Germany."

(Hertslett, vol. xiv, p. 1058.)

Treaty between Great Britain, Belgium, Denmark, France, Germany and the Netherlands for regulating the police of the North Sea fisheries.   May 6, 1882.

2. Les pêcheurs nationaux jouiront du droit exclusif de pêche dans le rayon de 3 milles, à partir de la laisse de basse mer, le long de toute l'étendue des côtes de leurs pays respectifs, ainsi que des îles et des bancs qui en dépendent.

Pour les baies le rayon de 3 milles sera mesuré à partir d'une ligne droite, tirée, en travers de la baie, dans la partie la plus rapprochée de l'entrée, au premier point où l'ouverture n'excédera pas 10 milles.

(Hertslett, vol. xv, p. 794.)

British Order in Council, October 23rd, 1877.

Prescribes the obligation of not concealing or effacing numbers or marks on boats, employed in fishing or dredging for purposes of sale on the coasts of England, Wales, Scotland and the Islands of Guernsey, Jersey, Alderney, Sark and Man, and not going outside;

(a) The distance of 3 miles from low water mark along the whole extent of the said coasts;

(b) In cases of bays less than 10 miles wide the line joining the headlands of said bays.

(Hertslett, vol. xiv, p. 1032.)

To this list may be added the unratified treaty of 1888 between Great Britain and the United States which is so familiar to the tribunal. Such unratified treaty contains an authoritative interpretation of the Convention of October 20th, 1818, *sub-judice:* "The three marine miles mentioned in Article 1 of the Convention of October 20th, 1818, shall be measured seaward from low-water mark; but at every bay, creek or harbor, not otherwise specifically provided for in this treaty, such three marine miles shall be measured seaward from a straight line drawn across the bay, creek or harbor, in the part nearest the entrance at the first point where the width does not exceed ten marine miles," which is recognizing the exceptional bays as aforesaid and laying the rule for the general and common bays.

It has been suggested that the treaty of 1818 ought not to be studied as hereabove in the light of any treaties of a later date, but rather be referred to such British international conventions as preceded it and clearly illustrate, according to this view, what were, at the time, the principles maintained by Great Britain as to their sovereignty over the sea and over the coast and the adjacent territorial waters. In this connection the treaties of 1686 and 1713 with France and of 1763 with France and Spain have been recited and offered as examples also of exclusion of nations by agreement from fishery rights on the high seas. I cannot partake of such a view. The treaties of 1686, 1713 and 1763 can hardly be understood with respect to this, otherwise than as examples of the wild, obsolete claims over the common ocean which all nations have of old abandoned with the progress of an enlightened civilization. And if certain nations accepted long ago to be excluded by convention from fishing on what is to-day considered a common sea, it is precisely because it was then understood that such tracts of water, now free and open to all, were the exclusive property of a particular power, who, being the owners, admitted or excluded others from their use. The treaty of 1818 is in the meantime one of the few which mark an era in the diplomacy of the world. As a matter of fact it is the very first which commuted the rule of the cannon-shot into the three marine miles of coastal jurisdiction. And it really would appear unjustified to explain such historic document, by referring it to international agreements of a hundred and two hundred years before when the doctrine of Selden's *Mare Clausum* was at its height and when the coastal waters were fixed at such distances as sixty miles, or a hundred miles, or two days' journey from the shore and the like. It seems very appropriate, on the contrary, to explain the meaning of the treaty of 1818 by comparing it with those which immediately followed and established the same limit of coastal jurisdiction. As a general rule a treaty of a former date may be very safely construed by referring it to the provisions of like treaties made by the same nation on the same matter at a later time. Much more so when, as occurs in the present case, the later conventions, with no exception, starting from the same premise of the three miles coastal jurisdiction arrive always to an uniform policy and line of action in what refers to bays. As a matter of fact all authorities approach and connect the modern fishery treaties of Great Britain and refer them to the treaty of 1818. The second edition of Kluber, for instance, quotes in the same sentence the treaties of October 20th, 1818, and August 2, 1839, as fixing a distance of three miles from low water mark for coastal jurisdiction. And Fiori, the well-known Italian jurist, referring to the same marine miles of coastal jurisdiction, says: "This rule recognized as early as the treaty of 1818 between the United States and Great Britain, and that betwen Great Britain and France in 1839, has again been admitted in the treaty of 1867." (*Nouveau Droit International Public,* Paris, 1885, section 803.)

This is only a recognition of the permanency and the continuity of States. The treaty of 1818 is not a separate fact unconnected with the later policy of Great Britain. Its negotiators were not parties to such international convention and their powers disappeared as soon as they signed the document on behalf of their countries. The parties to the treaty of 1818 were the United States and Great

Britain, and what Great Britain meant in 1818 about bays and fisheries, when they for the first time fixed a marginal jurisdiction of three miles, can be very well explained by what Great Britain, the same permanent political entity, understood in 1839, 1843, 1867, 1874, 1878 and 1882, when fixing the very same zone of territorial waters. That a bay in Europe should be considered as different from a bay in America and subject to other principles of international law can not be admitted in the face of it. What the practice of Great Britain has been outside the treaties is very well known to the tribunal, and the examples might be multiplied of the cases in which that nation has ordered its subordinates to apply to the bays on these fisheries the ten mile entrance rule or the six miles according to the occasion. It has been repeatedly said that such have been only relaxations of the strict right, assented to by Great Britain in order to avoid friction on certain special occasions. That may be. But it may also be asserted that such relaxations have been very many and that the constant, uniform, never contradicted, practice of concluding fishery treaties from 1839 down to the present day, in all of which the ten miles entrance bays are recognized, is the clear sign of a policy. This policy has but very lately found a most public, solemn and unequivocal expression. "On a question asked in Parliament on the 21st of February, 1907," says Pitt Cobbett, a distinguished English writer, with respect to the Moray Firth Case, "it was stated that, according to the view of the Foreign Office, the Admiralty, the Colonial Office, the Board of Trade and the Board of Agriculture and Fisheries, the term 'territorial waters' was deemed to include waters extending from the coast line of any part of the territory of a State to three miles from the low-water mark of such coast line and the waters of all bays, the entrance to which is not more than *six miles,* and of which the entire land boundary forms part of the territory of the same state." (*Pitt Cobbett Cases and Opinions on International Law,* vol. 1, p. 143.)

Is there a contradiction between these six miles and the ten miles of the treaties just referred to? Not at all. The six miles are the consequence of the three miles marginal belt of territorial waters in their coincidence from both sides at the inlets of the coast and the ten miles far from being an arbitrary measure are simply an extension, a margin given for convenience to the strict six miles with fishery purposes. Where the miles represent sixty to a degree in latitude the ten miles are besides the sixth part of the same degree. The American Government in reply to the observations made to Secretary Bayard's memorandum of 1888, said very precisely: "The width of ten miles was proposed not only because it had been followed in conventions between many other Powers, but also because it was deemed reasonable and just in the present case; this Government recognizing the fact that while it might have claimed a width of six miles as a basis of settlement, fishing within bays and harbors only slightly wider would be confined to areas so narrow as to render it practically valueless and almost necessarily expose the fishermen to constant danger of carrying their operations into forbidden waters." (British Case Appendix, page 416.) And Professor John Bassett Moore, a recognized authority on international law, in a communication addressed to the Institute of International Law, said very forcibly: "Since you observe that there does not appear to be any convincing reason to prefer the ten mile line in such a case to that of double three miles, I may say that there have been supposed to exist reasons both of convenience and of safety. The ten-mile line has been adopted in the cases referred to as a practical rule. The transgression of an encroachment upon territorial waters by fishing vessels is generally a grave offense, involving in many instances the forfeiture of the offending vessel, and it is obvious that the narrower the space in which it is permissible to fish the more likely the offense is to be committed. In order, therefore, that fishing may be practicable and safe and not constantly attended with the risk of violating territorial waters, it has been thought to be expedient not to allow it where the extent of free waters between the three miles drawn on each side of the bay is less than four miles. This is the reason of the ten-mile line. Its intention is not to hamper or restrict the right to fish, but to render its exercise practicable and safe. When fishermen fall in with a shoal of fish, the impulse to follow it is so strong as to make the possibilities of transgression very serious within narrow limits of free waters. Hence it has been deemed wiser to exclude them from space less than four miles each way from the forbidden lines. In spaces less than this operations are not only hazardous, but so circumscribed as to render them of little practical value." (*Annuaire de l'Institut de Droit International*, 1894, p. 146.)

So the use of the ten mile bays so constantly put into practice by Great Britain in its fishery treaties has its root and connection with the marginal belt of three miles for the territorial waters. So much so that the tribunal having decided not to adjudicate in this case the ten miles entrance to the bays of the treaty of 1818, this will be the only one exception in which the ten miles of the bays do not follow as a consequence the strip of three miles of territorial waters, the historical bays and estuaries always excepted.

And it is for that reason that an usage so firmly and for so long a time established ought, in my opinion, be applied to the construction of the treaty under consideration, much more so, when custom, one of the recognized sources of law, international as well as municipal, is supported in this case by reason and by the acquiescence and the practice of many nations.

The tribunal has decided that: "In case of bays the 3 miles (of the treaty) are to be measured from a straight line drawn across the body of water at the place where it ceases to have the configuration characteristic of a bay. At all other places the three miles are to be measured following the sinuosities of the coast." But no rule is laid out or general principle evolved for the parties to know what the nature of such configuration is or by what methods the points should be ascertained from which the bay should lose the characteristics of such. There lies the whole contention and the whole difficulty, not satisfactorily solved, to my mind, by simply recommending, without the scope of the award and as a system of procedure for resolving future contestations under Article 4 of the treaty of arbitration, a series of lines, which practical as they may be supposed to be, can not be adopted by the parties without concluding a new treaty.

These are the reasons for my dissent, which I much regret, on Question 5.

Done at The Hague, September 7th, 1910

LUIS M. DRAGO

ADDITIONAL DOCUMENTS

Modus vivendi between the United States and Great Britain in regard to inshore fisheries on the treaty coast of Newfoundland—Agreement effected by exchange of notes at London, October 6/8, 1906 [1]

AMERICAN EMBASSY,
London, October 6, 1906.

SIR: I am authorized by my Government to ratify a *modus vivendi* in regard to the Newfoundland fishery question on the basis of the Foreign Office memorandum, dated the 25th of September, 1906, in which you accept the arrangement set out in my memorandum of the 12th of September and consent accordingly to the use of purse seines by American fishermen during the ensuing season, subject, of course, to due regard being paid in the use of such implements to other modes of fishery, which, as you state, is only intended to secure that there shall be the same spirit of give and take and of respect for common rights between the users of purse seines and the users of stationary nets as would be expected to exist if both sets of fishermen employed the same gear.

My Government understand by this that the use of purse seines by American fishermen is not to be interfered with, and that the shipment of Newfoundlanders by American fishermen outside the 3-mile limit is not to be made the basis of interference or to be penalized; at the same time they are glad to assure His Majesty's Government, should such shipments be found necessary, that they will be made far enough from the exact 3-mile limit to avoid any reasonable doubt.

On the other hand, it is also understood that our fishermen are to be advised by my Government, and to agree, not to fish on Sunday.

It is further understood that His Majesty's Government will not bring into force the Newfoundland foreign fishing vessels Act of 1906 which imposes on American fishing vessels certain restrictions in addition to those imposed by the Act of 1905, and also that the provisions of the first part of section 1 of the Act of 1905, as to boarding and bringing into port, and also the whole of section 3 of the same Act, will not be regarded as applying to American fishing vessels.

It also being understood that our fishermen will gladly pay light dues if they are not deprived of their rights to fish, and that our fishermen are not unwilling to comply with the provisions of the

---

[1] *Foreign Relations of the United States*, 1906, pt. 1, p. 701.

colonial customs law as to reporting at a custom-house when physically possible to do so.

I need not add that my Government are most anxious that the provisions of the *modus vivendi* should be made effective at the earliest possible moment. I am glad to be assured by you that this note will be considered as sufficient ratification of the *modus vivendi* on the part of my Government.

I have the honor to be, with the highest consideration, sir,

Your most obedient, humble servant,

WHITELAW REID

The Right Honorable SIR EDWARD GREY, BT.,

Etc., etc., etc.

FOREIGN OFFICE, *October 8, 1906.*

YOUR EXCELLENCY: I have received with satisfaction the note of the 6th instant in which your Excellency states that you have been authorized by your Government to ratify a *modus vivendi* in regard to the Newfoundland fishery question on the basis of the memorandum which I had the honor to communicate to you on the 25th ultimo, and I am glad to assure your Excellency that the note in question will be considered by His Majesty's Government as a sufficient ratification of that arrangement on the part of the United States Government.

His Majesty's Government fully share the desire of your Government that the provisions of the *modus vivendi* should be made effective at the earliest moment possible, and the necessary instructions for its observance were accordingly sent to the Government of Newfoundland immediately on receipt of your Excellency's communication.

I have the honor to be, with the highest consideration, your Excellency's most obedient, humble servant,

(In the absence of the Secretary of State)

E. GORST

His Excellency the Honorable WHITELAW REID,

Etc., etc., etc.

Memorandum of the American Embassy of September 12, 1906[1]

My Government hears with the greatest concern and regret that in the opinion of His Majesty's Government there is so wide a divergence of views with regard to the Newfoundland fisheries that an immediate settlement is hopeless.

But it is much gratified with His Majesty's Government's desire

---

[1]*Foreign Relations of the United States*, 1906, pt. 1, p. 702.

to reach a *modus vivendi* for this season, and appreciates the readiness to waive the foreign fishing vessels Act of 1906. This and other restrictive legislation had compelled our fishermen to use purse seines or abandon their treaty rights.

My Government sees in the offer not to apply section 3, Act of 1905, and that part of section 1 relating to boarding fishing vessels and bringing them into port fresh proof of a cordial disposition not to press unduly this kind of regulation.

Our fishermen will also gladly pay light dues, if not hindered in their right to fish. They are not unwilling, either, to comply with the regulation to report at custom-houses, when possible. It is sometimes physically impossible, however, to break through the ice for that purpose.

Most unfortunately the remaining proposals, those as to purse seining and Sunday fishing, present very grave difficulties.

We appreciate perfectly the desire of His Majesty's Government to prevent Sunday fishing. But if both this and purse seine fishing are taken away, as things stand there might be no opportunity for profitable fishing left under our treaty rights. We are convinced that purse seines are no more injurious to the common fishery than the gill nets commonly used—are not, in fact, so destructive and do not tend to change the migratory course of the herring as gill nets do, through the death of a large percentage of the catch and consequent pollution of the water.

The small amount of purse seining this season could not, of course, materially affect the common fishery anyway. Besides many of our fishermen have already sailed, with purse seines as usual, and the others are already provided with them. This use of the purse seine was not the free choice of our fishermen. They have been driven to it by local regulations, and the continued use of it at this late date this year seems vital.

But we will renounce Sunday fishing for this season if His Majesty's Government will consent to the use of purse seines, and we can not too strongly urge an acceptance of this solution.

AMERICAN EMBASSY, *London, September 12, 1906.*

Memorandum of the British Foreign Office of September 25, 1906[1]

His Majesty's Government have considered, after consultation with the Government of Newfoundland, the proposals put forward in the

---

[1] *Foreign Relations of the United States,* 1906, pt. 1, p. 703.

memorandum communicated by the United States Ambassador on the 12th instant, respecting the suggested *modus vivendi* in regard to the Newfoundland fishery question.

They are glad to be able to state that they accept the arrangement set out in the above memorandum and consent accordingly to the use of purse seines by United States fishermen during the ensuing season, subject, of course, to due regard being paid, in the use of such implements, to other modes of fishery.

His Majesty's Government trust that the United States Government will raise no objection to such a stipulation, which is only intended to secure that there shall be the same spirit of give and take and of respect of common rights between the users of purse seines and the users of stationary nets as would be expected to exist if both sets of fishermen employed the same gear.

They further hope that, in view of this temporary authorization of the purse seines, the United States Government will see their way to arranging that the practice of engaging Newfoundland fishermen just outside the three-mile limit, which, to some extent, prevailed last year, should not be resorted to this year.

An arrangement to this effect would save both His Majesty's Government and the Newfoundland Government from embarrassment which, it is conceived, having regard to the circumstances in which the *modus vivendi* is being settled, the United States Government would not willingly impose upon them. Moreover, it is not in itself unreasonable, seeing that the unwillingness of the United States Government to forego the use of purse seines appears to be largely based upon the inability of their fishermen to engage local men to work the form of net recognized by the colonial fishery regulations.

The United States Government assured His Majesty's late Government in November last that they would not countenance a specified evasion of the Newfoundland foreign fishing vessels Act, 1905, and the proposed arrangement would appear to be in accordance with the spirit which prompted that assurance.

FOREIGN OFFICE, *September 25, 1906.*

*Modus vivendi between the United States and Great Britain in re-
gard to inshore fisheries on the treaty coast of Newfoundland—
Agreement effected by exchange of notes at London, September
4/6, 1907*[1]

AMERICAN EMBASSY,
London, September 4, 1907.

SIR: I am authorized by my Government to ratify a *modus vivendi*
in regard to the Newfoundland fishery question, as follows:

It is agreed that the fisheries shall be carried on during the present
year substantially as they were actually carried on for the most of
the time by mutual agreement, under the *modus vivendi* of 1906.

(1) It it understood that His Majesty's Government will not bring
into force the Newfoundland foreign fishing vessels Act of 1906,
which imposes on American fishing vessels certain restrictions in
addition to those imposed by the Act of 1905, and also that the provisions of the first part of section 1 of the Act of 1905, as to boarding and bringing into port, and also the whole of section three of the
same Act, will not be regarded as applying to American fishing vessels.

(2) In consideration of the fact that the shipment of Newfoundlanders by American fishermen outside the three-mile limit is not to
be made the basis of interference or to be penalized, my Government
waives the use of purse seines by American fishermen during the term
governed by this agreement, and also waives the right to fish on
Sundays.

(3) It is understood that American fishing vessels will make their
shipment of Newfoundlanders, as fishermen, sufficiently far from the
exact three-mile limit to avoid reasonable doubt.

(4) It is further understood that American fishermen will pay light
dues when not deprived of their rights to fish, and will comply with
the provisions of the colonial customs law as to reporting at a custom-house when physically possible to do so.

I need not add that my Government is most anxious that the provisions of this *modus vivendi* should be made effective at the earliest
possible moment, and that, in view of this, and of the actual presence
of our fishing fleet on the treaty shore, we do not feel that an exchange
of ratifications should be longer delayed. But my Government has
every desire to make the arrangement, pending arbitration, as agreeable as possible to the Newfoundland authorities, consistent with the
due safeguarding of treaty rights which we have enjoyed for nearly

---

[1] *Foreign Relations of the United States,* 1907, pt. 1, p. 531.

a century. If, therefore, the proposals you have recently shown me from the Premier of Newfoundland or any other changes in the above *modus vivendi* should be proposed by mutual agreement between the Newfoundland authorities and our fishermen, having due regard to the losses that might be incurred by a change of plans so long after preparations for the season's fishing had been made and the voyage begun, my Government will be ready to consider such changes with you in the most friendly spirit, and if found not to compromise our rights, to unite with you in ratifying them at once.

I am glad to be assured by you that this note will be considered as sufficient ratification of the *modus vivendi* on the part of my Government.

I have the honor to be, with the highest consideration, sir, your most obedient humble servant,

WHITELAW REID

The Right Honorable SIR EDWARD GREY, Baronet, etc., etc., etc.

FOREIGN OFFICE, *September 6, 1907.*

YOUR EXCELLENCY: I have the honor to acknowledge the receipt of your Excellency's note of the 4th instant, containing the terms of the *modus vivendi* with regard to the Newfoundland fisheries—which you are authorized by your Government to ratify.

I am glad to assure your Excellency that His Majesty's Government agrees to the terms of the *modus vivendi* and that your Excellency's note will be considered by His Majesty's Government as a sufficient ratification of that arrangement on the part of His Majesty's Government.

His Majesty's Government fully shares the desire of your Government that the provisions of the *modus vivendi* should be made effective at the earliest possible moment, and the necessary steps will be taken by His Majesty's Government to secure its observance.

His Majesty's Government takes note of the conciliatory offer of the United States Government to consider in a most friendly spirit any changes in the *modus vivendi* which may be agreed upon locally between the Newfoundland authorities and the United States fishermen and which may be acceptable both to the United States Government and to His Majesty's Government.

I have the honor to be, with the highest consideration, your Excellency's most obedient humble servant,

E. GREY

His Excellency the Honorable WHITELAW REID, etc., etc., etc.

Modus vivendi between the United States and Great Britain in re-
gard to inshore fisheries on the treaty coast of Newfoundland—
Agreement effected by exchange of notes signed at London, July
15/23, 1908[1]

FOREIGN OFFICE, *July 15, 1908.*

YOUR EXCELLENCY: On the 18th ultimo your Excellency proposed
on behalf of the United States Government that, as arbitration in regard to the Newfoundland fisheries question could not be arranged
before the forthcoming fishery season, the *modus vivendi* of last
year should be renewed with the same elasticity as before for the parties concerned to make local arrangements satisfactory to both sides.

I have the honor to inform your Excellency that the Newfoundland
Government, having been consulted on the subject, have expressed the
desire that the herring fishery during the ensuing season should be
conducted on the same principles as in the season of 1907, and formally undertake to permit during this year the conduct of the herring
fishery as last year.

As the arrangements for last year were admittedly satisfactory to
all concerned in the fishing, His Majesty's Government hope that the
United States Government will see their way to accept this formal
assurance on the part of the Newfoundland Government as a satisfactory arrangement for the season of 1908. If this course be adopted
it would seem unnecessary to enter into any further formal arrangements, seeing that the communication of this assurance to the United
States Government and its acceptance by them would be tantamount
to a *modus vivendi*.

I have the honor to be, with the highest consideration, your Excellency's most obedient, humble servant,

LOUIS MALLET

(For SIR EDWARD GREY)

His Excellency the Honorable WHITELAW REID, etc., etc., etc.

AMERICAN EMBASSY,
London, July 23, 1908.

SIR: The reply, in your letter of July 15, 1908, to my proposal of
June 18th, for a renewal of last year's *modus vivendi* for the approaching Newfoundland fisheries season, with the same elasticity as
before for local arrangements, has been duly considered.

I am gratified to learn that the Newfoundland Government was so
well satisfied with the result of these arrangements under the *modus*

---

[1] *Foreign Relations of the United States*, 1908, p. 378.

vivendi for last year that it offers a formal undertaking that the American fishermen shall be permitted to conduct the herring fisheries this year in the same way.

It is proper to observe that our fishermen would have preferred last year, and would prefer now to work the fisheries with purse seines, as heretofore, as provided in the *modus vivendi* of 1906. But they yielded last year to the strong wishes of the Newfoundland Government in this matter, and joined in the arrangement under the elastic clause at the close of the *modus vivendi* of 1907 by which, with the approval of the British and American Governments, they gave up also other claims in return for certain concessions. I must reserve their right to these and to purse seines, as heretofore enjoyed, as not now abandoned, and therefore to be duly considered in the pending arbitration before the Hague tribunal.

But with this reservation, and with the approval of my Government, I now have pleasure in accepting the offer that the herring fishery during the ensuing season shall be conducted on the same principles as in the season of 1907, and the formal undertaking against interference with this by the Newfoundland Government, as a substantial agreement on my proposal of June 18th.

We unite also with you in regarding this exchange of letters as constituting in itself a satisfactory agreement for the season of 1908, without the necessity for any further formal correspondence.

I am glad to add that Mr. Alexander, of the United States Fish Commission, will be sent again this year to the treaty shore, and that my Government feels sure that, through his influence, there will be general willingness to carry out the spirit of the understanding, and work on the lines of least resistance.

I have the honor to be, with the highest consideration, sir, your most obedient, humble servant,

WHITELAW REID

The Right Honorable SIR EDWARD GREY, Bart., etc., etc., etc.

Correspondence of January 27–March 4, 1909, Supplementary to the Agreement for Arbitration [1]

DEPARTMENT OF STATE,
Washington, January 27, 1909.

EXCELLENCY: In order to place officially on record the understanding already arrived at by us in preparing the special agreement which

---

[1] Malloy, *Treaties, Conventions, etc., between the United States and Other Powers,* vol. 1, p. 841. For the agreement for arbitration, see *ante,* p. 147.

we have signed to-day for the submission of questions relating to fisheries on the north Atlantic coast under the general treaty of arbitration concluded between the United States and Great Britain on the fourth day of April, 1908, I have the honor to declare on behalf of the Government of the United States that Question 5 of the series submitted, namely, "From where must be measured the 'three marine miles of any of the coasts, bays, creeks, or harbors' referred to in the said article" is submitted in its present form with the agreed understanding that no question as to the Bay of Fundy, considered as a whole apart from its bays or creeks, or as to innocent passage through the Gut of Canso is included in this question as one to be raised in the present arbitration; it being the intention of the parties that their respective views or contentions on either subject shall be in no wise prejudiced by anything in the present arbitration.

I have the honor to be, with the highest respect, your Excellency's most obedient servant,

ELIHU ROOT

His Excellency The Right Honorable
   JAMES BRYCE, O.M.,
      Ambassador of Great Britain.

BRITISH EMBASSY,
Washington, January 27, 1909.

SIR: I have the honor to acknowledge your note of to-day's date and in reply have to declare on behalf of His Majesty's Government, in order to place officially on record the understanding already arrived at by us in preparing the special agreement which we have signed to-day for the submission of questions relating to fisheries on the north Atlantic coast under the general treaty of arbitration concluded between Great Britain and the United States on the 4th day of April, 1908, that Question 5 of the series submitted, namely, "From where must be measured the 'three marine miles of any of the coasts, bays, creeks or harbors' referred to in the said article" is submitted in its present form with the agreed understanding that no question as to the Bay of Fundy, considered as a whole apart from its bays and creeks, or as to innocent passage through the Gut of Canso is included in this question as one to be raised in the present arbitration; it being the intention of the parties that their respective views or contentions on either subject shall be in no wise prejudiced by anything in the present arbitration.

I have the honor to be, with the highest consideration, sir, your most obedient, humble servant,

JAMES BRYCE

The Honorable ELIHU ROOT,
   Etc., etc., etc.,
    Secretary of State.

DEPARTMENT OF STATE,
Washington, February 21, 1909.

EXCELLENCY: I have the honor to inform you that the Senate, by its resolution of the 18th instant, gave its advice and consent to the ratification of the special agreement between the United States and Great Britain, signed on January 27, 1909, for the submission to the Permanent Court of Arbitration at The Hague of questions relating to fisheries on the north Atlantic coast.

In giving this advice and consent to the ratification of the special agreement, and as a part of the act of ratification, the Senate states in the resolution its understanding—"that it is agreed by the United States and Great Britain that Question 5 of the series submitted, namely, 'from where must be measured the three marine miles of any of the coasts, bays, creeks, or harbors referred to in said article?' does not include any question as to the Bay of Fundy, considered as a whole apart from its bays or creeks, or as to innocent passage through the Gut of Canso, and that the respective views or contentions of the United States and Great Britain on either subject shall be in no wise prejudiced by anything in the present arbitration, and that this agreement on the part of the United States will be mentioned in the ratification of the special agreement and will, in effect, form part of this special agreement."

In thus formally confirming what I stated to you orally, I have the honor to express the hope that you will in like manner formally confirm the assent of His Majesty's Government to this understanding which you heretofore stated to me orally, and that you will be prepared at an early day to exchange the notes confirming the special agreement as provided for therein and in the general arbitration convention of June 5, 1908.

I have the honor to be, with the highest consideration, your Excellency's most obedient servant,

ROBERT BACON

His Excellency The Right Honorable
   JAMES BRYCE, O.M.,
    Ambassador of Great Britain.

BRITISH EMBASSY,
Washington, March 4, 1909.

SIR: I have the honor to acknowledge the receipt of your note informing me that the Senate of the United States has approved the special agreement for the reference to arbitration of the questions relating to the fisheries on the north Atlantic coast and of the terms of the resolution in which that approval is given.

It is now my duty to inform you that the Government of His Britannic Majesty confirms the special agreement aforesaid and in so doing confirms also the understanding arrived at by us that Question 5 of the series of questions submitted for arbitration, namely, from where must be measured the "three marine miles of any of the coasts, bays, creeks, or harbors" referred to in the said article, is submitted in its present form with the agreed understanding that no question as to the Bay of Fundy considered as a whole apart from its bays or creeks, or as to innocent passage through the Gut of Canso, is included in this question as one to be raised in the present arbitration, it being the intention of the parties that their respective views or contentions on either subject shall be in nowise prejudiced by anything in the present arbitration.

This understanding is that which was embodied in notes exchanged between your predecessor and myself on January 27th, and is that expressed in the above-mentioned resolution of the Senate of the United States.

I have the honor to be, with the highest respect, sir, your most obedient, humble servant,

JAMES BRYCE

The Honorable ROBERT BACON,
Secretary of State.

DEPARTMENT OF STATE,
Washington, March 4, 1909.

EXCELLENCY: I have the honor to acknowledge the receipt of your note of the 4th instant in which you confirm the understanding in the matter of the special agreement submitting to arbitration the differences between the Governments of the United States and Great Britain concerning the north Atlantic fisheries, as expressed in the resolution of the Senate of February 18, 1909, and as previously agreed upon by the interchange of notes with my predecessor of January 27, 1909.

I therefore have the honor to inform you that this Government considers the special agreement as in full force and effect from and after the 4th day of March, 1909.

I have the honor to be, with the highest consideration, your Excellency's most obedient servant,

ROBERT BACON

His Excellency The Right Honorable
JAMES BRYCE, O.M.,
Ambassador of Great Britain.

Resolution of the United States Senate concerning Newfoundland Fisheries[1]

February 18, 1909.

Resolved (two-thirds of the Senators present concurring therein), That the Senate advise and consent to the ratification of a special agreement between the United States and Great Britain for the submission to the Permanent Court of Arbitration at The Hague of questions relating to fisheries on the north Atlantic coast, signed on the 27th day of January, 1909.

In giving this advice and consent to the ratification of the said special agreement, and as a part of the act of ratification, the Senate understands that it is agreed by the United States and Great Britain that Question 5 of the series submitted, namely, "from where must be measured the 'three marine miles of any of the coasts, bays, creeks, or harbors' referred to in the said article," does not include any question as to the Bay of Fundy, considered as a whole apart from its bays, or creeks, or as to innocent passage through the Gut of Canso, and that the respective views or contentions of the United States and Great Britain on either subject shall be in nowise prejudiced by anything in the present arbitration, and that this agreement on the part of the United States will be mentioned in the ratification of the special agreement and will, in effect, form part of this special agreement.

---

[1] Malloy, *Treaties, Conventions, etc., between the United States and Other Powers,* vol. 1, p. 843.

*Modus vivendi between the United States and Great Britain in re-
gard to inshore fisheries on the treaty coast of Newfoundland—
Agreement effected by exchange of notes signed at London, July
22/September 8, 1909*[1]

AMERICAN EMBASSY,
London, July 22, 1909.

Inasmuch as under the provisions of the special agreement, dated
January 27, 1909, between the United States and Great Britain for
the submission to arbitration of certain questions arising with respect
to the north Atlantic coast fisheries, the decision of the tribunal on
such questions will not be rendered before the summer of 1910, and
inasmuch as the *modus vivendi* entered into with Great Britain last
July with respect to the Newfoundland fisheries does not in terms
extend beyond the season of 1908, my Government thinks it desirable
that the *modus* of last year should be renewed for the coming season,
and, if possible, until the termination of the arbitration proceedings for
the settlement of these questions.

I am therefore instructed to propose such a renewal to His Majesty's Government, the understanding on both sides originally having
been, as you may remember, that the *modus* was entered into pending
arbitration.

I have the honor to be, with the highest consideration, sir, your most
obedient, humble servant,

WHITELAW REID

The Right Honorable SIR EDWARD GREY, Bt., etc., etc., etc.

FOREIGN OFFICE, *September 8, 1909.*

SIR: In reply to Mr. Whitelaw Reid's note of July 22 last I have
the honor to state that His Majesty's Government agree to the renewal of the *modus vivendi* of 1908 for the regulation of the Newfoundland fisheries, until the termination of the arbitration proceedings before the Hague tribunal for the settlement of the Atlantic
fisheries questions.

His Majesty's Government suggest that Mr. Whitelaw Reid's note
of July 22 and my present reply should be regarded as constituting
a sufficient ratification of the above understanding without the necessity
for embodying it in a more formal document.

I have the honor to be, with high consideration, sir, your most
obedient, humble servant,

E. GREY

J. R. CARTER, ESQ., etc., etc., etc.

---

[1] *Foreign Relations of the United States*, 1909, p. 283.

Agreement between the United States and Great Britain adopting with certain modifications the rules and method of procedure recommended in the award of September 7, 1910, of the north Atlantic coast fisheries arbitration.—Signed at Washington, July 20, 1912.[1]

The United States of America and His Majesty the King of the United Kingdom of Great Britain and Ireland and of the British Dominions beyond the Seas, Emperor of India, being desirous of concluding an agreement regarding the exercise of the liberties referred to in Article 1 of the treaty of October 20, 1818, have for this purpose named as their plenipotentiaries:

The President of the United States of America:

Chandler P. Anderson, Counselor for the Department of State of the United States;

His Britannic Majesty:

Alfred Mitchell Innes, *Chargé d'Affaires* of His Majesty's Embassy at Washington;

Who, having communicated to each other their respective full powers, which were found to be in due and proper form, have agreed to and concluded the following articles:

ARTICLE 1

Whereas the award of the Hague tribunal of September 7, 1910, recommended for the consideration of the parties certain rules and a method of procedure under which all questions which may arise in the future regarding the exercise of the liberties referred to in Article 1 of the treaty of October 20, 1818, may be determined in accordance with the principles laid down in the award, and the parties having agreed to make certain modifications therein, the rules and method of procedure so modified are hereby accepted by the parties in the following form:

1. All future municipal laws, ordinances, or rules for the regulation of the fisheries by Great Britain, Canada, or Newfoundland in respect of (1) the hours, days, or seasons when fish may be taken on the treaty coasts; (2) the method, means, and implements used in the taking of fish or in carrying on fishing operations; (3) any other regulations of a similar character; and all alterations or amendments of such laws, ordinances, or rules shall be promulgated and come into operation within the first fifteen days of November in each year; provided, however, in so far as any such law, ordinance, or rule

---

[1] *U. S. Statutes at Large*, vol. 37, pt. 2, p. 1634.

shall apply to a fishery conducted between the 1st day of November and the 1st day of February, the same shall be promulgated at least six months before the 1st day of November in each year.

Such laws, ordinances, or rules by Great Britain shall be promulgated by publication in the London *Gazette,* by Canada in the Canada *Gazette,* and by Newfoundland in the Newfoundland *Gazette.*

After the expiration of ten years from the date of this agreement. and so on at intervals of ten years thereafter, either party may propose to the other that the dates fixed for promulgation be revised in consequence of the varying conditions due to changes in the habits of the fish or other natural causes; and if there shall be a difference of opinion as to whether the conditions have so varied as to render a revision desirable, such difference shall be referred for decision to a commission possessing expert knowledge, such as the permanent mixed fishery commission hereinafter mentioned.

2. If the Government of the United States considers any such laws or regulations inconsistent with the treaty of 1818, it is entitled so to notify the Government of Great Britain within forty-five days after the publication above referred to, and may require that the same be submitted to and their reasonableness, within the meaning of the award, be determined by the permanent mixed fishery commission constituted as hereinafter provided.

3. Any law or regulation not so notified within the said period of forty-five days, or which, having been so notified, has been declared reasonable and consistent with the treaty of 1818 (as interpreted by the said award) by the permanent mixed fishery commission, shall be held to be reasonable within the meaning of the award; but if declared by the said commission to be unreasonable and inconsistent with the treaty of 1818, it shall not be applicable to the inhabitants of the United States exercising their fishing liberties under the treaty of 1818.

4. Permanent mixed fishery commissions for Canada and Newfoundland, respectively, shall be established for the decision of such questions as to the reasonableness of future regulations, as contemplated by Article 4 of the special agreement of January 27, 1909. These commissions shall consist of an expert national, appointed by each party for five years; the third member shall not be a national of either party. He shall be nominated for five years by agreement of the parties, or, failing such agreement, within two months from the date, when either of the parties to this agreement shall call upon the other

to agree upon such third member, he shall be nominated by Her Majesty the Queen of the Netherlands.

5. The two national members shall be summoned by the Government of Great Britain, and shall convene within thirty days from the date of notification by the Government of the United States. These two members having failed to agree on any or all of the questions submitted within thirty days after they have convened, or having before the expiration of that period notified the Government of Great Britain that they are unable to agree, the full commission, under the presidency of the umpire, is to be summoned by the Government of Great Britain, and shall convene within thirty days thereafter to decide all questions upon which the two national members had disagreed. The commission must deliver its decision, if the two Governments do not agree otherwise, within forty-five days after it has convened. The umpire shall conduct the procedure in accordance with that provided in Chapter IV of the Convention for the pacific settlement of international disputes, of October 18, 1907, except in so far as herein otherwise provided.

6. The form of convocation of the commission, including the terms of reference of the question at issue, shall be as follows:

> The provision hereinafter fully set forth of an act dated......
> published in the......Gazette, has been notified to the Government of Great Britain by the Government of the United States under date of......, as provided by the agreement entered into on July 20, 1912, pursuant to the award of the Hague tribunal of September 7, 1910.
> Pursuant to the provisions of that agreement the Government of Great Britain hereby summons the permanent mixed fishery commission for
> { Canada } composed of ....commissioner for the
> { Newfoundland }
> United States of America, and of......... commissioner for
> { Canada } who shall meet at Halifax, Nova Scotia, with
> { Newfoundland }
> power to hold subsequent meetings at such other place or places as they may determine, and render a decision within thirty days as to whether the provision so notified is reasonable and consistent with the treaty of 1818, as interpreted by the award of the Hague tribunal of September 7, 1910, and if not, in what respect it is unreasonable and inconsistent therewith.
> Failing an agreement on this question within thirty days, the commission shall so notify the Government of Great Britain in

order that the further action required by that award shall be taken for the decision of the above question.

The provision is as follows ....

7. The unanimous decision of the two national commissioners, or the majority decision of the umpire and one commissioner, shall be final and binding.

8. Any difference in regard to the regulations specified in Protocol XXX of the arbitration proceedings, which shall not have been disposed of by diplomatic methods, shall be referred not to the commission of expert specialists mentioned in the award but to the permanent mixed fishery commissions, to be constituted as hereinbefore provided, in the same manner as a difference in regard to future regulations would be so referred.

ARTICLE 2

And whereas the tribunal of arbitration in its award decided that—

In case of bays the three marine miles are to be measured from a straight line drawn across the body of water at the place where it ceases to have the configuration and characteristics of a bay. At all other places the three marine miles are to be measured following the sinuosities of the coast.

And whereas the tribunal made certain recommendations for the determination of the limits of the bays enumerated in the award;

Now, therefore, it is agreed that the recommendations, in so far as the same relate to bays contiguous to the territory of the Dominion of Canada, to which Question 5 of the special agreement is applicable, are hereby adopted, to wit:

In every bay not hereinafter specifically provided for, the limits of exclusion shall be drawn three miles seaward from a straight line across the bay in the part nearest the entrance at the first point where the width does not exceed ten miles.

For the Baie des Chaleurs the limits of exclusion shall be drawn from the line from the light at Birch Point on Miscou Island to Macquereau Point light; for the Bay of Miramichi, the line from the light at Point Escuminac to the light on the eastern point of Tabisintac Gully; for Egmont Bay, in Prince Edward Island, the line from the light of Cape Egmont to the light of West Point; and off St. Ann's Bay, in the Province of Nova Scotia, the line from the light at Point Anconi to the nearest point on the opposite shore of the mainland.

For or near the following bays the limits of exclusion shall be three marine miles seawards from the following lines, namely:

For or near Barrington Bay, in Nova Scotia, the line from the light on Stoddard Island to the light on the south point of Cape Sable, thence to the light at Baccaro Point; at Chedabucto and St. Peter's Bays, the line from Cranberry Island light to Green Island light, thence to Point Rouge; for Mira Bay, the line from the light on the east point of Scatary Island to the northeasterly point of Cape Morien.

Long Island and Bryer Island, on St. Mary's Bay, in Nova Scotia, shall, for the purpose of delimitation, be taken as the coasts of such bays.

It is understood that the award does not cover Hudson Bay.

ARTICLE 3

It is further agreed that the delimitation of all or any of the bays on the coast of Newfoundland, whether mentioned in the recommendations or not, does not require consideration at present.

ARTICLE 4

The present agreement shall be ratified by the President of the United States, by and with the advice and consent of the Senate thereof, and by His Britannic Majesty, and the ratifications shall be exchanged in Washington as soon as practicable.

In faith whereof the respective plenipotentiaries have signed this agreement in duplicate and have hereunto affixed their seals.

Done at Washington on the 20th day of July, one thousand nine hundred and twelve.

CHANDLER P. ANDERSON   [SEAL]

ALFRED MITCHELL INNES [SEAL]

THE ORINOCO STEAMSHIP COMPANY CASE

between

THE UNITED STATES *and* VENEZUELA

Decided October 25, 1910

Syllabus

This claim originated in a concession from Venezuela to one Ellis Grell, granted on January 17, 1894,[1] for the exclusive right to navigate the Orinoco River in steam vessels between Trinidad and Ciudad Bolívar. The contract embodying the concession contained the so-called Calvo clause, which provided that "questions and controversies which may arise with regard to the interpretation or execution of this contract shall be resolved by the tribunals of the Republic in accordance with its laws, and shall not in any case give occasion for international reclamations."

By subsequent assignment the Grell concession came into possession of the Orinoco Shipping and Trading Company, a British corporation, the majority of the stock and bonds of which was held by American citizens. The Government of Venezuela became indebted to this company for approximately half a million dollars for services rendered and damages sustained. An adjustment was effected on May 10, 1900, by which the concession was extended for a period of six years and the Government agreed to pay the company 100,000 bolivars ($19,200) in cash and a second sum of the same amount at a later date. The company, on its part, acknowledged as settled all its claims against the Government. The contract of settlement also contained the so-called Calvo clause. The first payment of 100,000 bolivars was duly made, but the second was not.

On October 5, 1900, Venezuela opened the navigation of the Orinoco River to the commerce of all nations, thus destroying the monopoly claimed by the company as assignee of the Grell concession. This was done by repealing a decree promulgated on July 1, 1893[2] a few months before the original concession was granted, which closed the Orinoco to foreign trade. On December 14, 1901, the Venezuelan Government further cancelled the extension of the concession granted in accordance with the contract of settlement of May 10, 1900. The company's efforts to obtain relief from the Government of Venezuela being unsuccessful, the matter was brought to the attention of the American and British Governments. Later, the American stock-

[1] *Post*, p. 258.   [2] *Post*, p. 253.

holders of the British company organized an American corporation known as the Orinoco Steamship Company, which took over the business, assets and liabilities of the former company. The claims of the corporation taken over from the company for the payment overdue under the agreement of May 10, 1900, for damages arising from the annulment of the exclusive concession, for services rendered, imposts illegally exacted, for the use and detention of and damages to vessels, loss of earnings and counsel fees, amounting to approximately $1,400,000, were presented to the United States and Venezuelan claims commission under the protocol of February 17, 1903.[1] The commission assumed jurisdiction of the claims under the wording of the protocol, which included "all claims owned by citizens of the United States," and the umpire, Dr. Barge, on February 22, 1904,[2] made an award in favor of the claimants, amounting to approximately $28,000, covering the detention and use of steamers, goods delivered to the Government and passages furnished it.

Although the protocol provided that the decision of the commission and of the umpire should be final and conclusive, the United States protested the award on the grounds that it disregarded the terms of the protocol and contained essential errors of law and fact such as invalidated it in accordance with the principles of international law.

After several years of negotiations about this and other claims, in the course of which diplomatic relations were severed, a protocol was signed on February 13, 1909,[3] which provided for the submission of the case to arbitration in the following form:

The arbitral tribunal shall first decide whether the decision of umpire Barge, in this case, in view of all the circumstances and under the principles of international law, is not void, and whether it must be considered so conclusive as to preclude a reexamination of the case on its merits. If the arbitral tribunal decides that said decision must be considered final, the case will be considered by the United States of America as closed; but on the other hand, if the arbitral tribunal decides that said decision of umpire Barge should not be considered as final, said tribunal shall then hear, examine and determine the case and render its decision on the merits.[4]

The tribunal, composed of three members selected from the Permanent Court of Arbitration at The Hague, none of whom could be a citizen of either of the contracting countries, was constituted as follows: Heinrich Lammasch of Austria, Auguste M. F. Beernaert of Belgium, and Gonzalo de Quesada of Cuba. Its sessions began September 28 and ended October 19, 1910, the decision being rendered on October 25, 1910.

The tribunal held that, while on principle an arbitral decision should be accepted, respected and carried out without any reservation, in

---

[1] *Ante*, p. 74.   [2] *Post*, p. 255.   [3] *Post*, p. 235.   [4] *Post*, p. 236.

this case the parties had admitted in the protocol of submission that excess of jurisdiction and essential error nullified an arbitral judgment, and called upon the tribunal to decide whether the judgment of umpire Barge was not void, and, if so, to reexamine the case on its merits. The tribunal further held that the nullity of one claim in an arbitral award embracing several independent claims does not nullify the others. The tribunal then proceeded to examine each item considered by the former award and decided as follows:

The decision upon the claims based upon the annulment of the concession was not vitiated by excess of authority or essential error, and was therefore not subject to revision.

In view of the express provisions of the agreement of submission of February 17, 1903, that the umpire was to decide according to absolute equity and without regard to objections of a technical nature or the provisions of local legislation, umpire Barge exceeded his jurisdiction in rejecting the claim for payment due under the contract of May 10, 1900, because of the failure of the claimants to appeal to the Venezuelan courts, in accordance with the Calvo clause of the contracts, and to notify the Government of the assignment of the claim, in accordance with local law. The claim was declared to be well founded and accordingly allowed.

The tribunal made the same holding with reference to claims for transportation of passengers and merchandise and for the retention and hire of steamers, which were disallowed by the former award because the claimants omitted to notify Venezuela of the assignment of them.

The balance of the former decision with reference to the remaining claims was held not subject to reexamination or revision, except that a portion of the amount claimed for counsel fees and expenses of litigation was allowed.

The claims allowed by the tribunal amounted to $64,412.59, in addition to the $28,224.93 allowed by the original decision, making a total recovery of $92,637.52, upon which interest was allowed at the rate of three per cent.

With the above exceptions, the decision of umpire Barge was held to remain in full force and effect.

AWARD OF THE TRIBUNAL

Award of the tribunal of arbitration constituted under an Agreement signed at Carácas, February 13, 1909, between the United States of America and the United States of Venezuela.—The Hague, October 25, 1910.[1]

By an agreement signed at Carácas the 13th of February, 1909,[2]

---

[1] Official report, p. 64. For the original French text, see Appendix, p. 504.
[2] *Post*, p. 235.

the United States of America and of Venezuela have agreed to submit to a tribunal of arbitration, composed of three arbitrators, chosen from the Permanent Court of Arbitration, a claim of the United States of America against the United States of Venezuela;

This agreement states:

The arbitral tribunal shall first decide whether the decision of umpire Barge,[1] in this case, in view of all the circumstances and under the principles of international law, is not void, and whether it must be considered to be so conclusive as to preclude a reexamination of the case on its merits. If the arbitral tribunal decides that said decision must be considered final, the case will be considered by the United States of America as closed; but on the other hand, if the arbitral tribunal decides that said decision of umpire Barge should not be considered as final, the said tribunal shall then hear, examine and determine the case and render its decisions on its merits.[2]

In virtue of said agreement, the two Governments respectively have named as arbitrators the following members of the Permanent Court of Arbitration:

His Excellency Gonzalo de Quesada Envoy Extraordinary and Minister Plenipotentiary of Cuba at Berlin, etc.;

His Excellency A. Beernaert, Minister of State, member of the Chamber of Representatives of Belgium, etc.;

And the arbitrators so designated, in virtue of said agreement, have named as umpire:

Mr. H. Lammasch, professor in the University of Vienna, member of the Upper House of the Austrian Parliament, etc.;

The cases, counter-cases and conclusions have been duly submitted to the arbitrators and communicated to the parties;

The parties have both pleaded and replied, both having pleaded the merits of the case, as well as the previous question, and the discussion was declared closed on October 19th, 1910;

Upon which the tribunal, after mature deliberation, pronounces as follows:

Whereas by the terms of an agreement dated February 17th,

---

[1]*Post*, p. 255.   [2]*Post*, p. 236.

1903,[1] a mixed commission was charged with the decision of all claims owned (*poseidas*) by citizens of the United States of America against the Republic of Venezuela, which shall not have been settled by a diplomatic agreement or by arbitration between the two Governments and which shall have been presented by the United States of America; an umpire, to be named by Her Majesty the Queen of the Netherlands, was eventually to give his final and conclusive decision (*definitiva y concluyente*) on any question upon which the commissioners might not have been able to agree;

Whereas the umpire thus appointed, Mr. Barge, has pronounced on the said claims on the 22nd of February 1904;

Whereas it is assuredly in the interest of peace and the development of the institution of international arbitration, so essential to the well-being of nations, that on principle, such a decision be accepted, respected and carried out by the parties without any reservation, as it is laid down in Article 81 of the Convention for the pacific settlement of international disputes of October 18th, 1907; and besides no jurisdiction whatever has been instituted for reconsidering similar decisions;

But whereas in the present case, it having been argued that the decision is void, the parties have entered into a new agreement under date of the 13th of February 1909, according to which, without considering the conclusive character of the first decision, this tribunal is called upon to decide whether the decision of umpire Barge, in virtue of the circumstances and in accordance with the principles of international law, be not void, and whether it must be considered so conclusive as to preclude a reexamination of the case on its merits;

Whereas by the agreement of February 13th, 1909,[2] both parties have at least implicitly admitted, as vices involving the nullity of an arbitral decision, excessive exercise of jurisdiction and essential error in the judgment (*exceso de poder y error esencial en el fallo*);

Whereas the plaintiff party alleges excessive exercise of jurisdiction and numerous errors in law and fact equivalent to essential error;

---

[1] An agreement providing for the creation of the mixed commission for the settlement of claims of citizens, corporations, etc., of the United States against Venezuela. See *ante*, p. 74.

[2] *Post*, p. 235.

Whereas, following the principles of equity in accordance with law, when an arbitral award embraces several independent claims, and consequently several decisions, the nullity of one is without influence on any of the others, more especially when, as in the present case, the integrity and the good faith of the arbitrator are not questioned; this being ground for pronouncing separat ly on each of the points at issue;

I. As regards the 1,209,701.04 dollars:

Whereas this tribunal is in the first place called upon to decide whether the award of the umpire is void, and whether it must be considered conclusive; and whereas this tribunal would have to decide on the merits of the case only if the umpire's award be declared void;

Whereas it is alleged that the umpire deviated from the terms of the agreement by giving an inexact account of the Grell contract and the claim based on it, and in consequence thereof fell into an essential error; but since the award reproduces said contract textually and in its entire tenor; whereas it is scarcely admissible that the umpire should have misunderstood the text and should have exceeded his authority by pronouncing on a claim which had not been submitted to him, by failing to appreciate the connection between the concession in question and exterior navigation, the umpire having decided *in terminis*, that "the permission to navigate these channels was only annexed to the permission to call at Trinidad";

Whereas the appreciation of the facts of the case and the interpretation of the documents were within the competence of the umpire and as his decisions, when based on such interpretation, are not subject to revision by this tribunal, whose duty it is not to say if the case had been well or ill judged, but whether the award must be annulled; that if an arbitral decision could be disputed on the ground of erroneous appreciation, appeal and revision, which the Conventions of The Hague of 1899 and 1907 made it their object to avert, would be the general rule;

Whereas the point of view from which the umpire considered the claim of $513,000 (afterwards reduced in the conclusions of the United States of America to $335,000, and being part of said sum of $1,209,701.04), is the consequence of his interpretation of the contract of May 10th, 1900, and of the relation between this contract and the decree of the same date;

Whereas the circumstance that the umpire, not content to have based his award on his interpretation of the contracts, which of itself should be deemed sufficient, has invoked other subsidiary reasons, of a rather more technical character, can not vitiate his decision;

II. As regards the 19,200 dollars (100,000 bolívares):

Whereas the agreement of February 17th, 1903, did not invest the arbitrators with discretionary powers, but obliged them to give their decision on a basis of absolute equity without regard to objections of a technical nature, or to the provisions of local legislation (*con arreglo absoluto á la equidad, sin reparar en objeciones técnicas, ni en las disposiciones de la legislación local*);

Whereas excessive exercise of power may consist, not only in deciding a question not submitted to the arbitrators, but also in misinterpreting the express provisions of the agreement in respect of the way in which they are to reach their decisions, notably with regard to the legislation or the principles of law to be applied;

Whereas the only motives for the rejection of the claim for 19,200 dollars are: 1st, the absence of all appeal to the Venezuelan courts of justice, and 2nd, the omission of any previous notification of cession to the debtor, it being evident that "the circumstance that the question might be asked if on the day this claim was filed, this indebtedness was proved compellable," could not serve as a justification of rejection;

Whereas it follows from the agreements of 1903 and 1909—on which the present arbitration is based—that the United States of Venezuela had by convention renounced invoking the provisions of Article 14 of the Grell contract and of Article 4 of the contract of May 10th, 1900, and as at the date of said arguments it was, in fact, certain that no lawsuit between the parties had been brought before the Venezuelan courts and as the maintenance of Venezuelan jurisdiction with regard to these claims would have been incompatible and irreconcilable with the arbitration which had been instituted;

Whereas there is a question not of the cession of a concession but of the cession of a debt, and as the omission to notify previously the cession of a debt constitutes but a failure to observe a prescription of local legislation, though a similar prescription also exists in other legislations, it can not be considered as required by absolute equity, at least when the debtor actually possessed knowledge of the cession and has paid neither the assignor nor the assignee;

III. As regards the 147,638.79 dollars:

Whereas with regard to the 1,053 dollars for the transport of passengers and merchandise in 1900 and the 25,845.20 dollars for the hire of the steamers *Delta, Socorro, Masparro, Guanare, Heroe,* from July 1900 to April 1902, the award of the umpire is based only on the omission of previous notification of the cession to the Government of Venezuela or of the acceptance by it, this means of defense being eliminated by the agreement, as mentioned before;

Whereas the same might be said of the claim for 19,571.34 dollars for the restitution of national taxes, said to have been collected contrary to law, and of that of 3,509.22 dollars on account of the retention of the *Bolívar;* but as it has not been proved on the one hand that the taxes here under discussion belonged to those from which the Orinoco Shipping and Trading Company was exempt, and on the other hand that the fact objected to proceeded from abuse of authority on the part of the Venezuelan consul; and as both claims must therefore be rejected on their merits, though on other grounds, the annulment of the award on this point would be without interest;

Whereas the decision of the umpire, allowing 27,692.31 dollars instead of 28,461.53 dollars for the retention and hire of the *Masparro* and *Socorro* from March 21st to September 18th, 1902, as regards the 769.22 dollars disallowed, is based here also only on the omission of notification of the cession of the debt;

Whereas the umpire's decision with regard to the other claims included under this head for the period after April 1st, 1902, is based on a consideration of facts and on an interpretation of legal principles which are subject neither to reëxamination nor to revision by this tribunal, the decisions awarded on these points not being void;

IV. As regards the 25,000 dollars:

Whereas the claim for 25,000 dollars for counsel fees and expenses of litigation has ben disallowed by the umpire in consequence of the rejection of the greater part of the claims of the United States of America, and as by the present award some of these claims having been admitted it seems equitable to allow part of this sum, which the tribunal fixes *ex aequo et bono* at 7,000 dollars;

Whereas the Venezuelan law fixes the legal interest at 3% and as, under these conditions, the tribunal, though aware of the insufficiency of this percentage, can not allow more;

For these reasons:

The tribunal declares void the award of umpire Barge dated February 22nd, 1904, on the four following points:

1°, as regards the   19,200   dollars;
2°, as regards the   1,053   dollars;
3°, as regards the   25,845.20 dollars;
4°, as regards the   769,22 dollars deducted from the claim for 28,461.53 dollars for the retention and hire of the *Masparro* and *Socorro;*

And deciding, in consequence of the nullity thus recognized and by reason of the elements submitted to its appreciation:

Declares these claims founded and allows to the United States of America, besides the sums allowed by the award of the umpire of February 22nd, 1904, the sums of:

1°, 19,200   dollars;   3°, 25,845.20 dollars;
2°, 1,053   dollars;   4°,   769.22 dollars;

the whole with interest at 3 per cent from the date of the claim (June 16th, 1903), the whole to be paid within two months after the date of the present award;

Allows besides for the indemnification of counsel fees and expenses of litigation 7,000 dollars;

Rejects the claim for the surplus, the award of umpire Barge of February 22nd, 1904, preserving, save for the above points, its full and entire effect.

Done at The Hague in the Permanent Court of Arbitration in triplicate original, October 25th, 1910.

The President: LAMMASCH
The Secretary General: MICHIELS VAN VERDUYNEN

AGREEMENT FOR ARBITRATION

Protocol of an agreement between the United States of America and the United States of Venezuela for the decision and adjustment of certain claims.—Signed at Carácas, February 13, 1909.[1]

William I. Buchanan, high commissioner, representing the President of the United States of America, and Doctor Francisco González Guinán, Minister for Foreign Affairs of the United States of Venezuela, duly authorized by General Juan Vicente Gomez, Vice-President of the United States of Venezuela, in charge of the Presidency of the Republic, having exhibited to each other and found in due form their respective powers, and animated by the spirit of sincere friendship that has always existed and should exist between the two nations they represent, having conferred during repeated and lengthy conferences concerning the manner of amicably and equitably adjusting the differences existing between their respective Governments with regard to the claims pending between them since neither the United States of America nor the United States of Venezuela aspires to anything other than sustaining that to which in justice and equity it is entitled; and as a result of these conferences have recognized the great importance of arbitration as a means toward maintaining the good understanding which should exist and increase between their respective nations, and to the end of avoiding hereafter, so far as possible, differences between them, they believe it is from every point of view desirable that a treaty of arbitration shall be adjusted between their respective Governments.

With respect to the claims that have been the subject of their long and friendly conferences, William I. Buchanan and Doctor Francisco González Guinán have found that the opinions and views concerning them sustained by their respective Governments have been, and are, so diametrically opposed and so different that they have found it difficult to adjust them by common accord; wherefore it is necessary to resort to the conciliatory means of arbitration, a measure to which the two nations they represent are mutually bound by their signatures to the treaties of the Second Peace Conference at The Hague in 1907, and one which is recognized by the entire civilized world as the only satisfactory means of terminating international disputes.

Being so convinced, and firm in their resolution not to permit, for any reason whatever, the cordiality that has always existed between

---

[1] Official report, p. 1. For the Spanish text, see Appendix, p 508.

their respective countries to be disturbed, the said William I. Buchanan and Doctor Francisco González Guinán, thereunto fully authorized, have adjusted, agreed to and signed the present protocol for the settlement of the said claims against the United States of Venezuela, which are as follows:

1. The claim of the United States of America on behalf of the Orinoco Steamship Company;

[Paragraphs Nos. 2 and 3 are omitted as they do not refer to the case of the Orinoco Steamship Company.]

ARTICLE 1

With respect to the first of these claims, that of the Orinoco Steamship Company, the United States of Venezuela has upheld the immutability of the arbitral decision of umpire Barge, rendered in this case, alleging that said decision does not suffer from any of the causes which by universal jurisprudence give rise to its nullity, but rather that it is of an unappealable character, since the *compromis* of arbitration can not be considered as void, nor has there been an excessive exercise of jurisdiction, nor can the corruption of the judges be alleged, nor an essential error in the judgment; while on the other hand, the United States of America, citing practical cases, among them the case of the revision, with the consent of the United States of America, of the arbitral awards rendered by the American-Venezuelan mixed commission created by the Convention of April 25, 1866, and basing itself on the circumstances of the case, considering the principles of international law and of universal jurisprudence, has upheld not only the admissibility but the necessity of the revision of said award; in consequence of this situation, William I. Buchanan and Doctor Francisco González Guinán, in the spirit that has marked their conferences, have agreed to submit this case to the elevated criterion of the arbitral tribunal created by this protocol, in the following form:

The arbitral tribunal shall first decide whether the decision of umpire Barge, in this case, in view of all the circumstances and under the principles of international law, is not void, and whether it must be considered so conclusive as to preclude a reexamination of the case on its merits. If the arbitral tribunal decides that said decision must be considered final, the case will be considered by the United States of America as closed; but on the other hand, if the arbitral tribunal decides that said decision of umpire Barge should not be considered as final, said arbitral tribunal shall then hear, examine and determine the case and render its decision on the merits.

[Articles 2 and 3 are omitted, as they do not refer to the case of the Orinoco Steamship Company.]

ARTICLE 4

The United States of America and the United States of Venezuela having, at the Second Peace Conference held at The Hague in 1907, accepted and recognized the Permanent Court of The Hague, it is agreed that the cases mentioned in Articles 1, 2 and 3 of this protocol, that is to say, the case of the Orinoco Steamship Company, that of the Orinoco Corporation and of its predecessors in interest and that of the United States and Venezuela Company, shall be submitted to the jurisdiction of an arbitral tribunal composed of three arbitrators chosen from the above-mentioned Permanent Court of The Hague.

No member of said Court who is a citizen of the United States of America or of the United States of Venezuela shall form part of said arbitral tribunal, and no member of said Court can appear as counsel for either nation before said tribunal.

This arbitral tribunal shall sit at The Hague.

ARTICLE 5

The said arbitral tribunal shall, in each case submitted to it, determine, decide and make its award, in accordance with justice and equity. Its decisions in each case shall be accepted and upheld by the United States of America and the United States of Venezuela as final and conclusive.

ARTICLE 6

In the presentation of the cases to the arbitral tribunal both parties may use the French, English or Spanish language.

ARTICLE 7

Within eight months from the date of this protocol, each of the parties shall present to the other and to each of the members of the arbitral tribunal, two printed copies of its case, with the documents and evidence on which it relies, together with the testimony of its respective witnesses.

Within an additional term of four months, either of the parties may in like manner present a counter-case with documents and additional evidence and depositions, in answer to the case, documents, evidence and depositions of the other party.

Within sixty days from the expiration of the time designated for the filing of the counter-cases, each Government may, through its representative, make its arguments before the arbitral tribunal, either orally or in writing, and each shall deliver to the other copies of any arguments thus made in writing, and each party shall have a right to reply in writing, provided such reply be submitted within the sixty days last named.

ARTICLE 8

All public records and documents under the control or at the disposal of either Government or in its possession, relating to the matters in litigation shall be accessible to the other, and, upon request, certified copies of them shall be furnished.   The documents which each party produces in evidence shall be authenticated by the respective Minister for Foreign Affairs.

ARTICLE 9

All pecuniary awards that the arbitral tribunal may make in said cases shall be in gold coin of the United States of America, or in its equivalent in Venezuelan money, and the arbitral tribunal shall fix the time of payment, after consultation with the representatives of the two countries.

ARTICLE 10

It is agreed that within six months from the date of this protocol, the Government of the United States of America and that of the United States of Venezuela shall communicate to each other, and to the Bureau of the Permanent Court at The Hague, the name of the arbitrator they select from among the members of the Permanent Court of Arbitration.

Within sixty days thereafter the arbitrators shall meet at The Hague and proceed to the choice of the third arbitrator in accordance with the provisions of Article 45 of The Hague Convention for the peaceful settlement of international disputes, referred to herein.

Within the same time each of the two Governments shall deposit with the said Bureau the sum of fifteen thousand francs on account of the expenses of the arbitration provided for herein, and from time to time thereafter they shall in like manner deposit such further sums as may be necessary to defray said expenses.

The arbitral tribunal shall meet at The Hague twelve months from the date of this protocol to begin its deliberations and to hear the arguments submitted to it. Within sixty days after the hearings are closed its decisions shall be rendered.

ARTICLE 11

Except as provided in this protocol the arbitral procedure shall conform to the provisions of the Convention for the peaceful settlement of international disputes, signed at The Hague on October 18, 1907, to which both parties are signatory, and especially to the provisions of Chapter III thereof.

ARTICLE 12

It is hereby understood and agreed that nothing herein contained shall preclude the United States of Venezuela, during the period of five months from the date of this protocol, from reaching an amicable adjustment with either or both of the claimant companies referred to in Articles 2 and 3 herein,[1] provided that in each case wherein a settlement may be reached, the respective company shall first have obtained the consent of the Government of the United States of America.

The undersigned, William I. Buchanan and Francisco González Guinán, in the capacity which each holds, thus consider their conferences with respect to the differences between the United States of America and the United States of Venezuela as closed, and sign two copies of this protocol of the same tenor and to one effect, in both the English and Spanish languages, at Carácas, on the thirteenth day of February one thousand nine hundred and nine.

WILLIAM I. BUCHANAN [SEAL]

F. GONZÁLEZ GUINÁN   [SEAL]

---

[1]Articles 2 and 3 not printed, as they have no bearing on the Orinoco Steamship Company Case.

ADDITIONAL DOCUMENTS

Opinion of Mr. Bainbridge, in the original Orinoco Steamship Company Case before the United States and Venezuelan Claims Commission of 1903.[1]

Inasmuch as, by reason of a disagreement between the commissioners, this claim is to be submitted to the umpire, to whom in such case the protocol exclusively confides its decision, the commissioner on the part of the United States limits himself to the consideration of certain questions which have been raised by the respondent Government, affecting the competency of the commission to determine this very important claim.

It may be presumed that in framing the convention establishing the commission, the high contracting parties had clearly in view the scope of the jurisdiction to be conferred upon it and deliberately chose, in order to define that scope, the words most appropriate to that end.

Article 1 of the protocol defines the jurisdiction of the commission in the following terms:

> All claims owned by citizens of the United States of America against the Republic of Venezuela which have not been settled by diplomatic agreement or by arbitration between the two Governments, and which shall have been presented to the commission hereinafter named by the Department of State of the United States or its legation at Carácas, shall be examined and decided by a mixed commission, which shall sit at Carácas, and which shall consist of two members, one of whom is to be appointed by the President of the United States and the other by the President of Venezuela. It is agreed that an umpire may be named by the Queen of the Netherlands.[2]

The protocol was signed at Washington on behalf of the respective Governments on the 17th of February, 1903. In view of the explicit language of the article quoted above, it would seem too clear for argument that the contracting parties contemplated and agreed to the submission to this tribunal of all claims, not theretofore settled by diplomatic agreement or by arbitration, which were *on that date* owned by citizens of the United States against the Republic of Venezuela.

The Orinoco Steamship Company is a corporation organized and existing under and by virtue of the laws of the State of New Jersey. It is the successor in interest, by deed of assignment dated April 1st,

---

[1] *United States and Venezuela Arbitration at The Hague, Appendix to the Case of the United States,* vol. i, p. 654.
[2] *Ante,* p. 74.

1902, of the Orinoco Shipping and Trading Company, Limited, a company limited by shares, organized under the English companies acts of 1862 to 1893, and duly registered in the office of the register of joint stock companies, London, England, on the 14th day of July, 1898. Among other of the assets transferred by the said deed of assignment were "all franchises, concessions, grants made in favor of the Orinoco Shipping and Trading Company, Limited, by the Republic of Venezuela, particularly the concession granted by the Government of Venezuela for navigation by steamer from Ciudad Bolívar to Maracaibo, made originally by the national Executive with Manuel Antonio Sanchez, and approved by Congress on the 8th day of June, 1894," and "all claims and demands existing in favor of the Orinoco Shipping and Trading Company, Limited, against the Republic of Venezuela." The claims and demands referred to constitute in the main the claim here presented on behalf of the Orinoco Steamship Company.

The learned counsel for Venezuela contends that:

> At the time when the acts occurred which are the basis of the claim, the Orinoco Steamship Company did not exist and could not have had any rights before coming into existence, and in order that it might be protected to-day by the United States of America it would be necessary, in accordance with the stipulations of the protocol, that the damages, in the event of being a fact, should have been suffered by an American citizen, not that they should have been suffered by a third party of different nationality and later transferred to an American citizen; such a proceeding is completely opposed to equity and to the spirit of the protocol.

In the case of Abbiatti vs. Venezuela before the United States and Venezuelan Claims Commission of 1890, the question arose whether the claimant, not having been a citizen of the United States at the time of the occurrences complained of, had a standing in court; and it was *held* that under the treaty claimants must have been citizens of the United States "at least when the claims arose." This was declared to be the "settled doctrine." Mr. Commissioner Little in his opinion says:

> As observed elsewhere, the infliction of a wrong upon a State's own citizen is an injury to it, and in securing redress it acts in discharge of its own obligations and, in a sense, in its own interest. This is the key—*subject, of course, to treaty terms*—for the determination of such jurisdictional questions: Was the plaintiff State injured? It was not, when the person wronged was at the time a citizen of another State. Naturalization transfers allegiance, but not existing State obligations.

It is to be observed that in attempting to lay down a rule applicable to the case, the commission is careful to make the significant reservation that the rule enunciated is "subject of course to treaty terms." It does not deny the competency of the high contracting parties to provide for the exercise of a wider jurisdiction by appropriate terms in a treaty. And that is precisely what has been done here. The unequivocal terms employed in the present protocol were manifestly chosen to confer jurisdiction of all claims *owned* (on February 17, 1903) by the citizens of the United States against the Republic of Venezuela, presented to the commission by the Department of State of the United States or its legation at Carácas. Under these treaty terms, the key to such a jurisdictional question as that under consideration is the *ownership* of the claim by a citizen of the United States of America on the date the protocol was signed.

The present claim, together with other assets of the Orinoco Shipping and Trading Company, Limited, was acquired by valid deed of assignment by the Orinoco Steamship Company, a citizen of the United States, on April 1st, 1902, long prior to the signing of the protocol, and is therefore clearly within the jurisdiction of this commission.

Pursuant to the requirement of the convention, the commissioners and the umpire, before assuming the functions of their office took a solemn oath carefully to examine and impartially decide according to justice and the provisions of the convention all claims submitted to them. Undoubtedly the first question to be determined in relation to each claim presented is whether or not it comes within the terms of the treaty. If it does, the jurisdiction of the commission attaches.

> Jurisdiction is the power to hear and determine a cause; it is *coram judice* whenever a case is presented which brings this power into action. United States *vs.* Arredondo, 6 Pet., 691.

Thenceforward the commission is directed by the protocol and is bound by its oath carefully to examine and impartially to decide in conformity with the principles of justice and the rules of equity all questions arising in the claim, and its decision is declared to be final and conclusive.

The jurisdiction exercised by this commission is derived from a solemn compact between independent nations. It supersedes all other jurisdictions in respect of all matters properly within its scope. It can not be limited or defeated by any prior agreement of the parties litigant to refer their contentions to the local tribunals. Local jurisdiction is displaced by international arbitration; private agreement is superseded by public law or treaty.

As to every claim fairly within the treaty terms, therefore, the functions of this commission, under its fundamental law and under its oath, are not fulfilled until to its careful examination there is added an impartial decision upon its merits. It can not deny the benefit of its jurisdiction to any claimant in whose behalf the high contracting parties have provided this international tribunal. Jurisdiction assumed, some *decision*, some final and conclusive action in the exercise of its judicial power is incumbent upon the commission. Mr. Commissioner Gore in the case of the *Betsy*, before the United States and British Commission of 1794, well said:

> To refrain from acting when our duty calls us to act, is as wrong as to act where we have no authority. We owe it to the respective Governments to refuse a decision in cases not submitted to us; we are under equal obligation to decide on those cases that are within the submission. 3 Moore, *Int. Arb.*, 2290.

Finally, the protocol imposes upon this tribunal the duty of deciding all claims "upon a basis of absolute equity, without regard to objections of a technical nature, or of the provisions of local legislation." Clearly the high contracting parties had in view the substance and not the shadow of justice. They sought to make the remedies to be afforded by the commission dependent not upon the niceties of legal refinement, but upon the very right of the case. The vital question in this, as in every other claim before this tribunal, is whether and to what extent citizens of the United States of America have suffered loss or injury; and whether and to what extent the Government of Venezuela is responsible therefor.

———

Opinion of Mr. Grisanti, in the original Orinoco Steamship Company Case before the United States and Venezuelan Claims Commission of 1903.[1]

The Orinoco Steamship Company, Limited, demands payment of the Government of Venezuela for four claims, as follows:

———

[1] *United States and Venezuela Arbitration at the Hague, Appendix to the Case of the United States,* vol. i, p. 670.

Attention is called to the fact that the amounts claimed (U. S. money) as here given differ from the amounts given in the arbitral award. This discrepancy is probably due to errors in calculation, the amounts in bolivars being identical in all cases.

1st.   For $1,209,701.05 which sum the claimant company reckons as due for damages and losses caused by the Executive decree of October 5, 1900, said decree having, as the company affirms, annulled its contract-concession celebrated on May 26, 1894.   The company deems as a reasonable value of the contract $82,432.78 per annum.

2nd.   For $147,638.79 at which the claimant company estimates the damages and losses sustained during the last revolution, including services rendered to the Government of the Republic.

3rd.   For 100,000 bolivars, or $19,219.19 overdue on account of the transaction celebrated on May 10, 1900.

4th.   For $25,000 for counsel fees and expenses incurred in carrying out said claims.

The forementioned claims are held by the Orinoco Steamship Company, a corporation of American citizenship, organized and existing under and pursuant to the provision of an act of the legislature of the State of New Jersey as assignee and successor of the Orinoco Shipping and Trading Company Limited, of English nationality, organized in conformity with the respective laws of Great Britain.

And in fact, it has always been the Orinoco Shipping and Trading Company Limited which has dealt and contracted with the Government of Venezuela, as evidenced by the documents and papers relating thereto.   In case the forementioned claims be considered just and correct, the rights from which they arise were originally invested in the juridical character (*persona juridica*) of the Orinoco Shipping and Trading Company Limited; and its claims are for the first time presented to this mixed commission by and on behalf of the Orinoco Steamship Company, as its assignee and successor, in virtue of an assignment and transfer which appears in Exhibit No. 3 annexed to the memorial in pages 51 to 59 of the same, and in the reference to which assignment we shall presently make some remarks.

Before stating an opinion in regard to the grounds of said claims, the Venezuelan commissioner holds that this commission has no jurisdiction to entertain them.   Said objection was made by the honorable agent for Venezuela prior to discussing the claims in themselves, and as the Venezuelan commissioner considers such objection perfectly well founded he adheres to it and will furthermore state the powerful reasons on which he considers said objection to be founded.

It is a principle of international law, universally admitted and practiced, that for collecting a claim protection can only be tendered by the Government of the nation belonging to the claimant who originally acquired the right to claim, or in other words that an international claim must be held by the person who has retained his own citizenship since said claim arose up to the date of its final settlement, and that only the government of such person's country is entitled to demand payment for the same, acting on behalf of the claimant. Furthermore, the original owner of the claims we are analyzing was the Orinoco Shipping and Trading Company Limited—an English company; and that which demands their payment is the Orinoco Steamship Company Limited—an American company; and as claims do not change nationality for the mere fact of their future owners having a different citizenship, it is as clear as daylight that this Venezuelan-American Mixed Commission has no jurisdiction for entertaining said claims. The doctrine which I hold has also been sustained by important decisions awarded by international arbitrators.

Albino Abbiatti applied to the Venezuelan-American Mixed Commission of 1890, claiming to be paid several amounts which in his opinion the Government of Venezuela owed him. The acts alleged as the grounds for the claims took place in 1863 and 1864, at which time Abbiatti was an Italian subject, and it appears that subsequently, in 1866, he became a United States citizen. The commission disallowed the claim, declaring its want of jurisdiction to entertain said claim for the following reasons:

> Has the claimant then, not having been a citizen of the United States at the time of the occurrences complained of, a standing here? The question is a jurisdictional one. The treaty provides: "All claims on the part of corporations, companies or individuals, citizens of the United States, upon the Government of Venezuela . . . shall be submitted to a new commission, etc." Citizens when? In claims like this they must have been citizens at least when the claims arose. Such is the settled doctrine. The plaintiff State is not a claim agent. As observed elsewhere, the infliction of a wrong upon a state's own citizen is an injury to it, and in securing redress it acts in discharge of its own obligation and, in a sense, in its own interest. This is the key—subject, of course, to treaty terms—for the determination of such jurisdictional questions: Was the plaintiff State injured? It was not, where the person wronged was at the time a citizen of another state, although afterwards becoming its own citizen. The injury there was to the other state. Naturalization transfers allegiance, but not existing state obligations. Abbiatti could not impose upon the United States, by becoming its citizen, Italy's existing duty toward him. This is not a case of uncompleted wrong at the time of citizenship, or of one continuous in its nature.
>
> The commission has no jurisdiction of the claim for want of required citizenship, and it is therefore dismissed. (*United States*

and Venezuelan Claims Committee. Claim of Albina Abbiatti
vs. The Republic of Venezuela, No. 34, p. 84.)

In the case mentioned Abbiatti had always owned the claim; but as
he was an Italian subject when the damage occurred, the commission
declared it had no jurisdiction to entertain said claim, notwithstanding that at the time of applying to the commission he had become a
citizen of the United States.

Article 1 of the protocol signed at Washington on February 17 of
the current year says, textually, as follows:

> *All claims owned by citizens of the United States of America
> against the Republic of Venezuela which have not been settled by
> diplomatic agreement or by arbitration between the two Govern-
> ments, and which shall have been presented to the commission
> hereinafter named by the Department of State* of the United States
> or its legation at Carácas, shall be examined and decided by a
> mixed commission, etc.

Owned when? we beg to ask, in our turn, as in the above-inserted
decision. Owned *ab initio,* that is to say, owned since the moment
when the right arose up to the moment of applying with it to this
mixed commission. The verb "to own" means *to possess,* and as
used in the protocol signifies *"being the original proprietor";* therefore
it will not suffice that the claim be possessed by a citizen of the United
States at the time the protocol was signed; the jurisdiction of this
commission requires that the right should have risen in the citizen of
the United States and that said citizen shall never have failed to be
the owner of such a right. Thus and thus only could the Government of the United States protect the claimant company; thus, and on
such conditions alone, would this commission have jurisdiction to
entertain said claims.

If the clause, "All claims owned by citizens of the United States
of America," etc., were considered doubtful, and consequently should
require interpretation, it ought undoubtedly to be given in accordance
with the forementioned universal principle—the basis of this statement—and not in opposition to it. Derogation of a principle of law
in a judicial document has to be most clearly expressed; otherwise, the
principle prevails, and the protocol must be interpreted accordingly.

> While in some of the earlier cases the decisions as to what con-
> stituted citizenship within the meaning of the convention were
> exceptional, it was uniformly held that such citizenship was nec-
> essary when the claim was presented as well as when it arose.

Numerous claims were dismissed on the ground that the claimant was not a citizen when the claim arose. The assignment of a claim to an American citizen was held not to give the commission jurisdiction.

An American woman who was married in July 1861 to a British subject in Mexico was held not to be competent to appear before the commission as a claimant in respect of damage done by the Mexican authorities in November 1861 to the estate of her former husband, though her second husband had in 1866 become a citizen of the United States by naturalization. On the other hand, where the nationality of the owner of a claim, originally American or Mexican, had for any cause changed, it was held that the claim could not be entertained. Thus, where the ancestor, who was the original owner, had died, it was held that the heir could not appear as a claimant unless his nationality was the same as that of his ancestor. The person who had the "right to the award" must, it was further held, be considered as the "real claimant" by the commission, and, whoever he might be, must "prove himself to be a citizen" of the government "by which the claim was presented." (Moore, *International Arbitrations,* vol. 2, p. 1353.)

In the memorial (No. 4) it is affirmed that 99 per cent of the total capital stock of the Orinoco Shipping and Trading Company, Limited, was owned by citizens of the United States of America, but this circumstance, even if it were proved, does not deprive said company of its British nationality, on account of its being organized, according to the referred-to memorial, under the English companies acts of 1862 to 1893 and duly registered in the office of the register of joint stock companies, London, on the 14th of July, 1898. The fact is that limited companies owe their existence to the law in conformity to which they have been organized, and consequently their nationality can be no other than that of said law. The conversion of said company, which is English, into the present claimant company, which is North American, can have no retroactive effect in giving this tribunal jurisdiction for entertaining claims which were originally owned by the first-mentioned company, as that would be to overthrow or infringe fundamental principles.

Naturalization not retroactive. Without discussing here the theory about the retroactive effect of naturalization for certain purposes, I believe it can be safely denied in the odious matter of injuries and damages. A government may resent an indignity or injustice done to one of its subjects, but it would be absurd to open an asylum to all who have, or believe they have, received some injury or damage at the hands of any existing government, to come and be naturalized for the effect of obtaining redress for all their grievances.   (Moore, work cited, vol. 3, p. 2483.)

The three quotations inserted hold and sanction the principle that, in order that the claimant might allege his rights before a mixed claims commission organized by the government of his country and that of the owing nation, it is necessary that the claim should always have belonged to him and that he should never have changed his nationality. And this principle demands that this commission should declare its want of jurisdiction, whether the two companies be considered as different juridical characters (*personas juridicas*) and that the claimant is a successor of the other, or whether they be considered as one and the same, having changed nationality.

I now beg to refer to another matter—to the analysis of the judicial value of the deed of assignment.

In the first number of the exhibit "The Orinoco Shipping and Trading Company" appears selling to "The Orinoco Steamship Company," which is the claimant, the nine steamships named, respectively, *Bolívar, Manzanares, Delta, Apure, Guanare, Socorro, Masparro, Heroe,* and *Morganito.* These steamships were destined for coastal service or *cabotaje,* some to navigate the rivers of Guanare, Cojedes, Portuguesa, and Masparro from Ciudad Bolívar up to the mouth of the Uribante River (Olachea contract of June 27, 1891), and others to navigate between said Ciudad Bolívar and Maracaibo, and to call at the ports of La Vela, Puerto Cabello, La Guaira, Guanta, Puerto Sucre, and Carúpano (Grell contract, June 8, 1894); this line was granted the option of calling at the ports of Curaçao and Trinidad while the Government fixes definitely the transshipment ports for merchandise from abroad, and while they are making the necessary installations.   (Article 12.)

However, the coastal trade can only be carried on by ships of Venezuelan nationality, in conformity with Article 1, Law XVIII, of the Financial Code, which provides that—

> Internal maritime trade of *cabotaje* or coastal service is that which is carried on between the open ports of Venezuela and other parts of the continent, as well as between the banks of its lakes and rivers, *in national ships,* whether laden with foreign merchandise for which duties have been paid, or with native goods or productions. (*Comercio de Cabotaje,* p. 87.)

—

And if we further add that the steamers were obliged to navigate under the Venezuelan flag (Article 2 of the Grell contract), as in fact they did, the result is that said steamers are Venezuelan by nationalization, wherefore the assignment of said steamers alleged by the Orinoco Shipping and Trading Company, Limited, to the claimant company is absolutely void and of no value, owing to the fact that the stipulations provided by the Venezuelan law (here inserted) for the validity of such an assignment were not fulfilled.

Law XXXIII (Financial Code) on the Nationalization of Ships

ARTICLE 1ST. The following alone will be held as national ships:
1ST. . . . .
2ND. . . . .
3RD. . . . .
4TH. Those nationalized according to law.
ARTICLE 6TH. . . . .
The guaranty given for the proper use of the flag must be to the satisfaction of the custom-house. The property deed must be registered at the office of the place where the purchase takes place, and if such purchase is made in a foreign country a certificate of the same, signed by the Venezuelan consul and by the harbor master, shall have to be sent, drawn on duly stamped paper.
ARTICLE 12TH. When a ship, or part thereof, is to be assigned, a new patent must be obtained by the assignee, after having presented the new title deeds to the custom-house and receiving therefrom the former patent, stating measurements and tonnage therein contained, in order to obtain said patent.

The assignment of the forementioned steamer is, to the Government of Venezuela, void and of no value or effect whatever.

In Exhibit No. 2 "The Orinoco Shipping and Trading Company Limited" appears as assigning several immovable properties situated in the *Territorio Federal Amazonas* of the Republic of Venezuela to the claimant company, and the title deed has not been registered at the sub-register office of said Territory, as prescribed by the Venezuelan Civil Code in the following provisions:

ARTICLE 1883. Registration must be made at the proper office of the department, district, or canton where the immovable property which has caused the deed is situated.
ARTICLE 1888. In addition to those deeds which, by special decree, are subject to the formalities of registration, the following must be registered:

1st. All acts between living beings, due to gratuitous, onerous, or assignment title deeds of immovable or other property or rights susceptible of hypothecation.

In Exhibit No. 3, the Orinoco Shipping and Trading Company Limited appears assigning the Olachea contract of June 27, 1891, and the Grell contract of June 8, 1894. In assigning the first of these the approval of the Venezuelan Government was not obtained, either before or after, thereby infringing the following provision:

This contract may be transferred wholly or in part to any other person or corporation *upon previous approval of the National Government.*

In assigning the second the stipulation provided in Article 13 of giving previous notice to the Government was infringed. If any argument could be made in regard to the annulment of the latter assignment, there is no doubt whatever in regard to the annulment of the former, whereas in the foregoing provision the Government reserves the right of being a contracting party in the assignment, and consequently said assignment, without the previous consent of the Government, is devoid of judicial efficacy.

The assignment of those contracts is, therefore, of no value for the Government of Venezuela.

The fifth paragraph of the same refers to the assignment which "The Orinoco Shipping and Trading Company Limited" intended to make to "The Orinoco Steamship Company" of all claims and demands existing in favor of the party of the first part, either against the Republic of Venezuela or against any individuals, firms, or corporations. This transfer of credits, which are not specified nor even declared, and which has not been notified to the Government, is absolutely irregular, and lacks judicial efficacy with regard to all parties except the assignor and assignee companies, in conformity with Article 1496 of the Civil Code, which provides as follows:

An assignee has no rights against third parties until after the assignment has been notified to the debtor, or when said debtor has accepted said assignment.

The foregoing article is, in substance, identical to Article 1690 of the French Civil Code, and in reference thereto Baudry-Lacantinerie says that—

Les formalités prescrites par l'art. 1690 ont pour but de donner à la cession une certaine publicité, et c'est pour ce motif que la loi fait de leur accomplissement une condition de l'investiture du cessionnaire à l'égard des tiers. Les tiers sont réputés ignorer la cession, tant qu'elle n'a pas été rendue publique par la signification du transport ou par l'acceptation authentique du cédé; voilà pourquoi elle ne leur devient opposable qu'à date de l'accomplissement de l'une ou de l'autre de ces formalités. (*Précis du Droit Civil.* Tome troisième, p. 394, numero 624.)

Quelles sont les personnes que l'article 1690 désigne sous le nom de tiers, et à l'égard desquelles le cessionnaire n'est saisi que par la notification ou l'acceptation authentique du transport? Ce sont tous ceux qui n'ont pas été parties à la cession et qui ont un intérêt légitime à la connaître et à la contester, c'est-à-dire: 1. le cédé; 2. tous ceux qui ont acquis du chef du cédant des droits sur la créance cédée; 3. les créanciers chirographaires du cédant.

1. *Le débiteur cédé.*—Jusqu'à ce que le transport lui ait été notifé ou qu'il l'ait accepté, le débiteur cédé a le droit de considérer le cédant comme étant le véritable titulaire de la créance. La loi nous fournit trois applications de ce principe. (Baudry-Lacantinerie, work and vol. quoted, p. 395. See also Laurent, *"Principes de Droit Civil,"* vol. 24, p. 472.)[1]

I do not expect that the foregoing arguments will be contested, having recourse to the following provision of the protocol:

The commissioners, or in case of their disagreement, the umpire, shall decide all claims upon a basis of absolute equity, without regaid to objections of a technical nature or of the provisions of local legislation.

---

[1]TRANSLATION: The formalities prescribed by Article 1690 are for the purpose of giving a certain publicity to the assignment, and it is for this reason that the law makes their fulfilment a condition to the investiture of the assignee as regards third parties. Third parties are supposed to know nothing of the assignment so long as it has not been made public by the notice of conveyance or by the authentic acceptance of the debtor whose debt is assigned; this is why it can be alleged against them only after the fulfilment of one or the other of these formalities.

Who are these persons designated by Article 1690 by the name of *third parties* and with respect to whom the debtor whose debt is assigned is only responsible upon notice or the authentic acceptance of the conveyance? They are all those who have not been parties to the assignment and who have a legitimate interest in knowing about it and opposing it; that is to say: (1) the debtor whose debt is assigned; (2) all those who have acquired through the assignor rights to the claim assigned; (3) the creditors holding debts against the assignor in writing.

The debtor whose debt is assigned. Until he has been notified of the conveyance or has accepted it the debtor whose debt is assigned has a right to consider the assignor as being the true owner of the claim. The law furnishes us three applications of this principle.

If such a broad sense were given to this clause in regard to all cases as to bar any consideration for Venezuelan law, it would not only be absurd, but monstrous. Such, however, can not be the case. How could a claim possibly be disallowed on the grounds of the claimant being a Venezuelan citizen without invoking the Venezuelan law, which bestows upon him said citizenship? How in certain commissions could Venezuela have been exempted from having to pay for damages caused by revolutionists if the judicial principles which establish such exemption had not been pleaded? Said clause provides that no regard shall be had to objections of a technical nature, or of the provisions of local legislation, whenever such objections impair principles of equity, but when, in compliance with said principles, to disregard those objections would be to overthrow equity itself, and equity has to be the basis for all the decisions of this commission. In the present instance conformity exists between the one and the others. And in merely adding that the majority of the cited provisions are in reference to contracts, it is understood that their basis has been equity and not rigorous law. On the other hand, if this commission were to decide upon paying an award for a claim which the claimant company is not properly entitled to, through not being the owner thereof, it would be a contention against the precepts of equity.

In view, therefore, of the substantial irregularities of the deed of assignment and transfer, the Government of Venezuela has a perfect right to consider "The Orinoco Shipping and Trading Company Limited" as the sole owner of the claims analyzed, and whereas said company is of British nationality, this Venezuelan-American Mixed Commission has no jurisdiction to entertain the claim mentioned.

The incompetency of this commission has been perfectly established. I shall now analyze the claims themselves. The Orinoco Steamship Company holds that the Executive decree promulgated on October 5, 1900, allowing the free navigation of the Macareo and Pedernales channels, annulled its contract concession of May 26, 1894, which contract the claimant company considered as granting it the exclusive right to carry on foreign trade through said channels. The company states as follows:

Since said 16th day of December, A. D. 1901, notwithstanding the binding contract and agreement between the United States of Venezuela and the Orinoco Shipping and Trading Company Limited, and your memorialist as assignee of said company, to the contrary, said United States of Venezuela, acting through its duly constituted officials, has authorized and permitted said Macareo and Pedernales channels of the river Orinoco to be used and navigated by vessels engaged in foreign trade other than those belonging to your memorialists or its predecessors in interest, and has thus enabled said vessels to do much of the business and to obtain the profits therefrom which, under the terms of said contract-concession of June 8, 1894, and the extension thereof of May 10, 1900, should have been done and obtained solely by your memorialist or its said predecessor in interest, and much of said business will continue to be done and the profits derivable therefrom will continue to be claimed and absorbed by persons and companies other than your memorialists, to its great detriment and damage. (Memorial, pp. 28 and 29.)

Let us state the facts such as they appear in the respective documents.

On July 1, 1893, the Executive power issued a decree in order to prevent contraband which was carried on in the several *bocos* (mouths) of the river Orinoco, to wit:

ARTICLE 1. Vessels engaged in foreign trade with Ciudad Bolívar shall be allowed to proceed only by way of the Boca Grande of the river Orinoco; the Macareo and Pedernales channels being reserved for the coastal service, navigation by the other channels of the said river being absolutely prohibited.

On May 26, 1894, the Executive power entered into a contract with Mr. Ellis Grell, represented by his attorney, Mr. Manuel Antonio Sanchez, wherein the contractor undertook to establish and maintain in force navigation by steamers between Ciudad Bolívar and Maracaibo in such manner that at least one journey per fortnight be made, touching at the ports of La Vela, Puerto Cabello, La Guaira, Guanta, Puerto Sucre, and Carúpano. Article 12 of this contract stipulates as follows:

While the Government fixes definitely the transshipment ports for merchandise from abroad, and while they are making the necessary installations, the steamers of this line shall be allowed to call at the ports of Curaçao and Trinidad and any one of the steamers leaving Trinidad may also navigate by the channels of the Macareo and Pedernales of the river Orinoco in conformity with the formalities which by special resolution may be imposed by the minister of finance in order to prevent contraband and to safeguard fiscal interests; to all which conditions the contractor agrees beforehand.

On October 5, 1900, the national Executive promulgated the following decree:

ARTICLE I. The decree of the 1st of July, 1893, which prohibited the free navigation of the Macareo, Pedernales, and other navigable waterways of the river Orinoco is abolished.

Did the 1894 contract grant the Orinoco Shipping and Trading Company Limited an exclusive privilege to engage in foreign trade with the use of said Macareo and Pedernales channels? The perusal of Article 12 above referred to will suffice without the least hesitation to answer this question negatively. The fact is that the company's contract-concession is for establishing the inward trade between the ports of the Republic, from Ciudad Bolívar to Maracaibo, and the company's steamers were only granted a temporary permission to call at Curaçao and Trinidad, *while the Government fixed definitely the transshipment ports for merchandise from abroad, and while they were making the necessary installations.*
It would be necessary to overthrow the most rudimental laws of logic in order to hold that a line of steamers established to engage in coastal trade or *cabotaje*, navigating on the Macareo and Pedernales channels, which are free for internal navigation, should have the privilege of engaging in foreign trade through the mentioned channels. The decree of July 1 of 1893, promulgated with a view to prevent contraband in the channels of the river Orinoco and on the coast of Paria, is not a stipulation of the contract concession of the Orinoco Shipping and Trading Company Limited, and therefore the Government of Venezuela could willingly abolish it, as, in fact, it did abolish it on October 5, 1900. Neither is it reasonable to suppose that the Government at the time of celebrating the referred-to contract alienated its legislative powers, which, owing to their nature, are inalienable. On the other hand, a privilege, being an exception to common law, must be most clearly established; otherwise it does not exist. Whenever interpretation is required by a contract it should be given in the sense of freedom, or, in other words, exclusive of privileges.
Furthermore, it is to be remarked that the Orinoco Shipping and Trading Company Limited has never complied with either of the two contracts (the Olachea and the Grell contracts) particularly as refers to the latter, as evidenced by a document issued by said company, a copy of which I shall present, and as evidenced also by the memorial (No. 15).
On May 10, 1900, a settlement was agreed to by the minister of internal affairs and the Orinoco Shipping and Trading Company Limited, in virtue whereof the Government undertook to pay the

company 200,000 bolivars for all its claims prior to said convention, having forthwith paid said company 100,000 bolivars, and at the same time a resolution was issued by said minister granting the Grell contract (May 26, 1894) a further extension of six years.

The company holds that the decree of October 5, 1900, annulled its contract and also annihilated the above-mentioned prorogation, and that, as the concession of said prorogation had been the principal basis of the settlement for the company to reduce its credits to 200,000 bolivars, said credits now arise in their original amount.

It has already been proved that the referred-to Executive decree of October 5, 1900, did not annul the Grell contract, and this will suffice to evidence the unreasonableness of such contention. It must, furthermore, be added that the settlement and the concession for prorogation are not the same act, nor do they appear in the same document; therefore it can not be contended that the one is a condition or stipulation of the other. Besides, the concession for prorogation accounts for itself without having to relate it to the settlement; whereas in the resolution relative to said prorogation the company on its part renounced its right to the subsidy of 4,000 bolivars which the Government had assigned to it in Article 7 of the contract.

The Venezuelan Commissioner considers that this commission has no jurisdiction to entertain the claim deduced by the Orinoco Steamship Company, and that, in case it had, said claims ought to be disallowed.

Award of Charles Augustinus Henri Barge, umpire in the original Orinoco Steamship Company Case before the United States and Venezuelan Claims Commission of 1903.—Carácas, February 22, 1904.[1]

A difference of opinion arising between the commissioners of the United States of North America and the United States of Venezuela, this case was duly referred to the umpire.

The umpire having fully taken into consideration the protocol, and also the documents, evidence and arguments, and also likewise all other communications made by the two parties, and having impartially and carefully examined the same, has arrived at the decision embodied in the present award.

---

[1] *United States and Venezuela Arbitration at the Hague, Appendix to the Case of the United States,* vol. i, p. 686. See *ante,* p. 243, note 1, 2nd paragraph.

Whereas the Orinoco Steamship Company demands payment of the Government of Venezuela for four claims, as follows:

1st. $1,209,700.05 as due for damages and losses caused by the Executive decree of October 5th, 1900, having [by] this decree annulled a contract concession celebrated on May 26th, 1894;

2nd. 100,000 bolivars, or $19,219.19 overdue on account of a transaction celebrated on May 10th, 1900;

3rd. $149,698.71 for damages and losses sustained during the last revolution, including services rendered to the Government of the Republic;

4th. $25,000 for counsel fees and expenses incurred in carrying out said claims;

And whereas the jurisdiction of this commission in this case is questioned, this question has in the first place to be investigated and decided;

Now, whereas the protocol (on which alone is based the right and the duty of this commission to examine and decide "upon a basis of absolute equity, without regard to the objections of a technical nature or of the provisions of local legislation"), gives this commission the right and imposes the duty to examine and decide "all claims owned by citizens of the United States of America against the Republic of Venezuela which have not been settled by diplomatic agreement or by arbitration between the two Governments, and which shall have been presented to the commission by the Department of State of the United States or its legation at Carácas," it has to be examined in how far this claim of the Orinoco Steamship Company possesses the essential qualities to fall under the jurisdiction of this commission;

Now, whereas this claim against the Venezuelan Government was presented to this commission by the Department of State of the United States of America through its agent;

And whereas it has not been settled by diplomatic agreement or arbitration;

And whereas the Orinoco Steamship Company, as evidence shows, is a corporation created and existing under and by virtue of the laws of the State of New Jersey, in the United States of America,

There only remains to be examined if the company owns the claim brought before the commission;

Now, whereas almost all the items of this claim—at all events those originated before the 1st of April, 1902—are claims that "the Orinoco Shipping and Trading Company, Limited," an English corporation, pretended to have against the Government of Venezuela;

And whereas on the said April 1st, 1902, the said English company, for the sum of $1,000,000, sold and transferred to the American company, the complainant [*claimant*], "all its claims and demands either against the Government of Venezuela or against individuals, firms and corporations," these claims from that date *prima facie* show themselves as owned by the claimant;

Whereas further on it is true that according to the admitted and practiced rule of international law, in perfect accordance with the general principles of justice and perfect equity, claims do not change nationality by the fact that their consecutive owners have a different citizenship, because a state is not a claim agent, but only, as the infliction of a wrong upon its citizens is an injury to the state itself, it may secure redress for the injury done to its citizens, and not for the injury done to the citizens of another state,

Still, this rule may be overseen or even purposely set aside by a treaty,

And as the protocol does not speak—as is generally done in such cases—of all claims *of* citizens, etc. (which would rightly be interpreted "all claims for *injuries done to citizens,* etc."), but uses the usual expression "all claims *owned* by citizens," it must be held that this uncommon expression was not used without a determined reason;

And whereas the evidence shows that the Department of State of the United States of America knew about these claims and took great interest in them (as is shown by the diplomatic correspondence about these claims presented to the commission in behalf of claimant), and that the plenipotentiary of Venezuela a short time before the signing of the protocol, in his character of United States envoy extraordinary and minister plenipotentiary, had corresponded with his Government about these claims, and that even as late as December 20th, 1902, and January 27th, 1903, one of the directors of the claimant company, J. van Vechten Olcott, wrote about these claims, in view of the event of arbitration, to the President of the United States of America, it is not to be accepted that the high contracting parties, anxious, as is shown by the history of the protocol, to set aside and to settle all questions about claims not yet settled between them, should have forgotten these very important claims when the protocol was redacted and signed,

And, therefore, it may safely be understood that it was the aim of the high contracting parties that claims [such] as these, being at the moment of the signing of the protocol *owned* by citizens of the United States of North America, should fall under the jurisdiction of the commission instituted to investigate and decide upon the claims the high contracting parties wished to see settled,

And, therefore, the jurisdiction of this commission to investigate and decide claims *owned* by citizens of the United States of North America at the moment of the signing of the protocol has to be recognized, without prejudice, naturally, of the judicial power of the commission, and its duty to decide upon a basis of absolute equity when judging about the rights the transfer of the ownership might give to claimant against third parties,

For all which reasons the claims presented to this commission on behalf of the American company, "the Orinoco Steamship Company," have to be investigated by this commission and a decision has to be given as to the right of the claimant company to claim what it does claim, and as to the duty of the Venezuelan Government to grant to the claimant company what this company claims for.

Now, as the claimant company in the first place claims for $1,209,-700.05 as due for damages and losses caused by the Executive decree of October 5th, 1900, this decree having annulled a contract concession celebrated on May 26th, 1894, this contract-concession and this decree have to be examined, and it has to be investigated:

Whether this decree annulled the contract-concession;

Whether this annulment, when stated, caused damages and losses;

Whether the Government of Venezuela is liable for those damages and losses;

And, in the case of this liability being proved, whether it is to claimant the Government of Venezuela is liable for these damages and losses.

And whereas the mentioned contract concession (a contract with Mr. Ellis Grell, transferred to the Venezuelan citizen, Manuel A. Sanchez, and approved by Congress of the United States of Venezuela on the 26th of May, 1894) reads as follows:

> The Congress of the United States of Venezuela, in view of the contract celebrated in this city on the 17th of January of the present year between the minister of the interior of the United States of Venezuela, duly authorized by the chief of the national executive, on the one part, and on the other, Edgar Peter Ganteaume, attorney for Ellis Grell, transferred to the citizen Manuel A. Sanchez, and the additional article of the same contract dated 10th of May instant, the tenor of which is as follows:
>
> Dr. Feliciano Acevedo, minister of the interior of the United States of Venezuela, duly authorized by the chief of the national executive, on the one part, and Edgar Peter Ganteaume, attorney

ior Ellis Grell, and in the latter's name and representation, who is resident in Port of Spain, on the other part, and with the affirmative vote of the government council have celebrated a contract set out in the following articles:

ARTICLE 1. Ellis Grell undertakes to establish and maintain in force; navigation by steamers between Ciudad Bolívar and Maracaibo within the term of six months, reckoned from the date of this contract, in such manner that at least one journey per fortnight be made, touching at the ports of La Vela, Puerto Cabello, La Guaira, Guanta, Puerto Sucre, and Carúpano, with power to extend the line to any duly established port of the Republic.

ARTICLE 2. The steamers shall navigate under the Venezuelan flag.

ARTICLE 3. The contractor undertakes to transport free of charge the packages of mail which may be placed on board the steamers by the authorities and merchants through the ordinary post-offices, the steamers thereby acquiring the character of mail steamers, and as such exonerated from all national dues.

ARTICLE 4. The contractor shall draw up a tariff of passages and freights by agreement with the Government.

ARTICLE 5. The company shall receive on board each steamer a Government employee with the character of fiscal postmaster, nominated by the minister of finance, with the object of looking after the proper treatment of the mails and other fiscal interests.

The company shall also transport public employees when in commission of the Government at half the price of the tariff, provided always that they produce an order signed by the minister of finance or by one of the presidents of the States. Military men on service and troops shall be carried for the fourth part of the tariff rates. The company undertakes also to carry gratis materials of war, and at half freights all other goods which may be shipped for account and by order of the National Government.

ARTICLE 6. The General Government undertakes to concede to no other line of steamers any of the benefits, concessions and exemptions contained in the present contract as compensation for the services which the company undertakes to render as well to national interests as those of private individuals.

ARTICLE 7. The Government of Venezuela will pay to the contractor a monthly subsidy of four thousand bolivars (4,000) so long as the conditions of the present contract are duly carried out.

ARTICLE 8. The National Government undertakes to exonerate from payment of import duties all machinery, tools, and accessories which may be imported for the use of the steamers and all other materials necessary for their repair, and also undertakes to permit the steamers to supply themselves with coal and provisions, etc., in the ports of Curaçao and Trinidad.

ARTICLE 9. The company shall have the right to cut from the national forests wood for the construction of steamers or necessary buildings and for fuel for the steamers of the line.

ARTICLE 10. The officers and crews of the steamers, as also the woodcutters and all other employees of the company, shall be exempt from military service, except in cases of international war.

ARTICLE 11. The steamers of the company shall enjoy in all the ports of the Republic the same freedom and preferences by law established as are enjoyed by the steamers of lines established with fixed itinerary.

ARTICLE 12. While the Government fixes definitely the transshipment ports for merchandise from abroad, and while they are making the necessary installations, the steamers of this line shall be allowed to call at the ports of Curaçao and Trinidad, and any one of the steamers leaving Trinidad may also navigate by the channels of the Macareo and Pedernales of the river Orinoco in conformity with the formalities which by special resolution may be imposed by the minister of finance, in order to prevent contraband and to safeguard fiscal interests; to all which conditions the contractor agrees beforehand.

ARTICLE 13. This contract shall remain in force for fifteen years, reckoned from the date of its approbation, and may be transferred by the contractor to another person or corporation upon previous notice to the Government.

ARTICLE 14. Disputes and controversies which may arise with regard to the interpretation or execution of this contract shall be resolved by the tribunals of the Republic in accordance with the laws of the nation, and shall not in any case be considered as a motive for international reclamations.

Two copies of this contract of the same tenor and effect were made in Carácas the seventeenth day of January, 1894.

(Signed) FELICIANO ACEVEDO
(Signed) EDWARD P. GANTEAUME

ADDITIONAL ARTICLE. Between the minister of the interior of the United States of Venezuela and citizen Manuel A. Sanchez, concessionnary of Mr. Ellis Grell, have agreed to modify the eighth article of the contract made on the 17th day of January of the present year for the coastal navigation between Ciudad Bolívar and Maracaibo on the following terms:

ARTICLE 8. The Government undertakes to exonerate from payment of import duties the machinery, tools and articles which may be imported for the steamers, and all other materials destined for the repairs of the steamers; while the Government fixes the points of transport and coaling ports. the contractor is hereby permitted to take coal and provisions for the crew in the ports of Curaçao and Trinidad.

Carácas, 10th May, 1894.

Signed: JOSÉ R. NUÑEZ
Signed: M. A. SANCHEZ

And whereas the mentioned executive decree of October 5th, 1900, reads as follows:

DECREE

ARTICLE 1. The decree of the 1st of July, 1893, which prohibited the free navigation of the Macareo, Pedernales, and other navigable waterways of the river Orinoco is abolished.

ARTICLE 2. The minister of interior relations is charged with the execution of the present decree.

Now whereas in regard to the said contract it has to be remarked that in almost all arguments, documents, memorials, etc., presented on behalf of the claimant it is designated as a concession for the exclusive navigation of the Orinoco River by the Macareo or Pedernales channels, whilst in claimant's memorial it is even said that "the chief and indeed only value of this contract was the exclusive right to navigate the Macareo and Pedernales channels of the river Orinoco, and that. according to claimant, this concession of exclusive right was annulled by the aforesaid decree, and that it is for the losses that were the consequence of the annullment of this concession of exclusive right that damages were claimed.

The main question to be examined is whether the Venezuelan Government by said contract gave a concession for the exclusive navigation of said channels of said river, and whether this concession of exclusive navigation was annulled by said degree.

And whereas the contract shows that Ellis Grell (the original contractor) pledged himself to establish and maintain in force navigation by steamers between Ciudad Bolívar and Maracaibo, touching at the ports of La Vela, Puerto Cabello, La Guaira, Guanta, Puerto Sucre, and Carúpano, and to fulfil the conditions mentioned in Articles 2, 3, 4 and 5, whilst the Venezuelan Government promised to grant to Grell the benefits, concessions and exemptions outlined in Articles 7, 8, 9, 11 and 12, and in Article 6 pledges itself to concede to no other line of steamers any of the benefits, concessions, and exemptions contained in the contract, the main object of the contract appears to be the assurance of a regular communication by steamer from Ciudad Bolívar to Maracaibo, touching the duly established Venezuelan ports between those two cities. For the navigation between these duly established ports no concession or permission was wanted, but in compensation to Grell's engagement to establish and maintain in force for fifteen years (Article 13) this communication, the Venezuelan Government ac-

corded him some privileges which it undertook to grant to no other line
of steamers.

Whereas therefore this contract in the whole does not show itself
as a concession for exclusive navigation of any waters, but as a contract to establish a regular communication by steamers between the
duly established principal ports of the Republic, the pretended concession for exclusive navigation of the Macareo and Pedernales channels
must be sought in Article 12 of the contract, the only article in the
whole contract in which mention of them is made.

And whereas this article in the English version in claimant's memorial, reads as follows:

> *While* the Government fixes definitely the transshipment ports
> for merchandise from abroad, and *while* they are making the
> necessary installations, the steamers of this line shall be allowed
> to call at the ports of Curaçao and Trinidad, and any one of the
> steamers leaving Trinidad may also navigate by the channels of
> the Macareo and Pedernales of the river Orinoco, etc.,

it seems clear that the permission in this article—by which article
the permission of navigating the said channels was not given to the
claimant in general terms and for all its ships indiscriminately but
only for the ships leaving Trinidad—would only have force for the
time till the Government would have fixed definitely the transshipment
ports, *which it might do at any moment* and *till* the necessary installations were made, and not for the whole term of the contract, which
according to Article 13 would remain in force for fifteen years;

And whereas this seems clear when reading the English version of
the contract as cited in the memorial, it seems, if possible, still more
evident when reading the original Spanish text of this article, of which
the above-mentioned English version gives not a quite correct translation, from which Spanish text reading as follows [*sic.*]:

> ART. 12. Mientras el Gobierno fija definitivamente los puertos
> de trasbordo para las mercancías procedentes del extranjero, y
> mientras hace las necesarias instalaciones, las será permitido á los
> buques de la línea, tocar en los puertos de Curaçao y de Trinidad,
> pudiendo además navegar el vapor que salga de la última Antilla
> por los caños de Macareo y de Pedernales del Río Orinoco, previas
> las formalidades que por resolución especial dictará el Ministerio
> de Hacienda para impedir el contrabando en resguardo de los inte-
> reses fiscales; y á las cuales de antemano se somete el contratista.

(The words *"el vapor que salga de la última Antilla,"* being given in the English version as *"any one* of the steamers leaving Trinidad.")

It can not be misunderstood that this *"el vapor"* is the steamer that had called at Trinidad according to the permission given for the special term that the "while" (*mientras*) would last; wherefore it seems impossible that the permission given in Article 12 only for the time there would exist circumstances which the other party might change at any moment could ever have been the main object, and, as is stated in the memorial, "the chief and, indeed, only value" of a contract that was first made for the term of fifteen years, which term later on even was prolonged to twenty-one years.

And whereas therefore it can not be seen how this contract concession for establishing and maintaining in force for *fifteen years* a communication between the duly established ports of Venezuela can be called a concession for the exclusive navigation of the said channels, when the permission to navigate these channels was only annexed to the permission to call at Trinidad and would end with that permission, whilst the obligation to navigate between the ports of Venezuela from Ciudad Bolívar to Maracaibo would last;

And whereas on the contrary all the stipulations of the contract are quite clear when holding in view the purpose why it was given, viz, to establish and maintain in force a communication between the duly established ports of Venezuela, *i. e.,* a regular coastal service by steamers,

Because to have and retain the character and the rights of ships bound to coastal service it was necessary that the ships should navigate under Venezuelan flag (Article 2), that they should have a special permission to call at Curaçao and Trinidad to supply themselves with coal and provisions (Article 8), which stipulation otherwise would seem without meaning and quite absurd, as no ship wants a special permission of any government to call at the ports of another government, and to call at the same foreign ports for transshipment while the government fixed definitely the transshipment ports (Article 12). In the same way *during that time* a special permission was necessary for *the* ship leaving Trinidad to hold and retain this one right of ships bound to coastal service—to navigate by the channels of Macareo and Pedernales—which special permission would not be necessitated any longer as soon as the Government could fix definitely the Venezuelan ports that would serve as transshipment ports, because then they would *per se* enjoy the right of all ships bound to coastal service, viz, to navigate through the mentioned channels.

What is called a concession for exclusive navigation of the mentioned channels is shown to be nothing but a permission to navigate these channels as long as certain circumstances should exist.

And whereas therefore the contract approved by decree of the 8th of June, 1894, never was a concession for the exclusive navigation of said channels of the Orinoco; and whereas the decree which reopened these channels for free navigation could not annul a contract that never existed;

All damages claimed for the annulling of a concession for exclusive navigation of the Macareo and Pedernales channels of the Orinoco River must be disallowed.

Now whereas it might be asked if the permission to navigate by those channels, given to the steamer that on its coastal trip left Trinidad, was not one of the "benefits, concessions and exemptions" that the Government in Article 6 promised not to concede to any other line of steamers;

It has not to be forgotten that in Article 12 the Government did not give a general permission to navigate by the said channels, but that this whole article is a temporal measure taken to save the character and the rights of coastal service, to the service which was the object of this contract, during the time the Government had not definitely fixed the transshipment ports; and that it was not an elementary part of the concession, that would last as long as the concession itself, but a mere arrangement by which temporarily the right of vessels bound to coastal service, viz., to navigate said channels, would be safeguarded for the vessel that left Trinidad as long as the vessels of this service would be obliged to call at this island, and that therefore the benefit and the exemption granted by this article was not *to navigate by said channels,* but *to hold the character and right of a coastal vessel, notwithstanding having called at the foreign port of Trinidad;* and as this privilege was not affected by the reopening of the channels to free navigation, and the Government by aforesaid decree did not give any benefit, concession and exemption granted to this concession to any other line of steamers, a claim for damages for the reopening of the channels based on Article 6 can not be allowed. It may be that the concessionary and his successors thought that during all the twenty-one years of this concession the Government of Venezuela would not definitely fix the transshipment ports, nor reopen the channels to free navigation, and [on] those thoughts based a hope that was not fulfilled and formed a plan that did not succeed; but it would be a strange appliance of absolute equity to make the government that grants a concession liable for the not realized dreams and vanished *"chateaux en Espagne"* of inventors, promoters, solicitors and purchasers of concessions.

But further on—even when it might be admitted that the reopening of the channels to free navigation might furnish a ground to base a claim on (*quod non*)—whilst investigating the right of claimant and the liability of the Venezuelan Government, it has not to be forgotten that, besides the already-mentioned articles, the contract has another article, viz., Article 14, by which the concessionary pledges himself not to submit any dispute or controversies which might arise with regard to the interpretation or execution of this contract to any other tribunal but to the tribunals of the Republic, and in no case to consider these disputes and controversies a motive for international reclamation, which article, as the evidence shows, was repeatedly disregarded and trespassed upon by asking and urging the intervention of the English and United States Governments without ever going for a decision to the tribunals of Venezuela;

And as the unwillingness to comply with this pledged duty is clearly shown by the fact that the English Government called party's attention to this article, and, quoting the article, added the following words, which certainly indicated the only just point of view from which such pledges should be regarded:

> Although the general international rights of His Majesty's Government are in no wise modified by the provisions of this document to which they were not a party, *the fact that the company, have so far as lay in their power, deliberately contracted themselves out of every remedial recourse in case of dispute, except that which is specified in Article 14 of the contract,* is undoubtedly an element to be taken into serious consideration when they subsequently appeal for the intervention of His Majesty's Government;

And whereas the force of this sentence is certainly in no wise weakened by the remark made against it on the side of the concessionary, that "the terms of Article 14 of the contract have absolutely no connection whatever with the matter at issue," because "no *doubt or controversy* has arisen with respect to the *interpretation and execution* of the contract," but that "what has happened is this, that the Venezuelan Government has, by a most dishonest and cunningly devised trick, defrauded the company to the extent of *entirely nullifying* a concession which it had legally acquired at a very heavy cost," whereas, on the contrary, it is quite clear that the only question at issue was whether in Article 12, in connection with Article 6, a concession for exclusive navigation was given or not—*ergo*, a question of doubt and controversy about the interpretation;

And whereas the following words of the English Government addressed to the concessionary may well be considered:

> The company does not appear to have exhausted the legal remedies at their disposal before the ordinary tribunals of the country and it would be contrary to international practice for His Majesty's Government formally to intervene in their behalf through the diplomatic channel unless and until they should be in a position to show that they had exhausted their ordinary remedies with a result that a *prima facie* case of failure or denial of justice remained;

For whereas, if in general this is the only just standpoint from which to view the right to ask and to grant the means of diplomatical intervention and in consequence *casu quo* of arbitration, how much the more where the recourse to the tribunals of the country was formally pledged and the right to ask for intervention solemnly renounced by contract, and where this breach of promise was formally pointed to by the government whose intervention was asked;

Whereas therefore the question imposes itself, whether absolute equity ever would permit that a contract be willingly and purposely trespassed upon by one party in view to force its binding power on the other party;

And whereas it has to be admitted that, even if the trick to change a contract for regular coastal service into a concession for exclusive navigation succeeded (*quod non*), in the face of absolute equity the trick of making the same contract a chain for one party and a screw-press for the other never can have success:

It must be concluded that Article 14 of the contract disables the contracting parties to base a claim on this contract before any other tribunal than that which they have freely and deliberately chosen, and to parties in such a contract must be applied the words of the Hon. Mr. Finley, United States Commissioner in the Claims Commission of 1889: "So they have made their bed and so they must lie in it."

But there is still more to consider.

For whereas it appears that the contract originally passed with Grell was legally transferred to Sanchez and later on to the English company "The Orinoco Shipping and Trading Company Limited," and on the 1st day of April, 1902, was sold by this company to the American company, the claimant;

But whereas Article 13 of the contract says that it might be transferred to another person or corporation *upon previous notice* to the Government, whilst the evidence shows that this notice has not been previously (indeed ever) given; the condition on which the contract might be transferred not being fulfilled, the "Orinoco Shipping and Trading Company Limited" had no right to transfer it, and this transfer of the contract without previous notice must be regarded as null and utterly worthless;

Wherefore, even if the contract might give a ground to the above-examined claim to "The Orinoco Shipping and Trading Company Limited" (once more *quod non*), the claimant company as quite alien to the contract could certainly never base a claim on it.

For all which reasons every claim of the Orinoco Steamship Company against the Republic of the United States of Venezuela for the annulment of a concession for the exclusive navigation of the Macareo and Pedernales channels of the Orinoco has to be disallowed.

As for the claim for 100,000 bolivars, or $19,219.19, overdue on a transaction celebrated on May 10th, 1900, between the Orinoco Shipping and Trading Company Limited and the Venezuelan Government:

Whereas these 100,000 bolivars are those mentioned in letter B, of Article 2 of said contract, reading as follows:

(B) One hundred thousand bolivars (100,000), which shall be paid in accordance with such arrangements as the parties hereto may agree upon on the day stipulated in the decree [of the] 23d of April, ultimo, relative to claims arising from damages caused during the war, or by other case whatever;

And whereas nothing whatever of any arrangement, in accordance with which it was stipulated to pay, appears in the evidence before the commission, it might be asked if, on the day this claim was filed, this indebtedness was proved compellable;

Whereas further on, in which way ever [*sic.*] this question may be decided, the contract has an Article 4, in which the contracting parties pledged themselves to the following: "All doubts and controversies which may arise with respect to the interpretation and the execution of this contract shall be decided by the tribunals of Venezuela and in conformity with the laws of the Republic, without such mode of settlement being considered motive of international claims," whilst it is shown in the diplomatic correspondence brought before the commission on behalf of claimant, that in December, 1902, a formal petition to make it [an] international claim was directed to the Government of the United States of America without the question having been brought before the tribunals of Venezuela, which fact certainly constitutes a flagrant breach of the contract on which the claim was based;

And whereas, in addition to everything that was said about such clauses here above it has to be considered what is the real meaning of such a stipulation;

And whereas when parties agree that doubts, disputes, and controversies shall only be decided by a certain designated third [person], they implicitly agree to recognize that there properly shall be no claim from one party against the other, but for what is due as a result of a decision on any doubts, disputes or controversies by that one designated third [person]; for which reason, in addition to everything that was said already upon this question heretofore, in questions on claims based on a contract wherein such a stipulation is made absolute equity does not allow to recognize such a claim between such parties before the conditions are realized, which in that contract they themselves made conditions *sine qua non* for the existence of a claim;

And whereas further on—even in the case the contract did not contain such a clause, and that the arrangements, in accordance to which it was stipulated to pay were communicated to and proved before this commission—it ought to be considered that if there existed here a recognized and compellable indebtedness, it would be a debt of the Government of Venezuela to the Orinoco Shipping and Trading Company;

For whereas it is true that evidence shows that on the 1st of April, 1902, all the credits of that company were transferred to the claimant company, it is not less true that, as shown by evidence, this transfer was never notified to the Government of Venezuela;

And whereas according to Venezuelan law, in perfect accordance with the principles of justice and equity recognized and proclaimed in the codes of almost all civilized nations, such a transfer gives no right against the debtor when it was not notified to or accepted by that debtor;

And whereas here it can not be objected that according to the protocol no regard has to be taken of provisions of local legislation, because the words "the commissioners or, in case of their disagreement, the umpire shall decide all claims upon a basis of absolute equity, without regard to *objections* of a technical nature, or of the provisions of local legislation," clearly have to be understood in the way that questions of technical nature or the provisions of local legislation should not be taken into regard when there were *objections*

against the rules of absolute equity; for, in case of any other interpretation, the fulfilling of the task of this commission would be an
impossibility, as the question of American citizenship could never be
proved without regard to the local legislation of the United States of
America, and this being prohibited by the protocol, all claims would
have to be disallowed, as the American citizenship of the claimant
would not be proved; and as to technical questions it might then be
maintained (as was done in one of the papers brought before this commission on behalf of a claimant in one of the filed claims) that the
question whether there was a *proof* that claimant had a right to a claim
was a mere technical question;

And whereas, if the provisions of local legislation far from being
objections to the rules of absolute equity are quite in conformity with
those rules, it would seem absolutely in contradiction with this equity
not to apply its rules, because they were recognized and proclaimed by
the local legislation of Venezuela;

And whereas, the transfer of credits from "The Orinoco Shipping
and Trading Company" to "The Orinoco Steamship Company" neither
was notified to, or accepted by the Venezuelan Government, it can not
give a right to a claim on behalf of the last-named company against
the Government of Venezuela:

For all which reasons the claim of the Orinoco Steamship Company,
Limited, against the Government of Venezuela, based on the transaction of May 10th, 1900, has to be disallowed.

In the next place the company claims $147,038.79, at which sum it
estimates the damages and losses sustained during the last revolution,
including services rendered to the Government of Venezuela.

Now, whereas this claim is for damages and losses suffered and for
services rendered from June 1900, whilst the existence of the company only dates from January 31st, 1902, and the transfer of the credits
of "the Orinoco Shipping and Trading Company, Limited," to claimant took place on the 1st of April of this same year, it is clear from
what heretofore was said about the transfer of these credits, that all
items of this claim, based on obligations originated before said April
1st, 1902, and claimed by claimant as indebtedness to the afore-named
company and transferred to claimant on said April 1st, have to be disallowed as the transfer was never notified to or accepted by the Venezuelan Government. As to the items dating after the 1st of April, 1902,
in the first place the claimant claims for detention and hire of the
steamship *Masparro* from May 1st to September 18th, 1902 (141
days), at 100 pesos daily, = 14,100 pesos, and for detention and hire of

the steamship *Socorro* from March 21st to November 5th, 1902 (229 days), 22,900 pesos, together 37,000 pesos, equal to $28,461.53;

And whereas it is proved by evidence that said steamers have been in service of the National Government for the time above stated;

And whereas nothing in the evidence shows any obligation on the part of the owners of the steamers to give this service gratis, even if it were in behalf of the commonwealth;

Whereas therefore a remuneration for that service is due to the owners of these steamers:

The Venezuelan Government owes a remuneration for that service to the owners of the steamers;

And whereas these steamers, by contract of April 1st, 1902, were bought by claimant, and claimant therefore from that day was owner of the steamers:

This remuneration from that date is due to claimant.

And whereas in this case it differs [*sic.*] not that the transfer of the steamers was not notified to the Venezuelan Government, as it was no transfer of a credit, but as the credit was born after the transfer, and as it was not in consequence of a contract between the Government and any particular person or company, but, as evidence shows, because the Government wanted the steamers' service in the interest of its cause against revolutionary forces; and whereas for this forced detention damages are due, those damages may be claimed by him who suffered them, in this case the owners of the steamers;

And whereas the argument of the Venezuelan Government, that it had counter-claims, can in no wise affect this claim, as those counter-claims the Venezuelan Government alludes to, and which it pursues before the tribunals of the country, appear to be claims against "The Orinoco Shipping and Trading Company," and not against claimant;

And whereas it differs not whether claimant, as the Government affirms and as evidence seems clearly to show, if not taking part in the revolution, at all events favored the revolutionary party, because the ships were not taken and confiscated as hostile ships, but were claimed by the Government, evidence shows, because it wanted them for the use of political interest, and after that use were returned to the owners: For all these reasons there is due to claimant from the side of the Venezuelan Government, a remuneration for the service of the steamers *Masparro* and *Socorro*, respectively, from May first to September 18th, 1902 (141 days), and from April 1st to November 5th, 1902 (219 days, together 360 days);

And whereas, according to evidence since 1894 these steamers might be hired by the Government for the price of 400 bolivars, or 100 pesos, daily, this price seems a fair award for the forced detention:

Wherefore for the detention and use of the steamers *Masparro* and *Socorro* the Venezuelan Government owes to claimant 36,000 (thirty-six thousand) pesos, or $27,692.31.

Further on claimant claims $2,520.50 for repairs to the *Masparro* and $2,932.98 for repairs to the *Socorro,* necessitated, as claimant assures, by the ill usage of the vessels whilst in the hands of the Venezuelan Government.

Now whereas evidence only shows that after being returned to claimant the steamers required repairs at this cost, but in no wise that those repairs were necessitated by ill usage on the side of the Government;

And whereas evidence does not show in what state they were received and in what state they were returned by the Government;

And whereas it is not proved that in consequence of this use by the Government they suffered more damages than those that are the consequence of common and lawful use during the time they were used by the Government, for which damages in case of hire the Government would not be responsible;

Where the price for which the steamers might be hired is allowed for the use, whilst no extraordinary damages are proved, equity will not allow to declare the Venezuelan Government liable for these repairs:

Wherefore this item of the claim has to be disallowed.

Evidence in the next place shows that, on May 29 and May 31, 1902, 20 bags of rice, 10 barrels potatoes, 10 barrels onions, 16 tins lard, and two tons coal were delivered to the Venezuelan authorities on their demand on behalf of the Government forces, and for these provisions, as expropriation for public benefit, the Venezuelan Government will have to pay;

And whereas the prices that are claimed, viz., $6 for a bag of rice, $5 for a barrel [of] potatoes, $7 for a barrel [of] onions, $3 for a tin [of] lard, and $10 for a ton [of] coal, when compared with the market prices at Carácas, do not seem unreasonable, the sum of $308 will have to be paid for them.

As for the further $106.60 claimed for provisions and ship stores, whereas there is given no proof of these provisions and stores being taken by or delivered to the Government, they cannot be allowed.

For passages since April 1st, 1902, claimant claims $224.62, and whereas evidence shows that all these passages were given on request of the Government, the claim has to be admitted, and whereas the prices charged are the same that formerly could be charged by the "Orinoco Shipping and Trading Company," these prices seemed equitable;

Wherefore, the Venezuelan Government will have to pay on this item the sum of $224.62.

As to the expenses caused by stoppage of the steamer *Bolívar* at San Felix when Ciudad Bolívar fell in the hands of the revolution—

Whereas this stoppage was necessitated in behalf of the defense of the Government against revolution;

And whereas no unlawful act was done nor any obligatory act was neglected by the Government, this stoppage has to be regarded, as every stoppage of commerce, industry. and communication during war and revolution, as a common calamity that must be commonly suffered and for which government can not be proclaimed liable,

Wherefore, this item of the claim has to be disallowed.

And now as for the claim of $61,336.20 for losses of revenue from June to November, 1902, caused by the blockade of the Orinoco:

Whereas a blockade is the occupation of a belligerent party on land and on sea of all the surroundings of a fortress, a port, a roadstead and even [of] all the coasts *of its enemy*, in order to prevent all communication with the exterior, with the right of *"transient" occupation* until it puts itself into real possession of that port of the hostile territory, the act of forbidding and preventing the entrance of a port or a river on [its] *own territory* in order to secure internal peace and to prevent communication with the place occupied by rebels or a revolutionary party can not properly be named a blockade, and would only be a blockade when the rebels and revolutionists were recognized as a belligerent party;

And whereas in absolute equity things should be judged by what they are and not by what they are called, such a prohibitive measure on [its] own territory can not be compared with blockade of a hostile place, and therefore the same rules can not be adopted;

And whereas the right to open and close, as a sovereign on its own territory, certain harbors, ports and rivers in order to prevent the trespassing of fiscal laws is not and could not be denied to the Venezuelan Government, much less this right can be denied when used in defense not only of some fiscal rights, but in defense of the very existence of the Government;

And whereas the temporary closing of the Orinoco River (the so-called "blockade") in reality was only a prohibition to navigate that river in order to prevent communication with the revolutionists in Ciudad Bolívar and on the shores of the river, this lawful act by itself could never give a right to claims for damages to the ships that used to navigate the river;

But whereas claimant does not found the claim on the closure itself of the Orinoco River, but on the fact that, notwithstanding this prohibition, other ships were allowed to navigate its waters and were dispatched for their trips by the Venezuelan consul at Trinidad, whilst this was refused to claimant's ships, which fact in the brief on behalf of the claimant is called "unlawful discrimination in the affairs of neutrals," it must be considered that whereas the revolutionists were not recognized belligerents there can not properly here be spoken of "neutrals" and "the rights of neutrals," but that

Whereas it here properly was a prohibition to navigate;

And whereas, where anything is prohibited, to him who held and used the right to prohibit can not be denied the right to permit in certain circumstances what as a rule is forbidden,

The Venezuelan Government, which prohibited the navigation of the Orinoco, could allow that navigation when it thought proper, and only evidence of unlawful discrimination, resulting in damages to third [parties], could make this permission a basis for a claim to third parties;

Now, whereas the aim of this prohibitive measure was to crush the rebels and revolutionists, or at least to prevent their being enforced, of course the permission that exempted from the prohibition might always be given where the use of the permission, far from endangering the aim of the prohibition, would tend to that same aim, as, for instance, in the case that the permission were given to strengthen the governmental forces or to provide in [for] the necessities of the loyal part of the population;

And whereas the inculpation of unlawful discrimination ought to be proved;

And whereas, on one side, it not only is not proved by evidence that the ships cleared by the Venezuelan consul during the period in question did not receive the permission to navigate the Orinoco in view of one of the aforesaid aims;

But whereas, on the other side, evidence, as was said before, shows that the Government had sufficient reasons to believe claimant, if not assisting the revolutionists, at least to be friendly and rather partial to them, it can not be recognized as a proof of unlawful discrimination that the Government, holding in view the aim of the prohibition and defending with all lawful measures its own existence, did not give to claimant the permission it thought fit to give to the above-mentioned ships;

And whereas therefore no unlawful act or culpable negligence on the part of the Venezuelan Government is proved that would make the Government liable for the damages claimant pretends to have suffered by the interruption of the navigation of the Orinoco River;

This item of the claim has to be disallowed.

The last item of this claim is for $25,000 for counsel fees and expenses incurred in carrying out the above-examined and decided claims;

But whereas the greater part of the items of the claim had to be disallowed;

And whereas in respect to those that were allowed it is in no way proved by evidence that they were presented [?] to and refused by the Government of the Republic of the United States of Venezuela, and whereas therefore the necessity to incur those fees and further expenses in consequence of an unlawful act or culpable negligence of the Venezuelan Government is not proved, this item has, of course, to be disallowed.

For all which reasons the Venezuelan Government owes to claimant:

	U. S. Gold
For detention and use of the steamers *Masparro* and *Socorro*, 36,000 pesos, or	$27,692.31
For goods delivered for use of the Government	308.00
For passages	224.62
Together total	28,224.93

While all the other items have to be disallowed.

THE SAVARKAR CASE

between

FRANCE *and* GREAT BRITAIN

Decided February 24, 1911

Syllabus

This case arose as the result of the escape of Savarkar, a Hindoo, who was being transported from England to India for trial on a charge of abetment of murder, and who at Marseilles on July 8, 1910, escaped to the shore from the *Morea*, a British merchant vessel, which was carrying him. While being pursued by Indian policemen from the vessel, he was captured by a French police officer, who returned him to the *Morea*, which sailed with the fugitive on board on the following day. Subsequently, France demanded the restitution of the fugitive on the ground that his delivery to the British officers on board the vessel was contrary to the rules of international law, and, upon Great Britain's refusal to comply, the questions of law and fact involved were, by a *compromis* signed October 25, 1910,[1] submitted to the arbitration of a tribunal composed of the following members of the Permanent Court of Arbitration: Auguste M. F. Beernaert of Belgium, Louis Renault of France, Gregors Gram of Norway, A. F. de Savornin Lohman of Holland and the Earl of Desart of England. The sessions began February 14, 1911, and ended February 17, 1911, the decision being rendered February 24, 1911.

The tribunal found that previously to the arrival of the *Morea* at Marseilles arrangements had been made between the British and French police to prevent the escape of the fugitive, and that, although the French officer who arrested him may have been ignorant of his identity, there was no fraud or force used to obtain possession of him and the failure of the French authorities to disavow the arrest and delivery before the ship sailed might naturally have led the British police to believe that the French officer acted in accordance with instructions or that his conduct was approved. The tribunal held that while an irregularity was committed in the arrest of Savarkar and his delivery to the British police, there is no rule of international law which imposes under these circumstances any obligation on the Power which has the custody of the prisoner to restore him because of a mistake made by the foreign agent who delivered him up.

---

[1]*Post*, p. 280.

AWARD OF THE TRIBUNAL

Award of the tribunal of arbitration in the case of Savarkar, between France and Great Britain.—The Hague, February 24, 1911.[1]

Whereas, by an agreement dated October 25th, 1910,[2] the Government of the French Republic and the Government of His Britannic Majesty agreed to submit to arbitration the questions of fact and law raised by the arrest and restoration to the mail steamer *Morea* at Marseilles, on July 8th, 1910, of the British Indian Savarkar, who had escaped from that vessel where he was in custody; and the demand made by the Government of the French Republic for the restitution of Savarkar;

The arbitral tribunal has been called upon to decide the following question:

Should Vinayak Damodar Savarkar, in conformity with the rules of international law, be restored or not be restored by His Britannic Majesty's Government to the Government of the French Republic?

Whereas, for the purpose of carrying out this agreement, the two Governments have respectively appointed as arbitrators:

His Excellency Monsieur Beernaert, Minister of State, member of the Belgian Chamber of Representatives, etc., president;

The Right Honorable, the Earl of Desart, formerly His Britannic Majesty's Procurator General;

Monsieur Louis Renault, professor at the University of Paris, Minister Plenipotentiary, Legal Adviser of the Department of Foreign Affairs;

Monsieur G. Gram, formerly Norwegian Minister of State, Provincial Governor;

His Excellency, the Jonkheer A. F. de Savornin Lohman, Minister of State, member of the Second Chamber of the States-General of the Netherlands.

And, further, the two Governments have respectively appointed as their agents,

The Government of the French Republic:

---

[1] Official report, p. 54. For the French text, see Appendix, p. 516.
[2] *Post*, p. 280.

Monsieur André Weiss, Assistant Legal Adviser of the Department of Foreign Affairs of the French Republic, professor of law at the University of Paris.

The Government of His Britannic Majesty:

Mr. Eyre Crowe, Counselor of Embassy, a senior clerk at the British Foreign Office.

Whereas, in accordance with the provisions of the agreement, cases, counter-cases and replies have been duly exchanged between the parties, and communicated to the arbitrators.

Whereas the tribunal met at The Hague on the 14th February, 1911.

Whereas, with regard to the facts which gave rise to the difference of opinion between the two Governments, it is established that, by a letter dated June 29th, 1910, the Commissioner of the Metropolitan Police in London informed the *Directeur de la Sûreté générale* at Paris, that the British-Indian Vinayak Damodar Savarkar was about to be sent to India, in order to be prosecuted for abetment of murder, etc., and that he would be on board the vessel *Morea* touching at Marseilles on the 7th or 8th July.

Whereas, in consequence of the receipt of this letter, the Ministry of the Interior informed the Prefect of the *Bouches-du-Rhône*, by a telegram dated the 4th July, 1910, that the British police was sending Savarkar to India on board the steamship *Morea*. This telegram states that some *"revolutionnaires hindous"* [Hindu revolutionaries] then on the continent might take advantage of this to further the escape of this foreigner, and the Prefect was requested to take the measures necessary to guard against any attempt of that kind.

Whereas the *Directeur de la Sûreté générale* replied by a letter dated the 9th July, 1910, to the letter of the Commissioner of the Metropolitan Police, stating that he had given the necessary instructions for the purpose of guarding against the occurrence of any incident during the presence at Marseilles of the said Vinayak Damodar Savarkar, on board the steamship *Morea*.

Whereas, on the 7th July, the *Morea* arrived at Marseilles. The following morning, between 6 and 7 o'clock, Savarkar, having succeeded in effecting his escape, swam ashore and began to run; he was arrested by a brigadier of the French maritime *gendarmerie* and taken back to the vessel. Three persons who had come ashore from the vessel assisted the brigadier in taking the fugitive back. On the 9th July, the *Morea* left Marseilles with Savarkar on board.

Whereas, from the statements made by the French brigadier to the police of Marseilles, it appears:

That he saw the fugitive, who was almost naked, get out of a porthole of the steamer, throw himself into the sea and swim to the quay;

That at the same moment some persons from the ship, who were shouting and gesticulating, rushed over the bridge leading to the shore, in order to pursue him;

That a number of people on the quay commenced to shout *"Arrêtez-le"*;

That the brigadier at once went in pursuit of the fugitive and, coming up to him after running about five hundred metres, arrested him.

Whereas the brigadier declares that he was altogether unaware of the identity of the person with whom he was dealing, that he only thought that the man who was escaping was one of the crew, who had possibly committed an offense on board the vessel.

Whereas, with regard to the assistance afforded him by one of the crew and two Indian policemen, it appears from the explanations given on this point, that these men came up after the arrest of Savarkar, and that their intervention was only auxiliary to the action of the brigadier. The brigadier had seized Savarkar by one arm for the purpose of taking him back to the ship, and the prisoner went peaceably with him. The brigadier, assisted by the above-mentioned persons, did not relax his hold till he reached the half deck of the vessel.

The brigadier said that he did not know English.

From what has been stated, it would appear that the incident did not occupy more than a few minutes.

Whereas it is alleged that the brigadier who effected the arrest was not ignorant of the presence of Savarkar on board the vessel, and that his orders, like those of all the French police [agents] and *gendarmes*, were to prevent any Hindu from coming on board who had not got a ticket.

Whereas these circumstances show that the persons on board in charge of Savarkar might well have believed that they could count on the assistance of the French police [*agents*].

Whereas it is established that a *commissaire* of the French police came on board the vessel shortly after her arrival at the port, and in accordance with the orders of the Prefect, placed himself at the disposal of the commander in respect of the watch to be kept;

That, in consequence, this *commissaire* was put into communication with the British police officer who, with other police officers, was in charge of the prisoner;

That the Prefect of Marseilles, as appears from a telegram dated the 13th July, 1910, addressed to the Minister of the Interior, stated that he had acted in this matter in accordance with instructions given by the *Sûreté générale* to make the necessary arrangements to prevent the escape of Savarkar.

Whereas, having regard to what has been stated, it is manifest that the case is not one of recourse to fraud or force in order to obtain possession of a person who had taken refuge in foreign territory, and that there was not, in the circumstances of the arrest and delivery of Savarkar to the British authorities and of his removal to India, anything in the nature of a violation of the sovereignty of France, and that all those who took part in the matter certainly acted in good faith and had no thought of doing anything unlawful.

Whereas, in the circumstances cited above, the conduct of the brigadier not having been disclaimed by his chiefs before the morning of the 9th July, that is to say, before the *Morea* left Marseilles, the British police might naturally have believed that the brigadier had acted in accordance with his instructions, or that his conduct had been approved.

Whereas, while admitting that an irregularity was committed by the arrest of Savarkar and by his being handed over to the British police, there is no rule of international law imposing, in circumstances such as those which have been set out above, any obligation on the Power which has in its custody a prisoner, to restore him because of a mistake committed by the foreign agent who delivered him up to that Power.

For these reasons: The arbitral tribunal decides that the Government of His Britannic Majesty is not required to restore the said Vinayak Damodar Savarkar to the Government of the French Republic.

Done at The Hague, at the Permanent Court of Arbitration, February 24th, 1911.

> *The President:* A. BEERNAERT
>
> *The Secretary General:* MICHIELS VAN VERDUYNEN

AGREEMENT FOR ARBITRATION

Agreement between the United Kingdom and France referring to arbitration the case of Vinayak Damodar Savarkar.—Signed at London, October 25, 1910.[1]

The Government of His Britannic Majesty and the Government of the French Republic, having agreed, by an exchange of notes dated the 4th and 5th October, 1910, to submit to arbitration, on the one hand, the questions of fact and law raised by the arrest and restoration to the mail steamer *Morea*, at Marseilles, on the 8th July, 1910, of the Indian, Vinayak Damodar Savarkar, who had escaped from that vessel, on board of which he was in custody; and on the other hand, the demand of the Government of the Republic with a view to the restitution to them of Savarkar;

The undersigned, duly authorized to this effect, have arrived at the following agreement:

ARTICLE 1

An arbitral tribunal, composed as hereinafter stated, shall undertake to decide the following question:

Should Vinayak Damodar Savarkar, in conformity with the rules of international law, be restored or not be restored by His Britannic Majesty's Government to the Government of the French Republic?

ARTICLE 2

The arbitral tribunal shall be composed of five arbitrators chosen from the members of the Permanent Court at The Hague. The two contracting Parties shall settle the composition of the tribunal. Each of them may choose as arbitrator one of their nationals.

---

[1] Official report, p. 7. For the French text, see Appendix, p. 519.

ARTICLE 3

On the 6th December, 1910, each of the high contracting Parties shall forward to the Bureau of the Permanent Court fifteen copies of its case, with duly certified copies of all documents which it proposes to put in. The Bureau will undertake without delay to forward them to the arbitrators and to each party: that is to say, two copies for each arbitrator and three copies for each party. Two copies will remain in the archives of the Bureau.

On the 17th January, 1911, the high contracting Parties will deposit in the same manner their counter-cases, with documents in support of them.

These counter-cases may necessitate replies, which must be presented within a period of fifteen days after the delivery of the counter-cases.

The periods fixed by the present agreement for the delivery of the cases, counter-cases, and replies may be extended by mutual agreement between the high contracting Parties.

ARTICLE 4

The tribunal shall meet at The Hague the 14th February, 1911.

Each party shall be represented by an agent, who shall serve as intermediary between it and the tribunal.

The arbitral tribunal may, if it thinks necessary, call upon one or other of the agents to furnish it with oral or written explanations, to which the agent of the other party shall have the right to reply.

It shall also have the right to order the attendance of witnesses.

ARTICLE 5

The parties may employ the French or English language. The members of the tribunal may, at their own choice, make use of the French or English language. The decisions of the tribunal shall be drawn up in the two languages.

ARTICLE 6

The award of the tribunal shall be given as soon as possible, and, in any case, within thirty days following the date of its meeting at The Hague or that of the delivery of the written explanations which may have been furnished at its request. This period may, however, be prolonged at the request of the tribunal if the two high contracting Parties agree.

Done in duplicate at London, October 25, 1910.

(L. S.)   E. GREY

(L. S.)   PAUL CAMBON

ADDITIONAL DOCUMENTS

Notes of October 25, 1910, of their Excellencies the Right Honorable Sir Edward Grey, Principal Secretary of State of His Britannic Majesty, and Mr. Paul Cambon, French Ambassador to London, supplementary to the Agreement for Arbitration of the same date.[1]

October 25, 1910.

YOUR EXCELLENCY: With reference to the agreement which we have concluded this day, for the purpose of submitting to arbitration certain matters in connection with the arrest and restitution of Vinayak Demodar Savarkar, at Marseilles, in July last, I have the honour to place on record the understanding that any points which may arise in the course of this arbitration which are not covered by the terms of the Agreement above referred to shall be determined by the provisions of the International Convention for the pacific settlement of International disputes signed at The Hague, on the 18th of October, 1907.

It is further understood that each party shall bear its own expenses and an equal share of the expenses of the Tribunal.

It have the honour, etc.

Signed: E. GREY

October 25, 1910.

MR. MINISTER: I have the honor to acknowledge your Excellency's note of this day relative to the agreement which we signed today for the purpose of submitting to arbitration certain matters concerning the arrest and restitution of Vinayak Damodar Savarkar, at Marseilles, July 8 last. I am authorized to confirm, with your Excellency, the understanding that all questions which may arise in the course of this arbitration, which are not covered by the terms of the agreement above referred to, shall be determined by the provisions

---

[1]Official report, pp. 9, 10. For the original text of the French note, see Appendix, p. 520.

of the Convention for the pacific settlement of international disputes signed at The Hague, October 18, 1907.

It is further understood that each party shall bear its own expenses and an equal part of the expenses of the tribunal.

Kindly accept, etc.

Signed : PAUL CAMBON

THE CANEVARO CASE

between

ITALY *and* PERU

Decided May 3, 1912

Syllabus

The claim of the Italian Government against Peru on behalf of Napoléon, Carlos and Rafael Canevaro originated as follows: It appears that on December 12, 1880, N. de Pierola, at the time dictator of Peru, issued a decree by virtue of which there were created, under date of December 23, 1880, pay checks (*bons de paiement, libramientos*) to the order of the firm of José Canevaro & Sons for the sum of 77,000 pounds sterling, payable at different periods; that these pay checks were not paid as they fell due; that in 1885, the father having died in 1883, the firm was reorganized with José Francisco, César and Rafael Canevaro, Peruvian citizens, as copartners, forming a Peruvian corporation; that in 1885 the Peruvian Government paid 35,000 pounds sterling on account, leaving due and outstanding to the firm the sum of 43,140 pounds sterling; that the firm remained in existence until it was dissolved in 1900 by the death of José Francisco Canevaro; and that the pay checks (*bons de paiement*) finally passed into possession of Napoléon and Carlos Canevaro, Italian subjects, and Rafael Canevaro, whose claim to Italian nationality was contested by Peru.

Differences arose between the claimants and Peru as to whether the pay checks should be paid in coin, or in one per cent bonds in accordance with the provisions of the Peruvian domestic debt law of June 12, 1889, as to the amount which the claimants had a right to demand, and as to the nationality of Rafael Canevaro. Peru contended that the debt was contracted by Peru with a Peruvian corporation and that therefore its settlement was entirely a domestic matter, but, finally, on April 25, 1910, as the result of diplomatic negotiations with Italy, a *compromis*[1] was signed, submitting the questions in dispute to a tribunal of the Permanent Court of Arbitration at The Hague composed of the following members: Louis Renault of France, Guido Fusinato of Italy and Manuel Alvarez Calderón of Peru. The sessions began April 20, 1912, and ended April 22, 1912, the decision being rendered May 3, 1912.

The tribunal first decided the status of Rafael Canevaro. It considered him as having a twofold nationality: first, by birth in Peru, and, secondly, as the child of an Italian father; but, because of his having acted as a Peruvian citizen, it held that the Government of

---

[1]*Post*, p. 294.

Peru had a right to consider him as such and to deny his status as an Italian claimant. His claim was therefore dismissed.

The tribunal found that the firm of Canevaro & Sons, reorganized in 1885 upon the death of the father, was composed of Peruvian citizens, so that it was Peruvian by domicile as well as by the nationality of its members, and that the firm remained in existence until it was dissolved in 1900 by the death of José Francisco Canevaro. The debt was therefore domestic in its origin and subject to the laws of Peru, especially to the act of 1889, which Canevaro & Sons had recognized by attempting to avail itself of some of the provisions thereof. Napoléon and Carlos Canevaro urged their Italian nationality as a reason why the act of 1889 should not affect their claim, but the tribunal held that their title was derivative and could be neither better nor worse than the right originally acquired by the firm through which they directly or indirectly claimed. Hence, instead of the sum of 43,143 pounds sterling, they were only entitled to the bonds issued in 1889 to meet this indebtedness. The decision as to the amount of the claim was settled by the tribunal's holding that it should be paid in bonds. As to the question of interest, the tribunal decided that the bonds or pay checks (*libramientos*) of 1880 bore four per cent until due, and after this period until payment the legal rate of six per cent. But, as the act of 1889 provided one per cent interest, the tribunal allowed four per cent upon the original outstanding indebtedness until the date of maturity, six per cent after that date until the first of January, 1889, and one per cent upon the bonds issued in 1889 until July 31, 1912, at which date the bonds were to be paid. The tribunal, however, provided further that payment might be delayed until the first of January, 1913, but that from the first of August, 1912, to the first of January, 1913, the debt should bear six per cent interest.

AWARD OF THE TRIBUNAL

Award of the arbitral tribunal charged with passing on the difference between Italy and Peru in regard to the claim of the Canevaro brothers.—The Hague, May 3, 1912.[1]

Whereas, by a *compromis* dated April 25, 1910,[2] the Italian and Peruvian Governments agreed to submit the following questions to arbitration:

Should the Peruvian Government pay in cash, or in accordance with the provisions of the Peruvian law of June 12, 1889, on the domestic debt, the bills of exchange (*cambiali, libramientos*) now in

---

[1]Translation. For the original French text, see Appendix, p. 522.
[2]*Post*, p. 294.

the possession of the brothers Napoléon, Carlos, and Rafael Canevaro, which were drawn by the Peruvian Government to the order of the firm of José Canevaro & Sons for the sum of 43,140 pounds sterling, plus the legal interest on the said amount?

Have the Canevaro brothers a right to demand the total amount claimed?

Has Count Rafael Canevaro a right to be considered as an Italian claimant?

Whereas, pursuant to this *compromis* the following persons were designated as arbitrators:

Mr. Louis Renault, Minister Plenipotentiary, member of the Institute, professor in the Faculty of Law at the University of Paris and at the School of Political Sciences, Counselor for the Ministry of Foreign Affairs, president;

Mr. Guido Fusinato, Doctor of Law, former Minister of Public Instruction, honorary professor of international law at the University of Turin, Deputy, Counselor of State;

His Excellency Mr. Manuel Alvarez Calderón, Doctor of Law, professor at the University of Lima, Envoy Extraordinary and Minister Plenipotentiary of Peru at Brussels and Berne.

Whereas, the two Governments have respectively appointed as counsel:

The Royal Italian Government: Professor Vittorio Scialoja, Senator of the Kingdom of Italy and as assistant counsel, Count Giuseppe Francesco Canevaro, Doctor of Law;

The Peruvian Government: Mr. Manuel Maria Mesones, Doctor of Law, attorney.

Whereas, in accordance with the terms of the *compromis*, the memorials and counter-memorials have been duly exchanged between the parties and communicated to the arbitrators;

Whereas, the tribunal met at The Hague on April 20, 1912.

Whereas, in order to simplify the following statement it is deemed best to pass first upon the third question contained in the *compromis*, that is, the question of the status of Rafael Canevaro;

Whereas, according to Peruvian legislation (Article 34 of the Constitution), Rafael Canevaro is a Peruvian by birth because born on Peruvian territory,

And, whereas, on the other hand, according to Italian legislation (Article 4 of the Civil Code) he is of Italian nationality because born of an Italian father;

Whereas, as a matter of fact, Rafael Canevaro has on several occasions acted as a Peruvian citizen, both by running as a candidate for the Senate, where none are admitted except Peruvian citizens and where he succeeded in defending his election, and, particularly, by accepting the office of Consul General for the Netherlands, after having secured the authorization of both the Peruvian Government and the Peruvian Congress;

Whereas, under these circumstances, whatever Rafael Canevaro's status as a national may be in Italy, the Government of Peru has a right to consider him a Peruvian citizen and to deny his status as an Italian claimant.

Whereas, the debt which gave rise to the claim submitted to the tribunal is the result of a decree of the dictator Pierola of December 12, 1880, by virtue of which there were issued, under date of the 23d of the same month, pay checks (*bons de paiement, libramientos*) to the order of the firm of José Canevaro & Sons for the sum of 77,000 pounds sterling, payable at different periods;

Whereas, these "checks" were not paid at the periods set, which periods were coincident with the period of enemy occupation;

Whereas, a payment on account of 35,000 pounds sterling was made at London in 1885, leaving a debt of 43,140 pounds sterling, regarding which a decision is necessary;

Whereas, it is shown from the facts of the case that the business firm of José Canevaro & Sons, established at Lima, was reorganized in 1885, after the death of its founder in 1883;

Whereas the firm name of José Canevaro & Sons was preserved though, in reality, as shown by the act of liquidation of February 6, 1905, the company was composed of José Francisco and César Canevaro, whose Peruvian nationality was never contested, and of Rafael Canevaro, whose Peruvian nationality, in accordance with Peruvian law, has just been recognized by the tribunal;

Whereas, this company, whose firm name was Peruvian and whose members were of Peruvian nationality, continued to exist until the death of José Francisco Canevaro, in 1900.

Whereas, it was during the existence of this company that the Peruvian laws of October 26, 1886, June 12, 1889, and December 17, 1898, were enacted, prescribing the gravest measures with regard to the debts of the Peruvian Government, which measures appeared to be necessary owing to the deplorable condition to which Peru had been reduced by the evils of foreign and civil war;

Whereas, it is not the place of the tribunal to pass judgment upon the provisions themselves of the laws of 1889 and 1898, which provisions were indeed very severe upon the creditors of Peru, but as these provisions were, without doubt, forced upon Peruvian individuals and corporations alike, the tribunal can but recognize the fact.

Whereas, on September 30, 1890, the Canevaro company, through its representative, Giacometti, applied to the Senate for payment of the 43,140 pounds sterling which had, according to it, been furnished to meet the needs of the war;

Whereas, on April 9, 1891, in a letter addressed to the President of the Tribunal of Accounts, Giacometti assigned a triple origin to the debt: a balance due the Canevaro firm from the Government in payment of armaments bought in Europe during the war; drafts drawn by the Government against a consignment of guano to the United States, protested and then paid by José Francisco Canevaro; money furnished for the army by General Canevaro;

Whereas, also, on April 1, 1891, the said Giacometti, addressing the President of the Tribunal of Accounts, had invoked Article 14 of the law of June 12, 1889, which he said Congress had passed "for the most patriotic purposes," in order to obtain a settlement of the debt;

Whereas, the representative of the Canevaro firm had at first assigned a manifestly erroneous origin to the debt, it having by no means been a question of supplies furnished or advances made in view of the war against Chile, but, as was recognized later on, solely a question of the repayment of previous drafts which, drawn by the Peruvian Government, had been protested and then paid by the Canevaro firm;

Whereas, this is the standpoint from which the matter should be examined.

Whereas, the Canevaro firm acknowledged in 1890 and 1891 that it was subject to the law on domestic debt, and merely sought to place itself in a position to take advantage of a favorable provision of this law instead of submitting to the common fate of the creditors;

Whereas, its claim does not come within the provisions of Article 14 of said law, which it invoked, as above stated; and whereas, this case is not a question of a deposit received by the Government, nor of bills of exchange drawn upon the Government, accepted by it, and acknowledged to be lawful by the "present" Government, but óf an operation connected with accounts, being not for the purpose of procuriñg resources for the Government, but for the purpose of settling a previous debt;

Whereas, the Canevaro claim does, on the contrary, come within the very comprehensive terms of Article 1, No. 4, of the law which mentions pay orders (*libramientos*), bonds (*bons*), checks, bills and other money orders issued by the national bureaus *up to January, 1880*; and whereas, we may, as a matter of fact, offer the objection that this phrase [*up to January, 1880*] would seem to exclude the Canevaro claim, which is of December 23, 1880; nevertheless it is important to remark that this limitation as to date was for the purpose of excluding claims arising from acts of the dictator Pierola, in accordance with the law of 1886, which declared all acts of the latter void; and whereas, thus construing literally the provision in question, the Canevaro claim could not be invoked on any score, even to obtain the slight portion allowed by the law of 1889;

But whereas, on the one hand, it appears from the circumstances and from the terms of the *compromis* that the Peruvian Government itself acknowledges that the annulment prescribed by the law of 1886 does not apply to the Canevaro claim; and, on the other hand, that the annulment prescribed by the Pierola decree would leave intact the previous claim arising from the payment of the drafts;

And that thus the claim arising from the bonds of 1880, delivered to the Canevaro firm, must be considered as coming within the category of the evidences of indebtedness enumerated in Article 1, No. 4, of the law;

And whereas, it has been held, in a general way, that the law of 1889 ought not to apply to the Canevaro claim, and that the claim ought not to be considered as falling within *the domestic debt,* since its very characteristics precluded this, the certificates of indebtedness being to order, made payable in pounds sterling, and belonging to Italians;

Whereas, apart from the nationality of the individuals, it is understood that financial measures adopted within a country do not affect transactions entered into abroad by means of which the Government has made a direct appeal for foreign credit; this, however, is not the case here; in the matter of the bills issued in December, 1880, we are clearly dealing with an arrangement of a domestic nature, with bills drawn in Lima, payable in Lima, in compensation for a payment made voluntarily in the interest of the Government of Peru;

And this is not impaired by the fact that the evidences of indebtedness were to order and payable in pounds sterling, which fact did not prevent the Peruvian law from being applicable to the debt created and payable in the territory in which the said law prevailed;

Whereas, the enumeration contained in Article 1, No. 4, as referred to above, comprises evidences of indebtedness payable to order, and Article 5 foresees that conversions of money may be necessary;

Whereas, finally, as has been stated before, when the financial measures which gave rise to the claim were taken, the claim belonged to a company which was incontestably Peruvian;

And whereas, the claim of 1880 belongs at present to three Canevaro brothers, two of whom are certainly Italians;

Whereas, it is justifiable to question whether or not this circumstance renders the law of 1889 inapplicable;

And whereas, it is unnecessary for the tribunal to consider the claim as one belonging to Italians at the time of the enactment of the law which reduced to such an extent the rights of Peruvian creditors, or to consider whether the same sacrifices could be imposed upon foreigners as upon natives;

But whereas, at present it is solely a question of ascertaining whether a position in which natives are placed, and from which for them there is no escape, is radically modified when, in one way or another, foreigners are substituted for them;

And whereas, such a modification could not easily be admitted, since it would be contrary to the plain proposition that an assignee has no greater rights than the assignor;

And whereas, the Canevaro brothers appear as holding the disputed evidences of indebtedness by virtue of an indorsement;

And whereas, there is invoked in their behalf the ordinary effect of indorsement, which is to make the bearer of a note to order the direct creditor of the debtor, enabling him to reject any exceptions which might be made against his indorser;

And whereas, if we reject the theory that, outside of negotiable paper, indorsement is a purely civil conveyance, then we must, in this instance, refuse to admit the effect of indorsement;

And while, in reality, the date of the indorsement of the evidences of indebtedness of 1880 is not known, it is an indisputable fact that this indorsement occurred long after the paper became due; and there is therefore ground for applying the provision of the Peruvian Code of Commerce of 1902 (Article 436), according to which indorsement subsequent to maturity has only the force of an ordinary conveyance;

And whereas, moreover, the rule invoked above in regard to the effect of indorsement does not prevent making exceptions against the bearer, drawn from the very nature of the paper, which he knew or ought to have known;

And whereas, it is useless to remark that the Canevaro brothers knew perfectly well the character of the papers indorsed in their behalf;

And whereas, while the Canevaro brothers can not, as possessors of the claim by virtue of an indorsement, acquire a more favorable status than that of the company from which they derived their rights, it is a question whether their status should not be different if they are regarded as heirs of José Francisco Canevaro, which they appear to be in a notarial declaration of February 6, 1905;

Whereas, as a matter of fact, there is this difference between a conveyance and an inheritance: in the latter case, the claim has not passed from one person to another by an act of pure will;

Whereas, nevertheless, no decisive reason is found for admitting that the situation has changed by virtue of the fact that Italians succeeded a Peruvian and that the heirs have a new title which enables them to avail themselves of the claim under more favorable conditions than the *de cujus;*

Whereas, it is a general rule that heirs receive property subject to the same conditions as obtained when it was in the possession of the deceased;

Whereas, it has been maintained that the Peruvian law of 1889 on domestic debt, did not modify the obligations existing against Peru, but only gave to the administration the authority to pay its debts in a certain manner when the creditors demanded payment thereof, and that it is to the moment when payment is demanded that we should look in order to ascertain whether the exceptions specified in the law may be invoked against all persons, and especially against foreigners;

Whereas, as the present owners of the claim are Italians, it would be proper for the tribunal to pass on the question whether the Peruvian law of 1889 may, in spite of its exceptional character, be imposed upon foreigners;

But whereas, this view appears at variance with the general terms and spirit of the law of 1889;

Whereas, Congress, whose acts are not here under examination, intended to settle entirely the financial situation of Peru, and substitute the bonds which it issued for the old bonds;

Whereas, this situation is not altered because some creditors apply earlier than others for the settlement of their claims;

Whereas, this was the situation with regard to the Canevaro firm, which was Peruvian when the law of 1889 went into effect;

And whereas, for the reasons already set forth, this situation has not been changed in law by the fact that the claim has passed into the hands of Italians by indorsement or by inheritance;

And whereas, finally, the allegation that the Peruvian Government should indemnify the claimants for the damages occasioned them by its delay in discharging the debt of 1880, and that the damage is measured by the difference between payment in gold and payment in bonds of the consolidated debt; and that thus the Peruvian Government would be bound to pay in gold the sum claimed, even though it be admitted that the law of 1889 was properly applied to the indebtedness;

And whereas, the tribunal considers that in following this line of reasoning it would be departing from the terms of the *compromis,* which stipulates that it shall decide only whether the Peruvian Government should pay in cash *or* in accordance with the provisions of the Peruvian law of June 12, 1889;

And whereas, since the tribunal has admitted the latter alternative, the former solution should be excluded;

And whereas, further, the tribunal is not charged with deciding what responsibility the Peruvian Government may have incurred on any other score, and with inquiring as to whether the delay in payment may or may not be condoned because of the trying circumstances in which Peru was placed, especially in view of the fact that the question would, in reality, be one as to the responsibility incurred toward a Peruvian firm, the creditor when the delay occurred;

And whereas, it is proper to estimate the amount of the Canevaro claim at the time the law of 1889 went into effect;

Whereas, it was composed primarily of the principal, amounting to 43,140 pounds sterling, to which must be added the interest which had accrued up to that time;

Whereas, the interest, which, according to the decree of December 23, 1880, was four per cent per annum up to the respective maturities of the bonds delivered (*délivrés*) and which was included in the amount of these bonds, should be calculated from the said maturity dates at the legal rate of six per cent (Article 1274 of the Peruvian Civil Code) up to January 1, 1889;

Whereas, we thus obtain the sum of 16,577 pounds, 2 shillings, 2 pence sterling, which must be added to the principal in order to make up the total amount to be repaid in certificates of the consolidated debt, yielding one per cent interest, payable in gold, from January 1, 1889, until final payment;

And whereas, according to the above decision in regard to the status of Rafael Canevaro, the tribunal is to pass judgment only in regard to his two brothers;

And whereas, it is the duty of the tribunal to regulate the mode of executing the award:

Therefore,

The arbitral tribunal decides that the Peruvian Government shall, on July 31, 1912, deliver to the Italian Legation at Lima, on account of the brothers Napoléon and Carlos Canevaro:

1. In one per cent bonds of the domestic debt of 1889, the nominal amount of 39,811 pounds, 8 shillings, 1 penny sterling upon the surrender of two-thirds of the bonds issued on December 23, 1880, to the firm of José Canevaro & Sons;

2. In gold, the sum of 9,388 pounds, 17 shillings, 1 penny sterling, the amount of interest at one per cent from January 1, 1889, to July 31, 1912.

The Peruvian Government may delay payment of this latter sum until January 1, 1913, provided it pays interest thereon at the rate of six per cent from August 1, 1912.

Done at The Hague, in the palace of the Permanent Court of Arbitration, on May 3, 1912.

LOUIS RENAULT, *President*
MICHIELS VAN VERDUYNEN, *Secretary General*

AGREEMENT FOR ARBITRATION

Protocol between Italy and Peru for the arbitration of the Canevaro claim.—Signed at Lima, April 25, 1910.[1]

Dr. Don Meliton F. Porras, Minister of Foreign Relations of Peru, and Count Giulio Bolognesi, Chargé d'Affaires of Italy, having met at the office of the former, have agreed upon the following:

The Government of the Peruvian Republic, and the Government of His Majesty, the King of Italy, not having succeeded in reaching an agreement in regard to the claim presented by the latter on behalf of Count Napoléon, Carlos and Rafael Canevaro, for the payment of the sum of forty-three thousand, one hundred and forty pounds sterling and the legal interest thereon, which they demand from the Government of Peru,

Have resolved, in accordance with Article 1 of the general treaty of arbitration in force between the two countries, to submit this controversy to the Permanent Court of Arbitration at The Hague, which Court shall decide in accordance with law the following points:

---

[1]*American Journal of International Law*, vol. 6, Supplement, p. 212. For the original Italian and Spanish texts, see Appendix, p. 528.

Should the Government of Peru pay in cash, or in accordance with the Peruvian law of June 12, 1889, on the domestic debt, the bills of exchange (*libramientos*) now in the possession of the brothers Napoléon, Carlos and Rafael Canevaro which were drawn by the Peruvian Government to the order of the firm of José Canevaro and Sons for the sum of 43,140 pounds sterling, plus the legal interest on the said amount?

Have the Canevaro brothers a right to demand the total amount claimed?

Has Don Rafael Canevaro a right to be considered as an Italian claimant?

The Government of the Republic of Peru and the Government of His Majesty, the King of Italy, pledge themselves to designate, within four months from the date of this protocol, the members who are to constitute the arbitral tribunal.

Seven months after said arbitral tribunal has been organized, both Governments shall submit to the same a complete statement of the controversy, together with all the documents, evidence, briefs and arguments in the case, each Government being entitled to a period of five months in order to file its answer to the other Government, and in said answer they shall only be allowed to refer to the allegations contained in the statement of the other side.

The controversy shall then be deemed closed, unless the arbitral tribunal should require new documents, proofs, or briefs, in which case they must be presented within the term of four months from the time the arbitrator should demand the presentation of the same.

Should said documents, proofs or briefs not be presented within this period, an arbitral sentence shall be passed as if the same did not exist.

In witness whereof the undersigned put their names to the present protocol, drawn in Spanish and Italian, affixing their respective seals thereon.

Done in duplicate in Lima, the 25th day of April, 1910.

(L. S.)   M. F. PORRAS
(L. S.)   GIULIO BOLOGNESI

ADDITIONAL DOCUMENTS

Notes Concerning the Formation of the Arbitral Tribunal[1]

MINISTRY OF FOREIGN AFFAIRS,
Lima, April 27, 1910.

SIR: There being no stipulation in the protocol submitting to arbitration the claim presented against the Peruvian Government by the brothers Canevaro, in regard to the formation of the arbitral tribunal, it is a pleasure to me to propose to your Excellency that the same be made in accordance with Article 87 of the Convention for the pacific settlement of international disputes, signed at The Hague in 1907.

I reiterate to your Excellency the assurances of my highest consideration.

M. F. PORRAS

To COUNT GIULIO BOLOGNESI,
Chargé d'Affaires of Italy.

LEGATION OF HIS MAJESTY, THE KING OF ITALY,
Lima, April 27, 1910.

MR. MINISTER: I have the honor to acknowledge receipt of the note of your Excellency No. 18, of this date, and I am highly pleased to accept the proposal of your Excellency providing for the formation of the arbitral tribunal at The Hague to pass upon the Canevaro controversy, in accordance with the provisions of Article 87 of the Convention for the pacific settlement of international disputes signed at The Hague in 1907.

Be pleased, Mr. Minister, to accept the assurances of my highest and distinguished consideration.

GIULIO BOLOGNESI

To His Excellency,
DR. MELITON F. PORRAS,
Minister of Foreign Relations.

---

[1] *American Journal of International Law,* vol 6, Supplement, p. 214. For the original Spanish text, see Appendix, p. 530.

THE RUSSIAN INDEMNITY CASE

between

RUSSIA *and* TURKEY

Decided November 11, 1912

Syllabus

Article 5 of the treaty of Constantinople, concluded January 27/February 8, 1879, between Russia and Turkey, which ended the war of 1877-78 between those two countries, stipulated that "the claims of Russian subjects and institutions in Turkey for indemnity on account of damages sustained during the war shall be paid as soon as they are examined by the Russian Embassy at Constantinople and transmitted to the Sublime Porte."

The claims were duly examined by the Embassy and presented to the Turkish Government, but payments were delayed and only made under constant pressure from the Russian Government.

The claims amounted in all to 6,186,543 francs, of which sum 50,000 Turkish pounds were paid in 1884, 50,000 in 1889, 75,000 in 1893, 50,000 in 1894, and a trifle over 42,438 in 1902, leaving a balance of 1,539 Turkish pounds, which the Turkish Government deposited in the Ottoman Bank to the credit of Russia, but which the latter refused to receive on the ground that payment of the interest which Russia claimed for the delayed payments had not been made. The controversy over this interest was submitted by a *compromis* signed at Constantinople July 22/August 4, 1910,[1] to the arbitration of a tribunal composed of the following: Charles Édouard Lardy, of Switzerland; Baron Michel de Taube and André Mandelstam, of Russia, and Herante Abro Bey and Ahmed Réchid Bey, of Turkey. Of these members, only two, viz., Lardy and de Taube, were selected from the panel of the Permanent Court. The sessions began February 15, 1911, and ended November 6, 1912, the decision being rendered November 11, 1912.

On a preliminary question raised by Turkey—that the claims were due to certain specified subjects of Russia and not to the Russian Government, and that therefore Russia as such had no standing in the court—the tribunal found that the treaty was made with Russia for the benefit of its subjects, and rejected the Turkish contention.

On the main question the tribunal decided that Turkey was responsible in the same manner as a private debtor for the payment of interest, but was only responsible after demand had been made for the payment of the principal and interest upon such principal. The tri-

---

[1] *Post*, p. 324.

bunal found that Russia had made such a demand in proper form on December 31, 1890/January 12, 1891, but that subsequently the Russian Government, through its Embassy at Constantinople, repeatedly agreed to accept the balance as stated by Turkey, in which no interest was included. The tribunal considered this to be a renunciation of the claim for interest, and held that, after the principal had been paid in full to Russia or placed at its disposal, the Russian Government was, by the interpretation which had been accepted and practiced in its name by its Embassy, estopped from reopening the question.

AWARD OF THE TRIBUNAL

Award of the arbitral tribunal constituted by virtue of the arbitration agreement signed at Constantinople between Russia and Turkey, July 22/August 4, 1910.—The Hague; November 11, 1912.[1]

By a *compromis* signed at Constantinople, July 22/August 4, 1910,[2] the Imperial Government of Russia and the Imperial Ottoman Government agreed to submit to an arbitral tribunal the final decision of the following questions:

I. Whether or not the Imperial Ottoman Government must pay the Russian claimants interest-damages by reason of the dates on which the said Government made payment of the indemnities determined in pursuance of Article 5 of the Treaty of January 27/February 8, 1879, as well as of the protocol of the same date?

II. In case the first question is decided in the affirmative, what should be the amount of these interest-damages?

The arbitral tribunal was composed of:

His Excellency Monsieur Lardy, Doctor of Laws, member and former president of the Institute of International Law, Envoy Extraordinary and Minister Plenipotentiary of Switzerland at Paris, member of the Permanent Court of Arbitration, umpire;

His Excellency Baron Michel de Taube, Assistant Minister of Public Instruction of Russia, Councilor of State, Doctor of Laws, associate of the Institute of International Law, member of the Permanent Court of Arbitration;

---

[1]*American Journal of International Law*, vol. 7., p. 178. For the original French text, see Appendix, p. 532.
[2]*Post*, p. 324.

Mr. André Mandelstam, First Dragoman of the Imperial Embassy of Russia at Constantinople, Councilor of State, Doctor of International Law, associate of the Institute of International Law;

Herante Abro Bey, Licentiate in Law, Legal Counselor of the Sublime Porte; and

Ahmed Réchid Bey, Licentiate in Law, Legal Counselor of the Sublime Porte.

Mr. Henri Fromageot, Doctor of Laws, associate of the Institute of International Law, advocate in the Court of Appeals of Paris, acted as agent of the Imperial Russian Government and was assisted by

Mr. Francis Rey, Doctor of Laws, Secretary of the European Commission of the Danube, in the capacity of secretary;

Mr. Édouard Clunet, advocate in the Court of Appeals of Paris, member and former president of the Institute of International Law, acted as agent of the Imperial Ottoman Government and was assisted by

Mr. Ernest Roguin, professor of comparative legislation in the University of Lausanne, member of the Institute of International Law, in the capacity of counsel to the Ottoman Government;

Mr. André Hesse, Doctor of Laws, advocate in the Court of Appeals of Paris, in the capacity of counsel to the Ottoman Government;

Youssouf Kémâl Bey, professor in the Faculty of Law of Constantinople, former deputy, director of the Ottoman Commission of Juridical Studies; in the capacity of counsel to the Ottoman Government;

Mr. C. Campinchi, Advocate in the Court of Appeals of Paris, in the capacity of secretary to the agent of the Ottoman Government;

Baron Michiels van Verduynen, secretary general of the International Bureau of the Permanent Court of Arbitration, acted as secretary general, and

Jonkheer W. Röell, first secretary of the International Bureau of the Court, attended to the secretariat.

After a first session at The Hague on February 15, 1911, to arrange certain questions of procedure, the cases and counter-cases were duly exchanged by the parties and communicated to the arbitrators, who declared respectively, as well as the agents of the parties, that they waived the right to ask for further information.

The arbitral tribunal met again at The Hague on October 28, 29, 30, 31, November 2, 5, and 6, 1912, and after having heard the oral arguments of the agents and counsel of the parties, made the following award:

PRELIMINARY QUESTION

In view of the preliminary request of the Imperial Ottoman Government that the claim of the Imperial Russian Government be declared inadmissible without examining the principal question, the tribunal, considering that the Imperial Ottoman Government bases this preliminary request, in its written demands, upon the fact

That the direct creditors for the principal sums adjudged to them were the Russian subjects individually, benefiting by a stipulation made in their names, either in the preliminaries of peace signed at San Stefano, February 19/March 3, 1878, or by Article 5 of the treaty of Constantinople of January 27/ February 8, 1879, or by the protocol of the same date, and that their titles in this respect were established by the designative decisions of the commission *ad hoc* which met at the Russian Embassy at Constantinople, which decisions were communicated to the Sublime Porte;

That, under these circumstances, the Imperial Russian Government should have proved the survival of the rights of each claimant and the identity of the persons entitled at the present time to avail themselves of these rights, especially since the transfer of certain of these rights has been reported to the Imperial Ottoman Government;

That, even admitting that the Russian State was the only direct creditor as to the indemnities, the Imperial Russian Government should have, nevertheless, made such proof, inasmuch as the said Government could not deny its duty to transmit to the claimants or their assigns the sums which it might obtain in the present suit as moratory interest-damages, the claimants appearing, upon this supposition, as beneficiaries of the stipulation made in their interest, if not as creditors.

That, however, the Imperial Russian Government furnished no proof as to the identity of the claimants or of their assigns, or as to the survival of their claims (Counter-reply of Turkey, pp. 81 and 82) ;

Considering that the Imperial Russian Government maintains, on the contrary, in its written demands

That the debt specified in the treaty of 1879 is, none the less, a debt of State to State; that it could not be otherwise as to the responsibility resulting from the failure to pay the said debt; that consequently the Imperial Russian Government alone is qualified to receipt for it, and for that reason to receive the sums to be paid to the claimants; that, moreover, the Imperial Ottoman Government does not dispute the Russian Government's title of direct creditor of the Sublime Porte;

That the Imperial Russian Government is acting by virtue of a right which it possesses in claiming the interest-damages on account of the non-fulfilment of an engagement made with it directly;

That it fully proves its rights by establishing the non-fulfilment of this engagement, which, moreover, is not disputed, and by presenting its title, which is the treaty of 1879 . . .;

That the Sublime Porte, provided with the receipt regularly delivered to it by the Imperial Russian Government has no concern in the allotment of the sums distributed or to be distributed by the said Government among its subjects entitled to indemnity; that this is a question of a domestic nature with which the Imperial Ottoman Government has nothing to do (Reply of Russia, pp. 49 and 50) ;

Considering that the origin of the claim goes back to a war and an international fact in the first degree; that the source of the indemnity is not only an international treaty but a treaty of peace and the agreements made with a view to the execution of this treaty of peace; that this treaty and these agreements were between Russia and Turkey, settling between themselves, State to State, as public and sovereign Powers, a question of international law; that the preliminaries of peace included in the indemnities "which His Majesty the Emperor of Russia claims that the Sublime Porte bound itself to pay to him" the ten million roubles allowed as damages and interest to Russian subjects who were victims of the war in Turkey; that this condition of debt from State to State has been confirmed by the fact that the claims were to be examined by a purely Russian commission; that the Imperial Russian Government has full authority in the matter of conferring, collecting and distributing the indemnities, in its capacity as sole creditor; that whether, in theory, Russia has acted by virtue of its right to protect its nationals or by some other right is a matter of little moment, since it is with the Imperial Russian Government alone that the Sublime Porte entered into or undertook the engagement the fulfilment of which is demanded;

Considering that the fulfilment of engagements between States, as between individuals, is the surest commentary on the effectiveness of these engagements;

That, upon the attempt of the Ottoman financial department in 1885 to impose the proportional stamp-tax required from individuals by the Ottoman laws, upon a receipt given by the Russian Embassy at Constantinople for a payment on account, Russia immediately protested and maintained "that the debt was one contracted by the Ottoman to the Russian Government" . . . and "not a simple debt between individuals arising from a private engagement or contract" (Russian note of March 15/27, 1885, Russian memorandum, appendix No. 19, p. 19); that the Sublime Porte did not insist, and that in fact the two parties have constantly acted in practice, for more than fifteen years, as if Russia was the creditor of Turkey and not of private claimants;

That the Sublime Porte has made, without a single exception, all the successive payments upon the receipt alone of the Russian Embassy at Constantinople, acting in behalf of its Government;

That the Sublime Porte has never asked, upon payments on account, if the beneficiaries were still living or who were their assigns at the time, or according to what method the payments on account were divided among them, leaving this duty entirely to the Imperial Russian Government;

Considering that the Sublime Porte contends, in the main, in the present litigation, that it is fully released by the payments which it has, in fact, made to the Imperial Russian Government alone represented by its Embassy, without the participation of the claimants;

For these reasons decides that

The preliminary request is set aside.

Passing then upon the main question, the arbitral tribunal renders the following decision:

I

IN THE MATTER OF FACT

The protocol signed at Adrianople, January 19/31, 1878, which put an end by an armistice to hostilities between Russia and Turkey, contains the following stipulation:

> 5. The Sublime Porte engages to indemnify Russia for the cost of the war and the losses that it has been forced to suffer. The character of this indemnity, whether pecuniary, territorial or other, will be arranged later.

Article 19 of the preliminaries of peace signed at San Stefano, February 19/March 3, 1878, is in these terms:

> The war indemnities and the losses suffered by Russia which His Majesty the Emperor of Russia claims, and which the Sublime Porte has engaged to pay to him, consist of: (a) 900 million roubles, war expenses; (b) 400 million roubles, damages upon the southern coast; (c) 100 million roubles, damages in the Caucasus; (d) ten million roubles, damages and interest to Russian subjects and institutions in Turkey; total, 1400 million roubles.

And further on:

> The ten million roubles claimed as indemnity for Russian subjects and institutions in Turkey shall be paid as soon as the claims of those interested have been examined by the Russian Embassy at Constantinople and transmitted to the Sublime Porte.

At the Congress of Berlin, at the session of July 2, 1878, protocol No. 11, it was agreed that the ten million roubles in question did not concern Europe but only the two interested States, and that they would not be mentioned in the treaty between the Powers represented at Berlin. Consequently the question was again taken up directly between Russia and Turkey, who stipulated, in the final treaty of peace signed at Constantinople, January 27/February 8, 1879, as follows:

> Article 5. The claims of Russian subjects and institutions in Turkey for indemnity on account of damages suffered during the war will be paid as soon as they are examined by the Russian Embassy at Constantinople and transmitted to the Sublime Porte.
>
> The total of these claims shall in no case exceed 26,750,000 francs.
>
> Claims may be presented to the Sublime Porte beginning one year from the date on which ratifications are exchanged, and no claims will be admitted which are presented after the expiration of two years from that date.

The same day, January 27/February 8, 1879, in the protocol to the treaty of peace, the Russian plenipotentiary, Prince Lobanow, declared that the sum of 26,750,000 francs specified in Article 5 constitutes a maximum which the claims could probably never reach; he adds that a commission *ad hoc* will be formed at the Russian Embassy to examine scrupulously the claims which are presented to it, and that, according to the instructions of his Government, an Ottoman delegate can take part in the examination of these claims.

Ratifications of the treaty of peace were exchanged at St. Petersburg, February 9/21, 1879.

The commission established at the Russian Embassy and composed of three Russian officials immediately began its labors. The Ottoman commissioner generally abstained from taking part. The total losses of Russian subjects was fixed by the commission at 6,186,543 francs. This was communicated to the Sublime Porte between October 22/November 3, 1880, and January 29/February 10, 1881. The sum was not contested and the Russian Embassy made claim for the payment at the same time that it transmitted the final decisions of the commission.

On September 23, 1881, the Embassy transmitted a "petition" of the lawyer Rossolato, "special attorney of several Russian subjects" who were to receive indemnities, which petition was addressed to the Embassy and demanded that the Ottoman Government should come to an understanding with the Embassy "within eight days from notification, as to the method of payment," declaring that the said Ottoman Government was "held now and henceforth responsible for all interest-damages, especially the moratory interest."

By a convention signed at Constantinople May 2/14, 1882, the two Governments agreed (Article 1) that the war indemnity, the amount of which was fixed at 802,500,000 francs by Article 4 of the treaty of peace of 1879 after deducting the value of the territory ceded by Turkey, should bear no interest and should be paid in one hundred annual instalments of 350,000 Turkish pounds, approximately 8,000,000 francs.

On June 19/July 1, 1884, no sum having been paid for the claimants, the embassy "makes formal claim for full payment of the indemnities which were adjudged to Russian subjects . . .; it will be obliged, otherwise, to acknowledge their right to claim, in addition to the principal, interest proportional to the delay in the settlement of their claims."

On December 19, 1884, the Sublime Porte made a first payment on account, of 50,000 Turkish pounds, approximately 1,150,000 francs.

In 1885 the union of Bulgaria and Eastern Roumelia occurred, as well as the Serbo-Bulgarian war. Turkey made no further payment on account. A reminding note having been sent in January, 1886, without result, the embassy insisted, on February 15/27, 1887. It transmitted a "petition" sent to it by Russian claimants, in which they hold the Ottoman Government "responsible for this increase of damages caused them by the delay in the payment of their indemnities," and the Embassy adds: "Further postponements will force the Imperial Government to make claim in behalf of its nationals for interest on account of the delays in settling their claims."

Reminding notes of July and December, 1887, being without effect, the Embassy complained on January 26/February 7, 1888, that Turkey has paid various debts incurred subsequent to its obligations to Russian claimants. It recalled the fact that "the arrears amount to the sum of about 215,000 Turkish pounds, a single payment of 50,000 Turkish pounds having been made out of a total of 265,000 Turkish pounds awarded"; it therefore requested "urgently . . . that the sums due Russian subjects be immediately,

and before every other payment, levied upon the amount paid by
X . . ." (a debtor of the Imperial Ottoman Government).

On April 22, 1889, Turkey made a second payment on account,
of 50,000 pounds.

On December 31, 1890/January 12, 1891, the Embassy, stating
that it has been paid only 100,000 pounds out of a total of 265,000,
wrote to the Sublime Porte that the delay in the settlement of this
debt is causing the Russian nationals to suffer losses that are con-
tinually increasing; it believes, therefore, that it is its duty to request the Sublime Porte "to have immediate orders issued by the
proper persons so that the sum due may be paid without delay, *as
well as the legal interest* in regard to which (the Embassy) had the
honor of notifying the Sublime Porte by its note of February 15/
27, 1887."

In August, 1891, a further reminder was sent. In October/No-
vember, 1892, the Embassy wrote "that matters can not continue
indefinitely in this way"; that "the requests of Russian subjects are
becoming more and more urgent," that "it is the duty of the Embassy to act energetically in their behalf . . . that it is a question of
an indisputable obligation and an international duty to be performed
. . ." that "the Ottoman Government can no longer offer as ex-
cuse the precarious state of its finances," and concluded by demanding a "prompt and final settlement of the debt."

April 2/14, 1893, a third instalment of 75,000 Turkish pounds
was paid; the Sublime Porte, in giving notice of this payment on
March 27, adds that, as to the balance, half of it will be included in
the current budget and the other half in the next budget; "the
question thus settled happily ends the incidents to which it had
given rise." The Porte hoped, therefore, that the Embassy would
be willing, because of its sincere friendly sentiments towards Turkey, to accept definitively the *tumbeki* monopoly following the example of the other Powers.

On this occasion, and recalling the fact that the Imperial Russian Government "has always shown itself friendly and conciliating
in all its business pertaining to the financial interests of the Ottoman Empire," the Embassy acted on the 30th of the same month in
accordance with the terms announced in view of the payment, and

consented to subject Russians engaged in the *tumbeki* trade in Turkey to the newly created arrangement.

A year later, May 23/June 4, 1894, not having received another instalment, the Ambassador, after having stated the non-performance of the "arrangement" to which he had "consented in order to facilitate the fulfilment of its obligation by the Ottoman Government," declared that he was "placed in a position which renders it impossible for him to accept further promises, arrangements or postponements," and, "obliged to insist *that the total of the balance* due to Russian subjects, *which amounts to 91,000 Turkish pounds,* be, without further delay, paid to the Embassy. . . . Recent financial operations have just placed at the disposal (of the Sublime Porte) large sums."

On October 27 of the same year, 1894, an instalment of 50,000 Turkish pounds was paid, and the Sublime Porte wrote, as early as the third of the same month, to the Embassy: "As to the balance of 41,000 Turkish pounds, the Ottoman Bank will guarantee payment in the near future."

In 1896, there was an exchange of correspondence between the Sublime Porte and the Embassy as to whether the revenues upon which the Ottoman Bank was to levy the balance were not already pledged to Russia for payment of the war indemnity, properly so-called, or whether that portion of the revenues over and above the annuity affected by the war indemnity could not be used to indemnify Russian subjects who were victims of the events of 1877-8. In the course of this correspondence, the Sublime Porte pointed out, in the notes which it addressed to the Embassy on February 11 and May 28, 1896, that the balance due amounted to the sum of 43,978 Turkish pounds.

From 1895 to 1899, serious events occurring in Asia Minor obliged Turkey to seek an extension in behalf of the Ottoman Bank, at its request; the insurrection of the Druses, the insurrection in Crete which was followed by the Graeco-Turkish war of 1897, and insurrections in Macedonia, caused Turkey repeatedly to mobilize troops and even armies.

For three years no correspondence was exchanged and when it was resumed the Sublime Porte, in notes it addressed to the Embassy, July 19, 1899, and July 5, 1900, again specified 43,978 Turkish pounds as the amount of the balance of the indemnities. On its part, the Embassy, in its notes of April 25/May 8, 1900, and March 3/16, 1901, specified the same figure, but complained that the orders given in various provinces "for the payment of the 43,978 Turkish pounds, the amount of the balance of the indemnity due Russian subjects," have not been carried out, and that the Ottoman Bank has paid nothing; it urgently requests the Sublime Porte kindly to give categorical orders to the proper person for the payment, without further delay, of the above-mentioned sums."

After the Sublime Porte had announced in May, 1901, that the Department of Finance had been urged to settle the balance of the indemnity during the course of the month, the Ottoman Bank at last advised the Russian Embassy on February 24 and May 26, 1902, that it had received and was holding at the disposal of the Embassy 42,438 Turkish pounds of the balance of 43,978 pounds.

The Embassy in acknowledging receipt of this notice two months later, June 23/July 6, 1902, remarked to the Sublime Porte, "that the Imperial Ottoman Government has taken more than twenty years to liquidate, and incompletely at that, a debt the immediate settlement of which was required from every point of view, a balance of 1,539 Turkish pounds still remaining unpaid. Referring, therefore, to its notes of September 23, 1881, February 15/27, 1887, and December 31, 1890/January 12, 1891, in regard to the interest to run on the said debt, remaining so long in suspense," the Embassy transmitted a petition in which the claimants demand, in substance, compound interest at 12% from January 1, 1881, to March 15, 1887, and at 9% from the latter date, when the legal rate of interest was reduced by an Ottoman law. The sum claimed by the petitioners amounted in the spring of 1902 to some twenty million francs on an original principal of about 6,200,000 francs. The note concluded as follows:

> The Imperial Embassy is pleased to believe that the Sublime Porte will not hesitate to admit in principle the just grounds for the claim set forth in this petition. In case, however, the Sublime Porte should raise objections to the amount of the sum claimed by the Russian subjects, the Imperial Embassy

sees no reason why examination of the details should not be deferred to a commission composed of Russian and Ottoman delegates.

The Sublime Porte replied on the 17th of the same month, July, 1902, that Article 5 of the treaty of peace of 1879 and the protocol of the same date do not provide for interest, and that in the light of the diplomatic negotiations which have taken place on the subject, it was far from expecting that the claimants would make such demands at the last moment, the effect of which would be to re-open a question which was happily closed. The Embassy replied on February 3/16, 1903, insisting "upon payment of the interest-damages claimed by its subjects. Only the amount of the damages could be a matter for investigation." In reply to a reminding note dated August 2/15, 1903, the Sublime Porte maintained its point of view, declaring itself, however, willing to submit the question to arbitration at The Hague, in case the claim should be insisted upon.

At the end of four years the Embassy accepted this suggestion by a note of March 19/April 1, 1908.

The arbitration agreement was signed at Constantinople, July 22/August 4, 1910.

As to the small sum of 1,539 Turkish pounds, it was, in December, 1902, placed by the Ottoman Bank at the disposal of the Russian Embassy, which refused it, and it remains deposited at the disposal of the Embassy.

II

IN THE MATTER OF LAW

1. The Imperial Russian Government bases its demand upon "the responsibility of States for the non-payment of pecuniary debts"; this responsibility implies, according to it, "obligation to pay interest-damages and especially interest on sums unduly withheld"; "the obligation to pay moratory interest" is "practical proof, in the matter of money debts," of the responsibility of States (Reply of Russia, pp. 27 and 51). "Failure to recognize these principles would be as contrary to the very conception of international law as it would be dangerous to the safety of peaceful relations; in fact, by declaring a debtor State irresponsible for the delay which it

causes its creditor, it would be admitted by that very fact that it need only follow its own whim in making payments; . . . the creditor State, on the other hand, would be obliged to resort to violence against such a contention . . . and to expect nothing from a pretended international law incapable of compelling the promiser to keep his word" (Russian Case, p. 29).

In other words, and still in the opinion of the Imperial Russian Government, "it is not a question of conventional interest, that is to say, interest arising from a particular stipulation . . ." but that "the obligation incumbent upon the Imperial Ottoman Government to pay moratory interest arises from the delay in the performance of the act, that is to say, the partial non-fulfilment of the stipulations of the treaty of peace; this obligation arose indeed, it is true, from the treaty of 1879, but it proceeds *ex post facto* from a new and accidental cause, namely, the failure of the Sublime Porte to carry out its contract as it pledged itself to do" (Russian Case, p. 29; Russian Reply, pp. 22 and 27).

2. The Imperial Ottoman Government, while admitting in explicit terms the general principle of the responsibility of States in the matter of the non-fulfilment of their engagements (Counter-reply, p. 29, No. 286, note, and p. 52, No. 358), maintains, on the contrary, that in public international law moratory interest does not exist "unless expressly stipulated" (Ottoman Counter-case, p. 31, No. 83, and p. 34, No. 95); that a State "is not a debtor like other debtors" (*ibid,* p. 33, No. 90), and that, without attempting to maintain "that no principle which is observed between individuals can be applied between States" (Ottoman Counter-reply, p. 26, No. 275), the position *sui generis* of the State as a public Power must be taken into account; that various legislative acts (for example, the French law of 1831, which establishes a period of five years for the outlawing of State debts; the Roman law which lays down the principle *Fiscus ex suis contractibus usuras non dat,* Lex 17, par. 5, *Digest* 22, 1) admit that the debtor State stands in a privileged position (Ottoman Counter-reply, p. 33, No. 92); that in admitting against a State an implied obligation, not expressly stipulated, in extending, for example, to a debtor State the principles of a formal demand for payment and its effect in private law, this State would be made a "debtor to a greater extent than it would have desired.

and there would be the risk of compromising the political life of the State, injuring its vital interests, upsetting its budget, preventing it from defending itself against an insurrection of foreign attack" (Ottoman Counter-case, p. 33, No. 91).

Contingently, in case responsibility should attach to it, the Imperial Ottoman Government concludes that this responsibility consists solely in moratory interest, that interest being due only from the date of the regular formal demand for payment (Ottoman Counter-reply, pp. 71, *et scq.*, Nos. 410, *et seq.*).

It presents in opposition, moreover, the exceptions of *res judicata,* of *force majeure,* of the gift character of the indemnities, and of the tacit or express renunciation by Russia of the benefit of the legal demand for payment.

3. The questions of law involved in the present litigation, which has arisen between States as public Powers subject to international law, and these questions being within the province of public law, the law to be applied is public international law, or the law of nations, and the parties rightly agree upon this point (Russian Case, p. 32; Ottoman Counter-case, Nos. 47 to 54, p. 18; Russian reply, p. 18; Ottoman Counter-reply, p. 17, Nos. 244 and 245).

4. The demand of the Imperial Russian Government is based upon the general principle of the responsibility of States, in support of which it has cited a large number of arbitral awards.

The Sublime Porte, without disputing this general principle, contends that it is not subject to its application, but that States have the right to an exceptional and privileged position in the special case of responsibility in the matter of money debts.

It declares that the majority of the arbitral precedents cited are of no force, as they do not apply to this special category.

The Imperial Ottoman Government remarks, in support of its point of view, that in theory there is a distinction between various responsibilites, according to their origin and according to their scope. These shades of difference occur especially in the theory of responsibilities in the Roman law and in systems of law inspired by the Roman law. In the Ottoman Case attention is called to the following distinctions, some of which are classic: Responsibilities are, in the first place, divided into two categories, according as they arise from an act of violence or a quasi-act of violence, or from a

contract.   Among contractual responsibilities there is a further distinction, according as it is a question of obligations concerning a
prestation of some kind other than a sum of money, or a question of
prestations of a purely pecuniary nature, of a money debt properly
so-called.   These various categories of responsibilities are not appreciated in civil law in absolutely the same manner, the circumstances giving rise to the responsibility as well as its consequences
being variable.   While in the matter of responsibilities arising from
acts of violence no formality whatever is necessary, in the matter
of contractual responsibilities a demand in due form of law is
always required.   While in the matter of obligations concerning a
prestation other than one involving a sum of money, as likewise
in the matter of acts of violence the reparation for the damage is
complete (*lucrum cessans* and *damnum emergens*), this reparation,
in the matter of money debts, is restricted legally to interest on the
sum due, which interest runs only from the date of the demand in
due form of law.   The *interest-damages* are called *compensatory,*
when they are compensation for damage resulting from the act of
violence or the non-fulfilment of an obligation.   They are *moratory
interest-damages* when they are caused by delay in the fulfilment of
an obligation.   Finally, writers call *moratory interest* interest legally
allowed in case of delay in the payment of money debts, thus dis-
tinguishing it from other interest which is sometimes added to the
money valuation of damages, to fix the total amount of an indemnity, this last being called *compensatory interest.*

These distinctions in civil law can be explained : in the matter of
contractual responsibility one has the right to require greater
promptness on the part of the other contracting party than the
victim of an unforeseen act of violence could expect.   In the matter of money debts, the difficulty of estimating the consequences of
the demand explains why the amount of the damages has been fixed
legally.

The argument of the Imperial Ottoman Government consists in
maintaining that in public international law special responsibility,
consisting in the payment of moratory interest in case of delay in
the settlement of a money debt, does not exist so far as a debtor State
is concerned.   The Sublime Porte does not dispute the responsibility
of States if it is a question of compensatory interest, or of interest

that might enter into the calculation of these compensatory interest-damages. The responsibility which the Sublime Porte refuses to acknowledge is the interest which may result, in the form of interest for delay or moratory interest, in the restricted sense, from delay in the fulfilment of a pecuniary obligation.

It is necessary to investigate whether these various terms, these appellations invented by commentators, correspond to intrinsic differences in the very nature of law, differences essentially juridical in the conception of responsibility. The tribunal is of the opinion that all interest-damages are always reparation, compensation for culpability. From this point of view all interest-damages are compensatory, whatever name they may be given. Legal interest allowed a creditor for a sum of money from the date of the demand in due form of law is the legal compensation for the delinquency of a tardy debtor exactly as interest-damages or interest allowed in case of an act of violence, of a quasi-act of violence, of the non-fulfilment of an obligation, are compensation for the injury suffered by the creditor, the money value of the responsibility of the delinquent debtor. Exaggeration of the consequences of civil-law distinctions in responsibility is the more inadmissible because in much recent legislation there appears a tendency to lessen or abolish the mitigation which the Roman law and its derivatives admitted in the matter of responsibility as to money debts. It is certain, indeed, that all culpability, whatever may be its origin, is finally valued in money and transformed into obligation to pay; it all ends or can end, in the last analysis, in a money debt. The tribunal, therefore, can not possibly perceive essential differences between various responsibilities. Identical in their origin—culpability—they are the same in their consequences—reparation in money.

The tribunal is, therefore, of the opinion that the general principle of the responsibility of States implies a special responsibility in the matter of delay in the payment of a money debt, unless the existence of a contrary international custom is proven.

The Imperial Russian Government and the Sublime Porte brought into their arguments a series of arbitral decisions, which have admitted, affirmed and sanctioned the principle of the responsibility of States. The Sublime Porte considers nearly all of these decisions without any bearing on the present case, and eliminates even those in which the arbitrator has expressly allowed interest on sums of money. The Imperial Ottoman Government is of the opinion that in these cases it is a question of compensatory interest and sets them aside as having no bearing on the present litigation. The tribunal, for the reasons indicated above, is of the opinion, on the contrary, that there is no reason why the great analogy which exists between the different forms of responsibility should not be taken into account; this analogy appears particularly close between interest called *moratory* and interest called *compensatory*. The analogy appears to be complete between the allowance of interest from a certain date upon valuing the responsibility in money, and the allowance of interest on the principal determined by agreement and remaining unpaid by a delinquent debtor. The only difference is that, in one case the interest is allowed by the judge, since the debt was not exigible, and in the other case the amount of the debt was determined by agreement and the interest becomes exigible automatically in case of demand in due form of law.

To weaken this close analogy, the Sublime Porte must prove the existence of a custom—of precedents in accordance with which moratory interest in the restricted sense of the word had been refused *because it was moratory interest,*—or the existence of a custom derogatory, in the matter of a pecuniary debt, to the general principles of responsibility. The tribunal is of the opinion that such proof not only has not been given, but, on the contrary, the Imperial Russian Government has been able to reinforce its position by several arbitral awards in which moratory interest has been allowed to States, in some cases, it is true, with shades of difference, and to a certain extent debatable (Mexico-Venezuela, October 2, 1903. Russian Case, p. 28, and note 5; Ottoman Counter-case, p. 38, No. 107; Columbia-Italy, April 9, 1904. Russian Reply, p. 28 and note 7; Ottoman Counter-reply, p. 58, No. 368; United States-Choctaws. Russian Reply, p. 29, Ottoman Counter-reply, p. 59, No. 369; United States-Venezuela, December 5, 1885. Russian Reply, p. 28, and note 5). To these cases should be added the award made on July 2, 1881, by His Majesty the Emperor of Austria in the Mosquito affair, in the sense that the arbitrator in no wise refused moratory interest as such, but simply declared that the principal being in the nature of a gift, interest for deferred payment should not, in the judgment of the arbitrator, be allowed (Russian Reply, p. 28, note 4; Ottoman Counter-reply, p. 55, No. 365, note).

It remains to examine the question whether the Sublime Porte has any grounds for maintaining that a debtor State is not like other debtors, that it can not be a "debtor to a greater extent than it may have wished," and that by binding it with obligations which it has not stipulated, for example, the responsibilities of a private debtor, there is the risk of compromising its finances and even its political existence.

When the tribunal has admitted that no essential differences distinguish the various responsibilities of States from each other, that all are resolved or finally may be resolved into the payment of a sum of money, and that international custom and precedents accord with these principles, it must be concluded that the responsibility of States can be denied or admitted only in its entirety and not in part; thenceforth it would not be possible for the tribunal to declare this responsibility inapplicable in the matter of money debts without extending this inapplicability to all the other categories of responsibilities.

If a State is condemned to compensatory interest-damages because of an act of violence or the non-fulfilment of an obligation, it is a debtor to a degree which it may not have voluntarily stipulated, even more so than in case of delay in the payment of a conventional money debt. As to the effects of these responsibilities upon the finances of a debtor State, they might indeed be just as serious, if not more so, if it were a question of interest-damages which the Sublime Porte calls compensatory, as when it is simply a question of moratory interest in the restricted sense of the word. Moreover, however little the responsibility may imperil the existence of the State, it would constitute a case of *force majeure* which could be pleaded in public international law as well as by a private debtor.

The tribunal is, therefore, of the opinion that the Sublime Porte, which has explicitly accepted the principle of the responsibility of States, has no grounds for demanding an exception to this responsibility in the matter of money debts by pleading its character of public Power and the political and financial consequences of this responsibility.

5. To determine in what this special responsibility, which is incumbent upon a State debtor for a clear and exigible conventional debt, consists, it is now necessary to examine, proceeding by analogy as in the case of the arbitral awards which have been pleaded, the general principles of public and private law in this matter, as much from the point of view of the extent of this responsibility as of the contrary exceptions.

All the private legislation of the States forming the European concert admits, as did formerly the Roman law, the obligation to pay at least interest for delayed payments as legal indemnity when it is a question of the non-fulfilment of an obligation consisting in the payment of a sum of money fixed by convention, clear and exigible, such interest to be paid at least from the date of the demand made upon the debtor in due form of law. Some of this legislation goes farther and considers that such demand is already made upon the debtor on the date when the debt falls due, or admits complete reparation for damages instead of simple legal interest.

If most legislation, following the example of the Roman law, requires an express demand in due form of law, it is because the creditor on his part is in default for lack of diligence inasmuch as he does not demand payment of a clear and exigible sum.

The Imperial Russian Government (Case, p. 32) itself admits, in favor of the necessity of a demand in due form of law, that, in equity, it may be expedient "not to take by surprise a debtor State liable to moratory interest, when no notice had been given to remind it to carry out its engagements." Writers (for example, Heffter, *International Law of Europe*, paragraph 94) remark that, in "the execution of a public treaty, we must proceed with moderation and equity, according to the maxim that we must treat others as we wish to be treated ourselves. We must, therefore, grant reasonable extensions, so that the obligated party may suffer the least possible injury. The obligated party may await the creditor's demand in due form of law before being held responsible for delay, provided it is not a question of prestations, the performance of which it expressly stipulated for a fixed time." (See also Mérignhac, *Treatise on International Arbitration*, Paris, 1895, p. 290.)

A number of international arbitral awards have admitted that, even when it is a question of interest-damages for deferred payments, there is no occasion to have it run from the date of the damageable fact (United States *v.* Venezuela, Orinoco—Hague award of October 25, 1910, protocols, p. 59; United States *v.* Chile, May 15, 1863—award of His Majesty the King of the Belgians, Leopold I. La Fontaine, *Pasicrisie,* p. 36, column 2 and page 37, column 1; Germany *v.* Venezuela—Arrangement of May 7, 1903. Ralston & Doyle, *Venezuelan Arbitrations,* Washington, 1904, pp. 520 to 523; United States *v.* Venezuela, December 5, 1885. Moore, *Digest of International Arbitrations,* pp. 3545 and 3567, vol. 4, etc.).

Hence there is no occasion, and it would be contrary to equity, to assume that a debtor State is subject to stricter responsibility than a private debtor in most European legislation. Equity requires, as its theory indicates and as the Imperial Russian Government itself admits, that there shall be notice, demand in due form of law addressed to the debtor, for a sum which does not bear interest. The same reasons require that the demand in due form of law shall mention expressly the interest, and combine to set aside responsibility for more than simple legal interest.

It is seen from the correspondence submitted, that the Imperial Russian Government has expressly and in absolutely categorical terms demanded payment from the Sublime Porte of the principal and "interest," by the note of its Embassy at Constantinople, dated December 31, 1890/January 12, 1891. Diplomatic channels are the normal and regular means of communication between States in their relations governed by international law. This demand for payment is, therefore, regular and in due form.

The Imperial Ottoman Government must, consequently, be held responsible for the interest for delayed payments from the date of the receipt of this demand in due form of law.

The Imperial Ottoman Government pleads, in case responsibility is imposed upon it, various exceptions, the scope of which remains to be examined:

6. *The exception of "force majeure,"* cited as of the first importance, may be pleaded in opposition in public as well as in private international law. International law must adapt itself to political necessities. The Imperial Russian Government expressly admits (Russian Reply, p. 33 and note 2) that the obligation of a State to

carry out treaties may give way "if the very existence of the State should be in danger, if the observance of the international duty is . . . 'self-destructive.' "

It is incontestable that the Sublime Porte proves, by means of the exception of *force majeure* (Ottoman Counter-reply, p. 43, Nos. 119 to 128, Ottoman Counter-reply, p. 64, Nos. 382 to 398 and p. 87) that Turkey was, from 1881 to 1902, in the midst of financial difficulties of the utmost seriousness, increased by domestic and foreign events (insurrections and wars) which forced it to make special application of a large part of its revenues, to undergo foreign control as to part of its finances, to grant even a *moratorium* to the Ottoman Bank, and, in general, it was placed in a position where it could meet its engagements only with delay and postponements, and even then at great sacrifice. But it is asserted, on the other hand, that during this same period and especially following the creation of the Ottoman Bank, Turkey was able to obtain loans at favorable rates, redeem other loans, and, finally, pay off a large part of its public debt, estimated at 350,000,000 francs (Russian Reply, p. 37). It would clearly be exaggeration to admit that the payment (or obtaining of a loan for the payment) of the comparatively small sum of about six million francs due the Russian claimants would imperil the existence of the Ottoman Empire or seriously compromise its internal or external situation. The exception of *force majeure* can not, therefore, be admitted.

7. The Sublime Porte maintains then "that the acknowledgement of a principal debt to the Russian claimants constituted a *gift* agreed upon in their interest between the two Governments" (Counter-reply, No. 253, p. 19; No. 331, p. 44; No. 365, p. 55, and conclusions, p. 87). It remarks that the German civil code, paragraph 522, the Germanic common law, Austrian jurisprudence and the Roman law, pleaded on suppletory grounds (Law 16, *praemium, Digest* 22. 1) forbid the imposition of moratory interest in the case of a donation. It cites, especially, the arbitral award made on July 2, 1881, by His Majesty the Emperor of Austria in the Mosquito affair between Great Britain and Nicaragua.

In this affair Great Britain had renounced by a treaty of 1860 its protectorate over Mosquito, had given up the city of Grey Town (San Juan del Norte) and had recognized the sovereignty of Nicaragua over Mosquito, stipulating that this republic should pay for ten years to the chief of the Mosquitos an annual sum of 5,000 dollars, to facilitate the establishment of self-government in his territories. It was not long before this annuity ceased to be paid. In the opinion of the arbitrator, the chief of the Mosquitos was receiving the benefit of a veritable gift, claimed in his behalf from Nicaragua by the British Government, which had made political sacrifices in giving up its protectorate and the port of Grey Town.

In the opinion of the tribunal, the Russian claimants suffered damages—were victims of acts of war. Turkey bound itself to reimburse the amount of these damages to all the Russian victims who might prove their injury to the satisfaction of the commission established at the Russian Embassy at Constantinople. The decisions of this commission were not contested and it is not incumbent upon the arbitral tribunal to examine into them again or to decide whether or not they were too liberal. If the indemnification by Turkey of the Russian victims of war operations was not compulsory in the common law of nations, it is in nowise contrary to that law and can be considered as the transformation of a moral duty into a juridical obligation by a treaty of peace, under conditions analogous to a war indemnity properly so called. In all the thirty years' diplomatic correspondence over this affair, the Russian victims of war operations have always been considered by the two parties signatory to the agreements of 1878–1879 as claimants and not as donees. Finally, Turkey has obtained value received for its pretended gift by the fact that hostilities have ceased (Russian Reply, p. 50, paragraph 2). It is, therefore, not possible to admit the existence of an act of generosity, and still less of a gift, and it is consequently superfluous to inquire whether in public international law donors should receive the benefit of exemption from moratory interest, established for their benefit by certain private legislation.

8. The Sublime Porte pleads the exception of *res judicata*, supporting its position upon the fact that three claimants have asked the commission established at the Russian Embassy at Constantinople for interest to the time of complete payment, that the commission set aside their request, and that this negative action would certainly have intervened in the case of the other claimants who have not demanded such interest. (Ottoman Counter-reply, p. 86.)

This exception can not be admitted because, even granting that the Constantinople commission may be considered as a tribunal, the question now pending is whether interest-damages are due, *a posteriori*, by reason of the dates on which the indemnities fixed from 1878–81 by the commission were paid. But that commission did not decide and could not have decided this question.

9. The Sublime Porte pleads, as a last exception, the fact "that it was understood, tacitly and indeed expressly, in the course of the eleven or twelve last years of diplomatic correspondence, that Russia did not claim interest or interest-damages of any kind which would have been a burden to the Ottoman Empire," and "that the Imperial Russian Government, when once the entire principal was placed at its disposal, could not validly bring up again in a one-sided manner the understanding agreed to by it" (Ottoman Counter-reply, pp. 89-91).

The Imperial Ottoman Government remarks, and justly, that if Russia sent to Constantinople through diplomatic channels, on December 31, 1890/January 12, 1891, a regular demand for payment of the principal and interest it follows, on the other hand, from the subsequent correspondence, that at the time of the payments on account, no interest reservation appeared in the receipts given by the Embassy, and the Embassy never considered the sums received as interest. It also follows that the parties not only mapped out plans to bring about payment, but abstained from mentioning interest during a period of some ten years. It follows, above all, that the two Governments interpreted in the same manner the term *balance of the indemnity;* that this term, used for the first time by the Ottoman Ministry of Foreign Affairs in its communication of March 27, 1893, frequently recurs thereafter; that the two Governments have constantly meant by the word balance the portion of the principal remaining due on the date the notes were exchanged, which sets aside moratory interest; that the Russian Ambassador at Constantinople wrote on May 23/June 4, 1894: "I am obliged to insist that the total of the balance due Russian subjects, which amounts to 91,000 Turkish pounds, be paid to the Embassy without further delay, in order to give satisfaction to the just complaints and claims of those interested . . . and thus really put an end—to use your Excellency's expression—to the incidents to which it had given rise," that this sum of 91,000 Turkish pounds was exactly the sum which was then due on the principal and that thus moratory interest was not considered; that on October 3d of the same year, 1894, Turkey, about to make a payment on account, of 50,000 pounds, announced to the Embassy, without meeting with any objections, that the Ottoman Bank "will guarantee payment of the balance of 41,000 Turkish pounds"; that on January 13/25, 1896, the Embassy again used the same term, *balance of the indemnity*, in protesting against the handing over by Turkey to the Ottoman Bank assignments of revenues which were already pledged to the Imperial Russian Government for the payment of the war indemnity; that on February 11th of the same year, 1896, at the time of the discussion of the resources to be furnished to the Ottoman Bank, the Sublime Porte mentioned, in a note addressed to the Embassy, "the 43,978 Turkish pounds, representing the balance of the indemnity"; that a few days later, February 10/22, the Embassy replied, making use of the same words *balance of the indemnity;* and that on May 28th the Ottoman Ministry of Foreign Affairs mentioned once more "the sum of 43,978 Turkish pounds representing the said balance"; that the same was true of a note of the Embassy dated April 25/May 8, 1900, although more than four years had elapsed between this communication and the communication of 1896, and that the question of interest should have been again called to attention in some way after so long an interval; that this same expression, *balance of the indemnity*, appears in the note of the Sublime Porte of July 5, 1900; that, finally, on March 3/16, 1901, the Russian Embassy, after having stated that the Ottoman Bank had not supplied further funds "for the payment of the 43,978 Turkish pounds, the amount of the balance of the indemnity due to Russian subjects," asked that categorical orders be sent to the proper person "for the payment without further delay 'of the above-mentioned sums' "; that this balance, or practically this amount, having been held by the Ottoman Bank at the disposal of the Embassy, it was not until several months later, June 23/July 6, that the Embassy transmitted to the Sublime Porte a request of "those interested," demanding payment of some twenty million francs for interest on account of delayed payments, expressing the hope that the Sublime Porte "will not hesitate to recognize in principle the just grounds for the claim," except "to refer the examination of the details to a" mixed Russo-Turkish "commission"; that in short, for eleven years and more, and up to a date after the payment of the balance of the principal, there had not only been no question of interest between the two Governments, but mention had been made again and again of only the balance of the principal.

When the tribunal recognized that, according to the general principles and custom of public international law, there was a similarity between the condition of a State and that of an individual, which are debtors for a clear and exigible conventional sum, it is equitable and juridical also to apply by analogy the principles of private law common to cases where the demand for payment must be considered as removed and the benefit to be derived therefrom as eliminated. In private law, the effects of demand for payment are eliminated when the creditor, after having made legal demand upon the debtor, grants one or more extensions for the payment of the principal obligation, without reserving the rights acquired by the legal demand (Toullier-Duvergier, *Droit français*, vol. iii, p. 159, No. 256), or again, when "the creditor does not follow up the summons to the debtor," and "these rules apply to interest-damages, and also to interest due for the non-fulfilment of an obligation .   .   .   or for delay in its fulfilment" (Duranton, *Droit français*, x, p. 470; Aubry and Rau, *Droit Civil*, 1871, iv, p. 99; Berney, *De la demeure*, etc., Lausanne, 1886, p. 62; Windscheid, *Lehrbuch des Pandektenrechts*, 1879, p. 99; Demolombe, x, p. 49; Laronbière i, art. 1139, No. 22, etc.).

In the relations between the Imperial Russian Government and the Sublime Porte, Russia therefore renounced its right to interest, since its Embassy repeatedly accepted without discussion or reservation and mentioned again and again in its own diplomatic correspondence the amount of the balance of the indemnity as identical with the amount of the balance of the principal.   In other words, the correspondence of the last few years proves that the two parties interpreted, in fact, the acts of 1879 as implying that the payment of the balance of the principal and the payment of the balance to which the claimants had a right were identical, and this implied the relinquishment of the right to interest or moratory interest-damages.

The Imperial Russian Government can not, when the principal of the indemnity has been paid or placed at its disposal, validly reconsider one-sidedly an interpretation accepted and practised in its name by its Embassy.

III

IN CONCLUSION

The arbitral tribunal, basing its conclusion upon the statements of law and fact which precede, is of the opinion

That in principle the Imperial Ottoman Government was liable to moratory indemnities to the Imperial Russian Government from December 31, 1890/January 12, 1891, the date of the receipt of the explicit and regular demand for payment.

But that, in fact, the benefit to the Imperial Russian Government of this legal demand having ceased as a result of the subsequent relinquishment by its Embassy at Constantinople, the Imperial Ottoman Government is not held liable to pay interest-damages by reason of the dates on which the payment of the indemnities was made.

And, consequently, decides that a negative reply is made to question 1 of Article 3 of the *compromis,* thus stated: "Whether or not the Imperial Ottoman Government must pay the Russian claimants interest-damages by reason of the dates on which the said Government made payment of the indemnities determined in pursuance of Article 5 of the treaty of January 27/February 8, 1879, as well as of the protocol of the same date?"

Done at The Hague, in the building of the Permanent Court of Arbitration, November 11, 1912.

> *President:* LARDY
> *Secretary General:* MICHIELS VAN VERDUYNEN
> *Secretary:* RÖELL

AGREEMENT FOR ARBITRATION

Compromis of arbitration between the Imperial Russian Government and the Imperial Ottoman Government.—Signed at Constantinople, July 22/August 4, 1910.[1]

The Imperial Russian Government and the Imperial Ottoman Government, co-signatories of the Hague Convention of October 18, 1907, for the pacific settlement of international disputes:

Considering the provisions of Article 5 of the treaty signed at Constantinople between Russia and Turkey, January 27/February 8, 1879, as follows:

> The claims of Russian subjects and institutions in Turkey for indemnity on account of damages suffered during the war will be paid as soon as they are examined by the Russian Embassy at Constantinople and transmitted to the Sublime Porte.
>
> The total of these claims shall in no case exceed 26,750,000 francs.
>
> Claims may be presented to the Sublime Porte beginning one year from the date on which ratifications are exchanged, and no claims will be admitted which are presented after the expiration of two years from that date;

Considering the additional explanation contained in the protocol bearing the same date:

> As to the expiration of one year, fixed by this article as the date from which claims may be presented to the Sublime Porte, it is understood that one exception will be made in favor of the Russian Hospital's claim, amounting to 11,200 pounds sterling;

Considering that a disagreement has arisen between the Imperial Russian Government and the Imperial Ottoman Government as to the questions of law arising from the dates on which the Imperial Ottoman Government made the following payments on the amounts of the indemnities regularly presented in pursuance of the said Article 5, to wit:

	Turkish pounds	Piastres	Paras
In 1884	50,000	..	..
In 1889	50,000	..	..
In 1893	75,000	..	..
In 1894	50,000	..	..
In 1902	42,438	67	$\frac{22}{40}$

---

[1] *American Journal of International Law*, vol. 7, Supplement, p. 62. For the original French text, see Appendix, p. 551.

Considering that the Imperial Russian Government holds that the Imperial Ottoman Government is responsible to the Russian claimants for interest-damages because of the delay in settling its debt;

Considering that the Imperial Ottoman Government contests, both in fact and in law, the grounds of the Imperial Russian Government's contention;

Considering that it had not been possible to settle the dispute through diplomatic channels;

And having resolved, in conformity with the stipulations of the said Hague Convention, to end this controversy by submitting the question to arbitration;

Have authorized to this effect their representatives designated below, to wit:

For Russia,

His Excellency Monsieur Tcharikow, Ambassador of His Majesty the Emperor of Russia at Constantinople;

For Turkey,

His Excellency Rifaat Pasha, Minister of Foreign Affairs, to conclude the following *compromis:*

ARTICLE 1

The Powers in controversy decide that the arbitral tribunal to which the question will be submitted as a last resort shall be composed of five members, who shall be appointed in the following manner:

Each party must name, as soon as possible and within two months from the date of this *compromis,* two arbitrators, and the four arbitrators thus appointed shall choose an umpire. In case the four arbitrators shall not, within two months of their appointment, have chosen an umpire either unanimously or by a majority, the choice of an umpire devolves upon a third party agreed upon by the parties. If, after the lapse of two more months, an agreement is not reached upon this question, each party designates a different Power and the umpire is chosen by the Powers thus designated.

If, after the lapse of two more months, these two Powers have not been able to agree, each of them presents two candidates selected from the list of members of the Permanent Court, exclusive of the members of the said Court selected by the two Powers or by the parties and being nationals neither of the former nor of the latter. These candidates, moreover, can not belong to the nationality of the arbitrators appointed by the parties in the present arbitration. The umpire is chosen by lot from the two candidates thus presented.

The drawing of lots will be done by the International Bureau of the Permanent Court at The Hague.

ARTICLE 2

The Powers in controversy will be represented before the arbitral tribunal by agents, counsel or advocates, in conformity with the provisions of Article 62 of the Hague Convention of 1907 for the pacific settlement of international disputes.

These agents, counsel or advocates will be appointed by the parties in ample time to prevent any delay in the arbitration.

ARTICLE 3

The questions in dispute and upon which the parties ask the arbitral tribunal to render a definitive decision are as follows:

I. Whether or not the Imperial Ottoman Government must pay the Russian claimants interest-damages by reason of the dates on which the said Government made payment of the indemnities determined in pursuance of Article 5 of the treaty of January 27/February 8, 1879, as well as of the protocol of the same date?

II. In case the first question is decided in the affirmative, what should be the amount of these interest-damages?

ARTICLE 4

The arbitral tribunal, as soon as it is constituted, shall meet at The Hague at a date to be determined by the arbitrators and within one month from the appointment of the umpire. After settling, in conformity with the letter and the spirit of the Hague Convention of 1907, all questions of procedure which may arise and which are not provided for in the present *compromis*, the said tribunal shall determine the date of its next meeting.

However, it is agreed that the tribunal can not open the arguments on the questions in dispute, either before the expiration of two months or after the expiration of three months from the filing of the counter-case or the counter-reply provided for by Article 6 and, later, by the arrangements set forth in Article 8.

ARTICLE 5

The arbitral procedure will include two distinct phases : the written statement of the case ; and the arguments which will consist in the oral development of the pleas of the parties before the tribunal.

French is the only language which the tribunal will use and which may be used before it.

ARTICLE 6

Within eight months at most after the date of the present *compromis*, the Imperial Russian Government must deliver to each of the members of the arbitral tribunal one complete copy, and to the Imperial Ottoman Government ten complete copies, written or printed, of its case, containing every argument in support of its claim with reference to the two questions mentioned in Article 3.

Within eight months at most after this delivery, the Imperial Ottoman Government must deliver to each of the members of the tribunal, as well as to the Imperial Russian Government, the same number, as specified above, of complete copies, written or printed, of its counter-case, with all supporting arguments, but confining itself to question 1 of Article 3.

Within one month after this delivery the Imperial Russian Government will inform the president of the arbitral tribunal whether it intends to present a reply. In that case, it will have an extension of three months at most from the date of such notification in which to communicate the said reply under the same conditions as the case. The Imperial Ottoman Government will then have an extension of four months from the date of this communication to present its counter-reply, under the same conditions as the counter-case.

The extension fixed by the present article may be lengthened if agreed to by both parties, or if the tribunal deems it necessary in order to reach a just decision.

But the tribunal will not take into consideration cases, counter-cases or other communications which are presented to it by the parties after the expiration of the last extension which it has granted.

ARTICLE 7

If in the cases or other papers exchanged either of the parties has referred or alluded to a document or paper of which it alone is in possession and of which it has not furnished a copy, it must furnish the other party with a copy, if the other party so requests, within thirty days.

ARTICLE 8

In case the arbitral tribunal decides question 1 of Article 3 in the affirmative, it must, before taking up question 2 of the same article, grant the parties further extensions, which may not be less than three months each, for the presentation and exchange of their demands and arguments in support of them.

ARTICLE 9

The decisions of the tribunal on the first, and contingently on the second question at issue, shall be rendered, in so far as possible, within one month from the closing by the president of the arguments relating to each of these questions.

ARTICLE 10

The judgment of the arbitral tribunal shall be final and must be executed strictly and without any delay.

ARTICLE 11

Each party bears its own expenses and half of the expenses of the tribunal.

ARTICLE 12

Whatever questions arise in this arbitration which are not provided for by the present *compromis* shall be governed by the stipulations of the Hague Convention for the pacific settlement of international disputes, except, however, those articles the acceptance of which has been reserved by the Imperial Ottoman Government.

Done at Constantinople, July 22/August 4, 1910.

(Signed) RIFAAT
(Signed) N. TCHARYKOW

THE CARTHAGE CASE

between

FRANCE *and* ITALY

Decided May 6, 1913

Syllabus

During the Turko-Italian war in Africa in 1912, the Italians established a strict watch against the possibility of military supplies or reinforcements of any kind reaching the Turks in Tripoli by way of Tunis. As the result, on January 16, 1912, the *Carthage,* a steamer belonging to the *Compagnie Générale Transatlantique,* was stopped by an Italian war vessel while on its way from Marseilles to Tunis, on account of having on board an aeroplane and parts of another, destined to a private consignee in Tunis, which the Italians claimed was contraband of war. It being impossible to transfer the aeroplane from one ship to another, the *Carthage* was conveyed to Cagliari, where it was detained until January 20, 1912. The release of the vessel was demanded by the French Ambassador at Rome. The aeroplane and parts were landed by order of the company and the *Carthage* was allowed to resume her voyage.

Upon assurance to the Italian Government that the aeroplane was intended purely for exhibition purposes and that there was no intention on the part of the owner to offer his services to the Ottoman Government, the aeroplane was released on January 21, 1912. The French Government demanded in addition reparation for the insult to the French flag and for the violation of international law and conventions between the two Governments and damages for the injury to the private parties interested in the vessel and its voyage. The Italian Government made a counter-claim against France for the amount of the expenses caused by the seizure of the *Carthage.*

The controversy was referred for settlement to a tribunal selected from the members of the Permanent Court of Arbitration at The Hague, under a *compromis* dated March 6, 1912.[1] The tribunal was composed of K. Hj. L. Hammarskjöld of Denmark; Louis Renault of France; Guido Fusinato of Italy; J. Kriege of Germany, and Baron Michel de Taube of Russia. Its sessions began March 31, 1913, and ended May 6, 1913, the decision being rendered on the latter date. The tribunal held that, while belligerents have as a general rule the right of visit and search, to determine if contraband is carried by neutral vessels, the legality of acts committed after the search depends upon the presence of contraband or sufficient legal reasons to believe

---

[1] *Post,* p. 336.

that it exists; that the information in the possession of the Italian authorities as to the hostile destination of the aeroplane, which was an essential element to establish its contraband nature, was not legally sufficient and that, therefore, the capture of the vessel and its convoy to Cagliari and detention there were illegal. The French Government was awarded the sum of 160,000 francs in satisfaction for the damages suffered by the private parties interested in the vessel and its voyage. The national claims of the respective Governments were, however, disallowed.

AWARD OF THE TRIBUNAL

Award of the arbitral tribunal in the case of the French mail steamer "Carthage."—The Hague, May 6, 1913.[1]

Considering that, by an agreement dated January 26, 1912,[2] and by a *compromis* dated the following 6th of March,[3] the Government of the French Republic and the Royal Italian Government have agreed to submit to an arbitral tribunal composed of five members the decision of the following questions:

1. Were the Italian naval authorities within their rights in proceeding, as they did, to the capture and temporary detention of the French mail steamer *Carthage?*

2. What should be the pecuniary or other consequences, following the decision of the preceding question?

Considering that, in accordance with this *compromis*, the two Governments have chosen, by common consent, the following members of the Permanent Court of Arbitration to constitute the arbitral tribunal:

His Excellency Guido Fusinato, Doctor of Law, Minister of State, former Minister of Public Instruction, honorary professor of international law in the University of Turin, Deputy, Councilor of State;

Mr. Knut Hjalmar Leonard Hammarskjöld, Doctor of Law, formerly Minister of Justice, formerly Minister of Public Worship and Instruction, formerly Envoy Extraordinary and Minister Plenipotentiary at Copenhagen, formerly President of the Court of Ap-

---

[1] *American Journal of International Law*, vol. 7, p. 623. For the original French text, see Appendix, p. 556.
[2] *Post*, p. 337.   [3] *Post*, p. 336.

peals of Jönköping, formerly professor in the Faculty of Law of Upsala, Governor of the Province of Upsala;

Mr. Kriege, Doctor of Law, at present Confidential Counselor of Legation and Director in the Department of Foreign Affairs, Plenipotentiary in the German Federal Council;

Mr. Louis Renault, Minister Plenipotentiary, member of the Institute, professor in the Faculty of Law of the University of Paris and of the *École Libre des Sciences Politiques*, Jurisconsult in the Ministry of Foreign Affairs;

His Excellency Baron Michel de Taube, Doctor of Law, Assistant Minister of Public Instruction of Russia, Councilor of State;

That the two Governments have, at the same time designated Mr. Hammarskjöld to perform the duties of president.

Considering that, in accordance with the *compromis* of March 6, 1912, the cases and counter-cases have been duly exchanged by the parties and communicated to the arbitrators;

Considering that the tribunal, constituted as above, met at The Hague on March 31, 1913;

That the two Governments have respectively appointed as agents and counsel,

The Government of the French Republic:

Mr. Henri Fromageot, advocate in the Court of Appeals of Paris, assistant jurisconsult in the Ministry of Foreign Affairs, counsel in international law for the Navy Department, agent;

Mr. André Hesse, advocate in the Court of Appeals of Paris, member of the Chamber of Deputies, counsel;

The Royal Italian Government:

Mr. Arturo Ricci-Busatti, Envoy Extraordinary and Minister Plenipotentiary, Chief of the Bureau of Disputed Claims and Legislation of the Royal Ministry of Foreign Affairs, agent;

Mr. Dionisio Anzilotti, professor of international law in the University of Rome, counsel.

Considering that the agents of the parties have presented the following demands to the tribunal, to-wit,

The agent of the Government of the French Republic:
May it please the tribunal
As to the first question propounded by the *compromis*,

To say that the Italian naval authorities were not within their rights in proceeding as they did to the capture and temporary detention of the French mail steamer *Carthage;*

In consequence and as to the second question,

To say that the Royal Italian Government shall be obliged to pay to the Government of the French Republic as damages:

1. The sum of one franc for the offense against the French flag;

2. The sum of one hundred thousand francs as reparation for the moral and political injury resulting from the failure to observe international common law and conventions binding upon both Italy and France;

3. The sum of five hundred and seventy-six thousand, seven hundred and thirty-eight francs, twenty-three centimes, the total amount of the losses and damages claimed by private parties interested in the steamer and its voyage;

To say that the above-mentioned sum of one hundred thousand francs shall be paid to the Government of the Republic for the benefit of such work or institution of international interest as it may please the tribunal to indicate;

In the second place, and in case the tribunal does not consider itself at present sufficiently informed as to the grounds for the individual claims,

To say that one or more of its members to whom it may be pleased to entrust this duty, shall proceed, in the presence of the agents and counsel of the two Governments, in the chamber where its deliberations take place, to the examination of each of the said individual claims;

In all cases, and by the application of Article 9 of the *compromis,*

To say that, after the expiration of three months from the day of the award, the sums to be paid by the Royal Italian Government and not yet paid shall bear interest at the rate of four per cent per annum.

And the agent of the Royal Italian Government:

May it please the tribunal

As to the first question propounded by the *compromis,*

To say and decide that the Italian naval authorities were entirely within their rights in proceeding, as they did, to the capture and temporary detention of the French mail steamer *Carthage;*

In consequence and as to the second question,

To say and decide that the French Government shall be obliged to pay to the Italian Government the sum of two thousand and seventy-two francs, twenty-five centimes, the amount of expense caused by the seizure of the *Carthage;*

To say, that, upon the expiration of three months from the day of the award, the sum to be paid by the Government of the French Republic will, if it has not yet been paid, bear interest at the rate of four per cent per annum.

Considering that, after the tribunal had heard the oral statements of the agents of the parties and the explanations which they furnished upon its request, the arguments were duly declared closed.

IN THE MATTER OF FACT

Considering that the French mail steamer *Carthage*, of the *Compagnie Générale Transatlantique*, in the course of a regular trip between Marseilles and Tunis, was stopped on January 16, 1912, at 6:30 a.m., in the open sea, seventeen miles from the coast of Sardinia, by the destroyer *Agordat* of the Royal Italian Navy;

That the commander of the *Agordat,* having ascertained that there was on board the *Carthage* an aeroplane belonging to one Duval, a French aviator, and consigned to his address at Tunis, declared to the captain of the *Carthage* that the aeroplane in question was considered by the Italian Government contraband of war;

That, as it was impossible to transfer the aeroplane from one vessel to the other, the captain of the *Carthage* received the order to follow the *Agordat* to Cagliari, where he was detained until January 20;

IN THE MATTER OF LAW

Considering that, according to the principles universally acknowledged, a belligerent war-ship has, as a general rule and except under special circumstances, the right to stop a neutral commercial vessel in the open sea and proceed to search it to see whether it is observing the rules of neutrality, especially as to contraband;

Considering, on the other hand, that the legality of every act which goes beyond a mere search depends upon the existence either of a trade in contraband or of sufficient reasons to believe that such a trade exists,

That, in this respect, the reasons must be of a juridical nature;

Considering that in this case the *Carthage* was not only stopped and searched by the *Agordat;* but also taken to Cagliari, sequestrated and detained for a certain time, after which it was released by the administrative authority;

Considering that the purpose of the measures taken against the French mail steamer was to prevent the transportation of the aeroplane belonging to one Duval, and shipped on the *Carthage* to the address of this same Duval at Tunis;

That this aeroplane was considered by the Italian authorities contraband of war, both by its nature and by its destination, which in reality might have been for the Ottoman forces in Tripolitana;

Considering, in so far as concerns the hostile destination of the aeroplane, an essential element of its seizability,

That the information possessed by the Italian authorities was of too general a nature and had too little connection with the aeroplane in question to constitute sufficient juridical reasons to believe in a hostile destination and, consequently, to justify the capture of the vessel which was transporting the aeroplane;

That the despatch from Marseilles, relating certain remarks of the mechanician of Mr. Duval, did not reach the Italian authorities until after the *Carthage* had been stopped and taken to Cagliari and could not, therefore, have caused these measures; that, moreover, the despatch could not in any case have been considered a sufficient reason, in the light of what has previously been said;

Considering that, this conclusion being reached, the tribunal is not called upon to inquire whether or not the aeroplane should by its nature be included in articles of contraband, either conditional or absolute, or to examine whether the theory of a continuous voyage should or should not be applicable in this case;

Considering that the tribunal finds it likewise superfluous to examine the question whether, at the time of the measures taken against the *Carthage* there were irregularities of form, and if, in case there were, these irregularities were of a kind to vitiate measures which would otherwise have been legal;

Considering that the Italian authorities demanded surrender of the mail only that it might reach its destination as quickly as possible,

That this demand, which apparently was at first misunderstood by the captain of the *Carthage,* was in conformity with the Convention of October 18, 1907, relative to certain restrictions in the exercise of the right of capture, which, however, was not ratified by the belligerents.

Upon the request that the Royal Italian Government be condemned to pay to the Government of the French Republic as damages:

1. The sum of one franc for the offense against the French flag;

2. The sum of one hundred thousand francs as reparation for the moral and political injury resulting from the failure to observe international common law and conventions binding upon both France and Italy,

Considering that, in case a Power should fail to fulfil its obligations, whether general or special, to another Power, the establishment of this fact, especially in an arbitral award, constitutes in itself a serious penalty;

That this penalty is made heavier in such case by the payment of damages for material losses;

That, as a general rule and excluding special circumstances, these penalties appear to be sufficient;

That, also, as a general rule, the introduction of a further pecuniary penalty appears to be superfluous and to go beyond the purposes of international jurisdiction;

Considering that, by the application of what has just been said, the circumstances of the present case are not such as to call for such a supplementary penalty; that, without further examination, there is no occasion to comply with the above-mentioned request.

Upon the request of the French agent that the Italian Government be condemned to pay the sum of five hundred and seventy-six thousand seven hundred and thirty-eight francs, twenty-three centimes, the total amount of the losses and damages claimed by private parties interested in the vessel and its voyage,

Considering that the request for indemnity is, in principle, justified;

Considering that the tribunal, after having heard the concurring explanations of two of its members charged by it to investigate the said claims, has fixed the amount due the *Compagnie Générale Transatlantique* at seventy-five thousand francs, the amount due the aviator Duval and his associates at twenty-five thousand francs; and, finally, the amount due the passengers and shippers at sixty thousand francs; making a total of one hundred and sixty thousand francs to be paid by the Italian Government to the French Government.

For these reasons

The arbitral tribunal declares and pronounces as follows:

The Italian naval authorities were not within their rights in proceeding, as they did, to the capture and temporary detention of the French mail steamer *Carthage*.

The Royal Italian Government shall be obliged, within three months from the present award, to pay to the Government of the French Republic the sum of one hundred and sixty thousand francs, the amount of the losses and damages suffered, by reason of the capture and seizure of the *Carthage*, by the private parties interested in the vessel and its voyage.

There is no occasion to give effect to the other claims contained in the demands of the two parties.

Done at The Hague, in the building of the Permanent Court of Arbitration, the 6th day of May, 1913.

President:	HJ. L. HAMMARSKJÖLD
Secretary General:	MICHIELS VAN VERDUYNEN
Secretary:	RÖELL

AGREEMENT FOR ARBITRATION

Compromis of arbitration relative to the question raised by the capture and temporary detention of the French mail steamer "Carthage."—Signed at Paris, March 6, 1912.[1]

The Government of the French Republic and the Royal Italian

---

[1] Translation. For the original French text, see Appendix, p. 561.

Government, having agreed, on January 26, 1912,[1] in application of the arbitration convention of December 25, 1903, which was renewed on December 24, 1908, to entrust an arbitral tribunal with the examination of the capture and temporary detention of the French mail steamer *Carthage* by the Italian naval authorities, as well as with the duty of deciding the consequences which should follow,

The undersigned, duly authorized for that purpose, have agreed upon the following *compromis:*

ARTICLE 1

An arbitral tribunal, composed as is hereinafter stipulated, is charged with the settling of the following questions:

1. Were the Italian naval authorities within their rights in proceeding, as they did, to the capture and temporary detention of the French mail steamer *Carthage?*

2. What pecuniary or other consequences should follow the decision of the preceding question?

ARTICLE 2

The tribunal shall be composed of five arbitrators which the two Governments shall choose from among the members of the Permanent Court of Arbitration at The Hague, appointing one of them to exercise the functions of umpire.[2]

ARTICLE 3

On June 15, 1912, each party shall deposit with the Bureau of the Permanent Court of Arbitration fifteen copies of its memorial, with certified copies of all papers and documents which it intends to present in the case.

The Bureau shall guarantee their transmission to the arbitrators and parties, to wit: two copies for each arbitrator; three copies for each party; two copies shall remain in the archives of the Bureau.

On August 15, 1912, each party shall deposit in the same manner as above its counter-memorial with the papers appertaining thereto, and its final conclusions.

ARTICLE 4

Each of the parties shall deposit with the Bureau of the Permanent Court of Arbitration at The Hague, at the same time that it deposits

[1]See *post*, p. 339.
[2]See supplementary agreement of April 4, 1912, *post*, p. 340.

its memorial, a sum for the purpose of expenses, which shall be fixed by mutual agreement.

ARTICLE 5

The tribunal shall meet at The Hague, upon the convocation of its president, in the second fortnight of the month of September, 1912.

ARTICLE 6

Each party shall be represented by an agent whose duty it shall be to serve as intermediary between it and the tribunal.

The tribunal may demand that either agent furnish it, if necessary, with oral or written explanations, to which the agent of the opposing party shall have the right to reply.

ARTICLE 7

The French language shall be used by the tribunal. Each party may use its own language.

ARTICLE 8

The award of the tribunal shall be rendered with the least possible delay and in any case within the thirty days following the closing of the debates. However, this period may be extended upon the demand of the tribunal and the consent of the parties.

ARTICLE 9

The tribunal is competent to regulate the conditions for the execution of its award.

ARTICLE 10

On all points not covered by the present *compromis,* the stipulations of the Hague Convention for the pacific settlement of international disputes, of October 18, 1907, shall be applicable to the present arbitration.

Done, in duplicate, at Paris, March 6, 1912.

(Signed)   L. RENAULT
(Signed)   G. FUSINATO

ADDITIONAL DOCUMENTS

Joint Note of the French Ambassador and the Italian Minister of Foreign Affairs, concerning the settlement of the questions arising out of the arrest of the French steamers "Carthage" and "Manouba."[1]—Signed January 26, 1912.[2]

The Ambassador of France and the Minister of Foreign Affairs of Italy, having investigated in the most friendly spirit the circumstances which preceded and followed the arrest and search by an Italian cruiser of two French steamers proceeding from Marseilles to Tunis, are happy to report, in thorough accord and before every other consideration, that in neither of the two countries has there arisen as a result of these incidents any feeling contrary to the sentiments of sincere and constant friendship which unite them.

This report has led the two Governments without difficulty to decide:

1. That the questions arising from the capture and temporary detention of the steamer *Carthage* shall be referred to the Court of Arbitration at The Hague for examination, under the Franco-Italian arbitration convention of December 23, 1903, renewed December 24, 1908.

2. That in the matter of the seizure of the *Manouba* and of the Ottoman passengers who were on board, as this action, according to the Italian Government, was taken by virtue of the rights which it declares it possesses according to the general principles of international law and Article 47 of the Declaration of London of 1909, the circumstances under which this action was taken and the consequences thereof shall likewise be submitted for examination to the high international Court established at The Hague; that, in order to restore the *statu quo ante*, in so far as concerns the Ottoman passengers who were seized, the latter shall be delivered to the French consul at Cagliari, who shall see that they are taken back to the place from which they sailed, upon the responsibility of the French Government, which Government shall take the necessary measures to prevent Ottoman passengers not belonging to the "Red Crescent" but to fighting forces, from sailing from a French port to Tunis or to the scene of military operations.

---

[1] For the *Manouba* Case, see *post*, p. 341.
[2] *American Journal of International Law*, vol. 7, Supplement, p. 176. For the original French text, see Appendix, p. 562.

Franco-Italian Agreement Signed at Paris, April 4, 1912[1]

The Government of the French Republic and the Royal Italian Government, having in mind the two *compromis* negotiated March 6, 1912,[2] by Messrs. Louis Renault and Fusinato, for the purpose of settling by arbitration of the Permanent Court at The Hague the incidents relative to the seizure of the *Carthage* and of the *Manouba*, declaring their approval of the terms, and considering themselves bound by their texts;

Have appointed by common accord the following members of the Permanent Court of Arbitration to constitute the arbitral tribunal:

Mr. Guido Fusinato, Doctor of Law, former Minister of Public Instruction, former professor of international law at the University of Turin, Deputy, Councilor of State;

Mr. Knut Hjalmar Léonard Hammarskjöld, Doctor of Law, former Minister of Justice, former Minister of Public Worship and Instruction, former Envoy Extraordinary and Minister Plenipotentiary at Copenhagen, former President of the Court of Appeals of Jönköping, former professor in the Faculty of Law of Upsala, Governor of the province of Upsala;

Mr. Kriege, Doctor of Law, Confidential Counselor of Legation, Director of the Department of Foreign Affairs;

Mr. Louis Renault, Minister Plenipotentiary, professor in the Faculty of Law of Paris, Counselor to the Minister of Foreign Affairs;

Baron Taube, permanent member of the Council of the Minister of Foreign Affairs, professor of international law in the Imperial University of St. Petersburg, Councilor of State;

Mr. Hammarskjöld shall perform the duties of umpire or president of the tribunal.

The two Governments agree to fix at 3,000 Netherland florins the sum to be deposited by each of them, conformably to Article 4 of each *compromis,* it being understood that the said sum is to serve as provision for all business with which the above-mentioned arbitral tribunal is charged.

The two Governments reserve the right to modify by mutual agreement Article 5 of each of the *compromis* with respect to the date of the meeting of the arbitral tribunal.

Done at Paris, April 4, 1912.

                         (L. S.) Signed: R. Poincaré
                         (L. S.) Signed: M. Ruspoli

---

[1]Translation. For the original French text, see Appendix, p. 563.
[2]*Ante*, p. 336; *post*, p. 351.

THE MANOUBA CASE

between

FRANCE *and* ITALY

Decided May 6, 1913

Syllabus

On January 5, 1912, during the war between Turkey and Italy over Tripoli and Cyrenaica, the Ottoman Government requested the French Government to provide facilities for a Turkish Red Crescent Mission to reach the seat of the war *via* Tunis, which the French Government agreed to do. The Italian Ambassador in Paris protested against the proposed action, but the French Government assured him that the Turks in question were members of the Red Crescent Mission and also sent instructions that the Tunis authorities should confirm this fact before allowing the Turks to proceed. This information and proceeding satisfied the Ambassador and he communicated with his Government. Before his message arrived, however, the *Manouba*, a French vessel, upon which the Turks were being transported, was captured on January 18, 1912, by an Italian war vessel, and taken to Cagliari, at which port it arrived on the same day. The Italians, claiming that the Turks were carrying arms and money for the use of the Ottoman forces in Tripoli, demanded their surrender, and, on the refusal of the captain of the *Manouba* to comply, seized the vessel. The French Embassy was advised of what had occurred, and, in view of assurances of the Italians that the Turks were belligerents, directed the vice-consul at Cagliari to order their removal from the *Manouba*. This was done in the afternoon of January 19, 1912, and the vessel proceeded on her voyage. Notwithstanding the action of the French Embassy, vigorous representations were immediately made to the Italian Government by the French Government, which demanded the release of the Turks, reparation for the offense to the French flag, the violation of the conventional engagements between the two countries, particularly Article 2 of the Hague Convention of 1907 relative to certain restrictions on the right of capture in maritime warfare, and Article 9 of the Geneva Convention of July 6, 1906, for the amelioration of the condition of the sick and wounded in the field, and the verbal agreement between the two Governments relative to the passengers on the *Manouba*. Indemnities to the private individuals interested in the steamer and its voyage were also demanded. The Italian Government agreed to deliver the Turkish subjects to the French consul at Cagliari to be returned upon the responsibility of France to the place from which they sailed. It took issue, however, with the other French demands, and made a counter-claim for the violation of its belligerent right under international law to ascertain the character of individuals suspected of being soldiers of the enemy found on board neutral commercial vessels, and for reimbursement of expenses incurred on account of the seizure of the vessel.

The controversy was referred under a *compromis* dated March 6, 1912,[1] to an arbitral tribunal selected from the members of the Permanent Court of Arbitration at The Hague. The tribunal was composed of K. Hj. L. Hammarskjöld of Sweden; Louis Renault of France; Guido Fusinato of Italy; J. Kriege of Germany, and Baron Michel de Taube of Russia. Its sessions began March 31, 1913, and ended May 6, 1913. In an award rendered on the latter date, the tribunal held that there was a misunderstanding between the two Governments as to the exemption of the vessel which carried these passengers from the right of search, and that, in the absence of a special understanding, the Italian naval authorities were justified in acting according to the common international law; that they had sufficient reasons to believe that some of the passengers were enemy soldiers and had a right to demand and compel their surrender, but that they had no right to capture the vessel and force it to leave its course unless for the purpose of arresting the captain for failure to comply with such demand; that no such demand having been made, the capture and conveyance of the ship to Cagliari were illegal. The tribunal further held, however, that the illegality of the capture did not affect the right of the Italian authorities at Cagliari to demand and compel the surrender of the Turkish passengers and to arrest them, and upon refusal of the demand by the captain to detain the vessel until it was complied with. The detention of the vessel at Cagliari and the arrest of the passengers were therefore held to be legal. The national claims of both Governments were disallowed, but a small indemnity was awarded to France for the losses sustained by the private individuals interested in the vessel and its voyage by reason of its illegal capture and convoy to Cagliari, from which indemnity the tribunal deducted the amount of expenses incurred by the Italian Government in guarding the vessel during its sequestration at Cagliari to compel the surrender of the passengers.

AWARD OF THE TRIBUNAL

Award of the arbitral tribunal in the case of the French mail steamer "Manouba."—The Hague, May 6, 1913.[2]

Considering that by an agreement dated January 26, 1912,[3] and

---

[1] *Post*, p. 351.
[2] *American Journal of International Law*, vol 7, p. 629. For the original French text, see Appendix, p. 565.
[3] *Ante*, p. 339.

by a *compromis* dated the 6th of March following,[1] the Government of the French Republic and the Royal Italian Government have agreed to submit to an arbitral tribunal composed of five members the decision of the following questions:

1. Were the Italian naval authorities, in general and in the special circumstances under which the act was committed, within their rights in proceeding, as they did, to the capture and the temporary detention of the French mail steamer *Manouba*, as well as to the arrest of the twenty-nine Ottoman passengers who were on board?

2. What should be the pecuniary or other consequences following the decision of the preceding question?

Considering that, in accordance with this *compromis* the two Governments have chosen, by common consent, the following members of the Permanent Court of Arbitration to constitute the arbitral tribunal:

His Excellency Guido Fusinato, Doctor of Law, Minister of State, formerly Minister of Public Instruction, honorary professor of international law in the University of Turin, Deputy, Councilor of State;

Mr. Knut Hjalmar Leonard Hammarskjöld, Doctor of Law, formerly Minister of Justice, formerly Minister of Public Worship and Instruction, formerly Envoy Extraordinary and Minister Plenipotentiary at Copenhagen, formerly President of the Court of Appeals of Jönköping, formerly professor in the Faculty of Law of Upsala, Governor of the Province of Upsala;

Mr. Kriege, Doctor of Law, at present Confidential Counsel of Legation and Director in the Department of Foreign Affairs, Plenipotentiary in the German Federal Council;

Mr. Louis Renault, Minister Plenipotentiary, member of the Institute, professor in the Faculty of Law of the University of Paris and of the *École Libre des Sciences Politiques*, Jurisconsult of the Ministry of Foreign Affairs;

His Excellency Baron Michel de Taube, Doctor of Law, Assistant to the Minister of Public Instruction of Russia, Councilor of State;

That the two Governments have, at the same time, designated Mr. Hammarskjöld to perform the duties of president.

---

[1] *Post.* p. 351.

Considering that, in accordance with the *compromis* of March 6, 1912, the cases and counter-cases have been duly exchanged by the parties and communicated to the arbitrators;

Considering that the tribunal, constituted as specified above, met at The Hague on March 31, 1913;

That the two Governments, respectively, have appointed as agents and counsel,

The Government of the French Republic:

Mr. Henri Fromageot, advocate in the Court of Appeal of Paris, assistant jurisconsult in the Ministry of Foreign Affairs, Counselor in international law of the Navy Department, agent;

Mr. André Hesse, advocate in the Court of Appeal of Paris, member of the Chamber of Deputies, counsel;

The Royal Italian Government:

Mr. Arturo Ricci-Busatti, Envoy Extraordinary and Minister Plenipotentiary, Chief of the Bureau of Disputed Claims and of Legislation of the Royal Ministry of Foreign Affairs, agent;

Dr. Dionisio Anzilotti, professor of international law in the University of Rome, counsel.

Considering that the agents of the parties have presented the following demands to the tribunal, to wit:

The agent of the Government of the French Republic:

May it please the tribunal

As to the first question propounded by the *compromis,*

To say and decide that the Italian naval authorities were not, in general and in the special circumstances under which the act was committed, within their rights in proceeding, as they did, to the capture and temporary detention of the French mail steamer *Manouba,* as well as to the arrest of the twenty-nine Ottoman passengers who were on board.

As to the second question propounded by the *compromis,*

To say that the Royal Italian Government shall be obliged to pay to the Government of the French Republic the sum of one franc damages, as moral reparation for the offense against the honor of the French flag;

To say that the Royal Italian Government shall be obliged to pay to the Government of the French Republic the sum of one hundred thousand francs, as penalty and reparation for the political and moral injury resulting from the violation by the Royal Italian Government of its general and special conventional engagements, particularly the Convention of The Hague of October 18, 1907, relative to certain restrictions on the right of capture in maritime warfare, Article 2; the Geneva Convention of July 6, 1906, for the amelioration of the condition of the wounded and sick in armies in the field, Article 9; and the verbal agreement between the two Governments of January 17, 1912, relative to the control of the passengers on board the steamer *Manouba;*

To say that the said sum will be paid to the Government of the Republic for the benefit of such work or institution of international interest as it shall please the tribunal to designate;

To say that the Royal Italian Government shall be obliged to pay to the Government of the French Republic the sum of one hundred and eight thousand, six hundred and one francs, seventy centimes, the amount of the indemnities claimed by the private individuals interested either in the steamer *Manouba* or in its voyage;

Further, and in case the tribunal does not consider itself sufficiently enlightened upon this last count,

To say, before coming to a decision, that one or more of its members, whom it shall commission for that purpose, shall proceed, in the chamber where its deliberations take place, to examine the claims of the private individuals interested;

In any case, and by the application of Article 9 of the *compromis,*

To say that, upon the expiration of three months from the date of the award, the sums which the Royal Italian Government is to pay and which shall not have been paid shall bear interest at the rate of four per cent per annum.

And the agent of the Royal Italian Government:

May it please the tribunal

As to the first question propounded by the *compromis,*

To say and decide that the Italian naval authorities were fully within their rights in proceeding, as they did, to the capture and temporary detention of the French mail steamer *Manouba,* as well as to the arrest of the twenty-nine Ottoman passengers who were suspected of being soldiers and whose true character the Italian Government had the right to ascertain.

Consequently and as to the second question,

To say and decide that no pecuniary or other consequences should be imposed upon the Italian Government because of the capture and temporary detention of the French mail steamer *Manouba;*

To say and decide that the French Government was wrong in its contention that the Ottoman passengers who fell legally into the hands of the Italian authorities should be surrendered to the French Government;

To say that the Government of the French Republic shall be obliged to pay to the Royal Government the sum of one hundred thousand francs as a penalty and reparation for the material and moral injury resulting from the violation of international law, especially in so far as the right of the belligerent to ascertain the character of individuals suspected of being soldiers of the enemy, who were found on board neutral commercial vessels, is concerned;

To say that the said sum shall be paid to the Royal Italian Government, to be devoted to such work or such institution of international interest as it shall please the tribunal to indicate;

Further and in case the tribunal should not consider that this kind of penalty should be admitted;

To say that the Government of the Republic shall be bound to make amends for the wrong done the Royal Italian Government in such manner as it shall please the tribunal to indicate;

In any event,

To say that the Government of the Republic shall be obliged to pay to the Royal Italian Government the sum of four hundred and fourteen francs, forty-five centimes, the expenses incurred on account of the seizure of the *Manouba;*

To say that, upon the expiration of three months from the date of the award, the sums to be paid by the Government of the Republic and not yet paid shall bear interest at the rate of four per cent per annum.

Considering that, after the tribunal had heard the oral statements of the agents of the parties and the explanations which they furnished at its request, the arguments were duly declared closed.

In the Matter of Fact

Considering that the French mail steamer *Manouba*, of the *Compagnie de Navigation Mixte*, in the course of a regular trip between Marseilles and Tunis, was stopped off the Island of San Pietro on the 18th of January, 1912, about eight o'clock in the morning by the torpedo boat destroyer *Agordat* of the Royal Italian Navy;

Considering that, after ascertaining the presence of twenty-nine Turkish passengers on board the said steamer, which passengers were suspected of belonging to the Ottoman army, the *Manouba* was captured and conducted to Cagliari;

Considering that, having arrived at this port on the same day, about five o'clock in the evening, the captain of the *Manouba* was summoned to deliver the above-mentioned passengers to the Italian authorities and that, upon his refusal, these authorities proceeded to seize the steamer;

Considering, finally, that, upon the request of the vice-consul of France at Cagliari, the twenty-nine Turkish passengers were delivered to the Italian authorities on January 19 at half-past four in the afternoon, and that the *Manouba* was then released and resumed its trip to Tunis on the same day at 7:20 p.m.

In the Matter of Law

Considering that, if the French Government believed, given the circumstances under which the presence of Ottoman passengers on board the *Manouba* was made known to it, that, taking into consideration the promise that the character of said passengers would be verified, the *Manouba* was exempted from the right of search or coercion on the part of the Italian naval authorities, it is established that the Italian Government did not in good faith understand the matter in the same way;

That, consequently, in the absence of a special agreement between the two Governments, the Italian naval authorities were justified in acting according to the common law;

Considering that, according to the tenor of the *compromis*, the proceeding of the Italian Government includes three successive phases, to wit: the capture, the temporary detention of the *Manouba*, and the arrest of the twenty-nine Turkish passengers who were on board;

That it is proper to examine in the first place the legality of each of these three phases, considered as isolated acts and independent of the above-mentioned proceeding as a whole;

In this order of things,

Considering that the Italian naval authorities had, at the time of the capture of the *Manouba*, sufficient reason to believe that the Ottoman passengers who were on board were, some of them at least, military persons enrolled in the enemy's army;

That, consequently, these authorities had the right to compel the surrender of these passengers to them;

Considering that they had a right to summon the captain to deliver them, as well as to take the measures necessary to compel him to do so, or to take possession of these passengers in case of his refusal;

Considering, on the other hand, that, even admitting that there might have been grounds for believing that the Ottoman passengers formed a military troop or detachment, there was no reason for calling in question the good faith of the owner and of the captain of the *Manouba*;

Considering that, under these circumstances, the Italian naval authorities were not within their rights in capturing the *Manouba* and in compelling it to leave its course and follow the *Agordat* to Cagliari, unless it were for the purpose of arrest after the captain had refused to obey a summons to surrender the Ottoman passengers;

That no summons of that kind having been made before the capture, the act of capturing the *Manouba* and taking it to Cagliari, was not legal;

Considering that, as the summons made at Cagliari was without immediate effect, the Italian naval authorities had the right to take the necessary measures of compulsion, and specifically, to detain the *Manouba* until the Ottoman passengers were delivered to them;

That the detention effected was legal only to the extent of a temporary and conditional sequestration;

Considering, finally, that the Italian naval authorities had the right to compel the surrender of the Ottoman passengers and to arrest them.

In so far as the proceeding as a whole is concerned,

Considering that the three phases, of which the single proceeding provided for by the *compromis* is composed, should be judged by themselves, and the illegality of any one of them should not, in this case, have any bearing on the regularity of the others;

That the illegality in capturing and taking the *Manouba* to Cagliari did not vitiate the successive phases of the act;

Considering, moreover, that the capture could not be legalized by the regularity, relative or absolute, of these last phases considered separately.

Upon the request that the Royal Italian Government be condemned to pay as damages:

1. The sum of one franc for the offense against the French flag;

2. The sum of one hundred thousand francs as reparation for the moral and political injury resulting from the failure to observe international common law and the conventions which are mutually binding upon both Italy and France,

And upon the request that the Government of the French Republic be condemned to pay the sum of one hundred thousand francs as a penalty and reparation for the material and moral injury resulting from the violation of international law, specifically in so far as concerns the right of the belligerent to verify the character of individuals suspected of being soldiers of the enemy, who are found on board neutral vessels of commerce,

Considering that, in case a Power has failed to fulfil its obligations, whether general or special, to another Power, the establishment of this fact, especially in an arbitral award, constitutes in itself a severe penalty;

That this penalty is increased, if there be occasion, by the payment of damages for material losses;

That, as a general proposition and leaving out of consideration special circumstances, these penalties appear to be sufficient;

That, also as a general rule, the imposition of a further pecuniary penalty appears to be superfluous and to go beyond the objects of international jurisdiction;

Considering that, by the application of what has been stated, the circumstances of the present case do not justify such supplementary penalty; that, without further examination, there is no reason for complying with the above-mentioned requests.

Upon the request of the French agent that the Royal Italian Government be compelled to pay to the Government of the French Republic the sum of one hundred and eight thousand, six hundred and one francs, seventy centimes, the amount of the indemnities claimed by private individuals interested either in the steamer *Manouba* or in its voyage;

Considering that an indemnity is due on account of the delay occasioned to the *Manouba* by its unwarranted capture and its convoy to Cagliari, but the delay caused by the illegal refusal of the captain to surrender the twenty-nine Turkish passengers at Cagliari, as well as the fact that the vessel was not taken entirely out of its course to Tunis, should be taken into account;

Considering that, if the Italian naval authorities effected the detention of the *Manouba* instead of the temporary and conditional sequestration, which was legal, it appears that in this matter the interested parties suffered no losses and damages;

Considering that, taking account of these circumstances and also of the expense incurred by the Italian Government in guarding the detained vessel, the tribunal, after having heard the concurring explanations of two of its members charged by it with the investigation of the said claims, has decided upon four thousand francs as the amount due all those interested in the vessel and its voyage.

For these reasons the arbitral tribunal declares and pronounces as follows:

In so far as the proceeding as a whole, which is covered by the first question propounded by the *compromis*, is concerned,

The different phases of this proceeding should not be considered as connected with each other in the sense that the character of any one of them, in this case, should not affect the character of the others.

In so far as the various phases of the said proceeding considered separately are concerned,

The Italian naval authorities were not, in general and in the special circumstances under which the act was committed, within their rights in proceeding, as they did, to the capture of the French mail steamer *Manouba* and its convoy to Cagliari;

When once the *Manouba* was captured and taken to Cagliari, the Italian naval authorities were, in general and in the special circumstances under which the act was committed, within their rights in proceeding, as they did, to the arrest of the twenty-nine Ottoman passengers who were on board.

In so far as concerns the second question propounded by the *compromis*,

The Royal Italian Government shall be obliged, within three months from the present award, to pay to the Government of the French Republic the sum of four thousand francs, which, after deducting the amount due the Italian Government for guarding the *Manouba* is the amount of the losses and damages sustained, by reason of the capture of the *Manouba* and its convoy to Cagliari, by the private individuals interested in the vessel and its voyage. There is no occasion to comply with the other claims contained in the demands of the two parties.

Done at The Hague, in the building of the Permanent Court of Arbitration, May 6, 1913.

President: HJ. L. HAMMARSKJÖLD
Secretary General: MICHIELS VAN VERDUYNEN
Secretary: RÖELL

AGREEMENT FOR ARBITRATION

Compromis of arbitration relative to the questions raised by the capture and temporary detention of the French mail steamer "Manouba."— Signed at Paris, March 6, 1912.[1]

The Government of the French Republic and the Royal Italian Government, having agreed, on January 26, 1912,[2] in application of the Franco-Italian arbitration convention of December 25, 1903, which was renewed December 24, 1908, to entrust an arbitral tribunal with the examination of the capture and temporary detention of the French mail steamer *Manouba* by the Italian naval authorities, particularly in the special circumstances under which that act was committed, and of the arrest of the twenty-nine Ottoman passengers who were on board, as well as with the duty of deciding the consequences which should follow,

---

[1] Translation. For the original French text, see Appendix, p. 571.
[2] See *ante*, p. 339.

The undersigned, duly authorized for that purpose, have agreed upon the following *compromis:*

ARTICLE 1

An arbitral tribunal, composed as hereinafter stipulated, is charged with the settling of the following questions:

1. Were the Italian naval authorities, in general and in the special circumstances under which the act was committed, within their rights in proceeding, as they did, to the capture and temporary detention of the French mail steamer *Manouba,* as well as to the arrest of the twenty-nine Ottoman passengers who were on board?

2. What should be the pecuniary or other consequences, following the decision of the preceding question?

ARTICLE 2

The tribunal shall be composed of five arbitrators which the two Governments shall choose from among the members of the Permanent Court of Arbitration at The Hague, one of whom shall perform the duties of umpire.[1]

ARTICLE 3

On June 15, 1912, each party shall deposit with the Bureau of the Permanent Court of Arbitration fifteen copies of its memorial, with certified copies of all documents and papers which it intends to present in the case.

The Bureau shall guarantee their transmission without delay to the arbitrators and parties, to wit: two copies for each arbitrator, three copies for each opposing party; two copies shall remain in the archives of the Bureau.

On August 15, 1912, each party shall deposit in the same manner as above, its counter-memorial with the papers appertaining thereto, and its final conclusions.

ARTICLE 4

Each of the parties shall deposit with the Bureau of the Permanent Court of Arbitration at The Hague at the same time that it deposits its memorial, a sum for the purpose of expenses, which shall be fixed by mutual agreement.

---

[1] See the supplementary agreement of April 4, 1912, *ante*, p. 340.

ARTICLE 5

The tribunal shall meet at The Hague, upon the convocation of its president, in the second fortnight of the month of September, 1912.

ARTICLE 6

Each party shall be represented by an agent whose duty it shall be to serve as intermediary between it and the tribunal.

The tribunal may demand that either agent furnish it, if necessary, with oral or written explanations, to which the agent of the opposing party shall have the right to reply.

ARTICLE 7

The French language shall be used by the tribunal. Each party may use its own language.

ARTICLE 8

The award of the tribunal shall be rendered with the least possible delay and in any case within thirty days following the closing of the debates. However, this period may be extended upon the demand of the tribunal and the consent of the parties.

ARTICLE 9

The tribunal is competent to regulate the conditions for the execution of its award.

ARTICLE 10

On all points not covered by the present *compromis*, the stipulations of the Hague Convention for the pacific settlement of international disputes, of October 18, 1907, shall be applicable to the present arbitration.

Done, in duplicate, at Paris, March 6, 1912.

(Signed) L. RENAULT
(Signed) G. FUSINATO

THE ISLAND OF TIMOR CASE

between

THE NETHERLANDS *and* PORTUGAL

Decided June 25, 1914

Syllabus

This arbitration grew out of a dispute between the Netherlands and Portugal over the boundaries of their respective possessions in the Island of Timor, which was partitioned between them by a treaty of April 20, 1859.[1] In order to avoid the division of native tribes this treaty had left certain Dutch territory within the boundaries assigned to Portugal and *vice versa,* but as it later appeared desirable to abolish these so-called "enclaves," a convention was signed on June 10, 1893,[2] for that purpose and for the establishing of the boundary in the clearest manner. A commission acting under this convention reached an agreement upon most of the boundary in 1898–1899, and the disputed points were referred to a conference at The Hague, which on July 3, 1902, agreed upon a solution which was transformed into a diplomatic convention on October 1, 1904.[3] This convention settled the remainder of the boundary with the exception of a part of the Portuguese enclave formerly within Dutch territory. As to this a theoretical line was drawn and a mixed commission appointed to survey and mark it. The commissioners after starting upon their work were unable to agree upon some of the geographical points which had been laid down for their guidance, and their labors were suspended. After a lengthy diplomatic correspondence between the foreign offices of the respective Governments an agreement was signed at The Hague on April 3, 1913,[4] referring the disputed boundary to the decision of an arbitrator, according to the data to be furnished by the parties and on the basis of the general principles of international law.

Mr. Charles Édouard Lardy, the Swiss Minister to France, was selected as arbitrator. He rendered an award on June 25, 1914, fixing the boundary in accordance with the contentions of the Netherlands.

---

[1]*Post*, p. 390. [2]*Post*, p. 393. [3]*Post*, p. 396. [4]*Post*, p. 387.

AWARD OF THE TRIBUNAL

Arbitral award rendered in execution of the compromis signed at The Hague, April 3, 1913, between the Netherlands and Portugal concerning the boundary of a part of their possessions in the Island of Timor.—Paris, June 25, 1914.[1]

A dispute having arisen between the Royal Government of the Netherlands and that of the Portuguese Republic concerning the subject of the boundary of a part of their respective possessions in the Island of Timor, the two Governments, by a convention signed at The Hague, April 3, 1913,[2] of which ratifications were exchanged in the same city on July 31st following, decided as a last resort to refer its solution to an arbitrator, and accordingly by common accord designated the undersigned.

To understand the sense and scope of the *compromis* of April 3, 1913, there is need succinctly to explain the negotiations that preceded that *compromis*.

I. HISTORICAL

The Island of Timor, the farthest east of the continuous series of the Sonde Islands and the nearest to Australia, was discovered by the Portuguese in the sixteenth century; the island measures about 500 kilometers in length from west to east by a maximum width of 100 kilometers. A lofty chain of mountains, certain summits of which reach an altitude of nearly 3,000 meters, divides this island lengthwise into two slopes. The eastern part of the island, with an approximate area of 19,000 square kilometers, and a population of about 300,000 inhabitants, is Portuguese. The western part, with a population estimated in 1907 of 131,000 inhabitants and an area of about 20,000 square kilometers, is under the sovereignty of the Netherlands, with the exception of the "Kingdom of Okussi and Ambeno," situate on the northwest coast and surrounded on all sides by Dutch territory except on the shore.

The name of "kings" given by the Portuguese to the chieftains of tribes is explained by the fact that in the native tongue they are called *leorey;* the final syllable of this word has been translated into

---

[1] *American Journal of International Law,* vol 9, p. 240. For the original French text, see Appendix, p. 574.
[2] *Post,* p. 387.

Portuguese by the word *Rey*.   The Dutch give these chieftains the more modest title of *radjahs*.

This territorial partition between the Netherlands and Portugal rests on the following agreements:

April 20, 1859,[1] a treaty signed at Lisbon and duly ratified in the course of the summer of 1860, had defined the respective frontiers of the middle of the island, but had left existing (Article 2) the Dutch enclave of Maucatar in the midst of Portuguese territory, and the Portuguese enclave of Oikoussi in the midst of Dutch territory in the west of the island.   It was stipulated (Article 3) that the enclave of Oikoussi consists of the State of Ambenu wherever the "Portuguese flag is raised, the State of Oikoussi proper and that of Noimuti."   See annex A, page 31.[1]

By another convention signed at Lisbon June 10, 1893,[2] and duly ratified, the two Governments, "desiring to settle on conditions most favorable to the development of civilization and commerce" their relations in the archipelago of Timor, agreed "to establish the boundary of their possessions in the clearest and most exact fashion" in that island and "to cause the enclaves now existing to disappear" (Preamble and Article 1).   A commission of experts was to be designated to the end of "formulating a proposition capable of serving as the basis for the conclusion of a further convention fixing the new boundary line in the said island" (Article 2).   In case of difficulties the two parties engaged "to submit to the decision of an   .   .   .   arbitrator" (Article 7).   See annex B, page 34.[2]

This mixed commission repaired to the premises and agreed in 1898-1899 on most of the boundary.   Notwithstanding, a considerable number of divergencies persisted as to the principal frontier in the middle of the Island of Timor as well as to the frontier of the Kingdom of Okussi-Ambenu in the western part of the island. The map annexed[3] under No. II indicates the respective claims. A conference was assembled at The Hague from June 23 to July 3, 1902, to attempt their solution.   It decreed July 3, 1902, a plan

---

[1] *Post*, p. 390.   [2] *Post*, p. 393.
[3] For annexed maps, see opposite p. 386.

which was transformed into a diplomatic convention signed at The Hague, October 1, 1904, and duly ratified. See annex C, page 37.[1]

A summary of the results of the Convention of 1904 is shown on the transparent map annexed under No. I; the superposition of the transparent map No. I on the map No. II shows what Portugal obtained, in the center of the Island of Timor, the Dutch enclave of Maukatar, and what the Netherlands obtained in the same region, Tahakay, and Tamira Ailala. On the other hand, in the northwest of the Island of Timor and to the south of the territory designated by the treaty of 1859, under the name of Oikussi enclave, the Netherlands obtained Noimuti. Finally, the controverted eastern limit of the territory of Oikussi-Ambeno is fixed theoretically according to a line A-C, which was to be surveyed and indicated on the grounds within the shortest possible delay" (Acts of the conference of 1902, sessions of June 27, pages 10 and 11, and of June 28, page 12; convention of October 1, 1904, Article 4). The line A-C allowed by the conference was fixed in Article 3, No. 10 of the convention of 1904 in the following terms: "From this point" (the confluence of the Noël Bilomi with the Oè-Sunan) "the boundary follows the thalweg of the Oè-Sunan, runs as much as possible across Nipani and Kelali (Keli), strikes the source of the Noël Meto, and follows the thalweg of that river to its mouth."

All seemed ended, when the boundary commissioners, having arrived at the premises in June 1909, for the work of setting the metes of the eastern frontier of Oikussi-Ambeno could not agree and decided to refer the matter to their Governments. The two Governments were none the more able to agree and decided to have recourse to arbitration. What was this difficulty that the boundary commissioners encountered?

II. The Difficulty Which Instigated the Arbitration

In proceeding to the work of bounding the eastern frontier of Oikussi-Ambeno the commissioners had commenced in the north, on the coast, and ascended in a southerly direction the course of the Noël Meto river, which was to serve as a frontier from its mouth

---

[1]Post, p. 396.

to its source. These operations took place between the 1st and the 10th of June, 1909, and a mete was placed at the source of the Noèl Meto. The source being obstructed by some steep cliffs impossible to cross, the commissioners decided on a general reconnaissance between the northern and southern parts of the country still to be bounded, that is to say, between the source of the Noèl Meto, in the north, and of the Noèl Bilomi, in the south.

A disagreement first arose in the north: The map (see annex III) signed in 1904, at the same time as the convention, bore the name *Kelali* accompanied between parentheses by the word *Keli*. The Dutch delegates maintained the word Keli meant on the summit of Mount Kelali, a particular point, situated to the west of the Noèl Meto between two "peaked" rocks, and which had been indicated by the natives of Tumbaba (Dutch) as the boundary between them and the natives (Portuguese) of Ambeno; according to the Dutch commissioners this point is a "magnificent" natural boundary which nearly follows the limit described on the map of 1904. The Portuguese commissioners, on the contrary, propose "to follow. . . . some thalwegs in the country to the east of the line proposed by the Dutch delegates, starting from the same mete" placed at the source of the Noèl Meto. The commission decided to survey the two lines and to leave the solution to superior authorities.

In the southern part, on the Bilomi river, the commissioners state, in their session of June 17, 1909, that they followed west to east the course of the Nono Nisi (or Nise), then the course of the Noèl Bilomi, and that they now *"reached the spot* (where the commission of 1899 had terminated its work) *where the survey must be continued to the north."* That point had been designated in the convention of 1904, Article 3, Nos. 9 and 10, and on the map annexed, as the confluence of the Noèl Bilomi and the Oè Sunan. "The four delegates state that *at that place there are two affluents coming from the north, but neither is called the Oè Sunan."*

The Dutch delegates then explain that the country situated between the two affluents is called Sunan, that moreover, they do not recognize any affluent of the Noèl Bilomi bearing the name of Oè Sunan and that none exists; thus they insist the frontier line be surveyed toward the north, starting from the point designated on the maps of 1899 and 1904.

The Portuguese delegates observe that a river called Oè Sunan or Oil Sunan, which is not, it is true, an affluent of the Bilomi, exists farther to the east and has its source "hard by the Bilomi."

The commissioners unanimously decided to survey the two lines, *"starting from a point"* indicated on the maps of 1899 and 1904, and *"where the commission of 1899 terminated its work,"* that is, the line proposed by the Dutch delegates in a northerly direction and the line desired by the Portuguese in an easterly direction (session of June 17, 1909, First Portuguese Case, page 27).

At the session of June 21, 1909, and during the course of the survey of the frontier line proposed by the Portuguese delegates in the easterly direction ascending the Noèl Bilomi river, "the four delegates state uanimously that they have not met an affluent (of the Noèl Bilomi) called the Oè-Sunan." The Dutch delegates observe that the Bilomi has changed its name, in this region, to which their Portuguese colleagues answer "that the Bilomi river still exists, but that, following the native customs, it bears the name of the country it crosses." Finally and above all, the Portuguese delegates observe that a short distance from the Bilomi, on the north bank, is one Mount Kinapua, on the opposite slope of which is a river bearing the name of Oè Sunan, and which flows north. It would suffice to follow the course of that river, then to ascend the Noi Fulan river and finally to connect the source of the latter with the source of the Noèl Meto already recognized by the mixed commission.

The Dutch delegates declare it useless to proceed to a reconnaissance on this river, for Mount Kinapua and the boundary that would result from the Portuguese proposition would be outside the territory which was disputed in 1899; Mount Tasona figures on the map of 1899 on the extreme eastern limit of the Portuguese *claims* of that time, claims which the treaty of 1904 threw aside; thus there could be no question of a boundary going still farther east.

The labors of the mixed commission were suspended and the question, brought within the domain of diplomacy, gave place to a long exchange of correspondence between the cabinets of The Hague and Lisbon.

This correspondence ended in the agreement of 1913,[1] entrusting the arbitrator with the commission of deciding, according to "the data furnished by the parties" and "on the basis of the general principles of international law, how ought to be fixed conformably with Article 3, No. 10 of the convention concluded at The Hague, October 1, 1904, ...the boundary starting from the Noèl Bilomi to the source of the Noèl Meto." See annex D, page 41.[1]

III. THE PORTUGUESE POINT OF VIEW

The principal arguments invoked by the Government of the Portuguese Republic in favor of the thesis supported by its boundary commissioners can be summarized as follows:

1. At the point where the work of the 1899 boundary was stopped, and where, according to the treaty of 1904 and according to the map annexed thereto, the Noèl Bilomi should receive an affluent with the name of Oè Sunan, it is recognized by common agreement that no affluent by that name exists.

2. There exists, on the contrary, farther to the east, a river Oè Sunan, which is not, it is true, an affluent of the Bilomi, but which takes its source on the north slope of Kinapua Mountain very close to the river Bilomi; on Mount Kinapua there is a mete proclaimed by numerous native chieftains as having served as the recognized boundary between the Portuguese Ambenos and the Dutch Tumbabas. From the same Mount Kinapua a brook runs toward the Bilomi, and these two water-courses seem to continue each other from the summit. According to the native chieftains, the course of this river Oè-Sunan is the historical and natural boundary between the Portuguese Ambenos on one side, and the Dutch Tumbabas and Amakonos on the other side.

3. The same native chieftains include in Ambeno all that region comprised between the river Oè Sunan on the east, the river Ni Fullan on the north and the incontestibly Portuguese territory of Oikoussi-Ambeno west of Mounts Kelali and Netton. On a private map published at Batavia the name Ambeno is found inscribed altogether in that part wrongly claimed to-day by the Netherlands.

---

[1] *Post*, p. 387.

4. The treaty of 1859 rests on the principle that native States should not be separated, parcelled out; the boundary-line proposed by the Netherlands cuts the Ambenos' territory and would deprive those natives of their pasture and garden lands that are located to the east of the frontier and in Dutch territory.

5. Nothing proves that the boundary to be effected ought necessarily to commence where the work of bounding had been suspended in 1899, following hostilities among the natives, and marked on the maps at the confluence of the Bilomi and the Oè Sunan brook, which in reality does not exist at that spot. There are two affluents at that spot; the Kamboun and the Nono-Offi. Why follow the course of the Kamboun to the north rather than that of the Nono-Offi, which comes from the northeast and spills into the Bilomi at that point?

By the maps of 1899 and 1904, in the opinion of the Portuguese Government, it was desired to give the boundary commissioners only "a drawing designed to fix ideas, and a vague and simple indication of what ought to be settled later."

The true intention of the signatories of the treaty of 1904 was to follow the course of the Oè Sunan, where it is in reality, that is to say, farther east. Thus, in the sense of the treaty, nothing hinders ascending the Bilomi to the point nearest the source of the true Oè Sunan, a source so near the course of the Bilomi that it is almost an affluent.

6. The line proposed by the Netherlands, which according to the treaty of 1904 ought "to cross Nipani and Kelali (Keli) as much as possible," does not cross Nipani but touches only Fatu Nipani, that is to say, the western extremity of Nipani. Hence it does not correspond to the program of 1904.

7. The line proposed by the Netherlands does not constitute a natural frontier, while that suggested by Portugal follows watercourses nearly all the way.

IV. THE DUTCH POINT OF VIEW

The principal arguments of the Royal Government of the Netherlands may be summarized as follows:

1. The treaty of 1859 did not prescribe in any imperative way

that native territories ought not to be divided or parcelled. On the contrary, it assigned to Portugal "the State of Ambenu wherever the Portuguese flag is raised there," thus sanctioning not only the division of a native State, but precisely the division of the very State of Ambenu, and that in the following terms: "The Netherlands cedes to . . . Portugal *that part* of the State of Ambenu or Ambeno which for several years has flown the Portuguese flag."

More than this, the treaty of 1859 could have been, and has been modified effectively by the subsequent treaties, treaties which alone ought to be taken into consideration to-day in those places where they have modified the treaty of 1859.

2. No uncertainty exists as to the point where the boundary commissioners of 1899 stopped. That point served as a basis for the negotiations of 1902, and was marked on the map (annex III) signed at that time by the negotiators of the two countries as to be adjoined to the draft of the treaty. That draft of 1902 became the treaty of 1904. From this point and no other begins line A-C, admitted in 1902 as properly placing the frontier (map annex I) That line A-C extends from this point north as far as the source of the river Noèl Meto, and the frontier ought then to follow that water-course as far as its embouchure into the sea in the north.

The location of the source of the Noèl Meto was recognized contradictorily in 1909: a mete was placed there by common agreement. The discussion concerned only the survey between that source and point A situate at the spot where the commissioners stopped in 1899.

3. On the official map of 1899 (annex IV), as on the official map of 1904 (annex III), an affluent, to which, by an error that the Netherlands does not contest, has been given the name of Oè Sunan, is represented as coming from the north to the point in question. This river, which in reality bears among the Tumbabas the name of Kabun, and among the Ambenos that of Lèos, corresponds wholly to the intention of the contracting parties, which was to follow, beginning with point A, an affluent coming from the north in the direction A-C. The error of name has the less significance since very frequently in that region the water-courses have several names, or change their names, or bear the name of the country they traverse: the region east of Kabun, or Lèos (the Oè Sunan

of 1904) has, according to the Portuguese Government, the name of Hue-Son, of analogous sound, and, according to the Dutch commissioners, that of Sunan, which explains the error of the commissioners.

4. The native chieftains of Amakono (Dutch) declared (mixed commission, session of February 21, 1899) that their country comprises all the region "situated between the Oè Sunan, Nipani, Kelali-Keli, and the Noèl Meto (on the west), the sea of Timor (on the north), the Noèl Boll Bass, the Humusu and Kin Napua summits (on the east), Tasona, the Noèl Boho and the Noèl Bilomi (on the south)." Now the western frontier here described and indicated in 1899 as separating the Amakanos (Dutch) from Ambeno (Portuguese) is precisely that sanctioned by the treaty of 1904. The Oè Sunan which figures there can be only the water-course to which mistakenly but by common agreement this name was given in the official maps of 1899 and 1904, that is to say, a water-course situated *west* of the disputed territory, and not the pretended Oè Sunan now pleaded by Portugal, which is situated on the *eastern* frontier of the disputed territory. Hence this is the very water-course, no matter what its name, situated to the west of the said territory, which the parties agreed to adopt as a boundary.

The proof that Portugal could not have had in view in 1899 and 1904 the eastern stream to which it now gives the name of Oè Sunan, is furnished by the fact that in the session of February 21, 1899, its commissioners proposed as a boundary a line starting from the point where the stream called Oè Sunan spills into the Bilomi and then ascending the Noèl Bilomi easterly as far as Nunkalaï (next crossing Tasona and from Kin Napua proceeding northerly as far as Humusu and to the source of the Noèl Boll Bass, of which the course would have served as a frontier as far as its embouchure into the sea). This Portuguese proposition of 1899 would be unintelligible if there were a question of any other stream than that figuring on the official maps of 1899 and 1904 with the name of Oè Sunan; how could there be a question of another river Oè Sunan situated *east* of Nunkalaï since Nunkalaï is really *west* and not east of this new Oè Sunan discovered by the Portuguese?

5. Two inquiries recently instituted by the Dutch authorities of the Island of Timor confirmed, moreover, that no river by the name of Oè Sunan rises on Mount Kinapua; the stream that rises on the north slope, at a certain distance from the summit, has the names Poeamesse and Noilpolan, and at Fatoe Metassa (Fatu Mutassa of the Portuguese) spills into the Noèl Manama, the Ni-Fullan of the Portuguese maps (second Dutch Case, No. VII, page 6).

6. Quite precisely, the line proposed by the Netherlands does not traverse the territory of Nipani, but the treaty of 1904 does not require that. It stipulates that the line designed to unite the sources of the Oè Sunan and the source of the Noèl Meto shall cross "Nipani as much as possible." As the territory to be bounded was unexplored, the words "as much as possible" were justified; in fact, the line suggested by the Netherlands, if at all it crosses the territory of Nipani, crosses the western extremity called Fatu Nipani. Now, according to the declarations recorded in the *procès-verbal* of the boundary of February 21, 1899, the natives, in designating the Oè-Sunan, Nipani, Kelali, and the Noèl Meto as the eastern frontier of Okussi-Ambeno (Portuguese) and as the western frontier of Amakono (Dutch) had in view the rocky pile of Fatu Nipani, forming the western end of Nipani.

7. The frontier proposed by the Netherlands is a natural frontier formed by a chain of mountains separating the water-courses all the way.

It was never prescribed or recommended in 1902-1904 absolutely to follow water-courses as a boundary, and, on the northern frontier of Okussi-Ambeno, bounds have been placed by common agreement in several places, notably when the line passes from one river basin into another. (See especially Article 3 of the convention of 1904, Nos. 2, 3, and 4.[1])

A few metes will suffice to designate the frontier on the ridge line proposed by the Netherlands.

The survey claimed by Portugal, moreover, would itself also require metes in the region of Mount Kinapua, between the Bilomi and the pretended new Oè Sunan, and elsewhere in the region between the source of the Noèl Meto and the stream to which the

---

[1]*Post,* p. 397.

Portuguese give the name Ni-Fullan, that is to say, at the two ends of the Portuguese survey.

8. The line that Portugal proposes to-day reproduces the substance of its claims of 1899 and 1902 in that region. Now, it is incontestable that by accepting the line A-C in the conference of 1902 and incorporating it in the treaty of 1904 Portugal ceded the territory to which formerly it made pretensions. Equitably it could not claim that same territory to-day.

V. THE RULES OF LAW APPLICABLE

According to Article 2 of the *compromis,* the arbitrator is to base his decision not only on the treaties in force between the Netherlands and Portugal relative to the boundary of their possessions in the Island of Timor, but also on the "general principles of international law."

It is almost superfluous to call these principles to mind.

Heffter, *Völkerrecht,* section 94, for example, is of this opinion: "Every treaty binds to a complete and loyal execution not only of what literally has been promised but that to which a party has bound itself, and also of what is conformable to the essence of any treaty whatsoever as to the harmonious intention of the contracting Parties (that is to say, what is called the spirit of treaties)." Heffter adds, section 95: "In case of doubt, treaties ought to be interpreted conformably with the real mutual intention, and conformably to what can be presumed, between parties acting loyally and with reason, was promised by one to the other according to the words used."

Rivier, *Principes du droit des gens,* II, No. 157, expresses the same thought in these terms: "Above all the common intention of the parties must be established: *id quod actum est* . . . Good faith prevailing throughout this subject, treaties ought not to be interpreted exclusively according to their letter, but according to their spirit. . . . Principles of treaty interpretation are, by and large, and *mutatis mutandis,* those of the interpretation of agreements *between individuals,* principles of common sense and experience, already formulated by the Prudents of Rome." (Ulpien, L. 34, in Digest de R. J. 50. 17: *"Semper in stipulationibus et in cetius contractibus id sequimur quod actum est."*)

Between individuals, the rules reverted to by Rivier were formulated in the principal codes in terms sufficiently precise to be used as commentaries:

Code civil français, neerlandais, etc., Articles 1156-1157. "In conventions one should *seek to find what the common intention of the contracting parties was, rather than to stop with the literal sense of the words.* When a clause is susceptible of two meanings it should be interpreted in that meaning which gives it some effect, rather than in that meaning which produces no effect." *German Civil Code* of 1896, Article 133: "To interpret a declaration of will, it is necessary *to seek the actual will and not to be content with the literal meaning of the expression"* (*Bei der Auslegung einer Willenserklärung ist der wirkliche Wille zu erforschen und nicht an dem buchstäblichen Sinne des Ausdrucks "zu haften"*). *Portuguese Civil Code of 1867,* Article 684. *Swiss Code des Obligations of 1911,* Article 18: "To appreciate the character and clauses of a contract, there is occasion to *look for the actual common intention of the parties, without dwelling on inexact names or expressions of which use might have been made, either erroneously,* or to disguise the true nature of the convention." It is useless to dwell on the entire coincidence of private and international law in this point.

It now remains only to apply these rules to the circumstances of the case and to seek to find what the actual and mutual intention of the Netherlands and Portugal was at the time of the negotiations of 1902 that ended in the convention of 1904.

VI. The Intention of the Parties in Signing the Convention of 1904

1. The purpose of the treaty of Lisbon of June 10, 1893, had been to seek to establish a clearer and more exact boundary of the respective possessions in the Island of Timor, and to cause "the enclaves now existing" to disappear (Article 1). The "enclaves" figuring under this name in the previous treaty signed at Lisbon, April 20, 1859, were those of Maucatar (Article 2, paragraph 1) and of Oi Koussi (Article 2, paragraph 2, and Article 3, paragraph 1).

When in June, 1902, the delegates of both Governments met at

The Hague to seek to reconcile the diverging propositions of the boundary commissioners sent to the premises in 1898-1899, the delegates immediately agreed to grant Portugal the Dutch enclave of Maucatar at the center of the Island of Timor, and to the Netherlands the Portuguese enclave of Noimuti to the south of the "kingdom" of Ambeno.   In the session of June 26th the Portuguese demanded, in the middle of the island, all the part of the territory of Fialarang, situate east of the river Mota Bankarna (see map annex II) ; they maintained further that the Kingdom of Ambeno, being bounded by the sea, could not be considered as an enclave any more than Belgium, Portugal, or the Netherlands, and so this unquestionably could not be granted to the Netherlands ; they also claimed for Ambeno all the hinterland of the coast between the mouths of the Noèl Meto and the Noèl Boll Bass.   This hinterland was to extend southerly as far as the river Bilomi and follow that river from west to east between the point at which the boundary commissioners stopped, in the west, in 1899 and, in the east, a place called Nunkalai on the map at that time drawn up in common by the boundary commissioners of the two countries.   The limits of the disputed territory having been designated by the four letters A, B, C, D on a map (see annex II) presented by the Dutch delegates to the conference of 1902, the discussion turned to the western line A-C, hallowed by the Netherlands, and the eastern line B-D claimed by Portugal.

On the map annexed here under No. IV the respective claims have been shown, as they result from the map signed in common by all the boundary commissioners at Koepang, February 16, 1899.

The Dutch delegates declared at the conference of June 26, 1902, that the chieftains of the territory of Fialarang, in the middle of the Island of Timor, refused absolutely to pass under the sovereignty of Portugal, so that it was not, or no longer was, possible to cut off that point which Dutch territory makes into Portuguese territory in that region (see map II).

The first Portuguese delegate replied that it was not necessary "to allow oneself to be guided too much by humanitarian motives toward the people of the Island of Timor; for petty causes these tribes quit their native soil to set up elsewhere, and several times they have left the Dutch territory to establish themselves in Portuguese territory, and *vice versa.*" Finally the Portuguese delegate renounced the territory of Fiamarangs in the middle of the Island of Timor, but asked that the western frontier of Oikoussi be fixed "according to the proposition of the Dutch commissioners of 1899." (See this proposition in the *procès-verbal* of the session held at Koepang, February 8, 1899, in the first Portuguese Case, p. 24.)

The next day, June 27th, the Dutch delegate accepted the Portuguese proposition, but, to avoid all misunderstanding, claimed for his Government "*absolute* certitude that the eastern limit of Okussi *represented by the line A-C* shall be designated as much as possible on the land itself."

In fact, there was a misunderstanding, for the first Portuguese delegate replied that the proposition of the day before "did not say that the frontier east of Okussi shall be formed by the line A-C, but on the contrary by the line proposed by the mixed commission of 1899 and indicated by the letters A-B."

The first Dutch delegate immediately replied that "if the line A-C is not accepted as the frontier east of Oikoussi (and if the Dutch demands for the frontier in the center of Timor are not accepted) . . . the Dutch delegates withdraw their consent to the Portuguese proposition. . . . They would never be able to submit to their Government a plan which did not satisfy these conditions." The Dutch delegate ended by declaring that if a friendly agreement on this basis could not be reached, the Netherlands would have recourse to the arbitration foreseen by the convention of 1893 on the "enclave question," thus giving it to be understood that in the case of the line A-C being refused for the eastern frontier of Ambeno, the Netherlands would raise the much greater question of whether the whole of Ambeno was not an enclave that logically might revert to the Netherlands, since several times in the treaty of 1859 Ambeno had been designated as an enclave, and since one of the objects of the convention of 1893 was the "suppression of enclaves."

At the session of June 28th, the Portuguese delegates "having seriously examined the proposition of the Dutch delegates, put forward in the session of June 27th, resolved to accept that proposition, as well as the terms advanced by them (by the Dutch delegates) on that subject."

It is important to reproduce this discussion in detail, since it throws positive light on the real and mutual intention of the parties. Portugal declared herself satisfied with the conditions offered to her. In the middle of the Island of Timor she acquired the large enclave of Maukatar; if she did not there acquire the country of the Fialarangs, she kept Oikussi Ambeno in the west of the Island of Timor, and avoided discussing before arbitrators the delicate question of whether this enclave was or was not an enclave susceptible of being granted in its entirety to the Netherlands; Portugal preferred under these circumstances to renounce the debated eastern part of Oikussi Ambeno rather than to risk losing more or even all in that locality. In a word, throughout the negotiations she found compensations deemed sufficient by her for abandoning the line B-D and the intermediate line A-B that she claimed. She finally accepted the line A-C claimed by the Netherlands *sine qua non*.

Thus it is certain that this line A-C should be considered, in the intention of the parties, as a *concession* made by Portugal to the Netherlands, and that fact was proclaimed by the Portuguese delegates themselves, in the case which they presented at the session of June 26, 1902, during the conferences at The Hague, in these terms: "These territories represent a *considerable reduction* of the frontiers of the kingdom of Ocussi-Ambenou."

2. What is line A-C?

(a) First, where is point C? At the embouchure of the Noèl Meto river into the Sea of Timor in the northern part of the island. No dispute exists on this subject, and the convention of 1904, Article 3, No. 10, expressly stipulates that the frontier follows the thalweg of the Noèl Meto from its source to its mouth. Between 1899 and 1902–1904 Portugal on the contrary claimed all that territory east of the Noèl Meto as far as the river Noèl Boll Bass; the mouth of the Noèl Boll Bass was point B, the northern end of the A-B line claimed by Portugal (Portuguese proposition, session of February 21, 1899, second Dutch Case annex II, *procès-verbaux*

of The Hague conferences, 1902, page 10, and maps here annexed
I and II).

If the location of point C is not disputed, it is nevertheless useful
to state that the adoption in 1904 of the course of the Noèl Meto
rather than the course of the Noèl Boll Bass, as a boundary line,
proves the general intention of restoring the frontier toward the
west.

(*b*) The location of the source of the Noèl Meto was determined
and a mete was set there by common agreement (*procès-verbal* of
June 14, 1909, first Portuguese Case, page 26). All that part of
the survey is thus definitely settled. (See map annex VI.)

(*c*) Now, where is the other end of the line, point A, acknowledged in the conference of 1902? The Netherlands maintain this
point A is found where the reconnaissance of 1899 ended and where
the commissioners had to stop their work because of hostilities between the native tribes, that is to say at the point where the commissioners, having followed the Nono Balena, the Nono Nive and the
Noèl Bilomi, reached the confluence of this last river with another
coming from the north and to which by common agreement the
name of Oè Sunan was allotted.

All the boundary line in the western and lower part of the basin
of the Bilomi was sanctioned and definitely admitted as frontier
by the treaty of 1904. Article 3, No. 9. At the time of the subsequent reconnaissance of June 17, 1909, it is stated in the *procès-
verbal* that this point is not doubtful: "It is decided *unanimously*
that the survey shall be followed from this point, *that is to say, the
point where the commission of 1899 stopped its work.*" (First
Dutch Case, annex III, page 4; first Portuguese Case, page 27.)
The disagreement comes only as to what is to be done *from this
point on,* whether toward the north (Dutch claim) or in the easterly
direction (Portuguese claim). Now this point, at which the work
was suspended in 1899, starting from which the disagreement had
arisen in 1899 and 1902, was marked on the official map signed in
a contradictory manner by the boundary commissioners of the two
nations February 16, 1899. It is this very point which was considered when in the conference at The Hague of 1902, the dele-

gates of the two States solved the dispute by pronouncing in favor of a frontier extending toward the north and designated by the name of line A-C. In drawing up this map of February 16, 1899 (annex IV appended here) under the map annexed to the convention of 1904 (annex III, appended here), they state that there is absolute agreement between them as to the location of the point in question.

The Portuguese Government, moreover, does not contest very sharply the location of point A, for in its first case it expresses itself as follows, page 10: "There is no pretension to deny that the line starts from point A. What is debated is the subordinate inflexions . . . ," and farther on page 15: "There is no denial that the frontier concerned starts from the point where the surveyors were prevented from going farther; what is denied is that they had the intention of running it north *from there*."

From the above it results that the arbitrator is certain that three points of the line A-C have been duly established incontestably, and not even contested: point C in the north, the source of the Noèl Meto in the middle, and point A in the south, at the spot where the boundary work was suspended in 1899. These three points certainly correspond to the intention of the parties when they negotiated the project of the convention of 1902 and transformed it into the convention of 1904. To admit another solution as to the location of point A, moreover, would again place in question the frontier of the lower course of the Noèl Bilomi agreed upon by No. 9 of Article 3 of the treaty of 1904; now, No. 9 is not contested and is not in litigation.

3. There now remains to examine the part of line A-C comprised between point A in the south and the source of the Noèl Meto in the middle of line A-C.

Here again, and always, we must look for the real and harmonious intention of the parties when they bound themselves:

In 1902 two propositions were in sight: That of Portugal had been formulated as follows in the *procès-verbal* of the session of the boundary commissioners held at Koepang, February 21, 1899 (annex II in the second Dutch Case): "From this last point (point

A), the length of the Noèl Bilomi as far as Nunkalai, from there crossing Tasona, Kin Napua, Humusu, as far as the source of the Noèl Boll Bass; then the length of that river as far as its mouth." At the conferences of The Hague of 1902, this survey (D-B) was abandoned at the session of June 26th by the Portuguese delegation and replaced by the demand for an intermediate and diagonal sur- vey A-B, which would have the course of the Noèl Boll Bass as a frontier in the northwest instead of the Noèl Meto (see Map II here appended).   On the 28th of June the Portuguese delegation abandoned this retreating line (*ligne de retraite*) A-B, moved back westerly from the Noèl Boll Bass to the Noèl Meto, and accepted line A-C claimed by the Netherlands.   This line A-C was immedi- ately traced on a map which officially had been annexed to the treaty of 1904 (see map annexed III).

On this map the frontier, starting from point A where the undis- puted frontier of the lower course of the Noèl Bilomi ends, as- cends a northerly direction the course of a small affluent called Oè Sunan by common agreement, then continues northerly as far as the location, then not known, of the source of the Noèl Meto.   This survey on the map was defined and commented on as follows in the treaty, Article 3, No. 10: "Starting from this point (A) the boun- dary follows the thalweg of the Oè Sunan, crosses Nipani and Kelali (Keli) as much as possible, strikes the source of the Noèl Meto and follows the thalweg of that river as far as its mouth." Now this text, made definitive in the treaty of 1904, *reproduces word for word the text proposed by the Dutch commissioners* at that same session at Koepang, February 21, 1899, in opposition to what the Portuguese claimed at that time.   Simply calling to attention these two maps and the fact that in 1902–1904, the Portuguese pro- posal was ignored totally and the Dutch proposal inserted word for word, suffices to establish by evidence the intention of the contract- ing parties: when they negotiated and signed the agreement of 1904 they adopted the Dutch survey and threw aside the survey desired by Portugal on that part of the frontier of the two States in the Island of Timor.   Thus, in the mind of the arbitrator, the two par- ties had a *real and harmonious wish to adopt the most western sur-*

vey, not only on the northern slope of the island between the Noèl Boll Bass and the Noèl Meto, but also in the center of the island, between the source of the Noèl Bilomi and the source of the Noèl Meto.

It is now fitting to enter into the details of examining the most western survey :

4. Portugal observes to-day that the water-course marked Oè Sunan on the official maps of 1899 and 1904, and in Article 3, No. 9 of the treaty of 1904, does not exist; that really this water-course bears the name of Kabun among the members of the Tumbabas tribe or of Lèos among the members of the tribe of Ambenos, and that the true Oè Sunan is to be found six or seven kilometers farther to the east. It is true, the Portuguese Government adds, that this other Oè Sunan is not an affluent of the Bilomi river, that it takes its source at a certain distance from that river, on the north slope of Mount Kinapua, but this other Oè Sunan and Mount Kinapua are claimed by the Ambenos (Portuguese) as from ancient date forming the frontier between them on the west and the Dutch Amakonos on the east : So it is this other Oè Sunan, in the opinion of the Portuguese Government, that the two Governments had in mind, when in Article 3, No. 10 of the treaty of 1904 they stipulated that the frontier would follow the course of the Oè Sunan.

To appreciate the scope of this allegation there is reason to recollect that, on the map prepared by the boundary commissioners of the two nations at Koepang, February 16, 1899 (map annex IV) the frontier then demanded by Portugal is indicated by a dotted line *following the presumed course of the Noèl Bilomi upstream* in an easterly direction starting from the point (A) where the said commissioners had to stop their work at that time, that is to say, starting from the confluence of the Noèl Bilomi with what then by common agreement was called the Oè Sunan; in the map of 1899 care was taken to have the dotted line followed with the words "Noèl Bilomi" so as to indicate well the Portuguese commissioners desire to follow the course of the river while ascending it.

On the other hand, at the time of the treaty of 1904, all of the dotted line east of the point where a halt was made in 1899 was suppressed, to show clearly that there was no longer reason to ascend in an easterly direction the then unexplored course of the Noèl Bilomi, and that on the contrary the frontier should proceed toward the north (see transparent map annex III). This implies, in the mind of the arbitrator, the harmonious intention to grant, from point A upstream, *both banks* of the Noèl Bilomi to the Netherlands.

Another fact which to the arbitrator seems to imply the harmonious intention of the parties at the time of the signature of the convention of 1904, is that, in the description of the frontier proposed by the Portuguese commissioners in 1899, they suggested the following survey *west to east*: "From this last point (the confluence of the Noèl Bilomi with the affluent at that time named Oè Sunan) the length of the Noèl Bilomi *as far as Nunkelaï*, from there crossing Tasona, Kinapua . . .;" according to this Portuguese description Nunkalaï is to be found east of the river Oè-Sunan and west of Kinapua. Now, the other Oè-Sunan river, now claimed by Portugal as a frontier, is situate several kilometers *east*, and not west, of Nunkalaï, from which results the impossibility that this river had been considered by the Portuguese delegates in their proposals of that time.

What further confirms this impression of the arbitrator is the fact that the new Oè Sunan, this one which, six kilometers to the east, has its source on the northern watershed of Mount Kinapua, is not an *affluent* of the Noèl Bilomi.

Finally, this other Oè Sunan does not proceed "toward Nipani and Kelali (Keli)" as the treaty of 1904 prescribes it, but is very quickly confused with other rivers flowing east and finally ends in regions incontestably Dutch.

Together all of these concordant circumstances lead the arbitrator to the conviction that there is no need to pause on the mistake of name made by the boundary commissioners in 1899 and by the negotiators of the international acts of 1902 and 1904 when they gave the name of Oè Sunan to Kabun or Lèos, and that, on the contrary, there is reason to admit that it is this very Kabun or Lèos that the parties intended to consider as properly to serve as a frontier from point A north. This mutual error of the commissioners of both nations is explained, moreover, when one states that most of the water-courses of that region bear several names or bear the name of the country which they cross and that a region neighboring to Kabun or Lèos has the name Sunan the sound of which resembles that of Oè Sunan.

To admit any other solution, to accept a survey mounting the course of the Noèl Bilomi as far as Mount Kinapua, then passing into the basin of another Oè Sunan which is not an affluent of the Bilomi, and which does not proceed toward Nipani and Kelali, would be contrary to the whole spirit of the negotiation of 1902–1904, and irreconcilable with the map annexed to the convention of 1904.

Portugal could not, at this late time, claim equitably between the Noèl Bilomi and the source of the Noèl Meto and, in connection with a setting of metes, almost exactly the territory which it renounced expressly in 1902–1904 for compensations deemed sufficient by her or because she wished to avoid an appeal on the part of the Netherlands to arbitration or to more extensive claims in the Okussi region (see map annexes V and VI).

In other words, there develops from what has gone before the conviction that the will of the contracting Parties ought to be interpreted in the sense that, starting from point A situate on the Bilomi river, the frontier follows in a northerly direction the thalweg of the river Kabun or Leos as far as the source of this last watercourse wrongly called Oè Sunan in 1899, 1902 and 1904.

The reasoning elucidated above under No. 4 would be superfluous if, as the Government of the Netherlands affirms (second Case, No. VIII, page 6), the last reconnaissances made on the premises established that this new Oè Sunan does not exist and that the watercourse to which this name has been given by the Portuguese is in reality called Noèl Polan or Poeamesse.

5. We have now but to seek the intention of the parties for that region included between the source of the Kabun or Lèos river (wrongly called Oè Sunan in 1899–1904) and the source of the Noèl Meto.

The convention of 1904 is expressed as follows: "The thalweg of the Oè Sunan, (recognized above under No. 4 as rightfully called Kabun or Lèos) crosses Nepani and Kelali (Keli) *as much as possible*, (and)strikes the source of the Noèl Meto. . . ."

The Dutch boundary commissioners and their Government propose to connect the sources of the Kabun and Noèl Meto rivers by following almost exactly the dividing line of the streams, that is to say, a series of peaks of which the principal ones, from north to south, have the names of Netton, Adjausene, Niseu, or Nisene, Wanat or Vanate, Fatu Nipani or Fatoe Nipani, Fatu Kabi (Fatoe Kabi) and Kelali (Keli).

This proposal is contested by the Portuguese Government because it would be contrary to the intention of the parties whose aim was, at the time of the conclusion of the treaties between the two Governments, not to divide the native States; now, that line detaches the whole eastern part from Portuguese Ambeno. In its first Case, and especially in the annexes to the second, the Portuguese Government invokes the depositions of numerous native chieftains to prove, in substance, that the whole space which would be attributed to the Netherlands is a part of Ambeno and belongs to the Ambenos. Besides this they invoke a private map edited at Batavia on which the Ambenos are indicated as occupying the territory claimed by the Netherlands. The Portuguese Government is of the opinion that Ambenu-Oïkussi was granted incontestably to Portugal by the treaty of 1859, and that the tribe of Ambenos could not be partitioned between two sovereignties.

Once again must the arbitrator seek to reconstitute the will of the parties. Now according to the test of the treaty of 1859 Portugal obtained only the "part" of the State of Ambeno that "has raised the Portuguese flag;" that certain parts of Ambeno were considered, since 1859, as remaining under the sovereignty of the Netherlands, would be nothing anomalous. Further than this, the private map edited at Batavia could not be weighed in value with the two official maps signed by the commissioners or delegates of the two States in 1899 and 1904, and on these two official maps (annexes III and IV) the name Ambeno does not figure within the disputed territory; both put that name west and outside the disputed territory. Moreover, it results from the document at hand that since

1899 the Dutch commissioners produced declarations of the native Tumbaba and Amakano chieftains assuring that this territory belonged to them and was not a part of Ambeno (annex III in the second Dutch Case, declaration made at the session held at Koepang, February 21, 1899). Thus we find ourselves in the presence of contradictory assertions of natives. The latter in 1899 had been fighting for more than twenty years (first Portuguese Case, page 22) at the time of the arrival of the boundary commissioners in that region, and the Portuguese Government (in its first Case, page 9) acknowledged it as "certain that the peoples east of Oikussi Ambeno have disputed the contiguous territories for a long time and that these peoples are so intermingled that it is difficult to distinguish what really does belong to them." See also in the second Portuguese Case, page 10, the deposition of the Ambeno chief, Béne Necat: "The eastern part of Oikussi and Ambeno was inhabited by the Tumbaba people who were driven out of there three generations ago .   .   .   by the Ambenos.   .   .   .   Since then that region has been desert, although it has been overrun by both Tumbabas and Ambenos."

The intention of the parties at the time of the negotiation of 1902 is found documented in the *procès-verbal* of the session of June 26th (*procès-verbaux*, page 7) during the course of which the first Portuguese delegate himself advised "not to allow one's self to be guided too much in this business by humanitarian motives toward the peoples of the Island of Timor; for petty causes these tribes quit their native soil to set up elsewhere, and several times they have left Dutch territory to establish themselves in Portuguese territory, and *vice versa.*" The next day, *procès-verbaux*, page 11, the first Dutch delegate observed that his Government was making "a great concession" in not claiming the whole of Ambeno, "considering that according to his opinion the convention of 1893 implied the disappearance of the enclave of Oikussi"; he declared that if the two Governments were not able to come to an arrangement on the basis of the line A-C proposed by the Netherlands, the latter would consider itself bound to have recourse to arbitration to decide whether Ambeno was an enclave that ought to be granted to it entirely, and then, June 28th, the Portuguese delegation accepted line A-C

without restriction or reservation as had been claimed by the Dutch
delegation.

From all these facts there results the conviction of the arbitrator
that in 1902–1904 an agreement was reached without taking into
account the chance of detaching such or such a parcel claimed by
the Ambenos, the Tumbabas, or the Amakonos, and expressly stating that there would be no preoccupation with the claims, contradictory as they were, of the natives. In other terms, from the
procès-verbaux of 1902 there results the conviction of the arbitrator that Portugal accepted line A-C as it was claimed *by the Netherlands*, precisely because Portugal preferred to abandon claims of a
secondary order to the east, in order to save the big piece, that is
to say, in order to save what the treaty of 1859 calls the "enclave"
of Ambenu-Okussi. The Government of the Netherlands, in the
mind of the arbitrator, also correctly maintains in its second Case,
page 2, that nothing in the treaty of 1859 prevented the division
of the kingdom of Ambeno, and adds: "Even if the treaty of
1859 did not sanction such a division, the Portuguese Government
legitimately could not oppose such a division *now*. Such objections
would come too late, and ought to have been raised *before* the conclusion of the treaty of 1904."

The arbitrator observes, moreover, on the two official maps of
1899 and 1904 (annexes III and IV) that Nipani is indicated as
being very close and slightly to the east of line A-C, a short distance from the source of the Oè Sunan (recognized at present as
rightfully called Kabun or Lèos) ; if the survey now claimed by
Portugal were adopted, that survey would pass very far to the east
and north of Nipani, and consequently would "cross" that territory
still less than the survey proposed by the Netherlands. It is true
that the Portuguese Government locates Nipani (see the map annexed under No. VI of the first Dutch Case and the word
Nipani written *in blue* on the map here appended, annex IV)
northwest of the disputed territory, but this unilateral Portuguese
map could not be weighed in opposition to the two official maps
of 1899 and 1904 (annexes III and IV), signed by the delegates
of the two States; besides, even on this exclusively Portuguese map,
the frontier desired by Portugal seems surveyed to the north of
Nipani and does not appear to "cross" that territory.

6. The Government of the Portuguese Republic finally objects to this survey of a line almost due north and south between the source of the Kabun or Lèos river and the source of the Noèl Meto, since it is a land frontier, necessitating the placing of metes, while the eastern line suggested by Portugal is formed essentially by a succession of streams, which is preferable in order to avoid conflicts among the natives.   In the mind of the arbitrator, this objection rests on no information resulting from the negotiations of 1899 or 1904.   On the southern frontier of Okussi-Ambeno, the frontier adopted in 1904 in not a few points is independent of water-courses and ought to have been or would have been marked on land by metes.   The very survey suggested by Portugal would also admit of being in part on land and necessitating the setting of metes, notably at the southeast angle (in the environs of Mount Kinapua, between the course of the Bilomi river and the river called Oè Sunan by the Portuguese), and at the northeast angle (between the sources of the river by the Portuguese called Ni-Fullan and the source of the Noèl Meto).

The survey suggested by the Dutch boundary commissioners would appear to the arbitrator to constitute a frontier sufficiently natural easily to be bounded on land.

It consists of a continuous series of rather high summits, from north to south, bearing the names of Netton, Loamitoe, Adjausene, Niseu, Wanat, Fatoe-Nipani, Kelali or Keli, of which the altitude is indicated as from 500 to 1,000 meters.   This range serves as a watershed, and the rivers east of that line run east.   Thus it does not seem that it would be difficult technically to proceed to the boundary along that range of elevations, the general direction of which corresponds entirely to the theoretical line A-C adopted by common agreement in 1904.

VII. Conclusions

The preceding considerations of fact and law lead the arbitrator to the following conclusions:

1. The treaty of 1859 had granted to Portugal in the eastern part of the Island of Timor, the Oikussi-Ambenu enclave, and

at that time the Netherlands ceded to Portugal *"that part* of Ambenu which, for several years, has raised the Portuguese flag."

2. The purpose of the convention of 1893 was "to establish in the clearest and most exact manner the boundary" of the respective possessions in Timor and "to abolish the enclaves existing" there "at the present time."

3. The convention of 1904 rectified the frontier in the center of the island by granting Portugal the Dutch enclave of Maukatar and other disputed territory, and in the southwestern part of the island the Portuguese enclave of Noemuti to the Netherlands. On the other hand, during the negotiations of 1902 the Netherlands renounced raising the greater question of whether Oikussi Ambenu was, as the treaty of 1859 indicated it, an enclave rightfully reverting to them. This agreement was reached under the condition, expressly accepted by Portugal, of adopting for the eastern frontier of the kingdom of Oikussi (Ambenu) line A-C claimed by the Netherlands during the negotiations of 1902. This line A-C was established by the treaty of 1904. (See map annexes I and II.)

4. Point C of this line is not disputed; it is located on the north coast of the Island of Timor, at the embouchure of the Noèl Meto into the sea, the course of which river was substituted in 1902–1904 for the course of the Noèl Boll Bass river, located farther east and claimed by Portugal.

The course of the Noèl Meto, of which the thalweg was to serve as the frontier as far as the source, was recognized, is not disputed, and a mete was set contradictorily at its source.

5. Point A at the southern end of the line agreed on in 1904, is the point where the boundary work was interrupted in 1899. This has not been disputed seriously by Portugal, who twice in the first Case uses the words: "It can not be denied that the line starts from point A, to which the *procès-verbaux* of the negotiations refer (p. 10). . . . It is not disputed that the frontier concerned does not start from the point where the surveyors of 1899 were hindered from going any farther" (p. 15). To dispute the location of point A would again put in question the boundary of the lower course of the Noèl Bilomi down-stream from that point; now, that part of the frontier was settled definitely by No. 9 of Article 3 of

the treaty of 1904; moreover, point A was marked contradictorily on the official maps of 1899 and 1904 (see annexes III and IV).

6. Starting from point A the negotiators of 1902–1904 found themselves confronted with two proposals. One, the Portuguese proposal, consisted in ascending the Noèl Bilomi river as a frontier in an easterly direction as far as Nunkalaï, then directing the frontier to the north, through Humusu, finally striking the source of the Noèl Boll Bass spilling into the sea east of the Noèl Meto (line B-D). The other, the Dutch proposal, said A-C line, consisted in striking north from point A as far as the sources of the Noèl Meto. The negotiators clearly and categorically repudiated the first Portuguese survey to accept the second line A-C claimed by the Netherlands; on the map annexed to the treaty of 1904 they granted to the Netherlands *both banks* of the Noèl Meto upstream from point A, at which the boundary runners had stopped their work in 1899 (see maps III and IV).

7. The descriptions of this line A-C in the treaty of 1904, Article 3, No. 10, the maps contradictorily sketched in 1899, and on which the negotiators of 1902 deliberated, and finally the official map annexed to the treaty of 1904, mention an affluent at point A as properly forming a boundary in a northerly direction, to which all parties gave the name of Oè-Sunan from 1899 to 1909. To-day all parties agree this affluent really bears the name of Kabun or Lèos. Another river subsequently discovered about six kilometers farther east bears the name of Oe Sunan according to the Portuguese, and rises north of Kinapua, a mountain situate very near the north bank of the Bilomi. The existence of this Oè Sunan stream is contested by the Netherlands, in their second Case, following two recent reconnaissances: this alleged Oè-Sunan really would be called Poeamesse or Noèl Polan.

In the mind of the arbitrator it is impossible that this other Oè Sunan river, if it exist, could have been the one the negotiators of 1899 and of 1902—1904 had in view, for

(*a*) It is not an affluent of the Noèl Bilomi;

(*b*) The frontier *proposed by Portugal* at this period and *mapped* by common agreement in 1902–1904 was, starting from point A and proceeding *easterly*, to pass through *Nunkalaï* then through Kinapua; now Nunkalaï is situated many kilometers west of Mount Kinapua and *west* of the source of this new river called Oè Sunan by the Portuguese;

(*c*) *Both* banks of the Noèl Bilomi upstream to the east of point A having been granted to the Netherlands in 1904, the affluent that is to serve as a frontier in a northerly direction cannot be sought upstream and east of point A.

General principles for the interpretation of conventions demand that account be taken "of the real and mutual intention of the parties without pausing on inexact expressions or terms which possibly they have used erroneously." It is true that the parties erred in giving the name Oè Sunan to the affluent coming to point A from the north, but this is the only affluent (then erroneously called Oè Sunan) which, in the harmonious thinking of the parties, was necessarily the point at which the frontier ought to leave the Noèl Bilomi to proceed north,—and not any other river to which the Portuguese give the name Oè Sunan and which would be located six kilometers farther east. In other words, the thalweg of the river to-day called Kabun or Lèos is what ought to serve as the frontier from point A north.

8. Starting south from the source of this Kabun or Lèos river (wrongly called Oè Sunan from 1899 to 1909) the frontier, according to the tenor of Article 3, No. 10, of the treaty of 1904, ought "to cross Nipani and Kelali (Keli) as much as possible" to reach the source of the Noèl Meto to the north.

The boundary proposed by the Portuguese would go completely around that region designated under the name of Nipani on the official map of 1904 and according to that map situated near the source of the Kabun or Lèos; the frontier would be several kilometers distant from Nipani in an easterly direction. Even if, as does a Portuguese map which has no character because being contradictorily acknowledged, one gives the name of Nipani to a region located much more to the north, east of the sources of the Noèl Meto, the frontier claimed by Portugal would not the more cross Nipani, but would go around it to the north.

The treaty of 1904 prescribes the crossing of Nipani "as much as possible." The survey suggested by the Netherlands runs along the western part of Nipani and is nearer to it than the survey proposed by Portugal.

9. Portugal objects that the line due north and south between the sources of the Kabun and the Noèl Meto rivers would parcel the territory of the Ambenos, granting part to the Netherlands and part to Portugal; this parcelling would be contrary to the treaty of 1859.

In the mind of the arbitrator, this objection is not established in the sense that already in 1859 a "part" of Ambeno was placed incontestably under the sovereignty of the Netherlands. Besides, in the course of the negotiations from 1899 to 1904, contradictory declarations of the natives were produced, the Dutch Amakonos and Tumbabas claiming the disputed territory, and the Portuguese Ambenos claiming it from their side. Thus the alleged parcelling is not demonstrated. More, it was understood in the conferences of 1902, on the observation of the first Portuguese delegate himself, that there was no need to be extensively preoccupied with the pretensions of the tribes who frequently displaced each other and passed successively from the territory of one of the States to that of the other. The objection that the territories of even one tribe should not be parcelled could not be entertained by the arbitrator, for it would need to have been presented during the course of the negotiations from 1902-1904; at this time it is too late, because the treaty of 1904, Article 3, No. 10 (all that the arbitrator had to interpret), makes no mention of any intention of the parties never to divide native populations; on the contrary, that treaty ran the boundary line according to the conferences in the course of which it was understood that considerations of that kind ought not to be preponderant.

10. The summit line proposed by the Government of the Netherlands between the source of the river Kabun (Lèos) to the south, and the source of the Noèl Meto to the north, is sufficiently natural to be surveyed on land without great practical difficulties. It offers the advantage that the water-courses uniformly descend from that summit line toward the territories placed wholly under Dutch sovereignty. The survey suggested by the Portuguese Government,

384 THE HAGUE COURT REPORTS

on the contrary, would attribute the upper and the lower part of these several streams to different sovereignties.

11. In a general way, in fact, the demand of Portugal reproduces completely, for all the territory between the Noèl Bilomi to the south and the Noèl Meto to the north, the line that that State claimed in 1902 and abandoned at the end of the conference of 1902 and in the treaty of 1904. If the present Portuguese claim were established, it would not be explained why the Netherlands in 1902 made a *sine qua non* condition of the rejection of this Portuguese demand. Conventions between States, like those between individuals, ought to be interpreted "rather in the sense in which they can have some effect than in the sense in which they can produce none." The Dutch threat to break off the negotiations in 1902 would have meant nothing if the intention had been to grant Portugal precisely the territory claimed by the Netherlands as a condition for agreement.

12. Finally, if we take the point of view of equity, which it is important not to lose sight of in international relations, the summit line proposed by the Netherlands is not contrary to equity, in the sense that Portugal will receive more territory than it had reason to hope for according to the theoretical line A-C, to which she consented in 1904, before the land could be explored. Line A-C is wholly inside the territory that will revert to Portugal; the Portuguese Republic, in fact, will receive a better share than it ought to expect there (see map appended VII). If, on the contrary, the eastern survey suggested by the Portuguese Government were adopted, the Netherlands could rightfully allege that they were being deprived of almost all the territory which theoretically was granted to them in 1904 as compensation for abandoning the enclave of Maukatar in the center of the Island of Timor and in compensation for abandoning Dutch claims to the whole of the Ambeno enclave.

Consequently,

The arbitrator, considering the two treaties signed at Lisbon, April 20, 1859, and June 10, 1893, and the treaty signed at The Hague, October 1, 1904, between the Netherlands and Portugal for the boundary of their respective possessions in the Island of Timor;

Considering the *compromis* of arbitration signed at The Hague, April 3, 1913, and notably Article 2 thus couched: "The arbitrator, acting upon the data furnished by the parties, shall decide, on the basis of the treaties and the general principles of international law, conformably to Article 3, No. 10 of the convention concluded at The Hague, October 1, 1904, concerning the boundary of the Dutch and Portuguese possessions in the Island of Timor, how the boundary-line should be fixed, starting from the Noèl Bilomi, up to the source of the Noèl Meto";

Considering the diplomatic notes designating the undersigned as arbitrator through the application of Article 1 of the *compromis;*

Considering the first and second Cases deposited in due time by each of the high contracting Parties, as well as the maps and documents annexed to the said Cases;

Considering the statements of fact and of law formulated above under Nos. I to VII;

Considering the convention signed at The Hague, October 18, 1907, for the pacific settlement of international disputes; makes the following

AWARD

Article 3, No. 10, of the convention concluded at The Hague, October 1, 1904, concerning the boundary of Dutch and Portuguese possessions in the Island of Timor, ought to be interpreted conformably with the conclusions of the Royal Government of the Netherlands for the boundary, starting from the Noèl Bilomi, up to the source of the Noèl Meto; consequently, it will proceed to the survey of that part of the frontier on the basis of the map scaled at 1/50,000 annexed under No. IV of the first Case deposited with the arbitrator by the Dutch Government. A reproduction of this map signed by the arbitrator is appended as annex VII to the present award of which it shall be an integral part.

Expenses, fixed at 2,000 francs, have been deducted from the sum of 4,000 francs consigned to the hands of the arbitrator in execution of Article 8 of the *compromis* of April 3, 1913; the remainder, or 2,000 francs, shall be remitted in equal shares to the two parties, and receipted, at the moment of the notification of the award.

Done in three originals, of which one shall be deposited and receipt therefor taken by the secretary general of the International Bureau of the Permanent Court of Arbitration at The Hague, with his Excellency the Minister of Foreign Affairs of the Netherlands as notification to the Royal Government of the Netherlands, and of which the second shall be deposited on the same day and in the same form with his Excellency the Envoy Extraordinary and Minister Plenipotentiary of the Portuguese Republic near Her Majesty the Queen of the Netherlands, as notification to the Government of the Portuguese Republic. The third original shall be deposited in the archives of the International Bureau of the Permanent Court of Arbitration.

Paris, June 25, 1914.   LARDY

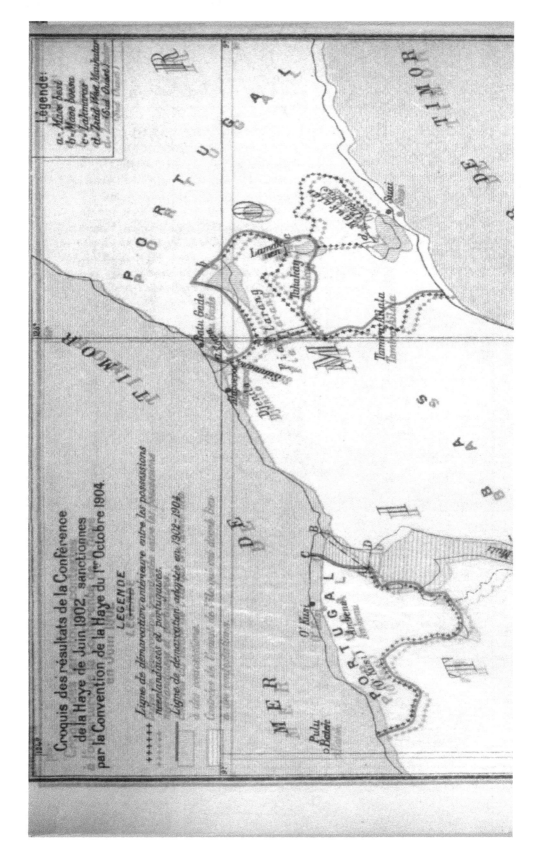

Croquis des résultats de la Conférence
de la Haye de Juin 1902, sanctionnés
par la Convention de la Haye du 1er Octobre 1904.

LÉGENDE

+++++ Ligne de démarcation antérieure entre les possessions
néerlandaises et portugaises.

.... Ligne de démarcation adoptée en 1902-1904.

Légende:
a.- Māūe Poēil
b.- Māūe Poēau
c.- Laktmīras
d.- Zuid West Maukatar
(Sud Ouest)

PORTUGAIR

TIMOR

PORTUGAL

MER DE TIMOR

DE TIMOR

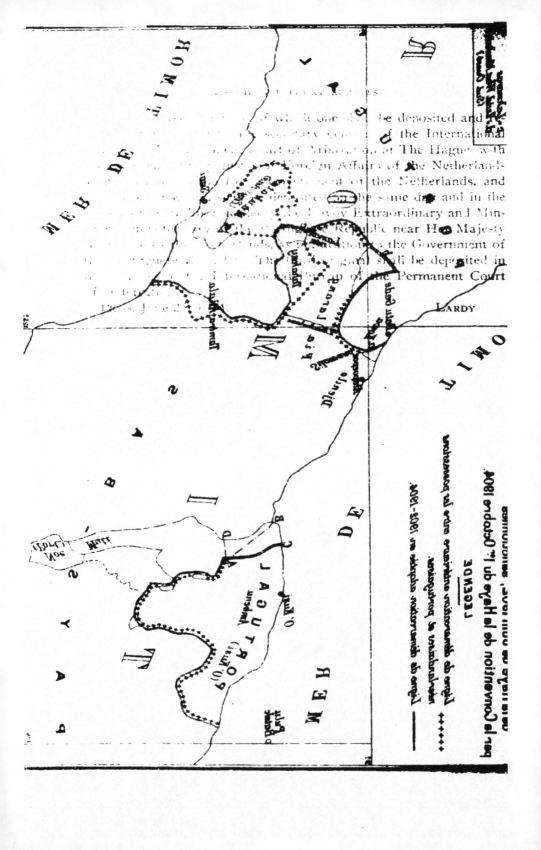

Croquis des territoires contestés
à l'ouverture de la Conférence de la Haye
en Juin 1902

LÉGENDE

++++++ Ligne de démarcation incontestée entre les possessions
néerlandaises et portugaises.

Contrées du centre de l'île qui ont donné lieu
à des contestations.

Contrées de l'ouest de l'île qui ont donné lieu
à des contestations.

Légende:
a - Maoe besi
b - Maoe bonan
c - Lakmaras
d - Zaïd Wehat Maubatar
(Sud Ouest)

PORTUGAL

TIMOR

TIMOR DE

MER DE

P O R T U G A L

Batu Gade

Lamaknen

Tambas Alala

Tshakroy

Silawang

Fialarang

Djenilo

Alapoepoe

Nenang

Suai

Mauk clat
(Tafos-Bac)

Palu o Batek

O Kusi
P. (O'Kusi)
Ambenu

TIMOR

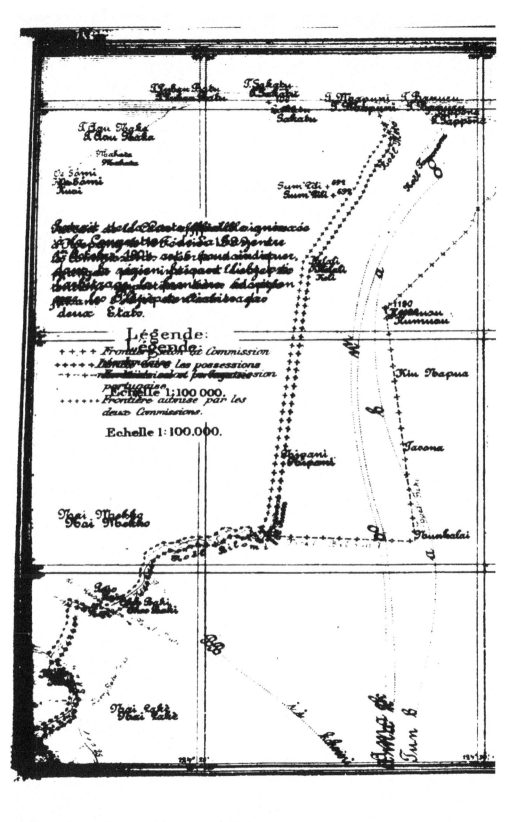

Extrait de la Carte officielle signée aux
du Congo le 14 Octobre 1886, entre
le Octobre 1885, ainsi fait conduire,
dans la région intéressé l'Objet de
ce litige par la frontière adoptée
par les Plénipotentiaires des
deux États.

Légende:
+ + + + Frontière selon la Commission
+++++ limite entre les possessions
−+−−− administrée par la mission
portugaise.
Echelle 1:100 000.
+++++ Frontière admise par les
deux Commissions.

Echelle 1: 100.000.

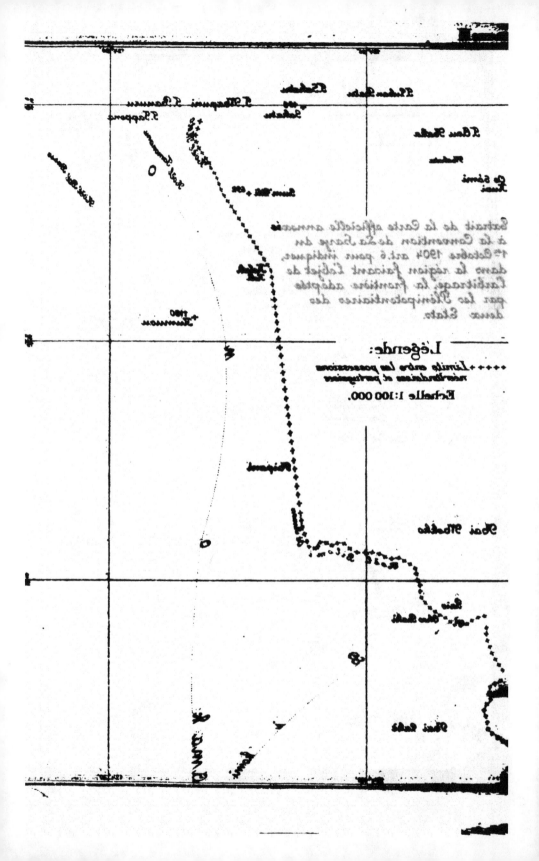

Extrait de la Carte officielle signée à Koepang le 16 Février 1899 entre les Commissaires néerlandais et portugais pour indiquer leurs prétentions respectives dans la région faisant l'objet de l'arbitrage

Légende:

++++ Frontière selon la Commission néerlandaise.

−+−+− Frontière selon la Commission portugaise.

++++++ Frontière admise par les deux Commissions.

Echelle 1:100.000.

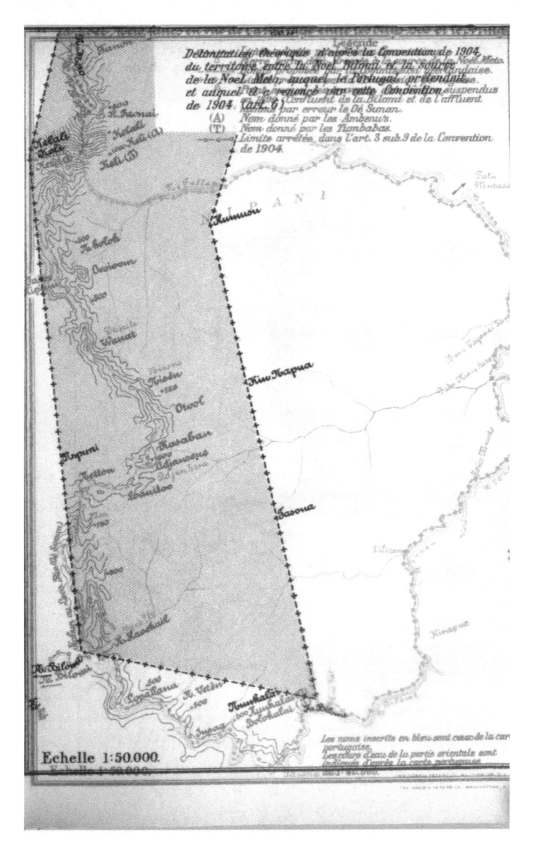

Légende

Délimitation théorique d'après la Convention de 1904 du territoire entre la Noël Bilomi et la source de la Noël Metor, auquel le Portugal prétendait et auquel il a renoncé par cette Convention de 1904. (art. 6.)

(A) Nom donné par les Ambenu's.
(T) Nom donné par les Tombabas.

Limite arrêtée dans l'art. 3 sub. 9 de la Convention de 1904.

Echelle 1:50.000.

Les noms inscrits en bleu sont ceux de la carte portugaise.

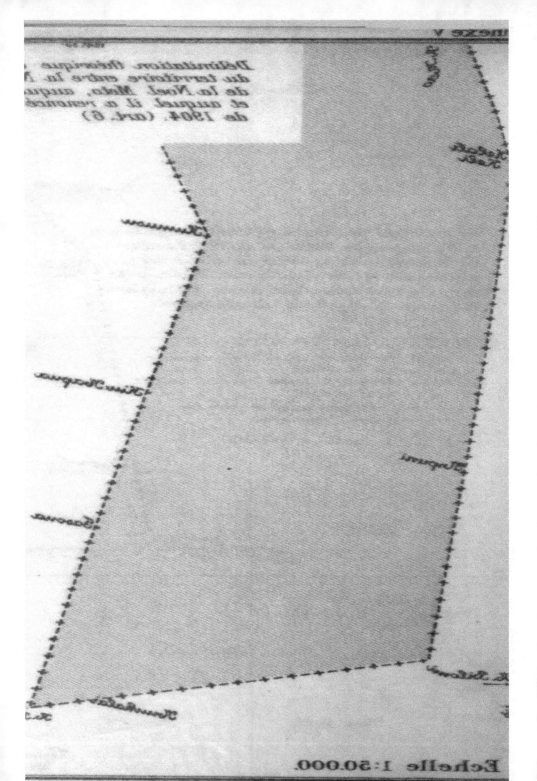

Légende

++++++   Limite adoptée par les deux Commissions.
   ö   Pierre borne déjà dressée à la source de la Noël Meto.
‒ ‒ ‒ ‒   Limite proposée par la Commission néerlandaise.
•‒•‒•‒   Limite proposée par la Commission portugaise.
  A   Point auquel les travaux ont dû être suspendus
           en 1899 (Confluent de la Bilomi et de l'affluent
           nommé par erreur le Oé Sunan.
(A)   Nom donné par les Ambenu's.
(T)   Nom donné par les Tumbabas.
‒o‒o‒o   Limite arrêtée dans l'art. 3 sub.3 de la Convention
           de 1904.

Banon

Kelali
Kelali (A)
Kelali (T)

N. Iuonai
Kelali
Keli (A)
Keli (T)

N I P A N I

N. Bolok
Oeoioem
Tatin Nipani

Densile
Wanat

Tioén
Otvol
Kasaban
Adjansene
Netton
Loanitoe

Saluan ou Loes Riw (Oé Sunan)

N. Kaoshail
N. Bilomi
Lopa Lana
N. Velén
Inoaa
Tunkalai (A)
Bolokalai (T)
Tasena

Kinapua

Les noms inscrits en bleu sont ceux de la carte
portugaise.
Les cours d'eau de la partie orientale sont
indiqués d'après la carte portugaise
au 1:40.000.

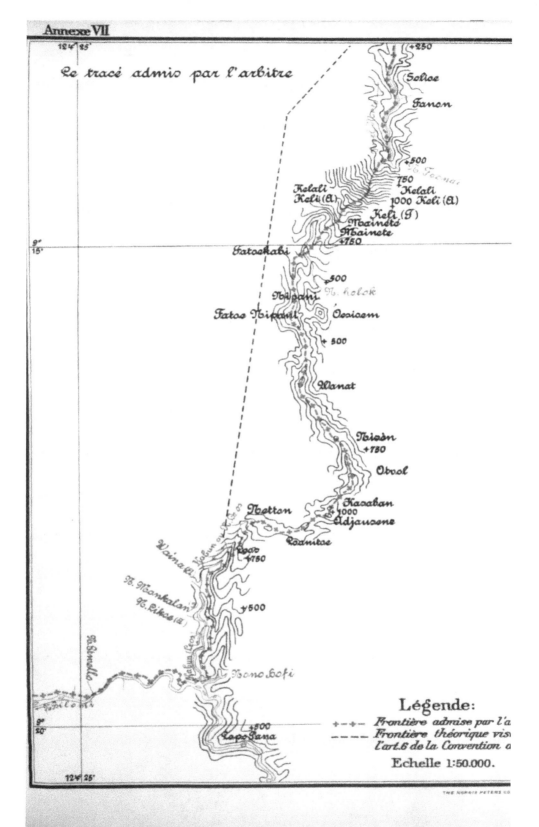

Le tracé admis par l'arbitre

Légende:

+-+- Frontière admise par l'a
---- Frontière théorique vis
l'art.6 de la Convention a

Echelle 1:50.000.

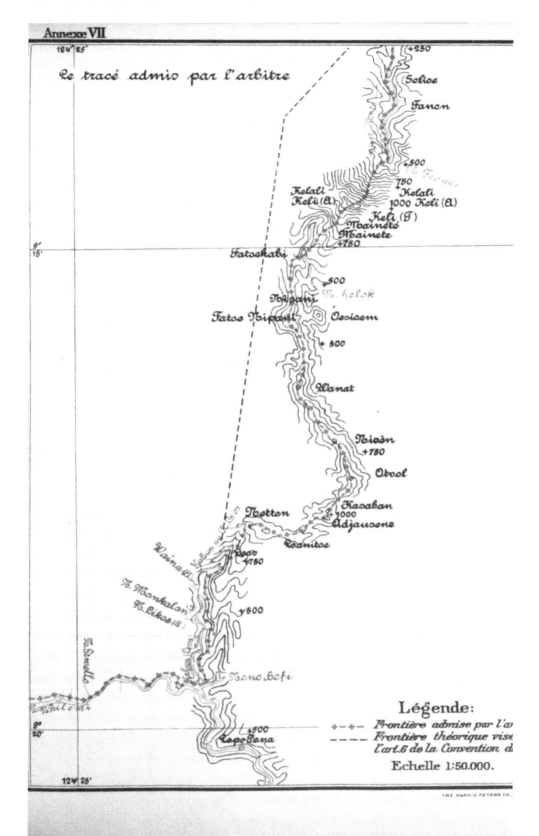

Le tracé admis par l'arbitre

Légende:

+−+−+ Frontière admise par l'a...

− − − Frontière théorique vise...

l'art.6 de la Convention d...

Echelle 1:50.000.

AGREEMENT FOR ARBITRATION

Compromis for the settling of differences in the interpretation of the treaty of October 1, 1904, relative to the boundary in the Island of Timor.—Signed at The Hague, April 3, 1913.[1]

Her Majesty the Queen of the Netherlands and the President of the Republic of Portugal, considering that the execution of the convention concluded between the Netherlands and Portugal at The Hague, October 1, 1904,[2] regarding the delimitation of the Dutch and Portuguese possessions in the Island of Timor, has led to a dispute concerning the surveying of that part of the boundary referred to under Article 3, No. 10, of the said convention;

Desiring to settle this dispute in a friendly manner;

In view of Article 14 of the said convention and of Article 38 of the convention for the pacific settlement of international disputes, concluded at The Hague, October 18, 1907;

Have designated as their plenipotentiaries, to wit:

. . . .

Who, duly authorized to that end, have agreed upon the following articles:

ARTICLE 1

The Government of Her Majesty the Queen of the Netherlands and the Government of the Portuguese Republic agree to submit the aforementioned dispute to a sole arbitrator to be chosen from the membership of the Permanent Court of Arbitration.

If the two Governments should not agree upon the selection of the said arbitrator, they shall request the President of the Swiss Confederation to designate him.

ARTICLE 2

The arbitrator, acting upon the data furnished by the parties, shall decide on the basis of the treaties and the general principles of international law, conformably to Article 3, No. 10, of the convention concluded at The Hague, October 1, 1904, concerning the boundary of the Dutch and Portuguese possessions in the Island of Timor, how

---

[1] Translation. For the original French text, see Appendix, p. 596.
[2] *Post*, p. 396.

the boundary-line should be fixed starting from the Noèl Bilomi, up to the source of the Noèl Meto.

ARTICLE 3

Through the intermediary of the International Bureau of the Permanent Court of Arbitration, each of the parties shall transmit to the arbitrator, within three months after the exchange of the ratifications of the present convention, a memoir containing an exposition of its rights and the documents in support thereof, and shall immediately forward a certified copy thereof to the other party.

Upon the expiration of the period herein stated, each of the parties shall be entitled to another period of three months to transmit, if it deems it expedient, to the arbitrator, through the intermediary hereinbefore indicated, a second memoir of which it transmit a certified copy to the other party.

The arbitrator is authorized to grant to each of the parties so desiring, a prorogation of two months regarding the periods mentioned in this article. He shall give notification of each prorogation to the adverse party.[1]

ARTICLE 4

After the exchange of these memoirs, no communication, either written or verbal shall be made to the arbitrator, unless the latter requests of one or both of the parties additional information in writing.

The party furnishing such information shall immediately forward a certified copy thereof to the other party, and the latter may, in its discretion, within a period of two months after the receipt of the said copy, communicate in writing to the arbitrator, such observations as may be necessary. A certified copy of these observations shall also be communicated immediately to the adverse party.

ARTICLE 5

The arbitrator shall render his decision in a place to be designated by him.

ARTICLE 6

The arbitrator shall use the French language both in rendering his decision and in the communications that he may have occasion to

---

[1] A prorogation of two months was granted to the parties by the arbitrator for the transmittal of their *second* memoirs.

address to the parties in the course of the procedure. Memoirs and other communications coming from the parties themselves shall be written in the same language.

ARTICLE 7

The arbitrator shall decide all questions that might arise with regard to procedure during the course of the litigation.

ARTICLE 8

Immediately after the ratifications of the present convention, each of the parties shall deposit with the arbitrator, in advance, the sum of 2,000 francs to cover the expenses of the procedure.

ARTICLE 9

The decision shall be communicated in writing by the arbitrator to the parties.

It shall state the reasons upon which it is based.

In his decision, the arbitrator shall state the amount of the expenses of the procedure. Each party shall bear its own personal expenses and one-half each the said expenses of procedure.

ARTICLE 10

The parties obligate themselves to accept as final the decision rendered by the arbitrator in accordance with the provisions of the present convention and to abide by it without any reservation whatever.

The dispute concerning the execution of the decision shall be referred to the arbitrator.

ARTICLE 11

The present convention shall be ratified and shall become binding immediately after the exchange of ratifications, which shall take place at The Hague as soon as possible.

In faith of which, the respective plenipotentiaries have signed the present convention and have affixed their seals thereto.

Done in duplicate at The Hague, April 3, 1913.

(L. S.) (Signed) R. DE MAREÈS VAN SWINDEREN
(L. S.) (Signed) ANTONIO MARIA BARTHOLOMEU FERREIRA

ADDITIONAL DOCUMENTS

Agreement between the Netherlands and Portugal relative to the boundary of their possessions in the archipelago of Timor and Solor.—Signed at Lisbon, April 20, 1859.[1]

His Majesty the King of the Netherlands, His Majesty the King of Portugal and the Algarves, believing it to be necessary finally to settle the existing incertitudes regarding the boundaries of Dutch and Portuguese possessions in the archipelago of Timor and Solor, and desiring to prevent forever any misunderstanding that might arise because of ill-defined boundaries and too numerous enclaves, have with that end in view, conferred their full power, to wit:

.   .   .   .

Who, after having communicated to each other the said full powers, found in good and due form, have agreed to conclude a treaty of demarkation and exchange, containing the following articles:

ARTICLE 1

The boundaries between the Dutch and Portuguese possessions in the Island of Timor shall be on the north, the frontiers separating Cova from Juanilo; and on the south, those that separate Sua from Lakecune.

Between these two points, the boundaries of the two possessions shall be the same as those between the contiguous Dutch and Portuguese States.

These States are as follows:

Contiguous States under the Sovereignty of the Netherlands	*Contiguous States under the Sovereignty of Portugal*
Juanilo	Cova
Silawang	Balibo
Fialarang (Fialara)	Lamakitu
Lamaksanulu	Tafakaij ou Takaij
Lamakanée	Tatumea
Naitimu (Nartimu)	Lanken
Manden	Dacolo
Dirma	Tamiru Eulalang (Eulaleng)
Lakecune	Suai

ARTICLE 2

The Netherlands recognizes the sovereignty of Portugal over all the States to the east of the boundaries thus defined, excepting the

---

[1]Translation. For the orginal French text, see Appendix, p. 599.

Dutch State of Maucatar or Caluninème (Coluninène), which extends into the Portuguese States of Lamakitu, Tanterine, Follafaix (Follefait) and Suai.

Portugal recognizes the sovereignty of the Netherlands over all the States west of these boundaries, excepting the extensional territory of Oikoussi, which remains Portuguese.

ARTICLE 3

The enclave of Oikoussi includes the State of Ambenu wherever the Portuguese flag flies, the State of Oikoussi itself and the State of Noimuti.

The boundaries of this enclave are the frontiers between Ambenu and Amfoang to the west, of Insana and Reboki (Beboki) including Cicale on the east, and Sonnebait, including Amakono and Tunebaba (Timebaba) on the south.

ARTICLE 4

On the Island of Timor, Portugal recognizes therefore the sovereignty of the Netherlands over the States of Amarassi, Bibico (Traijnico, Waijniko), Buboque (Reboki), Derima (Dirma), Fialara (Fialarang), Lamakanée, Nira (Lidak), Juanilo, Mena and Fulgarite or Folgarita (dependencies of the State of Harnenno).

ARTICLE 5

The Netherlands yields to Portugal the kingdom of Moubara (Maubara) and that portion of Ambenu (Sutrana) which, for several years past, has flown the Portuguese flag.

Immediately after the exchange of ratifications of this treaty by Their Majesties the King of the Netherlands and the King of Portugal shall have taken place, the Government of the Netherlands shall direct the superior authorities of the Dutch Indies to convey the kingdom of Moubara (Maubara) to the superior authorities of Timor Dilly.

ARTICLE 6

The Netherlands disclaims any pretension whatever over the Island of Kambing (Pulo Kambing), on the north of Dilly, and recognizes Portuguese sovereignty over this island.

ARTICLE 7

Portugal yields to the Netherlands the following possessions:

On the island of Flores, the States of Larantuca, Sicca, Paga, with their dependencies;

On the island of Adenara, the State of Wouré;

On the island of Solor, the State of Pamangkaju.

Portugal disclaims all pretensions it might possibly have entertained with regard to other States or localities situate on the above-named islands, or upon those of Lomblen, Pantar and Ombaij, whether these States fly the Dutch or Portuguese flag.

ARTICLE 8

By reason of the provisions of the preceding article, the Netherlands obtains full and undivided possession of all islands situate on the north of Timor, to wit: those of Flores, Adenara, Solor, Lomblen, Pantar (Quantar) and Ombaij, together with the near islands belonging to the archipelago of Solor.

ARTICLE 9

And as compensation for what Portugal might lose by the exchange of the above-mentioned respective possessions, the Government of the Netherlands:

1. Shall give to the Portuguese Government a complete quit-claim to the sum of 80,000 florins, borrowed in 1851 from the Government of the Dutch Indies by the Government of the Portuguese possessions in the archipelago of Timor;

2. Shall deliver in addition to the Portuguese Government a sum of 120,000 Netherland florins.

This amount shall be payable one month after the exchange of ratifications of the present treaty.

ARTICLE 10

The freedom of worship is mutually guaranteed to the inhabitants of the territories exchanged in virtue of the present treaty.

ARTICLE 11

The present treaty, which in conformity with the rules prescribed by the fundamental laws in force in the kingdoms of the Netherlands and Portugal, shall be submitted to the legislative powers for ratification, and the ratifications shall be exchanged at Lisbon, within a period of eight months from the date of its signature, or sooner if possible.

In faith of which the respective plenipotentiaries have signed the present treaty and affixed thereto the seal of their arms.

Done at Lisbon, April 20, 1859.

> (L. S.) (Signed) A. M. DE FONTES PEREIRA DE MELLO
> (L. S.) (Signed) M. HELDEWIER

Convention between the Netherlands and Portugal relative to commerce, navigation, boundaries, and mutual rights of preëmption as regards their respective possessions in the Timor and Solor archipelago.—Signed at Lisbon, June 10, 1893.[1]

Her Majesty the Queen of the Netherlands and in her name Her Majesty the Queen Regent of the Kingdom and

His Majesty the King of Portugal and the Algarves, realizing the community of interests existing between their possessions in the archipelago of Timor and Solor and desiring by mutual good-will to determine the conditions most favorable for the advancement of civilization and commerce in their possessions, have resolved to conclude a special convention and to that end have designated their plenipotentiaries, to wit:

.   .   .   .

Who, after having communicated to each other their respective full powers, found in good and due form, have agreed upon the following articles:

ARTICLE 1

In order to facilitate the exercise of their rights of sovereignty, the high contracting parties, believe it to be necessary to establish in the clearest and most exact manner the boundary of their possessions on the island of Timor and to abolish the enclaves existing at the present time.

ARTICLE 2

The high contracting Parties shall appoint to that end a commission of experts whose duty it shall be to formulate a proposition which may serve as a basis for the conclusion of a subsequent convention determining the new boundary lines in the said island.

---

[1] Translation. For the original French text, see Appendix, p. 601.

This convention shall be submitted to the approbation of the legislatures of the two countries.

ARTICLE 3

Within the Island of Timor there shall be granted to fishing vessels belonging to the subjects of each of the high contracting Parties, as well as to their crews, the same protection on the part of the respective authorities as that enjoyed by their respective subjects.

The commerce, industry and navigation of the two countries shall enjoy there the treatment of the most favored foreign nation, excepting the special treatment respectively accorded by the high contracting Parties to the indigenous States.

ARTICLE 4

The high contracting Parties decide that the importation and exportation of firearms or parts thereof, or cartridges, capsules or other ammunition intended for them, are prohibited within their possessions in the archipelago of Timor and Solor.

Independent of measures directly adopted by the Governments for the arming of their public force and the organization of their defense, individual exceptions may be made with regard to their European subjects, sufficient guarantee being given that the particular weapons and ammunition that might be furnished them shall not pass into the hands of or be sold to third parties, and in case of foreign travelers, the latter shall be provided with a declaration of their Government stating that the weapon and the ammunition are exclusively intended for their personal defense.

ARTICLE 5

The superior authorities of the Dutch party and of the Portuguese party in the Island of Timor shall nevertheless be authorized to determine annually by mutual agreement the number and kind of unperfected firearms and the amount of ammunition that may be received in the course of the same year, as well as the conditions under which such importations may be granted.

Such importation, may, however, take place only through the intermediary of certain persons or agents residing in the island itself, who in respect to this matter shall have obtained special authorization from the respective superior administration.

In case such authorization is abused, it shall be withdrawn immediately and may not be renewed.

ARTICLE 6

As a proof of its desire of establishing good neighborly relations, the Dutch Government hereby declares to relinquish its claim to indemnification to which it believes itself entitled as a result of certain treatment to which Dutch-Indian fishermen were subjected from 1889–1892 on the part of the Timor-Portuguese authorities.

ARTICLE 7

In case difficulties should arise with regard to their intercolonial relations in the archipelago of Timor and Solor or with regard to the interpretation of the present convention, the high contracting Parties agree to submit such difficulties to the decision of an arbitral commission.

This commission shall be composed of an equal number of arbitrators chosen by the high contracting Parties and of an arbitrator designated by these arbitrators.

ARTICLE 8

The present convention shall be ratified and the ratifications exchanged at Lisbon.

In faith of which, the plenipotentiaries have signed the same and affixed their seals thereto.

Done in duplicate at Lisbon, June 10, 1893.

> (L. S.) (Signed) CAREL VAN HEECKEREN
> (L. S.) (Signed) ERNESTO RODOLPHO HINTZE RIBEIRO

Declaration Signed at Lisbon, July 1, 1893, regarding Cession of Territory[1]

The undersigned plenipotentiaries of the Governments of the signatories of the convention of June 10, 1893,[2] have agreed upon the following declaration:

In order to insure the result of their common action tending espe-

---

[1]Translation. For the original French text, see Appendix, p. 603.
[2]_Ante_, p. 393.

cially to encourage the commerce and industry of their nationals by guarantees of security and stability, the high contracting Parties declare that in case of cession in part or in whole of their territories or of their rights of sovereignty in the archipelago of Timor and Solor, they mutually recognize the right of preference regarding terms similar or equivalent to those which shall have been offered. Cases of disagreement as to these terms are likewise subject to the application of Article 7 of the aforesaid convention.

The present declaration which shall be ratified at the same time as the convention concluded at Lisbon, June 10, 1893, shall be regarded as an integral part of the said convention, and shall have the same force and value.

In faith of which the respective plenipotentiaries have signed the present declaration and affixed their seals thereto.

Done in duplicate at Lisbon, July 1, 1893.

> (L. S.) (Signed) Carel van Heeckeren
> (L. S.) (Signed) Ernesto Rodolpho Ribeiro

Convention between the Governments of the Netherlands and Portugal for the settlement of the boundary between their possessions in the Island of Timor.—Signed at The Hague, October 1, 1904.[1]

Her Majesty the Queen of the Netherlands and His Majesty the King of Portugal and the Algarves, etc., etc.

Recognizing the community of interests existing between their possessions in the archipelago of Timor and of Solor, and desiring to define a clear and exact boundary of these possessions in the Island of Timor, after having informed themselves of the result of the labors of the mixed commission appointed for the regularization of the Dutch and Portuguese frontiers in the Island of Timor, established by the respective Governments in virtue of Article 2 of the convention concluded between the high contracting Parties at Lisbon, June 10, 1893,[2] have resolved to conclude a convention to that effect and have designated as their plenipotentiaries:

.   .   .   .

Who, after having communicated to each other their full powers, found in good and due form, have agreed upon the following:

---

[1] Translation. For the original French text, see Appendix, p. 604.
[2] *Ante*, p. 393.

ARTICLE 1

The Netherlands conveys Maucatar to Portugal.

ARTICLE 2

Portugal conveys Noimuti, Tahakay and Tamiru Ailala to the Netherlands.

ARTICLE 3

The boundary between Ambenu-Oikussi, belonging to Portugal, and the Dutch possessions in the Island of Timor is formed by a line:

1. Starting from the mouth of the (river) Noèl Besi whence the highest point on the (island) Pulu-Batek is seen under an astronomical azimuth of 30', 47" northwest, following the thalweg of the Noèl Besi, that of the Noèl Niema and that of the Bidjael Sunan to its source ;

2. Ascending from this point to the summit of the Bidjael Sunan, and descending down the thalweg of the Noèl Miu Mavo to the point situate on the southwest of the village Oben ;

3. From thence passing on the west of this village along the summits Banat and Kita to the summit Nivo Nun Po ; from thence following the thalweg of the rivers Nono Boni and Noèl Pasab to its affluent the Nono Susu, and ascending the Nono Susu to its source ;

4. Passing the Klus (Crus) to the point where the frontier between Abani and Nai Bobbo crosses the river Fatu Basin, from thence to the point called Subina ;

5. Descending thence by the thalweg of the Fatu Basin to the Kè An ; thence to the Nai Naõ ;

6. Crossing the Nai Naö and descending into Tut Nonie, along the thalweg of the Tut Nonie to the Noèl Ekan ;

7. Following the thalweg of the Noèl Ekan to the affluent the Sonau ; along the thalweg of this affluent to its source, and thence to the river Nivo Nono ;

8. Ascending along the thalweg of this river to its source, and passing the point called Ohoè Baki, ending at the source of the Nono Balena ;

9. Following the thalweg of this river, the thalweg of the Nono Nisè and that of the Noèl Bilomi to the affluent of the latter, the Oè Sunan ;

10. From this point, the boundary follows the thalweg of the Oè Sunan, crosses as much as possible Nipani and Kelali (Keli) and,

extending to the source of the Noèl Meto, it follows the thalweg of the latter river even to its mouth.

ARTICLE 4

That part of the boundary between Ambenu-Oikussi and the Dutch possessions defined under Article 3, No. 10, shall be surveyed and demarkated on the ground as soon as possible.

The survey of the said part of the boundary and its demarkation on the land shall be attested by a *procès-verbal* accompanied by a map to be traced in duplicate which shall be submitted for the approval of the high contracting Parties; after their approval, the said documents shall be signed in the name of the respective Governments.

Only after the said documents have been signed, the high contracting Parties shall acquire sovereignty over the regions mentioned under Articles 1 and 2.

ARTICLE 5

The boundary between the Dutch possessions in the western part and of the Portuguese possessions in the eastern part of the Island of Timor shall from the north to the south follow a line:

1. Starting from the mouth of the Mota Biku (Silaba) along the thalweg of this river to its affluent the We Bedain, along the thalweg of the We Bedain, to the Mota Asudaät (Assudat), along the thalweg of this river to its source, and following thence in the direction north to south the hills of the Kleek Teruïn (Klin Teruïn) and of the Berènis (Birènis) Kakótun;

2. Thence to the river Muda Sorun, following the thalweg of this river and that of the Tuah Naruk even to the river Telau (Talau);

3. Following the thalweg of the Telau to the river Malibaka along the thalweg of this river, the thalweg of the Mautilu and that of the Pepies to the mountain Bulu Hulu (Bulu Bulu);

4. From there to Karawa Kotun, from the latter along the thalweg of the river Tafara along the thalweg of this river to its source called Mota Tiborok (Tibor), and ascending from there to the summit Dato Miet and descending to the Mota Alun;

5. Along the thalweg of the Mota Alun, along the thalweg of the Mota Sukaër (Sukar), and that of the Mota Baukama even to the affluent of the latter called Kalan-Féhan;

6. Passing across the mountains Tahi Fehu, Fatu Suta, Fatu Rusa, passing the large tree called Halifea and the summit Uas Lulik, then crossing the river We Merak where the latter receives its affluent

the We Nu, thence crossing the large boulder called Fatu Rokon and the summits Fitun Monu, Debu Kasabauk, Ainin Matan and Lak Fuin;

7. From Lak Fuin to the point where the Hali Sobuk connects with the Mota Haliboï and along the thalweg of this river to its source;

8. From this source even to that of the Mota Bebulu, along the thalweg of this river to the We Diek, ascending to the summits Ai Kakar and Takis, descending into the Mota Masin and following the thalweg of the Mota Masin and of its mouth called Mota Talas.

ARTICLE 6

With the exception of the provisions of Article 4, the boundaries defined under Articles 3 and 5 are traced on the maps annexed to the present convention and signed by the respective plenipotentiaries.

ARTICLE 7

The territories respectively conveyed shall be vacated and the demarkation thereon entrusted to competent authorities within six months after the approval of the *procès-verbal* referred to under Article 4.

ARTICLE 8

The archives, maps and other documents relating to the territories transferred shall be transmitted to the new authorities at the same time as the territories themselves. ·

ARTICLE 9

Navigation upon the rivers forming the boundaries shall be free to the subjects of the two high contracting Parties, except for the transportation of firearms and ammunition.

ARTICLE 10

When the territory shall have been transferred, stone posts indicating the year of the present convention, of a form and dimensions proper to the object that they are intended to fulfil, shall with due solemnity be set at a proper place on the bank near the mouth of the rivers hereinafter named. The Dutch posts shall be set on the western banks of the Mota Biku and the Mota Masin, and the Portuguese posts upon the eastern banks of the said rivers. Four stone posts shall be provided by the Dutch Government at the expense of the two Governments and the Dutch Government shall place a vessel of the royal navy at the disposal of the respective authorities for the solemn transfer of the territories conveyed and for the setting of the posts

Furthermore, where it is not formed by natural limits, the boundary shall by mutual agreement be demarkated on the ground by the local authorities.

ARTICLE 11

With the exception of the provisions of Article 4, a *procès-verbal* shall be drawn up in the French language recording the transfer of the territories and the setting of the posts.

The *procès-verbal* shall be drawn up in duplicate and signed by the respective authorities of the two countries.

ARTICLE 12

Freedom of worship is mutually guaranteed to the inhabitants of the territories exchanged by the present convention.

ARTICLE 13

The high contracting Parties mutually recognize, in case of cession in part or in whole of their territories or of their rights of sovereignty in the archipelago of Timor and Solor, the right of preference regarding terms similar or equivalent to those which shall have been offered.

ARTICLE 14

All disputes regarding the interpretation or the execution of the present convention, if they can not be settled in a friendly manner, shall be referred to the Permanent Court of Arbitration in conformity with the provisions set forth in Chapter II of the international Convention of July 29, 1899, for the pacific settlement of international disputes.

ARTICLE 15

The present convention shall be ratified and the ratifications thereof exchanged as soon as possible after the approbation by the legislatures of the two countries.

In faith of which the respective plenipotentiaries have signed the present convention and affixed their seals thereto.

Done in duplicate at The Hague, October 1, 1904

(L. S.) (Signed) BN MELVIL DE LYNDEN
(L. S.) (Signed) IDENBURG
(L. S.) (Signed) CONDE DE SELIR

REPORTS

HAGUE COMMISSIONS OF INQUIRY

THE NORTH SEA or DOGGER BANK CASE[1]

between

GREAT BRITAIN *and* RUSSIA

Findings Reported February 26, 1905

Syllabus

In October, 1904, during the Russo-Japanese war, the Admiral of the Russian Baltic fleet, then coaling off the coast of Norway, received rumors from several sources of the presence of Japanese torpedo boats in the vicinity, and on this account the fleet set sail for the Far East twenty-four hours ahead of schedule. As the last division of the fleet, in immediate charge of the Admiral, was passing through the North Sea in the early hours of the morning of October 9, 1904, it came upon what afterwards proved to be an English fishing fleet from Hull, England. The Russians, under a misapprehension that the English vessels were the Japanese torpedo boats, opened fire, with the result that one fishing boat was sunk and others damaged, while two fishermen were killed and six injured.

In order to prevent serious results from this incident, France suggested resort to an international commission of inquiry, as provided for in the convention for the pacific settlement of international disputes, adopted by the Hague Conference of 1899. The suggestion was accepted by Great Britain and Russia, and an agreement was signed on November 25, 1904,[2] which invested a commission composed of admirals from the British, Russian, United States, French and Austrian navies with authority to find the facts in dispute and to fix responsibility. The commission held sessions at Paris from December 22, 1904, to February 26, 1905, on which date its report was rendered.

The conclusion reached was that there were no torpedo boats either among the trawlers or anywhere near and that the opening of fire by the Russian Admiral was not justified. His action under the circumstances was not, however, such as to cast discredit upon his military abilities or humanity or that of the personnel of his squadron. Russia accepted the decision and paid damages to the extent of about $300,000.

---

[1]This case is also known as "The Hull Incident."
[2]*Post*, p. 410.

REPORT OF THE COMMISSION

Report of the commissioners, drawn up in accordance with Article 6 of the declaration of St. Petersburg of November 12/25, 1904.—Paris, February 26, 1905.[1]

1. The commissioners, after a minute and prolonged examination of the whole of the facts brought to their knowledge in regard to the incident submitted to them for inquiry by the declaration of St. Petersburg of the 12th (25th) November, 1904,[2] have proceeded to make, in this report, an analysis of these facts in their logical sequence.

By making known the prevailing opinion of the commission on each important or decisive point of this summary, they consider that they have made sufficiently clear the causes and the consequences of the incident in question, as well as the deductions which are to be drawn from them with regard to the question of responsibility.

2. The second Russian squadron of the Pacific fleet, under the command-in-chief of Vice-Admiral Aide-de-camp General Rojdestvensky, anchored on the 7th (20th) October, 1904, off Cape Skagen, with the purpose of coaling before continuing its voyage to the Far East.

It appears, from the depositions made, that, from the time of the departure of the squadron from the roadstead of Réval, Admiral Rojdestvensky had had the vessels under his charge take minute precautions in order to be fully prepared for a night attack by torpedo boats, either at sea or at anchor.

These precautions seemed to be justified by the numerous reports of the agents of the Imperial Government regarding possible hostile attacks, which in all likelihood would take the form of torpedo boat attacks.

Moreover, during his stay at Skagen, Admiral Rojdestvensky had been warned of the presence of suspect vessels on the coast of Norway. He had learned, also, from the commander of the transport *Bakan* coming from the north, that he had seen on the previous night four torpedo boats, carrying a single light only, and that at the masthead.

---

[1] *American Journal of International Law*, vol. 2, p. 931. For the original French text, see Appendix, p. 609.
[2] *Post*, p. 410.

This news made the Admiral decide to start twenty-four hours earlier.

3. Consequently, each of the six distinct divisions of the fleet got under way, separately and in turn, and reached the North Sea independently, in the order indicated in Admiral Rojdestvensky's report; that flag-officer commanding in person the last division, formed by the four new battleships *Prince Souvoroff, Emperor Alexander III, Borodino, Orel,* and the transport *Anadyr.*

This division left Skagen on the 7th (20th) October at 10 o'clock in the evening.

A speed of twelve knots was ordered for the first two divisions, and of ten knots for the following divisions.

4. Between 1:30 and 4:15 on the afternoon of the next day, the 8th (21st) October, all the divisions of the squadron passed in turn the English steamer *Zero,* whose captain examined the different units so attentively that they could be recognized from his description of them.

The results of his observations are, moreover, in general agreement with the statements in Admiral Rojdestvensky's report.

5. The last vessel to pass the *Zero* was, according to his description of her, the *Kamchatka.*

This transport, which originally was in a division with the *Dmitri Donskoi* and the *Aurora,* was, therefore, left behind and isolated about ten miles to the rear of the squadron. She had been obliged to slaken speed in consequence of damage to her engines.

This accidental delay was, perhaps, incidentally the cause of the events which followed.

6. Toward 8 o'clock in the evening this transport did, in fact, meet the Swedish vessel *Aldebaran* and other unknown vessels and open fire on them, doubtless in consequence of the anxiety due to the circumstances of her momentary isolation, her damaged engines, and her poor fighting ability.

However this may be, the commander of the *Kamchatka,* at 8:45 o'clock, sent a message by wireless telegraphy to his commander-in-chief regarding this encounter, stating that he was "attacked on all sides by torpedo boats."

7. In order to understand the effect which this news had on Admiral Rojdestvensky's subsequent decisions, it must be remem-

bered that, in his opinion, the attacking torpedo boats, of whose presence fifty miles to the rear of the division which he commanded, he was thus, rightly or wrongly, informed, might overtake and attack him about 1 o'clock in the morning.

This information led Admiral Rojdestvensky to signal to his ships about 10 o'clock in the evening to redouble their vigilance and look out for an attack by torpedo boats.

8. On board the *Souvoroff* the admiral deemed it essential that one of the two superior officers of his staff should be on watch on the captain's bridge during the night in order to observe, in his place, the progress of the squadron and to warn him at once if any incident occurred.

On board all the ships, moreover, the Admiral's standing orders to the officer of the watch were to open fire in case of an evident and imminent attack by torpedo boats.

If the attack were from the front he should open fire on his own initiative, and, in the contrary case, which would be much less pressing, he should refer to his commanding officer.

With regard to these orders, the majority of the commissioners consider that they were in no way excessive in time of war, and particularly in the circumstances, which Admiral Rojdestvensky had every reason to consider very alarming, seeing that it was impossible for him to verify the accuracy of the warnings that he had received from the agents of his Government.

9. Toward 1 o'clock in the morning of the 9th (22d) October, 1904, the night was rather dark, a slight, low fog partly clouding the air. The moon only showed intermittently between the clouds. A moderate wind blew from the southeast, raising a long swell, which gave the ships a roll of 5° on each side.

The course followed by the squadron toward the southwest would have taken the last two divisions, as the event proved, close past the usual fishing ground[1] of the fleet of Hull trawlers, which was composed of some thirty of these small steamboats, and was spread over an area of several miles.

It appears from the concordant testimony of the British witnesses that all these boats carried their proper lights, and were trawling in accordance with their usual rules, under the direction of their

---

[1] Dogger Bank.

"admiral," and in obedience to the signals given by the conventional rockets.

10. Judging from the communications received by wireless telegraphy, the divisions which preceded that of Admiral Rojdestvensky across these waters had signaled nothing unusual.

It became known afterward, in particular, that Admiral Folkersam, having been led to pass round the fishing fleet on the north, threw his electric searchlight on the nearest trawlers at close quarters, and, having seen them to be harmless vessels, quietly continued his voyage.

11. A short time afterwards the last division of the squadron, led by the *Souvoroff* flying Admiral Rojdestvensky's flag, arrived in its turn close to the spot where the trawlers were fishing.

The direction in which this division was sailing led it nearly toward the main body of the fleet of trawlers, round which and to the south of which it would therefore be obliged to sail, when the attention of the officers of the watch on the bridges of the *Souvoroff* was attracted by a green rocket, which put them on their guard. This rocket, sent up by the "admiral" of the fishing fleet, indicated in reality, according to regulation, that the trawlers were to trawl on the starboard tack.

Almost immediately after this first alarm, and as shown by the evidence, the lookout men, who, from the bridges of the *Souvoroff,* were scanning the horizon with their night glasses, discovered "on the crest of the waves on the starboard bow, at an approximate distance of eighteen to twenty cables," a vessel which aroused their suspicions because they saw no light, and because she appeared to be bearing down upon them.

When the suspicious-looking vessel was shown up by the searchlight, the lookout men thought they recognized a torpedo boat proceeding at great speed.

It was on account of these appearances that Admiral Rojdestvensky ordered fire to be opened on this unknown vessel.

The majority of the commissioners express the opinion, on this subject, that the responsibility for this action and the results of the fire to which the fishing fleet was exposed are to be attributed to Admiral Rojdestvensky.

12. Almost immediately after fire was opened to starboard, the

Souvoroff caught sight of a little boat on her bow barring the way, and was obliged to turn sharply to the left to avoid running it down. This boat, however, on being lit up by the searchlight, was seen to be a trawler.

To prevent the fire of the ships being directed against this harmless vessel, the searchlight was immediately thrown up at an angle of 45°.

The admiral then made the signal to the squadron "not to fire on the trawlers."

But at the same time that the searchlight had lit up this fishing vessel, according to the evidence of witnesses, the lookout men on board the *Souvoroff* perceived to port another vessel, which appeared suspicious from the fact of its presenting the same features as were presented by the object of their fire to starboard.

Fire was immediately opened on this second object, and was, therefore, being kept up on both sides of the ship, the line of ships having resumed their original course by a correcting movement without changing speed.

13. According to the standing orders of the fleet, the Admiral indicated the objects against which the fire should be directed by throwing his searchlight upon them; but as each vessel swept the horizon in every direction with her own searchlights to avoid being taken by surprise, it was difficult to prevent confusion.

The fire, which lasted from ten to twelve minutes, caused great loss to the trawlers. Two men were killed and six others wounded; the *Crane* sank; the *Snipe*, the *Mino*, the *Moulmein*, the *Gull*, and the *Majestic* were more or less damaged.

On the other hand, the cruiser *Aurora* was hit by several shots.

The majority of the commissioners observe that they have not sufficiently precise details to determine what was the object fired on by the vessels; but the commissioners recognize unanimously that the vessels of the fishing fleet did not commit any hostile act; and, the majority of the commissioners being of opinion that there were no torpedo boats either among the trawlers nor anywhere near, the opening of the fire by Admiral Rojdestvensky was not justifiable.

The Russian commissioner, not considering himself justified in sharing this opinion, expresses the conviction that it was precisely the suspicious-looking vessels approaching the squadron with hostile intent which provoked the fire.

14. With reference to the real objectives of this nocturnal firing, the fact that the *Aurora* was hit by several 47-millimeter and 75-millimeter shells would lead to the supposition that this cruiser, and perhaps even some other Russian vessels, left behind on the route followed by the *Souvoroff* unknown to that vessel, might have provoked and been the object of the first few shots.

This mistake might have been caused by the fact that this vessel, seen from astern, was apparently showing no light, and by a nocturnal optical illusion which deceived the lookout on the flagship.

On this head the commissioners find that they are without important information which would enable them to determine the reasons why the fire on the port side was continued.

According to their conjecture, certain distant trawlers might have been mistaken for the original objectives, and thus fired upon directly. Others, on the contrary, might have been struck by a fire directed against more distant objectives.

These considerations, moreover, are not in contradiction with the impressions formed by certain of the trawlers, who, finding that they were struck by projectiles and remained under the rays of the searchlights, might believe that they were the object of a direct fire.

15. The time during which the firing lasted on the starboard side, even taking the point of view of the Russian version, seems to the majority of the commissioners to have been longer than was necessary.

But that majority considers that, as has already been said, they have not before them sufficient data as to why the fire on the port side was continued.

In any case, the commissioners take pleasure in recognizing, unanimously, that Admiral Rojdestvensky personally did everything he could, from beginning to end of the incident, to prevent trawlers, recognized as such, from being fired upon by the squadron.

16. Finally, the *Dmitri Donskoi* having signaled her number, the Admiral decided to give the general signal for "cease firing." The line of his ships then continued on their way, and disappeared to the southwest without having stopped.

On this point the commissioners recognize, unanimously, that after the circumstances which preceded the incident and those which produced it, there was, at the cessation of fire, sufficient uncertainty with regard to the danger to which the division of vessels was exposed to induce the Admiral to proceed on his way.

Nevertheless, the majority of the commissioners regret that Admiral Rojdestvensky, in passing the Straits of Dover, did not take care to inform the authorities of the neighboring maritime Powers, that, as he had been led to open fire near a group of trawlers, these boats, of unknown nationality, stood in need of assistance.

17. In concluding this report, the commissioners declare that their findings, which are therein formulated, are not, in their opinion, of a nature to cast any discredit upon the military qualities or the humanity of Admiral Rojdestvensky, or of the personnel of his squadron.

SPAUN
FOURNIER
DOUBASSOFF
LEWIS BEAUMONT
CHARLES HENRY DAVIS

AGREEMENT FOR INQUIRY

Declaration between Great Britain and Russia, relating to the constitution of an international commission of inquiry on the subject of the North Sea incident.—Signed at St. Petersburg, November 12/25, 1904.[1]

His Britannic Majesty's Government and the Imperial Russian Government having agreed to entrust to an international commission of inquiry, assembled conformably to Articles 9 to 14 of the Hague Convention of the 29th (17th) July, 1899, for the pacific settlement of international disputes, the task of elucidating by means of an impartial and conscientious investigation the questions of fact connected with the incident which occurred during the night of the 21st-22d (8th-9th) October, 1904, in the North Sea (on which occasion the firing of the guns of the Russian fleet caused the loss of a boat and the death of two persons belonging to a British fishing fleet, as well as damages to

---

[1] *American Journal of International Law*, vol. 2, p. 929. For the original French text, see Appendix, p. 614.

other boats of that fleet and injuries to the crews of some of those boats), the undersigned, being duly authorized thereto, have agreed upon the following provisions:

ARTICLE 1

The international commission of inquiry shall be composed of five members (commissioners), of whom two shall be officers of high rank in the British and Imperial Russian navies, respectively. The Governments of France and of the United States of America shall each be requested to select one of their naval officers of high rank as a member of the commission. The fifth member shall be chosen by agreement between the four members above-mentioned.

In the event of no agreement being arrived at between the four commissioners as to the selection of the fifth member of the commission, His Imperial and Royal Majesty the Emperor of Austria, King of Hungary, shall be invited to select him.

Each of the two high contracting parties shall likewise appoint a legal assessor to advise the commissioners, and an agent officially enpowered to take part in the labors of the commission.

ARTICLE 2

The commission shall inquire into and report on all the circumstances relative to the North Sea incident, and particularly on the question as to where the responsibility lies and the degree of blame attaching to the subjects of the two high contracting Parties or to the subjects of other countries in the event of their responsibility being established by the inquiry.

ARTICLE 3

The commission shall settle the details of the procedure which it will follow for the purpose of accomplishing the task with which it has been entrusted.

ARTICLE 4

The two high contracting Parties undertake to supply the international commission of inquiry, to the greatest possible extent, with all the means and facilities necessary to enable it to thoroughly investigate and correctly estimate the matters in dispute.

ARTICLE 5

The commission shall assemble at Paris as soon as possible after the signature of this agreement.

ARTICLE 6

The commission shall present its report to the two high contracting Parties signed by all the members of the commission.

ARTICLE 7

The commission shall arrive at all its decisions by a majority vote of the five commissioners.

ARTICLE 8

The two high contracting Parties undertake to bear, each on its part, the expenses of the inquiry made by it previously to the assembly of the commission. The expenses incurred by the international commission, after the date of its assembly, in organizing its staff and in conducting the investigations which it will have to make, shall be shared equally by the two Governments.

In witness whereof the undersigned have signed the present declaration and have affixed their seals thereto.

Done in duplicate at St. Petersburg, November 25 (12), 1904.

(Signed)   CHARLES HARDINGE
(Signed)   COUNT LAMSDORFF

ADDITIONAL DOCUMENT

Supplementary protocol to the Declaration between Great Britain and Russia relative to the constitution of an international commission of inquiry on the subject of the North Sea incident.—Signed at St. Petersburg, November 12/25, 1904.[1]

The undersigned have met to-day in the building of the Imperial Ministry of Foreign Affairs to proceed to the signature of the declaration between the Government of His Britannic Majesty and the Imperial Russian Government, concerning the institution of a commission of inquiry on the subject of the North Sea incident.

After the reading of the respective instruments, found in good and due form, the signature of the said declaration took place in the usual manner.

In faith of which the undersigned have drawn up the present protocol and attached the seals of their arms.

Done in duplicate at St. Petersburg, November 12 (25), 1904.

(L. S.) CHARLES HARDINGE
(L. S.) COUNT LAMSDORFF

---

[1] Translation. For the original French text, see Appendix, p. 615.

THE TAVIGNANO, CAMOUNA AND GAULOIS CASES

between

FRANCE *and* ITALY
Findings Reported May 2, 1913

Syllabus

On January 25, 1912, during the Turco-Italian war, the French mail steamer *Tavignano* was seized by the Italian torpedo boat *Fulmine* off the coast of Tunis and conducted to Tripoli under suspicion of having on board contraband of war. The suspicion proved to be unwarranted and the vessel was released on the following day.

On the same date, in the same waters, the two Tunisian mahones, *Camouna* and *Gaulois,* were fired upon by the Italian torpedo boat *Canopo.*

The French Government claimed indemnity for these acts from the Italian Government on the ground that the vessels when encountered were within the territorial waters of Tunis and were not, according to international law, subject to either attack or capture. On the other hand, Italy maintained that the acts complained of took place on the high seas and that no rule of international law had been violated.

The cases were submitted to a commission of inquiry by agreements signed April 15 and May 20, 1912.[1] The commission made its report on July 23d, but as no definite conclusion was reached a *compromis* was signed on November 8th[2] submitting the case for arbitration to the tribunal in charge of the *Carthage* and *Manouba* cases.[3] No decision was rendered by the tribunal, the matter being finally settled out of court by a special agreement dated May 2, 1913,[4] according to the terms of which Italy agreed to pay an indemnity to the French Government of five thousand francs for distribution among the various individuals who had sustained losses.

REPORT OF THE COMMISSION

Report of the commission of inquiry constituted in virtue of the agreement for inquiry signed at Rome between France and Italy, May 20, 1912.—Malte, July 23, 1912.[5]

The commissioners, after having examined and compared all data gathered both from the documents presented by the two parties

---

[1]*Post*, pp. 417, 419.   [2]*Post*, p. 419.   [3]*Ante*, pp. 329, 341.
[4]*Post*, p. 421.
[5]Translation. For the original French text, see Appendix, p. 616.

and from the evidence in the case; after having done the important
part, which was the weighing of all this evidence; and after having
taken into consideration the degree of uncertainty appertaining
thereto, has reached the following conclusions:

I

The evidence and documents presented are not of a nature to
permit of determination of the exact geographical points where occurred the various acts which have been submitted to inquiry, but
simply of the zones in which they occurred, it being impossible to
decide upon an exact point in the zones.

1. Regarding the point where the *Tavignano* stopped.

This point is within the area of a rectilinear quadrilateral set off
by the following four apexes:

> Apex C...Latitude   33°29'20" North,
>   Longitude   8°56'40" East of Paris.
> Apex B...Latitude   33°29'10" North,
>   Longitude   8°55'10" East of Paris.
> Apex A...Latitude   33°26'30" North,
>   Longitude   8°54'40" East of Paris.
> Apex D...Latitude   33°26'30" North,
>   Longitude   8°56'20" East of Paris.

2. Regarding the pursuit of the mahones:

A. By the *Fulmine*.

The *Fulmine*, setting out from an indeterminate point in the zone
above defined, pursued the mahones, perhaps going out of that
zone, in a direction impossible to determine definitely but which
was either southeast or southwest by south.

The pursued mahones were located at the following points, which
are the centers of inexact circles of half-mile radii:

> *Camouna*..Latitude   33°24'10" North,
>   Longitude   9°00'15" East of Paris.
>
> *Gaulois*... Latitude   33°22'40" North,
>   Longitude   8°59'55" East of Paris.

After this pursuit the *Fulmine* returned to moor near the *Tavig-nano*, at point *H*, which the commission has chosen as the center of an inexact circle of a half-mile radius.

B. The *Canopo* cannonaded the *Gaulois* when that mahone was at a point indicated above and when it (the *Canopo*) was proceeding in a northerly direction from the point indicated in its log-book by

Latitude   33°20′45″ North,
Longitude   9°00′50″ East of Paris.

which point the commission has also adopted as the center of an inexact circle of a half-mile radius.

The commission, after its visit to the localities and after verification in the waters of Zarzis, decided, in reporting, to use for the hydrography, configuration and nature of the coast and neighboring banks the French Hydrographic Service Card No. 4247. The commission recalls the fact that its verification was the object of the *procès-verbal* of July 15, 1912, which is numbered 68.

The president having read the present report to the commissioners, the report and its conclusions have been unanimously adopted.

Done at Malte, in triplicate, July 23, 1912.

Commissioners: GUISEPPE GENOESE ZERBI
SOMBORN
SEGRAVE

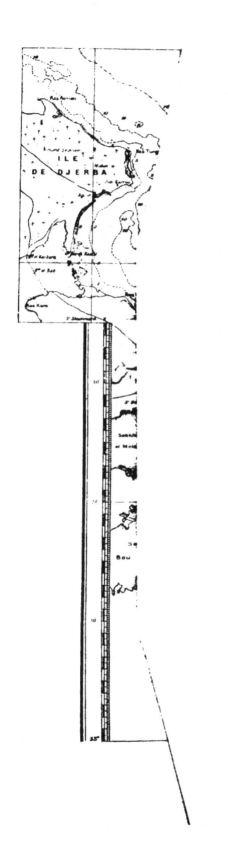

AGREEMENT FOR INQUIRY

Convention of Inquiry in the "Tavignano," "Camouna" and "Gaulois" Cases.—Signed at Rome, May 20, 1912.[1]

The Government of the French Republic and the Royal Italian Government, equally desirous of settling the dispute caused by the capture and temporary detention of the French mail steamer *Tavignano*, on January 25, 1912, by the Royal Italian naval vessel *Fulmine*, as well as the firing upon the mahones *Camouna* and *Gaulois*, on January 25, 1912, by the Italian torpedo boat *Canopo;*

Have resolved, conformably to Part III of the Hague Convention of October 18, 1907, for the pacific settlement of international disputes, to confide to an international commission of inquiry the task of clearing up the actual circumstances under which the said capture and detention, and the said firing took place;

And have, to this end, agreed upon the following provisions:

ARTICLE 1

An international commission of inquiry, composed as hereinafter stipulated, is entrusted:

I. To investigate, mark and determine the exact geographic point where occurred: (1) the capture of the French mail steamer *Tavignano* by the Royal Italian naval vessel *Fulmine*, on January 25, 1912; (2) the pursuit of the mahones *Camouna* and *Gaulois* by the same vessel and also by the Royal Italian naval vessel *Canopo,* and the firing by the latter upon the said mahones;

II. To determine exactly the hydrography, configuration and nature of the coast and of the neighboring banks, the distance between any points which one or the other of the commissioners might deem useful to mark, and the distance from these points to those where the above-mentioned deeds occurred;

III. To make a written report of the result of its investigation.

ARTICLE 2

The international commission of inquiry shall be composed of three commissioners, of which two shall be national naval officers of France

---

[1] Translation. For the original French text, see Appendix, p. 617.

and Italy, of a rank at least equal to that of captain.   The Government of His Britannic Majesty shall be asked to choose the third commissioner from among his naval officers, of a higher or the highest rank. The latter shall assume the office of president.

Two secretaries shall be appointed, one by the Government of the French Republic and the other by the Royal Italian Government, as registrars of the commission, and they shall assist it in its operations.

ARTICLE 3

The international commission of inquiry shall be qualified to secure all information, interrogate and hear all witnesses, to examine all papers on board either of the said ships, vessels and mahones, to proceed, if necessary, with sounding, and, in general, to resort to all sources of information calculated to bring out the truth.

The two Governments agree in this respect to furnish the commission with all possible means and facilities, particularly those of transportation, to enable it to accomplish its task.

ARTICLE 4

The international commission of inquiry shall meet at Malte as soon as possible and shall have the power to change its place of meeting conformably to Article 20 of the Hague Convention of October 18, 1907, for the pacific settlement of international disputes.

ARTICLE 5

The French language shall be used by the international commission of inquiry; however, in their deliberations the commissioners may use their respective languages.

ARTICLE 6

Within a period not to exceed fifteen days from the date of its first meeting the international commission of inquiry shall arrive at the conclusions of its report and shall communicate them to each of the two Governments.

ARTICLE 7

Each party shall pay its own expenses and an equal share of the expenses of the commission.

ARTICLE 8

All points not covered by the present convention of inquiry, especially those relating to the procedure of inquiry, shall be regulated by the provisions of the Hague Convention of October 18, 1907, for the pacific settlement of international disputes.

Done in duplicate, at Rome, May 20, 1912.

Signed: CAMILLE BARRÈRE
DI SAN GIULIANO

ADDITIONAL DOCUMENTS

Agreement between France and Italy relative to the "Tavignano," "Camouna" and "Gaulois" Cases.—Signed at Rome, April 15, 1912.[1]

The French and Italian Governments have decided to submit to an international commission of inquiry the questions of fact raised:

1. On the subject of the seizure of the French steamer *Tavignano* by the Italian torpedo boat *Fulmine,* on January 25, 1912, in the waters of Ras-Zira;

2. On the subject of the cannon shots fired by the torpedo boat *Canopo,* on the same day and in the same waters, upon the two Tunisian mahones *Camouna* and *Gaulois.*

After the said commission shall have terminated its investigation, the result shall be transmitted, if it is deemed necessary, to the arbitral tribunal charged with the settling of the *Carthage* and *Manouba* affairs, in order that it may decide the question of law, fix the responsibility and determine the moral and material reparation which are due.

Rome, April 15, 1912.

Signed: CAMILLE BARRÈRE
DI SAN GIULIANO

Compromis of arbitration relative to the questions raised on the subject of the seizure of the French steamer "Tavignano" and on the subject of the cannon shots fired by an Italian torpedo boat upon two Tunisian mahones.—Signed at Paris, November 8, 1912.[2]

The Government of the French Republic and the Royal Italian Government, having agreed, on April 15, 1912:[3]

1. To submit to an international commission of inquiry the questions raised on the subject of the seizure of the French steamer *Tavignano*

---

[1]Translation. For the original French text, see Appendix, p. 621.
[2]*Id.* This controversy was settled out of court by a special agreement, see *post,* p. 421.
[3]See *supra.*

by the Italian torpedo boat *Fulmine* on January 25, 1912, in the waters
of Raz-Zira and on the subject of the cannon shots fired by the Italian
torpedo boat *Canopo* on the same day and in the same waters, upon
the two Tunisian mahones *Camouna* and *Gaulois;*

2. To transmit, if necessary, the result of the inquiry to the arbitral
tribunal charged with the settling of the *Carthage* and *Manouba* affairs, in order that it may decide the question of law, fix the responsibility and determine the moral and material reparation which are due ;

Having taken recognition of the report presented July 23, 1912, by
the said international commission of inquiry ;

The undersigned, duly authorized for that purpose, have agreed
upon the following *compromis:*

ARTICLE 1

The arbitral tribunal charged with the settling of the affairs of the
Carthage and *Manouba* is also authorized to pronounce upon the incidents concerning the seizure of the French steamer *Tavignano* and the
cannon shots fired upon the Tunisian mahones, as well as to decide the
questions of law, fix the responsibility and determine the moral and
material reparation which are due.

ARTICLE 2

In all that concerns the questions of fact raised by the two incidents,
the arbitral tribunal must make use of the report presented by the
international commission of inquiry of July 23, 1912, as well as the
procès-verbaux of the said commission.

The said report and *procès-verbaux* shall be printed at the expense
and under the supervision of both parties and with the least possible
delay.

ARTICLE 3

On January 25, 1913, each party shall deposit with the Bureau of
the Permanent Court of Arbitration fifteen copies of its memorial,
with certified copies of all documents and papers which it intends to
submit in the case.

The Bureau shall guarantee their transmission without delay to the
arbitrators and parties, to wit: two copies for each arbitrator; three
copies for each party; two copies shall remain in the archives of the
Bureau.

On March 1, 1913, each party shall deposit, under the same conditions as above, its counter-memorial, with the papers appertaining thereto, and its final conclusions.

The tribunal shall meet at The Hague, in the second fortnight of March, upon the convocation of its president.

ARTICLE 4

For all points not covered by the present *compromis*, the stipulations of the *compromis* of March 6, 1912,[1] and of the agreement of April 4, 1912,[2] shall be applicable to the present litigation.

Done at Paris, November 8, 1912.

(Signed)   L. RENAULT
(Signed)   G. FUSINATO

Agreement between France and Italy settling definitively the "Tavignano," "Camouna" and "Gaulois" controversy.—Signed at The Hague, May 2, 1913.[3]

As the two affairs of the *Carthage* and the *Manouba* are about to be settled by arbitral award, the Government of the French Republic and the Royal Italian Government consider that a direct settlement of the affair concerning the *Tavignano* and the two Tunisian mahones is particularly desirable because of the similar nature of the dispute. The two Governments are especially desirous of taking this course which gives them another opportunity to show the spirit of cordial friendship which mutually animates them. To this end they have agreed that it will be equitable to indemnify the individuals for the losses sustained by them. The Royal Italian Government having declared itself willing to pay the sum of five thousand francs for this purpose, the Government of the French Republic has declared that it will accept the same and consider this affair thus definitively settled.

The undersigned have testified to the agreement of their Governments by the present act, which shall have the force of law.

Signed: L. RENAULT
G. FUSINATO

---

[1] *Ante*, pp. 336, 351.   [2] *Ante*, p. 340.
[3] Translation. For the original French text, see Appendix, p. 623.

TABULAR STATEMENT

OF

AWARDS AND REPORTS

OF THE

HAGUE TRIBUNALS

AND

COMMISSIONS OF INQUIRY

Case	Parties
The Pious Fund Case	Mexico *vs.* United States
The Venezuelan Preferential Case	Germany, Great Britain, Italy *vs.* Venezuela *et al.*
The Japanese House Tax Case	France, Germany, Great Britain *vs.* Japan
The Muscat Dhows Case	France *vs.* Great Britain
The Casablanca Case	France *vs.* Germany
The Grisbadarna Case	Norway *vs.* Sweden
The North Atlantic Coast Fisheries Case	Great Britain *vs.* United States
The Orinoco Steamship Company Case	United States *vs.* Venezuela
The Savarkar Case	France *vs.* Great Britain
The Canevaro Case	Italy *vs.* Peru
The Russian Indemnity Case	Russia *vs.* Turkey
The *Carthage* Case ⎱ The *Manouba* Case ⎰	France *vs.* Italy
The Island of Timor Case	Netherlands *vs.* Portugal

Case	Parties
The North Sea or Dogger Bank Case	Great Britain *vs.* Russia
The *Tavignano, Camouna* and *Gaulois* Cases[2]	France *vs.* Italy

[1]The name of the president of the tribunal appears first in this list. [2]Not a member of the Perma-
in charge of the *Carthage* and *Manouba* cases, but they were finally settled out of court by a special agree-

THE HAGUE TRIBUNALS OF ARBITRATION

Date of Agreement	Date of Award	Arbitrators[1]
May 22, 1902	October 14, 1902	Matzen, Sir Edward Fry, Martens, Asser, de Savornin Lohman
May 7, 1903	February 22, 1904	Mourawieff, Lammasch, Martens
August 28, 1902	May 22, 1905	Gram, Renault, Motono
October 13, 1904	August 8, 1905	Lammasch, Melville W. Fuller, de Savornin Lohman
November 10, 1908	May 22, 1909	Hammarskjöld, Sir Edward Fry, Fusinato, Kriege, Renault
March 14, 1908	October 23, 1909	Loeff,[2] Beichmann,[2] Hammarskjöld
January 27, 1909	September 7, 1910	Lammasch, de Savornin Lohman, George Gray, Sir Charles Fitzpatrick, Drago
February 13, 1909	October 25, 1910	Lammasch, Beernaert, de Quesada
October 25, 1910	February 24, 1911	Beernaert, Renault, Lord Desart, Gram, de Savornin Lohman
April 25, 1910	May 3, 1912	Renault, Fusinato, Calderón
July 22/August 4, 1910	November 11, 1912	Lardy, Baron de Taube, Mandelstam,[2] Herante Abro Bey,[2] Ahmed Réchid Bey[2]
March 6, 1912	May 6, 1913	Hammarskjöld, Renault, Fusinato, Kriege, Baron de Taube
April 3, 1913	June 25, 1914	Lardy

HAGUE COMMISSIONS OF INQUIRY

Date of Agreement	Date of Report	Commissioners
November 12/25, 1904	February 26, 1905	Admirals, Spaum, Doubassoff, Beaumont, Fournier, Davis
April 25, 1912	July 23, 1912	Captains James Segrave, Sombron, Zerbi

nent Court. [2]These cases were also referred, by *compromis* of November 8, 1912, to the Hague tribunal ment of May 2, 1913.

APPENDIX

THE PIOUS FUND CASE

Award of the Tribunal, October 14, 1902[1]

Le Tribunal d'Arbitrage, constitué en vertu du Traité conclu à Washington, le 22 mai 1902, entre les Etats-Unis d'Amérique et les Etats-Unis Mexicains;

Attendu que, par un compromis, rédigé sous forme de *Protocole*, entre les Etats-Unis d'Amérique et les Etats-Unis Mexicains, signé à Washington le 22 mai 1902, il a été convenu et réglé que le différend, qui a surgi entre les Etats-Unis d'Amérique et les Etats-Unis Mexicains au sujet du *"Fonds Pieux des Californies"* dont les annuités étaient réclamées par les Etats-Unis d'Amérique, au profit de l'Archevêque de San Francisco et de l'Evêque de Monterey, au Gouvernement de la République Mexicaine, serait soumis à un Tribunal d'Arbitrage, constitué sur les bases de la *Convention pour le règlement pacifique des conflits internationaux*, signée à La Haye le 29 juillet 1899, qui serait composé de la manière suivante, savoir:

Le Président des Etats-Unis d'Amérique désignerait deux Arbitres non-nationaux et le Président des Etats-Unis Mexicains également deux Arbitres non-nationaux. Ces quatre Arbitres devraient se réunir le 1 septembre 1902 à La Haye afin de nommer le Surarbitre qui, en même temps, serait de droit le Président du Tribunal d'Arbitrage.

Attendu que le Président des Etats-Unis d'Amérique a nommé comme Arbitres:

Le très honorable Sir Edward Fry, Docteur en droit, autrefois siégeant à la Cour d'Appel, Membre du Conseil Privé de Sa Majesté Britannique, Membre de la Cour permanente d'Arbitrage et

Son Excellence Monsieur de Martens, Docteur en Droit, Conseiller Privé, Membre du Conseil du Ministère Impérial des affaires Etrangères de Russie, Membre de l'Institut de France, Membre de la Cour permanente d'Arbitrage;

Attendu que le Président des Etats-Unis Mexicains a nommé comme Arbitres:

Monsieur T. M. C. Asser, Docteur en Droit, Membre du Conseil d'Etat des Pays-Bas, ancien Professeur à l'Université d'Amsterdam, Membre de la Cour permanente d'Arbitrage et

Monsieur le Jonkheer A. F. de Savornin Lohman, Docteur en Droit, ancien Ministre de l'Intérieur des Pays-Bas, ancien Professeur à l'Université libre d'Amsterdam, Membre de la Seconde Chambre des Etats-Généraux, Membre de la Court permanente d'Arbitrage;

Lesquels Arbitres, dans leur réunion du 1 septembre 1902, ont élu, conformément aux Articles XXXII–XXXIV de la Convention de La

---

[1] Official report, p 107.

Haye du 29 juillet 1899, comme Surarbitre et Président de droit du Tribunal d'Arbitrage:

Monsieur Henning Matzen, Docteur en Droit, Professeur à l'Université de Copenhague, Conseiller extraordinaire à la Cour Suprême, Président du Landsthing, Membre de la Cour permanente d'Arbitrage.

Et attendu, qu'en vertu du Protocole de Washington du 22 mai 1902, les susnommés Arbitres, réunis en Tribunal d'Arbitrage, devraient décider:

1°. Si la dite réclamation des Etats-Unis d'Amérique au profit de l'Archevêque de San Francisco et de l'Evêque de Monterey est régie par le principe de la *res judicata,* en vertu de la sentence arbitral du 11 novembre 1875, prononcée par Sir Edward Thornton, en qualité de Surarbitre;

2°. Si *non,* si la dite réclamation est juste, avec pouvoir de rendre tel jugement qui leur semblera juste et équitable;

Attendu que les susnommés Arbitres, ayant examiné avec impartialité et soin tous les documents et actes, présentés au Tribunal d'Arbitrage par les Agents des Etats-Unis d'Amérique et des Etats-Unis Mexicains, et ayant entendu avec la plus grande attention les plaidoiries orales, présentées devant le Tribunal par les Agents et les Conseils des deux Parties en litige;

Considérant que le litige, soumis à la décision du Tribunal d'Arbitrage, consiste dans un conflit entre les Etats-Unis d'Amérique et les Etats-Unis Mexicains qui ne saurait être règlé que sur la base des traités internationaux et des principes du droit international;

Considérant que les Traités internationaux, conclus depuis l'année 1848 jusqu'au compromis du 22 mai 1902, entre les deux Puissances en litige, constatent le caractère éminemment international de ce conflit;

Considérant que toutes les parties d'un jugement ou d'un arrêt concernant les points débattus au litige s'éclairent et se complètent mutuellement et qu'elles servent toutes à préciser le sens et la portée du dispositif, à déterminer les points sur lesquels il y a chose jugée et qui partant ne peuvent être remis en question;

Considérant que cette règle ne s'applique pas seulement aux jugements des tribunaux institués par l'Etat, mais également aux sentences arbitrales, rendues dans les limites de la compétence fixées par le compromis;

Considérant que ce même principe doit, à plus forte raison, être appliqué aux arbitrages internationaux;

Considérant que la Convention du 4 juillet 1868, conclue entre les deux Etats en litige, avait accordé aux Commissions Mixtes, nommées par ces Etats, ainsi qu'au Surarbitre à désigner éventuellement, le droit de statuer sur leur propre compétence;

Considérant que dans le litige, soumis à la décisions du Tribunal d'Arbitrage, en vertu du compromis du 22 mai 1902, il y a, non seulement identité des parties en litige, mais également identité de la matière, jugée par la sentence arbitrale de Sir Edward Thornton comme Surarbitre en 1875 et amendée par lui le 24 octobre 1876;

Considérant que le Gouvernement des Etats-Unis Mexicains a consciencieusement exécuté la sentence arbitrale de 1875 et 1876, en payant les annuités adjugées par le Surarbitre ;

Considérant que, depuis 1869, trente-trois annuités n'ont pas été payées par le Gouvernement des Etats-Unis Mexicains au Gouvernement des Etats-Unis d'Amérique et que les règles de la prescription, étant exclusivement du domaine du droit civil, ne sauraient être appliquées au présent conflit entre les deux Etats en litige ;

Considérant, en ce qui concerne la monnaie, dans laquelle le paiement de la rente annuelle doit avoir lieu, que le dollar d'argent, ayant cours légal au Mexique, le paiement en or ne peut être exigé qu'en vertu d'une stipulation expresse ;

Que, dans l'espèce, telle stipulation n'existant pas, la Partie défenderesse a le droit de se libérer en argent ;

Que, par rapport à ce point, la sentence de Sir Edward Thornton n'a pas autrement force de chose jugée que pour les vingt et une annuités à l'égard desquelles le surarbitre a décidé que le paiement devait avoir lieu en dollars d'or Mexicains, puisque la question du mode de paiement ne concerne pas le fond du droit en litige mais seulement l'exécution de la sentence ;

Considérant, que d'après l'Article X du Protocole de Washington du 22 mai 1902, le présent Tribunal d'Arbitrage aura à statuer, en cas de condamnation de la République du Mexique, dans quelle monnaie le paiement devra avoir lieu ;

Par ces motifs le Tribunal d'Arbitrage décide et prononce à l'unanimité ce qui suit :

1°. Que la dite réclamation des Etats-Unis d'Amérique au profit de l'Archevêque de San Francisco et de l'Evêque de Monterey est régie par le principe de la *res judicata,* en vertu de la sentence arbitrale de Sir Edward Thornton du 11 novembre 1875 amendée par lui le 24 octobre 1876 ;

2°. Que, conformément à cette sentence arbitrale, le Gouvernement de la Républiqe des Etats-Unis Mexicains devra payer au Gouvernement des Etats-Unis d'Amérique la somme *d'un million quatre cent vingt mille six cent quatre vingt deux Dollars du Mexique et soixante sept cents* (1,420,682.67/100 *Dollars du Mexique*) en monnaie ayant cours légal au Mexique, dans le délai fixé par l'Article X du Protocole de Washington du 22 mai 1902.

Cette somme d'un million quatre cent vingt mille six cent quatre vingt deux Dollars et soixante sept cents (1,420,682.67/100 Dollars) constituera le versement total des annuités échues et non payées par le Gouvernement de la République Mexicaine, savoir de la rente annuelle de *quarante trois mille cinquante Dollars du Mexique et quatre vingt dix neuf cents* (43,050.99/100 Dollars du Mexique) depuis le 2 février 1869 jusqu'au 2 février 1902 ;

3°. Le Gouvernement de la République des Etats-Unis Mexicains paiera au Gouvernement des Etats-Unis d'Amérique le 2 février 1903, et chaque année suivante à cette même date du 2 février, à perpétuité la rente annuelle de *quarante trois mille cinquante Dollars du Mexique*

et quatre vingt dix neuf cents (43,050.99/100 Dollars du Mexique)
en monnaie ayant cours légal au Mexique.

Fait à La Haye, dans l'Hôtel de la Cour permanente d'Arbitrage,
en triple original, le 14 octobre 1902.

HENNING MATZEN
EDW. FRY
MARTENS
T. M. C. ASSER
A. F. DE SAVORNIN LOHMAN

Agreement for Arbitration, May 22, 1902[1]

Por cuanto, en virtud de las disposiciones de una Convención ajus-
tada entre las Altas Partes Contratantes arriba mencionadas, con fecha
4 de Julio de 1868, y siguientes convenciones suplementarias de ella,
fué sometida á la Comisión Mixta establecida por dicha Convención
una reclamación presentada por parte y en favor de los prelados de la
Iglesia Católica Romana de California contra la República de México,
por réditos anuales de cierto fondo llamado el "Fondo Piadoso de las
Californias," los cuales réditos se consideraron devengados desde el
2 de Febrero de 1848, fecha de la firma del tratado de Guadalupe
Hidalgo, hasta el 1º. de Febrero de 1869, fecha del canje de las ratificaciones de la Convención arriba referida; y

Por cuanto la indicada Comisión Mixta, después de examinar dicha
reclamación, que fué señalada en el libro de registro con el número
493 é intitulada "Thaddeus Amat Obispo Católico Romano de Mon-
terrey, por la corporación unitaria que representa, y Joseph S. Alemany Obispo Católico Romano de San Francisco, por la corporación
unitaria que representa, contra la República de México" decidió la
reclamación contra la República de México, y en favor de dichos reclamantes, dando un laudo por novecientos cuatro mil setecientos pesos
noventa y nueve centavos ($904,700.99); los cuales, como se expresa
en la exposición de dicho tribunal, fueron el importe de réditos venci-
dos en veintiún años á razón de cuarenta y tres mil ochenta pesos
noventa y nueve centavos ($43,080.99) anuales sobre la suma de sete-
cientos diez y ocho mil diez y seis pesos cincuenta centavos ($718,-
016.50) y habían de pagarse en oro mexicano; y dicha suma de novecientos cuatro mil setecientos pesos noventa y nueve centavos ($904,-
700.99) fué completamente pagada y finiquitada en conformidad con
los términos de dicha Convención; v

Por cuanto los Estados Unidos de América por los Obispos Cató-
licos Romanos arriba nombrados y sus sucesores con el mismo título
é interés han reclamado á México después de dicho laudo los sucesi-
vos vencimientos de dichos réditos y han insistido en que la expresada
reclamación fué definitivamente juzgada y su monto fijado en contra
de México y á favor de los primitivos reclamantes y de sus sucesores

---

[1] *U. S. Statutes at Large*, vol. 32, p. 1916.

con el mismo título é interés, conforme á la primera Convención mencionada de 1868, en virtud de dicho laudo como *res judicata;* y han sostenido además que independientemente de tal laudo su reclamación contra México era justa ; aserciones ambas que han sido controvertidas é impugnadas por la República de México, y las Altas Partes signatarias de este Compromiso, animadas de un vivo deseo de que la controversia así suscitada sea amigable, satisfactoria y justamente resuelta, han convenido en someter dicha controversia á la decisión de árbitros, quienes se ajustarán en todo lo que no se disponga de otro modo por el presente instrumento, á las prevenciones de la Convención internacional para el arreglo pacífico de controversias internacionales comunmente denominada "Convención de La Haya" y estarán facultados para resolver:

1º. Si dicha reclamación como consecuencia del laudo anterior está regida por el principio de *res judicata;* y

2º. De no estarlo, si es justa la misma reclamación.

Y para pronunciar un fallo ó laudo tal que sea adecuado y conveniente a todas las circunstancias del caso:

Por tanto, se conviene entre los Estados Unidos de América, representados por John Hay, Secretario de Estado de los Estados Unidos de América, y la República de México, representada por Manuel de Azpíroz, Embajador Extraordinario y Plenipotenciario de la República de México en los Estados Unidos de América, en lo siguiente:

I

Las referidas cuestiones serán sometidas al tribunal especial que en seguida se autoriza para examinarlas, determinarlas y fallarlas.

II

El tribunal especial constituido por este instrumento se compondrá de cuatro árbitros, debiendo ser dos nombrados por cada una de las altas partes contratantes y un árbitro superior que será elegido con arreglo á las disposiciones de la Convención de La Haya. Los árbitros nombrados, como se ha dicho, por cada una de las Altas Partes Contratantes serán dados á conocer por la parte que los nombró á la otra parte dentro de sesenta días que correrán desde la fecha de este protocolo. Ninguno de los árbitros nombrados como se ha dicho será oriundo ó ciudadano de las partes contratantes. El laudo podrá ser pronunciado por mayoría de votos de dicho tribunal. Todas las vacantes que ocurran entre los miembros de dicho tribunal por causa de muerte, separación ó inhabilidad que provenga de causa anterior al pronunciamiento del laudo serán cubiertas del mismo modo que fué nombrado el miembro cesante, como se dispone en la Convención de La Haya, y si ocurrieren después que dicho tribunal se haya instalado podrán justificar, á juicio del tribunal, una prórroga del término señalado para la audiencia ó resolución, según sea el caso, con tal que ella no pase de treinta días.

III

Todas las alegaciones, testimonios, pruebas, informes en derecho y conclusiones ó laudos de los Comisionados ó del tercero en discordia, presentados ante la Comisión Mixta arriba referida ó acordados por ella, son de aducirse como pruebas ante el tribunal que ahora se nombra, juntamente con toda la correspondencia habida entre los dos países concerniente á los puntos comprendidos en este arbitramento; exhibiéndose al nuevo tribunal dichos documentos originales ó copias de ellos debidamente certificados por los Departamentos de Estado respectivos de las Altas Partes Contratantes. Cuando cualquiera de las dos partes cite libros impresos por vía de prueba, la que ofrezca tal prueba especificará el volumen, edición y página de la parte que quiera se lea, y proporcionará al tribunal impresos los pasajes que deseare hacer valer, cuya exactitud será comprobada con testimonio legal; y si la obra original no está ya formando parte del archivo de la primera Comisión Mixta, el libro mismo será puesto á disposición de la parte contraria, en los despachos respectivos del Secretario de Estado ó del Embajador de México en Washington, según sea el caso, treinta días antes de la reunión del tribunal que aquí se nombra.

IV

Cada parte podrá pedir á la otra que dé á conócer cualquier hecho ó documento considerado como prueba ó que contenga materia de prueba interesante ó la parte que la solicita; debiendo ser descrito el documento deseado con suficiente exactitud para su identificación; y se dará la noticia se hará la exhibición pedida, mediante una relación del hecho, ó el depósito de una copia de dicho documento (certificada por quien lo tenga legalmente en guarda si es un documento público, y autorizada por su poseedor si el documento fuere privado) y á la parte contraria se deberá dar la oportunidad de examinar el original en la ciudad de Washington en el Departamento de Estado ó en el despacho del Embajador de México según fuere el caso. Si la noticia ó exhibición deseada se obtuviere demasiado tarde para que pueda ser contestada diez días antes que el tribunal aquí establecido abra la audencia, en tal caso la contestación que se dé al pedimento, ó el documento que se produzca, se presentará al tribunal aquí establecido, tan pronto como fuere posible.

V

Todo testimonio oral que no conste en el archivo del primer arbitramento podrá rendirse por cualquiera de las partes ante algún juez ó secretario de juzgado de letras ó notario público, de la manera, con las precauciones y bajo las condiciones prescritas para tal caso en las reglas de la Comisión Mixta de México y los Estados Unidos de América, y adoptadas por dicho tribunal el 10 de Agosto de 1869, en todo lo que sean aplicables. Cuando el testimonio se extienda por escrito, firmado que sea por el testigo y legalizado por el funcionario ante quien se haya rendido, deberá ser sellado, dirigido al tribunal que aquí se establece, y así sellado se entregará en depósito en el Despacho de Relaciones exteriores de México ó en el Departamento de Estado de los Estados Unidos á fin de que sea remitido al tribunal que aquí se establece cuando el mismo se reúna.

VI

Dentro de sesenta días desde la fecha de este instrumento la parte de los Estados Unidos de América, por medio de su agente ó abogado, deberá preparar y entregar al Departamento de Estado arriba dicho un memorial impreso del origen y monto de la reclamación, acompañado de las citas de libros impresos y de aquellas partes de las pruebas ó piezas del archivo del primer arbitramento, en que quiera fundar su reclamación, dando copias de los mismos documentos á la Embajada de la República Mexicana en Wáshington para uso del agente ó abogado de México.

VII

Dentro de cuarenta días después de la entrega del memorial á la Embajada Mexicana, el agente ó abogado de la República de México entregará al Departamento de Estado de los Estados Unidos de América, de la misma manera y con iguales referencias, un memorial de sus alegaciones y razones de oposición á la reclamación dicha.

VIII

Las prevenciones de los párrafos VI y VII no impedirán á los agentes ó abogados de las partes contratantes reforzar oralmente ó por escrito sus argumentos citando cualesquiera documentos probatorios ú otras pruebas que consideren útiles y les haya sido dado conocer y examinar en un período subsiguiente á los términos señalados para el traslado del memorial y la contestación.

IX

La primera reunión del tribunal arbitral arriba nombrado se verificará con objeto de elejir un árbitro superior el 1º. de Septiembre de 1902 en la Haya en el local que al efecto destine la Oficina Internacional de la Haya constituida en virtud de la convención de la Haya, antes referida y para dar principio á las audiencias del tribunal se designa el 15 de Septiembre de 1902, ó si en esa fecha no estuviere ya electo el árbitro superior, las audiencias comenzarán tan pronto como sea posible y no después del 15 de Octubre de 1902, en cuyo tiempo y lugar ó en otras fechas que el tribunal disponga (y en Bruselas, si el tribunal determinare no tener sus sesiones en la Haya) explicaciones y alegatos, que se presenten según lo determine el tribunal, y el caso le quedará sometido. Esta sumisión con todos los alegatos, relación de hechos y presentación de documentos estará concluida dentro de los treinta días siguientes al término señalado para las audiencias del tribunal (á no ser que este acuerde una prórroga que no excederá de treinta días) y el laudo se pronunciará dentro de treinta días después de cerradas las audiencias. Copias certificadas del laudo se darán á los agentes ó abogados de las respectivas partes y se enviarán al Embajador de México en Wáshington y al Secretario de Estado de los Estados Unidos, así como al Ministro de Negocios Extranjeros de los Países Bajos para su archivo.

X

Si el laudo del tribunal fuere adverso á la República Mexicana, sus conclusiones expresarán la suma, la especie de moneda en que ha de ser pagada, y la suma será la que se considere justa conforme á lo probado y alegado. La suma, si alguna fuere definitivamente fallada, será pagada al Secretario de Estado de los Estados Unidos de América dentro de ocho meses desde la fecha del laudo.

XI

Los agentes de abogados de las respectivas partes podrán convenir en la admisión de cualesquiera hechos, y tal convenio debidamente firmado será admitido como prueba de los mismos hechos.

XII

Cada una de las partes contratantes pagará sus propios gastos y la mitad de los comunes del arbitraje, incluyendo la remuneración de los árbitros; mas estas costas no constituirán parte de la suma fallada.

XIII

Habrá lugar á revisión conforme á lo prevenido en el artículo 55 de la Convención de La Haya, si fuere promovida dentro de ocho días desde la notificación del laudo. Las pruebas admisibles en este recurso se presentarán dentro de diez días desde la fecha en que se concediere (el cual solamente se otorgará, si así se acordare, dentro de cinco días después de su promoción) y las pruebas de la parte contraria dentro de los diez días siguientes á no ser que se conceda mayor plazo por el tribunal. Los alegatos se producirán dentro de diez días después de la presentación de todas las pruebas, y el fallo ó laudo se dará dentro de los diez días siguientes. Todas las disposiciones aplicables al fallo ó laudo recurrido se aplicarán en lo posible el fallo ó laudo de revisión, bien entendido que en los procedimientos de este recurso se empleará la lengua francesa.

XIV

El laudo último dado conforme á este compromiso será definitivo y concluyente en todos los puntos propuestos á la consideración del tribunal.

Hecho por duplicado en inglés y en español en Washington hoy día 22 de Mayo, A. D. 1902.

JOHN HAY   [SEAL]
M. DE AZPIROZ   [SEAL]

Convention of July 4, 1868, between the United States of America and the Republic of Mexico for the Adjustment of Claims[1]

Considerando que es conveniente mantener y ensanchar los sentimientos amistosos entre la república Mexicana y los Estados Unidos, y afianzar así el sistema y principios de gobierno republicano en el continente Americano; y considerando que con posterioridad á la celebración del tratado de Guadalupe Hidalgo, de 2 de Febrero de 1848, ciudadanos de la república Mexicana han hecho reclamaciones y presentado quejas, con motivo de perjuicios sufridos en sus personas ó sus propiedades, por autoridades de los Estados Unidos, y reclamaciones y quejas semejantes se han hecho y presentado con motivo de perjuicios sufridos por ciudadanos de los Estados Unidos, en sus personas ó sus propiedades por autoridades de la república Mexicana, [el Presidente de la república Mexicana] y el Presidente de los Estados Unidos de América han determinado concluir una convención para el arreglo de dichas reclamaciones y quejas, y han nombrados sus plenipotenciarios; el Presidente de la república Mexicana, á Matias Romero, acreditado como Enviado Extraordinario y Ministro plenipotenciario de la república Mexicana en los Estados Unidos; y el Presidente de los Estados Unidos, á William H. Seward, Secretario de Estado, quienes después de haberse mostrado sus respectivos plenos poderes y encontradolos en buena y debida forma, han convenido en los Artículos siguientes:

ARTÍCULO I

Todas las reclamaciones hechas por corporaciones, compañías ó individuos particulares, ciudadanos de la república Mexicana, procedentes de perjuicios sufridos en sus personas ó en sus propiedades, por autoridades de los Estados Unidos, y todas las reclamaciones hechas por corporaciones, compañías ó individuos particulares, ciudadanos de los Estados Unidos, procedentes de perjuicios sufridos en sus personas ó en sus propiedades, por autoridades de la república Mexicana, que hayan sido presentadas á cualquiera de los dos gobiernos, solicitando su interposición para con el otro, con posterioridad á la celebración del tratado de Guadalupe Hidalgo entre la república Mexicana y los Estados Unidos, de 2 de Febrero de 1848, y que aún permanecen pendientes, de la misma manera que cualesquiera otras reclamaciones que se presentaren dentro del tiempo que mas adelante se especificará, se referiran á dos comisionados, uno de los cuales será nombrado por el Presidente de la república Mexicana y el otro por el Presidente de los Estados Unidos, con el consejo y aprobación del Senado. En caso de muerte, ausencia ó incapacidad de alguno de los comisionados, ó en caso de que alguno de los comisionados cese de funcionar como tal, ó suspenda el ejercicio de sus funciones, el Presidente de la república Mexicana ó el Presidente de los Estados Unidos respectivamente, nombraran desde luego otra persona que haga de comisionado en lugar del que originalmente fué nombrado.

---

[1] *U. S. Statutes at Large*, vol. 15, p. 679.

Los comisionados nombrados de esta manera, se reuniran en Washington dentro de seis meses, después de cangeadas las ratificaciones de esta convención, y antes de desempeñar sus funciones, haran y suscribiran una declaración solemne de que examinaran y decidiran imparcial y cuidadosamente, segun su mejor saber, y conforme con el derecho público, la justicia y equidad, y sin temor ó afección á su respectivo pais, sobre todas las reclamaciones antes especificadas, que se les sometan por los gobiernos de la república Mexicana y de los Estados Unidos respectivamente, y dicha declaración se asentará en la acta de sus procedimientos.

Los comisionados procederan entonces á nombrar una tercera persona que hará de árbitro en el caso ó casos en que difieran de opinión.

Si no pudieren convenir en el nombre de esta tercera persona, cada uno de ellos nombrará una persona, y en todos y cada uno de los casos en que los comisionados difieran de opinión respecto de la decisión que deban dar, se determinará por suerte quien de las dos personas así nombradas hará de árbitro en ese caso particular. La persona ó personas que se eligieren de esa manera, para ser árbitros, haran y suscribirán, ántes de obrar como tales, en cualquier caso, una declaración solemne en una forma semejante á la que deberá haber sido ya hecha y suscrita por los comisionados, la cual se asentará también en la acta de los procedimientos. En caso de muerte, ausencia ó incapacidad de la persona ó personas nombradas árbitros, ó en caso de que suspendan el ejercicio de sus funciones, se rehusen á desempeñarlas ó cesen en ellas, otra persona será nombrado árbitro de la manera que queda dicha, en lugar de la persona originalmente nombrada, y hará y suscribirá la declaración ántes mencionada.

Artículo II

En seguida procederan juntamente los comisionados á la investigación y decisión de las reclamaciones que se les presenten, en el órden y de la manera que de comun acuerdo creyeren conveniente, pero recibiendo solamente las pruebas ó informes que se les ministren por los respectivos gobiernos ó en su nombre. Tendran obligación de recibir y leer todas las manifestaciones ó documentos escritos que se les presenten por sus gobiernos respectivos, ó en su nombre, en apoyo ó respuesta á cualquiera reclamación, y de oir, si se les pidiere, á una persona por cada lado, en nombre de cada gobierno, en todas y cada una de las reclamaciones separadamente. Si dejaren de convenir sobre alguna reclamación particular, llamaran en su ausilio al árbitro que hayan nombrado de comun acuerdo, ó á quien la suerte haya designado segun fuere el caso, y el árbitro, después de haber examinado las pruebas producidas en favor y en contra de la reclamación, y después de haber oido, si se le pidiere, á una persona por cada lado, como queda dicho, y consultado con los comisionados, decidirá sobre ella finalmente y sin apelación. La decisión de los comisionados y del árbitro se dará en cada reclamación por escrito, especificará si la suma que se concediere se pagará en oro ó en moneda corriente de los Estados Unidos, y será firmada por ellos respectivamente. Cada gobierno podrá nombrar una persona que concurra á la comisión en nombre del gobierno respectivo, como agente; que presente ó defienda las reclamaciones en nombre del mismo gobierno, y que responda á las reclamaciones hechas contra el, y que le represente en general en todos los negocios que tengan relación con la investigación y decisión de reclamaciones.

El Presidente de la República Mexicana y el Presidente de los Estados Unidos de América se comprometen solemne y sinceramente en esta convención, á considerar la decisión de los comisionados de acuerdo, ó del árbitro, segun fuere el caso, como absolutamente final y definitiva, respecto de cada una de las reclamaciones falladas por los comisionados ó el árbitro respectivamente, y á dar entero cumplimiento á tales decisiones sin objeción, evasión ni dilación ninguno. Se conviene que ninguna reclamación que emane de acontecimientos de fecha anterior al 2 de Febrero de 1848, se admeterá con arreglo á esta convención.

Artículo III

Todas las reclamaciones se presentaran á los comisionados dentro de ocho meses contados desde el día de su primera reunión, á no ser en los casos en que se manifieste que haya habido razones para dilatarlas, siendo estas satisfactorias para los comisionados ó para el árbitro, si los comisionados no se convinieren, y en ese y otros casos semejantes el período para la presentación de las reclamaciones podrá estenderse por un plazo que no exceda de tres meses.

Los comisionados tendran la obligación de examinar y decidir todas las reclamaciones dentro de dos años y seis meses, contados desde el día re su primera reunión. Los comisionados de comun acuerdo ó el árbitro, si ellos difirieren podran decidir en cada caso, si una reclamación ha sido ó no debidamente hecha, comunicada y sometida á la comisión, ya sea en su totalidad ó en parte y cual sea esta, con arreglo al verdadero espíritu y á la letra de esta convención.

Artículo IV

Cuando los comisionados y el árbitro hayan decidido todos los casos que les hayan sido debidamente sometidos, la suma total fallada en todos los casos decididos en favor de los ciudadanos de una parte, se deducirá de la suma total fallada en favor de los ciudadanos de la otra parte, y la diferencia hasta la cantidad de trescientos mil pesos en oro, ó su equivalente, se pagará en la ciudad de México ó en la ciudad de Wáshington, al gobierno en favor de cuyos ciudadanos se haya fallado la mayor cantidad, sin interes, ni otra deducción que la especificada en el Artículo VI de esta convención. El resto de dicha diferencia se pagará en abonos anuales que no escedan de trescientos mil pesos en oro ó su equivalente, hasta que se haya pagado el total de la diferencia.

ARTÍCULO V

Las altas partes contratantes convienen en considerar el resultado de los procedimientos de esta comisión, como arreglo completo, perfecto y final, de toda reclamación contra cualquiera gobierno, que proceda de acontecimientos de fecha anterior al canje de las ratificaciones de la presente convención; y se comprometen ademas á que toda reclamación, ya sea que se haya presentado ó no á la referida comisión, sera considerada y tratada, concluidos los procedimientos de dicha comisión, como finalmente arreglada, desechada y para siempre inadmisible.

ARTÍCULO VI

Los comisionados y el árbitro llevaran una relación fiel y actas exactas de sus procedimientos con especificación de las fechas; con este objeto nombrarán dos secretarios versados en las lenguas de ambos países, para que les ayuden en el arreglo de los asuntos de la comisión. Cada gobierno pagará á su comisionado un sueldo que no exceda de cuatro mil quinientos pesos al año, en moneda corriente de los Estados Unidos, cuya cantidad será la misma para ambos gobiernos. La compensación que haya de pagarse al árbitro se determinará por consentimiento mútuo, al terminarse la comisión; pero podrán hacerse por cada gobierno adelantos necesarios y razonables en virtud de la recomendación de los dos comisionados. El sueldo de los secretarios no excederá de la suma de dos mil quinientos pesos al año, en moneda corriente de los Estados Unidos. Los gastos todos de la comisión, incluyendo los contingentes, se pagarán con una reducción proporcional de la cantidad total fallada por los comisionados, siempre que tal deducción no exceda del cinco por ciento de las cantidades falladas. Si hubiere algún deficiente, lo cubrirán ambos gobiernos por mitad.

ARTÍCULO VII

La presente convención será ratificada por el Presidente de la república Mexicana, con aprobación del Congreso de la misma, y por el Presidente de los Estados Unidos, con el consejo y aprobación del Senado de los mismos, y las ratificaciones se cangearán en Wáshington dentro de nueve meses contados desde la fecha de la convención, ó antes, si fuere posible.

En fé de lo cual, los respectivos plenipotenciarios la hemos firmado y sellado con nuestros sellos respectivos.

Hecho en Wáshington el día cuatro de Julio, del año del Señor mil ochocientos sesenta y ocho.

M. ROMERO [L. S.]
WILLIAM H. SEWARD [L. S.]

THE VENEZUELAN PREFERENTIAL CASE

Award of the Tribunal, February 22, 1904[1]

Le Tribunal d'Arbitrage, constitué en vertu des Protocoles, signés à Washington, le 7 mai 1903, entre l'Allemagne, la Grande-Bretagne et l'Italie d'une part, et le Vénézuela d'autre part ;

Considérant que d'autres Protocoles ont été signés à cet effet entre la Belgique, l'Espagne, les Etats-Unis d'Amérique, la France, le Mexique, les Pays-Bas, la Suède et Norvège d'une part, et le Vénézuela d'autre part ;

Considérant que tous ces Actes constatent l'accord le toutes les Parties contractantes relativement au règlement des réclamations contre le Gouvernement Vénézuélien ;

Considérant que diverses autres questions, résultant de l'action des Gouvernements d'Allemagne, de Grande-Bretagne et d'Italie concernant le règlement des réclamations, n'étaient pas susceptibles d'une solution par la voie diplomatique ordinaire ;

Considérant que les Puissances intéressées ont décidé de résoudre ces questions en les soumettant à l'arbitrage, conformément aux dispositions de la Convention, signée à La Haye le 29 juillet 1899, pour le règlement pacifique des conflits internationaux ;

Considérant qu'en vertu de l'Article III des Protocoles de Washington du 7 mai 1903, Sa Majesté l'Empereur de Russie a été invité par toutes les Puissances intéressées à désigner parmi les membres de la Cour Permanente d'Arbitrage de La Haye trois Arbitres, qui formeront le Tribunal d'Arbitrage chargé de résoudre et de régler les questions qui lui seront soumises en vertu des Protocoles susmentionnés ;

Attendu qu'aucun des Arbitres ainsi désignés ne pourrait être citoyen ou sujet de l'une quelconque des Puissances signataires ou créancières, et que le Tribunal devrait se réunir à La Haye le 1er septembre 1903 et rendre sa sentence dans le délai de six mois ;

Sa Majesté l'Empereur de Russie, en se rendant au désir de toutes les Puissances signataires des Protocoles susmentionnés de Washington du 7 mai 1903, a daigné nommer comme Arbitres les membres suivants de la Cour Permanente d'Arbitrage à La Haye :

Son Excellence Monsieur N. V. Mourawieff, Secrétaire d'Etat de Sa Majesté l'Empereur de Russie, Conseiller Privé Actuel, Ministre de la Justice et Procureur-Général de l'Empire de Russie ;

Monsieur H. Lammasch, Professeur de Droit Pénal et de Droit International à l'Université de Vienne, Membre de la Chambre des Seigneurs du Parlement autrichien, et

Son Excellence Monsieur F. De Martens, Docteur en Droit, Con-

---

[1] Official report, p. 129.

seiller Privé, Membre Permanent du Conseil du Ministère des Affaires Etrangères de Russie, Membre de l'Institut de France ;

Attendu que par des circonstances imprévues le Tribunal d'Arbitrage ne put être constitué définitivement que le 1ᵉʳ octobre 1903, les Arbitres, dans leur première réunion du même jour, en procédant conformément à l'Article XXXIV de la Convention du 29 juillet 1899, à la nomination du Président du Tribunal, ont élu comme tel Son Excellence Monsier Mourawieff, Ministre de la Justice ;

Et attendu qu'en vertu des Protocoles de Washington du 7 mai 1903, les susmentionnés Arbitres, réunis en Tribunal d'Arbitrage, lègalement constitué, devaient décider, conformément à l'Article I des Protocoles de Washington du 7 mai 1903, ce qui suit :

"La question de savoir, si l'Allemagne, la Grande-Bretagne et l'Italie ont, ou n'ont pas, droit à un traitement préférentiel ou séparé pour le paiement de leurs réclamations contre le Vénézuela et la trancher sans appel ;

Le Vénézuela ayant consenti à mettre de côté 30 pour cent de revenu des douanes de La Guayra et de Puerto Cabello pour le paiement des réclamations de toutes les nations contre le Vénézuela, le Tribunal de La Haye décidera comment ces recettes seront réparties entre les Puissances qui ont effectué le blocus d'une part, et les autres Puissances créancières d'autre part, et sa décision sera sans appel.

Si un traitement préférentiel ou séparé n'est pas accordé aux Puissances bloquantes, le Tribunal décidera comment les susdits revenus seront répartis entre toutes les Puissances créancières ; et les Parties conviennent que, dans ce cas, le Tribunal prendra en considération, par rapport aux paiements à effectuer au moyen de 30 pour cent tout droit de préférence ou de gage sur les revenus dont serait titulaire l'une quelconque des Puissances créancières, et le Tribunal tranchera en conséquence la question de répartition de façon qu'aucune Puissance ne jouisse d'un traitement préférentiel, et sa décision sera sans appel."

Attendu que les susmentionnés Arbitres, ayant examiné avec impartialité et soin tous les documents et actes, présentés au Tribunal d'Arbitrage par les Agents des Puissances intéressées dans ce litige, et ayant entendu avec la plus grande attention les plaidoiries orales, prononcées devant le Tribunal, par les Agents et Conseils der Parties en litige ;

Considérant que le Tribunal, en examinant le présent litige devait se règler d'après les principes du droit international et les notions de la justice ;

Considérant que les différents Protocoles signés à Washington depuis le 13 février 1903 et particulièrement les Protocoles du 7 mai 1903, dont la force obligatoire ne saurait être mise en doute, forment la base légale de la sentence arbitrale ;

Considérant que le Tribunal d'Arbitrage n'est nullement compétent ni pour contester la juridiction des commissions mixtes arbitrales, établies à Caracas, ni pour juger leur action ;

Considérant que le Tribunal ne se reconnait absolument aucune compétence pour porter un jugement sur le caractère ou la nature des opérations militaires entreprises par l'Allemagne, la Grande-Bretagne et l'Italie contre le Vénézuela;

Considérant que le Tribunal d'Arbitrage n'était non plus appelé à décider si les trois Puissances bloquantes avaient épuisé dans leur conflit avec le Vénézuela tous les moyens pacifiques, afin de prévenir l'emploi de la force;

Qu'il peut seulement constater le fait que depuis 1901 le Gouvernement du Vénézuela refusait catégoriquement de soumettre son conflit avec l'Allemagne et la Grande-Bretagne à l'arbitrage, proposé à plusieurs reprises et tout spécialement par la Note du Gouvernement Allemand du 16 juillet 1901;

Considérant qu'après la guerre entre l'Allemagne, la Grande-Bretagne et l'Italie d'une part, et le Vénézuela d'autre part, aucun traité formel de paix no fut conclu entre les Puissances belligérantes;

Considérant que les Protocoles, signés à Washington le 13 février 1903, n'avaient point règlé toutes les questions en litige entre les Parties belligérantes, en laissant particulièrement ouverte la question de la répartition des recettes des douanes de La Guayra et de Puerto Cabello;

Considérant que les Puissances belligérantes, en soumettant la question du traitement préférentiel par rapport à ces recettes au jugement du Tribunal d'Arbitrage, sont tombées d'accord que la sentence arbitrale doit servir à complèter cette lacune et à assurer le rétablissement définitif de la paix entre elles;

Considérant d'une part que les opérations de guerre des trois grandes Puissances européenes contre le Vénézuela ont céssé avant qu'elles eussent reçu satisfaction sur toutes leurs réclamations, et d'autre part, que la question du traitement préférentiel a été soumise à l'arbitrage, le Tribunal doit reconnaître dans ces faits un témoignage précieux en faveur du grand principe de l'arbitrage dans toutes les phases des conflits internationaux;

Considérant que les Puissances bloquantes, en admettant l'adhésion aux stipulations des Protocoles du 13 février 1903 des autres Puissances ayant des réclamations à l'egard du Vénézuela, ne pouvaient évidemment avoir l'intention de renoncer ni à leurs droits acquis, ni à leur position privilégiée de fait;

Considérant que le Gouvernement du Vénézuela dans les Protocoles du 13 février (article I) reconnait lui-même *en principe le bien-fondé des réclamations,* présentées contre lui par les Gouvernements d'Allemagne, de Grande-Bretagne et d'Italie;

Tandis que dans les Protocoles, signés entre le Vénézuela et les Puissances dites neutres ou pacifiques, le bien-fondé des réclamations de ces dernières n'a point été reconnu en principe;

Considérant que le Gouvernement du Vénézuela jusqu'à la fin de janvier 1903 ne protestait nullement contre la prétention des Puissances bloquantes d'exiger des gages spéciaux pour le règlement de leurs réclamations;

Considérant que le Vénézuela lui-même faisait toujours durant les négociations diplomatiques une distinction formelle entre *"les Puissances alliée,"* et *"les Puissances neutres ou pacifiques"*;

Considérant que les Puissances neutres, qui réclament actuellement devant le Tribunal d'Arbitrage l'égalité dans la répartition de 30 pour cent des recettes des douanes de La Guayra et de Puerto Cabello, n'ont pas protesté contre la prétention des Puissances bloquantes à un traitement préférentiel, ni au moment de la cessation de la guerre contre le Vénézuela, ni immédiatement après la signature des Protocoles du 13 février 1903 ;

Considérant qu'il résulte des négociations diplomatiques, ayant abouti à la signature des Protocoles du 13 février et 7 mai 1903, que les Gouvernements Allemand et Britannique insistaient constamment sur ce qu'il leur soit donné des garanties pour *"a sufficient and punctual discharge of the obligations"* (Mémorandum Britannique du 23 décembre 1902, communiqué au Gouvernement des Etats-Unis d'Amérique) ;

Considérant que le Plénipotentiaire du Gouvernement du Vénézuela accepta ces réserves de la part des Puissances alliées sans la moindre protestation ;

Considérant que le Gouvernement du Vénézuela ne s'engagea, qu'à l'égard des Puissances alliées, à offrir des garanties spéciales pour l'accomplissement des engagements pris par lui ;

Considérant que la bonne foi qui doit régir les relations internationales impose le devoir de constater que les mots *"all claims"* employés par le Représentant du Gouvernement du Vénézuela dans ses pourparlers avec les Représentants des Puissances alliées (Statement left in the hands of Sir Michael H. Herbert by Mr. H. Bowen of 23 January, 1903), ne pouvaient viser que les réclamations de ces dernières et ne pouvaient se rapporter qu'à celles-ci ;

Considérant que les Puissances neutres, n'ayant pris aucune part aux opérations de guerre contre le Vénézuela, pourraient sous quelque rapport profiter des circonstances créées par ces opérations, sans toutefais acquérir des droits nouveaux ;

Considérant que les droits acquis des Puissances neutres ou pacifiques à l'égard du Vénézuela restent à l'avenir absolument intacts et garantis par des arrangements internationaux respectifs ;

Considérant qu'en vertu de l'Article V des Protocoles du 7 mai 1903, signés à Washington, le Tribunal "décidera aussi suivant la disposition générale, formulée par l'Article LVII de la Convention internationale du 29 juillet 1899, comment, quand et par qui les frais du présent arbitrage seront payés";

Par ces motifs:

Le Tribunal d'Arbitrage décide et prononce à l'unanimité ce qui suit :

1°. L'Allemagne, la Grande-Bretagne et l'Italie ont droit à un traitement préférentiel pour le paiement de leurs réclamations contre le Vénézuela ;

2°. Le Vénézuela ayant consenti à mettre de côté 30 pour cent du revenu des douanes de La Guayra et de Puerto Cabello pour le paiement des réclamations de toutes les nations contre le Vénézuela, les trois Puissances susmentionées ont un droit de préférence au paiement de leurs réclamations au moyen de ces 30 pour cent des recettes des deux ports vénézuéliens sus-indiqués;

3°. Chaque Partie en litige supporte ses propres frais et une part égale des frais du Tribunal.

Le Gouvernement des Etats-Unis d'Amérique est chargé de veiller à l'exécution de cette dernière disposition dans le délai de trois mois.

Fait à la Haye, dans l'Hôtel de la Cour Permanente d'Arbitrage, le 22 février 1904.

(Signé)   N. Mourawieff
(")   H. Lammasch
(")   Martens

Agreement for Arbitration, May 7, 1903[1]

Von dem Kaiserlich Deutschen Gesandten Herrn Freiherrn Speck von Sternburg als Bevollmächtigten der Kaiserlich Deutschen Regierung und dem Gesandten der Vereinigten Staaten von Amerika Herrn Herbert W. Bowen als Bevollmächtigten der Venezolanischen Regierung ist zur Ausführung der Artikel 3 und 4 des deutsch-venezolanischen Protokolls vom 13. Februar 1903 nachstehendes Abkommen über die zur Feststellung der deutschen Reklamationen berufene gemischte Kommission unterzeichnet worden:

Artikel I

Die von der Kaiserlich Deutschen und der Venezolanischen Regierung zu ernennenden Mitglieder der gemischten Kommission treten am 1. Juni 1903 in Carácas zusammen. Der von dem Präsidenten der Vereinigten Staaten von Amerika zu ernennende Obmann tritt sobald als möglich, spätestens aber am 1. Juni 1903 in die Kommission ein.

Der Obmann ist zu den Verhandlungen und Entscheidungen zuzuziehen, sobald das deutsche und das venezolanische Mitglied sich über eine Frage nicht einigen können oder es sonst für angezeigt erachten. Bei Zuziehung des Obmanns führt dieser den Vorsitz.

Wenn nach dem Zusammentritte der Kommission der Obmann oder eines der beiden anderen Mitglieder in Wegfall kommt, so soll dessen Nachfolger sofort in derselben Weise wie das weggefallene Mitglied ernannt werden.

Das deutsche und das venezolanische Mitglied haben zu ihrer Unterstützung bei den Kommissionsarbeiten je einen der deutschen und der spanischen Sprache mächtigen Sekretär zu ernennen.

---

[1]Official records of the Imperial German Embassy at Washington, D. C.

Artikel II

Vor Beginn ihrer Thätigkeit sollen der Obmann und die beiden anderen Mitglieder in feierlicher Weise einen Eid oder eine eidesstattliche Versicherung dahin ableisten, dass sie die ihnen unterbreiteten Reklamationen sorgfältig prüfen und unparteiisch nach den Grundsätzen der Gerechtigkeit sowie nach den Bestimmungen des Protokolls vom 13. Februar 1903 und des vorliegenden Abkommens entscheiden werden. Die Ableistung des Eides oder der eidesstattlichen Versicherung ist durch die Protokolle der Kommission festzustellen.

Die Entscheidungen der Kommission über die Reklamationen sollen auf der Grundlage vollkommener Billigkeit sowie ohne Rücksicht auf Einwendungen technischer Art oder auf die Bestimmungen der Landesgesetzgebung erfolgen. Sie sind schriftlich in deutscher und spanischer Sprache abzufassen. Die zuerkannten Entschädigungsbeträge müssen angegeben werden als zahlbar in deutschem Golde oder dem Gegenwert in Silber, wie sich solcher zur Zeit der effektiven Zahlung in Carácas stellen wird.

Artikel III

Die Reklamationen sind bei der Kommission von dem Kaiserlich Deutschen Gesandten in Carácas bis zum 1. Juli 1903 anzumelden. Diese Frist kann von der Kommission in geeigneten Fällen angemessen verlängert werden. Die Kommission hat über die einzelnen Reklamationen binnen sechs Monaten nach deren Anmeldung und sofern das deutsche und das venezolanische Mitglied sich nicht einigen, binnen sechs Monaten nach Zuziehung des Obmanns zu entscheiden.

Die Kommission ist verpflichtet, vor der Entscheidung das ihr von dem Kaiserlich Deutschen Gesandten in Carácas und der Venezolanischen Regierung vorgelegte Beweismaterial sowie mündliche oder schriftliche Ausführungen etwaiger Bevollmächtigten des Gesandten oder der Regierung entgegenzunehmen und einer sorgfältigen Prüfung zu unterziehen.

Über die Verhandlungen der Kommission haben die in Artikel 1 Absatz 4 bezeichneten Sekretäre genaue Protokolle in zwei gleichlautenden Ausfertigungen zu führen, die von ihnen und den an der Verhandlung beteiligten Mitgliedern der Kommission zu unterzeichnen sind. Nach Beendigung der Kommissionsarbeiten ist je eine Ausfertigung dieser Protokolle der Kaiserlich Deutschen und der Venezolanischen Regierung zur Verfügung zu stellen.

Artikel IV

Soweit nicht die vorstehenden Artikel besondere Bestimmungen enthalten, kann die Kommission selbst das Verfahren in der ihr geeignet scheinenden Weise regeln. Insbesondere ist sie befugt, selbst die Erklärungen der Reklamanten oder ihrer etwaigen Bevollmächtigten entgegenzunehmen und die erforderlichen Beweise zu erheben.

Artikel V

Der Obmann bezieht für seine Mühewaltung und Auslagen eine angemessene Entschädigung, die ebenso wie etwaige gemeinsame Kosten der Kommission von der Kaiserlich Deutschen und der Venezolanischen Regierung zu gleichem Anteile getragen wird.

Die Entschädigungen, die den beiden anderen Mitgliedern und den Sekretären der Kommission zu gewähren sind, werden von der Regierung getragen, von deren Seite diese Personen bestellt sind. Ebenso trägt jede Regierung die ihr sonsst etwa erwachsenden eigenen Kosten.

So geschehen in doppelter Ausfertigung in deutscher und englischer Sprache zu Washington am siebten Mai. Eintausend neunhundert und drei.

(L. S.) (gez.) STERNBURG
(L. S.) (gez.) HERBERT W. BOWEN

Protocol of February 13, 1903, between Germany and Venezuela for the Adjustment of Claims[1]

Protokoll Zwischen dem Kaiserlich Deutschen Ausserordentlichen Gesandten und bevollmächtigten Minister Herrn Freiherrn Speck von Sternburg als Bevollmächtigten der Kaiserlich Deutschen Regierung und dem Gesandten der Vereinigten Staaten von Amerika Herrn Bowen als Bevollmächtigten der Venezolanischen Regierung ist zur Beilegung der zwischen Deutschland und Venezuela entstandenen Streitigkeiten nachstehendes Protokoll abgeschlossen worden:

Artikel I

Die Venezolanische Regierung erkennt im Prinzip die von der Kaiserlich Deutschen Regierung erhobenen Reklamationen deutscher Untertanen als berechtigt an.

Artikel II

Die deutschen Reklamationen aus den venezolanischen Bürgerkriegen von 1898 bis 1900 belaufen sich auf 1,718,815.67 Bolivares. Die Venezolanische Regierung verpflichtet sich von diesem Betrag Pf. Sterling 5,500 = 137,500 Bolivares (Fünftausend fünfhundert Pfund Sterling = Einhundert sieben und dreissig tausend fünfhundert Bolivares) sofort bar zu bezahlen und zur Tilgung des Restes fünf am 15 März, 15 April, 15 Mai, 15 Juni und 15 Juli 1903 an den Kaiserlich Deutschen Gesandten in Carácas zahlbare Wechsel über entsprechende Teilbeträge einzulösen, die Herr Bowen sofort ausstellen und Herrn Freiherrn von Sternburg übergeben wird. Sollte die Venezolanische

---

[1] Official records of the Imperial German Embassy at Washington, D. C.

Regierung diese Wechsel nicht einlösen, so soll die Zahlung aus den Zolleinkünften von La Guaira und Puerto Cabello erfolgen, und soll die Zollverwaltung in den beiden Häfen bis zur vollständigen Tilgung der erwähnten Schulden belgischen Zollbeamten übertragen werden.

Artikel III

Die in den Artikeln II und VI nicht erwähnten deutschen Reklamationen, insbesondere die Reklamationen, welche aus dem gegenwärtigen venezolanischen Bürgerkriege herrühren, ferner die Ansprüche der Deutschen Grossen Venezuela Eisenbahn-Gesellschaft gegen die Venezolanische Regierung wegen Beförderung von Personen und Gütern sowie die aus dem Bau eines Schlachthauses in Carácas entstandenen Forderungen en des Ingenieurs Karl Henckel in Hamburg und der Aktiengesellschaft für Beton-und Monierban in Berlin werden einer gemischten Kommission überwiesen.

Diese Kommission hat sowohl über materielle Berechtigung der einzelnen Forderungen wie über deren Höhe zu entscheiden. Bei den Reklamationen wegen widerrechtlicher Beschädigung oder Wegnahme von Eigentum erkennt überdies die Venezolanische Regierung ihre Haftpflicht im Prinzip an, dergestalt, dass die Kommission nicht über die Frage der Haftpflicht, sondern lediglich über die Widerrechtlichkeit der Beschädigung oder Wegnahme sowie über die Höhe der Entschädigung zu befinden hat.

Artikel IV

Die im Artikel III erwähnte gemischte Kommission hat ihren Sitz in Carácas. Sie setzt sich zusammen aus je einem von der Kaiserlich Deutschen und der Venezolanischen Regierung zu ernennenden Mitglied. Die Ernennung hat bis zum 1, Mai 1903 zu erfolgen. Soweit sich die beiden Mitglieder über die erhobenen Ansprüche einigen, ist ihre Entscheidung als entgültig anzusehen, soweit eine Einigung unter ihnen nicht zu stande kommt, ist zur Entscheidung ein Obmann zuzuziehen, der von dem Präsidenten der Vereinigten Staaten von Amerika ernannt wird.

Artikel V

Zur Befriedigung der im Artikel III bezeichneten Reklamationen sowie der gleichartigen Forderungen anderer Mächte wird die Venezolanische Regierung vom 1 März 1903, ab monatlich 30% der Zolleinkunfte von La Guaira und Puerto Cabello unter Ausschluss jeder anderen Verfügung dem Vertreter der Bank von England in Carácas überweisen. Sollte die Venezolanische Regierung dieser Verpflichtung nicht nachkommen, so soll die Zollverwaltung in den beiden Häfen bis zur vollständigen Befriedigung der vorstehend erwähnten Forderungen belgischen Zollbeamten übertragen werden.

Alle Streitfragen in Ansehung der Verteilung der im Absatz 1 bezeichneten Zolleinkünfte sowie in Ansehung des Rechts Deutschlands, Gross-Britanniens und Italiens auf gesonderte Befriedigung ihrer

Reklamationen sollen in Ermangelung eines anderweitigen Abkommens durch den ständigen Schiedshof im Haag entschieden werden. An dem Schiedsverfahren können sich alle anderen interessierten Staaten den genannten drei Mächten gegenüber als Partei beteiligen.

Artikel VI

Die Venezolanische Regierung verpflichtet sich, die zum grössten Teil in deutschen Händen befindliche 5 prozentige venezolanische Anleihe von 1896 zugleich mit ihrer gesamten auswärtigen Schuld in befriedigender Weise neu zu regeln. Bei dieser Regelung sollen die für den Schuldendienst zu verwendenden Staatseinkünfte unbeschadet der diesbezüglich bereits bestehenden Verpflichtungen bestimmt werden.

Artikel VII

Die von den deutschen Seestreitkräften weggenommenen venezolanischen Kriegs-und Handelsfahrzeuge werden in dem Zustande, in dem sie sich gegenwärtig befinden, der Venezolanischen Regierung zurückgegeben. Aus der Wegnahme dieser Schiffe wie aus deren Aufbewahrung können keine Entschädigungsanprüche hergeleitet werden. Auch wird ein Ersatz für Beschädigung oder Vernichtung der Schiffe nicht gewährt.

Artikel VIII

Nach Unterzeichnung dieses Protokolles soll die über die venezolanischen Häfen verhängte Blockade gemeinsam mit den Regierungen Gross-Britanniens und Italiens aufgehoben werden. Auch werden die diplomatischen Beziehungen zwischen der Kaiserlich Deutschen und der Venezolanischen Regierung wieder aufgenommen.

So geschehen in doppelter Ausfertigung in deutscher und englischer Sprache zu Washington am dreizehnten Februar Eintausend neunhundert und drei.

(L. S.) (gez.) Herbert W. Bowen
(L. S.) (gez.) H. Sternburg

Protocol of February 17, 1903, between the United States of America and Venezuela for the Adjustment of Claims[1]

Los Estados Unidos de América y la República de Venezuela, por medio de sus representantes, John Hay, Secretario de Estado de los Estados Unidos de América, y Herbert W. Bowen, Plenipotenciario de la República de Venezuela, han convenido en el siguiente protócolo, que han firmado.

Artículo I

Todas las reclamaciones poseídas por ciudadanos de los Estados Unidos de América contra la República de Venezuela, que no hayan

---

[1] *United States Treaty Series*, No. 420.

sido arregladas por la vía diplomática ó por arbitraje entre los dos Gobiernos, y que hubieren sido presentadas por el Departamento de Estado de los Estados Unidos ó por su Legación en Caracas á la Comisión abajo mencionada, serán examinadas y decididas por una Comisión Mixta, que celebrará sus sesiones en Caracas, y que se compondrá de dos miembros, uno de los cuales será nombrado por el Presidente de los Estados Unidos, y el otro por el Presidente de Venezuela.

Se conviene en que tercero en discordia podrá ser nombrado por la Reina de los Países Bajos. Si uno de dichos comisionados ó el tercero en discordia dejare de ejercer sus funciones, será nombrado en el acto su sucesor del mismo modo que el antecesor de éste. Dichos comisionados y tercero en discordia deben ser nombrados antes del día primero de mayo de 1903.

Los comisionados y el tercero en discordia se reunirán en la ciudad de Caracas el día primero de junio de 1903. El tercero en discordia presidirá sus deliberaciones, y tendrá facultad para dirimir cualquier cuestión sobre la que no puedan avenirse los comisionados. Antes de empezar á ejercer las funciones de su cargo, los comisionados y el tercero en discordia prestarán solemne juramento de examinar con cuidado, y de decidir imparcialmente, con arreglo á la justicia y á las estipulaciones de esta convención, todas las reclamaciones que se les sometieren, y tales juramentos se asentarán en su libro de actas. Los comisionados, ó en caso de que éstos no puedan avenirse, el tercero en discordia decidirá todas las reclamaciones con arreglo absoluto a la equidad, sin reparar en objeciones técnicas, ni en las disposiciones de la legislación local.

Las decisiones de la comisión, y en caso de su desavenencia, las del tercero en discordia, serán definitivas y concluyentes. Se estenderán por escrito. Todas las cantidades falladas serán pagaderas en moneda de oro de los Estados Unidos ó en su equivalente en plata.

Artículo II

Los comisionados ó el tercero en discordia, según el caso, investigarán y decidirán tales reclamaciones con arreglo únicamente á las pruebas ó informes suministrados por los respectivos Gobiernos, ó en nombre de éstos. Tendrán obligación de recibir y considerar todos los documentos ó exposiciones escritas que les fueren presentadas por los respectivos Gobiernos, ó en su nombre, en apoyo ó en refutación de cualquiera reclamación, y de oir los argumentos orales ó escritos que hiciere el agente de cada Gobierno sobre cada reclamación. En caso de que dejen de avenirse sus opiniones sobre cualquiera reclamación, decidirá el tercero en discordia.

Cada reclamación se presentará formalmente á los comisionados dentro de treinta días contados desde la fecha de su primera reunión, á menos que los comisionados ó el tercero en discordia prorroguen, en algún caso, por un término que no exceda de tres meses, el período concedido para presentar la reclamación. Los comisionados tendrán obligación de examinar y decidir todas las reclamaciones dentro de seis meses contados desde el día en que hubieren sido formalmente presentadas por primera vez, y en caso de su desavenencia, examinará y decidirá el tercero en discordia dentro de un período correspondiente contado desde la fecha de tal desavenencia.

Artículo III

Los comisionados y el tercero en discordia llevarán un registro exacto de todas sus deliberaciones y acuerdos. Para ese objeto, cada comisionado nombrará un secretario versado en el idioma de cada país para que le ayude en el despacho de los negocios que pendieren ante la comisión. Salvo las estipulaciones del presente protócolo, toda cuestión de procedimiento se remitirá á la resolución de la comisión, ó en caso de su desavenencia, á la del tercero en discordia.

Artículo IV

Una retribución equitativa será pagada por las partes contratantes, en partes iguales, á los comisionados y al tercero en discordia por sus servicios y gastos, y también se satisfaran de la misma manera, los demás gastos del arbitraje.

Artículo V

Con el fin de pagar el importe total de las reclamaciones que se hayan de decidir de la manera que queda dicha, y otras reclamaciones de ciudadanos ó súbditos de otros Estados, el Gobierno de Venezuela reservará, y no enajenará para ningún otro objeto (empezando desde el mes de marzo de 1903) un treinta por ciento, en pagos mensuales, de las rentas aduanales de la Guaira y Puerto Cabello, y el dinero así reservado será distribuido con arreglo al fallo del Tribunal de la Haya.

En caso de que no se cumpla el susodicho convenio, empleados belgas quedarán encargados del cobro de los derechos de aduana de ambos puertos, y los administrarán hasta que se hayan cumpeido las obligaciones del Gobierno de Venezuela respecto de las referidas reclamaciones. La remisión al Tribunal de la Haya de la cuestión arriba expuesta será objeto de un protócolo separado.

Artículo VI

Todas las sumas falladas á favor de ciudadanos de los Estados Unidos, que no se hayan satisfecho, serán pagadas con puntualidad, conforme á las disposiciones de los respectivos fallos.

Wáshington, D. C. February 17, 1903.

JOHN HAY [SEAL]
HERBERT W. BOWEN [SEAL]

THE JAPANESE HOUSE TAX CASE

Award of the Tribunal, May 22, 1905[1]

Attendu qu'aux termes de Protocoles, signés à Tokyo le 28 août 1902, un désaccord s'est produit, entre le Gouvernement du Japon d'une part et les Gouvernements d'Allemagne, de France et de Grande-Bretagne d'autre part, touchant le sens réel et la portée des dispositions suivantes des traités respectifs et autres engagements existant entre eux, c'est-à-dire:

Paragraphe 4 de l'Article XVIII du Traité de Commerce et de Navigation du 4 avril 1896 entre le Japon et l'Allemagne: "Sobald diese Einverleibung erfolgt" [c'est-à-dire: quand les divers quartiers étrangers qui existent au Japon auront été incorporés dans les communes respectives du Japon] "sollen die bestehenden, zeitlich unbegrenzten Ueberlassungsverträge, unter welchen jetzt in den gedachten Niederlassungen Grundstücke besessen werden, bestätigt und hinsichtlich dieser Grundstücke sollen keine Bedingungen irgend einer anderen Art auferlegt werden, als sie in den bestehenden Ueberlassungsverträgen enthalten sind";—et § 3 de la communication complementaire de même date du Secrétaire d'Etat des Affaires Etrangères de l'Empire d'Allemagne au Ministre du Japon à Berlin: "3. dass, da das Eigenthum an den im Artikel XVIII des Vertrages erwähnten Niederlassungsgrundstücken dem Japanischen Staate verbleibt, die Besitzer oder deren Rechtsnachfolger für ihre Grundstücke ausser dem kontraktmässigen Grundzins Abgaben oder Steuern irgend welcher Art nicht zu entrichten haben werden," et l'alinéa suivant de la réponse du Ministre du Japon de même date à la précédente communication: "dass die darin unter Nummer 1 bis 4 zum Ausdruck gebrachten Voraussetzungen, welche den Erwerb dinglicher Rechte an Grundstücken, die Errichtung von Waaren haüsern, die Steuerfreiheit der Grundstücke in den Fremdenniederlassungen und die Erhaltung wohlerworbener Rechte nach Ablauf des Vertrages zum Gegenstande haben, in allen Punkten zutreffend sind";

Paragraphe 4 de l'Article XXI du Traité revisé du 4 août 1896 entre le Japon et la France: "Lorsque les changements ci-dessus indiqués auront été effectués" [c'est-à-dire: lorsque les divers quartiers étrangers qui existent au Japon auront été incorporés aux communes respectives du Japon et feront dès lors partie du système municipal du Japon; et lorsque les autorités japonais compétentes auront assumé toutes les obligations et tous les devoirs municipaux, et que les fonds et biens municipaux qui pourraient appartenir à ces quartiers auront été transférés aux dites autorités], "les baux à perpétuité en vertu desquels les étrangers possèdent actuellement des

[1] Official report, p. 43.

propriétés dans les quartiers seront confirmés, et les propriétés de cette nature ne donneront lieu à aucuns impôts, taxes, charges, contributions ou conditions quelconques autres que ceux expressément stipulés dans les baux en question";

Paragraphe 4 de l'Article XVIII du Traité revisé du 16 juillet 1894 entre le Japon et la Grande-Bretagne: "When such incorporation takes place" [c'est-à-dire: quand les divers quartiers étrangers qui existent au Japon auront été incorporés aux communes respectives du Japon], "existing leases in perpetuity under which property is now held in the said settlements shall be confirmed, and no conditions whatsoever other than those contained in such existing leases shall be imposed in respect of such property";

Attendu que les Puissances en litige sont tombées d'accord pour soumettre leur différend à la décision d'un Tribunal d'Arbitrage,

qu'en vertu des Protocoles susmentionnés,

les Gouvernements d'Allemagne, de France et de Grande-Bretagne ont désigné pour Arbitre Monsieur Louis Renault, Ministre Plénipotentiaire, Membre de l'Institut de France, Professeur à la Faculté de droit de Paris, Jurisconsulte du Département des Affaires Etrangères, et

le Gouvernement du Japon a désigné pour Arbitre Son Excellence Monsieur Itchiro Motono, Envoyé Extraordinaire et Ministre Plénipotentiaire de Sa Majesté l'Empereur du Japon à Paris, Docteur en droit,

que les deux Arbitres sus-nommés ont choisi pour Surarbitre Monsieur Gregers Gram, ancien Ministre d'Etat de Norvège, Gouverneur de Province;

Attendu que le Tribunal ainsi composé a pour mission de statuer, en dernier ressort, sur la question suivante:

Oui ou non, les dispositions des traités et autres engagements ci-dessus mentionnés exemptent-elles seulement les terrains possédés en vertu des baux perpétuels concédés par le Gouvernement Japonais ou en son nom,—ou bien exemptent-elles les terrains et les bâtiments de toute nature construits ou qui pourraient être construits sur ces terrains,—de tous impôts, taxes, charges, contributions ou conditions quelconques autres que ceux expressément stipulés dans les baux en question?

Attendu que le Gouvernement Japonais soutient que les terrains seuls sont, dans la mesure qui vient d'être indiquée, exemptés du paiement d'impôts et autres charges,

que les Gouvernements d'Allemagne, de France et de Grande-Bretagne prétendent, au contraire, que les bâtiments, construits sur ces terrains, jouissent de la même exemption,

Attendu que, pour se rendre compte de la nature et de l'étendue des engagements contractés de part et d'autre par les baux à perpétuité, il faut recourir à divers arrangements et conventions intervenus, sous le régime des anciens traités, entre les autorités japonaises et les représentants de plusieurs Puissances,

Attendu que de ces actes et des stipulations insérées dans les baux il résulte :

que le Gouvernement Japonais avait consenti à prêter son concours à la création de quartiers étrangers dans certaines villes et ports du Japon, ouverts aux ressortissants d'autres nations,

que, sur les terrains désignés à l'usage des étrangers dans les différentes localités, le Gouvernement Japonais a exécuté, à ses frais, des travaux en vue de faciliter l'occupation urbaine,

que les étrangers n'étant pas, d'après les principes du droit japonais, admis à acquérir la propriété de terrains situés dans le pays, le Gouvernement leur a donné les terrains en location à perpétuité,

que les baux déterminent l'étendue des lots de terre loués et stipulent une rente annuelle fixe, calculée à raison de l'espace loué,

qu'il fut convenue qu'en principe les quartiers étrangers resteraient en dehors du système municipal du Japon, mais qu'au reste, ils n'étaient pas soumis à une organisation uniforme,

qu'il était arrêté, par voie de règlements, comment il serait pourvu aux diverses fonctions de l'administration et qu'il était prescrit que les détenteurs des terrains seraient tenus de subvenir partiellement aux frais de la municipalité à l'aide de redevances dont le montant et le mode de perception étaient déterminés,

Attendu qu'on s'expliquerait bien le soin apporté dans la rédaction des dits actes en vue de préciser les obligations de toute nature incombant aux étrangers vis à vis du Gouvernement Japonais, s'il était entendu que la rente annuelle représentât, non seulement le prix de la location, mais aussi la contrepartie des impôts dont les preneurs eussent été redevables à raison de la situation créée à leur profit par les baux et que, par conséquent, ils n'auraient, en cette qualité, a supporter que les impôts et charges qui étaient expressément mentionnés dans les dits baux,

Attendu qu'au reste, il n'est pas contesté que ce ne soit là le véritable sens de ces actes, en tant qu'il s'agit des terrains, mais que le Gouvernement Japonais allègue que les baux n'avaient pour objet que les terrains nus et qu'il n'admet pas que les constructions, élevées sur les terrains, fussent comprises dans les stipulations sur lesquelles l'exemption des impôts serait fondée,

qu'il a allégué que les terrains seuls appartenaient au Gouvernement, les constructions étant, au contraire, la propriété des preneurs, et qu'en conséquence l'immunité dont il est question ne pouvait s'étendre qu'aux immeubles qui n'étaient pas sortis du patrimoine de l'Etat,

Attendu que, toutefois, la question qu'il s'agit de décider est celle de savoir si, au point de vue fiscal, les constructions élevées sur les terrains loués étaient, de commun accord, considérées comme accessoires de ces terrains, ou non, et que a solution de cette question ne dépend pas de distinctions tirées d'une prétendue différence quant à la propriété des immeubles,

que le Tribunal ne saurait donc s'arrêter à la discussion engagée à ce sujet et fondée sur les principes du droit civil,

Attendu que les terrains étaient loués pour y construire des maisons, ce qui est indiqué, à la fois, par la situation des immeubles et par la nature des aménagements effectués par le Gouvernement Japonais,

que l'obligation d'ériger des bâtiments était, dans certaines localités, imposée sous peine de déchéance, que les baux contenaient souvent une clause, aux termes de laquelle les bâtiments, qui se trouveraient sur les terrains, deviendraient la propriété du Gouvernement Japonais, au cas où le preneur aurait manqué à ses engagements,

Attendu qu'il faut admettre que les circonstances qui viennent d'être relatées offrent des arguments à l'encontre de la prétention que le sol et les constructions constituent, dans les relations entre les parties et au point de vue fiscal, des objets entièrement distincts,

Attendu qu'en intervenant aux dits actes, le Gouvernement du Japon a agi, non seulement en propriétaire des terrains donnés en location, mais aussi comme investi du pouvoir souverain du pays,

Attendu que la volonté des parties faisait, par conséquent, la loi en la matière et que, pour établir comment les actes ont été réellement interprétés, il faut s'en rapporter au traitement auquel les détenteurs des terrains ont été, au point de vue des impôts, soumis, en fait, dans les différentes localités,

Attendu, à cet égard, qu'il est constant que, suivant une pratique qui n'a pas varié et qui a existé durant une longue série d'années, non seulement les terrains en question, mais aussi les bâtiments élevés sur ces terrains, ont été exemptés de tous impôts, taxes, charges, contributions ou conditions autres que ceux expressément stipulés dans les baux à perpétuité,

Attendu que le Gouvernement du Japon soutient, il est vrai, que cet état de choses, de même que l'immunité fiscale dont jouissaient en général les étrangers dans le pays, n'était dû qu'à la circonstance que les tribunaux consulaires refusaient de donner la sanction nécessaire aux lois fiscales du pays,

Attendu que, toutefois, cette prétention est dépourvue de preuves et qu'il n'est pas même allégué que le Gouvernement Japonais ait jamais fait, vis à vis des Gouvernements d'Allemagne, de France et de Grande-Bretagne, des réserves à l'effet de maintenir les droits qu'il dit avoir été lésés,

que, bien qu'il ait été allégué que l'immunité dont les étrangers jouissaient, en fait, au point de vue des impôts, sous le régime des anciens traités, était générale et qu'elle s'étendait aux étrangers résidant en dehors des concessions en question, il résulte pourtant des renseignements fournis au sujet de détenteurs d'immeubles—terrains et maisons—à Hiogo, que ladite règle n'a pas été d'une application universelle,

que, dans tous les cas, la situation de fait n'est pas douteuse, de quelque façon qu'on l'explique,

Attendu, au point de vue de l'interprétation des dispositions des nouveaux traités au sujet desquels il y a contestation entre les Parties, que la rédaction de l'article 18 du traité entre la Grande-Bretagne et le Japon—traité antérieur aux deux autres—avait été précédée de propositions tendant à mettre les étrangers, détenteurs de terrains, sur le même pied que les sujets japonais, tant au point de vue de la propriété des immeubles qui leur avaient été concédés en location que pour ce qui concerne le paiement de taxes et d'impôts, mais qu'on est ensuite tombé d'accord sur le maintien du régime qui jusqu'alors avait été pratiqué,

que le Gouvernement Japonais prétend, il est vrai, que la question de maintenir le *status quo* ne se rapportait qu'aux terrains, mais que cette prétention ne se trouve pas justifiée par les expressions employées au cours des négociations,

qu'au contraire, le représentant du Gouvernement Japonais qui a pris l'initiative pour arriver à un accord dans ce sens s'est borné à proposer le maintien du *status quo* dans les concessions étrangères (*maintenance of the status quo in the foreign settlements*),

qu'il n'est pas à présumer que le délégué de la Grande-Bretagne, en présentant un projet élaboré sur la base de ladite proposition, ait entendu faire une restriction concernant les constructions, que cela ne résulte, ni des mots insérés dans le procès-verbal, ni du contenu de l'article par lui proposé,

que, pour maintenir intégralement le *status quo,* il ne suffirait pas d'admettre que l'immunité fiscale, qui jusqu'à cette époque s'étendait, tant sur les terrains que sur les constructions, dans les quartiers étrangers, serait maintenue pour le sol seulement et qu'elle cesserait d'exister pour ce qui concerne les maisons,

qu'il doit surtout en être ainsi lorsqu'on considère que, pour se conformer à ce qui était convenu, les Parties ne se sont pas bornées à formuler une disposition au sujet de la confirmation des baux, mais qu'elles ont ajouté qu'aucunes conditions, sauf celles contenues dans les baux en vigueur, ne seront imposées relativement à une telle propriété (*no conditions whatsoever other than those contained in such existing leases shall be imposed in respect of such property*),

que cette dernière clause et rédigée d'une façon encore plus explicite dans le traité avec la France,

Attendu qu'au surplus, dans les clauses dont il s'agit, les Puissances n'ont pas parlé de terrains, comme elles auraient dû nécessairement le faire si l'immunité, contrairement à ce qui avait été pratiqué jusque là, avait dû être restreinte aux terrains,

qu'elles ont, au contraire, employé des expressions assez larges pour comprendre dans son ensemble la situation faite par les baux aux preneurs,

Attendu que le Tribunal ne saurait, non plus, admettre que les notes échangées entre les Gouvernements d'Allemagne et du Japon, au moment de la conclusion du nouveau traité, contiennent des explications de nature à placer l'Allemagne dans des conditions moins avantageuses que les deux autres Puissances,

que le Gouvernement du Japon a surtout voulu tirer argument de ce que le Gouvernement Allemand a fondé l'immunité fiscale sur ce qu'il est interdit aux étrangers d'acquérir la propriété de terrains situés au Japon, mais qu'à cet égard il faut considérer qu'en fait les constructions avaient toujours eu le caractère de dépendances des terrains au point de vue des impôts, et qu'il n'est pas à présumer que le Gouvernement Allemand ait entendu renoncer aux avantages consentis en faveur de la Grande-Bretagne par le nouveau traité, ce qui serait d'ailleurs en contradiction avec la clause assurant à l'Allemagne le traitement de la nation la plus favorisée,

PAR CES MOTIFS:

Le Tribunal d'Arbitrage, à la majorité des voix, décide et déclare:

Les dispositions des traités et autres engagements mentionnés dans les protocoles d'arbitrage n'exemptent pas seulement les terrains possédés en vertu des baux perpétuels concédés par le Gouvernement Japonais ou en son nom, mais elles exemptent les terrains et les bâtiments de toute nature construits ou qui pourraient être construits sur ces terrains, de tous impôts, taxes, charges, contributions ou conditions quelconques autres que ceux expressément stipulés dans les baux en question.

Fait à la Haye, dans l'Hôtel de la Cour permanente d'Arbitrage, le 22 mai 1905.

(Signé) G. GRAM
(") L. RENAULT

Au moment de procéder à la signature de la présente Sentence arbitrale, usant de la faculté que me confère l'article 52, alinéa 2, de la *Convention pour le règlement pacifique des conflits internationaux*, conclue à la Haye le 29 juillet 1899, je tiens à constater mon dissentiment absolu avec la majorité du Tribunal, en ce qui concerne les motifs comme le dispositif de la Sentence.

(Signé) I. MOTONO

Agreement for Arbitration between Germany and Japan, August 28, 1902[1]

In der Erwägung,

dass zwischen den Regierungen von Deutschland, Frankreich und Grossbritannien einerseits und der Japanischen Regierung andrerseits ein Streitfall über den wahren Sinn und die Bedeutung der nachstehend aufgeführten Bestimmungen der zwischen ihnen abgeschlossenen Verträge und anderen Vereinbarungen entstanden ist, nämlich:

Artikel XVIII, Absatz 4, des Handels—und Schiffahrtsvertrages zwischen dem Deutschen Reich und Japan vom 4. April, 1896:

"Sobald diese Einverleibung erfolgt" [das heisst, sobald die ein-

---

[1]Official report, p. 5.

zelnen Fremdenniederlassungen in Japan den betreffenden Japanischen Gemeinden einverleibt sein werden], "sollen die bestehenden, zeitlich umbegrenzten Ueberlassungsverträge, unter welchen jetzt in den gedachten Niederlassungen Grundstücke besessen werden, bestätigt und hinsichtlich dieser Grundstücke sollen keine Bedingungen irgend einer anderen Art Auferlegt werden, als sie in den bestehenden Ueberlassungsverträgen enthalten sind";

ferner, Ziffer 3 der Note des Kaiserlich Deutschen Staatssekretärs des Auswärtigen Amts vom selben Tage an den Kaiserlich Japanischen Gesandten in Berlin:

"3. dass, da das Eigenthum an den im Artikel XVIII des Vertrages erwähnten Niederlassungsgrundstücken dem Japanischen Staate verbleibt, die Besitzer oder deren Rechtsnachfolger für ihre Grundstücke ausser dem kontraktmässigen Grundzins Abgaben oder Steuern irgend welcher Art nicht zu entrichten haben werden";

Und im Absatz 1 der Erwiderung des Japanischen Gesandten vom selben Tage auf die vorhergehende Note:

"das die darin unter Nummer 1 bis 4 zum Ausdruck gebrachten Voraussetzungen, welche den Erwerb dinglicher Rechte an Grundstücken, die Errichtung von Waarenhäusern, die Steuerfreiheit der Grundstücke in den Fremdenniederlassungen und die Erhaltung wohlerworbener Rechte nach Ablauf des Vertrages zum Gegenstande haben, in allen Punkten zutreffend sind";

Artikel XXI, Absatz 4, des revidirten Vertrages Zwischen Frankreich und Japan vom 4. August, 1896:

"Lorsque les changements ci-dessus indiqués auront été efectués" [das heisst: sobald die einzelnen Fremdenniederlassungen in Japan den betreffenden Japanischen Gemeinden einverleibt sein und Bestandtheile der Japanischen Gemeinden bilden werden; und sobald die zuständigen Japanischen Behörden alle municipalen Verbindlichkeiten und Verpflichtungen übernommen haben un die municipalen Gelder und Vermögensgegenstände, welche diesen Niederlassungen gehören, den genannten Japanischen Behörden übergeben sein werden], "les baux à perpétuité en vertu desquels les étrangers possèdent actuellement des propriétés dans les quartiers seront confirmés, et les propriétés de cette nature ne donneront lieu à aucuns impôts, taxes, charges, contributions ou conditions quelconques autres que ceux expressément stipulés dans les baux en question"; und

Artikel XVIII, Absatz 4, des revidirten Vertrages vom 16. Juli, 1894, zwischen Grossbritannien und Japan:

"When such incorporation takes place" [das heisst: sobald die einzelnen Fremdenniederlassungen in Japan den betreffenden Japanischen Gemeinden einverleibt sein werden], "existing leases in perpetuity under which property is now held in the said Settlements shall be confirmed, and no conditions whatsoever other than those contained in such existing leases shall be imposed in respect of such property";

In der Erwägung,
dass der Streitfall auf gewöhnlichem diplomatischen Wege nicht erledigt werden kann;

Und in der Erwägung,

dass die betheiligten Mächte, welche Signatarmächte des Haager Abkommens zur friedlichen Erledigung internationaler Streitfälle sind, beschlossen haben, den Streitfall dadurch zu erledigen, dass sie denselben in Gemässheit der Bestimmungen des vorerwähnten Abkommens einem unparteiischen Schiedsgericht unterbreiten;

haben die genannten Regierungen zur Ausführung dieses Entschlusses die nachstehenden Vertreter, nämlich:

die Regierung von Deutschland:

den Ausserordentlichen Gesandten und Bevollmächtigten Minister Seiner Majestät des Deutschen Kaisers, Königs von Preussen, Herrn Grafen von Arco Valley;

die Regierung von Frankreich:

den Bevollmächtigten Minister, Geschäftsträger von Frankreich, Herrn G. Dubail;

die Regierung von Grossbritannien:

den Ausserordentlichen Gesandten und Bevollmächtigten Minister Seiner Majestät des Königs von Grossbritannien, Sir Claude Maxwell Macdonald, G.C.M.G., K.C.B.;

die Regierung von Japan:

den Minister der Auswärtigen Angelegenheiten Seiner Majestät des Kaisers von Japan, Herrn Baron Komura Jutaro;

ermächtigt, das nachstehende Protokoll abzuschliessen:

I. Die an dem Streitfall betheiligten Regierungen kommen dahin überein, dass das Schiedsgericht, welchem der Streitfall zur endgültigen Entscheidung vorzulegen ist, aus drei Mitgliedern bestehen soll, die dem ständigen Schiedshof im Haag angehören und in nachstehender Weise zu bestimmen sind:

Jede Partei hat sobald wie möglich, jedenfalls nicht später als zwei Monate nach dem Datum dieses Protokolls, einen Schiedsrichter zu ernennen, und die beiden so ernannten Schiedsrichter haben gemeinschaftlich einen Obmann zu wählen. Wenn die beiden Schiedsrichter zwei Monate nach ihrer Ernennung einen Obmann noch nicht gewählt haben, so soll Seine Majestät der König von Schweden und Norwegen gebeten werden, einen Obmann zu ernennen.

II. Die Streitfrage, über welche die in diesem Schiedsverfahren streitenden Parteien eine endgültige Entscheidung des Schiedsgerichts erbitten, ist folgende:

Befreien die vorerwähnten Bestimmungen der Verträge und übrigen Vereinbarungen lediglich den Grund und Boden, welcher unter den zeitlich unbegrenzten, von der Japanischen Regierung oder für dieselbe abgeschlossenen Ueberlassungsverträgen besessen wird, oder befreien sie Grund und Boden *und* Gebäude jeglicher Art, welche auf diesem Grund und Boden errichtet sind oder in der Folge errichtet werden sollten, von allen Abgaben, Steuern, Lastern, Contributionen oder Bedingungen jeder Art, welche nicht ausdrücklich in den betreffenden Ueberlassungsverträgen festgesetzt sind?

III. Innerhalb von acht Monaten, vom Datum dieses Protokolls an gerechnet, soll jede Partei den einzelnen Mitgliedern des Schiedsgerichts und der Gegenpartei in je einem Exemplar eine vollständige, geschriebene oder gedruckte Darstellung des Streitfalls, ihrer Gründe und des Beweismaterials überreichen, auf welche sie sich in dem gegenwärtigen Schiedsverfahren stützt. Innerhalb von weiteren sechs Monaten haben beide Parteien in gleicher Weise in geschriebener oder gedruckter Form ihre Gegenvorstellungen nebst deren schliesslicher Begründung sowie das ergänzende Beweismaterial einzureichen; diese Gegenvorstellungen, deren Begründung und das ergänzende Beweismaterial sollen indessen lediglich eine Erwiderung auf die von der Gegenpartei eingereichte Darstellung des Streitfalls, auf dessen Begründung und auf das darauf bezügliche Beweismaterial enthalten.

IV. Jeder Partei steht das Recht zu, dem Schiedsgericht als Beweismaterial alle diejenigen Urkunden, Schriftstücke, amtlichen Correspondenzen und anderen offiziellen oder öffentlichen Erklärungen und Akten über den Streitgegenstand zu unterbreiten, deren Vorlegung sie als nothwendig erachtet. Wenn aber eine Partei in ihrer Darstellung des Streitfalls, ihrer Gegenvorstellung oder Begründung ein in ihrem ausschliesslichen Besitz befindliches Schriftstück erwähnt oder auf ein solches Bezug nimmt, ohne eine Abschrift beizufügen, so ist sie verpflichtet, der Gegenpartei auf deren Verlangen innerhalb von dreissig Tagen nach Stellung des bezüglichen Antrags eine Abschrift des betreffenden Schriftsücks auszuhändigen.

V. Jede Partei ist berechtigt, vorbehaltlich des Rechts einer Erwiderung seitens der Gegenpartei, dem Schiedsgericht innerhalb einer von ihm zu bestimmenden Frist zur geeigneten Verwerthung eine Aufzeichnung derjenigen Einwendungen vorzulegen, die sie bezüglich der von der anderen Partei eingereichten Gegenvorstellung, deren Begründung und des ergänzenden Beweismaterials erhebt, wenn sie der Ansicht ist, dass die betreffenden Schriftstücke oder einige derselben unerheblich oder unrichtig sind, oder sich nicht genau in den Grenzen einer Erwiderung auf die Darstellung des Streitfalls, deren Begründung oder auf das Beweismaterial halten.

VI. Abgesehen von den unter Nummer III und V dieses Protokolls aufgeführten, sollen keine Schriftstücke oder Mittheilungen in schriftlicher oder mündlicher Form in dem Schiedsverfahren zugelassen oder berücksichtigt werden, es sei denn, dass das Schiedsgericht von einer Partei neue oder ergänzende, in schriftlicher Form abzugebende Erläuterungen oder Aufschlüsse verlangt. Sind diese Erläuterungen oder Aufschlüsse gegeben, so soll die Gegenpartei berechtigt sein, sich hierauf innerhalb einer vom dem Schiedsgericht zu bestimmenden Frist schriftlich zu äussern.

VII. Das Gericht soll an einem später von den Parteien zu bezeichnenden Ort so bald wie thunlich zusammentreten, aber nicht eher als zwei Monate und nicht später als drei Monate nach Einreichung der Gegenvorstellung gemäss Nummer III dieses Protokolls; es soll den Streitfall unparteiisch und sorgfältig prüfen und entscheiden. Die Entscheidung des Gerichtes soll, wenn möglich, innerhalb eines Monats nach dem Zeitpunkt verkündet werden, an dem der Präsident die Verhandlung für geschlossen erklärt hat.

VIII. In dem Schiedsverfahren ist die Japanische Regierung als die eine Partei anzusehen, während die Regierungen von Deutschland, Frankreich und Grossbritannien zusammen als die andere Partei gelten.

IX. Sofern in diesem Protokoll nichts anderes vorgesehen ist, sollen in dem gegenwärtigen Schiedsverfahren die Vorschriften des Haager Abkommens zur friedlichen Erledigung internationaler Streitfälle zur Anwendung kommen.

So geschehen in Tôkiô am 28. August, 1902 (28. Tag des 8. Monats des 35. Jahres Meiji).

GEZ. GRAF VON ARCO VALLEY
GEZ. JUTARO KOMURA

Agreement for Arbitration between France and Japan, August 28, 1902[1]

Attendu qu'un désaccord s'est produit entre le Gouvernement du Japon d'une part, et les Gouvernements de France, d'Allemagne et de Grande-Bretagne d'autre part, touchant le sens réel et la portée des dispositions suivantes des Traités respectifs et autres engagements existant entre eux, c'est-à-dire:

Paragraphe 4 de l'Article XVIII du Traité de Commerce et de Navigation du 4 Avril, 1896, entre le Japon et l'Allemagne: "Sobald diese Einverleibung erfolgt" [c'est-à-dire: quand les divers quartiers étrangers qui existent au Japon auron été incorporés dans les Communes respectives du Japon], "sollen die bestehenden, zeitlich unbegrenzten Ueberlassungsverträge, unter welchen jetzt in den gedachten Niederlassungen Grundstücke besessen werden, bestätigt und hinsichtlich dieser Grundstücke sollen keine Bedingungen irgend einer anderen Art auferlegt werden, als sie in den bestehenden Ueberlassungsverträgen enthalten sind"; et §3 de la communication complémentaire de même date du Secrétaire d'Etat des Affaires Etrangères de l'Empire d'Allemagne au Ministre du Japon à Berlin: "3. dass, da das Eigenthum an den im Artikel XVIII des Vertrages erwähnten Niederlassungsgrundstücken dem Japanischen Staate verbleibt, die Besitzer oder deren Rechtsnachfolger für ihre Grundstücke ausser dem kontraktmässigen Grundzins Abgaben oder Steuern irgend welcher Art nicht zu entrichten haben werden," et l'alinéa suivant de la réponse du Ministre du Japon de même date à la précédente communication: "dass die darin unter Nummer 1 bis 4 zum Ausdruck gebrachten Voraussetzungen, welche den Erwerb dinglicher Rechte an Grundstücken, die Errichtung von Waarenhäusern, die Steuerfreiheit der Grundstücke in den Fremdenniederlassungen und die Erhaltung wohlerworbener Rechte nach Ablauf des Vertrages zum Gegenstande haben, in allen Punkten zutreffend sind";

Paragraphe 4 de l'Article XXI du Traité revisé de 4 Août, 1896,

---

[1] Official report, p. 9.

entre le Japon et la France: "Lorsque les changements ci-dessus indiqués auront été effectués" [c'est-à-dire: lorsque les divers quartiers étrangers qui existent au Japon auront été incorporés aux Communes respectives du Japon et feront dès lors partie de système municipal du Japon; et lorsque les Autorités Japonaises compétentes auront assumé toutes les obligations et tous les devoirs municipaux, et que les fonds et biens municipaux qui pourraient appartenir à ces quartiers auront été transférés aux dites autorités], "les baux à perpétuité en vertu desquels les étrangers possèdent actuellement des propriétés dans les quartiers seront confirmés, et les propriétés de cette nature ne donneront lieu à aucuns impôts, taxes, charges, contributions ou conditions quelconques autres que ceux expressément stipulés dans les baux en question";

Paragraphe 4 de l'Article XVIII du Traité revisé du 16 Juillet, 1894, entre le Japon et la Grande-Bretagne: "When such incorporation takes place" [c'est-à-dire: quand les divers quartiers étrangers que existent au Japon auront été incorporés aux Communes respectives du Japon], "existing leases in perpetuity under which property is now held in the said Settlements shall be confirmed, and no conditions whatsoever other than those contained in such existing leases shall be imposed in respect of such property";

Attendu que le litige n'est pas susceptible d'être réglé par la voie diplomatique;

Attendu que les Puissances en désaccord, co-Signataires de la Convention de La Haye pour le règlement pacifique des conflits internationaux, ont résolu de terminer ce différend, en soumettant la question à un arbitrage impartial suivant les stipulations de la dite Convention;

Les dites Puissances ont, dans le but de réaliser ces vues, autorisé les Représentants ci-dessous désignés, à savoir:

Le Gouvernement Français: M. G. Dubail, Ministre Plénipotentiaire, Chargé d'Affaires de la République Française;

Le Gouvernement Allemand: M. le Comte d'Arco Valley, Envoyé Extraordinaire et Ministre Plénipotentiaire de Sa Majesté l'Empereur d'Allemagne, Roi de Prusse;

Le Gouvernement de Grande-Bretagne: Sir Claude Maxwell Macdonald, G.C.M.G., K.C.B., Envoyé Extraordinaire et Ministre Plénipotentiaire de Sa Majesté le Roi de Grande-Bretagne;

Le Gouvernement du Japon: M. le Baron Komura Jutaro, Ministre des Affaires Etrangères de Sa Majesté l'Empereur du Japon;

à conclure le Protocole suivant:

I. Les Puissances en litige décident que le Tribunal Arbitral auquel la question sera soumise en dernier ressort sera composé de trois membres pris parmi les Membres de la Cour Permanente d'Arbitrage de La Haye et qui seront désignés de la manière suivante:

Chaque Partie, aussitôt que possible, et dans un délai qui n'excèdera pas deux mois à partir de la date de ce Protocole, devra nommer un Arbitre, et les deux Arbitres ainsi désignés choisiront ensemble un sur-Arbitre. Dans le cas où les deux Arbitres n'auront pas, dans le délai de deux mois après leur désignation, choisi un sur-Arbitre, Sa Majesté le Roi de Suède et Norvège sera prié de nommer un sur-Arbitre.

II. La question en litige sur laquelle les Parties demandent au Tribunal Arbitral de prononcer une décision définitive est la suivante:

Oui ou non, les dispositions des Traités et autres engagements ci-dessus mentionnés, exemptent-elles seulement les terrains possédés en vertu des baux perpétuels concédés par le Gouvernement Japonais ou en son nom, ou bien exemptent-elles les terrains et les bâtiments de toute nature construits ou qui pourraient être construits sur ces terrains, de tous impôts, taxes, charges, contributions ou conditions quelconques autres que ceux expressément stipulés dans les baux en question?

III. Dans le délai de huit mois après la date de ce Protocole, chaque Partie devra remettre aux différents membres du Tribunal et à l'autre Partie, les copies complètes, écrites ou imprimées, de son Mémoire contenant toutes pièces à l'appui et arguments produits par elle au présent Arbitrage. Dans un délai de six mois au plus après cette remise, une communication semblable sera faite des copies manuscrites ou imprimées, des Contre-Mémoires, pièces à l'appui et conclusions finales des deux Parties: il est bien entendu que ces répliques, documents additionnels et conclusions finales devront se limiter à répondre au Mémoire principal et aux argumentations produites précédemment.

IV. Chaque Partie aura le droit de soumettre au Tribunal Arbitral comme instruments à faire valoir, tous les documents, Mémoires, correspondances officielles, déclarations ou actes officiels ou publics se rapportant à l'objet de l'Arbitrage et qu'elle jugera nécessaire. Mais si, dans les Mémoires, Contre-Mémoires ou arguments soumis au Tribunal, l'une ou l'autre Partie s'est référée ou a fait allusion à un document ou papier en sa possession exclusive dont elle n'aura pas joint la copie, elle sera tenue, si l'autre Partie le juge convenable, de lui en donner la copie dans les trente jours qui en suivront la demande.

V. Chacune des Parties peut, si elle le juge convenable, mais sous la réserve d'un droit de réponse de la part de l'autre Partie, dans un temps qui sera fixé par le Tribunal Arbitral, présenter, à telles fins que celui-ci jugera utiles, un état de ces objections aux Contre-Mémoires, instruments additionnels, et conclusions finales de l'autre Partie, dans le cas où ces documents ou l'un d'eux n'auraient pas trait à la question, seraient erronnés ou ne se limiteraient pas à répondre strictement au Mémoire principal et à son argumentation.

VI. Ni papiers, ni communications, soit écrites, soit orales, autres que ceux prévus par les paragraphes III et V de ce Protocole ne devront être acceptés ou pris en considération dans le présent Arbitrage à moins que le Tribunal ne demande à l'une ou l'autre Partie une explication ou information supplémentaire qui devra être donnée par écrit. Dans ce cas, l'autre Partie aura le droit de présenter une réponse écrite dans un délai à fixer par le Tribunal.

VII. Le Tribunal se réunira en un lieu indiqué plus tard par les Parties, aussitôt que possible, mais ni avant deux mois, ni plus tard que trois mois à dater de la remise des Contre-Mémoires prévue au Paragraphe III de ce Protocole; il procèdera avec impartialité et soin à l'examen et au jugement du litige. Le jugement du Tribunal sera prononcé autant que possible dans le délai d'un mois après la clôture par le Président des débats de l'Arbitrage.

VIII. Dans cet Arbitrage, le Gouvernement Japonais sera considéré comme étant l'une des Parties, et les Gouvernements Français, Allemand, et de la Grande-Bretagne conjointement comme étant l'autre Partie.

IX. En tout ce qui n'est pas prévu par le présent Protocole, les stipulations de la Convention de La Haye pour le règlement pacifique des conflits internationaux seront appliquées à cet Arbitrage.

Fait à Tôkiô le 28 Août, 1902, correspondant au 28ème jour du 8ème mois de la 35ème année de Meiji.

Signé: G. DUBAIL
Signé: JUTARO KOMURA

Extract from the Treaty of Commerce and Navigation of April 4, 1896, between Germany and Japan[1]

ART. 18. Die vertragschliessenden Theile sind über Folgendes einverstanden:

Die einzelnen Fremdenniederlassungen in Japan sollen den betreffenden japanischen Gemeinden einverleibt werden und hinfort Bestandtheile der japanischen Gemeinden bilden.

Die zuständigen japanischen Behörden sollen demnach mit Bezug auf dieselben alle Verbindlichkeiten und Verpflichtungen übernehmen, welche ihnen hinsichtlich der Gemeinden obliegen, und gleichzeitig sollen die öffentlichen Gelder und Vermögensgegenstände, welche diesen Niederlassungen gehören, den genannten japanischen Behörden übergeben werden.

Sobald diese Einverleibung erfolgt, sollen die bestehenden, zeitlich unbegrenzten Ueberlassungsverträge, unter welchen jetzt in den gedachten Niederlassungen Grundstücke besessen werden, bestätigt und hinsichtlich dieser Grundstücke sollen keine Bedingungen irgend einer anderen Art auferlegt werden, als sie in den bestehenden Ueberlassungsverträgen enthalten sind.

Die Besitzrechte an diesen Niederlassungsgrundstücken können in Zukunft von ihren Besitzern frei und, ohne dass es dazu, wie bisher in gewissen Fällen, der Genehmigung der konsularischen oder japanischen Behörden bedarf, an Inländer oder Auslander veräussert werden.

Im Uebrigen gehen die nach den ursprünglichen Ueberlassungsverträgen den Konsularbehörden zustehenden Funktionen auf die japanischen Behörden uber.

---

[1] Martens, *Nouveau Recueil Général de Traités*, 2d series, vol. 23, p. 275.

Alle Ländereien, welche von de japanischen Regierung für öffentliche Zwecke der Fremdenniederlassung bisher zinsfrei hergegeben worden sind, sollen, unbeschadet der aus der Gebietshoheit sich ergebenden Rechte, frei von allen Steuern und Lasten den öffentlichen Zwecken, für welche sie ursprunglich bestimmt worden, dauernd erhalten bleiben.

ART. 19. Der gegenwärtige Vertrag erstreckt sich auch auf die mit einem der vertragschliessenden Theile gegenwärtig oder künftig zollgeeinten Gebiete.

ART. 20. Der gegenwärtige Vertrag tritt vom Tage seines vollen Inkrafttretens ab an die Stelle des Vertrages vom 20. Februar 1869, sowie derjenigen Abkommen und Uebereinkünfte, welche in Ergänzung des letzteren Vertrages abgeschlossen sind oder bestehen. Von demselben Tage ab verlieren jene früheren Vereinbarungen ihre Wirksamkeit, und demgemäss hört alsdann die bis dahin in Japan ausgeübte Gerichtsbarkeit deutscher Gerichtsbehörden auf und erreichen alle ausnahmsweisen Privilegien, Befreiungen und Immunitäten, die bis dahin die deutschen Reichsangehörigen als einen Bestandtheil oder einen Ausfluss dieser Gerichtsbarkeit genossen, ohne Weiteres ihre Endschaft. Diese Gerichtsbarkeit wird alsdann von japanischen Gerichten übernommen und ausgeübt werden.

Extract from the Treaty of Commerce and Navigation of August 4, 1896, between France and Japan[1]

XXI. Le Gouvernement de la République Française donne, en ce qui le concerne, son adhésion à l'arrangement suivant:

Les divers quartiers étrangers qui existent au Japon seront incorporés aux communes respectives du Japon et feront dès lors partie du système municipal du Japon.

Les autorités Japonaises compétentes assumeront en conséquence toutes les obligations et tous les devoirs municipaux qui résultent de ce nouvel état de choses, et les fonds et biens municipaux qui pourraient appartenir à ces quartiers seront, de plein droit, transférées aux dites autorités Japonaises.

Lorsque les changements ci-dessus indiqués auront été effectués, les baux à perpétuité, en vertu desquels les étrangers possèdent actuellement des propriétés dans les quartiers seront confirmés, et les propriétés de cette nature ne donneront lieu à aucuns impôts, taxes, charges, contributions, ou conditions quelconques autres que ceux expressément stipulés dans les baux en question. Il est entendu toutefois qu'aux autorités Consulaires dont il y est fait mention seront substituées les autorités Japonaises.

Les terrains que le Gouvernement Japonais aurait concédés exempts de rentes, vu l'usage public auquel ils étaient affectés, resteront, sous la réserve de droits de la souveraineté territoriale, affranchis d'une

---

[1]*British and Foreign State Papers.* vol. 88, p. 536.

manière permanente de tous impôts, taxes, et charges; et ils ne seront point détournés de l'usage auquel its étainet primitivement destinés.

XXII. Les dispositions du présent Traité sont applicables à l'Algérie. Il est entendu qu'elles deviendraient en outre applicables aux Colonies Françaises pour lesquelles le Gouvernement Français en réclamerait le bénéfice. Le Représentant de la République Française à Tôkiô aurait à cet effet à le notifier au Gouvernement Japonais dans un délai de deux ans à dater du jour de l'échange des ratifications du présent Traité.

XXIII. A dater de la mise en vigueur du présent Traité seront abrogés le Traité du 9 Octobre, 1858, la Convention du 25 Juin, 1866, et en général tous les arrangements conclus entre las Hautes Parties Contractantes existant antérieurement à cette date. En conséquence, la juridiction Française au Japon et les privilèges, exemptions, ou immunités dont les Français jouissaient en matière juridictionnelle seront supprimés de plein droit et sans qu'il soit besoin de notification, du jour de la mise en vigueur du présent Traité; et les Français seront dès lors soumis à la juridiction des Tribunaux Japonais,

THE MUSCAT DHOWS CASE

Award of the Tribunal, August 8, 1905[1]

Le Tribunal d'Arbitrage constitué en vertu du Compromis conclu à Londres le 13 octobre 1904, entre la France et la Grande Bretagne;

Attendu que le Gouvernement Français et celui de Sa Majesté Britannique ont jugé convenable, par la Déclaration du 10 mars 1862, "de s'engager réciproquement à respecter l'indépendance" de Sa Hautesse le Sultan de Mascate,

Attendu que des difficultés se sont élevées sur la portée de cette Déclaration relativement à la délivrance, par la République Française, à certains sujets de Sa Hautesse le Sultan de Mascate de pièces les autorisant à arborer le pavillon Français, ainsi qu'au sujet de la nature des privilèges et immunités revendiqués par les sujets de Sa Hautesse, propriétaires ou commandants de boutres ("dhows") qui sont en possession de semblables pièces ou qui sont membres de l'équipage de ces boutres et leurs familles, particulièrement en ce qui concerne le mode suivant lequel ces privilèges et ces immunités affectent le droit de juridiction de Sa Hautesse le Sultan sur ses dits sujets,

Attendu que les deux Gouvernements sont tombés d'accord par le Compromis du 13 octobre 1904 de faire décider ces difficultés par voie d'arbitrage conformément à l'article 1 de la Convention conclue par les deux Puissances le 14 octobre 1903,

Attendu qu'en exécution de ce Compromis ont été nommés Arbitres, par le Gouvernement de Sa Majesté Britannique:

Monsieur Melville W. Fuller, Chief Justice des Etats-Unis d'Amérique, et

par le Gouvernement de la République Française:

Monsieur le Jonkheer A. F. de Savornin Lohman, Docteur en droit, ancien Ministre de l'Intérieur des Pays-Bas, ancien Professeur à l'Université libre à Amsterdam, Membre de la Seconde Chambre des Etats-Généraux,

Attendu que ces Arbitres n'étant pas tombés d'accord dans le délai d'un mois à partir de leur nomination sur le choix d'un Surarbitre, ce choix étant dévolu dès lors en vertu de l'article 1 du Compromis au Roi d'Italie, Sa Majesté a nommé comme Surarbitre:

Monsieur Henri Lammasch, Docteur en droit, Professeur de droit international à l'Université à Vienne, Membre de la Chambre des Seigneurs du Parlement Autrichien,

Attendu que les Mémoires, Contre-Mémoires et Conclusions ont été dûment communiqués au Tribunal et aux Parties,

Attendu que le Tribunal a examiné avec soin ces documents, et les

---

[1] Official report, p. 61.

observations supplémentaires qui leur ont été présentées par les deux Parties ;

QUANT À LA PREMIÈRE QUESTION :

Considérant, qu'en général il appartient à tout Souverain de décider à qui il accordera le droit d'arborer son pavillon et de fixer les règles auxquelles l'octroi de ce droit sera soumis, et considérant qu'en conséquence l'octroi du pavillon Français à des sujets de Sa Hautesse le Sultan de Mascate ne constitue en soi aucune atteinte à l'indépendance du Sultan,

Considérant que néanmoins un Souverain peut être limité dans l'exercice de ce droit par des traités, et considérant que le Tribunal en vertu de l'article 48 de la Convention pour le règlement pacifique des conflits internationaux du 29 juillet 1899 et de l'article 5 du Compromis du 13 octobre 1904, "est autorisé à déterminer sa compétence en interprétant le compromis ainsi que les autres traités qui peuvent être invoqués dans la matière, et en appliquant les principes du droit international," et qu'en conséquence la question se pose sous quelles conditions les Puissances qui ont accédé à l'Acte Général de la Conférence de Bruxelles du 2 juillet 1890 concernant la suppression de la traite des esclaves africaine, spécialement à l'article 32 de cet Acte, ont le droit d'autoriser des navires indigènes à arborer leurs pavillons,

Considérant que par l'article 32 de cet Acte la faculté des Puissances Signataires d'octroyer leur pavillon à des navires indigènes a été limitée dans le but de supprimer la traite des esclaves et dans les intérêts généraux de l'humanité, sans faire aucune distinction si celui qui sollicite le droit d'arborer le pavillon appartient à un état signataire ou non, et considérant qu'en tout cas la France est liée vis à vis de la Grande Bretagne de n'octroyer son pavillon que sous les conditions prescrites par cet Acte,

Considérant que pour atteindre le but susdit les Puissances Signataires de l'Acte de Bruxelles sont convenues par l'article 32, que l'autorisation d'arborer le pavillon d'une des dites Puissances ne sera accordée à l'avenir qu'aux bâtiments indigènes qui satisferont à la fois aux trois conditions suivantes:

1°. Les armateurs ou propriétaires devront être sujets ou protégés de la Puissance dont ils demandent à porter les couleurs,

2°. Ils seront tenus d'établir qu'ils possèdent des biensfonds dans la circonscription de l'autorité à qui est adressée leur demande, ou de fournir une caution solvable pour la garantie des amendes qui pourraient être éventuellement encourues.

3°. Les dits armateurs ou propriétaires, ainsi que le capitaine du bâtiment, devront fournir la preuve qu'ils jouissent d'une bonne réputation et notamment n'avoir jamais été l'objet d'une condamnation pour faits de traite,

Considérant qu'à défaut d'une definition du terme "protégé" dans l'Acte Général de la Conférence de Bruxelles, il faut entendre ce terme dans le sens qui correspond le mieux tant aux intentions élevées de cette Conférence et de l'Acte Final qui en est résulté, qu'aux principes du droit international tels qu'ils ont été exprimés dans les conventions en vigueur à cette époque, dans la législation nationale en tant qu'elle a obtenu une reconnaissance internationale et dans la pratique du droit des gens,

Considérant que le but de l'article 32 susdit est de n'admettre à la navigation dans ces mers infestées par la traite des esclaves que ceux des navires indigènes qui sont soumis à la plus stricte surveillance des Puissances Signataires, condition dont l'accomplissement ne peut être assuré que si les propriétaires, armateurs et équipages de ces navires sont exclusivement soumis à la souveraineté et à la juridiction de l'Etat, sous le pavillon duquel ils exercent la navigation,

Considérant que depuis la restriction que le terme "protégé" a subie en vertu de la législation de la Porte Ottomane en 1863, 1865 et 1869, spécialement de la loi Ottomane du 23 sefer 1280 (août 1863), implicitement acceptée par les Puissances qui jouissent du droit des capitulations, et depuis le traité conclu entre la France et le Maroc en 1863, auquel ont accédé un grand nombre d'autres Puissances et qui a obtenu la sanction de la Convention de Madrid du 30 juillet 1880, le terme "protégé" n'embrasse par rapport aux Etats à capitulations que les catégories suivantes : 1°. les personnes sujets d'un pays qui est sous le protectorat de la Puissance dont elles réclament la protection, 2°. les individus qui correspondent aux catégories énumérées dans les traités avec le Maroc de 1863 et de 1880 et dans la loi Ottomane de 1863, 3°. les personnes, qui par un traité spécial ont été reconnues comme "protégés," telles que celles énumérées par l'article 4 de la Convention Franco-Mascataise de 1844 et 4°. les individus qui peuvent établir qu'ils ont été considérés et traités comme protégés par la Puissance en question avant l'année dans laquelle la création de nouveaux protégés fut réglée et limitée, c'est-à-dire avant l'année 1863, ces individus n'ayant pas perdu leur *status* une fois légitimement acquis,

Considérant que, quoique les Puissances n'aient renoncé *expressis verbis* à l'exercice du prétendu droit de créer des protégés en nombre illimité que par rapport à la Turquie et au Maroc, néanmoins l'exercice de ce prétendu droit a été abandonné de même par rapport aux autres Etats Orientaux, l'analogie ayant toujours été reconnue comme un moyen de compléter les dispositions écrites très défectueuses des capitulations, en tant que les circonstances sont analogues,

Considérant d'autre part que la concession *de facto* de la part de la Turquie, de transmettre le *status* de "protégés" aux descendants de personnes qui en 1863 avaient joui de la protection d'une Puissance Chrétienne, ne peut être étendue par analogie à Mascate, les circonstances étant entièrement différentes, puisque les protégés des Etats Chrétiens en Turquie sont d'une race, nationalité et religion différentes de celles de leurs maîtres Ottomans, tandis que les habitants de Sour et les autres Mascatais qui pourraient solliciter le pavillon Français, se trouvent à tous ces égards entièrement dans la même condition que les autres sujets du Sultan de Mascate,

Considérant que les dispositions de l'article 4 du Traité Franco-Mascatais de 1844 s'appliquent seulement aux personnes qui sont *bona fide* au service des Français, mais pas aux personnes qui demandent des titres de navires dans le but d'exercer quelque commerce,

Considérant que le fait d'avoir donné avant la ratification de la Convention de Bruxelles le 2 janvier 1892 des autorisations d'arborer le pavillon Français à des navires indigènes ne répondant pas aux conditions prescrites par l'article 32 de cet Acte n'était pas en contradiction avec une obligation internationale de la France,

PAR CES MOTIFS,

décide et prononce ce qui suit:

1°. avant le 2 janvier 1892 la France avait le droit d'autoriser des navires appartenant à des sujets de Sa Hautesse le Sultan de Mascate à arborer le pavillon Français, n'étant liée que par ses propres lois et règlements administratifs;

2°. les boutriers, qui avant 1892 avaient été autorisés par la France à arborer le pavillon Français, conservent cette autorisation aussi longtemps que la France la continue à celui qui l'avait obtenue;

3°. après le 2 janvier 1892 la France n'avait pas le droit d'autoriser des navires appartenant à des sujets de Sa Hautesse le Sultan de Mascate à arborer de pavillon Français, que sous condition que leurs propriétaires ou armateurs avaient ou auraient établi qu'ils ont été considérés et traités par la France comme ses "protégés" avant l'année 1863;

QUANT A LA 2ᵐᵉ QUESTION:

Considérant que la situation légale de navires portant des pavillons étrangers et des propriétaires de ces navires dans les eaux territoriales d'un Etat Oriental est déterminée par les principes généraux de juridiction, par les capitulations ou autres traités et par la pratique qui en est résultée,

Considérant que les termes du Traité d'Amitié et de Commerce entre la France et l'Iman de Mascate du 17 novembre 1844 sont, surtout en raison des expressions employées dans l'article 3 "Nul ne pourra, sous aucun prétexte, pénétrer dans les maisons, magasins et autres propriétés, possédés ou occupés par des Français ou par des personnes au service des Français, ni les visiter sans le consentement de l'occupant, à moins que ce ne soit avec l'intervention du Consul de France," assez larges pour embrasser aussi bien des navires que d'autres propriétés,

Considérant que, quoiqu'il ne saurait être nié qu'en admettant le droit de la France d'octroyer dans certaines circonstances son pavillon à des navires indigènes et de soustraire ces navires à la visite par les autorités du Sultan ou en son nom, la traite des esclaves est facilitée, parce que les marchands d'esclaves pour se soustraire à la recherche peuvent facilement abuser du pavillon Français, la possibilité d'un tel abus, qui peut être entièrement supprimé par l'accession de toutes les Puissances à l'article 42 de l'Acte de Bruxelles, ne peut exercer aucune influence sur la décision de cette affaire, qui ne doit être fondée que sur des motifs d'ordre juridique,

Considérant qu'en vertu des articles 31–41 de l'Acte de Bruxelles l'octroi du pavillon à un navire indigène est strictement limité à ce navire et à son propriétaire et que dès lors il ne peut être transmis ou transféré à quelque autre personne ni à quelque autre navire, même si celui-ci appartenait au même propriétaire,

Considérant que l'article 4 du Traité Franco-Mascatais assure aux sujets de Sa Hautesse le Sultan de Mascate "qui seront au service des Français" la même protection qu'aux Français eux-mêmes, mais considérant que les propriétaires, commandants et équipages des boutres autorisés à arborer le pavillon Français n'appartiennent pas à cette catégorie de personnes et encore moins les membres de leurs familles,

Considérant que le fait de soustraire ces personnes à la souveraineté, spécialement à la juridiction, de Sa Hautesse le Sultan de Mascate serait en contradiction avec la Déclaration du 10 mars 1862, par laquelle la France et la Grande Bretagne se sont engagées réciproquement à respecter l'indépendance de ce Prince,

Par ces Motifs,

décide et prononce ce qui suit :

1°. les boutres ("dhows") de Mascate qui ont été autorisés, ainsi qu'il a été indiqué ci-dessus, à arborer le pavillon Français, ont dans les eaux territoriales de Mascate le droit à l'inviolabilité, réglée par le Traité Franco-Mascatais du 17 novembre 1844 ;

2°. l'autorisation d'arborer le pavillon Français ne peut être transmise ou transférée à quelque autre personne ou à quelque autre boutre ("dhow"), même si celui-ci appartenait au même propriétaire ;

3°. les sujets du Sultan de Mascate, qui sont propriétaires ou commandants de boutres ("dhows") autorisés à arborer le pavillon Français ou qui sont membres des équipages de tels boutres ou qui appartiennent à leurs familles ne jouissent en conséquence de ce fait d'aucun droit d'exterritorialité, qui pourrait les exempter de la souveraineté, spécialement de la juridiction, de Sa Hautesse le Sultan de Mascate.

Fait à *La Haye,* dans l'Hôtel de la Cour permanente d'Arbitrage, le 8 août 1905.

(Signé) H. Lammasch
" Melville W. Fuller
" A. F. de Savornin Lohman

Agreement for Arbitration, October 13, 1904[1]

Attendu que le Gouvernement Français et celui de Sa Majesté Britannique ont jugé convenable, par la Déclaration du 10 mars 1862, "de s'engager réciproquement à respecter l'indépendance" de Sa Hautesse le Sultan de Mascate ;

---

[1]Official report, p. 5.

Attendu que des difficultés se sont élevées sur la portée de cette Déclaration relativement à la délivrance, par la République Française, à certains sujets de Sa Hautesse le Sultan de Mascate de piéces les autorisant à arborer le pavillon Français, ainsi qu'au sujet de la nature des privilèges et immunités revendiqués par les sujets de Sa Hautesse, propriétaires ou commandants de boutres ("dhows") qui sont en possession de semblables pièces ou qui sont membres de l'équipage de ces boutres et leurs familles, particulièrement en ce qui concerne le mode suivant lequel ces privilèges et ces immunités affectent le droit de juridiction de Sa Hautesse le Sultan sur ses dits sujets :

Les soussignés, dûment autorisés à cet effet par leurs Gouvernements respectifs, conviennent, par les présentes, que ces difficultés seront tranchées par voie d'arbitrage conformément à l'Article I de la Convention intervenue entre les deux pays, le 14 octobre dernier, et que la décision du Tribunal de La Haye sera définitive.

Il est aussi convenu par les présentes de ce qui suit :

ARTICLE I

Chacune des Hautes Parties Contractantes nommera un Arbitre, et ces deux Arbitres ensemble choisiront un Surarbitre ; si, dans le délai d'un mois à partir de leur nomination, ils ne peuvent tomber d'accord, le choix d'un Surarbitre sera confié à Sa Majesté le Roi d'Italie. Les Arbitres et le Surarbitre ne seront pas sujets ou citoyens de l'une ou l'autre des Hautes Parties Contractantes et seront choisis parmi les membres de la Cour de La Haye.

ARTICLE II

Chacune des Hautes Parties Contractantes devra, dans un délai de trois mois après la signature du présent Compromis, remettre à chaque membre du Tribunal constitué par les présentes, et à l'autre Partie, un Mémoire écrit ou imprimé exposant et motivant sa réclamation et un dossier écrit ou imprimé contenant les documents ou toutes autres pièces probantes écrites ou imprimées sur lesquelles il s'appuie.

Dans les trois mois de la remise des dits Mémoires, chacune des Hautes Parties remettra à chaque membre du Tribunal et à l'autre Partie un Contre-Mémoire écrit ou imprimé, avec les pièces à l'appui.

Dans le mois de la remise des Contre-Mémoires, chaque Partie pourra remettre à chaque Arbitre et à l'autre Partie des conclusions écrites ou imprimées, à l'appui des propositions qu'elle aurait mises en avant.

Les délais fixés par le présent Compromis pour la remise du Mémoire, du Contre-Mémoire, et des conclusions pourront être prolongés d'un commun accord par les Parties Contractantes.

ARTICLE III

Le Tribunal se réunira à La Haye, dans la quinzaine de la remise des Arguments.

Chaque Partie sera représentée par un Agent.

Le Tribunal pourra, s'il juge nécessaire de plus amples éclaircissements en ce qui regarde un point quelconque, demander, à chaque Agent, une explication orale ou par écrit ; mais, en pareil cas, l'autre Partie aura le droit de répliquer.

ARTICLE IV

La décision du Tribunal sera rendue dans les trente jours qui suivront sa réunion à La Haye ou la remise des explications qui auraient été fournies à sa demande, à moins que, à la requête du Tribunal, les Parties Contractantes ne conviennent de prolonger le délai.

ARTICLE V

Les dispositions de la Convention de La Haye, du 29 juillet 1899, s'appliqueront à tous les points non prévus par le présent Compromis.
Fait, en double exemplaire, à Londres, le 13 octobre 1904.

(L.-S.) PAUL CAMBON
(L.-S.) LANSDOWNE

Extract from the Treaty of Friendship and Commerce of November 17, 1844, between France and the Iman of Muscat[1]

III. Les Français auront la faculté d'acheter, de vendre ou de prendre à bail des terres, maisons, magasins, dans les Etats de Son Altesse le Sultan de Mascate. Nul ne pourra, sous aucun prétexte pénétrer dans les maisons, magasins et autres propriétés, possédés ou occupés par des Français ou par des personnes au service des Français, ni les visiter sans le consentement de l'occupant, à moins que ce ne soit avec l'intervention du Consul de France.

Les Français ne pourront, sous aucun prétexte, être retenus contre leur volonté dans les Etats du Sultan de Mascate.

IV. Les sujets de Son Altesse le Sultan de Mascate qui seront au service des Français jouiront de la même protection que les Français eux-mêmes ; mais, si les sujets de Son Altesse sont convaincus de quelque crime ou infraction punissable par la loi, ils seront congédiés par les Français au service desquels ils se trouverait, et livrés aux autorités locales.

Declaration of March 10, 1862, between France and Great Britain respecting the Independence of the Sultans of Muscat and Zanzibar[2]

S. M. l'Empereur des Français et S. M. la Reine du Royaume-Uni de la Grande-Bretagne et d'Irlande, prenant en considération l'importance qui s'attache au maintien de l'indépendance du Sultan de Mascate

[1] *British and Foreign State Papers*, vol. 35, p. 1011.
[2] Martens, *Nouveau Recueil Général de Traités*, 3d series, vol. 4, p. 768.

d'une part, et du Sultan de Zanzibar de l'autre, ont jugé convenable de s'engager réciproquement à respecter l'indépendance de ces deux Princes.

Les soussignés Ministre des Affairs Etrangères de S. M. l'Empereur des Français et Ambassadeur Extraordinaire de S. M. Britannique près la Cour de France, étant munis de pouvoirs à cet effet, déclarent en conséquence, par le présent acte, que leurs dites Majestés prennent réciproquement l'engagement indiqué ci-dessus.

En foi de quoi, les soussignés ont signé en double la présente déclaration et y ont apposé le cachet de leurs armes.

Fait à Paris, le 10 mars 1862.

E. Thouvenel   Cowley

Extract from the General Act of Brussels of July 2, 1890, for the Suppression of the African Slave Trade[1]

Section II. Règlement Concernant l'Usage du Pavillon et la Surveillance des Croiseurs

1. Règles Pour la Concession du Pavillon aux Bâtiments Indigènes, le Rôle d'Equipage, et le Manifeste des Passagers Noirs

XXX. Les Puissances Signataires s'engagent à exercer une surveillance rigoureuse sur les bâtiments indigènes autorisés à porter leur pavillon dans la zone indiquée à l'Article XXI, et sur les opérations commerciales effectuées par ces bâtiments.

XXXI. La qualification de bâtiment indigène s'applique aux navires qui remplissent une des deux conditions suivantes:

1. Présenter les signes extérieurs d'une construction ou d'un gréement indigène.

2. Etre montés par un équipage dont le capitaine et la majorité des matelots soient originaires d'un des pays baignés par les eaux de l'Océan Indien, de la Mer Rouge, ou du Golfe Persique.

XXXII. L'autorisation d'aborder le pavillon d'une des dites Puissances ne sera accordée à l'avenir qu'aux bâtiments indigènes qui satisferont à la fois aux trois conditions suivantes:

1. Les armateurs ou propriétaires devront être sujets ou protégés de la Puissance dont ils demandent à porter les couleurs;

2. Ils seront tenus d'établir qu'ils possèdent des biens-fonds dans la circonscription de l'autorité à qui est adressée leur demande, ou de fournir une caution solvable pour la garantie des amendes qui pourraient être éventuellement encourues;

3. Les dits armateurs ou propriétaires, ainsi que le capitaine du bâtiment, devront fournir la preuve qu'ils jouissent d'une bonne réputation et notamment n'avoir jamais été l'objet d'une condamnation pour faits de Traite.

---

[1] *British and Foreign State Papers*, vol. 82, p. 65.

XXXIII. L'autorisation accordée devra être renouvelée chaque année. Elle pourra toujours être suspendue ou retirée par les autorités de la Puissance dont le bâtiment porte les couleurs.

XXXIV. L'acte d'autorisation portera les indications nécessaires pour établir l'identité du navire. Le capitaine en sera détenteur. Le nom du bâtiment indigène et l'indication de son tonnage devront être incrustés et peints en caractères Latins à la poupe, et la ou les lettres initiales de son port d'attache, ainsi que le numéro d'enregistrement dans la série des numéros de ce port, seront imprimés en noir sur les voiles.

XXXV. Un rôle d'équipage sera délivré au capitaine du bâtiment au port de départ par l'autorité de la Puissance dont il porte le pavillon. Il sera renouvelé à chaque armement du bâtiment ou, au plus tard, au bout d'une année, et conformément aux dispositions suivantes :

1. Le rôle sera, au moment du départ, visé par l'autorité qui l'a délivré.

2. Aucun noir ne pourra être engagé comme matelot sur un bâtiment sans qu'il ait été préalablement interrogé par l'autorité de la Puissance dont ce bâtiment porte le pavillon, ou, à défaut de celle-ci, par l'autorité territoriale, à l'effet d'établir qu'il contracte un engagement libre.

3. Cette autorité tiendra la main à ce que la proportion des matelots ou mousses ne soit pas anormale par rapport au tonnage ou au gréement des bâtiments.

4. L'autorité qui aura interrogé les hommes préalablement à leur départ les inscrira sur le rôle d'équipage, où ils figureront avec le signalement sommaire de chacun d'eux en regard de son nom.

5. Afin d'empêcher plus sûrement les substitutions, les matelots pourront, en outre, être pourvus d'une marque distinctive.

XXXVI. Lorsque le capitaine du bâtiment désirera embarquer des passagers noirs, il devra en faire la déclaration à l'autorité de la Puissance dont il porte le pavillon, ou, à défaut de celle-ci, à l'autorité territoriale. Les passagers seront interrogés, et, quand il aura été constaté qu'ils s'embarquent librement, ils seront inscrits sur un manifeste spécial donnant le signalement de chacun d'eux en regard de son nom, et indiquant notamment le sexe et la taille. Les enfants noirs ne pourront être admis comme passagers qu'autant qu'ils seront accompagnés de leurs parents ou de personnes dont l'honorabilité serait notoire. Au départ le manifeste des passagers sera visé par l'autorité indiquée ci-dessus, après qu'il aura été procédé à un appel. S'il n'y a pas de passagers à bord, mention expresse en sera faite sur le rôle d'équipage.

XXXVII. A l'arrivée dans tout port de relâche ou de destination, le capitaine du bâtiment produira devant l'autorité de la Puissance dont il porte le pavillon, ou, à défaut de celle-ci, devant l'autorité territoriale, le rôle d'équipage et, s'il y a lieu, les manifestes de passagers antérieurement délivrés. L'autorité contrôlera les passagers arrivés à destination ou s'arrêtant dans un port de relâche, et fera mention de leur débarquement sur le manifeste. Au départ, la même autorité apposera de nouveau son visa au rôle et au manifeste, et fera l'appel des passagers.

XXXVIII. Sur le littoral Africain et dans les îles adjacentes, aucun passager noir ne sera embarqué à bord d'un bâtiment indigène en dehors des localités où réside une autorité relevant d'une des Puissances Signataires.

Dans toute l'étendue de la zone prévue à l'Article XXI, aucun passager noir ne pourra être débarqué d'un bâtiment indigène hors d'une localité où réside une autorité relevant d'une des Hautes Parties Contractantes et sans que cette autorité assiste au débarquement.

Les cas de force majeure qui auraient déterminé l'infraction à ces dispositions devront être examinés par l'autorité de la Puissance dont le bâtiment porte les couleurs, ou, à défaut de celle-ci, par l'autorité territoriale du port dans lequel le bâtiment inculpé fait relâche.

XXXIX. Les prescriptions des Articles XXXV, XXXVI, XXXVII, et XXXVIII ne sont pas applicables aux bateaux non pontés entièrement, ayant un maximum de 10 hommes d'équipage, et qui satisferont à l'une des deux conditions suivantes :

1. S'adonner exclusivement à la pêche dans les eaux territoriales;
2. Se livrer au petit cabotage entre les différentes ports de la même Puissance territoriale, sans s'éloigner de la côte à plus de 5 milles.

Ces différents bateaux recevront, suivant les cas, de l'autorité territoriales ou de l'autorité Consulaire, une licence spéciale, renouvelable chaque année et révocable dans les conditions prévues à l'Article XL, et dont le modèle uniforme, annexé au présent Acte Général, sera communiqué au Bureau International de Renseignements.

XL. Tout acte ou tentative de Traite, légalement constaté à la charge du capitaine, armateur, ou propriétaire d'un bâtiment autorisé à porter le pavillon d'une des Puissances Signataires, ou ayant obtenu la licence prévue à l'Article XXXIX, entraînera le retrait immédiat de cette autorisation ou de cette licence. Toutes les infractions aux prescriptions du paragraphe 2 du Chapitre III seront punies, en outre, des pénalités édictées par les Lois et Ordonnances spéciales à chacune des Puissances Contractantes.

XLI. Les Puissances Signataires s'engagent à déposer au Bureau International de Renseignements les modèles types des documents ci-après :

1. Titre autorisant le port du pavillon.
2. Rôle d'équipage.
3. Manifeste des passagers noirs.

Ces documents, dont la teneur peut varier suivant les Règlements propres à chaque pays, devront renfermer obligatoirement les renseignements suivants, libellés dans une langue Européenne :

1. En ce qui concerne l'autorisation de porter le pavillon :

(a) Le nom, le tonnage, le gréement, et les dimensions principales du bâtiment ;

(b) Le numéro d'inscription et la lettre signalétique du port d'attache ;

(c) La date de l'obtention du permis et la qualité du fonctionnaire qui l'a délivré.

2. En ce qui concerne le rôle d'équipage:
(a) Le nom du bâtiment, du capitaine, et de l'armateur ou des propriétaires;
(b) Le tonnage du bâtiment;
(c) Le numéro d'inscription et le port d'attache du navire, sa destination, ainsi que les renseignements spécifiés à l'Article XXV.
3. En ce qui concerne le manifeste des passagers noirs:
Le nom du bâtiment qui les transporte et les renseignements indiqués à l'Article XXXVI, et destinés à bien identifier les passagers.

Les Puissances Signataires prendront les mesures nécessaires pour que les autorités territoriales, ou leurs Consuls, envoient au même Bureau des copies certifiées de toute autorisation d'arborer leur pavillon, dès qu'elle aura été accordée, ainsi que l'avis du retrait dont ces autorisations auraient été l'objet.

Les dispositions du présent Article ne concernent que les papiers destinés aux bâtiments indigènes.

Supplementary Agreement of January 13, 1905, to the Agreement for Arbitration[1]

La constitution du Tribunal Arbitral institué par le Compromis signé à Londres le 13 Octobre, 1904, ayant été retardée de quelques jours par suite de circonstances indépendantes de la volonté des Hautes Parties Contractantes, le Gouvernement de Sa Majesté Britannique et le Gouvernement de la République Française ont jugé utile, d'un commun accord, d'user de la faculté qui leur est accordée dans le 4e paragraphe de l'Article II du dit Compromis de prolonger le délai fixé pour la remise du Mémoire.

Ils conviennent, en conséquence, par les présentes, de fixer au 1er Février la date à laquelle les membres du Tribunal Arbitral et les deux Gouvernements intéressés recevront communication du Mémoire ou du dossier présenté par les Parties.

Il est également entendu que les délais successifs prévus à l'Article II du Compromis pour la procédure Arbitrale courront du 1er Février au lieu du 13 Janvier, date qui résultait des termes de l'Accord signé le 13 Octobre, 1904, par M. Paul Cambon et Lord Lansdowne.

Fait à Londres, en double exemplaire, le 13 Janvier, 1905.

(L. S.) PAUL CAMBON
(L. S.) LANSDOWNE

Supplementary Agreement of May 19, 1905 to the Agreement for Arbitration[2]

La constitution du Tribunal Arbitral institué par le Compromis signé à Londres le 13 Octobre, 1904, ayant été retardée de quelques jours par suite de circonstances indépendantes de la volonté des

[1]Official report, p. 9.
[2]Ibid., p. 11.

Hautes Parties Contractantes, le Gouvernement de la République Française et le Gouvernement de Sa Majesté Britannique ont jugé utile, d'un commun accord, d'user de la faculté qui leur est accordée par le quatrième paragraphe de l'Article II dudit Compromis de prolonger le délai fixé pour la remise des Conclusions.

Ils conviennent, en conséquence, par les présentes, de laisser au Tribunal Arbitral le soin de fixer. la date à laquelle les membres dudit Tribunal et les deux Gouvernements intéressés recevront communication des Conclusions présentées par les Parties.

Cet Accord additionnel sera communiqué au Tribunal Arbitral par les soins du Bureau International de la Cour Permanente d'Arbitrage.

Fait à Londres, en double exemplaire, le 19 Mai, 1905.

(L. S.)   PAUL CAMBON
(L. S.)   LANSDOWNE

THE CASABLANCA CASE

Award of the Tribunal, May 22, 1909[1]

Considérant que, par un Protocole du 10 novembre 1908 et par un Compromis du 24 du même mois, le Gouvernement de la République française et le Gouvernement impérial allemand se sont mis d'accord pour charger un Tribunal arbitral, composé de cinq membres, de résoudre les questions de fait et de droit que soulèvent les événements qui se sont produits à Casablanca, le 25 septembre 1908, entre des agents des deux pays ;

Considérant que, en exécution de ce Compromis, les deux Gouvernements ont désigné respectivement comme Arbitres,

le Gouvernement de la République française : le très honorable Sir Edward Fry, Docteur en droit, autrefois siégeant à la Cour d'appel, Membre du Conseil privé du Roi, Membre de la Cour permanente d'Arbitrage, et M. Louis Renault, Membre de l'Institut de France, Ministre plénipotentiaire, Professeur à la Faculté de droit de Paris, Jurisconsulte du Ministère des Affaires Etrangères, Membre de la Cour permanente d'Arbitrage ;

et le Gouvernement impérial allemand : M. Guido Fusinato, Docteur en droit, ancien Ministre de l'Instruction publique, ancien Professeur de droit international à l'Université de Turin, Député au Parlement italien, Conseiller d'Etat, Membre de la Cour permanente d'Arbitrage, et M. Kriege, Docteur en droit, Conseiller actuel intime de Légation, Conseiller rapporteur et Jurisconsulte au Département des Affaires Etrangères, Membre de la Cour permanente d'Arbitrage ;

Que les Arbitres ainsi désignés chargés, de nommer un Surarbitre, ont choisi comme tel M. K. Hj. L. de Hammarskjöld, Docteur en droit, ancien Ministre de la Justice, ancien Ministre des Cultes et de l'Instruction publique, ancien Envoyé extraordinaire et Ministre plénipotentiaire à Copenhague, ancien Président de la Cour d'Appel de Jönköping, ancien Professeur à la Faculté de droit d'Upsal, Gouverneur de la Province d'Upsal, Membre de la Cour permanente d'Arbitrage ;

Considérant que, conformément aux dispositions du Compromis du 24 novembre 1908, les mémoires et contre-mémoires ont été dûment échangés entre les Parties et communiqués aux Arbitres ;

Considérant que le Tribunal, constitué comme il est dit ci-dessus, s'est réuni à La Haye le 1ᵉʳ mai 1909 ;

Que les deux Gouvernements ont respectivement désigné comme Agents,

le Gouvernement de la République française : M. André Weiss, Professeur à la Faculté de droit de Paris, Jurisconsulte adjoint du Ministère des Affaires Etrangères,

---

[1] Official report, p. 153.

et le Gouvernement impérial allemand: M. Albrecht Lentze, Docteur en droit, Conseiller intime de Légation, Conseiller rapporteur au Département des Affaires Etrangères;

Considérant que les Agents des Parties ont présenté au Tribunal les conclusions suivantes:

savoir, l'Agent du Gouvernement de la République française:

PLAISE AU TRIBUNAL,

Dire et juger que c'est à tort que le Consul et les agents du Consulat impérial allemand à Casablanca ont tenté de faire embarquer sur un navire allemand des déserteurs de la Légion étrangère française, ne ressortissant pas à la nationalité allemande;

Dire et juger que c'est à tort que le même Consul et les mêmes agents ont, dans les mêmes conditions, accordé, sur le territoire occupé par le corps de débarquement français à Casablanca, leur protection et leur assistance matérielle à trois autres légionnaires, qu'ils croyaient ou qu'ils pouvaient croire Allemands, méconnaissant ainsi les droits exclusifs de juridiction qui appartiennent à l'Etat occupant, en territoire étranger, même en pays de Capitulations, au regard des soldats de l'armée d'occupation, et des actes, quels qu'ils soient et d'où qu'ils viennent, qui sont de nature à compromettre sa sécurité;

Dire et juger qu'aucune atteinte n'a été portée, en la personne de M. Just, chancelier du Consulate impérial à Casablanca, et du soldat marocain Abd-el-Kerim ben Mansour, à l'inviolabilité consulaire, par les officiers, soldats et marins français qui ont procédé à l'arrestation des déserteurs; et qu'en repoussant les attaques et les voies de fait dirigées contre eux, lesdits officiers, soldats et marins se sont bornés à user du droit de légitime défense.

Et l'Agent du Gouvernement impérial allemand (*conclusions traduites*),

PLAISE AU TRIBUNAL,

1°. En ce qui concerne les questions de fait,

Déclarer que trois individus qui avaient antérieurement servi dans la Légion étrangère française, Walter Bens, Heinrich Heinemann et Julius Meyer, tous trois Allemands, ont, le 25 septembre 1908, au port de Casablanca, pendant qu'ils étaient accompagnés par des agents de l'Allemagne, été violemment arrachés à ces derniers et arrêtés par des agents de la France; qu'à cette occasion des agents de l'Allemagne ont été attaqués, maltraités, outragés et menacés par des agents de la France;

2°. En ce qui concerne les questions de droit,

Déclarer que les trois individus mentionnés au No. 1 étaient, au 25 septembre 1908, soumis exclusivement à la juridiction et à la protection du Consulat impérial allemand à Casablanca; que des agents de la France n'étaient pas alors autorisés à entraver l'exercice par des agents de l'Allemagne de la protection allemande sur ces trois individus et à revendiquer de leur côté sur eux un droit de juridiction;

3°. En ce qui concerne la situation des individus arrêtés le 25 septembre 1908 au sujet de laquelle il y a contestation,

Décider que le Gouvernement de la République française, aussitôt que possible, se dessaisira des trois Allemands désignés au No. 1 et les mettra à la disposition du Gouvernement allemand.

Considérant que l'Agent de la République française a, dans l'audience du 17 mai 1909, déclaré que, dans ses conclusions, il ne s'agit, soit pour les déserteurs de nationalité allemande, soit pour les autres, que des mesures prises par des agents allemands après la désertion et en vue de faire embarquer les déserteurs ;

Considérant qu'après que le Tribunal eut entendu les exposés oraux des Agents des Parties et les explications qu'ils lui ont fournies sur sa demande, les débats ont été déclarés clos dans l'audience du 17 mai 1909 ;

Considérant que, d'après le régime des Capitulations en vigueur au Maroc, l'autorité consulaire allemande exerce, en règle générale, une juridiction exclusive sur tous les ressortissants allemands qui se trouvent dans ce pays ;

Considérant que, d'autre part, un corps d'occupation exerce aussi, en règle générale, une juridiction exclusive sur toutes les personnes appartenant audit corps d'occupation ;

Que ce droit de juridiction doit être reconnu, toujours en règle générale, même dans les pays soumis au régime des Capitulations ;

Considérant que, dans le cas où des ressortissants d'une Puissance qui bénéficie au Maroc du régime des Capitulations appartiennent au corps d'occupation envoyé dans ce pays par une autre Puissance, il se produit, par la force des choses, un conflit entre les deux juridictions sus-indiquées ;

Considérant que le Gouvernement français n'a pas fait connaître la composition du corps expéditionnaire et n'a pas déclaré que le fait de l'occupation militaire modifiait la juridiction consulaire exclusive découlant du régime des Capitulations ; que, d'autre part, le Gouvernement allemand n'a pas réclamé au sujet de l'emploi au Maroc de la Légion étrangère qui, notoirement, est, pour une certaine partie, composée de ressortissants allemands ;

Considérant qu'il n'appartient pas à ce Tribunal d'émettre une opinion sur l'organisation de la Légion étrangère ou sur son emploi au Maroc ;

Considérant que le conflit de juridictions dont il a été parlé ne saurait être décidé par une règle absolue qui accorderait d'une manière générale la préférence, soit à l'une, soit à l'autre des deux juridictions concurrentes ;

Que, dans chaque cas particulier, il faut tenir compte des circonstances de fait qui sont de nature à déterminer la préférence ;

Considérant que la juridiction du corps d'occupation doit, en cas de conflit, avoir la préférence, lorsque les personnes appartenant à ce corps n'ont pas quitté le territoire placé sous la domination immédiate, durable et effective de la force armée ;

Considérant qu'à l'époque dont il s'agit, la ville fortifiée de Casablanca était militairement occupée et gardée par des forces militaires françaises qui constituaient la garnison de cette ville et se trouvaient, soit dans la ville même, soit dans les camps environnants;

Considérant que, dans ces conditions, les déserteurs de nationalité allemande, appartenant aux forces militaires de l'un de ces camps et étant dans l'enceinte de la ville, restaient soumis à la juridiction militaire exclusive;

Considérant, d'autre part, que, la question de la compétence respective en pays de Capitulations, de la juridiction consulaire et de la juridiction militaire étant très compliquée et n'ayant pas reçu de solution expresse nette et universellement reconnue, l'autorité consulaire allemande ne saurait encourir aucun blâme pour avoir accordé sa protection aux déserteurs susnommés, qui l'avaient sollicitée;

Considérant que le Consul allemand à Casablanca n'a pas accordé la protection du Consulat aux déserteurs de nationalité non allemande et que le drogman du Consulat n'a pas non plus dépassé à ce sujet les limites de sa compétence;

Considérant que le fait que le Consul a signé, sans le lire, le sauf-conduit portant *six* personnes au lieu de *trois* et omettant l'indication de la nationalité allemande, telle qu'il l'avait lui-même prescrite, ne peut lui être imputé que comme une faute non intentionnelle;

Considérant que le soldat marocain du Consulat, en contribuant à l'embarquement des déserteurs, n'a fait qu'agir d'après les ordres de ses supérieurs et que, à raison de sa situation inférieure, aucune responsabilité personnelle ne saurait peser sur lui;

Considérant que le Secrétaire du Consulat a intentionnellement cherché à faire embarquer des déserteurs de nationalité non allemande comme jouissant de la protection du Consulat;

Qu'à cette fin, il a, de propos délibéré, amené le Consul à signer le sauf-conduit mentionné ci-dessus; et que, dans la même intention, il a pris des mesures tant pour conduire au port que pour faire embarquer ces déserteurs;

Qu'en agissant ainsi, il est sorti des limites de sa compétence et a commis une violation grave et manifeste de ses devoirs;

Considérant que les déserteurs de nationalité allemande se sont trouvés au port sous la protection de fait de l'autorité consulaire allemande et que cette protection n'était pas manifestement illégale;

Considérant que cette situation de fait aurait dû, dans la mesure du possible, être respectée par l'autorité militaire française;

Considérant que les déserteurs de nationalité allemande ont été arrêtés par cette autorité malgré les protestations faites au nom du Consulat;

Considérant que l'autorité militaire aurait pu et, par conséquent, dû se borner à empêcher l'embarquement et la fuite de ces déserteurs et, avant de procéder à leur arrestation et à leur emprisonnement, à offrir de les laisser en séquestre au Consulate allemand, jusqu'à ce que la question de la juridiction compétente eût été résolue;

Que cette manière de procéder aurait aussi été de nature à maintenir le prestige de l'autorité consulaire, conformément aux intérêts communs de tous les Européens vivant au Maroc ;

Considérant que, même si l'on admet la légalité de l'arrestation, les circonstances ne justifiaient, de la part de militaires français, ni la menace faite à l'aide d'un revolver, ni la prolongation des coups portés au soldat marocain du Consulat même après que sa résistance avait été brisée ;

Considérant que, quant aux autres outrages ou voies de fait allégués de part et d'autre, l'enchaînement et la nature exacte des événements sont impossibles à établir ;

Considérant que, conformément à ce qui a été dit plus haut, les déserteurs de nationalité allemande auraient dû être remis au Consulat pour rétablir la situation de fait troublée par leur arrestation ;

Que cette restitution aurait aussi été désirable envue de maintenir le prestige consulaire ;

Mais, considérant que, dans l'état actuel des choses, ce Tribunal étant appelé à déterminer la situation définitive des déserteurs, il n'y a plus lieu d'ordonner la remise provisoire et temporaire qui aurait dû s'effectuer.

PAR CES MOTIFS,

Le Tribunal arbitral déclare et prononce ce qui suit :

C'est à tort et par une faute grave et manifeste que le Secrétaire du Consulat impérial allemand à Casablanca a tenté de faire embarquer, sur un vapeur allemand, des déserteurs de la Légion étrangère française qui n'étaient pas de nationalité allemande.

Le Consul allemand et les autres agents du Consulat ne sont pas responsables de ce chef, toutefois, en signant le sauf-conduit qui lui a été présenté, le Consul a commis une faute non intentionelle.

Le Consulat allemand n'avait pas, dans les conditions de l'espèce, le droit d'accorder sa protection aux déserteurs de nationalité allemande ; toutefois, l'erreur de droit commise sur ce point par les fonctionnaires du Consulat ne saurait leur être imputée comme une faute, soit intentionelle, soit non intentionelle.

C'est à tort que les autorités militaires françaises n'ont pas, dans la mesure du possible, respecté la protection de fait exercée sur ces déserteurs au nom du Consulat allemand.

Même abstraction faite du devoir de respecter la protection consulaire, les circonstances ne justifiaient, de la part de militaires français, ni la menace faite à l'aide d'un revolver, ni la prolongation des coups donnés au soldat marocain du Consulat.

Il n'y a pas lieu de donner suite aux autres réclamations contenues dans les conclusions des deux Parties.

Fait à La Haye, dans l'Hôtel de la Cour permanente d'Arbitrage, le 22 mai 1909.

Le Président: Hj. L. HAMMARSKJÖLD
Le Secrétaire général: MICHIELS VAN VERDUYNEN

Agreement for Arbitration, November 24, 1908[1]

Le Gouvernement de la République Française et le Gouvernement Impérial Allemand s'étant mis d'accord, le 10 novembre 1908, pour soumettre à l'arbitrage l'ensemble des questions soulevées par les événements qui se sont produits à Casablanca, le 25 septembre dernier, les soussignés, dûment autorisés à cet effet, sont convenus du compromis suivant :

Art. 1. Un Tribunal arbitral, constitué comme il est dit ci-après, est chargé de résoudre les questions de fait et de droit que soulèvent les événements qui se sont produits à Casablanca, le 25 septembre dernier, entre les agents des deux pays.

2. Le tribunal arbitral sera composé de cinq arbitres pris parmi les membres de la Cour permanente d'Arbitrage de La Haye.

Chaque Gouvernement, aussitôt que possible et dans un délai qui n'excédera pas quinze jours à partir de la date du présent compromis, choisira deux arbitres dont un seul pourra être son national. Les quatre arbitres ainsi désignés choisiront un surarbitre dans la quinzaine du jour où leur désignation leur aura été notifiée.

3. Le 1er février 1909, chaque partie remettra au Bureau de la Cour permanente dix-huit exemplaires de son Mémoire avec les copies certifiées conformes de toutes pièces et documents qu'elle compte invoquer dans la cause. Le Bureau en assurera sans retard la transmission aux arbitres et aux parties, savoir, de deux exemplaires pour chaque arbitre, de trois exemplaires pour chaque partie. Deux exemplaires resteront dans les archives du Bureau. Le 1er avril 1909, les parties déposeront dans la même forme leurs contre-Mémoires avec les pièces à l'appui de leurs conclusions finales.

4. Chaque partie devra déposer au Bureau International, au plus tard le 15 avril 1909, la somme de 3,000 florins néerlandais, à titre d'avance pour les frais du litige.

5. Le tribunal se réunira à La Haye le 1er mai 1909 et procédera immédiatement à l'examen du litige. Il aura la faculté de se transporter momentanément ou de déléguer un ou plusieurs de ses membres pour se transporter en tel lieu qu'il lui semblerait utile, en vue de procéder à des mesures d'information dans les conditions de l'article XX de la Convention du 18 octobre 1907, pour le règlement pacifique des conflits internationaux.

6. Les parties peuvent faire usage de la langue française ou de la langue allemande. Les membres de tribunal peuvent se servir, à leur choix, de la langue française ou de la langue allemande. Les décisions du Tribunal seront rédigées dans les deux langues.

7. Chaque partie sera représentée par un agent spécial avec mission de servir d'intermédiaire entre elle et le Tribunal. Ces agents donneront les éclaircissements qui leur seront demandés par le Tribunal et pourront présenter les moyens qu'ils jugeraient utiles à la défense de leur cause.

[1]*British and Foreign State Papers*, vol. 102, p. 916.

8. Pour tout ce qui n'est pas prévu par le présent compromis, les stipulations de la Convention précitée du 18 octobre 1907, dont la ratification n'a pas encore eu lieu, mais qui a été signée également par la France et l'Allemagne, seront applicables au présent arbitrage.

9. Après que le Tribunal arbitral aura résolu les questions de fait et de droit qui lui sont soumises, il réglera en conséquence la situation des individus arrêtés le 25 septembre dernier au sujet de laquelle il y a contestation.

Fait en double à Berlin, le 24 novembre 1908.

(L. S.) JULES CAMBON
(L. S.) KIDERLEN

Protocol of November 10, 1908, between France and Germany containing a Formula of Regrets for Events which occurred at Casablanca on the 25th September, 1908[1]

Les deux Gouvernements, regrettant les événements qui se sont produits à Casablanca le 25 septembre dernier et qui ont amené des agents subalternes à des violences et à de fâcheuses voies de fait, décident de soumettre l'ensemble des questions soulevées à ce sujet à l'arbitrage.

D'un commun accord, chacun des deux Gouvernements s'engage à exprimer ses regrets sur les actes de ces agents, suivant le jugement que les arbitres auront porté sur les faits et sur la question de droit.

Berlin, le 10 novembre, 1908.

JULES CAMBON
KIDERLEN

Procès-verbal of Regrets of May 29, 1909[2]

Le Gouvernement de la République et le Gouvernement Impérial étant convenus, le 10 novembre dernier, de soumettre l'ensemble des questions soulevées par les événements qui se sont produits a Casablanca, le 25 septembre précédent, à un tribunal arbitral convoqué à cet effet, et les deux Gouvernements s'étant engagés à s'exprimer mutuellement des regrets sur les actes de leurs agents, suivant le jugement que les arbitres auraient porté sur les faits et sur la question de droit; et le Tribunal arbitral ayant, à La Haye, le 22 mai, 1909, déclaré et prononcé ce qui suit:

"C'est à tort et par une faute grave et manifeste que le secrétaire du consulat Impérial allemand à Casablanca a tenté de faire embarquer sur un vapeur allemand des déserteurs de la Légion étrangère française, qui n'étaient pas de nationalité allemande. Le consul allemand et les autres agents du consulat ne sont pas responsables de ce chef; toutefois, en signant le sauf-conduit qui lui a été présenté, le consul a

[1] *British and Foreign State Papers*, vol. 102, p. 916.
[2] *Ibid.*, p. 602.

commis une faute non intentionnelle. Le consulat allemand n'avait pas, dans les conditions de l'espéce, le droit d'accorder sa protection, aux déserteurs de nationalité allemande; toutfois, l'erreur de droit commise sur ce point par les fonctionnaires du consulat ne saurait leur être imputée comme une faute, soit intentionnelle, soit non intentionnelle. C'est à tort que les autorités militaires françaises n'ont pas, dans la mesure du possible, respecté la protection de fait exercée sur ces déserteurs au nom du consulat allemand. Même abstraction faite du devoir de respecter la protection consulaire, les circonstances ne justifiaient, de la part de militaires français, ni la menace faite à l'aide d'un revolver, ni la prolongation des coups donnés au soldat marocain du consulat. Il n'y a pas lieu de donner suite aux autres réclamations contenues dans les réclamations des deux parties."

Le Gouvernement de la République française et le Gouvernement Impérial d'Allemagne déclarent, chacun en ce qui le concerne, exprimer les regrets que comportent les actes relevés à la charge de leurs agents par la décision arbitrale.

Fait à Berlin, en deux exemplaires, le 29 mai, 1909.

Von Schoen
Baron de Berckheim

THE GRISBADARNA CASE

Award of the Tribunal, October 23, 1909[1]

Considérant que, par une Convention du 14 mars 1908, la Norvège et la Suède se sont mises d'accord pour soumettre à la décision définitive d'un Tribunal arbitral, composé d'un Président qui ne sera ni sujet d'aucune des Parties contractantes ni domicilié dans l'un des deux pays, et de deux autres Membres, dont l'un sera Norvégien et l'autre Suédois, la question de la frontière maritime entre la Norvège et la Suède, en tant que cette frontière n'a pas été réglée par la Résolution Royale du 15 mars 1904;

Considérant que, en exécution de cette Convention, les deux Gouvernements ont désignée respectivement comme Président et Arbitres:

Monsieur J. A. Loeff, Docteur en droit et en sciences politiques ancien Ministre de la Justice, Membre de la Seconde Chambre des Etats-Généraux des Pays-Bas;

Monsieur F. V. N. Beichmann, Président de la Cour d'appel de Trondhjem, et

Monsieur K. Hj. L. de Hammarskjöld, Docteur en droit, ancien Ministre de la Justice, ancien Ministre des Cultes et de l'Instruction publique, ancien Envoyé extraordinaire et Ministre plénipotentiaire à Copenhague, ancien Président de la Cour d'appel de Jönköping, ancien Professeur à la Faculté de droit d'Upsal, Gouverneur de la Province d'Upsal, Membre de la Cour permanente d'Arbitrage;

Considérant que, conformément aux dispositions de la Convention, les Mémoires, Contre-Mémoires et Répliques ont été dûment échangés entre les Parties et communiqués aux Arbitres dans les délais fixés par le Président du Tribunal;

Que les deux Gouvernements ont respectivement désigné comme Agents,

le Gouvernement de la Norvège: Monsieur Kristen Johanssen, Avocat à la Cour suprème de Norvège,

et le Gouvernement de la Suède: Monsieur C. O. Montan, ancien Membre de la Cour d'appel de Svea, Juge au Tribunal mixte d'Alexandrie;

Considérant qu'il a été convenu, par l'article II de la Convention:

1°. que le Tribunal arbitral déterminera la ligne frontière dans les eaux à partir du point indiqué sous XVIII sur la carte annexée au projet des Commissaires norvégiens et suédois du 18 août 1897, dans la mer jusqu'à la limite des eaux territoriales;

---

[1] Official report, *in fine*.

2°. que les lignes limitant la zone, qui peut être l'objet du litige par suite des conclusions des Parties et dans la quelle la ligne frontière sera par conséquent établie, ne doivent pas être tracées de façon à comprendre ni des îles, ni des îlots, ni des récifs, qui ne sont pas constamment sous l'eau ;

Considérant qu'il a été également convenu, par l'article III de ladite Convention :

1°. que le Tribunal arbitral aura à décider si la ligne frontière doit être considérée, soit entièrement soit en partie, comme fixée par le Traité de délimitation de 1661 avec la carte y annexée et de quelle manière la ligne ainsi établie doit être tracée ;

2°. que, pour autant que la ligne frontière ne sera pas considérée comme fixée par ce traité et cette carte, le Tribunal aura à fixer cette ligne frontière entenant compte des circonstances de fait et des principes du droit international ;

Considérant que les Agents des Parties ont présenté au Tribunal les Conclusions suivantes (*conclusions traduites*),

l'Agent du Gouvernement Norvégien :

que la frontière entre la Norvège et la Suède, dans la zone qui forme l'objet de la décision arbitrale, soit déterminée en conformité avec la ligne indiquée sur la carte, annexée sous numero 35 au Mémoire présenté au nom du Gouvernement Norvégien ;

et l'Agent du Gouvernement Suédois :

I. en ce qui concerne la question préliminaire :

Plaise au Tribunal arbitral de déclarer, que la ligne de frontière litigieuse, quant à l'espace entre le point XVIII déjà fixé sur la carte des Commissaires de l'année 1897 et le point A sur la carte du Traité de frontière de l'année 1661, n'est établie qu'incomplètement par ledit traité et la carte du traité, en tant que la situation exacte de ce point-ci n'en ressort pas clairement, et, en ce qui regarde le reste de l'espace, s'étendant vers l'ouest à partir du même point A jusqu'à la limite territoriale, que la ligne de frontière n'a pas du tout été établie par ces documents ;

II. en ce qui concerne la question principale :

1. Plaise au Tribunal de vouloir bien, en se laissant diriger par le Traité et la carte de l'année 1661, et en tenant compte des circonstances de fait et des principes du droit des gens, déterminer la ligne de frontière maritime litigieuse entre la Suède et la Norvège à partir du point XVIII, déjà fixé, de telle façon, que d'abord la ligne de frontière soit tracée en ligne droite jusqu'à un point qui forme le point de milieu d'une ligne droite, reliant le récif le plus septentrional des Röskären, faisant partie des îles de Koster, c'est-à-dire celui indiqué sur la table 5 du Rapport de l'année 1906 comme entouré des chiffres de profondeur 9, 10 et 10, et le récif qui est le plus méridional des Svartskjär, faisant partie des îles de Tisler, et qui est muni d'une balise, point indiqué sur la même table 5 comme point XIX ;

2. Plaise au Tribunal de vouloir bien en outre, en tenant compte des circonstances de fait et des principes du droit des gens, établir le reste de la frontière litigieuse de telle façon, que

a. à partir du point fixé selon les conclusions sub 1 et désigné comme point XIX, la ligne de frontière soit tracée en ligne droite jusqu'à un point situé au milieu d'une ligne droite, reliant le récif le plus septentrional des récifs indiqués par le nom Stora Drammen, du côté suédois, et le rocher Hejeknub situé au sud-est de l'île Heja, du côté norvégien, point indiqué sur ladite table 5 comme point XX, et

b. à partir du point nommé en dernier lieu, la frontière soit tracée en ligne droite vers le vrai ouest aussi loin dans la mer que les territoires maritimes des deux Etats sont censés s'étendre;

Considérant que la ligne mentionnée dans les conclusions de l'Agent Norvégien est tracée comme suit:

du point XVIII indiqué sur la carte des Commissaires de 1897 en ligne droite jusqu'à un point XIX situé au milieu d'une ligne tirée entre le récif le plus méridional des Svartskjär—celui qui est muni d'une balise—et le récif le plus septentrional des Röskären,

de ce point XIX en ligne droite jusqu'à un point XX situé au milieu d'une ligne tirée entre le récif le plus méridional des Heiefluer (söndre Heieflu) et le récif le plus septentrional des récifs compris sous la dénomination de Stora Drammen,

de ce point XX jusqu'à un point XX*a* en suivant la perpendiculaire tirée au milieu de la ligne nommée en dernier lieu,

de ce point XX*a* jusqu'à un point XX*b* en suivant la perpendiculaire tirée au milieu d'une ligne reliant ledit récif le plus méridional des Heiefluer au récif le plus méridional des récifs compris sous la dénomination de Stora Drammen,

de ce point XX*b* jusqu'à un point XX*c* en suivant la perpendiculaire tirée au milieu d'une ligne reliant le söndre Heieflu au petit récif situé au Nord de l'îlot Klöfningen près de Mörholmen,

de ce point XX*c* jusqu'à un point XX*d* en suivant la perpendiculaire tirée au milieu d'une ligne reliant le midtre Heieflu au dit récif au Nord de l'îlot Klöfningen,

de ce point XX*d* en suivant la perpendiculaire tirée au milieu de la ligne reliant le midtre Heieflu à un petit récif situé à l'Ouest du dit Klöfningen jusqu'à un point XXI où se croisent les cercles tirés avec un rayon de 4 milles marins (à 60 au degré) autor des dits récifs,

Considérant, qu'après que le Tribunal eut visité la zone litigieuse, examiné les documents et les cartes qui lui ont été présentés, et entendu les plaidoyers et les répliques ainsi que les explications qui lui ont été fournies sur sa demande, les débats ont été déclarés clos dans la séance du 18 octobre 1909;

Considérant, en ce qui concerne l'interprétation de certaines expressions dont s'est servi la Convention et sur lesquelles les deux Parties, au cours des débats, ont émis des opinions différentes,

Que—en premier lieu—le Tribunal est d'avis, que la clause d'après laquelle il déterminera la ligne frontière dans la mer *jusqu'à la limite des eaux territoriales* n'a d'autre but que d'exclure l'éventualité d'une détermination incomplète, qui, dans l'avenir, pourrait être cause d'un nouveau litige de frontière;

que, de toute évidence, il a été absolument étranger aux intentions des Parties de fixer d'avance le point final de la frontière, de sorte que le Tribunal n'aurait qu'à déterminer la direction entre deux points donnés;

Que—en second lieu—la clause, d'après laquelle les lignes, limitant la zone, qui peut être l'objet du litige par suite des conclusions des Parties, *ne doivent pas être tracées de façon à comprendre, ni des îles, ni des îlots, ni des récifs, qui ne sont pas constamment sous l'eau* ne saurait être interprétée de manière à impliquer, que les îles, îlots et récifs susindiqués devraient être pris nécessairement comme points de départ pour la détermination de la frontière;

Considérant donc que, sous les deux rapports susmentionnés, le Tribunal conserve toute sa liberté de statuer sur la frontière dans les bornes des prétentions respectives;

Considérant, que d'après les termes de la Convention, la tâche du Tribunal consiste à déterminer la ligne frontière dans les eaux à partir du point indiqué sous XVIII, sur la carte annexée au projet des Commissaires Norvégiens et Suédois du 18 août 1897, dans ia mer, jusqu'à la limite des eaux territoriales;

Considérant, quant à la question "si la ligne frontière doit être considérée, soit entièrement soit en partie, comme fixée par le Traité de délimitation de 1661 avec la carte y annexée,"

que la réponse à cette question doit être négative, du moins en ce qui concerne la ligne frontière au delà du point A sur la carte susindiquée;

Considérant que la situation exacte, que le point A occupe sur cette carte ne peut être précisée d'une manière absolue, mais que, en tout cas, il correspond à un point situé entre le point XIX et le point XX, comme ces deux points seront fixés ci-après;

Considérant que les Parties en litige sont d'accord en ce qui concerne la ligne frontière du point indiqué sous XVIII sur la carte du 18 août 1897 jusqu'au point indiqué sous XIX dans les conclusions suédoises;

Considérant que, en ce qui concerne la ligne frontière du dit point XIX jusqu'à un point indiqué sous XX sur des cartes annexées aux mémoires, les Parties sont également d'accord, sauf la seule différence dépendant de la question de savoir si, pour déterminer le point XX, il faut prendre les Heiefluer ou bien le Heieknub comme point de départ du côté norvégien;

Considérant, à ce sujet,

que les Parties ont adopté, en pratique du moins, le principe du partage par la ligne médiane, tirée entre les îles, îlots et récifs, situés des deux côtés et n'étant pas constamment submergés, comme ayant été, à leur avis, le principe qui avait été appliqué en deçà du point A, par le Traité de 1661;

qu'une adoption de principe inspirée par de pareils motifs—abstraction faite de la question, si le principe invoqué a été réellement appliqué par ledit traité—doit avoir pour conséquence logique que, en l'appliquant de nos jours, on tienne compte en même temps des circonstances de fait ayant existé à l'époque du traité ;

Considérant que les Heiefluer sont des récifs dont, à un degré suffisant de certitude, on peut prétendre que, au temps du traité de délimitation de 1661, ils n'émergeaient pas de l'eau,

que, par conséquent, à cette époque là ils n'auraient pu servir comme point de départ pour une délimitation de frontière ;

Considérant donc que, au point de vue mentionné plus haut, le Heieknub doit être préféré aux Heiefluer ;

Considérant que le point XX étant fixé, il reste à déterminer la ligne frontière à partir de ce point XX jusqu'à la limite des eaux territoriales ;

Considérant que le point XX est situé, sans aucun doute, au delà du point A, indiqué sur la carte annexée au Traité de délimitation de 1661 ;

Considérant que la Norvège a soutenu la thèse, qui du reste n'a pas été rejetée par la Suède, que par le seul fait de la paix de Roskilde en 1658 le territoire maritime dont il s'agit a été partagé automatiquement entre Elle et la Suède ;

Considérant que le Tribunal se rallie complètement à cette opinion ;

Considérant que cette opinion est conforme aux principes fondamentaux du droit des gens, tant ancien que moderne, d'après lesquels le territoire maritime est une dépendance nécessaire d'un territoire terrestre, ce dont il suit, qu'au moment que, en 1658, le territoire terrestre nommé le Bohuslän fut cédé à la Suède, le rayon de territoire maritime formant la dépendance inséparable de ce territoire terrestre dut faire automatiquement partie de cette cession ;

Considérant que de ce raisonnement il résulte, que, pour constater quelle peut avoir été la ligne automatique de division de 1658, il faut avoir recours aux principes de droit en vigueur à cette époque ;

Considérant que la Norvège prétend, que, en deçà de la ligne Koster-Tisler le principe des documents de frontière de 1661 ayant été que la frontière devrait suivre la ligne médiane entre les îles, îlots et récifs des deux côtés, le même principe doit être appliqué quant à la frontière au delà de cette ligne ;

Considérant qu'il n'est pas établi, que la ligne de frontière déterminée par le traité et tracée sur la carte de délimitation ait été basée sur ce principe ;

qu'il y a des détails et des particularités dans la ligne suivie, qui font même surgir des doutes sérieux à ce sujet ;

que, même si l'on admettait pour la ligne de frontière déterminée par le traité, l'existence de ce principe, il ne s'ensuivrait pas que le même principe aurait du être appliqué pour la détermination de la frontière dans le territoire extérieur ;

Considérant, à ce sujet,

que le Traité de délimitation de 1661 et la carte de ce traité font *commencer* la ligne de frontière entre les îles de Koster et de Tisler ;

que, en déterminant la ligne de frontière, on est allé dans la direction de la mer vers la côte et non de la côte vers la mer ;

que l'on ne saurait donc même parler d'une continuation possible de cette ligne de frontière dans la direction vers le large;

que, par conséquent, le trait-d'union manque pour pouvoir présumer, sans preuve décisive, l'application simultanée du même principe aux territoires situés en deçà et à ceux situés au delà de la ligne Koster-Tisler;

Considérant en outre,

que ni le traité de délimitation, ni la carte y appartenant ne font mention d'îles, îlots ou récifs situés au delà de la ligne Koster-Tisler;

que donc, pour rester dans les intentions probable de ces documents, il faut faire abstraction de tels îles, îlots et récifs;

Considérant en plus,

que le territoire maritime, correspondant à une zone d'une certaine largeur, présente de nombreuses particularités qui le distinguent du territoire terrestre et des espaces maritimes plus ou moins complètement environnés de ces territoires;

Considérant au même sujet encore,

que les règles sur le territoire maritime ne sauraient servir de directives pour la détermination de la frontière entre deux pays limitrophes, d'autant moins qu'il s'agit dans l'espèce de la détermination d'une frontière, qui doit s'être automatiquement tracée en 1658, tandis que les règles invoquées datent de siècles postérieurs;

qu'il en est de même pour les règles du droit interne Norvégien, concernant la délimitation soit entre les propriétés privées, soit entre les unités administratives;

Considérant que, par tous ces motifs, on ne saurait adopter la méthode d'après laquelle la Norvège a proposé de déterminer la frontière du point XX jusqu'à la limite territoriale;

Considérant que le principe d'une ligne médiane à tirer au milieu des terres habitées ne trouve pas d'appui suffisant dans le droit des gens en vigueur au XVII° siècle;

Considérant qu'il en est de même pour le principe du thalweg ou du chenal le plus important, principe dont l'application à l'espèce ne se trouve pas non plus établie par les documents invoqués à cet effet;

Considérant que l'on est bien plus en concordance avec les idées du XVII° siècle et avec les notions de droit en vigueur à cette époque en admettant que la division automatique du territoire en question a du s'effectuer d'après la direction générale du territoire terrestre duquel le territoire maritime formait une appartenance et, en appliquant par conséquent, pour arriver à une détermination légitime et justifiée de la frontière, de nos jours ce même principe;

Considérant que, par suite, la ligne automatique de partage de 1658 doit être déterminée, ou—ce qui en d'autres termes est exactement la même chose—le partage d'aujourd'hui doit être fait en traçant une ligne perpendiculairement à la direction générale de la côte, tout en tenant compte de la nécessité d'indiquer la frontière d'une manière claire et indubitable et d'en faciliter, autant que possible, l'observation de la part des intéressés;

Considérant que, pour savoir quelle est cette direction, il faut, d'une manière égale, tenir compte de la direction de la côte située des deux côtés de la frontière ;

Considérant que la direction générale de la côte, d'après l'expertise consciencieuse du Tribunal, décline du vrai Nord d'environ 20 degrés vers l'Ouest ;

que, par conséquent, la ligne perpendiculaire doit se diriger vers l'Ouest, à environ 20 degrés au Sud ;

Considérant que les Parties sont d'accord à reconnaître le grand inconvénient qu'il y aurait à tracer la ligne frontière à travers des bancs importants ;

qu'une ligne de frontière, tracée du point XX dans la direction de l'Ouest, à 19 degrés au Sud, éviterait complètement cet inconvénient puisqu'elle passerait juste au Nord des Grisbådarna et au Sud des Skjöttegrunde et qu'elle no couperait non plus aucun autre banc important ;

que, par conséquent, la ligne frontière doit être tracée du point XX dans la direction de l'Ouest, à 19 degrés au Sud, de manière qu'elle passe au milieu des bancs Grisbådarna d'un côté et des bancs Skjöttegrunde de l'autre ;

Considérant que, bien que les Parties n'aient pas indiqué de marques d'alignement pour une ligne de frontière ainsi tracée, il y a lieu de croire que ce ne soit pas impossible d'en trouver ;

Considérant d'autre part que, le cas échéant, on pourrait avoir recours à d'autres méthodes connues de marquer la frontière ;

Considérant qu'une démarcation qui attribue les Grisbådarna à la Suède se trouve appuyée par l'ensemble de plusieurs circonstances de fait, qui ont été relevées aux cours des débats, et dont les principales sont les suivantes :

a. la circonstance que la pêche aux homards aux basfonds de Grisbådarna a été exercée depuis un temps bien plus reculé, dans une bien plus large mesure et avec un bien plus grand nombre de pêcheurs par les ressortissants de la Suède que par ceux de la Norvège ;

b. la circonstance que la Suède a affectué dans les parages de Grisbådarna, surtout dans les derniers temps, des actes multiples émanés de sa conviction que ces parages étaient suédois, comme, par exemple, le balisage, le mesurage de la mer et l'installation d'un bateau-phare, lesquels actes en trainaient des frais considérables et par lesquels elle ne croyait pas seulement exercer un droit mais bien plus encore accomplir un devoir ; tandis que la Norvège, de son propre aveu, sous ces divers rapports s'est soucié bien moins ou presque pas du tout de ces parages ;

Considérant, en ce qui concerne la circonstance de fait mentionnée sous *a,*

que, dans le droit des gens, c'est un principe bien établi, qu'il faut s'abstenir autant que possible de modifier l'état des choses existant de fait et depuis longtemps ;

que ce principe trouve une application toute particulière lorsqu'il s'agit d'intérêts privés, qui, une fois mis en souffrance, ne sauraient être sauvegardés d'une manière efficace même par des sacrifices quelconques de l'Etat, auquel appartiennent les intéressés ;

que c'est la pêche aux homards, qui, aux bancs de Grisbâdarna est de beaucoup la plus importante et que c'est surtout cette pêche qui donne aux bancs leur valeur, comme place de pêche ;

que, sans conteste, les Suédois ont été les premiers à pêcher aux homards à l'aide des engins et des embarcations nécessaires pour l'exercice de la pêche aussi loin dans la mer que sont situés les bancs en question ;

que la pêche en général a plus d'importance pour les habitantes de Koster que pour ceux de Hvaler et que, au moins jusqu'à un temps assez peu reculé, ceux-ci se sont adonnés plutôt à la navigation qu'à la pêche ;

que de ces diverses circonstances il ressort déjà avec une probabilité équivalente à un haut degré de certitude, que les Suédois ont, beaucoup plus tôt et d'une manière beaucoup plus efficace que les Norvégiens, exploité les bancs en question ;

que les dépositions et les déclarations des témoins sont en général en pleine concordance avec cette conclusion ;

que, également, la Convention d'arbitrage est en pleine concordance avec la même conclusion ;

que, d'après cette convention, il existe une certaine connexité entre la jouissance de la pêche des Grisbâdarna et l'entretien du bateau-phare et que, la Suède étant obligée d'entretenir le bateau-phare aussi longtemps que continuera l'état actuel, cela démontre que, d'après les raisons de cette clause, la jouissance principale en revient aujourd'hui à la Suède ;

Considérant, en ce qui concerne les circonstances de fait, mentionnés sous *b*,

Quant au balisage et au stationnement d'un bateau-phare,

que le stationnement d'un bateau-phare, nécessaire à la sécurité de la navigation dans les parages de Grisbâdarna, a été effectué par la Suède sans rencontrer de protestation et sur l'initiative même de la Norvège et que, également, l'établissement d'un assez grand nombre de balises y a été opéré sans soulever des protestations ;

que ce bateau-phare et ces balises sont maintenus toujours par les soins et aux frais de la Suède ;

que la Norvège n'a pris de mesures en quelque manière correspondantes qu'en y plaçant à une époque postérieure au balisage et pour un court laps de temps une bouée sonore, dont les frais d'établissement et d'entretien ne pourraient même être comparés à ceux du balisage et du bateau-phare ;

que de ce qui précède ressort que la Suède n'a pas douté de son droit aux Grisbâdarna et qu'Elle n'a pas hésité d'encourir les frais incombant au propriétaire et possesseur de ces bancs jusque même à un montant très-considérable ;

Quant aux mesurages de mer,

que la Suède a procédé la première et une trentaine d'années avant
le commencement de toute contestation, à des mesurages exacts, la-
borieux et coûteux des parages de Grisbådarna, tandis que les mesurages faits quelques années plus tard par les soins de la Norvège n'ont
même pas atteint les limites des mesurages Suédois;

Considérant donc qu'il n'est pas douteux du tout que l'attribution
des bancs de Grisbådarna à la Suède est en parfaite concordance avec
les circonstances les plus importantes de fait;

Considérant, qu'une demarcation qui attribues les Skjöttegrunde—
la partie la moins importante du territoire litigieux—à la Norvège se
trouve suffisamment appuyée, de son côté, par la circonstance de fait
sérieuse que, quoiqu'on doive conclure des divers documents et témoignages, que les pêcheurs, Suédois—comme il a été dit plus haut—
ont exercé la pêche dans les parages en litige depuis un temps plus reculé,
dans une plus large mesure et en plus grand nombre, il est certain
d'autre part que les pêcheurs Norvégiens n'y ont été jamais exclus de
la pêche;

que, en outre, il est avéré qu'aux Skjöttegrunde, les pêcheurs Norvégiens ont presque de tout temps, et d'une manière relativement bien
plus efficace qu'aux Grisbådarna, pris part à la pêche aux homards.

Par ces Motifs

Le Tribunal décide et prononce:

Que la frontière maritime entre la Norvège et la Suède, entant
qu'elle n'a pas été réglée par la Résolution royale du 15 mars 1904 est
déterminée comme suit:

du point XVIII, situé comme il est indiqué sur la carte annexée au
projet des commissaires Norvégiens et Suédois du 18 août 1897, une
ligne droite est tracée au point XIX, formant le point de milieu d'une
ligne droite tirée du récif le plus septentrional des Röskären au récif
le plus méridional des Svartskjär, celui qui est muni d'une balise,

du point XIX ainsi fixé une ligne droite est tracée au point XX,
formant le point de milieu d'une ligne droite tirée du récif le plus
septentrional du groupe des récifs Stora Drammen au récif le
Hejeknub situé au Sud-est de l'île Heja,

du point XX une ligne droite est tracée dans une direction Ouest,
19 degrés au Sud, laquelle ligne passe au milieu entre les Grisbådarna
et le Skjöttegrund Sud et se prolonge dans la même direction jusqu'à
ce qu'elle aura atteint la mer libre.

Fait à La Haye, le 23 octobre 1909 dans l'Hôtel de la Cour permanente d'arbitrage.

Le Président: J. A. Loeff
Le Secrétaire général: Michiels van Verduynen
Le Secrétaire: Röell

Agreement for Arbitration, March 14, 1908[1]

Hans Majestät Konungen af Sverige och hans Majestät Konungen af Norge, som funnit, att frågan om sjögränsen mellan Sverige och Norge, i den mån denna gräns icke redan blifvit bestämd genom kungl. beslutet den 15 mars 1904, bör hänskjutas till skiljedom, hafva för detta ändamål till Sina fullmäktige utsett:

Hans Majestät Konungen af Sverige:

Sin minister för utrikes ärendena Eric Birger Trolle;

Hans Majestät Konungen af Norge:

Sin envoyé extraordinaire och ministre plénipotentiare Paul Benjamin Vogt,

hvilka, efter att hafva meddelat hvarandra sina fullmakter, som befunnits i god och behörig form, öfverenskommit om följande bestämmelser:

ART. 1

Parterna förbinda sig att i nedan angifna omfång öfverlämna frågan om sjögränsen mellan Sverige och Norge till slutligt afgörande genom en skiljedomstol, bestående af en ordförande, som icke är någondera partens undersåte eller bosatt i någotdera landet, samt af två andra ledamöter, en svensk och en norsk.

Ordföranden utses af Hennes Majestät Drottningen af Nederländerna, de öfriga ledamöterna en af hvardera parten. Parterna förbehålla sig dock att, i händelse de därom kunna enas, genom en särskild öfverenskommelse utse

Hans Majestaet Kongen av Sverige og Hans Majestaet Kongen av Norge, som har fundet, at spörsmaalet om sjögraensen mellem Sverige och Norge i den utstraekning, hvori den ikke er blevet bestemt ved resolution av 15 mars 1904, bör henskytes til avgjörelse ved voldgift, har i dette öiemed opnaevnt som sine befuldmaegtigede:

Hans Majestaet Kongen av Sverige:

Sin minister for de utenrikske anliggender, Eric Birger Trolle;

Hans Majestaet Kongen av Norge:

Sin overordentlige utsending og befuldmaegtigede minister i Stockholm Paul Benjamin Vogt,

hvilke, efter at ha meddelt hinanden sine fuldmagter, som fandtes i god og behörig form, er kommet overens om fölgende artikler:

ART. 1

Parterne forpligter sig til i den nedenfor angivne utstraekning at undergi spörsmaalet om sjögraensen mellen Sverige og Norge endelig avgjörelse av en voldgiftsret, bestaaende av en praesidet, som ikke er nogen av parternes undersaat eller bosat i noget av de to lande, samt av to andre medlemmer, en svensk og en norsk.

Praesidenten vaelges av Hendes Majestaet Dronningen av Nederlandene, de övrige medlemmer en av hver part. Parterne forbeholder sig dog i tilfaelde av, at de derom kan enes, ved saerskilt overenskomst at utse enten

---

[1]Martens, *Nouveau Recueil Général de Traités*, 3d series, vol. 2, p. 761.

vare sig blott ordföranden eller skiljedomstolens samtliga ledamöter. Framställning till Hennes Majestät Drottningen af Nederländerna eller skiljedomare, som må blifva utsedd genom öfverenskommelse, skall göras af båda parterna gemensamt.

Art. 2

Skiljedomstolen skall, efter pröfning af parternas yrkanden samt till stöd därför anförda skäl och bevis, fastställa gränslinjen i vattnet från punkt XVIII å den vid de svenska och norska kommissariernas förslag af 18 augusti 1897 fogade karta ut i hafvet intill territorialgränsen. Det är öfverenskommet, att ytterlinjerna för det område, som genom parternas yrkande kan göras till föremål för tvist och inom hvilket gränsen alltså skall fastställas, icke må dragas så att däraf omfattas öar, holmar och skär, som ej ständigt öfversköljas af vattnet.

Art. 3

Skiljedomstolen äger att afgöra, huruvida gränslinjen bör anses vara, helt eller till viss sträckning, bestämd genom gränstraktaten af 1661 med därtill hörande karta och huru den sålunda bestämda gränslinjen bör uppdragas, samt att, för så vidt gränslinjen anses ej vara genom ifrågavarande traktat och karta bestämd, fastställa densamma med afseende på faktiska förhållanden och folkrättsliga principer.

Art. 4

Intill utgången af tredje kalenderåret efter det, hvarunder skiljedomstolens slutliga beslut

alene praesidenten eller voldgiftsrettens samtlige medlemmer. Henvendelse till Hendes Majaestaet Dronningen av Nederlandene eller til voldgiftsdommer, som maate bli utseet gjennem overenskomst, skal rettes av begge parter i faellesskap.

Art. 2

Voldgiftsretten skal efter ad ha prövet parternes paastande og de til stötte derfor anförte grunde og bevisligheter fastsaette graensellinjen i vandet fra punkt XVIII paa det kart, som er bilagt de svenske og norske kommissaerers forslag av 18 august 1897, ut i havet indtil territorialgraensen. Det er overenskommet, at yderlinjerne for det omraade, som ved parternes paastande kan gjöres til gjenstand for tvist, og indenfor hvilket graensen altsaa skal fastsaettes, ikke maa drages saaledes, at deri indbefattes öer, holmer og skjaer, som ikke stadig overskylles av vandet.

Art. 3

Voldgiftsretten har at avgjöre, hvorvidt graenselinjen bör ansees for at vaere helt eller paa en vis straekning fastslaaet ved graensetraktaten av 1661 med dertil hörende kart, og hvorledes den saaledes bestemte graenselinje bör optraekkes, samt forsaavidt graenselinjen ikke ansees at vaere bestemt ved omhandlede traktat og kart, at fastsaette samme under hensyn til faktiske forhold og folkeretslige principer.

Art. 4

Indtil utgangen av det tredje kalenderaar efter det, i hvilket voldgiftsrettens endelige beslut-

meddelas, må oberoende af den gränslinje, som genom berörda beslut fastställes, fiske inom det område, som enligt art. 2 kan vara föremål för tvist, idkas af hvartdera rikets undersåtar i samma omfattning som under femårsperioden 1901–05. Vid bedömande af fiskets omfattning tages hänsyn till de fiskandes antal, fiskets art och fångstsättet.

ART. 5

Det är öfverenskommet, att det rike, på hvars sida om den blifvande gränslinjen fiskegrundet Grisebådarne är beläget, icke gentemot det andra riket äger något anspråk på deltagande i kostnaden för fyrskepp eller liknande anordningar på eller i närheten af nämnda grund.

Sverige förbinder sig att bibehålla det nuvarande, utanför territorialgränsen utlagda fyrskeppet intill utgången af den i art. 4 nämnda tid.

ART. 6

Skiljedomstolens ordförande utsätter tid och ort för domstolens första sammanträde och kallar till detta sammanträde de öfriga ledamöterna.

Tid och ort för ytterligare sammanträden bestämmas af skiljedomstolen.

ART. 7

Det officiella språk, som af skiljedomstolen användes, skall vara engelska, franska eller tyska, enligt bestämmande, som träffas af ordföranden efter samråd med de öfriga ledamöterna.

Parterna må dessutom i inlagor,

---

ning meddeles, skal uten hensyn til den graenselinje, som gjennem naevnte beslutning fastaettes, fiske kunne drives av hvert rikes undersaatter indenfor det omraade, som efter art. II kan vaere gjenstand for tvist, i samme utstraekning som under femaarsperioden 1901–1905. Ved bedömmelsen av fiskets utstraekning tages hensyn til de fiskendes antal, fiskets art og fangstmaaten.

ART. 5

Det er overenskommet, at det rike, paa hvis side av den blivende g r a e n s e l i n j e fiskegrunderne "Grisebaaerne" er beliggende, ikke overfor det andet rike har krav paa deltagelse i omkostninger til fyrskib eller lignende foranstaltninger paa eller i naerheten av naevnte grunder.

Sverige forpligter sig til at bibeholde det nuvaerende utenfor territorialgraensen anlagte fyrskib indtil utgangen av den i art. IV naevnte overgangstid.

ART. 6

Voldgiftsrettens praesident bestemmer tid og sted for rettens förste sammentraede og varsler de övrige medlemmer om dette sammentraede.

Tid og sted for videre sammentraede bestemmes av voldgiftsretten.

ART. 7

Det officielle sprog, som af voldgiftsretten blir at anvende, skal vaere engelsk, fransk eller tysk overensstemmende med beslutning, som fattes av praesidenten efter samraad med de övrige medlemmer.

Parterne kan desuten i indlaeg,

beviscmedel och anföranden begagna någotdera landets språk, skiljedomstolen obetaget att låta verkställa öfversättning.

ART. 8

I afseende å förfarandet och omkostnaderna skola i tillämpliga delar gälla de bestämmelser, som innefattas i art. 62–85 af den på andra fredskonferensen i Haag 1907 antagna reviderade konvention för afgörandet på fredlig väg af internationella tvister.

Inlagor, repliker och bevismedel, som afses i art. 63 mom. 2 af nämnda konvention, skola delgifvas inom tider, som af skiljedomstolens ordförande bestämmas, och sist före den 1 mars 1909. Härigenom verkas ej rubbning i föreskrifterna om förfarandets andra afdelning, särskildt icke i bestämmelserna i art. 68–72 och 74 af samma konvention.

Skiljedomstolen äger, när den för sakens upplysning finner nödigt, anordna förhör, i båda parternas närvaro, med vittnen eller sakkunniga samt föreskrifva verkställandet af gemensamma hydrografiska undersökningar beträffande det tvistiga området.

ART. 9

Denna konvention skall ratificeras och ratifikationerna utväxlas i Stockholm snarast möjligt.

Till bekräftelse häraf hafva vederbörande fullmäktige undertecknat denna konvention och försett den med sina sigill.

Utfärdad i två exemplar på svenska och norska i Stockholm den 14 mars 1908.

(L. S.) Eric Trolle

bevismidler og anförsler benytte hvert av de to landes sprog, idet det er voldgiftsretten forbeholdt at foranstalte oversaettelse.

ART. 8

Med hensyn til proceduren og omkostningerne kommer til anvendelse, forsaavidt de kan tillempes, de bestemmelser, som indeholdes i artiklerne 62 till 85 i den paa den anden fredskonference i Haag i 1907 vedtagne reviderede konvention om fredelig avgjörelse av internationale stridigheter.

Indlaeg, repliker og bevismidler, hvortil sigtes i art. 63, 2 avsnit, i naevnte konvention, skal meddeles inden de tidsfrister, som av voldgiftsrettens praesident bestemmes, og senest inden 1 mars 1909. Herved sker ingen aendring i reglerne for procedurens anden avdeling, specielt ikke i bestemmelserne i art. 68–72 og 74 i samme konvention.

Voldgiftsretten har adgang til, naar den for sakens oplysning finder det nödvendigt, at foranstalte avhörelse i begge parters naervaer av vidner og sakkyndige samt til at beslutte iverksaettelse av faelles hydrografiske undersökelser vedrörende det omtvistede omraade.

ART. 9

Denne konvention skal ratificeres og ratifikationerne utvexles i Stockholm snarest mulig.

Til bekraeftelse herav har de respektive befuldmaegtigede undertegnet denne konvention og forsynet den med sine segl.

Udfaerdiget i to exemplarer paa svensk og norsk in Stockholm den 14 mars 1908.

(L. S.) Benjamin Vogt

Royal Resolution of March 26, 1904, with accompanying Protocol of March 15, 1904, concerning the Maritime Boundary between Norway and Sweden[1]

Under åberopande af bilagda protokoll i sammansatt norskt och svenskt statsråd den 15 mars 1904 äfvensom utdrag af statsrådsprotokollet öfver civilärenden för denna dag vill Kungl. Maj:t härmed föreslå Riksdagen medgifva, att frågan om sträckningen af sjögränsen emellan Sverige och Norge från den i förenämnda protokoll omförmälda punkt XVIII ut i hafvet, så långt territorialgränsen går, må hänskjutas till afgörande af en särskild skiljedomstol, i öfverensstämmelse med hvad i protokollen är anfördt.

De till ärendet hörande handlingar skola Riksdagens vederbörande utskott tillhandahållas; och Kungl. Maj:t förblifver Riksdagen med all kungl. nåd och ynnest städse välbevågen.

Under Hans Maj:ts, Min Allernådigste Konungs och Herres frånvaro:

GUSTAF

HJALMAR WESTRING

PROTOKOLL, HÅLLET I SAMMANSATT NORSKT OCH SVENSKT STATSRÅD INFÖR HANS KUNGL. HÖGHET KRONPRINSEN-REGENTEN Å KRISTIANIA SLOTT DEN 15 MARS 1904

Närvarande: Hans excellens herr statsministern Hagerup, Hans excellens herr statsministern Ibsen, Hans excellens herr statsministern Boström, Hans excellens herr ministern för utrikes ärendena Lagerheim, Statsråden: Kildal, Strugstad, Hauge, Schöning, Vogt, Mathiesen och Svenska statsrådet Westring.

Chefen för handels- och industridepartementet, statsrådet Schöning föredrog i underdånighet följande:

Departementet tillåter sig att inkomma med underdånigt betänkande angående åtgärder till närmare bestämmelse af riksgränsen i vattnet mellan Sverige och Norge.

Sjögränsen mellan de tvänne länderna, som löper från det inre af Idefjorden och ut till hafvet, är fastställd genom en gränsreglering af den 26 oktober 1661, ʹföretagen i öfverensstämmelse med fredstraktaterna i Roskilde af den 26 februari–9 mars 1658 och i Köpenhamn af den 27 maj–6 juni 1660.

Det har under tidernas lopp härskat osäkerhet om denna gränslinje beträffande flera punkter, i det att den icke någon gång under den långa tiʹsperioden mellan 1661 och 1897 har gjorts till föremål för gemensam besiktning och undersökning.

År 1897 vidtogo norska inredepartementet och svenska civildepartementet åtgärd för att söka få gränsens rätta sträckning klargjord, och under augusti månad nämnda år sammanträdde

[1] Sweden. *Royal Resolution No. 70, 1904.*

därefter två norska och två svenska kommissarier för att, efter genomgående af handlingar och undersökningar på platsen o. s. v., afgifva förslag till bestämmande och angifvande på kartorna af gränslinjen mellan Norge och Sverige från det inre af Idefjorden och ut till hafvet.

De norska kommissarierna voro expeditionssekreteraren Hroar Olsen och kommendören A. Rieck; de svenska kommissarierna voro kommendören E. Oldberg och assessoren H. Westring.

Kommissarierna framlade den 18 augusti 1897 som resultat af sina förhandlingar och undersökningar "kungl. svenska och norska kommissionens förslag till och beskrifning af sjögränsen mellan Norge och Sverige från det inre af Idefjorden ut till hafvet."

Det framgår af denna handling, som är undertecknad af samtliga fyra kommissarierna, att enighet rådde mellan dessa om gränslinjen från det inre af Idefjorden till en punkt mellan Jylte kummel (norsk) och en holme nordväst om Norra Hellsö (svensk)—hvilken punkt är betecknad som XVIII på en förslaget bilagd karta—så att Helleholmen hänföres till Sverige, Knivsöarna till Norge.

Med hänsyn till granslinjens sträckning från nämnda punkt XVIII och ut till hafvet uppnåddes däremot icke enighet inom kommissionen. De norska och de svenska medlemmarna framställde för denna del hvar sitt särskilda förslag, i enlighet hvarmed Grisbådarna tillika med några norr om Koster liggande skär och grund skulle tillfalla respektive Norge eller Sverige.

Kommissariernas förslag tillika med två därtill hörande kartor biläggas.

Departementet är af den åsikt, att den af de norska och de svenska kommissarierna gemensamt föreslagna linjen från det inre af Idefjorden till punkt XVIII på de förslaget medföljande kartor bör anses som den riktiga gränslinjen. I dett att med hänsyn till den närmare beskrifningen af denna linje hänvisas till kommissariernas förslag, tillåter departementet sig att hemställa, att linjen af Eders Maj :t godkännes såsom den rätta gränsen mellan rikena.

Så framt Eders Maj :t behagade fatta beslut i öfverensstämmelse melse härmed, förutsätter departementet, att därefter kungl. kungörelser angående den godkända gränslinjen utfärdas i hvartdera rikets särskilda statsråd.

Det torde vidare böra framhållas, att det är af betydelse, att snarast möjligt ett utmärkande af den här omhandlade delen af sjögränsen må äga rum. Den ändamålsenligaste ordningen synes vara att en kommissarie för hvart rike utses att företaga detta utmärkande, och departementet tillstyrker därför Eders Maj :t att bifalla detta, i det att departementet utgår ifrån att i så fall i hvartdera rikets särskilda statsråd utnämnas, respektive en norsk och en svensk kommissarie.

Som ofvan anförts, uppnådde de norska och de svenska kommissarierna icke enighet med afseende å frågan om gränsens rätta sträckning från omförmälda punkt XVIII ut till hafvet.

Här nedan lämnas en närmare beskrifning å den omtvistade gränslinjen, sådan som den från norsk och från svensk sida är afsedd att böra gå.

DE NORSKA KOMMISSARIERNAS UPPFATTNING

Från den som punkt XVIII betecknade punkten mellan Jylte kummel och en holme nordväst om Norra Hellsö bör gränsen dragas i rät linje ut i öppna hafvet genom midtpunkten af en rät linje, dragen från sydspetsen af den sydligaste norska Tislarön, Klöveren, till nordspetsen af norra Kosterö (svensk), så att gränslinjen går öfver Båtshakegrundet och att alla norr om denna gränslinje liggande holmar, skär och grund, däribland Grisbådarna, blifva norska.

Linjen är på kommissariernas karta betecknad med ful färg, och den omnämnda punkten mellan Klöveren och norra Kosterö betecknad som punkt XIX.

DE SVENSKA KOMMISSARIERNAS UPPFATTNING

Från punkt XVIII bör gränsen dragas i rät linje ut till öppna hafvet genom en punkt omkring 300 meter norr om Rödskärs Nordgrund och därefter ungefär midt mellan Grisbådarna och Sköttegrunden så, att alla söder om denna linje liggande holmar, skär och grund, däribland Grisbådarna, blifva svenska.

Linjen är på kommissariernas karta betecknad med gul färg, och den nämnda punkten norr om Rödskars Nordgrund betecknad som punkt XIX.

Detta departement tillåter sig underdånigst att föreslå, att frågan om den omtvistade gränslinjen hänskjutes till afgörande genom skiljedom af en särskild domstol, sedan samtycke härtill gifvits af bägge rikenas representationer, och att man härvid förfar på följande sätt:

I hvartdera rikets särskilda statsråd utses två skiljemän.

Skiljemännen välja gemensamt på förhand en femte skiljeman, som tillika fungerar som domstolens ordförande. Vid lika röstetal anförtros valet af femte skiljeman till det främmande statsöfverhufvud, som Hans Maj:t Konungen därom anmodar.

Reglerna för domstolens arbetsordning och för förhandlingarna afvensom för dess säte bestämmas af domstolen själf.

Den i behörig ordning afkunnade skiljedomen angående den omtvistade gränslinjens rätta sträckning skall vara slutligt bindande för bägge parterna.

Hvartdera riket bestrider de omkostnader för skiljedomen, som angå det allena, hvaremot de gemensamma utgifterna såsom till den femte skiljemannen o. s. v. fördelas med hälften på hvartdera riket.

I öfverensstämmelse med ofvanstående tillåter sig departementet underdånigst hemställa:

att Eders Maj:t behagade i nader bestämma:

1°.) att den af de norska och de svenska kommissarierna år 1897 gemensamt föreslagna gränslinjen mellan Norge och Sverige från det inre af Idefjorden till punkt XVIII på två, kommissariernas förslag bifogade kartor godkännes;

2°.) att utmärkande af denna gränslinje skall företagas af därtill utsedda kommissarier, en från hvartdera riket;

3°.) att frågan om gränslinjen mellan Norge och Sverige från ofvannämnda punkt XVIII ut i hafvet, så långt territorialgränsen går, hänskjutes till afgörande af en särskild skiljedomstol, i öfverensstämmelse med hvad här ofvan anförts, för såvidt de två rikenas representationer därtill gifva sitt samtycke.

De svenska ledamöterna af statsrådet instämde i hvad föredraganden hemställt beträffande godkännande af den utaf de svenska och de norska kommissarierna föreslagna gränslinjen från det inre af Idefjorden till den nämnda punkten XVIII samt denna gränslinjes utmärkande.

Hvad angick gränsens sträckning från punkten XVIII ut i hafvet intill territorialgränsen, anmälde dessa ledamöter, att uti flera i ärendet inkomma utlåtanden framställts förslag till gränslinjens bestämmande sålunda, att denna linje delvis komme att dragas ännu något nordligare än de svenska kommissarierna föreslagit. Under uttalande, med hänsyn härtill, af den uppfattning att förslaget om öfverlämnande till en särskild skiljedomstol att afgöra frågan om gränsens sträckning i denna del innebure, att parterna å ömse sidor skulle äga att, utan att vara bundna enhvar af sina kommissariers förslag, inför domstolen framställa de påståenden i nämnda hänseende, hvartill de kunde finna sig befogade, biträdde dessa ledamöter föredragandems förslag jämväl i denna del.

De norska medlemmarna af statsrådet hade intet att anmärka mot ofvanstående anförande, som öfverensstämde med hvad som också från norsk sida hade förutsatts.

I enlighet med hvad statsrådets ledamöter sålunda tillstyrkt, behagade Hans Kungl. Höghet Kronprinsen-Regenten bifalla det af chefen för norska handels och industridepartementet framställda förslaget.

THE ORINOCO STEAMSHIP COMPANY CASE

Award of the Tribunal, October 25, 1910[1]

Par un Compromis signé à Caracas le 13 février 1909, les Etats-Unis d'Amérique et du Vénézuela se sont mis d'accord pour soumettre à un Tribunal arbitral, composé de trois Arbitres choisis parmi les Membres de la Cour permanente d'Arbitrage, une réclamation des Etats-Unis d'Amérique envers les Etats-Unis du Vénézuela ;

Ce compromis porte :

"Le Tribunal arbitral décidera d'abord si la Sentence du Surarbitre Barge en cette affaire, en vue de toutes les circonstances et d'après les principes de droit international, n'est pas entachée de nullité et si elle doit être considérée comme concluante au point d'exclure un nouvel examen du cas sur le fond. Si le Tribunal arbitral décide que la dite Sentence doit être considérée comme définitive, l'affaire sera considérée par les Etats-Unis d'Amérique comme terminée ; mais si, par contre, le Tribunal arbitral décide que la dite Sentence du Surarbitre Barge ne doit pas être considérée comme définitive, le dit Tribunal arbitral devra alors entendre, examiner et résoudre l'affaire et rendre sa décision sur le fond ;"

En exécution du dit Compromis, les deux Gouvernements ont respectivement nommé Arbitres les Membres suivants de la Cour permanente d'Arbitrage :

Son Excellence Monsieur Gonzalo de Quesada, Envoyé extraordinaire et Ministre plénipotentiaire de Cuba à Berlin, etc. ;

Son Excellence Monsieur A. Beernaert, Ministre d'Etat, Membre de la Chambre des Représentants Belge, etc. ;

Et en vertu du dit Compromis, les Arbitres ainsi désignés ont nommé Surarbitre :

Monsieur H. Lammasch, Professeur à l'Université de Vienne, Membre de la Chambre des Seigneurs du Parlement Autrichien, etc. ;

Les Mémoires, Contre-Mémoires et Conclusions ont été dûment soumis aux Arbitres et communiqués aux Parties ;

Les Parties ont plaidé et répliqué ; l'une et l'autre ont plaidé le fond en même temps que la question préalable et les débats ont été déclarés clos le 19 octobre 1910 ;

Sur quoi, le Tribunal après en avoir mûrement délibéré, rend la Sentence suivante :

Considérant qu'aux termes d'un Compromis en date du 17 février 1903 une Commission Mixte a été chargée de décider toutes les réclamations exercées (owned—poseidas) par des citoyens des Etats-

---

[1]Official report, p. 54.

Unis d'Amérique à l'encontre des Etats-Unis du Vénézuela, qui n'auraient point été réglées par un accord diplomatique ou par un arbitrage entre les deux Gouvernements et qui seraient présentées par les Etats-Unis d'Amérique ; un Surarbitre, à désigner par Sa Majesté la Reine des Pays-Bas, devait éventuellement trancher toute question sur laquelle les Commissaires seraient en désaccord par une décision définitive (final and conclusive—definitiva y concluyente) ;

Considérant que le Surarbitre ainsi désigné, M. Barge, a statué sous la date du 22 février 1904, sur les dites réclamations ;

Considérant qu'il est assurément de l'intérêt de la paix et du développement de l'institution de l'arbitrage international si essentiel pour le bien-être des nations, qu'en principe semblable décision soit acceptée, respectée et exécutée par les Parties sans aucune réserve, ainsi qu'il est prescrit par l'article 81 de la Convention pour le règlement pacifique des conflits internationaux du 18 octobre 1907 que d'ailleurs, aucune juridiction n'est instituée pour reformer de semblables décisions ;

Mais considérant que dans l'espèce, la sentence ayant été arguée de nullité, il est advenu entre les Parties, sous la date du 13 février 1909, un nouveau Compromis, d'après lequel, sans tenir compte du caractère définitif de la première sentence, ce Tribunal est appelé à décider, si la sentence du Surarbitre Barge, en vertu de toutes les circonstances et d'après les principes du droit international, n'est pas entachée de nullité et si elle doit être considérée comme concluante au point d'exclure un nouvel examen au fond ;

Considérant que par le Compromis du 13 février 1909, les deux Parties admettent au moins implicitement, comme vices entrainant la nullité d'une sentence arbitrale, l'excès de pouvoir et l'erreur essentielle dans le jugement (excessive exercise of jurisdiction and essential error in the judgment—exceso de poder y error esencial en el fallo) ;

Considérant que la Partie demanderesse allègue l'excès de pouvoir et de nombreuses erreurs de droit et de fait équivalent à l'erreur essentielle ;

Considérant que, d'après les principes de l'équité d'accord avec le droit, lorsque une sentence arbitrale comporte divers chefs indépendants de demande et partant diverses décisions, la nullité éventuelle de l'une est sans influence quant aux autres et cela surtout lorsque, comme dans l'espèce l'intégrité et la bonne foi de l'arbitre ne sont pas en question ; qu'il y a donc lieu de statuer séparément sur chacun des points en litige ;

I. QUANT AUX 1,209,701.04 DOLLARS :

Considérant que ce Tribunal est appelé en premier lieu à décider si la sentence du Surarbitre est entachée de nullité et si elle doit être considérée comme concluante ; que dans le cas seulement où la sentence du Surarbitre serait déclarée nulle, le Tribunal aurait à statuer au fond ;

Considérant qu'il est allégué que le Surarbitre se serait écarté des termes du Compromis en relatant inexactement le contrat Grell et la prétention à laquelle celui-ci servait de base, et que par suite il serait tombé dans une erreur essentielle, mais que la sentence reproduit textuellement le dit contrat et dans son entière teneur; qu'il est d'autant moins admissible que le Surarbitre en aurait mal compris le texte et aurait excédé sa compétence et décidé sur une réclamation qui ne lui était pas soumise, en méconnaissant la relation de la concession en question à la navigation extérieure, alors qu'il a décidé in terminis, que le permis de naviguer par ces canaux (Marcareo et Pedernales) était seulement ajouté au permis de toucher à Trinidad ("when the permission to navigate these channels was only annexed to the permission to call at Trinidad") ;

Considérant que l'appréciation des faits de la cause et l'interprétation des documents était de la compétence du Surarbitre et que ses décisions en tant qu'elles sont fondées sur pareille interprétation ne sont pas sujettes à être revisées par ce Tribunal, qui n'a pas la mission de dire, s'il a été bien ou mal jugé, mais si le jugement doit être annulé; que si une sentence arbitrale pouvait être querellée du chef d'appréciation erronée, l'appel et la revision, que les Conventions de La Haye de 1899 et 1907 ont eu pour but d'écarter, seraient de règle générale ;

Considérant que le point de vue sous lequel le Surarbitre a envisagé la demande des $513,000—plus tard réduite dans les conclusions des Etats-Unis d'Amérique à $335,000 et partie de la prédite somme de $1,209,701.04—est la conséquence de son interprétation du contrat du 10 mai 1900 et de la relation de ce contrat au décret du même jour ;

Considérant que la circonstance que le Surarbitre, ne se contentant pas d'avoir fondé sa sentence sur son interprétation des contrats, motif qui en lui-même doit être considéré comme suffisant, a invoqué subsidiairement d'autres raisons d'un caractère plutôt technique, ne peut pas vicier sa décision ;

II. Quant aux 19,200 Dollars (100,000 Bolívares) :

Considérant que le Compromis du 17 février 1903 n'investissait pas les Arbitres d'un pouvoir discrétionnaire, mais les obligeait de rendre leur sentence sur la base de l'équité absolue sans tenir compte d'objections de nature technique ou de dispositions de la législation locale (con arreglo absoluto á la equidad, sin reparar en objeciones técnicas, ni en las disposiciones de la legislación local—upon a basis of absolute equity, without regard to objections of a technical nature, or of the provisions of local legislation) ;

Considérant que l'excès de pouvoir peut consister non seulement à décider une question non soumise aux Arbitres, mais aussi à méconnaître les dispositions impératives du Compromis quant à la voie d'après laquelle ils doivent arrêter leurs décisions, notamment en ce qui concerne la loi ou les principes de droit à appliquer ;

Considérant que le rejet de la demande des 19,200 dollars n'est motivé que 1°. par l'absence de tout appel à la Justice Vénézuélienne et 2°. par le défaut de notification préalable de la cession au débiteur, "la circonstance qu'on pourrait se demander si le jour où cette réclamation fut enregistrée, la dette était exigible" ne pouvant évidemment servir de justification au dit rejet;

Considérant qu'il résulte des Compromis de 1903 et de 1909—base du présent arbitrage—que les Etats-Unis du Vénézuela avaient renoncé conventionellement à faire valoir les dispositions de l'article 14 du contrat Grell et de l'article 4 du contrat du 10 mai 1900; qu'à la date des dits Compromis il était en effet constant qu'aucun litige entre ces Parties n'avait été déféré aux Tribunaux Vénézuéliens et que le maintien de la juridiction Vénézuélienne quant à ces réclamations eût été incompatible et inconciliable avec l'arbitrage institué;

Considérant qu'il ne s'agissait pas de la cession d'une concession, mais de la cession d'une créance, que le défaut de notification préalable de la cession d'une créance n'est que l'inobservation d'une prescription de la législation locale et bien que pareille prescription se trouve aussi dans d'autres législations, elle ne peut être considérée comme exigée par l'équité absolue, au moins lorsqu'en fait, le débiteur a eu connaissance de la cession et qu'il n'a pas plus payé sa dette au cédant qu'au cessionnaire;

III. QUANT AUX 147,638.79 DOLLARS:

Considérant qu'en ce qui concerne les 1,053 dollars pour transport de passagers et marchandises en 1900 et les 25,845.20 dollars pour loyer des bateaux à vapeur Delta, Socorro, Masparro, Guanare, Heroe de juillet 1900 à avril 1902, la sentence du Surarbitre ne se fonde que sur le défaut de notification préalable de la cession au Gouvernement du Vénézuela ou d'acceptation par lui, et que, comme il a été déjà dit, ce moyen de défense était écarté par le Compromis;

Considérant qu'on pourrait en dire autant de la demande des 19,571.34 dollars pour remboursement d'impôts nationaux qui auraient été illégalement perçus et de celle des 3,509.22 dollars du chef de la rétention du "Bolivar," mais qu'il n'est pas prouvé, d'une part que les impôts dont il s'agit étaient de ceux dont la Orinoco Shipping and Trading Company était exempte, d'autre part que le fait querellé procédait d'un abus d'autorité de la part du Consul Vénézuélien et qu'ainsi ces deux demandes devant être rejetées au fond, quoique par d'autres motifs, l'annullation de la sentence en ce point serait sans intérêt;

Considérant que la décision du Surarbitre allouant 27,692.31 dollars au lieu de 28,461.53 dollars pour rétention et loyer du Masparro et Socorro du 21 mars au 18 septembre 1902, est quant aux 769.22 dollars non alloués, ici encore uniquement fondée sur le défaut de notification de la cession de la créance;

Considérant que la décision du Surarbitre quant aux autres demandes rentrant dans ce chef pour la période postérieure au 1 avril 1902 est fondée sur des appréciations des faits et sur une interprétation de principes de droit qui ne sont pas sujettes ni à nouvel examen ni à revision par ce Tribunal, les décisions intervenues sur ces points n'étant pas entachées de nullité;

IV. Quant aux 25,000 Dollars:

Considérant que la demande de 25,000 dollars pour honoraires, dépenses et débours a été rejetée par le Surarbitre en conséquence du rejet de la plupart des réclamations des Etats-Unis d'Amérique, et que—par la présente sentence—quelques-unes de ces réclamations étant admises, il paraît équitable d'allouer une partie de cette somme, que le Tribunal fixe ex aequo et bono à 7,000 dollars ;

Considérant que la loi Vénézuélienne fixe l'intérêt légal à 3% et que, dans ces conditions, le Tribunal, tout en constatant en fait l'insuffisance de ce taux, ne peut allouer d'avantage ;

Par ces Motifs:

Le Tribunal déclare nulle la sentence du Surarbitre M. Barge en date du 22 février 1904, quant aux quatre points suivants :

1°. les 19,200 dollars ;
2°. les 1,053 dollars ;
3°. les 25,845.20 dollars ;
4°. les 769.22 dollars déduits da la réclamation des 28,461.53 dollars pour rétention et loyer du Masparro et Socorro ;

Et statuant, en conséquence de la nullité ainsi constatée, et à raison des éléments soumis à son appréciation :

Déclare ces chefs de demande fondés et alloue aux Etats-Unis d'Amérique, indépendamment des sommes allouées par la sentence du Surarbitre du 22 février 1904, les sommes de :

1°. 19,200 dollars ;   3°. 25,845.20 dollars ;
2°. 1,053 dollars ;   4°. 769.22 dollars ;

le tout avec intérêt à 3 pct. depuis la date de la demande (16 juin 1903) et à payer dans les deux mois de la présente sentence ;

alloue en outre à titre d'indemnité pour remboursement de frais et honoraires 7,000 dollars ;

rejette la demande pour le surplus ; la sentence du Surarbitre M. Barge du 22 février 1904 devant conserver en dehors des points ci-dessus, son plein et entier effet.

Fait à La Haye, dans l'Hôtel de la Cour permanente d'Arbitrage, en triple exemplaire, le 25 octobre 1910.

Le Président: Lammasch
Le Secrétaire général: Michiels van Verduynen

Agreement for Arbitration, February 13, 1909[1]

El Doctor Francisco González Guinán, Ministro de Relaciones Exteriores de los Estados Unidos de Venezuela, debidamente autorizado por el General Juan Vicente Gómez, Vicepresidente de los Estados Unidos de Venezuela, Encargado de la Presidencia de la República,

[1]Official report, p. 9.

y William I. Buchanan, Alto Comisionado, Representante del Presidente de los Estados Unidos de América, habiéndose exhibido y encontrado en forma sus respectivos poderes, y anomados del espíritu de franca amistad que siempre ha existido y debe existir entre las dos Naciones que representan, han tratado en repetidas y prolongadas conferencias de la manera de arreglar amistosa y equitativamente las diferencias que existen entre sus respectivos Gobiernos con respecto á las reclamaciones pendientes entre las dos Naciones, pues ni los Estados Unidos de Venezuela ni los Estados Unidos de América aspiran á otra cosa que al sostenimiento de lo que en justicia y equidad les corresponda; y como resultado de estas conferencias, han reconocido la grande importancia del arbitraje como medio de mantener la buena armonía que debe existir y desarrollarse entre sus respectivas Naciones y á fin de evitar en lo futuro, en todo lo posible, diferencias entre ellas, creen que es de todo punto conveniente que un Tratado de Arbitramento sea ajustado entre sus respectivos Gobiernos.

Con respecto á las reclamaciones que han sido el tema de sus largas y amistosas conferencias, el Doctor Francisco González Guinán y William I. Buchanan han encontrado que las opiniones y puntos de vista sostenidos por sus respectivos Gobiernos han sido y son tan diametralmente opuestos y distintos, que han encontrado difícil resolverlos de común acuerdo, por lo cual tienen que apelar á la medida conciliatoria del arbitraje, medida á la cual las dos Naciones que representan están ligadas entre sí por sus firmas á los tratados de la Segunda Conferencia de la Paz de La Haya de 1907, y que está reconocida por todo el mundo civilizado como el único modo satisfactorio para solucionar los conflictos internacionales.

Convencidos así y firmes en sus propósitos de no permitir que por ningún motivo se perturbe la cordialidad que siempre ha existido entre sus respectivos Países, los expresados Señores Doctor Francisco González Guinán y William I. Buchanan, ampliamente autorizados al efecto, han ajustado, convenido y firmado el Presente Protocolo para el arreglo de dichas reclamaciones contra los Estados Unidos de Venezuela, que son las siguientes:

1. La reclamación de los Estados Unidos de América en favor de la Orinoco Steamship Company;

2. La reclamación de los Estados Unidos de América en favor de la Orinoco Corporation y de sus causantes, The Manoa Company Limited, The Orinoco Company y The Orinoco Company Limited; y

3. La reclamación de los Estados Unidos de América en favor de la United States and Venezuela Company (también conocida como la reclamación Crichfield).

ARTÍCULO 1

Con respecto á la primera de esas reclamaciones, la de la Orinoco Steamship Company, los Estados Unidos de Venezuela han sostenido la inmutabilidad del fallo arbitral del Superárbitro Barge librado en este caso, alegando que dicho fallo no adolece de ninguna de las causales que por jurisprudencia universal dan lugar á nulidad, sino que antes bien reviste el carácter de inapelable, pues no puede tenerse por nulo el Compromiso de Arbitraje, ni ha habido exceso de poder, ni puede alegarse corrupción de jueces, ni error esencial en el fallo; y por otra parte, los Estados Unidos de América, alegando casos prácticos, entre ellos el caso de la revisión, por consentimiento de los Estados Unidos de América, de los fallos arbitrales dictados por la Comisión Mixta Venezolano—Americana, creada por la Convención del 25 de abril de 1866, y fundándose en las circunstancias del caso y considerando los preceptos de derecho internacional y de jurisprudencia universal, han sostenido no sólo la admisibilidad sino la necesidad de la revisión de dicho fallo; en consecuencia de esta situación, el Doctor Francisco González Guinán y William I. Buchanan con el espíritu que ha distinguido sus conferencias, han convenido en someter este caso al alto criterio del Tribunal Arbitral creado por este Protocolo, en la forma siguiente:

El Tribunal Arbitral debe decidir primero si el fallo del Superárbitro Barge, en este caso, bajo todas las circunstancias y los preceptos de derecho internacional, no está viciado de nulidad y tiene que considerarse concluyente hasta excluir un nuevo examen del caso en su fondo. Si el Tribunal Arbitral falla que debe considerarse dicho fallo concluyente, el caso será aceptado como concluido por los Estados Unidos de América; pero, si por otra parte, el Tribunal Arbitral decide que dicho fallo del Superárbitro Barge no debe considerarse definitivo, el mismo Tribunal Arbitral debe entonces examinar, oir y determinar el caso y librar su fallo en su fondo.

Artículo 2

En el curso de las muchas conferencias celebradas con respecto al asunto de los Estados Unidos de América por parte de la Orinoco Corporation y de sus causantes, contra los Estados Unidos de Venezuela, entre el Doctor Francisco González Guinán, Ministro de Relaciones Exteriores de Venezuela, y William I. Buchanan, Alto Comisionado, Representante del Presidente de los Estados Unidos de América, han encontrado que las opiniones y consideraciones sostenidas por sus respectivos Gobiernos con respecto á los derechos y reclamaciones de la Compañía reclamante son tan diametralmente opuestas entre sí, que hacen imposible conciliarlas por medio de negociaciones directas entre sus Gobiernos.

Entre éstas han encontrado que los Estados Unidos de América por parte de la Compañía reclamante sostienen que, tanto por el acto del Congreso Nacional de Venezuela como por Resoluciones y otros actos de su Poder Ejecutivo, los derechos y reclamaciones mantenidos y reclamados por los Estados Unidos de América por parte de la Compañía reclamante en la concesión Fitzgerald, origen del presente caso, y conforme á ella, son firmemente reconocidos y afirmados como subsistentes y válidos, y que el Gobierno de Venezuela ha insistido é insiste en que el fallo del Superárbitro Barge del 12 de abril de 1904, que Venezuela considera irrevocable, y la sentencia dictada por la

Corte Federal y de Casación de Venezuela, el 18 de marzo de 1908, son por sí una prueba concluyente de que no existen los derechos ni las pretensiones de la Compañía reclamante, pues la expresada Compañía, aun aceptando ser cesionaria de las otras, no llegó á constituirse de conformidad con las leyes de Venezuela, y aun habiéndose constituido, de antemano quedaba sometida á las leyes venezolanas y aceptado que éstas debían regir y decidir las contenciones y diferencias que pudieran ocurrir; mientras que los Estados Unidos de América por parte de la Compañía reclamante se han negado y se niegan á aceptar de manera alguna que ni el fallo del Superárbitro Barge ni el de la Corte Federal y de Casación de Venezuela puedan terminar ó hayan terminado ó eliminado los derechos y reclamaciones alegados por la Compañía reclamante de acuerdo con dicho contrato Fitzgerald, sino que por el contrario los derechos y reclamaciones alegados en esta materia por la Compañía reclamante son válidos y subsistentes.

En vista de estas y otras conclusiones igualmente contrarias, alcanzadas y persistentemente sostenidas por sus respectivos Gobiernos con respecto á este caso, los mencionados Representantes, animados por un firme propósito de hacer todo lo que esté á su alcance para conservar y fomentar una buena inteligencia entre sus Gobiernos, y con el deseo expreso de allegar los medios para un arreglo de las diferencias que entre ellos existen con respecto á este caso, en justicia y equidad, no pueden salirse de la conclusión de que ese mismo espíritu de cordialidad que ha venido privando en las numerosas conferencias ya efectuadas, recomienda é indica la conveniencia y la necesidad de someter este asunto á un Tribunal Internacional imparcial, á fin de que las diferencias que de él se derivan sean determinadas una vez por todas y concluyan de manera justa y equitativa.   Para llegar á este deseado fin, y de acuerdo con los principios arriba apuntados:

Queda convenido entre el Doctor Francisco González Guinán, Ministro de Relaciones Exteriores de los Estados Unidos de Venezuela, y William I. Buchanan, Alto Comisionado, Representante del Presidente de los Estados Unidos de América, debidamente autorizados á este efecto por sus respectivos Gobiernos, que el asunto de los Estados Unidos de América por parte de la Orinoco Corporation y de sus causantes, The Manoa Company Limited, The Orinoco Company y The Orinoco Company Limited, sea sometido al Tribunal Arbitral creado por este Protocolo.

Dicho Tribunal Arbitral examinará y decidirá:

1. Si el fallo del Superárbitro Barge del 12 de abril de 1904, bajo los preceptos de derecho internacional, no está viciado de nulidad y conserva el carácter de concluyente en el caso de las causantes de la Compañía reclamante contra Venezuela.

2. Si el Tribunal Arbitral sentencia que debe considerarse dicho fallo como concluyente, decidirá entonces, qué efecto tenía dicho fallo con respecto á la subsistencia del contrato Fitzgerald en aquella fecha, y con respecto á los derechos de la Compañía reclamante ó los de sus causantes en dicho contrato.

3. Si decide que el fallo de dicho Superárbitro Barge no debe

considerarse concluyente, dicho Tribunal Arbitral examinará en su fondo y fallará sobre las cuestiones sometidas á dicho Superárbitro por las causantes de la Compañía reclamante.

4. El Tribunal Arbitral examinará, considerará y decidirá si ha habido injusticia notoria contra la Compañía reclamante, ó sus causantes, respecto del contrato Fitzgerald, por el fallo de la Corte Federal y de Casación, librado el 18 de marzo de 1908 en el juicio seguido por el Gobierno de Venezuela contra las causantes· de la Compañía reclamante, ó por alguno de los actos de cualquiera de las autoridades del Gobierno de Venezuela.

Si el Tribunal Arbitral decide que ha habido tal injusticia, queda facultado para examinar el asunto de la Compañía reclamante y de sus causantes contra el Gobierno de Venezuela en su fondo, y para pronunciar fallo definitivo respecto de los derechos y las obligaciones de las partes, fijando los daños y perjuicios que en su alto criterio crea justos y equitativos.

En todo caso el Tribunal Arbitral decidirá:

(*a*). Qué efecto, si alguno, ha causado y tiene dicho fallo de la Corte Federal y de Casación, del 18 de marzo de 1908, en todo lo referente á los derechos de la Compañía reclamante como cesionaria del contrato Fitzgerald;

(*b*). Si dicho contrato Fitzgerald está vigente; y

(*c*). Si declara que dicho contrato está vigente, cuáles son, entonces, los derechos y las obligaciones de la Compañía reclamante por una parte, y del Gobierno de Venezuela por la otra.

ARTÍCULO 3

El Doctor Francisco González Guinán, Ministro de Relaciones Exteriores de los Estados Unidos de Venezuela, y William I. Buchanan, Alto Comisionado, Representante del Presidente de los Estados Unidos de América, han tratado cuidadosamente, en las conferencias que han celebrado, el asunto de los Estados Unidos de América, por parte de la United States and Venezuela Company contra los Estados Unidos de Venezuela, también conocido como asunto Crichfield, y observan que aunque los puntos que contienen differen en muchos respectos de los tratados con respecto á las reclamaciones que han sido consideradas, las mismas opiniones radicalmente opuestas prevalecen por parte de ambos Gobiernos.

A fin, pues, de que ningún asunto quede pendiente que no tienda á robustecer la buena inteligencia y amistad que existen entre los dos Gobiernos, sus Representantes arriba nombrados, el Doctor Francisco González Guinán y William I. Buchanan, convienen por el presente que dicho asunto de los Estados Unidos de América, por parte de la United States and Venezuela Company contra los Estados Unidos de Venezuela, sea sometido al Tribunal Arbitral creado por este Protocolo, y además que dicho Tribunal queda facultado para examinar, oír, considerar, determinar y fallar dicho asunto en su fondo en justicia y equidad.

Artículo 4

Los Estados Unidos de Venezuela y los Estados Unidos de América, habiendo en la Segunda Conferencia de la Paz efectuada en La Haya en 1907, aceptado y reconocido la Corte Permanente de La Haya, se conviene que todos los casos mencionados en los artículos I, II y III de este Protocol, es decir, el de la Orinoco Steamship Company, el de la Orinoco Corporation y de sus causantes, y el de la United States and Venezuela Company, se pongan bajo la jurisdicción de un Tribunal Arbitral compuesto de tres Arbitros escogidos de la Corte Permanente de La Haya ya citada.

No formará parte de este Tribunal Arbitral ninguno de los miembros de dicha Corte que sea ciudadano de los Estados Unidos de Venezuela ó de los Estados Unidos de América, y ningún miembro de dicha Corte podrá ser abogado ante dicho Tribunal por una ú otra Nación.

Este Tribunal Arbitral tendrá su asiento en La Haya.

Artículo 5

Dicho Tribunal Arbitral en cada caso que se le someta determinará decidirá y fallará de acuerdo con la justicia y la equidad. Sus decisiones serán en cada caso aceptadas y apoyadas por los Estados Unidos de Venezuela y por los Estados Unidos de América como definitivas y concluyentes.

Artículo 6

En la presentación de los casos al Tribunal Arbitral pueden ambas partes hacer uso de los idiomas francés, español ó inglés.

Artículo 7

Dentro de ocho meses, contados desde la fecha de este Protocolo, cada una de las partes presentará á la otra y á cada uno de los miembros del Tribunal Arbitral dos ejemplares impresos de su alegato con los documentos y pruebas en que se apoye, junto con el testimonio de sus testigos respectivos.

Dentro de un plazo adicional de cuatro meses, cualquiera de las partes puede, de la misma manera, presentar contra-alegato con documentos, pruebas y declaraciones adicionales en contestación al alegato, documentos, pruebas y declaraciones de la otra parte.

Dentro de sesenta días contados desde la expiración del plazo señalado para entregar los contra-alegatos, cada Gobierno puede, por medio de su Representante, hacer sus argumentos ante el Tribunal Arbitral, tanto verbalmente como por escrito, y cada uno entregará al otro copias de cualesquiera argumentos así hechos por escrito, y cada parte tendrá derecho á contestar por escrito, siempre que tal contestación sea sometida dentro de los sesenta días últimamente citados.

Artículo 8

Todos los archivos públicos y documentos bajo el control ó dirección de uno ú otro Gobierno ó en su posesión, relativos á los asuntos en litigio, serán accesibles al otro y, previa solicitud, se le darán las copias autenticadas de ellos. Los documentos que cada parte aduzca en sus pruebas deberán estar autenticados por el respectivo Ministro de Relaciones Exteriores.

Artículo 9

Todas las adjudicaciones pecuniarias que haga el Tribunal Arbitral en los dichos casos serán en moneda de oro de los Estados Unidos de América, ó su equivalente en moneda venezolana, debiendo el Tribunal Arbitral fijar el tiempo de los pagos, previa consulta con los Representantes de los dos Países.

Artículo 10

Queda convenido que, dentro de seis meses á contar desde la fecha de este Protocolo, el Gobierno de los Estados Unidos de Venezuela y el de los Estados Unidos de América se notificarán mutuamente, así como también notificarán á la Oficina de la Corte Permanente de La Haya, el nombre del Arbitro que escoja de entre los miembros de la Corte Permanente de Arbitraje.

Dentro de los sesenta días siguientes, los Arbitros arriba mencionados se reunirán en La Haya y procederán á escoger el Tercer Arbitro de acuerdo con las previsiones del artículo cuarenta y cinco de la Convención de La Haya para el Arreglo Pacífico de los Conflictos Internacionales arriba citada.

Dentro del mismo término cada uno de los dos Gobiernos depositará en dicha Oficina la suma de quince mil francos por cuenta de los gastos del arbitramento previsto por este Protocolo, y de cuando en cuando y de la misma manera serán depositadas las demás cantidades necesarias para cubrir dichos gastos.

El Tribunal Arbitral se reunirá en La Haya doce meses después de la fecha de este Protocolo para empezar sus deliberaciónes y oir los argumentos á él sometidos. Dentro de sesenta días después de cerradas las audiencias serán librados sus fallos.

Artículo 11

Con excepción de lo convenido en este Protocolo, el procedimiento arbitral se conformará á las previsiones de la Convención para el Arreglo Pacífico de los Conflictos Internacionales, de la cual ambas partes son signatarias, firmada en La Haya el 18 de octubre de 1907, y especialmente á las previsiones de su capítulo tercero.

Artículo 12

Queda entendido y pactado que nada de lo expuesto en este Protocolo será impedimento para que dentro del término de cinco meses,

á contar de la fecha de este Protocolo, los Estados Unidos de Venezuela puedan llegar á un arreglo amistoso con las dos ó cada una de
las Compañías reclamantes á que refieren los artículos II y III, siempre
que, en cada caso en que se llegare á un arreglo la respectiva Compañía
haya obtenido previamente el consentimiento del Gobierno de los
Estados Unidos de América.

Los signatarios, el Doctor Francisco González Guinán y William
I. Buchanan, con el carácter que cada uno inviste, de esta manera, dan
por terminadas sus conferencias con respecto á las diferencias entre
los Estados Unidos de Venezuela y los Estados Unidos de América
y firman dos ejemplares de este Protocolo de un mismo tenor y á un
solo efecto en cada uno de los idiomas español é inglés, en Caracas á
los trece días del mes de febrero del año de mil novecientos nueve.

(L. S.)   F. GONZÁLEZ GUINÁN
(L. S.)   WILLIAM I. BUCHANAN

THE SAVARKAR CASE

Award of the Tribunal, February 24, 1911[1]

Considérant que, par un Compromis en date du 25 octobre 1910, le Gouvernement de la République Française et le Gouvernement de Sa Majesté Britannique se sont mis d'accord à l'effet de soumettre à l'arbitrage, d'une part, les questions de fait et de droit soulevées par l'arrestation et la réintégration, à bord du paquebot "Morea," le 8 juillet 1910, à Marseille, du sujet britannique (British Indian) Savarkar, évadé de ce bâtiment où il était détenu ; d'autre part, la réclamation du Gouvernement de la République Française tendant à la restitution de Savarkar ;

que le Tribunal Arbitral a été chargé de décider la question suivante : Vinayak Damodar Savarkar doit-il, conformément aux règles du droit international, être ou non restitué par le Gouvernement de Sa Majesté Britannique au Gouvernement de la République Française ?

Considérant qu'en exécution de ce Compromis, les deux Gouvernements ont désigné respectivement comme Arbitres :

Son Excellence Monsieur Beernaert, Ministre d'Etat, Membre de la Chambre Belge des Représentants, etc., Président ;

Le Très Honorable Comte de Desart, ancien Procureur-Général de Sa Majesté Britannique ;

Monsieur Louis Renault, Professeur à l'Université de Paris, Ministre Plénipotentiaire, Jurisconsulte du Département des Affaires Etrangères ;

Monsieur G. Gram, ancien Ministre d'Etat de Norvège, Gouverneur de Province ;

Son Excellence Monsieur le Jonkheer A. F. de Savornin Lohman, Ministre d'Etat, Membre de la Seconde Chambre des Etats-Généraux des Pays-Bas ;

Considérant que les deux Gouvernements ont respectivement désigné comme Agents,

Le Gouvernement de la République Française :

Monsieur André Weiss, Jurisconsulte adjoint du Département des Affaires Etrangères de la République Française, Professeur à la Faculté de droit de Paris ;

Le Gouvernement de Sa Majesté Britannique :

Monsieur Eyre Crowe, Conseiller d'Ambassade, Chef de Section au Département des Affaires Etrangères de Sa Majesté Britannique.

Considérant que, conformément aux dispositions du Compromis, les Mémoires, Contre-Mémoires et Répliques ont été dûment échangés entre les Parties et communiqués aux Arbitres.

---

[1] Official report, p. 50.

Considérant que le Tribunal s'est réuni à La Haye le 1 février 1911,

Attendu, en ce qui concerne les faits qui ont donné lieu au différend entre les deux Gouvernements, qu'il est établi que, par une lettre du 29 juin 1910, le Chef de la Police Métropolitaine à Londres a fait savoir au Directeur de la Sûreté générale à Paris que le sujet Britannique Indien (British Indian) Vinayak Damodar Savarkar serait envoyé dans l'Inde à l'effet d'y être poursuivi pour une affaire d'assassinat, etc. (for abetment of murder, etc.), et qu'il serait à bord du navire "Morea," faisant escale à Marseille le 7 ou le 8 juillet.

Attendu qu'à la suite de cette lettre, le Ministère de l'Intérieur a, par un télégramme du 4 juillet 1910, averti le Préfet des Bouches-du-Rhône que la police britannique venait d'envoyer dans l'Inde Savarkar à bord du vapeur "Morea"; que ce télégramme mentionne que "quelques révolutionnaires hindous, actuellement sur le Continent, pourraient profiter de cette occasion pour faciliter l'evasion de cet étranger," et que le Préfet est prié "de vouloir bien prendre les dispositions nécessaires pour éviter toute tentative de ce genre."

Attendu que le Directeur de la Sûreté générale a, de son côté, répondu, le 9 juillet 1910, à la lettre du Chef de la Police à Londres, en lui faisant connaître qu'il a "donné les instructions nécessaires, en vue d'éviter tout incident à l'occasion du passage à Marseille du nommé Vinayak Damodar Savarkar, embarqué à bord du vapeur Morea."

Attendu que, le 7 juillet, le "Morea" arriva à Marseille; que, le lendemain entre 6 et 7 heures du matin, Savarkar, ayant réussi à s'échapper, a gagné la terre à la nage et s'est mis à courir; qu'il fut arrêté par un brigadier de la gendarmerie maritime français, et ramené à bord du navire; que trois personnes descendues du navire ont prêté assistance au brigadier pour reconduire le fugitif à bord; que, le 9 juillet, le "Morea" quitta Marseille emmenant ce dernier.

Attendu que des déclarations que le brigadier français a faites devant la police de Marseille, il résulte:

qu'il a vu le fugitif presque nu sortir par un hublot du vapeur se jeter à la mer et gagner le quai à la nage;

qu'au même instant, des personnes du bord se sont précipitées, en criant et en gesticulant, sur la passerelle conduisant à terre pour se mettre à la poursuite de cet homme;

que, d'autre part, de nombreuses personnes se trouvant sur le quai se mirent à crier, "Arrêtez-le";

que le brigadier s'élança aussitôt à la poursuite du fugitif, et, le rejoignant après un parcours de cinq cents mètres environ, l'arrêta.

Attendu que le brigadier déclare qu'il ignorait absolument à qui il avait eu affaire, qu'il a cru simplement que l'individu qui se sauvait, poursuivi par la clameur publique, était un homme de l'équipage ayant peut-être commis un délit à bord.

Attendu, quant à l'assistance que lui ont prêtée un homme de l'équipage et deux agents de la police indienne, qu'il résulte des explications fournies à ce sujet, qu'ils sont survenus après l'arrestation de Savarkar et que leur intervention n'a eu qu'un caractère secondaire;

que, le brigadier ayant pris Savarkar par un bras pour le ramener vers le navire, le prisonnier le suivit docilement et que le brigadier n'a pas cessé de le tenir, assisté des personnes susmentionnées, jusqu'à la coupée du navire;

qu'il a déclaré, du reste, qu'il ne connaissait pas la langue anglaise;

qu'à juger de ce qui a été relaté, tout l'incident n'a duré que quelques minutes.

Attendu qu'il est avéré que le brigadier qui opérait l'arrestation n'ignorait pas la présence de Savarkar à bord du navire et qu'il avait eu, comme tous les agents et gendarmes français, pour consigne d'empêcher de monter à bord tout Hindou qui ne serait pas porteur d'un billet de passage.

Attendu que les circonstances expliquent, du reste, que les personnes chargées à bord de surveiller Savarkar aient cru pouvoir compter sur l'assistance des agents français.

Attendu qu'il est établi qu'un Commissaire de la police française s'est présenté à bord du navire, peu de temps après son arrivée au port, et s'est mis, d'après l'ordre du Préfet, à la disposition du Commandant pour la surveillance à exercer;

que ce Commissaire a été, en conséquence, mis en relation avec l'officier de police britannique chargé, avec des agents, de la garde du prisonnier;

que le Préfet de Marseille, comme il résulte d'un télégramme du 13 juillet 1910 au Ministre de l'Intérieur, déclare avoir agi à cette occasion conformément aux instructions données par la Sûreté générale prescrivant de prendre les dispositions nécessaires pour empêcher l'evasion de Savarkar.

Attendu que, d'après ce qui précède, il est manifeste qu'il ne s'agit pas ici d'un cas où l'on aurait eu recours à des manœuvres frauduleuses ou à des actes de violence pour se mettre en possession d'une personne réfugiée sur un territoire étranger et qu'il n'y a eu, dans les faits de l'arrestation, de la livraison et de la conduite de Savarkar dans l'Inde, rien de nature à porter atteinte à la souveraineté de la France; que tous ceux qui ont pris part à l'incident ont été certainement de bonne foi et n'ont nullement cru s'écarter de la légalité.

Attendu que, dans les circonstances ci-dessus relatées, la conduite du brigadier n'ayant pas été désavouée par ses chefs avant le 9 juillet au matin, c'est-à-dire avant le départ du "Morea" de Marseille, les agents britanniques ont pu naturellement croire que le brigadier avait agi en conformité de ses instructions ou que sa conduite avait été approuvée.

Attendu qu'en admettant qu'une irrégularité ait été commise par l'arrestation et la remise de Savarkar aux agent britanniques, il n'existe pas, en droit international, de règle en vertu de laquelle la Puissance qui a, dans des conditions telles que celles qui ont été indiquées, un prisonnier en son pouvoir, devrait le rendre à raison d'une faute commise par l'agent étranger qui le lui a livré.

PAR CES MOTIFS:

Le Tribunal Arbitral décide que le Gouvernement de Sa Majesté Britannique n'est pas tenu de restituer le nommé Vinayak Damodar Savarkar au Gouvernement de la République française.

Fait à La Haye, dans l'Hôtel de la Cour Permanente d'Arbitrage, le 24 février 1911.

Le Président: A. BEERNAERT
Le Secrétaire général: MICHIELS VAN VERDUYNEN

Agreement for Arbitration, October 25, 1910[1]

Le Gouvernement de la République Française et le Gouvernement de Sa Majesté Britannique s'étant mis d'accord, par un échange de notes en date des 4 et 5 octobre 1910, à l'effet de soumettre à l'arbitrage, d'une part, les questions de fait et de droit soulevées par l'arrestation et la réintégration, à bord du paquebot *Morea,* le 8 Juillet 1910, à Marseille, de l'Indien Vinayak Damodar Savarkar, évadé de ce bâtiment, où il était détenu; d'autre part, la réclamation du Gouvernement de la République tendant à la restitution de Savarkar;

Les soussignés, dûment autorisés à cet effet, sont convenus du Compromis suivant:

ARTICLE PREMIER

Un Tribunal Arbitral, composé comme il est dit ci-après, sera chargé de décider la question suivante:

Vinayak Damodar Savarkar doit-il, conformément aux règles du droit international, être ou non restitué par le Gouvernement de Sa Majesté Britannique au Gouvernement de la République Française?

ART. 2

Le Tribunal Arbitral sera composé de cinq Arbitres pris parmi les membres de la Cour permanente de La Haye. Les deux Parties contractantes se mettront d'accord sur la composition du Tribunal. Chacune d'elles pourra désigner comme Arbitre un de ses nationaux.

ART. 3

Le 6 décembre 1910, chacune des Hautes Parties contractantes remettra, au Bureau de la Cour permanente, quinze exemplaires de son mémoire, avec les copies certifiées conformes de toutes pièces et documents qu'elle compte invoquer dans la cause. Le Bureau en assurera sans retard la transmission aux Arbitres et aux Parties: savoir, de deux exemplaires pour chaque Arbitre, de trois exemplaires pour chaque Partie. Deux exemplaires resteront dans les archives du Bureau.

---

[1] Official report, p. 5.

Le 17 janvier 1911, les Hautes Parties contractantes déposeront dans la même forme leurs contre-mémoires, avec pièces à l'appui.

Ces contre-mémoires pourront donner lieu à des répliques, qui devront être présentées dans un délai de quinze jours après la remise des contre-mémoires.

Les délais fixés par le présent Arrangement pour la remise des mémoires, contre-mémoires et répliques pourront être étendus par une entente mutuelle des Hautes Parties contractantes.

ART. 4

Le Tribunal se réunira à La Haye le 14 février 1911.

Chaque Partie sera représentée par un Agent, avec mission de servir d'intermédiaire entre elle et le Tribunal.

Le Tribunal Arbitral pourra, s'il l'estime nécessaire, demander à l'un ou à l'autre des Agents de lui fournir des explications orales ou écrites, auxquelles l'Agent de la Partie adverse aura le droit de répondre.

Il aura aussi la faculté d'ordonner la comparution de témoins.

ART. 5

Les Parties peuvent faire usage de la langue française ou de la langue anglaise. Les membres du Tribunal pourront se servir, à leur choix, de la langue française ou de la langue anglaise. Les décisions du Tribunal seront rédigées dans les deux langues.

ART. 6

La décision du Tribunal devra être rendue dans le plus bref délai possible, et dans tous les cas, dans les trente jours qui suivront la date de la réunion à La Haye ou celle de la remise des explications écrites qui lui auraient été fournies à sa requête. Ce délai pourrait, cependant, être prolongé à la demande du Tribunal si les deux Hautes Parties contractantes y consentaient.

Fait à Londres, en double exemplaire, le 25 octobre 1910.

(L. S.) Signé: PAUL CAMBON
(L. S.) Signé: E. GREY

Supplementary Note of October 25, 1910, to the Agreement for Arbitration, Addressed by His Excellency the Ambassador of the French Republic at London to His Excellency the Principal Secretary of State of His Britannic Majesty in the Department of Foreign Affairs[1]

25 Octobre 1910.

MONSIEUR LE MINISTRE: J'ai l'honneur d'accuser réception à Votre Excellence de sa note de ce jour relative à l'arrangement que nous avons signé aujourd'hui en vue de soumettre à l'arbitrage cer-

---
[1]Official report, p. 9.

taines questions concernant l'arrestation et la restitution de Vinayak Damodar Savarkar, à Marseille, le 8 juillet dernier. Je suis autorisé à constater, avec Votre Excellence, l'entente d'après laquelle toutes les questions qui pourraient s'élever au cours de cet arbitrage, et qui ne seraient pas prévues par le susdit arrangement, seront réglées conformément aux stipulations de la Convention, pour le règlement pacifique des conflicts internationaux, signée à la Haye le 18 octobre 1907.

Il est également entendu que chaque partie supportera ses propres frais et une part égale des dépenses du Tribunal.

Veuillez agréer, etc.

Signé: PAUL CAMBON

THE CANEVARO CASE

Award of the Tribunal, May 3, 1912[1]

Considérant que, par un Compromis en date du 25 avril 1910, le Gouvernement Italien et le Gouvernement du Pérou se sont mis d'accord à l'effet de soumettre à l'arbitrage les questions suivantes :

"Le Gouvernement du Pérou doit-il payer en espèces ou bien d'après les dispositions de la loi péruvienne sur la dette intérieure du 12 juin 1889 les lettres à ordre (*cambiali, libramientos*) dont sont actuellement possesseurs les frères Napoléon, Carlo et Raphaël Canevaro, qui furent tirées par le Gouvernement du Pérou à l'ordre de la maison José Canevaro é hijos pour le montant de 43,140 livres sterling plus les intérêts légaux du montant susdit ?"

"Les frères Canevaro ont-ils le droit d'exiger le total de la somme réclamée ?"

"Le comte Raphaël Canevaro a-t-il le droit d'être considéré comme réclamant italien ?"

Considérant qu'en exécution de ce Compromis, ont été désignés comme Arbitres :

Monsieur Louis Renault, Ministre plénipotentiaire, Membre de l'Institut, Professeur à la Faculté de droit de l'Université de Paris et à l'Ecole des sciences politiques, Jurisconsulte du Ministère des Affaires Etrangères, Président ;

Monsieur Guido Fusinato, Docteur en droit, ancien Ministre de l'Instruction publique, Professeur honoraire de droit international à l'Université de Turin, Député, Conseiller d'Etat ;

Son Excellence Monsieur Manuel Alvarez Calderon, Docteur en droit, Professeur à l'Université de Lima, Envoyé extraordinaire et Ministre plénipotentiaire du Pérou à Bruxelles et à Berne.

Considérant que les deux Gouvernements ont respectivement désigné comme Conseils :

Le Gouvernement Royal Italien :

Monsieur le Professeur Vittorio Scialoja, Sénateur du Royaume d'Italie et, comme conseil adjoint, le Comte Giuseppe Francesco Canevaro, Docteur en droit,

Le Gouvernement Péruvien :

Monsieur Manuel Maria Mesones, Docteur en droit, Avocat.

Considérant que, conformément aux dispositions du Compromis, les Mémoires et Contre-mémoires ont été dûment échangés entre les Parties et communiqués aux Arbitres ;

Considérant que le Tribunal s'est réuni à La Haye le 20 avril 1912.

Considérant que, pour la simplification de l'exposé que suivra, il

---

[1]Official report, p. 14.

vaut mieux statuer d'abord sur la troisième question posée par le Compromis, c'est-à-dire sur la qualité de Raphaël Canevaro;

Considérant que, d'après la législation péruvienne (Art. 34 de la Constitution), Raphaël Canevaro est Péruvien de naissance comme étant né sur le territoire péruvien,

Que, d'autre part, la législation italienne (Art. 4 du Code civil) lui attribue la nationalité italienne comme étant né d'un père italien;

Considérant qu'en fait, Raphaël Canevaro c'est, à plusieurs reprises, comporté comme citoyen péruvien, soit en posant sa candidature au Sénat où ne sont admis que les citoyens péruviens et où il est allé défendre son élection, soit surtout en acceptant les fonctions de Consul général des Pays-Bas, après avoir sollicité l'autorisation du Gouvernement, puis du Congrès péruvien;

Considérant que, dans ces circonstances, quelle que puisse être en Italie, au point de vue de la nationalité, la condition de Raphaël Canevaro, le Gouvernement du Pérou a le droit de le considérer comme citoyen péruvien et de lui dénier la qualité de réclamant italien.

Considérant que la créance qui a donné lieu à la réclamation soumise au Tribunal résulte d'un décret du dictateur Piérola du 12 décembre 1880, en vertu duquel ont été créés, à la date du 23 du même mois, des bons de paiement (libramientos) à l'ordre de la maison "José Canevaro é hijos" pour une somme de 77,000 livres sterling, payables à diverses échéances;

Que ces bons n'ont pas été payés aux échéances fixées, qui ont coïncidé avec l'occupation ennemie;

Qu'un acompte de 35,000 livres sterling ayant été payé à Londres en 1885, il reste une créance de 43,140 livres sterling sur le sort de laquelle il s'agit de statuer;

Considérant qu'il résulte des faits de la cause que la maison de commerce "Jose Canevaro é hijos," établie à Lima, a été reconstituée en 1885 après la mort de son fondateur, survenue en 1883;

Qu'elle a bien conservé la raison sociale "José Canevaro é hijos," mais qu'en réalité, comme le constate l'acte de liquidation du 6 février 1905, elle était composée de José Francisco et de César Canevaro, dont la nationalité péruvienne n'a jamais été contestée, et de Raphaël Canevaro, dont la même nationalité, aux termes de la loi du Pérou, vient d'être reconnue par le Tribunal;

Que cette société, péruvienne à un double titre et par son siège social et par la nationalité de ses membres, a subsisté jusqu'à la mort de José Francisco Canevaro, survenue en 1900;

Considérant que c'est au cours de l'existence de cette société que sont intervenues les lois péruviennes du 26 octobre 1886, du 12 juin 1889 et du 17 décembre 1898 qui ont édicté les mesures les plus graves en ce qui concerne les dettes de l'Etat péruvien, mesures qu'a paru nécessiter l'état désastreux auquel le Pérou avait été réduit par les malheurs de la guerre étrangère et de la guerre civile;

Considérant que, sans qu'il y ait lieu pour le Tribunal d'apprécier en elles-mêmes les dispositions des lois de 1889 et de 1898, certainement très rigoureuses pour les créanciers du Pérou, leurs dispositions s'imposaient sans aucun doute aux Péruviens individuellement comme aux sociétés péruviennes, qu'il y a là un pur fait que le Tribunal n'a qu'à constater.

Considérant que, le 30 septembre 1890, la Société Canevaro, par son représentant Giacometti, s'adressait au Sénat pour obtenir le paiement des 43,140 livres sterling qui auraient été, suivant lui, fournis pour satisfaire aux nécessités de la guerre ;

Que, le 9 avril 1891, dans une lettre adressée au Président du Tribunal des Comptes, Giacometti assignait une triple origine à la créance : un solde dû à la maison Canevaro par le Gouvernement comme prix d'armements achetés en Europe au temps de la guerre ; lettres tirées par le Gouvernement à la charge de la consignation du guano aux Etats-Unis, protestées et payées par José Francisco Canevaro ; argent fourni pour l'armée par le Général Canevaro ;

Qu'enfin, le 1ᵉʳ avril 1891, le même Giacometti, s'adressant encore au Président du Tribunal des Comptes, invoquait l'article 14 de la loi du 12 juin 1889 que, disait-il, le Congrès avait votée "animado del mas patriotico proposito," pour obtenir le règlement de la créance ;

Considérant que le représentant de la maison Canevaro avait d'abord assigné à la créance une origine manifestement erronée, qu'il ne s'agissait nullement de fournitures ou d'avances faites en vue de la guerre contre le Chili, mais, comme il a été reconnu plus tard, uniquement du remboursement de lettres de change antérieures qui, tirées par le Gouvernement péruvien, avaient été protestées, puis acquittées par la maison Canevaro ;

Que c'est en présence de cette situation qu'il convient de se placer ;

Considérant que la maison Canevaro reconnaissait bien, en 1890 et en 1891, qu'elle était soumise à la loi de 1889 sur la dette intérieure, qu'elle cherchait seulement à se placer dans le cas de profiter d'une disposition favorable de cette loi au lieu de subir le sort commun des créanciers ;

Que sa créance ne rentre pas dans les dispositions de l'article 14 de la dite loi qu'elle a invoquée, ainsi qu'il a été dit plus haut ; qu'il ne s'agit pas, dans l'espèce, d'un dépôt reçu par le Gouvernement, ni de lettres de change tirées sur le Gouvernement, acceptées par lui et reconnues légitimes par le Gouvernement "actuel," mais d'une opération de comptabilité n'ayant pas pour but de procurer des ressources à l'Etat, mais de règler une dette antérieure ;

Que la créance Canevaro rentre, au contraire, dans les termes très compréhensifs de l'article 1ᵉʳ, n°. 4 de la loi qui mentionnent les ordres de paiement (*libramientos*), bons, chèques, lettres et autres mandats de paiement émis par les bureaux nationaux *jusqu'en janvier 1880;* qu'on peut, à la vérité, objecter que ce membre de phrase semble devoir laisser en dehors le créance Canevaro qui est du 23 décembre 1880 ; mais qu'il importe de faire remarquer que cette limitation quant à la date avait pour but d'exclure les créances nées des actes du dictateur Piérola, conformément à la loi de 1886 qui a déclaré nuls tous les actes de ce dernier ; qu'ainsi, en prenant à la lettre la disposition dont il s'agit, la créance Canevaro ne pourrait être invoquée à aucun titre, même pour obtenir la faible proportion admise par la loi de 1889 ;

Mais considérant que, d'une part, il résulte des circonstances et des termes du Compromis que le Gouvernement péruvien reconnaît lui-même comme non applicable à la créance Canevaro la nullité édictée par la loi de 1886 ; que, d'autre part, la nullité du décret de Piérola laisserait subsister la créance antérieure née du paiement des lettres de change ;

Qu'ainsi, la créance résultant des bons de 1880 délivrés à la maison Canevaro doit être considérée comme rentrant dans la catégorie des titres énumérés dans l'article 1er, n°. 4, de la loi.

Considérant qu'il a été soutenu d'une manière générale que la dette Canevaro ne devait pas subir l'application de la loi de 1889, qu'elle ne pouvait être considérée comme rentrant dans *la dette intérieure,* parce que tous ses éléments y répugnaient, le titre étant à ordre, stipulé payable en livres sterling, appartenant à des Italiens ;

Considérant qu'en dehors de la nationalité des personnes, on comprend que des mesures financières, prises dans l'intérieur d'un pays, n'atteignent pas les actes intervenus au dehors par lesquels le Gouvernement a fait directement appel au crédit étranger ; mais que tel n'est pas le cas dans l'espèce : qu'il s'agit bien, dans les titres délivrés en décembre 1880, d'un règlement d'ordre intérieur, de titres créés à Lima, payables à Lima, en compensation d'un paiement fait volontairement dans l'intérêt du Gouvernement du Pérou ;

Que cela n'est pas infirmé par les circonstances que les titres étaient à ordre, payables en livres sterling, circonstances qui n'empêchaient pas la loi péruvienne de s'appliquer à des titres créés et payables sur le territoire où elle commandait ;

Que l'énumération de l'article 1er n°. 4 rappelée plus haut comprend des titres à ordre et que l'article 5 prévoit qu'il peut y avoir des conversions de monnaies à faire ;

Qu'enfin il a été constaté précédemment que, lorsque sont intervenues les mesures financières qui motivent la réclamation, la créance appartenait à une société incontestablement péruvienne.

Considérant que la créance de 1880 appartient actuellement aux trois frères Canevaro dont deux sont certainement Italiens ;

Qu'il convient de se demander si cette circonstance rend inapplicable la loi de 1889 ;

Considérant que le Tribunal n'a pas à rechercher ce qu'il faudrait décider si la créance avait appartenu à des Italiens au moment où intervenait la loi qui réduisait dans de si grandes proportions les droits des créanciers du Pérou et si les mêmes sacrifices pouvaient être imposés aux étrangers et aux nationaux ;

Mais qu'en ce moment, il s'agit uniquement de savoir si la situation faite aux nationaux, et qu'ils doivent subir, sera modifiée radicalement, parce qu'aux nationaux sont substitués des étrangers sous une forme ou sous une autre ;

Qu'une telle modification ne saurait être admise aisément, parce qu'elle serait contraire à cette idée simple que l'ayant-cause n'a pas plus de droit que son auteur.

Considérant que les frères Canevaro se présentent comme détenant les titres litigieux en vertu d'un endossement ;

Que l'on invoque à leur profit l'effet ordinaire de l'endossement qui est de faire considérer le porteur d'un titre à ordre comme créancier direct du débiteur, de telle sorte qu'il peut repousser les exceptions qui auraient été opposables à son endosseur ;

Considérant que, même en écartant la théorie d'après laquelle, en dehors des effets de commerce, l'endossement est une cession entièrement civile, il y a lieu, dans l'espèce, d'écarter l'effet attribué à l'endossement ;

Qu'en effet, si la date de l'endossement des titres de 1880 n'est pas connue, il est incontestable que cet endossement est de beaucoup postérieur à l'échéance ; qu'il y a lieu, dès lors, d'appliquer la disposition du Code de commerce péruvien de 1902 (art. 436) d'après laquelle l'endossement postérieur à l'échéance ne vaut que comme cession ordinaire ;

Que, d'ailleurs, le principe susrappelé au sujet de l'effet de l'endossement n'empêche pas d'opposer au porteur les exceptions tirées de la nature même du titre, qu'il a connues ou dû connaître ; qu'il est inutile de faire remarquer que les frères Canevaro connaissaient parfaitement le caractère des titres endossés à leur profit.

Considérant que, si les frères Canevaro ne peuvent, en tant que possesseur de la créance en vertu d'un endossement, prétendre à une condition plus favorable que celle de la société dont ils tiendraient leurs droits, il est permis de se demander si leur situation ne doit pas être différente en les envisageant en qualité d'héritiers de José Francisco Canevaro, comme les présente une déclaration notariée du 6 février 1905 ;

Qu'il y a, en effet, cette différence entre le cas de cession et le cas d'hérédité que, dans ce dernier, ce n'est pas par un acte de pure volonté que la créance a passé d'une tête sur une autre ;

Que, néanmoins, on ne trouve aucune raison décisive pour admettre que la situation a changé par ce fait que des Italiens ont succédé à un Péruvien et que les héritiers ont un titre nouveau qui leur permet de se prévaloir de la créance dans des conditions plus favorables que le *de cujus;*

Que c'est une règle générale que les héritiers prennent les biens dans l'état où ils se trouvaient entre les mains du défunt.

Considérant qu'enfin il a été soutenu que la loi péruvienne de 1889 sur la dette intérieure, sans changer les créances existantes contre le Pérou, avait seulement donné au Gouvernement la faculté de s'acquitter de ses dettes d'une certaine manière quand les créanciers en réclameraient le paiement, que c'est au moment où le paiement est réclamé qu'il faut se placer pour savoir si l'exception résultant de la loi peut être invoquée contre toutes personnes, spécialement contre les étrangers ;

Que, les propriétaires actuels de la créance étant des Italiens, il y aurait lieu pour le Tribunal de se prononcer sur le point de savoir si la loi péruvienne de 1889, malgré son caractère exceptionnel, peut être imposée aux étrangers;

Mais considérant que ce point de vue paraît en désaccord avec les termes généraux et l'esprit de la loi de 1889;

Que le Congrès, dont il ne s'agit pas d'apprécier l'œuvre en elle-même, a entendu liquider complètement la situation financière du Pérou, substituer les titres qu'il créait aux titres anciens;

Que cette situation ne peut être modifiée, parce que les créanciers se présentent plus ou moins tôt pour le règlement de leurs créances;

Que telle était la situation de la maison Canevaro, péruvienne au moment où la loi de 1889 entrait en vigueur, et que, pour les motifs déjà indiqués, cette situation n'a pas été changée en droit par le fait que la créance a, par endossement ou par héritage, passé à des Italiens.

Considérant, en dernier lieu, qu'il a été allégué que le Gouvernement péruvien doit indemniser les réclamants du préjudice que leur a occasionné son retard à s'aquitter de la dette de 1880, que le préjudice consiste dans la différence entre le paiement en or et le paiement en titres de la dette consolidée; qu'ainsi le Gouvernement péruvien serait tenu de payer en or la somme réclamée, en admettant même que la loi de 1889, se soit régulièrement appliquée à la créance;

Considérant que le Tribunal estime qu'en entrant dans cet ordre d'idées, il sortirait des termes du Compromis qui le charge seulement de décider si le Gouvernement du Pérou doit payer en argent comptant *ou* d'après les dispositions de la loi péruvienne du 12 juin 1889; que, le Tribunal ayant admis cette dernière alternative, la première solution doit être exclue; qu'il n'est pas chargé d'apprécier la responsabilité qu'aurait encourue à un autre titre le Gouvernement péruvien, de rechercher notamment si le retard à payer peut ou non être excusé par les circonstances difficiles dans lesquelles il se trouvait, étant donné surtout qu'il s'agirait en réalité d'une responsabilité encourue envers une maison péruvienne qui était créancière quand le retard s'est produit.

Considérant qu'il y a lieu de rechercher quel était le montant de la créance Canevaro au moment où est entrée en vigueur la loi de 1889;

Qu'elle se composait d'abord du capital de 43,140 livres sterling, mais qu'il faut y ajouter les intérêts ayant couru jusque là;

Que les intérêts qui étaient, d'après le décret du 23 décembre 1880, de 4% par an jusqu'aux échéances respectives des bons délivrés et qui étaient compris dans le montant de ces bons, doivent être, à partir de ces échéances, calculés au taux légal de 6% (Art. 1274 du Code civil péruvien) jusqu'au 1er janvier 1889;

Qu'on obtient ainsi une somme de £16,577.2.2 qui doit être jointe au principal pour former la somme globale devant être remboursée en titres de la dette consolidée et devant produire un intérêt de 1% payable en or à partir du 1er janvier 1889 jusqu'au paiement définitif;

Considérant que, d'après ce qui a été décidé plus haut relativement à la situation de Raphaël Canevaro, c'est seulement au sujet de ses deux frères que le Tribunal doit statuer.

Considérant qu'il appartient au Tribunal de régler le mode d'exécution de sa sentence.

PAR CES MOTIFS,

Le Tribunal arbitral décide que le Gouvernement Péruvien devra, le 31 juillet 1912, remettre à la Légation d'Italie à Lima pour le compte des frères Napoléon et Carlo Canevaro:

1°. en titres de la dette intérieure (1%) de 1889, le montant nominal de trente-neuf mille huit cent onze livres sterling huit sh. un p. (£39,811.8.1.) contre remise des deux tiers des titres délivrés de 23 décembre 1880 à la maison José Canevaro é hijos;

2°. en or, la somme de neuf mille trois cent quatre-vingt huit livres sterling dix-sept sh. un p. (£9,388.17.1.), correspondant à l'intérêt de 1% du 1er janvier 1889 au 31 juillet 1912.

Le Gouvernement péruvien pourra retarder le paiement de cette dernière somme jusqu'au 1er janvier 1913 à la charge d'en payer les intérêts à 6% à partir du 1er août 1912.

Fait à la Haye, dans l'Hôtel de la Cour Permanente d'Arbitrage, le 3 mai 1912.

Le Président: LOUIS RENAULT

Le Secrétaire général: MICHIELS VAN VERDUYNEN

Agreement for Arbitration, April 25, 1910[1]

Riuniti nel ministero delle relazioni estere del Perù i sottoscritti, conte Giulio Bolognesi, incaricato d'affari d'Italia, ed il dottor don Melitón F. Porras, ministro delle relazioni estere del Perù, hanno convenuto quanto segue:

Il governo di S. M. il Re d'Italia ed il governo della repubblica del Perù, non avendo potuto mettersi d'accordo riguardo al reclamo formulato dal primo in nome dei signori conti Napoleone, Carlo e Raffaele Canevaro per il pagamento della somma di quarantatre mila cento quaranta lire sterline, più gli interessi legali che essi sollecitano dal governo del Perù,

Hanno determinato, conformemente all'art. 1° del trattato per-

Reunidos en el Ministerio de Relaciones Exteriores del Perú, los infrascritos Señores Conte Giulio Bolognesi, Encargado de Negocios de Italia, y doctor don Melitón F. Porras, Ministro del Ramo, han convenido en lo siguiente:

El Gobierno de S. M. el Rey de Italia y el Gobierno de la Republica Peruana, no habiendo podido ponerse de acuerdo respecto de la reclamacion formulada por el primero á nombre de los Señores Condes Napoléon, Carlos y Rafael Canevaro, para el pago de la suma de cuarenta y tres mil ciento cuarenta libras esterlinas y sus intereses legales, que ellos solicitan del Gobierno del Perú,

Han determinado, de conformidad con el art. 1° del Tratado

[1] Official report, p. 5.

manente d'arbitrato esistente fra i due paesi, sottomettere questa controversia alla corte permanente d'arbitrato dell'Aja, la quale dovrà giudicare in diritto i seguenti punti :

Deve il governo del Perù pagare in effettivo o in base alle disposizioni della legge peruana del debito interno del 12 giugno 1889 le cambiali di cui sono attualmente possessori i fratelli Napoleone, Carlo e Raffaele Canevaro e che furono tratte dal governo del Perù all'ordine della Casa José Canevaro & Hijos per la somma di 43,140 lire sterline, più gli interessi legali di questa somma ?

Hanno i fratelli Canevaro diritto ad esigere la totalità della somma reclarata ?

Ha il conte Raffaele Canevaro diritto ad essere considerato reclamante italiano ?

Il governo di S. M. il Re d'Italia ed il governo della repubblica del Perù si obbligano a nominare, entro quattro mesi di questo protocollo, i membri della corte arbitrale.

Entro sette mesi dalla costituzione della corte arbitrale ambedue i governi le presenteranno l'esposizione completa della controversia, con tutti i documenti, prove, allegati e argomenti del caso; ogni governo potrà disporre di altri cinque mesi per presentare alla corte arbitrale la propria risposta all'altro governo, ed in questa sarà permesso soltanto di riferirsi alle argomentazioni contenute nell'esposizione della parte contraria.

Si considererà allora terminata la discussione, a meno che la corte arbitrale richieda nuovi

Permanente de Arbitraje existente entre los dos paises, someter esta controversia á la Corte Permanente de Arbitraje de La Haye, la cual deberá juzgar en derecho los siguientes puntos :

Debe el Gobierno del Perú pagar en efectivo, ó con aseglo á las disposiciones de la ley peruana de deuda interna de 12 Junio de 1889, los libramientos de que son actualmente posedores los hermanos Napoleón, Carlos y Rafael Canevaro y que fueron girados par el Gobierno Peruano á la orden de la Casa José Canevaro y Hijos para la suma de 43,140 libras esterlinas y ademas los intereses legales de dicha suma ?

Tienen los hermanos Canevaro derecho á exigir la totalidad de la suma reclamada ?

Tiene don Rafael Canevaro derecho á ser considerado como reclamante italiano ?

El Gobierno de S. M. el Rey de Italia y el Gobierno de la Republica Peruana se obligan á nombrar, dentro de cuatro meses contados desde la fecha de esto protocolo, los miembros de la Corte Arbitrale.

A los siete meses de la constitución de la Corte Arbitral, ambos Gobiernos le presentaran la exposición completa de la contraversia, con todos los documentos, pruebas, alegatos y argumentos del caso; cada Gobierno podrá disponer de otros cinco meses para presentar ante la Corte Arbitral su respuesta al otro Gobierno, y en dicha respuesta solamente será permitido referirse á las alegaciones contenidas en la exposición de la Parte Contraria.

Se considerará entonces terminada la discusión, á menos que la Corte Arbitral solicite neuvos

documenti, prove od allegati, che dovranno essere presentati entro quattro mesi contati dal momento in cui l'arbitro li chiede.

Se detti documenti, prove od allegati non vengono presentati entro questo termine, si pronuncierà la sentenza arbitrale, come se non esistessero.

In fede di che, i sottoscritti hanno firmato il presente protocollo, redatto in italiano ed in spagnuolo e vi hanno apposto i loro rispettivi sigilli.

Fatto in doppio esemplare, in Lima, il venticinque aprile millenovecentodieci.

documentos, pruebas ó alegatos, que deberán ser presentados dentro de cuatro meses contados desde el momento en que el Arbitro los pida.

Si dichos documentos, pruebas ó alegatos no se habiesen presentado en esto termino, se pronunciará la sentencia arbitral como si no existieren.

En fé de lo cual, los infrascritos firman el presente Protocolo, redacto en italiano y en español, poniendo en el sus respectivos sellos.

Hecho en doblo ejemplar, en Lima, el veinte y cinco de abril de mil noveciento dies.

GIULIO BOLOGNESI
M. F. PORRAS

Notes of April 27, 1910, concerning the Formation of the Tribunal[1]

MINISTERIO DE RELACIONES EXTERIORES
No. 18

Lima, *27 de abril de 1910.*

Señor encargado de negocios:

No habiéndose estipulado en el protocolo que somete á arbitraje la reclamación presentada contra el gobierno del Perú por los hermanos Canevaro, la forma de constitución de la corte arbitral, me es grato proponer á vuestra señoría que ella se haga de acuerdo con el articulo 87 de la convención para el arreglo pacífico de los conflictos internacionales, firmada en La Haya en 1907.

Renuevo á vuestra señoría, las seguridades de mi mayor consideración.

M. F. PORRAS

Al señor condé JULIO BOLOGNESI, encargado de negocios de Italia.

(TRADUCCIÓN)

LEGACIÓN DE S. M. EL REY DE ITALIA
No. 273

Lima, *27 de abril de 1910.*

Señor ministro:

Tengo el honor de acusar á V. E. recibo de su nota No. 18, fecha de hoy, y me es grato aceptar la propuesta de V. E. de constituir la

---

[1]*Boletín del Ministerio de Relaciones Exteriores* (Peru), No. xxxv, p. 263.

corte arbitral de La Haya que debe dar su fallo en la controversia
Canevaro, con arreglo á las disposiciones del artículo 87 de la convención para el arreglo pacífico de los conflictos internacionales firmada
en La Haya en 1907.

Quiera, señor ministro, aceptar las seguridades de mi mas alta y
distinguida consideración.

GIULIO BOLOGNESI

A S. E. el doctor don MELITON F. PORRAS, ministro de relaciones
exteriores.

THE RUSSIAN INDEMNITY CASE

Award of the Tribunal, November 11, 1912[1]

Par un Compromis signé à Constantinople le 22 juillet/4 août 1910, le Gouvernement Impérial de Russie et le Gouvernement Impérial Ottoman sont convenus de soumettre à un Tribunal arbitral la décision définitive des questions suivantes:

"I. Oui ou non, le Gouvernement Impérial Ottoman est-il tenu de payer aux indemnitaires russes des dommages-intérêts à raison des dates auxquelles ledit gouvernement a procédé au payement des indemnitiés fixées en exécution de l'article 5 du traité du 27 janvier/8 février 1879, ainsi que du Protocole de même date?"

"II. En cas de décision affirmative sur la première question, quel serait le montant de ces dommages-intérêts?"

Le Tribunal arbitral a été composé de

Son Excellence Monsieur Lardy, Docteur en droit, Membre et ancien Président de l'Institut de droit international, Envoyé extraordinaire et Ministre plénipotentiaire de Suisse à Paris, Membre de la Cour Permanente d'Arbitrage, Surarbitre;

Son Excellence le Baron Michel de Taube, Adjoint du Ministre de l'Instruction publique de Russie, Conseiller d'Etat actuel, Docteur en droit, associé de l'Institut de droit international, Membre de la Cour Permanente d'Arbitrage;

Monsieur André Mandelstam, Premier Drogman de l'Ambassade Impériale de Russie à Constantinople, Conseiller d'Etat, Docteur en droit international, associé de l'Institut de droit international;

Herante Abro Bey, Licencié en droit, Conseiller légiste de la Sublime-Porte;

et Ahmed Réchid Bey, Licencié en droit, Conseiller légiste de la Sublime-Porte;

Monsieur Henri Fromageot, Docteur en droit, associé de l'Institut de droit international, Avocat à la Cour d'Appel de Paris, a fonctionné comme Agent de Gouvernement Impérial Russe et a été assisté de

Monsieur Francis Rey, Docteur en droit, Secrétaire de la Commission Européenne du Danube, en qualité de Secrétaire;

Monsieur Edouard Clunet, Avocat à la Cour d'Appel de Paris, Membre et ancien Président de l'Institut de droit international, a fonctionné comme Agent du Gouvernement Impérial Ottoman et a été assisté de

Monsieur Ernest Roguin, Professeur de Législation comparée à l'Université de Lausanne, Membre de l'Institut de droit international, en qualité de Conseil du Gouvernement Ottoman;

---

[1] Official report, p. 79.

Monsieur André Hesse, Docteur en droit, Avocat à la Cour d'Appel de Paris, Député, en qualité de Conseil du Gouvernement Ottoman ;

Youssouf Kémâl Bey, Professeur à la Faculté de droit de Constantinople, ancien Député, Directeur de la Mission Ottomane d'études juridiques, en qualité de Conseil du Gouvernement Ottoman ;

Monsieur C. Campinchi, Avocat à la Cour d'Appel de Paris, en qualité de Secrétaire de l'Agent du Gouvernement Ottoman.

Le Baron Michiels van Verduynen, Secrétaire général du Bureau international de la Cour Permanente d'Arbitrage, a fonctionné comme Secrétaire général et

le Jonkheer W. Röell, Premier secrétaire du Bureau international de la Cour, a pourvu au Secrétariat.

Après une première séance à La Haye le 15 février 1911, pour régler certaines questions de procédure, les Mémoire, Contre-Mémoire, Réplique et Contre-Réplique ont été dûment échangé entre les Parties et communiqués aux Arbitres, qui ont respectivement déclaré, ainsi que les Agents des Parties, renoncer à demander des compléments de renseignements.

Le Tribunal arbitral s'est réuni de nouveau à La Haye les 28, 29, 30, 31 octobre, 1ᵉʳ, 2, 5 et 6 novembre 1912,

et après avoir entendu les conclusions orales des Agents et Conseils des Parties, il a rendu la Sentence suivante :

QUESTION PRÉJUDICIELLE

Vu la demande préjudicielle du Gouvernement Impérial Ottoman tendant à faire déclarer la réclamation du Gouvernement Impérial Russe non recevable sans examen du fond, le Tribunal

attendu que le Gouvernement Impérial Ottoman base cette demande préjudicielle, dans ses conclusions écrites, sur le fait "que, dans toute la correspondance diplomatique, ce sont les sujets russes individuellement qui, bénéficiant d'une stipulation faite en leurs noms, soit dans les Préliminaires de Paix signés à San Stéfano le 19 février 3 mars 1878, soit par l'article 5 du Traité de Constantinople du 27 janvier 8 février 1879, soit par le Protocole du même jour, ont été les créanciers directs des sommes capitales à eux adjugées, et que leurs titre à cet égard ont été constitués par les décisions nominatives prises par la Commission *ad hoc* réunie à l'Ambassade de Russie à Constantinople, décisions nominatives qui ont été notifiées à la Sublime-Porte ;

"Que, dans ces circonstances, le Gouvernement Impérial de Russie aurait dû justifier de la survivance des droits de chaque indemnitaire, et de l'individualité des personnes aptes à s'en prévaloir aujourd'hui, cela d'autant plus que la cession de certains de ces droits a été communiquée au Gouvernement Impérial Ottoman" ;

"Que le Gouvernement Impérial de Russie aurait dû agir de même, dans l'hypothèse aussi où l'Etat russe aurait été le créancier direct unique des indemnités ; cela parce que le dit Gouvernement ne saurait méconnaître son devoir de transmettre aux indemnitaires ou à leurs ayants-cause les sommes qu'il pourrait obtenir dans le procès actuel à titre de dommages-intérêts moratoires, les indemnitaires se présentant, dans cette supposition, comme les bénéficiaires, si non comme les créanciers, de la stipulation faite dans leur intérêt;

"Que cependant, le Gouvernement Impérial de Russie n'a fourni aucune justification quant à la personnalité des indemnitaires ou de leurs ayants-droit, ni quant à la survivance de leurs prétentions." (Contre-Réplique Ottomane, p. 81 et 82.)

Attendu que le Gouvernement Impérial de Russie soutient, au contraire, dans ses conclusions écrites,

"Que la dette stipulée dans le Traité de 1879 n'en est pas moins une dette d'Etat à Etat; qu'il n'en saurait être autrement de la responsabilité résultant de l'inexécution de la dite dette; qu'en conséquence le Gouvernement Impérial Russe est seul qualifié pour en donner quittance et, par là-même, pour toucher les sommes destinées à être payées aux indemnitaires; qu'au surplus, le Gouvernement Impérial Ottoman ne conteste pas au Gouvernement Impérial Russe la qualité de créancier direct de la Sublime-Porte;

"Que le Gouvernement Impérial Russe agit en vertu du droit qui lui est propre de réclamer des dommages-intérêts en raison de l'inexécution d'un engagement pris vis-à-vis de lui directement;

"Qu'il en justifie pleinement en établissant cette inexécution, qui n'est d'ailleur pas contestée, et en apportant son titre, qui est le Traité de 1879 . . .;

"Que la Sublime-Porte, nantie de la quittance à elle régulièrement délivrée par le Gouvernement Impérial Russe, n'a pas à s'immiscer dans la répartition des sommes distribuées ou à distribuer par ledit Gouvernement entre ses sujets indemnitaires; que c'est là une question d'ordre intérieur, dont le Gouvernement Impérial Ottoman n'a pas à connaître" (Réplique Russe, pages 49 et 50).

Considérant que l'origine de la réclamation remonte à une guerre, fait international au premier chef; que la source de l'indemnité est non seulement un Traité international mais un Traité de paix et les accords ayant pour objet l'exécution de ce Traité de paix; que ce traité et ces accords sont intervenus entre la Russie et la Turquie réglant entre elles, d'Etat à Etat, comme Puissances publiques et souveraines, une question de droit des gens; que les préliminaires de paix ont fait rentrer les 10 millions de roubles attribués à titre de dommages et intérêts aux sujets russes victimes des opérations de guerre en Turquie au nombre des indemnités "que S. M. l'Empereur de Russie réclame et que la Sublime-Porte s'est engagée à lui rembourser"; que ce caractère de créance d'Etat à Etat a été confirmé par le fait que les réclamations devaient être examinées par une Commission exclusivement russe; que le Gouvernement Impérial de Russie a conservé la haute main sur l'attribution, l'encaissement et la distribution des indemnités, en sa qualité de seul créancier; qu'il importe peu de savoir si, en théorie, la Russie a agi en vertu de son droit de protéger ses nationaux ou à un autre titre, du moment où c'est envers le Gouvernement Impérial Russe seul que la Sublime-Porte a pris ou a subi l'engagement réclamé d'elle:

Considérant que l'exécution des engagements est, entre Etats comme entre particuliers, le plus sûr commentaire du sens de ces engagements;

que, lors d'une tentative de l'administration Ottomane des Finances de percevoir, en 1885, sur une quittance donnée par l'Ambassade de Russie à Constantinople lors du payement d'un acompte, le timbre proportionnel exigé des particuliers par la législation ottomane, la Russie a immédiatement protesté et soutenu "que la dette était contractée par le Gouvernement Ottoman vis-à-vis celui de Russie" . . . et "non pas une simple créance de particuliers découlant d'un engagement ou contrat privé" (Note verbale russe du 15/27 mars 1885. Mémoire Russe, annexe N°. 19, page 19); que la Sublime-Porte n'a pas insisté, et qu'en fait, les deux Parties ont constamment, dans leur pratique de plus de quinze ans, agi comme si la Russie était la créancière de la Turquie à l'exclusion des indemnitaires privés;

que la Sublime-Porte a payé sans aucune exception tous les versements successifs sur la seule quittance de l'Ambassade de Russie à Constantinople agissant pour compte de son Gouvernement;

que la Sublime-Porte n'a jamais demandé, lors des versements d'acomptes, si les bénéficiaires existaient toujours ou quels étaient leurs ayants-cause du moment, ni d'après quelles normes les acomptes étaient répartis entre eux, laissant cette mission au seul Gouvernement Impérial de Russie;

Considérant que la Sublime-Porte prétend, au fond, dans le litige actuel, précisément être entièrement libérée par les payements qu'elle a, en fait, effectués en dehors de toute participation des indemnitaires entre les mains du seul Gouvernement Impérial de Russie représenté par son ambassade;

Par ces Motifs:

Arrête

la demande préjudicielle est écartée.

Statuant ensuite sur le fond le Tribunal arbitral a rendu la Sentence suivante:

I

En Fait

Dans le Protocole signé à Andrinople le 19/31 janvier 1878 et qui a mis fin par un armistice aux hostilités entre la Russie et la Turquie, se trouve la stipulation suivante:

"5°. La Sublime-Porte s'engage à dédommager la Russie des frais de la guerre et des pertes qu'elle a dû s'imposer. Le mode, soit pécuniaire, soit territorial ou autre, de cette indemnité sera réglé ultérieurement."

L'article 19 des Préliminaires de paix signés à San Stefano le 19 février/3 mars 1878 est ainsi conçu:

"Les indemnités de guerre et les pertes imposées à la Russie que S. M. l'Empereur de Russie réclame et que la Sublime-Porte s'est engagée à lui rembourser se composent de: a) 900 millions de roubles de frais de guerre . . . b) 400 millions de roubles de dommages infligés au littoral méridional . . . c) 100 millions de roubles de dommages causés au Caucase . . . d) *dix millions de roubles de dommages et intérêts aux sujets et institutions russes en Turquie:* total 1,400 millions de roubles."

Et plus loin: *"Les dix millions de roubles réclamés comme indemnité pour les sujets et institutions russes en Turquie seront payés à mesure que les réclamations des intéressés seront examinées par l'ambassade de Russie à Constantinople et transmises à la Sublime-Porte."*

Au congrès de Berlin, à la séance du 2 juillet 1878, protocole N°. 11, il fut entendu que les 10 millions de roubles dont il s'agit ne regardaient pas l'Europe, mais seulement les deux Etats intéressés, et qu'ils ne seraient pas insérés dans le traité entre les Puissances représentées à Berlin. En conséquence la question fut reprise directement entre la Russie et la Turquie, qui stipulèrent, dans le traité définitif de paix signé à Constantinople le 27 janvier/8 février 1879, la disposition suivante:

> Art. V. Les réclamations des sujets et institutions russes en Turquie à titre d'indemnité pour les dommages subis pendant la guerre seront payées à mesure qu'elles seront examinées par l'ambassade de Russie à Constantinople et transmises à la Sublime-Port. La totalité de ces réclamations ne pourra, en aucun cas, dépasser le chiffre de vingt-six millions sept cent cinquante mille francs. Le terme d'une année après l'échange des ratifications est fixé comme date à partir de laquelle les réclamations pourront être présentées à la Sublime-Porte, et celui de deux ans comme date après laquelle les réclamations ne seront plus admises.

Le même jour, 27 janvier/8 février 1879, dans le Protocole de signature du traité de paix, le Plénipotentiaire russe prince Lobanow déclara que la somme de 26,750,000 francs spécifiée à l'article V: "constitue un maximum auquel la totalité des réclamations ne pourra vraisemblablement jamais atteindre; il ajoute qu'une commission *ad hoc* sera instituée à l'ambassade de Russie pour examiner scrupuleusement les réclamations qui lui seront présentées, et que, d'après les instructions de son Gouvernement, un délégué ottoman pourra prendre part à l'examen de ces réclamations."

Les ratifications du traité de paix out été échangées à Saint-Pétersbourg le 9/21 février 1879.

La commission instituée à l'ambassade de Russie et composée de trois fonctionnaires russes commença aussitôt ses travaux. Le commissaire ottoman s'abstint généralement d'y prendre part. Le montant des pertes des sujets russes fut fixé par la commission à 6 millions 186,543 francs. Elles furent successivement notifiées à la Sublime-Porte entre le 22 octobre/3 novembre 1880 et le 29 janvier/10 février 1881; leur montant ne fut pas contesté et l'ambassade de Russie réclama le payement en même temps qu'elle transmettait à la Sublime-Porte les dernières décisions de la commission.

Le 23 septembre 1881, l'ambassade transmet une "pétition" de l'avocat Rossolato, "mandataire spécial de plusieurs sujets russes" ayant à toucher des indemnités, pétition adressée à l'ambassade et mettant le Gouvernement Ottoman en demeure de s'entendre avec lui "dans un délai de huit jours à partir de la signification, sur le mode de payement," déclarant "le tenir d'ores et déjà responsable de tous dommages-intérêts et notamment des intérêts moratoires."

Par convention signée à Constantinople le 2/14 mai 1882, les deux gouvernements conviennent, art. I⁰ʳ, que l'indemnité de guerre, dont le solde avait été fixé à 802,500,000 francs par l'art. IV du traité de paix de 1879 après défalcation de la valeur des territoires cédés par la Turquie, ne porterait pas d'intérêts et serait payée sous forme de cent versements annuels de 350,000 livres turques soit environ 8 millions de francs.

Le 19 juin/1ᵉʳ juillet 1884, aucune somme n'ayant été versée pour les indemnitaires, l'ambassade "réclame formellement le payement intégral des indemnités qui ont été adjugées aux sujets russes . . . .; elle se verra obligée, dans le cas contraire, à leur reconnaître la faculté de prétendre, outre le capital, à des intérêts proportionnés au retard que subit le règlement de leur créance."

Le 19 décembre 1884, la Sublime-Porte verse un premier acompte de 50,000 livres turques, soit environ 1,150,000 fr.

En 1885 se produit l'union de la Bulgarie et de la Roumélie orientale et la guerre serbo-bulgare. La Turquie ne paie aucun nouvel acompte. Une note de rappel en date de janvier 1886 ayant été sans résultat, l'ambassade insiste, le 15/27 février 1887 ; elle transmet une "pétition" qui lui est parvenue d'indemnitaires russes, dans laquelle ils tiennent le Gouvernement Ottoman "responsable de ce surcroît de dommages qui résulte pour eux du retard apporté au payement de leurs indemnités," et l'ambassade ajoute : "De nouveaux ajournements obligeraient le Gouvernement Impérial à réclamer en faveur de ses nationaux des intérêts pour les retards que subit le règlement de leurs créances."

Après des notes de rappel de juillet et décembre 1887 demeurées sans effet, l'ambassade se plaint le 26 janvier/7 février 1888, de ce que la Turquie ait payé diverses créances postérieures aux obligations contractées envers les indemnitaires russes. Elle rappelle que "les arriérés se montent à la somme d'environ 215,000 livres turques, un seul versement de 50,000 livres turques ayant été fait sur le total de 265,000 livres turques adjugées" ; elle demande donc "d'urgence . . . . que les sommes dues aux sujets russes soient immédiatement, et avant tout autre payement, prélevées sur celles qui seront payées par X . . . ." (un débiteur du Gouvernement Imperial Ottoman).

Le 22 avril 1889, la Turquie verse un second acompte de 50,000 livres.

Le 31 décembre 1890/12 janvier 1891, l'ambassade, constatant qu'il a été payé seulement 100,000 livres sur un total de 265,000, écrit à la Sublime-Porte que le retard apporté au règlement de cette créance fait subir des pertes toujours croissantes aux nationaux russes ; elle croit donc devoir prier la Sublime-Porte "de provoquer des ordres immédiats à qui de droit pour que la somme due . . . soit payée sans retard, *aussi bien que les intérêts légaux* au sujet desquels [l'ambassade] a eu l'honneur de prévenir la Sublime-Porte par note du 15/27 février 1887."

En août 1891 nouveau rappel. En octobre/novembre 1892, l'ambassade écrit "que cela ne peut durer indéfiniment ainsi"; que "les instances des sujets russes deviennent de plus en plus pressantes," que "l'ambassade a le devoir de s'en faire avec énergie l'interprète, . . . qu'il s'agit là d'une obligation indiscutable et d'un devoir international à remplir . . .," que "le Gouvernement Ottoman ne saurait plus invoquer pour s'y soustraire l'état précaire de ses finances," et conclut en demandant un "prompt et définitif règlement de la créance . . ."

Le 2/14 avril 1893, un troisième versement de 75,000 livres turques est effectué; la Sublime-Porte, en donnant avis de ce payement dès le 27 mars, ajoute que, pour le reliquat, la moitié en sera inscrite au budget courant et l'autre moitié au budget prochain; "la question ainsi réglée met heureusement fin aux incidents auxquels elle avait donné lieu." La Porte espère dès lors que l'ambassade voudra bien, dans ses sentiments d'amitié sincère à l'égard de la Turquie, accepter définitivement le monopole du tumbéki à l'instar des autres Puissances.

A cette occasion, et en rappelant que le Gouvernement Impérial Russe "s'est toujours montré amical et conciliant dans toutes les affaires touchant aux intérêts financiers de l'Empire ottoman," l'ambassade prend acte le 30 du même mois des dispositions annoncées en vue du payement et consent à ce que les Russes faisant en Turquie le commerce des tumbéki soient soumis au régime nouvellement créé.

Un an plus tard, le 23 mai/4 juin 1894, n'ayant reçu aucun versement nouveau, l'ambassadeur, après avoir constaté la non-exécution de "l'arrangement" auquel il avait "consenti afin de faciliter au Gouvernement Ottoman l'accomplissement de son obligation," se déclare "placé dans l'impossibilité d'accepter des promesses, des arrangements ou des atermoiements ultérieurs," et "obligé d'insister pour *que la totalité du reliquat* dû aux sujets russes, *qui monte à* 91,000 *livres turques,* soit, sans plus de retard, versé à l'ambassade . . . De récentes opérations financières viennent de mettre à la disposition [de la Sublime-Porte] des sommes importantes."

Le 27 octobre de la même année 1894, un versement de 50,000 livres turques est effectué, et la Sublime-Porte écrit, déjà le 3 du même mois, à l'ambassade: "Quant au reliquat de 41 mille livres turques, la Banque Ottomane en garantira le payement dans le cours de l'exercice prochain."

En 1896, une correspondance est échangée entre la Sublime-Porte et l'ambassade sur la question de savoir si les revenus sur lesquels la Banque Ottomane devait prélever le reliquat ne sont pas déjà engagés à la Russie pour le payement de l'indemnité de guerre proprement dite ou si la partie de ces revenus supérieure à l'annuité affectée à l'indemnité de guerre ne peut pas être employée à l'indemnisation des sujets russes victimes des événements de 1877/8. Au cours de cette correspondance, la Sublime-Porte indique, dans les notes qu'elle adresse à l'ambassade les 11 février et 28 mai 1896, que le reliquat dû s'élève à la somme de 43,978 livres turques.

De 1895 à 1899, de graves événements survenus en Asie-Mineure obligent la Turquie à provoquer un moratoire en faveur de la Banque Ottomane sur sa demande; l'insurrection des Druses, celle de la Crête qui est suivie de la guerre turco-grecque de 1897, des insurrections en Macédoine amènent à diverses reprises la Turquie à mobiliser des troupes et même des armées.

Pendant trois ans, aucune correspondance n'est échangée, et, lorsqu'elle reprend, la Sublime-Porte indique de nouveau le chiffre de 43,978 livres turques, comme le montant du reliquat des indemnités, dans les notes qu'elle adresse à l'ambassade les 19 juillet 1899 et 5 juillet 1900. A son tour, l'ambassade, dans ses notes de 25 avril/8 mai 1900 et 3/16 mars 1901, indique le même chiffre mais se plaint de ce que les ordres donnés dans diverses provinces "pour le payement des 43,978 livres turques, montant du reliquat de l'indemnité due aux sujets russes," n'ont pas été suivis d'effet, et de ce que la Banque Ottomane n'a rien versé; elle prie instamment la Sublime-Porte de vouloir bien donner à qui de droit des ordres catégoriques pour le payement, sans plus de retard, des sommes susmentionnées."

Après qu'en mai 1901 la Sublime-Porte eut annoncé que le Département des Finances avait été invité à régler dans le courant du mois le reliquat de l'indemnité, la Banque Ottomane avisait enfin, les 24 février et 26 mai 1902, l'ambassade de Russie qu'elle avait reçu et tenait à la disposition de l'ambassade 42,438 livres turques sur le reliquat de 43,978 livres.

L'ambassade, en accusant deux mois plus tard réception de cet envoi à la Sublime-Porte le 23 juin/6 juillet 1902, faisait observer "que le Gouvernement Impérial Ottoman a mis plus de vingt ans pour s'acquitter, et imparfaitement encore, d'une dette dont le règlement immédiat s'imposait à tous les points de vue, un solde de 1,539 livres turques restant toujours impayé. Se référant, par conséquent, à ses notes des 23 septembre 1881, 15/27 février 1887 et 31 décembre 1890/12 janvier 1891 au sujet des intérêts à courir sur la dite créance, restée si longtemps en souffrance" l'ambassade transmet une requête par laquelle les indemnitaires réclament, en substance, des intérêts composés à 12% depuis le 1er janvier 1881 jusqu'au 15 mars 1887, et à 9% depuis cette date, à laquelle le taux de l'intérêt légal a été abaissé par une loi ottomane. La somme réclamée par les signataires s'élevait à une vingtaine de millions de francs au printemps de 1902 pour un capital primitif de 6,200,000 francs environ. La note se terminait comme suit: "L'ambassade impériale se plaît à croire que la Sublime-Porte n'hésitera pas à reconnaître en principe le bien fondé de la réclamation exposée dans cette requête; dans le cas pourtant où la Sublime-Porte trouverait des objections à soulever contre le montant de la somme réclamée par les sujets russes, l'ambassade impériale ne verrait pas d'inconvénients à déférer l'examen des détails à une commission composée de délégués Russes et Ottomans."

La Sublime-Porte répond le 17 de ce même mois de juillet 1902 que l'art. V du Traité de paix de 1879 et le protocole de même date ne stipulent pas d'intérêts et qu'à la lumière des négociations diplomatiques qui ont eu lieu à ce sujet, elle était loin de s'attendre à voir formuler au dernier moment de la part des indemnitaires de telles demandes, dont l'effet serait de rouvrir une question qui se trouvait heureusement terminée.   L'ambassade réplique le 3/16 février 1903 en insistant "sur le payement des dommages-intérêts réclamés par ses ressortissants. Il n'y a que le montant de ces dommages qui pourrait faire l'objet d'une enquête."—Sur une note de rappel en date du 2/15 août 1903, la Sublime-Porte répond le 4 mai 1904 en maintenant sa manière de voir et en se déclarant toutefois disposée à déférer la question à un arbitrage à La Haye dans le cas où l'on insisterait sur la réclamation.

Au bout de quatre ans, l'ambassade accepte cette suggestion par note du 19 mars/1ᵉʳ avril 1908.

Le compromis d'arbitrage a été signé à Constantinople le 22 juillet/4 août 1910.

Quant au petit solde de 1,539 livres turques, il avait été mis par la Banque Ottomane en décembre 1902 à la disposition de l'ambassade de Russie qui l'a refusé et il demeure consigné à la disposition de l'ambassade.

II

En Droit

1. Le Gouvernement Impérial de Russie base sa demande sur "la responsabilité des Etats pour inexécution de dettes pécuniaires"; cette responsabilité implique, selon lui, "l'obligation de payer des dommages-intérêts et spécialement les intérêts des sommes indûment retenues"; "l'obligation de payer des intérêts moratoires" est "la manifestation pratique, en matière de dettes d'argent," de la responsabilité des Etats (Réplique Russe, pp. 27 et 51). "La méconnaissance de ces principes serait aussi contraire à la notion même du droit des gens que dangereuse pour la sécurité des relations pacifiques; en effet, en déclarant l'Etat débiteur irresponsable du délai qu'il inflige à son créancier, on lui reconnaîtrait, par là même, la liberté de n'écouter que son caprice pour s'exécuter; . . . on obligerait, d'autre part, l'Etat créancier à recourir à la violence contre une semblable prétention . . . et à ne rien attendre d'un prétendu droit des gens manifestement incapable d'assurer le respect de la parole donnée" (Mémoire Russe, p. 29).

En d'autres termes, et toujours dans l'opinion du Gouvernement Impérial de Russie, "il ne s'agit nullement ici d'intérêts conventionnels, c'est-à-dire nés d'une stipulation particulière . . ." mais "l'obligation incombant au Gouvernement Impérial Ottoman de payer des intérêts moratoires est née du retard à exécuter, c'est-à-dire de l'inexécution partielle du Traité de paix; cette obligation est bien née, il est vrai, à l'occasion du traité de 1879, mais elle provient *ex post facto* d'une cause nouvelle et accidentelle, qui est la faute de la Sublime-Porte à remplir ses engagements comme elle s'y était obligée." (Mémoire Russe, p. 29; Réplique Russe, pp. 22 et 27.)

2. Le Gouvernement Impérial Ottoman, tout en admettant en termes explicites le principe général de la responsabilité des Etats à raison de l'inexécution de leurs engagements (Contre-Réplique, p. 29, No. 286 Note et p. 52, No. 358), soutient, au contraire, qu'en droit international public, des intérêts moratoires n'existent pas "sans stipulation expresse" (Contre-Mémoire Ottoman, p. 31, No. 83, et p. 34, No. 95); qu'un Etat "n'est pas un débiteur comme un autre" (Ibidem, p. 33, No. 90), et que, sans songer à soutenir "qu'aucune règle observable entre particuliers ne puisse être appliquée entre Etats" (Contre-Réplique Ottomane, p. 26, No. 275), on doit tenir compte de la situation *sui generis* de l'Etat puissance publique; que diverses législation (par exemple la loi française de 1831 qui institue une prescription extinctive de cinq ans pour les dettes de l'Etat, le droit romain qui pose le principe *"Fiscus ex suis contractibus usuras non dat,"* Lex 17, paragr. 5, Digeste 22, 1) reconnaissent à l'Etat débiteur une situation privilégiée (Contre-Mémoire Ottoman, p. 33, No. 92); qu'en admettant contre un Etat une obligation implicite, non expressément stipulée, en étendant part exemple à un Etat débiteur les règles de la mise en demeure et ses effets en droit privé, on rendrait cet Etat "débiteur dans une mesure plus forte qu'il ne l'aurait voulu, risquerait de compromettre la vie politique de l'Etat, de nuire à ses intérêts primordiaux, de bouleverser son budget, de l'empêcher de se défendre contre une insurrection ou contre l'étranger." (Contre-Mémoire Ottoman, p. 33, No. 91.)

Eventuellement et pour le cas où une responsabilité devrait lui incomber, le Gouvernement Impérial Ottoman conclut à ce que cette responsabilité consiste uniquement en intérêts moratoires et cela seulement à partir d'une mise en demeure reconnue régulière. (Contre-Réplique Ottomane, pp. 71 et suivantes, Nos. 410 et suivants.)

Il oppose en outre les exceptions de la chose jugée, de la force majeure, du caractère de libéralité des indemnités, et de la renonciation tacite ou expresse de la Russie au bénéfice de la mise en demeure.

3. Les rapports de droit qui font l'objet du présent litige étant intervenus entre Etats Puissances publiques sujets du droit international et ces rapports rentrant dans le domaine du droit public, *le droit applicable est le droit international public* soit droit des gens et les Parties sont avec raison d'accord sur ce point. (Mémoire Russe, p. 32; Contre-Mémoire Ottoman, numéros 47 à 54, p. 18–20; Réplique Russe, p. 18; Contre-Réplique Ottomane, p. 17, numéros 244 et 245.)

4. La demande du Gouvernement Impérial de Russie est fondée sur le principe général de la responsabilité des Etats, à l'appui duquel il a invoqué un grand nombre de sentences arbitrales.

La Sublime-Porte, sans contester ce principe général, prétend échapper à son application en affirmant le droit des Etats à une situation exceptionnelle et privilégiée dans le cas spécial de la responsabilité en matière de dettes d'argent.

Elle déclare inopérants la plupart des précédents arbitraux invoqués, comme ne s'appliquant pas à cette catégorie spéciale.

Le Gouvernement Impérial Ottoman fait observer, à l'appui de sa manière de voir, qu'en doctrine, on distingue des responsabilités diverses selon leur origine et selon leur étendue. Ces nuances se rattachent surtout à la théorie des responsabilités en Droit romain et dans les législations inspirées du Droit romain. Les Mémoires Ottomans rappellent les distinctions suivantes dont quelques-unes sont classiques: Les responsabilités sont d'abord divisées en deux catégories, suivant qu'elles ont pour cause un délit ou quasi-délit (responsabilité délictuelle) ou un contrat (responsabilité contractuelle).—Parmi les responsabilités contractuelles, on distingue encore suivant q l'il s'agit d'obligations ayant pour objet une prestation quelconque au tre qu'une somme d'argent ou suivant qu'il s'agit de prestations d'un caractère exclusivement pécuniaire, d'une dette d'argent proprement dite. Ces diverses catégories de responsabilités ne sont pas appréciées en droit civil d'une manière absolument identique, les circonstances nécessaires à la naissance de la responsabilité ainsi que ces conséquences étant variables.—Tandis qu'en matière de responsabilités délictuelles aucune formalité quelconque n'est nécessaire, en matière contractuelle il faut toujours une mise en demeure. Tandis qu'en matière d'obligations ayant pour objet une prestation autre qu'une somme d'argent comme d'ailleurs en matière délictuelle, la réparation du dommage est complète (*lucrum cessans* et *damnum emergens*), cette réparation, en matière de dettes d'argent, est restreinte forfaitairement aux intérêts de la somme due, lesquels ne courront qu'à partir de la mise en demeure. Les *dommages-intérêts* sont appelés *compensatoires* quand ils sont la compensation du dommage résultant d'un délit ou de l'inexécution d'une obligation. Ils sont appelés *dommages-intérêts moratoires*, bien qu'ils représentent encore une compensation, lorsqu'ils sont la conséquence d'un retard dans l'exécution d'une obligation.—Les auteurs enfin appellent *intérêts moratoires* les intérêts forfaitairement alloués en cas de retard dans le payement de dettes d'argent, les distinguant ainsi d'autres intérêts ajoutés, parfois, pour fixer le montant total d'une indemnité, à l'évaluation en argent d'un dommage, ces derniers étant appelés *intérêts compensatoires*.

Ces distinctions du droit civil s'expliquent: En matière de responsabilité contractuelle en effet, on est en droit d'exiger d'un co-contractant une diligence dont la victime d'un délit imprévu ne saurait être tenue.—En matière de dettes d'argent, la difficulté d'évaluer les conséquences de la demeure explique qu'on ait fixé forfaitairement le montant du dommage.

La thèse du Gouvernement Impérial Ottoman consiste à soutenir qu'en droit international public, la responsabilité spéciale consistant au payement d'intérêts moratoires en cas de retard dans le règlement d'une dette d'argent liquide n'existe pas pour un Etat débiteur. La Sublime-Porte ne conteste pas la responsabilité des Etats s'il s'agit de dommages-intérêts compensatoires, ni des intérêts pouvant rentrer dans le calcul de ces dommages-intérêts compensatoires. La responsabilité que la Sublime-Porte décline, c'est celle pouvant résulter, sous forme d'intérêts de retard ou moratoires au sens restreint, du retard dans l'exécution d'une obligation pécuniaire.

Il importe de rechercher si ces dénominations variées, ces appellations créées par les commentateurs, correspondent à des différences intrinsèques dans la nature même du droit, à des différences dans l'essence juridique de la notion de responsabilité.—Le tribunal est d'avis que tous les dommages-intérêts sont toujours la réparation, la compensation d'une faute. A ce point de vue, tous les dommages-intérêts sont compensatoires, peu importe le nom qu'on leur donne. Les intérêts forfaitaires alloués au créancier d'une somme d'argent à partir de la mise en demeure sont la compensation forfaitaire de la faute du débiteur en retard exactement comme les dommages-intérêts ou les intérêts alloués en cas de délit, de quasi-délit ou d'inexécution d'une obligation de faire, sont la compensation du préjudice subi par le créancier, la représentation en argent de la responsabilité du débiteur fautif. —Exagérer les conséquences des distinctions faites en droit civil dans la responsabilité se légitimerait d'autant moins qu'il se dessine, dans plusieurs législations récentes, une tendance à atténuer ou à supprimer les adoucissements apportés par le Droit romain et ses dérivés à la responsabilité en matière de dettes d'argent.—Il est certain en effet que toutes les fautes, quelle qu'en soit l'origine, finissent par être évaluées en argent et transformées en obligation de payer; elles aboutissent toutes, ou peuvent aboutir, en dernière analyse, à une dette d'argent. —Il n'est donc pas possible au tribunal d'apercevoir des différences essentielles entre les diverses responsabilités. Identiques dans leur origine, la faute, elles sont les mêmes dans leurs conséquences, la réparation en argent.

Le Tribunal est donc de l'avis que le principe général de la responsabilité des Etats implique une responsabilité spéciale en matière de retard dans le payement d'une dette d'argent, à moins d'établir l'existence d'une coutume internationale contraire.

Le Gouvernement Impérial de Russie et la Sublime-Porte ont apporté au débat une série de sentences arbitrales qui ont admis, affirmé et consacré le principe de la responsabilité des Etats. La Sublime-Porte considère comme inopérantes la presque totalité de ces sentences et élimine même celles dans lesquelles l'arbitre a expressément alloué l'intérêt de sommes d'argent. Le Gouvernement Impérial Ottoman est d'avis qu'il s'agit là d'intérêts compensatoires et il les écarte comme sans application dans le litige actuel. Le Tribunal, pour les motifs indiqués plus haut, est au contraire de l'avis qu'il n'existe pas de raisons pour ne pas s'inspirer de la grande analogie qui existe entre les diverses formes de la responsabilité; cette analogie apparait comme particulièrement étroite entre les *intérêts* dits moratoires et les *intérêts* dits compensatoires; l'analogie parait complète entre allocation d'intérêts à partir d'une certaine date à l'occasion de l'évaluation de la responsabilité en capital, et l'allocation d'intérêts sur un capital fixé par conven-

tion et demeuré impayé par un débiteur en faute. La seule différence
est que, dans un des cas, les intérêts sont alloués par le juge puisque
la dette n'était pas exigible et que dans l'autre le montant de la dette
était fixé par convention et que les intérêts deviennent exigibles automatiquement en cas de mise en demeure.

Pour infirmer cette analogie très étroite, il faudrait que la Sublime-
Porte pût établir l'existence d'une coutume, de précédents d'après
lesquels des intérêts moratoires au sens restreint du mot auraient été
refusés *en tant qu'intérêts moratoires,* l'existence d'une coutume dé-
rogeant, en matière de dette pécuniaire, aux règles générales de la responsabilité.—Le Tribunal est d'avis que cette preuve, non seulement
n'a pas été faite, mais que le Gouvernement Impérial Russe a pu se
prévaloir, au contraire, de plusieurs sentences arbitrales dans lesquelles
des intérêts moratoires ont été, parfois il est vrai avec des nuances et
dans une mesure discutables, alloués à des Etats (*Mexique-Vénézuela*,
2 octobre 1903, Mémoire Russe, p. 28 et note 5; Contre-Mémoire Ottoman, p. 38, N°. 107; *Colombie-Italie*, 9 avril 1904, Réplique Russe, p.
28 et note 7; Contre-Réplique Ottomane, p. 58, N°. 368; *Etats-Unis-
Choctaws*, Réplique Russe, p. 29; Contre-Réplique Ottomane, p. 59,
N°. 369. *Etats-Unis-Vénézuela*, 5 décembre 1885, Réplique Russe, p.
28 et note 5). Il y a lieu d'ajouter à ces cas la sentence rendue le 2
juillet 1881 par S. M. l'Empereur d'Autriche dans l'affaire de la Mosquitia, en ce sens que l'arbitre n'a nullement refusé des intérêts moratoires comme tels, mais a simplement prononcé que l'allocation du
capital ayant le caractère d'une libéralité, cela excluait, dans la pensée
de l'arbitre, des intérêts de retard (Réplique Russe, p. 28, note 4;
Contre-Réplique Ottomane, p. 55, N°. 365, note).

Il reste à examiner si la Sublime-Porte est fondée à soutenir qu'un
Etat n'est pas un débiteur comme un autre, qu'il ne peut être "débiteur
dans une mesure plus forte qu'il ne l'aurait voulu," et qu'en lui im-
posant des obligations qu'il n'a pas stipulées, par exemple les responsabilités d'un débiteur privé, on risquerait de compromettre ses finances
et même son existence politique.

Dès l'instant où le Tribunal a admis que les diverses responsabilités
des Etats ne se distinguent pas les unes des autres par des différences
essentielles, que toutes se résolvent ou peuvent finir pas se résoudre
dans le payement d'une somme d'argent, et que la coutume internationale et les précédents concordent avec ces principes, il faut en conclure que la responsabilité des Etats ne saurait être niée ou admise
qu'entièrement et non pour partie; il ne serait dès lors pas possible au
tribunal de la déclarer inapplicable en matière de dettes d'argent sans
étendre cette inapplicabilité à toutes les autres catégories de responsabilités.

Si un Etat est condamné à des dommages-intérêts compensatoires
d'un délit ou de l'inexécution d'une obligation, il est, encore plus que
dans le cas de retard dans le payement d'une dette d'argent conventionnelle, débiteur dans une mesure qu'il n'aurait pas stipulée volontairement.—Quant aux conséquences de ces responsabilités pour les

finances de l'Etat débiteur, elles peuvent être au moins aussi graves, sinon davantage, s'il s'agit des dommages-intérêts appelés compensatoires par la Sublime-Porte, que s'il s'agit des simples intérêts moratoires au sens restreint du mot.   Pour peu d'ailleurs que la responsabilité mette en péril l'existence de l'Etat, elle constituerait un cas de force majeure qui pourrait être invoqué en droit international public aussi bien que par un débiteur privé.

Le Tribunal est donc d'avis que la Sublime-Porte, qui a accepté explicitement le principe de la responsabilité des Etats, n'est pas fondée à demander une exception à cette responsabilité en matière de dettes d'argent, en invoquant sa qualité de Puissance publique et les conséquences politiques et financières de cette responsabilité.

5. Pour établir en quoi consiste cette responsabilité spéciale incombant à l'Etat débiteur d'une dette conventionnelle liquide et exigible, il convient maintenant de rechercher, en procédant par analogie comme l'ont fait les sentences arbitrales invoquées, les principes généraux de droit public et privé en cette matière, tant au point de vue de l'étendue de cette responsabilité qu'à celui des exceptions opposables.

Les législations privées des Etats faisant partie du concert européen admettent toutes, comme le faisait autrefois le Droit romain, l'obligation de payer au moins des intérêts de retard à titre d'indemnité forfaitaire lorsqu'il s'agit de l'inexécution d'une obligation consistant dans le payement d'une somme d'argent fixée conventionnellement, liquide et exigible, et cela au moins à partir de la mise en demeure du débiteur.—Quelques législations vont plus loin et considèrent que le débiteur est déjà en demeure dès la date de l'échéance ou encore admettent la réparation complète des dommages au lieu des simples intérêts forfaitaires.

Si la plupart des législations ont, à l'exemple du Droit romain, exigé une mise en demeure expresse, c'est que le créancier est en faute de son côté par manque de diligence tant qu'il ne réclame pas le payement d'une somme liquide et exigible.

Le Gouvernement Impérial Russe (Mémoire, p. 32) admet lui-même, en faveur de la nécessité d'une mise en demeure, qu'en équité, il peut convenir "de ne pas prendre par surprise un Etat débiteur passible d'intérêts moratoires, alors qu'aucun avertissement ne l'a rappelé à l'observation de ses engagements."   Les auteurs (p. ex. Heffter, *Droit international de l'Europe*, paragr. 94), font observer que, lors de "l'exécution d'un traité public, il faut procéder avec modération et avec équité, d'après la maxime qu'on doit traiter les autres comme on voudrait être traité soi-même.   Il faut, en conséquence, accorder des délais convenables, afin que la partie obligée subisse le moins de préjudice possible.   L'obligé peut attendre la mise en demeure du créancier avant d'être responsable du retard, s'il ne s'agit pas de prestations dont l'exécution est rattachée d'une manière expresse à une époque déterminée."   Voir aussi Merignhac *Traité de l'arbitrage international*, Paris, 1895, p. 290.

D'assez nombreuses sentences arbitrales internationales ont admis, même lorsqu'il s'agissait de *dommages-intérêts* moratoires, qu'il n'y avait pas lieu de les faire courir toujours dès la date du fait dommageable (*Etats-Unis contre Vénésuela,* Orinoco, sentence de la Haye du 25 octobre 1910 protocoles, p. 59, *Etats-Unis contre Chili,* 15 mai 1863, sentence de S. M. le Roi des Belges Léopold I, Lafontaine, Pasicrisie, p. 36, colonne 2 et p. 37, colonne 1, *Allemagne contre Vénésuela,* Arrangement du 7 mai 1903, Ralston & Doyle, Venezuelan Arbitrations, Washington, 1904, p. 520 à 523, *Etats-Unis contre Vénésuela,* 5 décembre 1885, Moore, Digest of International Arbitrations, p. 3545 et p. 3567, Vol. 4, etc., etc.).

Il n'y a donc pas lieu, et il serait contraire à l'équité de présumer une responsabilité de l'Etat débiteur plus rigoureuse que celle imposée au débiteur privé dans un grand nombre de législations européennes. L'équité exige, comme l'indique la doctrine, et comme le Gouvernement Impérial Russe l'admet lui-même, qu'il y ait eu avertissement, mise en demeure adressée au débiteur d'une somme ne portant pas d'intérêts. Les mêmes motifs réclament que la mise en demeure mentionne expressément les intérêts, et concourent à faire écarter une responsabilité dépassant les simples intérêts forfaitaires.

Il résulte de la correspondance produite que le Gouvernement Impérial Russe a expressément et en termes absolument catégoriques, réclamé de la Sublime-Porte le payement du capital et "des intérêts" par note de son ambassade à Constantinople en date du 31 décembre 1890/12 janvier 1891. Entre Etats, la voie diplomatique constitue le mode de communication normal et régulier pour leurs relations de droit international public; cette mise en demeure est donc régulière en la forme.

Le Gouvernement Impérial Ottoman doit donc être tenu pour responsable des intérêts de retard à partir de la réception de cette mise en demeure.

Le Gouvernement Impérial Ottoman invoque, pour le cas où une responsabilité lui serait imposée, diverses *exceptions* dont il rest à examiner la portée:

6. *L'exception de la force majeure,* invoquée en première ligne, est opposable en droit international public aussi bien qu'en droit privé; le droit international doit s'adapter aux nécessités politiques. Le Gouvernement Impérial Russe admet expressément (Réplique Russe, p. 33 et note 2) que l'obligation pour un Etat d'exécuter les traités peut fléchir "si l'existence même de l'Etat vient à être en danger, si l'observation du devoir international est . . . self destructive."

Il est incontestable que la Sublime-Porte prouve, à l'appui de l'exception de la force majeure (Contre-Mémoire Ottoman, p. 43, Nos. 119 à 128, Contre-Réplique Ottomane, p. 64, Nos. 382 à 398 et p. 87) que la Turquie s'est trouvée de 1881 à 1902 aux prises avec des difficultés financières de la plus extrême gravité, cumulées avec des événements intérieurs et extérieurs (insurrections, guerres) qui l'ont obligée à donner des affectations spéciales à un grand nombre de ses revenus, à subir un contrôle étranger d'une partie de ses finances, à accorder même un moratoire à la Banque Ottomane, et, en général, à ne pouvoir faire face à ses engagements qu'avec des retards ou des lacunes et cela au prix de grands sacrifices. Mais il est avéré, d'autre part, que, pendant cette même période et notamment à la suite de la création de la Banque Ottomane, la Turquie a pu contracter des emprunts à des taux favorables, en convertir d'autres, et finalement amortir une partie importante, évaluée à 350 millions de francs, de sa dette publique (Réplique Russe, p. 37). Il serait manifestement exagéré d'admettre que le payement (ou la conclusion d'un emprunt pour le payement) de la somme relativement minime d'environ six millions de francs du aux indemnitaires russes aurait mis en péril l'existence de l'Empire Ottoman ou gravement compromis sa situation intérieure ou extérieure. *L'exception de la force majeure ne saurait donc être accueillie.*

7. La Sublime-Porte soutient ensuite "que la reconnaissance d'une créance de capital au profit des indemnitaires russes constituait une *libéralité* convenue dans leur intérêt entre les deux Gouvernements" (Contre-Réplique, No. 153, p. 19; No. 331, p. 44; No. 365, p. 55, et conclusions, p. 87)—Elle fait observer que le Code civil allemand, paragraphe 522, le Droit commun germanique, la jurisprudence autrichienne et le Droit romain invoqué à titre supplétoire (Loi 16 praemium, Digeste 22, 1) interdisent de frapper d'intérêts moratoires la donation.—Elle invoque surtout la sentence arbitrale rendue le 2 juillet 1881 par S. M. l'Empereur d'Autriche dans l'affaire de la Mosquitia entre la Grande-Bretagne et le Nicaragua.

Dans cette affaire, la Grande-Bretagne avait renoncé, par un traité de 1860, au protectorat sur la Mosquitia et à la ville de Grey Town (San Juan del Norte) et reconnu sur la Mosquitia la souveraineté du Nicaragua en stipulant que cette République payerait pendant dix ans au chef des Mosquitos, pour lui faciliter l'établissement du self-government dans ses territoires, une rente de 5,000 dollars qui ne tarda pas à demeurer impayée. Le chef des Mosquitos bénéficiait donc, dans la pensée de l'arbitre, d'une véritable libéralité, réclamée en sa faveur du Nicaragua par la Grande-Bretagne, qui, elle, avait fait des sacrifices politiques en renonçant à son protectorat et au port de Grey Town.— Dans l'opinion du Tribunal, les indemnitaires russes, eux, ont subi des dommages, ont été victimes de faits de guerre; la Turquie s'est engagée à rembourser le montant de ces dommages à toutes les victimes russes qui auraient fait évaluer leur préjudice par la commission instituée auprès de l'ambassade de Russie à Constantinople. Les décisions de cette commission n'ont pas été contestées et le Tribunal arbitral n'a pas à les reviser ni à apprécier si elles ont ou non été trop généreuses. Si l'indemnisation par la Turquie des Russes victimes des opérations de guerre n'était pas obligatoire en droit des gens commun, elle n'a rien de contraire à celui-ci et peut être considérée comme la transformation en obligation juridique d'un devoir moral par un traité de paix dans des conditions analogues à une indemnité de guerre proprement dite.—Dans toute la correspondance diplomatique échangée depuis trente ahs sur cette affaire, les Russes victimes des opérations de guerre ont toujours été considérés par les deux parties signataires des accords de 1878/1879 comme des indemnitaires et non comme des donataires. Enfin, la Turquie a reçu la contre-partie de sa prétendue libéralité dans le fait de la cessation des hostilités (Réplique Russe, p. 50, paragr. 2). *Il n'est donc pas possible d'admettre l'existence d'une libéralité* et encore moins une donation, et il devient, par suite, superflu de rechercher si, en droit international public, les donateurs doivent bénéficier de l'exemption d'intérêts moratoires établie à leur profit par certaines législations privées.

8. La Sublime-Porte invoque *l'exception de la chose jugée*, en s'appuyant sur le fait que trois indemnitaires ont demandé à la commission instituée auprès de l'ambassade de Russie à Constantinople des intérêts jusqu'à parfait payement, que la commission a écarté leur requête et que cette solution négative serait encore plus certainement intervenue à l'égard des autres indemnitaires qui n'ont pas réclamé de semblables intérêts. (Contre-Réplique Ottomane, p. 86).

Cette exception ne saurait être accueillie parce que, même en admettant que la commission de Constantinople puisse être considérée comme un tribunal, la question actuellement pendante est celle de savoir si des dommages-intérêts sont dus, *a posteriori* à raison des dates auxquelles ont été payées les indemnités évaluées en 1879/81 par la Commission; or celle-ci n'a pas jugé et n'a pu juger cette question.

9. La Sublime-Porte invoque, comme dernière exception, le fait "qu'il a été entendu, tacitement et même expressément, pendant tout le cours des onze ou douze dernières années de correspondances diplomatiques, que la Russie ne réclamait pas d'intérêts ni de dommages-intérêts d'aucune sorte qui auraient été à la charge de l'Empire Ottoman" et "que le Gouvernement Impérial de Russie, une fois le capital intégralement mis à sa disposition, ne pouvait pas valablement revenir d'une façon unilatérale sur l'entente convenue de sa part" (Contre-Réplique Ottomane, pp. 89–91).

Le Gouvernement Impérial Ottoman fait observer avec raison que si la Russie a fait parvenir à Constantinople, par la voie diplomatique, le 31 décembre 1890/12 janvier 1891, une mise en demeure régulière d'avoir à payer le capital et les intérêts, il résulte, d'autre part, de la correspondance *subséquente,* qu'à l'occasion du payement des acomptes, aucune réserve d'intérêts n'a figuré dans les reçus délivrés par l'ambassade, et que celle-ci n'a jamais imputé les sommes reçues sur les intérêts. Il en résulte aussi que les Parties ont non seulement ébauché des combinaisons pour arriver au payement, mais se sont abstenues de faire mention des intérêts pendant dix ans environ. Il en résulte surtout que les deux Gouvernements ont interprété de façon identique le terme de *reliquat* de l'indemnité; que ce terme, employé pour la première fois par le Ministère Ottoman des Affaires Etrangères dans une communication du 27 mars 1893, revient fréquemment dans la suite; que les deux Gouvernements ont visé constamment par le mot *reliquat* les fractions du capital restant dû à la date des notes échangées, ce qui laisse de côté les intérêts moratoires; que l'ambassadeur de Russie à Constantinople a écrit le 23 mai/4 juin 1894: "Je suis obligé d'insister pour que la *totalité du reliquat* dû aux sujets russes, *qui monte à 91,000 livres turques,* soit, sans plus de retard, versé à l'ambassade, afin de faire droit aux justes plaintes et réclamations des intéressés . . . et mettre ainsi réellement, selon l'expression de Votre Excellence, fin aux incidents auxquels elle avait donné lieu"; que cette somme de 91,000 livres turques était exactement celle qui demeurait alors due sur le capital et qu'ainsi les intérêts moratoires ont été laissés de côté;—que le 3 octobre de la même année 1894, la Turquie, sur le point de payer un acompte de 50,000 livres, a annoncé à l'ambassade, sans rencontrer d'objections, que la Banque Ottomane "garantira le payement du *reliquat de 41,000 livres turques*";—que le 13/25 janvier 1896, l'ambassade a repris le même terme de reliquat de l'indemnité tout en protestant contre l'affectation par la Turquie à la Banque Ottomane, de délégations sur des revenus déjà engagés au Gouvernement Impérial Russe pour le payement de l'indemnité de guerre;—que, le 11 février de cette même année 1896, à l'occasion de la discussion des ressources à fournir à la Banque Ottomane, la Sublime-Porte a mentionné, dans une note adressée à l'ambassade, "les 43,978 livres turques représentant *le reliquat de l'indemnité*";—que, quelques jours plus tard, le 10/22 février, l'ambassade a répondu en se servant des mêmes mots *"solde"* ou *"reliquat de l'indemnité,"* et, que le 28 mai, le Ministère Ottoman des Affaires Etrangères a mentionné derechef, "la somme de 43,978 livres turques représentant ledit reliquat";—qu'il en a été de même dans une note de l'ambassade datée du 25 avril/8 mai 1900, bien qu'il se fut écoulé près de quatre ans entre ces communications et celles de 1896 et qu'un rappel de la question des intérêts s'imposât en quelque sorte après un aussi long délai; que cette même expression "reliquat de l'indemnité" figure dans une note de la Sublime-Porte du 5 juillet 1900;—qu'enfin, le 3/16 mars 1901, l'Ambassade de Russie, après avoir constaté que la Banque Ottomane n'a pas fait de nouveaux versements "pour le payement des 43,978 livres turques, montant du *reliquat de l'indemnité* due aux sujets russes," a demandé l'envoi à qui de droit d'ordres "catégoriques pour le payement sans plus de retard des sommes susmentionnées";—que ce reliquat ayant, à un petit solde près, été tenu par la Banque Ottomane à la disposition de l'ambassade, c'est seulement au bout de plusieurs mois, le 23 juin/6 juillet, que cette dernière a transmis à la Sublime-Porte une demande "des intéressés" concluant au payement d'une vingtaine de millions de francs pour intérêts de retard, en exprimant l'espoir que la Sublime-Porte "n'hésitera pas à reconnaître, en principe, le bien fondé de la réclamation," sauf "à déférer l'examen des détails à une commission" mixte russo-turque;—qu'en résumé, depuis onze ans et davantage, et jusqu'à une date postérieure au payement du reliquat du capital, il n'avait non seulement plus été question d'intérêts entre les deux Gouvernements mais été à maintes reprises fait mention seulement du reliquat du capital.

Dès l'instant où le Tribunal a reconnu que, d'après les principes généraux et la coutume en droit international public, il y avait similitude des situations entre un Etat et un particulier débiteurs d'une somme conventionnelle liquide et exigible, il est équitable et juridique d'appliquer aussi par analogie les règles de droit privé commun aux cas où la demeure doit être considérée comme purgée et le bénéfice de celle-ci supprimée.—En droit privé, les effets de la demeure sont supprimés lorsque le créancier, après avoir constitué le débiteur en demeure, accorde un ou plusieurs délais pour satisfaire à l'obligation principale sans réserver les droits acquis par la demeure (*Toullier-Duvergier, Droit français*, tome III, p. 159, N°. 256), ou encore lorsque "le créancier ne donne pas suite à la sommation qu'il avait faite au débiteur," et "ces règles s'appliquent aux dommages intérêts et aussi aux intérêts dus pour l'inexécution de l'obligation * * * ou pour retard dans l'exécution" (*Duranton, Droit français*, X, p. 470, Aubry et Rau, *Droit Civil* 1871, IV, p. 99, Berney, *De la demeure*, etc., Lausanne, 1886, p. 62; Windscheid, *Lehrbuch des Pandektenrechts*, 1879, p. 99, Demolombe, X, p. 49; Larombière I, art. 1139, N°. 22, etc.).

Entre le Gouvernement Impérial Russe et la Sublime-Porte, il y a donc eu renonciation au intérêts de la part de la Russie, puisque son ambassade a successivement accepté sans discussion ni réserve et reproduit à maintes reprises dans sa propre correspondance diplomatique les chiffres du reliquat de l'indemnité comme indentiques aux chiffres du reliquat en capital.—En d'autres termes, la correspondance des dernières années établit que les deux Parties ont interprété, en fait, les actes de 1879 comme impliquant l'identité entre le payement du solde du capital et le payement du solde auquel avaient droit les indemnitaires, ce qui impliquait l'abandon des intérêts ou dommages-intérêts moratoires.

Le Gouvernement Impérial Russe ne peut, une fois le capital de l'indemnité intégralement versé ou mis à sa disposition, revenir valablement d'une façon unilatérale sur une interprétation acceptée et pratiquée en son nom par son ambassade.

III

En Conclusion

Le Tribunal arbitral, se basant sur les observations de droit et de fait qui précèdent, est d'avis

qu'en principe, le Gouvernement Impérial Ottoman était tenu, vis-à-vis du Gouvernement Impérial de Russie, à des indemnités moratoires à partir du 31 décembre 1890/12 janvier 1891, date de la réception d'une mise en demeure explicite et régulière,

mais que, de fait, le bénéfice de cette mise en demeure ayant cessé pour le Gouvernement Impérial de Russie par suite de la renonciation subséquente de son ambassade à Constantinople, le Gouvernement Impérial Ottoman n'est pas tenu ajourd'hui de lui payer des dommages-intérêts à raison des dates auxquelles a été effectué le payement des indemnités,

et, en conséquence,

ARRÊTE

il est répondu négativement à la question posée au chiffre 1 de l'article 3 du Compromis et ainsi conçue: "Oui ou non, le Gouvernement Impérial Ottoman est-il tenu de payer aux indemnitaires russes des dommages-intérêts à raison des dates auxquelles ledit Gouvernement a procédé au payement des indemnités fixées en exécution de l'article 5 du traité du 27 janvier/8 février 1879, ainsi que du Protocole de même date"?

Fait à La Haye, dans l'hôtel de la Cour Permanente d'Arbitrage, le 11 novembre 1912.

> *Le Président:* LARDY
> *Le Secrétaire général:* MICHIELS VAN VERDUYNEN
> *Le Secrétaire:* RÖELL

Agreement for Arbitration, July 22/August 4, 1910[1]

Le Gouvernement Impérial Russe et le Gouvernement Impérial Ottoman, cosignataires de la Convention de La Haye du 18 octobre 1907 pour le règlement pacifique des conflits internationaux:

Considérant les dispositions de l'Article 5 du Traité signe à Constantinople entre la Russie et la Turquie, le 27 janvier/8 février 1879, ainsi conçu:

"Les réclamations des sujets et institutions russes en Turquie à titre d'indemnité pour les dommages subis pendant la guerre seront payées à mesure qu'elles seront examinées par l'Ambassade de Russie à Constantinople et transmises à la Sublime Porte"

"La totalité de ces réclamations ne pourra en aucun cas dépasser le chiffre de 26,750,000 francs"

"Le terme d'une année après l'échange des ratifications est fixé comme date à partir de laquelle les réclamations pourront être présentées à la Sublime Porte, et celui de deux ans comme date après laquelle les réclamations ne seront plus admises";

Considérant l'explication additionelle insérée au Protocole de même date portant:

"Quant au terme d'une année fixé par cet Article comme date à partir de laquelle les réclamations pourront être présentées à la Sublime Porte, il est entendu qu'une exception y sera faite en faveur de la réclamation de l'Hôpital Russe s'élevant à la somme de 11,200 livres sterlings";

Considérant qu'un désaccord s'est élevé entre le Gouvernement Impérial Russe et le Gouvernement Impérial Ottoman relativement aux conséquences de droit résultant des dates auxquelles de Gouvernement

---

[1]Official report, p. 5.

Impérial Ottoman a effectué, sur les montants des indemnités règulière-
ment présentées en exécution dudit Article 5, les payements ci-après,
savoir :

	livr. turq.	pi.	par.
En 1884	50,000	—	—
En 1889	50,000	—	—
En 1893	75,000	—	—
En 1894	50,000	—	—
En 1902	42,438	67	31/40

Considérant que le Gouvernement Impérial Russe soutient que le
Gouvernement Impérial Ottoman est responsable de dommages-intérêts
à l'égard des indemnitaires russes pour le retard apporté au règlement
de sa dette ;
Considérant que le Gouvernement Impérial Ottoman conteste, tant
en fait qu'en droit, le bien-fondé de la prétention du Gouvernement
Impérial Russe ;
Considérant que le litige n'a pu être réglé par la voie diplomatique ;
Et ayant résolu, conformément aux stipulations de ladite Convention de La Haye, de terminer ce différend en soumettant la question à
un Arbitrage ;
Ont, à cet effet, autorisé leurs Représentants ci-dessous désignés,
savoir :
pour la Russie,
Son Excellence Monsieur Tcharykow, Ambassadeur de Sa Majesté
l'Empereur de Russie à Constantinople ;
pour la Turquie,
Son Excellence Rifaat Pacha, Ministre des Affaires étrangères,
A conclure le Compromis suivant :

ARTICLE PREMIER

Les Puissances en litige décident que le Tribunal Arbitral auquel la
question sera soumise en dernier ressort sera composé de cinq membres, lesquels seront désignés de la manière suivante :
Chaque Partie, aussitôt que possible, et dans un délai qui n'excédera
pas deux mois à partir de la date de ce Compromis, devra nommer
deux Arbitres, et les quatre Arbitres ainsi désignés choisiront ensemble
un Sur-Arbitre. Dans le cas où les quatre Arbitres n'auraient pas, dans
le délai de deux mois après leur désignation, choisi à l'unanimité ou à
la majorité un Sur-Arbitre, le choix du Sur-Arbitre est confié à une
Puissance tierce désignée de commun accord par les Parties. Si, dans
un délai de deux autres mois, l'accord ne s'établit pas à ce sujet,
chaque Partie désigne une Puissance différente et le choix du Sur-
Arbitre est fait de concert par les Puissances ainsi désignées.
Si, dans un délai de deux autres mois, ces deux Puissances n'ont
pu tomber d'accord, chacune d'elles présente deux candidats pris sur
la liste des membres de la Cour Permanente en dehors des membres

de ladite Cour désignés par ces deux Puissances ou par les Parties, et n'étant les nationaux ni des uns ni des autres. Ces candidats ne pourront, en plus, appartenir à la nationalité des Arbitres nommés par les Parties dans le présent Arbitrage. Le sort détermine lequel des candidats ainsi présentés sera le Sur-Arbitre.

Le tirage au sort sera effectué par les soins du Bureau International de la Cour Permanente de La Haye.

Art. 2

Les Puissances en litige se feront représenter auprès du Tribunal Arbitral par des agents, conseils ou avocats, en conformité desprévisions de l'Article 62 de la Convention de La Haye de 1907 pour le règlement pacifique des conflits internationaux.

Ces agents, conseils ou avocats seront désignés par les Parties à temps pour que le fonctionnement de l'Arbitrage ne subisse aucun retard.

Art. 3

Les questions en litige et sur lesquelles les Parties demandent au Tribunal Arbitral de prononcer une décisions définitive sont les suivantes:

I. Oui ou non, le Gouvernement Impérial Ottoman est-il tenu de payer aux indemnitaires russes des dommages-intérêts à raison des dates auxquelles ledit Gouvernement a procédé au payement des indemnités fixées en exécution de l'article 5 du Traité du 27 janvier/ 8 février 1879, ainsi que du Protocole de même date?

II. En cas de décision affirmative sur la première question, quel serait le montant de ces dommages-intérêts?

Art. 4

Le Tribunal Arbitral, une fois constitué, se réunira à La Haye à une date qui sera fixée par les Arbitres, et dans le délai d'un mois à partir de la nomination du Sur-Arbitre. Après le règlement—en conformité avec le texte et l'esprit de la Convention de La Haye de 1907— de toutes les questions de procédure qui pourraient surgir et qui ne seraient pas prévues par le présent Compromis, ledit Tribunal ajournera sa prochaine séance à la date qu'il fixera.

Toutefois, il reste convenue que le Tribunal ne pourra ouvrir les débats sur les questions en litige ni avant les deux mois, ni plus tard que les trois mois qui suivront la remise du Contre-Mémoire ou de la Contre-Réplique prévus par l'article 6 et éventuellement des conclusions stipulées à l'article 8.

Art. 5

La procédure arbitrale comprendra deux phases distinctes: l'instruction écrite et les débats qui consisteront dans le développement oral des moyens des Parties devant le Tribunal.

La seule langue dont fera usage le Tribunal et dont l'emploi sera autorisé devant lui sera la langue française.

Art. 6

Dans le délai de huit mois au plus après la date du présent Compromis, le Gouvernement Impérial Russe devra remettre à chacun des membres du Tribunal Arbitral, en un exemplaire, et au Gouvernement Impérial Ottoman, en dix exemplaires, les copies complètes, écrites ou imprimées, de son Mémoire contenant toutes pièces à l'appui de sa demande et pouvant se référer aux deux questions visées par l'article 3.

Dans un délai de huit mois au plus tard après cette remise, le Gouvernement Impérial Ottoman devra remettre à chacun des membres du Tribunal, ainsi qu'au Gouvernement Impérial Russe, en autant d'exemplaires que ci-dessus, les copies complètes, manuscrites ou imprimées, de son Contre-Mémoire, avec toutes pièces à l'appui, mais pouvant se borner à la question N°. I de l'article 3.

Dans de délai d'un mois après cette remise, le Gouvernement Impérial Russe notifiera au Président du Tribunal Arbitral s'il a l'intention de présenter une Réplique. Dans ce cas, il aura un délai de trois mois au plus, à compter de cette notification, pour communiquer ladite Réplique dans les mêmes conditions que le Mémoire. Le Gouvernement Impérial Ottoman aura alors un délai de quatre mois, à compter de cette communication, pour présenter sa Contre-Réplique, dans les mêmes conditions que le Contre-Mémoire.

Les délais fixés par le présent article pourront être prolongés de commun accord par les Parties, ou par le Tribunal, quand il le juge nécessaire, pour arriver à une décision juste.

Mais le Tribunal ne prendra pas en considération les Mémoires, Contre-Mémoires ou autres communications qui lui seront présentées par les Parties après l'expiration du dernier délai par lui fixé.

Art. 7

Si, dans les mémoires ou autres pièces échangés, l'une ou l'autre Partie s'est référée ou a fait allusion à un document ou papier en sa possession exclusive, dont elle n'aura pas joint la copie, elle sera tenue, si l'autre Partie le demande, de lui en donner la copie, au plus tard dans les trente jours.

Art. 8

Dans le cas où le Tribunal Arbitral aurait affirmativement statué sur la question posée au N°. I de l'article 3, il devra, avant d'aborder l'examen du N°. II du même article, donner aux Parties de nouveaux délais no pouvant être inférieurs à trois mois chacun, pour présenter et échanger leurs conclusions et arguments à l'appui.

Art. 9

Les décisions du Tribunal sur la première, et éventuellement sur la seconde question en litige, seront prononcées, autant que possible, dans le délai d'un mois après la clôture par le Président des débats relatifs à chacune de ces questions.

Art. 10

Le jugement du Tribunal Arbitral sera définitif et devra être exécuté strictement et sans aucun retard.

Art. 11

Chaque Partie supporte ses propres frais et une parte égale des frais du Tribunal.

Art. 12

En tout ce qui n'est pas prévu par le présent Compromis, les stipulations de la Convention de La Haye de 1907 pour le règlement pacifique des Conflits internationaux seront appliquées à cet Arbitrage, à l'exception, toutefois, des articles dont l'acceptation a été réservée par le Gouvernement Impérial Ottoman.

Fait à Constantinople, le 22 juillet/4 août 1910.

(Signé) :   N. Tcharykow
(Signé) :   Rifaat

THE CARTHAGE CASE

Award of the Tribunal, May 6, 1913[1]

Considérant que, par un Accord du 26 janvier 1912 et par un Compromis du 6 mars suivant, le Gouvernement de la République Française et le Gouvernement Royal Italien sont convenus de soumettre à un Tribunal Arbitral composé de cinq Membres la solution des questions suivantes:

1°. Les autorités navales italiennes étaient-elles en droit de procéder comme elles ont fait à la capture et à la saisie momentanée du vapeur postal français "Carthage"?

2°. Quelles conséquences pécuniaires ou autres doivent résulter de la solution donnée à la question précédente?

Considérant qu'en exécution de ce Compromis les deux Gouvernement ont choisi, d'un commun accord, pour constituer le Tribunal Arbitral les Membres suivants de la Cour Permanente d'Arbitrage:

Son Excellence Monsieur Guido Fusinato, Docteur en droit, Ministre d'Etat, ancien Ministre de l'Instruction publique, Professeur honoraire de droit international à l'Université de Turin, Député, Conseiller d'Etat;

Monsieur Knut Hjalmar Léonard de Hammarskjöld, Docteur en droit, ancien Ministre de la Justice, ancien Ministre des Cultes et de l'Instruction publique, ancien Envoyé extraordinaire et Ministre plénipotentiaire à Copenhague, ancien Président de la Cour d'appel de Jönköping, ancien Professeur à la Faculté de droit d'Upsal, Gouverneur de la province d'Upsal;

Monsieur Kriege, Docteur en droit, Conseiller actuel intime de Légation et Directeur au Département des Affaires Etrangères, Plénipotentiaire au Conseil Fédéral Allemand;

Monsieur Louis Renault, Ministre plénipotentiaire, Membre de l'Institut, Professeur à la Faculté de droit de l'Université de Paris et à l'Ecole libre des sciences politiques, Jurisconsulte du Ministère des Affaires Etrangères;

Son Excellence le Baron Michel de Taube, Docteur en droit, Adjoint du Ministre de l'Instruction publique de Russie, Conseiller d'Etat actuel;

que les deux Gouvernements ont, en même temps, désigné Monsieur de Hammarskjöld pour remplir les fonctions de Président.

Considérant que, en exécution du Compromis du 6 mars 1912, les Mémoires et Contre-Mémoires ont été dûment échangés entre les Parties et communiqués aux Arbitres;

Considérant que le Tribunal, constitué comme il est dit ci-dessus, s'est réuni à La Haye le 31 mars 1913;

[1]Official report, p. 112.

que les deux Gouvernements ont respectivement désigné comme Agents et Conseils,

le Gouvernement de la République Française:

Monsieur Henri Fromageot, Avocat à la Cour d'appel de Paris, Jurisconsulte suppléant du Ministère des Affaires Etrangères, Conseiller du Département de la Marine en droit international, Agent;

Monsieur André Hesse, Avocat à la Cour d'appel de Paris, Membre de la Chambre des Députés, Conseil;

Le Gouvernement Royal Italien:

Monsieur Arturo Ricci-Busatti, Envoyé extraordinaire et Ministre plénipotentiaire, Chef du Bureau du Contentieux et de la Législation au Ministère Royal des Affaires Etrangères, Agent;

Monsieur Dionisio Anzilotti, Professeur de droit international à l'Université de Rome, Conseil.

Considérant que les Agents des Parties ont présenté au Tribunal les conclusions suivantes, savoir,

l'Agent du Gouvernement de la République Française:

PLAISE AU TRIBUNAL,

Sur la première question posée par le Compromis,

Dire que les autorités navales italiennes n'étaient pas en droit de procéder comme elles ont fait à la capture et à la saisie momentanée du vapeur postal français "Carthage";

En conséquence et sur la seconde question,

Dire que le Gouvernement Royal Italien sera tenu de verser au Gouvernement de la République Française à titre de dommages-intérêts:

1°. La somme de *un franc* pour atteinte portée au pavillon français;

2°. La somme de cent mille francs pour réparation du préjudice moral et politique résultant de l'inobservation du droit commun international et des conventions réciproquement obligatoires pour l'Italie comme pour la France;

3°. La somme de cinq cent soixante-seize mille sept cent trente-huit francs vingt-trois centimes, montant total des pertes et dommages réclamés par les particuliers intéressés au navire et à son expédition;

Dire que la somme susdite de cent mille francs sera versée au Gouvernement de la République pour le bénéfice en être attribué à telle œuvre ou institution d'intérêt international qu'il plaira au Tribunal d'indiquer;

Subsidiairement et dans le cas où le Tribunal ne se croirait pas, dès à présent, suffisamment éclairé sur le bien fondé des réclamations particulières,

Dire que, par tel ou tels de ses membres qu'il lui plaira de commettre à cet effet, il sera, en présence des Agents et Conseils des deux Gouvernements, procédé, en la Chambre de ses délibérations, à l'examen de chacune desdites, réclamations particulières;

Dans tous les cas, et par application de l'article 9 du Compromis,

Dire que, à l'expiration d'un délai de trois mois à compter du jour de la sentence, les sommes mises à la charge du Gouvernement Royal Italien et non encore versées seront productives d'intérêts à raison de quatre pour cent par an.

Et l'Agent du Gouvernement Royal Italien:

PLAISE AU TRIBUNAL,

Sur la première question posée par le Compromis,

Dire et juger que les autorités navales italiennes étaient pleinement en droit de procéder comme elles ont fait à la capture et à la saisie momentanée du vapeur postal français "Carthage";

En conséquence et sur la seconde question,

Dire et juger qu'aucune conséquence pécuniaire ou autre ne saurait résulter, à la charge du Gouvernement Royal Italien, de la capture et de la saisie momentanée du vapeur postal français "Carthage";

Dire que le Gouvernement Français sera tenu de verser au Gouvernement Italien la somme de deux mille soixante-douze francs vingt-cinq centimes, montant des frais occasionnés par la saisie du "Carthage";

Dire que, à l'expiration d'un délai de trois mois à compter du jour de la sentence, la somme mise à la charge du Gouvernement de la République Française sera, si elle n'a pas encore été versée, productive d'intérêts à raison de quatre pour cent par an.

Considérant que, après que le Tribunal eut entendu les exposés oraux des Agents des Parties et les explications qu'ils lui ont fournies sur sa demande, les débats ont été dûment déclarés clos.

EN FAIT:

Considérant que le vapeur postal français "Carthage," de la Compagnie Générale Transatlantique, au cours d'un voyage régulier entre Marseille et Tunis, fut arrêté, le 16 janvier 1912, à 6 heures 30 du matin, en pleine mer, à 17 milles des côtes de Sardaigne, par le contre-torpilleur de la Marine Royale Italienne "Agordat";

que le commandant de l'"Agordat," ayant constaté le présence à bord du "Carthage" d'un aéroplane appartenant au sieur Duval, aviateur français, et expédié à Tunis à l'adresse de celui-ci, a déclaré au capitaine du "Carthage" que l'aéroplane en question était considéré par le Gouvernement Italien comme contrebande de guerre;

que, le transbordement de l'aéroplane n'ayant pu être opéré, le capitaine du "Carthage" a reçu l'ordre de suivre l'"Agordat" à Cagliari, où il a été retenu jusqu'au 20 janvier;

EN DROIT:

Considérant que, d'après les principes universellement admis, un bâtiment de guerre belligérant a, en thèse générale et sans conditions particulières, le droit d'arrêter en pleine mer un navire de commerce neutre et de procéder à la visite pour s'assurer s'il observe les règles sur la neutralité, spécialement au point de vue de la contrebande;

Considérant, d'autre part, que la légitimité de tout acte dépassant les limites de la visite dépend de l'existence, soit d'un trafic de contrebande, soit de motifs suffisants pour y croire, que, à cet égard, il faut s'en tenir aux motifs d'ordre juridique;

Considérant que, dans l'espèce, le "Carthage" n'a pas été seulement arrêté et visité par l'"Agordat," mais aussi amené à Cagliari, séquestré et retenu un certain temps, après lequel il a été relaxé par voie administrative;

Considérant que, le but poursuivi par les mesures prises contre le paquebot-poste français était d'empêcher le transport de l'aéroplane appartenant au sieur Duval, et embarqué sur le "Carthage" à l'adresse de ce même Duval, à Tunis;

que cet aéroplane était considéré par les autorités italiennes comme constituant de la contrebande de guerre, tant par sa nature que par sa destination qui, en réalité, aurait été pour les forces ottomanes en Tripolitaine;

Considérant, pour ce qui concerne la destination hostile de l'aéroplane, élément essentiel de la saisissabilité,

que les renseignements possédés par les autorités italiennes étaient d'une nature trop générale et avaient trop peu de connexité avec l'aéroplane dont il s'agit, pour constituer des motifs juridiques suffisants de croire à une destination hostile quelconque et, par conséquent, pour justifier la capture du navire qui transportait l'aéroplane;

que la dépêche de Marseille, relatant certains propos tenus par le mécanicien du sieur Duval, n'est parvenue aux autorités italiennes qu'après que le "Carthage" avait été arrêté et conduit à Cagliari et n'a pu, par suite, motiver ces mesures; que, d'ailleurs, elle n'aurait pu, dans tous les cas, fournir des motifs suffisants dans le sens de ce qui a été dit précédemment;

Considérant que, ce résultat acquis, il n'importe pas au Tribunal de rechercher si l'aéroplane devait ou non par sa nature être compris dans les articles de la contrebande, soit relative, soit absolue, pas plus que d'examiner si la théorie du voyage continu serait ou non applicable dans l'espèce;

Considérant que, le Tribunal trouve également superflu d'examiner s'il y a eu, lors des mesures prises contre le "Carthage," des irrégularités de forme et si, en cas d'affirmative, ces irrégularités étaient de nature à vicier des mesures autrement légitimes;

Considérant que, les autorités italiennes n'ont demandé la remise du *port postal* que pour le faire parvenir à destination le plus tôt possible,

que cette demande, qui paraît avoir été d'abord mal comprise par le capitaine du "Carthage," était conforme à la Convention du 18 octobre 1907 *relative à certaines restrictions à l'exercice du droit de capture*, qui, d'ailleurs, n'était pas ratifiée par les belligérants.

Sur la demande tendant à faire condamner le Gouvernement Royal Italien à verser au Gouvernement de la République Française à titre de dommages-intérêts:

1°. la somme de *un franc* pour atteinte portée au pavillon français;

2°. la somme de cent mille francs pour réparation du préjudice moral et politique résultant de l'inobservation du droit commun international et des conventions réciproquement obligatoires pour l'Italie comme pour la France,

Considérant que, pour le cas où une Puissance aurait manqué à remplir ses obligations, soit générales, soit spéciales, vis-à-vis d'une autre Puissance, la constatation de ce fait, surtout dans une sentence arbitrale, constitue déjà une sanction sérieuse;

que cette sanction est renforcée, le cas échéant, par le paiement de dommages-intérêts pour les pertes matérielles;

que, en thèse générale et abstraction faite de situations particulières, ces sanctions paraissent suffisantes;

que, également en thèse générale, l'introduction d'une autre sanction pécuniaire paraît être superflue et dépasser le but de la juridiction internationale;

Considérant que, par application de ce qui vient d'être dit, les circonstances de la cause présente ne sauraient motiver une telle sanction supplémentaire; que, sans autre examen, il n'y a donc pas lieu de donner suite à la demande susmentionnée.

Sur la demande de l'Agent français tendant à faire condamner le Gouvernement Italien à payer la somme de cinq cent soixante-seize mille sept cent trente-huit francs vingt-trois centimes, montant total des pertes et dommages réclamés par les particuliers intéressés au navire et à son expédition,

Considérant que, la demande d'une indemnité est, en principe, justifiée;

Considérant que, le Tribunal, après avoir entendu les explications concordantes de deux de ses membres chargés par lui de procéder à une enquête sur lesdites réclamations, a évalué à soixante-quinze mille francs le montant de l'indemnité due à la Compagnie générale transatlantique, à vingt-cinq mille francs le montant de l'indemnité due à l'aviateur Duval et consorts, enfin à soixante mille francs l'indemnité due à l'ensemble des passagers et chargeurs, soit à cent soixante mille francs la somme totale à payer par le Gouvernement Italien au Gouvernement Français.

PAR CES MOTIFS,

Le Tribunal Arbitral déclare et prononce ce qui suit:

Les autorités navales italiennes n'étaient pas en droit de procéder comme elles ont fait à la capture et à la saisie momentanée du vapeur postal français "Carthage."

Le Gouvernement Royal Italien sera tenu, dans les trois mois de la présente sentence, de verser au Gouvernement de la République Française la somme de cent soixante mille francs, montant des pertes et dommages éprouvés, à raison de la capture et de la saisie du "Carthage," par les particuliers intéressés au navire et à son expédition.

Il n'y a pas lieu de donner suite aux autres réclamations contenues dans les conclusions des deux Parties.

Fait à La Haye, dans l'Hôtel de la Cour Permanente d'Arbitrage, le 6 mai 1913.

Le Président: Hj. L. HAMMARSKJÖLD
Le Secrétaire général: MICHIELS VAN VERDUYNEN
Le Secrétaire: RÖELL

Agreement for Arbitration, March 6, 1912[1]

Le Gouvernement de la République Française et le Gouvernement Royal Italien, s'étant mis d'accord le 26 janvier 1912 par application de la Convention d'arbitrage du 25 décembre 1903, renouvelée le 24 décembre 1908 pour confier à un Tribunal d'arbitrage l'examen de la capture et de la saisie momentanée du vapeur postal français "Carthage" par les autorités navales italiennes, ainsi que la mission de se prononcer sur les conséquences qui en dérivent,

Les soussignés, dûment autorisés à cet effet, sont convenus du Compromis suivant:

ARTICLE 1

Un Tribunal arbitral, composé comme il est dit ci-après, est chargé de résoudre les questions suivantes:

1°. Les autorités navales italiennes étaient-elles en droit de procéder comme elles ont fait à la capture et à la saisie momentanée du vapeur postal français "Carthage"?

2°. Quelles conséquences pécuniaires ou autres doivent résulter de la solution donnée à la question précédente?

ARTICLE 2

Le Tribunal sera composé de cinq Arbitres que les deux Gouvernements choisiront parmi les Membres de la Cour permanente d'Arbitrage de La Haye, en désignant celui d'entre eux qui remplira les fonctions de Surarbitre.

ARTICLE 3

A la date du 15 juin 1912, chaque Partie déposera au Bureau de la Cour permanente d'Arbitrage quinze exemplaires de son mémoire, avec les copies certifiées conformes de tous les documents et pièces qu'elle compte invoquer dans la cause.

Le Bureau en assurera sans retard la transmission aux Arbitres et aux Parties, savoir deux exemplaires pour chaque Arbitre, trois exemplaires pour la Partie adverse; deux exemplaires resteront dans les archives du Bureau.

A la date du 15 août 1912, chaque Partie déposera dans les mêmes conditions que ci-dessus son contre-mémoire avec les pièces à l'appui et ses conclusions finales.

ARTICLE 4

Chacune des Parties déposera au Bureau de la Cour permanente d'Arbitrage de La Haye, en même temps que son mémoire et à titre de provision, une somme qui sera fixée d'un commun accord.

ARTICLE 5

Le Tribunal se réunira à La Haye, sur la convocation de son Président, dans la deuxième quinzaine du mois de septembre 1912.

---

[1] Official report, p. 5.

ARTICLE 6

Chaque Partie sera représentée par un Agent avec mission de servir d'intermédiaire entre elle et le Tribunal.

Le Tribunal pourra, s'il l'estime nécessaire, demander à l'un ou à l'autre des Agents de lui fournir des explications orales ou écrites auxquelles l'Agent de la Partie adverse aura le droit de répondre.

ARTICLE 7

La langue française est la langue du Tribunal. Chaque Partie pourra faire usage de sa propre langue.

ARTICLE 8

La sentence du Tribunal devra être rendue dans le plus bref délai possible et dans tous les cas dans les trente jours qui suivront la clôture des débats. Toutefois, ce délai pourra être prolongé à la demande du Tribunal et du consentement des Parties.

ARTICLE 9

Le Tribunal est compétent pour régler les conditions d'exécution de sa sentence.

ARTICLE 10

Pour tout ce qui n'est pas prévu par le présent Compromis, les dispositions de la Convention de La Haye du 18 octobre 1907 pour le règlement pacifique des conflits internationaux seront applicables au présent Arbitrage.

Fait en double à Paris, le 6 mars 1912.

Signé: L. RENAULT
Signé: G. FUSINATO

Joint Note of January 26, 1912, concerning the Settlement of the "Carthage" and "Manouba" Cases[1]

L'ambassadeur de France et le ministre des Affaires étrangères d'Italie ayant examiné dans l'esprit le plus cordiel les circonstances qui ont précédé et suivi l'arrêt et la visite par un croiseur italien de deux vapeurs français se rendant de Marseille à Tunis, ont été heureux de constater, d'un commun accord et avant toute autre considération, qu'il n'en résultait de la part d'aucun des deux pays aucune intention contraire aux sentiments de sincère et constante amité qui les unissent.

Cette constatation a amené sans difficulté les deux gouvernements a decider:

1°. Que les questions dérivant de la capture et de l'arrêt momentané du vapeur *Carthage*, seront déférées à l'examen de la cour d'arbi-

----

[1] *Le Mémorial Diplomatique*, January 28, 1912, p. 57.

trage de La Haye, en vertu de la convention d'arbitrage franco-
italienne du 23 décembre 1903, renouvelée le 24 décembre 1908;

2°. Qu'en ce qui concerne la saisie du vapeur *Manouba* et des
passagers ottomans qui y étaient embarqués, cette opération ayant été
effectuée, d'après le gouvernement italien, en vertu des droits qu'il
declare tenir des principes généraux du droit international et de l'article 47 de la déclaration de Londres de 1909, les circonstances spéciales
dans lesquelles cette opération a été faite et les conséquences qui en
découlent seront également soumises a l'éxamen de la haute juridiction
internationale instituée à La Haye; que dans le but de rétablir le
statu quo ante en ce qui concerne les personnes, les passagers ottomans
saisis, ces derniers seront remis au consul de France à Cagliari, pour
être reconduits par ses soins à leur lieu d'embarquement, sous la responsabilité du gouvernement français, qui prendra les mesures nécessaires pour empêcher que les passagers ottomans n'appartenant pas
au "Croissant Rouge," mais à des corps combattants, se rendent d'un
port français en Tunisie ou sur le théâtre des opérations militaires.

---

*Agreement of April 4, 1912, supplementary to the Agreements for
Arbitration in the "Carthage" and "Manouba" Cases*[1]

Le Gouvernement de la République Française et le Gouvernement
Royal Italien ayant pris connaissance des deux Compromis, établis
le 6 mars 1912 par MM. Louis Renault et Fusinato, en vue de régler
par l'arbitrage devant la Cour de la Haye les incidents relatifs à la
saisie du *Carthage* et à la saisie du *Manouba*, déclarent en approuver
les termes et se considèrent comme liés par leur texte;

Ils désignent, d'un commun accord, pour constituer le tribunal arbitral les membres suivants de la Cour d'arbitrage de La Haye:

M. Guido Fusinato, docteur en droit, ancien ministre de l'Instruction
Publique, ancien professeur de droit international à l'université de
Turin, député, conseiller d'État;

M. Knut Hjalmar Léonard de Hammarskjöld, docteur en droit,
ancien ministre de la Justice, ancien ministre des Cultes et de l'Instruction Publique, ancien envoyé extraordinaire et ministre plénipotentiaire à Copenhague, ancien président de la Cour d'appel de
Jönköping, ancien professeur à la faculté de droit d'Upsal, gouverneur
de la province d'Upsal;

M. Kriege, docteur en droit, conseiller intime actual de légation,
directeur au département des Affaires Étrangères;

M. Louis Renault, ministre plénipotentiaire, professeur à la faculté
de droit de Paris, jurisconsulte du ministère des Affaires Étrangères;

M. le baron Taube, membre permanent du Conseil du ministère des
Affaires Étrangères, professeur de droit international à l'Université
impériale de Saint-Pétersbourg, conseiller d'État;

---

[1] Official report, *Mémoire* of the French Republic, p. 7, note 2.

dent du tribunal.

M. de Hammarskjöld remplira les fonctions de Surarbitre ou Prési-

Les deux Gouvernements conviennent de fixer à 3,000 florins néerlandais la somme à déposer par chacun d'eux, conformément à l'article
4 de chaque Compromis, étant entendu que ladite somme est destinée
à servir de provision pour toutes les affaires dont le tribunal arbitral
ci-dessus désigné sera chargé de connaitre.

Les deux Gouvernements se réservent la faculté de modifier, d'un
commun accord, l'article 5 de chacun des Compromis en ce qui touche
la date de la réunion du tribunal arbitral.

Fait à Paris, le 4 avril 1912.

(L. S.) Signé: R. POINCARÉ
(L. S.) Signé: M. RUSPOLI

THE MANOUBA CASE

Award of the Tribunal, May 6, 1913[1]

Considérant que, par un Accord du 26 janvier 1912 et par un Compromis du 6 mars suivant, le Gouvernement de la République Française et le Gouvernement Royal Italien sont convenus de soumettre à un Tribunal Arbitral composé de cinq Membres la solution des questions suivantes:

1°. Les autorités navales italiennes étaient-elles, d'une façon générale et d'après les circonstances spéciales où l'opération a été accomplie, en droit de procéder comme elles ont fait à la capture et à la saisie momentanée du vapeur postal français "Manouba" ainsi qu'à arrestation des vingt-neuf passagers ottomans qui s'y trouvaient embarqués?

2°. Quelles conséquences pécuniaires ou autres doivent résulter de la solution donnée à la question précédente?

Considérant qu'en exécution de ce Compromis les deux Gouvernements ont choisi, d'un commun accord, pour constituer le Tribunal Arbitral les Membres suivants de la Cour Permanente d'Arbitrage:

Son Excellence Monsieur Guida Fusinato, Docteur en droit, Ministre d'Etat, ancien Ministre de l'Instruction publique, Professeur honoraire de droit international à l'Université de Turin, Député, Conseiller d'Etat;

Monsieur Knut Hjalmar Léonard de Hammarskjöld, Docteur en droit, ancien Ministre de la Justice, ancien Ministre des Cultes et de l'Instruction publique, ancien Envoyé extraordinaire et Ministre plénipotentiaire à Copenhague, ancien Président de la Cour d'appel de Jönköping, ancien Professeur à la Faculté de droit d'Upsal, Gouverneur de la province d'Upsal;

Monsieur Kriege, Docteur en droit, Conseiller actuel intime de Légation et Directeur au Département des Affaires Etrangères, Plénipotentiaire au Conseil Fédéral Allemand;

Monsieur Louis Renault, Ministre plénipotentiaire, Membre de l'Institut, Professeur à la Faculté de droit de l'Université de Paris et à l'Ecole libre des sciences politiques, Jurisconsulte du Ministère des Affaires Etrangères;

Son Excellence le Baron Michel de Taube, Docteur en droit, Adjoint du Ministre de l'Instruction publique de Russie, Conseiller d'Etat actuel;

que les deux Gouvernements ont, en même temps, désigné Monsieur de Hammarskjöld pour remplir les fonctions de Président.

Considérant que, en exécution du Compromis du 6 mars 1912, les Mémoires et Contre-Mémoires ont été dûment échangés entre les Parties et communiqués aux Arbitres;

[1] Official report, p. 119.

Considérant que le Tribunal, constitué comme il est dit ci-dessus, s'est réuni à La Haye le 31 mars 1913;

que les deux Gouvernements ont respectivement désigné comme Agents et Conseils,

le Gouvernement de la République Française:

Monsieur Henri Fromageot, Avocat à la Cour d'appel de Paris, Jurisconsulte suppléant du Ministère des Affaires Etrangères, Conseiller du Département de la Marine en droit international, Agent;

Monsieur André Hesse, Avocat à la Cour d'appel de Paris, Membre de la Chambre des Députés, Conseil;

Le Gouvernement Royal Italien:

Monsieur Arturo Ricci-Busatti, Envoyé extraordinaire et Ministre plénipotentiaire, Chef du Bureau du Contentieux et de la Législation au Ministère Royal des Affaires Etrangères, Agent;

Monsieur Dionisio Anzilotti, Professeur de droit international à l'Université de Rome, Conseil.

Considérant que les Agents des Parties ont présenté au Tribunal les conclusions suivantes, savoir,

l'Agent du Gouvernement de la République Française:

PLAISE AU TRIBUNAL,

Sur la première question posée par le Compromis,

Dire et juger que les autorités navales italiennes n'étaient pas, d'une façon générale et d'après les circonstances spéciales où l'opération a été accomplie, en droit de procéder comme elles ont fait à la capture et à la saisie momentanée du vapeur postal français "Manouba" ainsi qu'à l'arrestation des vingt-neuf passagers ottomans qui s'y trouvaient embarqués.

Sur la seconde question posée par le Compromis,

Dire que le Gouvernement Royal Italien sera tenu de verser au Gouvernement de la République Française la somme de *un franc* de dommages-intérêts, à titre de réparation morale de l'atteinte portée à l'honneur du pavillon français;

Dire que le Gouvernement Royal Italien sera tenu de verser au Gouvernement de la République la somme de cent mille francs, à titre de sanction et de réparation du préjudice politique et moral résultant de l'infraction par le Gouvernement Royal Italien à ses engagements conventionnels généraux et spéciaux et notamment à la Convention de la Haye du 18 octobre 1907 *relative à certaines restrictions au droit de capture dans la guerre maritime,* article 2, à la Convention de Genève du 6 juillet 1906 *pour l'amélioration du sort des blessés et malades dans les armées en campagne,* article 9, et à l'accord verbalement intervenu entre les deux Gouvernements, le 17 janvier 1912, relativement au contrôle des passagers embarqués sur le paquebot "Manouba";

Dire que ladite somme sera versée au Gouvernement de la République pour le bénéfice en être attribué à telle œuvre ou institution d'intérêt international qu'il plaira au Tribunal d'indiquer;

Dire que le Gouvernement Royal Italien sera tenu de verser au Gouvernement de la République Française la somme de cent huit mille six cent un francs soixante-dix centimes, montant des indemnités réclamées par les particuliers intéressés, soit dans le paquebot "Manouba," soit dans son expédition;

Subsidiairement et pour le cas où, sur ce dernier chef, le Tribunal ne se croirait pas suffisamment éclairée,

Dire, avant faire droit, que, par tel ou tels de ses membres qu'il commettra à cet effet, il sera procédé, dans la Chambre de ses délibérations et en présence des Agents et Conseils des deux Gouvernements, à l'examen des diverses réclamations des particuliers intéressés;

Dans tous les cas, et par application de l'article 9 du Compromis,

Dire que, à l'expiration d'un délai de trois mois à compter du jour de la sentence, les sommes mises à la charge du Gouvernement Royal Italien et non encore versées seront productives d'intérêts à raison de quatre pour cent par an.

Et l'Agent du Gouvernement Royal Italien:

PLAISE AU TRIBUNAL,

Sur la première question posée par le Compromis,

Dire et juger que les autorités navales italiennes étaient pleinement en droit de procéder comme elles ont fait à la capture et à la saisie momentanée du vapeur postal français "Manouba" ainsi qu'à l'arrestation des vingt-neuf passagers ottomans sur lesquels pesait le soupçon qu'ils étaient des militaires, et dont le Gouvernement Italien avait le droit de contrôler la véritable qualité.

En conséquence et sur la seconde question,

Dire et juger qu'aucune conséquence pécuniaire ou autre ne saurait résulter à la charge du Gouvernement Italien de la capture et de la saisie momentanée du vapeur postal français "Manouba";

Dire et juger que le Gouvernement Français a pretendu à tort qu'on lui remît les passagers ottomans qui se trouvaient légalement entre les mains des autorités italiennes;

Dire que le Gouvernement de la République sera tenu de verser au Gouvernement Royal la somme de cent mille francs à titre de sanction et de réparation du préjudice matériel et moral résultant de la violation du droit international, notamment en ce qui concerne le droit que le belligérant a de vérifier la qualité d'individus soupçonnés être des militaires ennemis, trouvés à bord de navires de commerce neutres;

Dire que ladite somme sera versée au Gouvernement Royal Italien pour être attribuée à telle œuvre ou institution d'intérêt international qu'il plaira au Tribunal d'indiquer;

Subsidiairement et pour le cas où le Tribunal ne croirait pas devoir admettre cette forme de sanction,

Dire que le Gouvernement de la République sera tenu de réparer le tort fait au Gouvernement Royal Italien de telle manière qu'il plaira au Tribunal d'indiquer;

Dans tous les cas,

Dire que le Gouvernement de la République sera tenu de verser au Gouvernement Royal Italien la somme de quatre cent quatorze francs quarante-cinq centimes, montant des frais occasionnés par la saisie du "Manouba";

Dire que, à l'expiration d'un délai de trois mois à compter du jour de la sentence, les sommes mises à la charge du Gouvernement de la République et non encore versées seront productives d'intérêts à raison de quatre pour cent par an.

Considérant que, après que le Tribunal eut entendu les exposés oraux des Agents des Parties et les explications qu'ils lui ont fournies sur sa demande, les débats ont été dûment déclarés clos.

EN FAIT:

Considérant que le vapeur postal français "Manouba," de la Compagnie de Navigation Mixte, au cours d'un voyage régulier entre Marseille et Tunis, fut arrêté dans les parages de l'île de San Pietro, le 18 janvier 1912, vers 8 heures du matin, par le contre-torpilleur de la Marine Royale Italienne "Agordat";

Considérant que, après constatation de la présence, à bord dudit vapeur, de vingt-neuf passagers turcs, soupçonnés d'appartenir à l'armée ottomane, le "Manouba" fut conduit sous capture à Cagliari;

Considérant que, arrivé dans ce port le même jour, vers 5 heures du soir, le capitaine du "Manouba" fut sommé de livrer les vingt-neuf passagers susmentionnés aux autorités italiennes et que, sur son refus, ces autorités procédèrent à la saisie du vapeur;

Considérant enfin que, sur l'invitation du Vice-Consul de France à Cagliari, les vingt-neuf passagers turcs furent livrés le 19 janvier, à 4 heures 30 de l'après-midi, aux autorités italiennes,

et que le "Manouba," alors relaxé, se remit en route sur Tunis le même jour, à 7 heures 20 du soir.

EN DROIT:

Considérant que, si le Gouvernement Français a dû penser, étant donné les circonstances dans lesquelles la présence de passagers ottomans à bord du "Manouba" lui était signalée, que, moyennant la promesse de faire vérifier le caractère desdits passagers, il exemptait le "Manouba" de toute mesure de visite ou de coercition de la part des autorités navales italiennes, il est établi qu'en toute bonne foi le Gouvernement Italien n'a pas entendu la chose de cette façon;

que, par suite, en l'absence d'un accord spécial entre les deux Gouvernements, les autorités navales italiennes ont pu agir conformément au droit commun;

Considérant que, d'après la teneur du Compromis, l'opération effectuée par les autorités navales italiennes renferme trois phases successives, savoir: la capture, la saisie momentanée du "Manouba" et l'arrestation des vingt-neuf passagers ottomans qui s'y trouvaient embarqués;

qu'il convient d'examiner d'abord la légitimité de chacune de ces trois phases, regardées comme des actes isolés et indépendants de l'ensemble de l'opération susmentionnée;

Dans cet ordre d'idées,

Considérant que les autorités navales italiennes avaient, lors de la capture du "Manouba," des motifs suffisants de croire que les passagers ottomans qui s'y trouvaient embarqués étaient, au moins en partie, des militaires enrôlés dans l'armée ennemie;

que ces autorités avaient, par conséquent, le droit de se les faire remettre;

Considérant qu'elles pouvaient, à cet effet, sommer le capitaine de les livrer, ainsi que prendre, en cas de refus, les mesures nécessaires pour l'y contraindre ou pour s'emparer de ces passagers;

Considérant, d'autre part, que, même étant admis que les passagers ottomans aient pu être considérés comme formant une troupe ou un détachement militaire, rien ne permettait de révoquer en doute l'entière bonne foi de l'armateur et du capitaine du "Manouba";

Considérant que, dans ces circonstances, les autorités navales italiennes n'étaient pas en droit de capturer le "Manouba," et de le faire dévier pour suivre l'"Agordat" à Cagliari, si ce n'est comme moyen de contrainte et après que le capitaine eût refusé d'obéir à une sommation de livrer les passagers ottomans;

que, aucune sommation de ce genre n'ayant eu lieu avant la capture, l'acte de capturer le "Manouba" et de l'amener à Cagliari n'était pas légitime;

Considérant que, la sommation faite à Cagliari étant restée sans effet immédiat' les autorités navales italiennes avaient le droit de prendre les mesures de contrainte nécessaires et, spécialement, de retenir le "Manouba" jusqu'à ce que les passagers ottomans fussent livrés;

que la saisie effectuée n'était légitime que dans les limites d'un séquestre temporaire et conditionnel;

Considérant enfin que les autorités navales italiennes avaient le droit de se faire livrer et d'arrêter les passagers ottomans.

Pour ce qui concerne l'ensemble de l'opération,

Considérant que les trois phases dont se compose l'opération unique prévue par le Compromis doivent être appréciées en elles-mêmes, sans que l'illégalité de l'une d'elles doive, dans l'espèce, influer sur la régularité des autres;

que l'illégalité de la capture et de la conduite du "Manouba" à Cagliari n'a pas vicié les phases postérieures de l'opération;

Considérant que la capture ne pourrait non plus être légitimée par la régularité, relative ou absolue, de ces dernières phases envisagées séparément.

Sur la demande tendant à faire condamner le Gouvernement Royal Italien à verser à titre de dommages-intérêts:

1°. la somme de *un franc* pour atteinte portée au pavillon français;

2°. la somme de cent mille francs pour réparation du préjudice moral et politique résultant de l'inobservation du droit commun international et des conventions réciproquement obligatoires pour l'Italie comme pour la France,

Et sur la demande tendant à faire condamner le Gouvernement de la République Française à verser la somme de cent mille francs à titre de sanction et de réparation du préjudice matériel et moral résultant de la violation du droit international, notamment en ce qui concerne le droit que le belligérant a de vérifier la qualité d'individus soupçonnés être des militaires ennemis, trouvés à bord de navires de commerce neutres,

Considérant que, pour le cas où une Puissance aurait manqué à remplir ses obligations, soit générales, soit spéciales, vis-à-vis d'une autre Puissance, la constatation de ce fait, surtout dans une sentence arbitrale, constitue déjà une sanction sérieuse;

que cette sanction est renforcée, le cas échéant, par le paiement de dommages-intérêts pour les pertes matérielles;

que, en thèse générale et abstraction faite de situations particulières, ces sanctions paraissent suffisantes;

que, également en thèse générale, l'introduction d'une autre sanction pécuniaire paraît être superflue et dépasser le but de la juridiction internationale;

Considérant que, par application de ce qui vient d'être dit, les circonstances de la cause présente ne sauraient motiver une telle sanction supplémentaire; que, sans autre examen, il n'y a donc pas lieu de donner suite aux demandes susmentionnées.

Sur la demande de l'Agent français tendant à ce que le Gouvernement Royal Italien soit tenu de verser au Gouvernement de la République Française la somme de cent huit mille six cent un francs soixante-dix centimes, montant des indemnités réclamées par les particuliers intéressés, soit dans le vapeur "Manouba," soit dans son expédition,

Considérant qu'une indemnité est due pour le retard occasionné au "Manouba" par sa capture non justifiée et sa conduite à Cagliari, mais qu'il y a lieu de tenir compte du retard provenant du refus non légitime du capitaine de livrer à Cagliari les vingt-neuf passagers turcs et aussi du fait que le navire n'a pas été entièrement détourné de sa route sur Tunis;

Considérant que, si les autorités navales italiennes ont opéré la saisie du "Manouba" au lieu du séquestre temporaire et conditionnel qui était légitime, il apparaît que, de ce chef, les intéressés n'ont pas éprouvé de pertes et dommages;

Considérant que, en faisant état de ces circonstances et aussi des frais occasionnés au Gouvernement Italien par la surveillance du navire retenu, le Tribunal, après avoir entendu les explications concordantes de deux de ses Membres chargés par lui de procéder à une enquête sur lesdites réclamations, a évalué à quatre mille francs la somme due à l'ensemble des intéressés au navire et à son expédition.

PAR CES MOTIFS,

Le Tribunal Arbitral déclare et prononce ce qui suit:

Pour ce qui concerne l'ensemble de l'opération visée dans le première question posée par le Compromis,

Les différentes phases de cette opération ne doivent pas être considérées comme connexes en ce sens que le caractère de l'une doive, dans l'espèce, influer sur le caractère des autres.

Pour ce qui concerne les différentes phases de ladite opération, appréciées séparément,

Les autorités navales italiennes n'étaient pas, d'une façon générale et d'après les circonstances spéciales où l'opération a été accomplie, en droit de procéder comme elles ont fait à la capture du vapeur postal français "Manouba" et à sa conduite à Cagliari;

Le "Manouba" une fois capturé et amené à Cagliari, les autorités navales italiennes étaient, d'une façon générale et d'après les circonstances spéciales où l'opération a été accomplie, en droit de procéder comme elles ont fait à la saisie momentanée du "Manouba," dans la mesure où cette saisie ne dépassait pas les limites d'un séquestre temporaire et conditionnel, ayant pour but de contraindre le capitaine du "Manouba" à livrer les vingt-neuf passagers ottomans qui s'y trouvaient embarqués;

Le "Manouba" une fois capturé, amené à Cagliari et saisi, les autorités navales italiennes étaient, d'une façon générale et d'après les circonstances spéciales où l'opération a été accomplie, en droit de procéder comme elles ont fait à l'arrestation des vingt-neuf passagers ottomans qui s'y trouvaient embarqués.

Pour ce qui concerne la seconde question posée par le Compromis,

Le Gouvernement Royal Italien sera tenu, dans les trois mois de la présente sentence, de verser au Gouvernement de la République Française la somme de quatre mille francs, qui, déduction faite des frais de surveillance du "Manouba" dûs au Gouvernement italien, forme le montant des pertes et dommages éprouvés, à raison de la capture et de la conduite du "Manouba" à Cagliari, par les particuliers intéressés au navire et à son expédition.

Il n'y a pas lieu de donner suite aux autres réclamations contenues dans les conclusions des deux Parties.

Fait à La Haye, dans l'Hôtel de la Cour Permanente d'Arbitrage, le 6 mai 1913.

Le Président: Hj. L. HAMMARSKJÖLD
Le Secrétaire général: MICHIELS VAN VERDUYNEN
Le Secrétaire: RÖELL

Agreement for Arbitration, March 6, 1912[1]

Le Gouvernement de la République Française et le Gouvernement Royal Italien, s'étant mis d'accord le 26 janvier 1912 par application de la Convention d'arbitrage franco-italienne du 25 décembre 1903, renouvelée le 24 décembre 1908 pour confier à un Tribunal d'arbitrage l'examen de la capture et de la saisie momentanée du vapeur postal français "Manouba" par les autorités navales italiennes notam-

---

[1] Official report, p. 9.

ment dans les circonstances spéciales où cette opération a été accomplie et de l'arrestation de vingt-neuf passagers ottomans qui s'y trouvaient embarqués, ainsi que la mission de se prononcer sur les conséquences qui en dérivent,

Les soussignés, dûment autorisés à cet effet, sont convenus du Compromis suivant:

ARTICLE 1

Un Tribunal arbitral, composé comme il est dit ci-après, est chargé de résoudre les questions suivantes:

1°. Les autorités navales italiennes étaient-elles, d'une façon générale et d'après les circonstances spéciales où l'opération a été accomplie, en droit de procéder comme elles ont fait à la capture et à la saisie momentanée du vapeur postal français "Manouba," ainsi qu'à l'arrestation des vingt-neuf passagers ottomans qui s'y trouvaient embarqués?

2°. Quelles conséquences pécuniaires ou autres doivent résulter de la solution donnée à la question précédente?

ARTICLE 2

Le Tribunal sera composé de cinq Arbitres que les deux Gouvernements choisiront parmi les Membres de la Cour permanente d'Arbitrage de La Haye, en désignant celui d'entre eux qui remplira les fonctions de Surarbitre.

ARTICLE 3

A la date du 15 juin 1912, chaque Partie déposera au Bureau de la Cour permanente d'Arbitrage quinze exemplaires de son mémoire, avec les copies certifiées conformes de tous les documents et pièces qu'elle compte invoquer dans la cause.

Le Bureau en assurera sans retard la transmission aux Arbitres et aux Parties, savoir deux exemplaires pour chaque Arbitre, trois exemplaires pour la Partie adverse; deux exemplaires resteront dans les archives du Bureau.

A la date du 15 août 1912, chaque Partie déposera dans les mêmes conditions que ci-dessus, son contre-mémoire avec les pièces à l'appui et ses conclusions finales.

ARTICLE 4

Chacune des Parties déposera au Bureau de la Cour permanente d'Arbitrage de La Haye, en même temps que son mémoire et à titre de provision, une somme qui sera fixée d'un commun accord.

ARTICLE 5

Le Tribunal se réunira à La Haye, sur la convocation de son Président, dans la deuxième quinzaine du mois de septembre 1912.

ARTICLE 6

Chaque Partie sera représentée par un Agent avec mission de servir d'intermédiaire entre elle et le Tribunal.

Le Tribunal pourra, s'il l'estime nécessaire, demander à l'un ou à l'autre des Agents de lui fournir des explications orales ou écrites, auxquelles l'Agent de la Partie adverse aura le droit de répondre.

ARTICLE 7

La langue française est la langue du Tribunal. Chaque Partie pourra faire usage de sa propre langue.

ARTICLE 8

La sentence du Tribunal sera rendue dans le plus bref délai possible et dans tous les cas dans les trente jours qui suivront la clôture des débats. Toutefois, ce délai pourra être prolongé à la demande du Tribunal et du consentement des Parties.

ARTICLE 9

Le Tribunal est compétent pour régler les conditions d'exécution de sa sentence.

ARTICLE 10

Pour tout ce qui n'est pas prévu par le présent Compromis, les dispositions de la Convention de La Haye du 18 octobre 1907 pour le règlement pacifique des conflits internationaux seront applicables au présent Arbitrage.

Fait en double à Paris, le 6 mars 1912.

Signé: L. RENAULT
Signé: G. FUSINATO

THE ISLAND OF TIMOR CASE

Award of the Tribunal, June 25, 1914[1]

Une contestation étant survenue entre le Gouvernement royal néer-landais et celui de la République portugaise au sujet de la délimitation d'une partie de leurs possessions respectives dans l'île de Timor, les deux Gouvernements ont décidé, par une Convention signée à La Haye le 3 avril 1913 et dont les ratifications ont été échangées dans la même ville le 31 juillet suivant, d'en remettre la solution en dernier ressort à un arbitre, et ont à cet effet désigné d'un commun accord le soussigné.

Pour comprendre le sens et la portée du compromis du 3 avril 1913, il y a lieu d'exposer succinctement les négociations qui ont précédé ce compromis.

I

HISTORIQUE

L'île de Timor, la dernière à l'orient de la série continue des îles de la Sonde et la plus rapprochée de l'Australie, fut découverte au XVIme siècle par les Portugais; cette île mesure environ 500 kilomètres de longueur de l'ouest à l'est sur une largeur de 100 kilomètres au maximum. Une haute chaîne de montagnes, dont certains sommets atteignent près de 3,000 mètres d'altitude, sépare l'île dans le sens de la longueur en deux versants.

La partie orientale de l'île, d'une superficie approximative de 19,000 kilomètres carrés avec une population d'environ 300,000 habitants, est portugaise. La partie occidentale, avec une population évaluée en 1907 à 131,000 habitants et une superficie d'environ 20,000 kilomètres carrés, est sous la souveraineté des Pays-Bas, à l'exception du "Royaume d'Okussi et d'Ambeno," situé sur la côte nord-ouest au milieu de territoires néerlandais de tous les côtés sauf du côté de la mer. Ce nom de "rois" donné par les Portugais aux chefs des tribus s'explique par le fait que, dans la langue indigène, on les appelle *Leorey;* la syllabe finale de ce mot a été traduite en portugais par le mot *Rey*. Les Néerlandais donnent à ces chefs le titre plus modeste de *radjahs*.

Cette répartition territoriale entre les Pays-Bas et le Portugal repose sur les Accords suivants:

Le 20 avril 1859, un traité signé à Lisbonne et dûment ratifié au cours de l'été de 1860, avait déterminé les frontières respectives par le milieu de l'île, mais avait laissé subsister (art. 2) "l'enclave" néer-landaise de Maucatar au milieu des territoires portugais et "l'enclave"

[1]Official report, p. 3.

portugaise d'Oikoussi au milieu des territoires néerlandais de l'ouest de l'île. Il fut stipulé (art. 3) que cette "enclave d'Oikoussi comprend l'Etat d'Ambenu partout où y est arboré le pavillon portugais, l'État d'Oikoussi proprement dit et celui de Noimuti."

Par une autre Convention signée à Lisbonne le 10 juin 1893 et dûment ratifiée, les deux Gouvernements, "desirant régler dans les conditions les plus favorables au développement de la civilisation et du commerce" leurs relations dans l'archipel de Timor, convinrent "d'établir d'une façon plus claire et plus exacte la démarcation de leurs possessions" dans cette île "et de faire disparaître les enclaves actuellement existantes" (Préambule et art. Iᵉʳ). Une commission d'experts devait être désignée à l'effet de "formuler une proposition pouvant servir de base à la conclusion d'une Convention ultérieure déterminant la nouvelle ligne de démarcation dans ladite île" (art. II). En cas de difficultés, les deux Parties s'engageaient "à se soumettre à la décision . . . d'arbitres" (art. VII).

Cette commission mixte se rendit sur les lieux et se mit d'accord en 1898–1899 sur la plus grande partie de la délimitation. Toutefois, tant sur la frontière principale au milieu de l'île de Timor que sur la frontière du Royaume d'Okussi-Ambenu dans la partie occidentale de l'île, d'assez nombreuses divergences persistaient. La carte annexée sous Nᵒ. II indique les prétentions respectives. Une Conférence fut réunie à La Haye du 23 juin au 3 juillet 1902 pour tâcher de les solutionner. Elle arrêta le 3 juillet 1902 un projet qui fut transformé en Convention diplomatique signée à La Haye le 1ᵉʳ octobre 1904 et dûment ratifiée.

Les résultats sommaires de cette Convention de 1904 sont figurés sur la carte transparente annexée sous Nᵒ. I; la superposition de la carte transparente Nᵒ. I sur la carte Nᵒ. II permet de constater que le Portugal a obtenu, au centre de l'île de Timor, l'enclave néerlandaise de Maukatar, et que les Pays-Bas ont obtenu dans cette même région le Tahakay et le Tamira Ailala. D'autre part, au nord-ouest de l'île de Timor et au sud du territoire désigné par le traité de 1859 sous le nom d'enclave d'Oikussi, les Pays-Bas obtiennent le Noimuti. Enfin la limite orientale contestée de ce territoire d'Oikussi-Ambeno est fixée théoriquement selon une ligne A–C qui devra être "arpentée et indiquée sur le terrain dans le plus court délai possible." (Actes de la Conférence de 1902, séances du 27 juin, pages 10 et 11, et du 28 juin, page 12; Convention du 1ᵉʳ octobre 1904, article 4.) La ligne A-C admise en Conférence fut définie à l'article 3 chiffre 10 de la Convention de 1904 dans les termes suivants: "A partir de ce point" (le confluent de la Noël Bilomi avec l'Oè-Sunan) "la limite suit le thalweg de l'Oè-Sounan, traverse autant que possible Nipani et Kelali (Keli), gagne la source de la Noël Meto et suit le thalweg de cette rivière jusqu'à son embouchure."

Tout semblait terminé, lorsque les commissaires délimitateurs arrivés sur les lieux en juin 1909 pour les opérations du bornage de la frontière orientale de l'Oikussi-Ambeno ne purent se mettre d'accord et décidèrent d'en référer à leurs Gouvernements. Les deux Gouvernements ne purent pas davantage se mettre d'accord et décidèrent de recourir à un arbitrage. Quelle était cette difficulté rencontrée par les commissaires délimitateurs?

II
LA DIFFICULTÉ QUI A PROVOQUÉ L'ARBITRAGE

En procédant aux trauvaux de délimitation de la frontière orientale de l'Oikussi-Ambeno, les commissaires avaient commencé au nord, sur la côte, et remonté dans la direction du sud le cours de la rivière Noèl Meto, qui devait servir de frontière de son embouchure à sa source. Ces opérations eurent lieu entre le 1er et le 10 juin 1909, et une borne fut placée à la source de la Noèl Meto. Cette source étant dominée par des falaises abruptes impossibles à franchir, les commissaires résolurent une reconnaissance générale du terrain entre la partie septentrionale et la partie méridionale du territoire encore à délimiter, c'est-à-dire entre la source de la Noèl Meto au nord et la rivière Noèl Bilomi au sud.

Au nord, un premier dissentiment surgit: La carte (voir annexe III) signée en 1904 en même temps que la Convention, portait le mot *Kelali* accompagné entre parenthèses du mot *Keli*. Les délégués néerlandais soutinrent que le mot Keli désigne, sur le sommet du mont Kelali, un point spécial situé à l'ouest de la source de la Noèl Meto entre deux pierres "en pic" et qui a été indiqué par les indigènes du Tumbaba (néerlandais) comme la limite entre eux et les indigènes (portugais) de l'Ambeno: ce point est, d'après les commissaires néerlandais, une "magnifique limite" naturelle qui suit à peu près la limite figurée sur la carte de 1904. Les commissaires portugais au contraire proposaient "de suivre . . . quelques thalwegs dans le terrain à l'est de la ligne proposée par les délégués néerlandais, en partant de la même borne" placée à la source de la Noèl Meto. La commission décida d'arpenter les deux lignes et de laisser la solution aux autorités supérieures.

Dans la partie sud, sur la rivière Bilomi, les commissaires constatent, dans leur séance du 17 juin 1909, qu'ils ont suivi de l'ouest à l'est le cours de la Nono Nisi (ou Nise) puis le cours de la Noèl Bilomi et qu'ils ont maintenant *"atteint l'endroit* (où la commission de 1889 avait terminé son travail) *où il faut continuer l'arpentage vers le nord."* Ce point avait été désigné dans la Convention de 1904, article 3, chiffres 9 et 10, et sur la carte y annexée, comme le confluent de la Noèl Bilomi et de l'Oè Sunan. "Les quatre délégués constatent *qu'à cet endroit, il y a deux affluents venant du nord, mais qu'aucun d'eux ne s'appelle l'Oè Sunan."*

Les délégués néerlandais exposent alors que la contrée située entre ces deux affluents est nommée Sunan, qu'ils ne connaissent d'ailleurs aucun affluent de la Noèl Bilomi portant le nom d'Oè Sunan et qu'il n'en existe pas; ils insistent donc pour que la ligne frontière soit arpentée vers le nord à partir du point désigné sur les cartes de 1899 et de 1904.

Les délégués portugais font observer qu'une rivière nommée Oè Sunan ou Oil Sunan, qui n'est, il est vrai, pas un affluent de la Bilomi, existe plus à l'est et a sa source "tout près du Bilomi."

Les commissaires décident à l'unanimité d'arpenter les deux lignes *"en partant du point"* indiqué sur les cartes de 1899 et de 1904 et *"où la commission de 1899 a terminé son travail,"* savoir la ligne proposée par les délégués néerlandais dans la direction du nord et la ligne désirée par les Portugais dans la direction de l'est (séance du 17 juin 1909, Premier Mémoire portugais, page 27).

A la séance du 21 juin 1909 et au cours de l'arpentage de la ligne frontière proposée par les délégués portugais dans la direction de l'est en remontant la rivière Noël Bilomi, "les quatre délégués constatent unanimement qu'ils n'ont pas rencontré un affluent (de la Noël Bilomi) nommé l'Oè-Sunan." Les Délégués néerlandais font observer que la Bilomi a, dans cette région, changé de nom, à quoi leurs collègues portugais répliquent "que la rivière de Bilomi continue toujours, mais que, suivant les usages indigènes, elle porte le nom de la contrée qu'elle traverse." Enfin et surtout, les délégués portugais font observer qu'à peu de distance de la Bilomi se trouve, sur la rive nord, un mont Kinapua, sur le versant opposé duquel se trouve une rivière portant le nom d'Oè Sunan et qui coule vers le nord. Il suffirait de suivre le cours de cette rivière, de remonter ensuite la rivière Noi Fulan et de relier enfin la source de celle-ci avec la source de la Noël Meto déjà reconnue par la commission mixte.

Les délégués néerlandais déclarent inutile de procéder à la reconnaissance de cette rivière, car le mont Kinapua et la limite qui résulterait de la proposition portugaise sont en dehors du territoire qui était contesté en 1899; le mont Tasona figure sur la carte de 1899 sur l'extrême limite orientale des *prétentions* portugaises d'alors, prétentions que le traité de 1904 a écartés; il ne saurait donc être question d'une délimitation allant encore plus loins vers l'est.

Les travaux de la Commission mixte furent suspendus et la question, portée sur le terrain diplomatique, donna lieu à un long échange de correspondances entre les cabinets de La Haye et de Lisbonne.

Ces correspondances ont abouti à l'accord de 1913 confiant à l'arbitre le mandat de décider, d'après "les données fournies par les parties," et, en se basant sur les principes généraux du droit, comment doit être fixée, conformément à l'art. 3, 10 de la Convention conclue à La Haye le 1ᵉʳ octobre 1904 . . ., la limite à partir de la Noël Bilomi jusqu'à la source de la Noël Meto."

III

LE POINT DE VUE PORTUGAIS

Les principaux arguments invoqués par le Gouvernement de la République portugaise en faveur de la thèse soutenue par ses commissaires délimitateurs peuvent être résumés comme suit:

1. Au point où les travaux de délimitation de 1899 ont été arrêtés

et où, d'après le traité de 1904 et d'après la carte y annexée, la Noël Bilomi doit recevoir un affluent du nom de l'Oè Sunan, il est reconnu d'un commun accord qu'il n'existe aucun affluent de ce nom.

2. Il existe au contraire, plus à l'est, une rivière Oè Sunan qui n'est pas, il est vrai, un affluent de la Bilomi, mais qui prend sa sources tres près de cette rivière Bilomi, sur le versant nord de la montagne Kinapua; sur le mont Kinapua se trouve une borne proclamée par de nombreux chefs indigènes comme ayant servi de limite reconnue entre les Ambenos portugais et les Tumbabas néerlandais. De ce même mont Kinapua descend vers la Bilomi un ruisseau, et, du sommet, ces deux cours d'eau semblent se continuer. D'après les chefs indigènes, le cours de cette rivière Oè Sunan est la limite historique et naturelle entre les Ambenos portugais d'une part et les Tumbabas et les Amakonos néerlandais d'autre part.

3. Les mêmes chefs indigènes font rentrer dans l'Ambeno toute la région comprise entre cette rivière d'Oè Sunan à l'est, la rivière Ni Fullan au nord, et le territoire incontestablement portugais de l'Oikoussi Ambeno à l'ouest des monts Kelalai et Netton. Sur une carte privée publiée à Batavia, le nom d'Ambeno se trouve même en entier inscrit dans la partie revendiquée à tort aujourd'hui par les Pays-Bas.

4. Le traité de 1859 pose en principe que les États indigènes ne doivent pas être séparés, morcelés; or la délimitation proposée par les Pays-Bas coupe le territoire des Ambenos et priverait ces indigènes de leurs pâturages et terrains maraichers qui se trouveraient par là situés à l'orient de la frontière et en territoire néerlandais.

5. Rien ne prouve que le bornage à effectuer doive nécessairement commencer au point où le travail de délimitation avait été suspendu en 1899 à la suite d'hostilités entre les indigènes et marqué sur les cartes au confluent de la Bilomi avec le ruisseau l'Oè Sunan qui n'existe pas en réalité à cet endroit. A cet endroit se trouvent deux affluents : le Kaboun et le Nono-Offi. Pourquoi suivre vers le nord le cours du Kaboun plutôt que celui du Nono-Offi qui vient du nord-est et qui se jette au même point dans la Bilomi?

Dans la pensée du Gouvernement portugais, on a voulu seulement donner dans les cartes de 1899 et 1904 aux commissaires délimitateurs "un graphique destiné à fixer les idées, et comme une vague et simple indication de ce qui devait être réglé plus tard."

La véritable intention des Signataires du traité de 1904 a été de suivre le cours de l'Oè Sunan, là où il est en réalité, c'est-à-dire beaucoup plus à l'est. Rien n'empêche donc, dans l'esprit du traité, de remonter la Bilomi jusqu'au point le plus rapproché de la source du vrai Oè Sunan, source si rapprochée du cours de la Bilomi qu'elle en [est] presque un affluent.

6. La ligne proposée par les Pays-Bas qui, d'après le traité de 1904, doit "traverser autant que possible Nipani et Kelalai (Keli)" ne *traverse* pas Nipani, mais touche seulement Fatu Nipani, c'est-à-dire l'extrémité occidentale de Nipani. Elle ne répond donc pas au programme de 1904.

7. La ligne proposée par les Pays-Bas ne constitue pas une frontière naturelle, tandis que celle suggérée par le Portugal suit des cours d'eau sur presque tout son parcours.

IV

LE POINT DE VUE NÉERLANDAIS

Les principaux arguments du Gouvernement royal néerlandais peuvent être résumés comme suit :

1. Le traité de 1859 n'avait nullement prescrit d'une façon impérative que les territoires indigènes ne doivent pas être devisés ou morcelés. Il a, au contraire, attribué au Portugal "l'État d'Ambenu partout où y est arboré le pavillon portugais," sanctionnant ainsi non seulement la division d'un État indigène, mais précisément la division de l'État d'Ambenu et cela dans les termes suivants : "La Néerlande cède au Portugal . . . *cette partie* de l'Etat d'Ambenu ou d'Ambeno qui, depuis plusieurs années, a arboré le pavillon portugais."

Au surplus, le traité de 1859 a pu être et a été effectivement modifié par les traités subséquents et ce sont les traités subséquents qui, aujourd'hui, doivent seuls être pris en considération là où ils ont modifié le traité de 1859.

2. Il n'existe aucune incertitude sur le point auquel les commissaires délimitateurs se sont arrêtés en 1899. Ce point a servi de base aux négociations de 1902 et a été repéré sur la carte (annexe III) signée alors par les négociateurs des deux Pays pour être jointe au projet de traité. Ce projet de 1902 est devenu le traité de 1904. C'est de ce point et non d'un autre que part la ligne A-C, admise en 1902 comme devant former la frontière (carte annexe I). Cette ligne A-C se dirige de ce point vers le nord jusqu'à la source de la rivière Noël Meto et la frontière doit suivre ensuite ce cours d'eau jusqu'à son embouchure dans la mer au nord.

L'emplacement de la source de la Noël Meto a été contradictoirement reconnu en 1909 ; une borne y a été plantée d'un commun accord. La discussion ne porte que sur le tracé entre cette source et le point A situé à l'endroit où les commissaires se sont arrêtés en 1899.

3. Sur la carte officielle de 1899 (annexe IV) comme sur la carte officielle de 1904 (annexe III), figure au point dont il s'agit un affluent venant du nord et auquel on a, par une erreur que les Pays-Bas ne contestent pas, donné à tort le nom d'Oè Sunan. Cet affluent, qui porte en réalité chez les Tumbabas le nom de Kabun et chez les Ambenos celui de Leos, répond entièrement à l'intention des Parties contractantes, qui était de suivre, à partir du point A, un affluent venant du nord dans la direction AC. L'erreur de nom a d'autant moins de portée que, très fréquemment dans la région, les cours d'eau portent plusieurs noms, ou changent de nom, ou portent le nom de la contrée qu'ils traversent ; or la région à l'est du Kabun ou Lèos (l'Oè Sunan de 1904) porte, d'après le Gouvernement portugais, le nom à consonnance analogue d'Hue Son, et d'après les commissaires néerlandais celui de Sunan, ce qui peut expliquer l'erreur des commissaires.

4. Les chefs indigènes de l'Amakono (néerlandais) ont déclaré (commission mixte, séance du 21 février 1899) que leur pays comprend toute la région "située entre l'Oè Sunan, Nipani, Kelali-Keli, et la Noèl Meto (à l'ouest), la mer de Timor (au nord), la Noèl Boll Bass, les sommets Humusu et Kin Napua (à l'est), Tasona, la Noèl Boho et la Noèl Bilomi (au sud)." Or la frontière occidentale décrite ici et indiquée dès 1899 comme séparant les Amakonos (néerlandais) de l'Ambeno (portugais) est précisément celle qui a été consacrée par le traité de 1904. L'Oè Sunan qui y figure ne peut être que le cours d'eau auquel on a donné à tort mais d'un commun accord ce nom dans les cartes officielles de 1899 et de 1904, c'est-à-dire un cours d'eau situé à *l'ouest* du territoire contesté, et non le prétendu Oè Sunan actuellement invoqué par le Portugal, et qui est situé sur la frontière *orientale* du territoire contesté. Le traité de 1904 a attribué aux Pays-Bas ce terri*oire contesté. C'est donc bien le cours d'eau, peu importe son nom, situé à l'ouest dudit territoire que les parties ont entendu adopter comme limite.

La preuve que le Portugal n'a pu, en 1899 et 1904, avoir en vue la rivière orientale à laquelle il donne maintenant le nom d'Oè Sunan, est fournie par le fait qu'à la séance du 21 février 1899, ses commissaires ont proposé comme limite une ligne partant du point où la rivière appelée alors Oè Sunan se jette dans la Bilomi et remontant ensuite vers l'est la Noèl Bilomi jusqu'à Nunkalaï (puis traversant Tasona et, à partir de Kin Napua se dirigeant vers le nord jusqu'à Humusu et à la source de la Noèl Boll Bass dont le cours aurait servi de frontière jusqu'à son embouchure dans la mer). Cette proposition portugaise de 1899 serait incompréhensible s'il s'agissait d'une rivière autre que celle figurant sur les cartes officielles de 1899 et 1904 sous le nom d'Oè Sunan; comment pourrait-il être question d'une autre rivière Oè Sunan située à l'*est* de Nunkalaï, alors que Nunkalaï est, en réalité, à l'*ouest* de ce nouvel Oè Sunan découvert par les Portugais et non pas à l'est?

5. Deux enquêtes récentes instituées par les autorités néerlandaises de l'île de Timor ont, d'ailleurs, confirmé qu'aucune rivière du nom d'Oè Sunan ne prend sa source sur le mont Kinapua; la rivière qui prend sa source sur le versant nord, à une certaine distance du sommet, porte les noms de Poeamesse ou de Noiepolan et se jette à Fatoe Metassa (Fatu Mutassa des Portugais) dans la Noèl Manama, la Ni Fullan des cartes portugaises (Second Mémoire néerlandais, chiffre VII, page 6).

6. Il est exact que la ligne proposée par les Pays-Bas ne traverse pas le territoire de Nipani, mais le traité de 1904 ne l'exige pas. Il stipule que la ligne destinée à relier la source de l'Oè Sunan à la source de la Noèl Meto traversera "autant que possible Nipani." Comme le territoire à délimiter était inexploré, les mots "autant que possible" étaient justifiés; en fait, la ligne suggérée par les Pays-Bas, si elle ne traverse pas tout le territoire de Nipani, en traverse l'extrémité occidentale appelée Fatu Nipani. Or, d'après les déclarations consignées au procès-

verbal de délimitation du 21 février 1899, les indigènes, en désignant l'Oè Sunan, Nipani, Kelali et la Noèl Meto comme la frontière orientale de l'Okussi Ambeno (portugais) et comme la frontière occidentale de l'Amakono (néerlandais), avaient eu en vue la masse rocheuse de Fatu Nipani formant l'extrémité occidentale de Nipani.

7. La frontière proposée par les Pays-Bas est une frontière naturelle formée par une chaîne de montagnes séparant partout les cours d'eau.

Il n'a jamais été prescrit ou recommandé en 1902–1904 de suivre avant tout des cours d'eau comme limite, et, sur la frontière méridionale de l'Okussi-Ambeno, on a, sur plusieurs points, notamment lorsque la ligne passait du bassin d'une rivière dans un autre, placé des bornes d'un commun accord (Voir notamment l'art. 3 de la Convention de 1904, chiffres 2, 3 et 4).

Il suffira aussi de quelques bornes pour délimiter la frontière sur la ligne de faîte proposée par les Pays-Bas.

Le tracé réclamé par le Portugal exigerait d'ailleurs lui aussi des bornes dans la région du mont Kinapua entre la Bilomi et le prétendu nouvel Oè Sunan, et en outre dans la région entre la source de la Noèl Meto et la rivière à laquelle les Portugais donnent le nom de Ni Fulan c'est-à-dire aux deux extrémités du tracé portugais.

8. La ligne que le Portugal propose aujourd'hui reproduit en substance ses prétentions de 1899 et de 1902 dans cette région. Or il est incontestable qu'en acceptant à la Conférence de 1902 et en consignant dans le traité de 1904 la ligne AC, le Portugal a cédé un territoire auquel il prétendait auparavant. Il ne saurait équitablement revendiquer aujourd'hui ce même territoire.

V

LES RÈGLES DE DROIT APPLICABLES

A teneur de l'article 2 du compromis, l'arbitre doit baser sa décision non seulement sur les traités en vigueur entre les Pays-Bas et le Portugal relatifs à la délimitation de leurs possessions dans l'île de Timor, mais aussi sur "les principes généraux du droit international."

Il est presque superflu de rappeler ces principes.

Heffter, *Völkerrechts,* § 94, s'exprime, par exemple, comme suit: "Tous les traités obligent à l'exécution loyale et complète, non pas seulement de ce qui a été littéralement promis, mais de ce à quoi on s'est engagé, et aussi de ce qui est conforme à l'essence de tout traité quelconque comme à l'intention concordante des contractants (c'est-à-dire à ce qu'on appelle l'esprit des traités)." Heffter ajoute § 95: "L'interprétation des traités doit, sans le doute, se faire conformément à l'intention réciproque constatable, et aussi conformément à ce qui peut être présumé, entre Parties agissant loyalement et raisonnablement, avoir été promis par l'une à l'autre à teneur des termes employés."

Rivier, *Principes du droit des gens,* II, N°. 157, formule les mêmes pénsees dans les termes suivants: "Il faut avant tout constater la commune intention des parties: *id quod actum est* . . . La bonne foi dominant toute cette matière, les traités doivent être interprétés non pas exclusivement selon leur lettre, mais selon leur esprit . . . Les principes de l'interprétation des traités sont, en somme, *et mutatis mutandis,* ceux de l'interprétation des conventions *entre particuliers,* principes de bon sens et d'expérience formulés déjà par les Prudents de Rome" (Ulpien, L. 34, au Digeste De R. J. 50.17: "Semper in stipu-lationibus et in ceteris contractibus id sequimur quod actum est").

Entre particuliers, les règles auxquelles Rivier renvoie ont été formulées dans les principaux codes en termes suffisamment précis pour se passer de commentaires:

Code civil français, néerlandais, etc., art. 1156–1157. "On doit dans les Conventions *rechercher quelle a été la commune intention des parties, plutôt que de s'arrêter au sens littéral des termes.* Lorsqu'une clause est susceptible de deux sens, on doit plutôt l'entendre dans celui avec lequel elle peut avoir quelque effet, que dans le sens avec lequel elle n'en pourrait produire aucun." *Code civil allemand* de 1896, art. 133: "Pour l'interprétation d'une déclaration de volonté, il faut *rechercher la volonté réelle et ne pas s'en tenir au sens littéral de l'ex-pression* (Bei der Auslegung einer Willenserklärung ist der wirkliche Wille zu erforschen und nicht an dem buchstäblichen Sinne des Aus-drucks *zu haften.*" Code civil portugais de 1867, art. 684. *Code suisse des obligations de 1911,* art. 18: "Pour apprécier la forme et les clauses d'un contrat, il y a lieu de *rechercher la réelle et commune intention des parties, sans s'arrêter aux expressions ou dénominations inexactes dont elles ont pu se servir, soit par erreur,* soit pour déguiser la nature véritable de la Convention."

Il est inutile d'insister, le droit des gens comme le droit privé étant sur ce point entièrement concordants.

Il ne reste plus qu'à faire application aux circonstances de la cause de ces règles et à rechercher quelle a été la réelle et commune intention des Pays-Bas et du Portugal lors des négociations de 1902 qui ont abouti à la Convention de 1904.

VI

L'INTENTION DES PARTIES EN SIGNANT LA CONVENTION DE 1904

1. Le traité de Lisbonne du 10 juin 1893 avait eu pour but de chercher à établir une démarcation plus claire et plus exacte des possessions respectives dans l'île de Timor et de faire disparaître les "enclaves actuellement existantes" (art. 1er). Les "enclaves" figurant sous ce nom au traité antérieur signé à Lisbonne le 20 avril 1859, étaient celles de Maucatar (art. 2, premier alinéa) et d'Oi Koussi (art. 2, second alinéa, et art. 3, premier alinéa).

Lorsqu'en juin 1902, les Délégués des deux Gouvernements se réunirent à La Haye pour chercher à concilier les propositions diver-gentes des commissaires délimitateurs envoyés sur les lieux en 1898–1899, les délégués furent immédiatement d'accord pour attribuer au

Portugal l'enclave néerlandaise de Maucatar au centre de l'île de Timor, et aux Pays-Bays l'enclave portugaise de Noimuti, au sud du "royaume" d'Ambeno. A la séance du 26 juin, les Portugais demande- rent, au milieu de l'île, toute la partie du territoire de Fialarang située à l'est de la rivière Mota Bankarna (voir la carte annexe II) ; ils soutinrent en outre que le royaume d'Ambeno confinant à la mer ne pouvait pas plus être considéré comme une enclave que la Belgique, le Portugal ou les Pays-Bas et qu'il ne pouvait donc être question de l'attribuer à la Néerlande ; ils revendiquèrent aussi pour l'Ambeno tout le Hinterland de la côte comprise au nord entre les embouchures de la Noël Meto et de la Noël Boll Bass. Ce Hinterland devait s'étendre au sud jusqu'à la rivière Noël Bilomi et suivre cette rivière de l'ouest à l'est entre le point auquel les commissaires délimitateurs s'étaient, à l'ouest, arrêtés en 1899 et, à l'est, un lieu dénommé Nunkalaï sur la carte dessinée alors en commun par les commissaires délimitateurs des deux Pays.—Les limites de ce territoire contesté ayant été dés- signées par les quatre lettres A B C D sur une carte (voir annexe II) présentée par les Délégués néerlandais à la Conférence de 1902 la dis- cussion s'engagea sur la ligne occidentale AC préconisée par les Pays- Bas, et la ligne orientale BD réclamée par le Portugal.

Sur la carte ci-annexée sous N°. IV, on a reproduit les prétentions respectives, telles qu'elles résultent de la carte signée en commun par tous les commissaires délimitateurs, à Kœpang, le 16 février 1899.

Les délégués néerlandais déclarèrent à la Conférence du 26 juin 1902 que les chefs du territoire de Fialarang, au milieu de l'île de Timor, se refusaient absolument à passer sous la souveraineté du Portugal, en sorte qu'il n'était pas ou n'était plus possible de supprimer cette pointe que le territoire néerlandais fait dans cette région en terri- toire portugais (Voir carte II).

Le premier délégué portugais répliqua qu'il ne fallait pas trop se "laisser guider par des préoccupations d'humanité envers les peuples de l'île de Timor ; pour des cas peu graves, ces tribus quittent leur sol natal pour s'établir ailleurs, et ils ont plusieurs fois quitté le territoire néerlandais pour s'établir dans le territoire portugais et inversement." Finalmente, le Délégué portugais renonça au territoires des Fialarangs au milieu de l'île de Timor, mais demanda que la frontière orientale de l'Oikoussi fût fixée "selon la proposition des commissaires néer- landais de 1899." (Voir cette proposition dans le procès-verbal de la séance tenue à Kœpang le 8 février 1899 dans le premier Mémoire por- tugais, p. 24.)

Le lendemain 27 juin, le premier Délégué néerlandais accepta la proposition portugaise, mais, pour èviter tout malentendu, réclama pour son Gouvernement "la certitude *absolue* que la limite orientale d'Okussi *représentée par la ligne A C* sera démarquée autant que pos- sible sur le terrain même."

Il y avait, en effet, malentendu, car le premier délégué portugais répondit que sa proposition de la veille "ne disait pas que la frontière à l'est d'Oikussi sera formée par la ligne A C, mais au contraire par la ligne proposée par la commission mixte de 1899 et indiquée par les lettres A B."

Le premier délégué néerlandais répliqua aussitôt que, "si la ligne AC n'est pas acceptée comme frontière à l'est d'Oikoussi (et si les demandes néerlandaises pour la frontière au centre de Timor ne sont pas agréées) . . . les délégués néerlandais retirent leurs consentement à la proposition portugaise . . . Jamais ils ne pourraient soumettre à leur Gouvernement un projet ne satisfaisant pas à ces conditions."—Le délégué néerlandais termina en déclarant que, si un accord amiable sur ces bases n'intervenait pas, les Pays-Bas recourraient à l'arbitrage prévu par la Convention de 1893 sur la "question des enclaves," donnant ainsi à entendre qu'en cas de refus de la ligne A C pour la frontière orientale de l'Ambeno, les Pays-Bas soulèveraient la question beaucoup plus vaste de savoir si la totalité de l'Ambeno n'était pas une enclave pouvant revenir logiquement à la Néerlande, puisque l'Ambeno avait été à plusieurs reprises désigné comme enclave dans le traité de 1859 et puisqu'un des buts de la Convention de 1893 était la "suppression des enclaves."

A la séance du 28 juin, les délégués portugais "ayant examiné sérieusement la proposition des délégués néerlandais, émise dans la séance du 27 juin, ont résolu d'accepter cette proposition, ainsi que les conditions posées par eux (par les délégués néerlandais) à ce sujet."

Il importait de reproduire avec détails cette discussion, parce qu'elle jette un jour décisif sur la réelle et commune intention des Parties.—Le Portugal s'est déclaré satisfait de la situation qui lui était offerte. Au milieu de l'île de Timor, il gagnait la grande enclave de Maukatar; s'il n'y gagnait pas le pays des Fialarangs, il conservait dans l'ouest de l'île de Timor l'Oikussi Ambeno et évitait d'avoir à discuter devant des arbitres la question délicate de savoir si ce royaume était ou non une "enclave" susceptible d'être attribuée en entier aux Pays-Bas; le Portugal a préféré dans ces circonstances renoncer à la partie orientale contestée de l'Oikussi Ambeno plutôt que de risquer d'y perdre davantage ou même d'y perdre tout; il a trouvé, en un mot, dans l'ensemble de la négociation, des compensations jugées par lui suffisantes à l'abandon de la ligne B D et de la ligne intermédiaire A B qu'il réclamait.—Il a finalement accepté la ligne A C réclamée *sine qua non* par les Pays-Bas.

Il est donc certain que cette ligne A C doit, dans l'intention des Parties, être considérée comme une *concession* faite par le Portugal aux Pays-Bas et ce fait a été proclamé par les Délégués portugais eux-mêmes dans le Mémoire qu'ils ont remis à la séance du 26 juin 1902, au cours des Conférences de La Haye, en ces termes: "ces territoires représentent une *réduction considérable* des frontières du royaume d'Ocussi-Ambenou."

2. Qu'est-ce que la ligne A C?

a) Et d'abord où est le point C? A l'embouchure de la rivière Noël Meto dans la mer de Timor au nord de l'île. Aucune contestation n'existe à ce sujet, et la Convention de 1904, article 3, chiffre 10, stipule expressément que la frontière suit le thalweg de la Noèl Meto de sa source à son embouchure.—Entre 1899 et 1902–1904, le Portugal prétendait au contraire à tout le territoire à l'est de la Noèl Meto jusqu'à la rivière Noèl Boll Bass; l'embouchure de la Noèl Boll Bass était le point B, terminus nord de la ligne A B revendiquée par le Portugal (Proposition portugaise, séance du 21 février 1899, 2ᵉ Mémoire néerlandais annexe II, Procès-verbaux des Conférences de La Haye 1902, page 10, et cartes ci-annexées I et II).

Si l'emplacement du point C n'est pas contesté, il est cependant utile de constater que l'adoption en 1904, comme ligne de démarcation, du cours de la Noèl Meto plutôt que du cours de la Noèl Boll Bass prouve l'intention générale de ramener la frontière vers l'ouest.

b) L'emplacement de la source de la Noèl Meto a été déterminé et une borne y a été plantée d'un commun accord (procès-verbal du 14 juin 1909, 1ᵉʳ Mémoire portugais, page 26). Toute cette partie du tracé est ainsi définitivement réglée. (Voir carte annexe VI.)

c) Où est maintenant, à l'autre extrémité de la ligne, le point A convenu à la Conférence de 1902? Les Pays-Bas soutiennent que ce point A se trouve là où se termina la reconnaissance de 1899 et où les commissaires durent arrêter leurs travaux à cause d'hostilité entre les tribus indigènes, c'est-à-dire au point où les commissaires après avoir suivi la Nono Balena, la Nono Nive et la Noèl Bilomi, ont atteint le confluent de cette dernière rivière avec une autre venant du nord et à laquelle avait été attribué d'un commun accord le nom d'Oè Sunan.

Toute la ligne de démarcation dans cette partie occidentale et inférieure du bassin de la Bilomi a été sanctionée et définitivement admise comme frontière par le traité de 1904, article 3, chiffre 9. Lors de la reconnaissance postérieure du 17 juin 1909, il est constaté au procès-verbal que ce point n'est pas douteux : "On décide *unanimement* que de ce point, *c'est-à-dire le point où la commission de 1899 a terminé son travail*, l'arpentage sera poursuivi." (1ᵉʳ Mémoire néerlandais, annexe III, page 4, 1ᵉʳ Mémoire portugais, page 27.) La divergence se produit seulement sur ce qu'il y a lieu de faire *à partir de ce point*, soit vers le nord (demande néerlandaise) soit dans la direction de l'est (demande portugaise). Or ce point, celui auquel les travaux avaient été suspendus en 1899, celui à partir duquel des divergences s'étaient produites entre 1899 et 1902, a été marqué sur la carte officielle signée contradictoirement par les commissaires délimitateurs des deux Pays le 16 février 1899 ; c'est ce même point qui a été envisagé lorsqu'à la Conférence de La Haye de 1902, les délégués des deux Etats ont solutionné le différend en se prononçant pour une frontière se dirigeant vers le nord et désignée sous le nom de ligne A C. En plaçant cette carte du 16 février 1899 (annexe IV ci-jointe) sous la carte annexée à la Convention de 1904 (annexe III ci-jointe), on constate qu'il y a concordance absolue entre elles quant à l'emplacement du point dont il s'agit.

Le Gouvernement portugais ne conteste d'ailleurs pas très vivement l'emplacement du point A, car dans son premier Mémoire il s'exprime comme suit, page 10: "On ne prétend pas nier que la ligne ne part du point A, auquel se rapportent les procès-verbaux des négociations, vers le point C. Ce qu'on discute, ce sont ses inflexions subordonnées . . ." et plus loin, page 15: "On ne conteste pas que la frontière dont il s'agit ne parte du point où les arpenteurs ont été empêchés d'aller plus loin: ce qu'on nie, c'est qu'on ait eu l'intention de la diriger *de là* directement vers le nord."

De ce qui précède, il résulte pour l'arbitre la certitude que trois points de la ligne A C sont dûment établis, incontestables et même incontestés: le point C au nord, la source de la Noël Meto au milieu et le point A au sud, à l'endroit où les travaux de délimitation ont été suspendus en 1899. Ces trois points correspondent certainement à l'intention des Parties lorsqu'elles ont négocié le projet de convention de 1902 et l'ont transformé en convention en 1904. Admettre une autre solution quant à l'emplacement du point A serait d'ailleurs remettre en question la frontière convenue pour le cours inférieur de la Noël Bilomi par le chiffre 9 de l'article 3 du traité de 1904; or ce chiffre 9 n'est pas contesté et n'est pas en cause.

3. Il reste à examiner maintenant la partie de la ligne A C comprise entre le point A au sud et la source de la Noël Meto au milieu de cette ligne A C.

Ici encore et toujours, il faut rechercher l'intention réelle et concordante des Parties au moment où elles ont contracté:

En 1902, deux propositions étaient en présence: Celle du Portugal avait été formulée comme suit dans le procès-verbal de la séance des commissaires délimitateurs tenue à Kœpang le 21 février 1899 (annexe II au 2ᵐᵉ Mémoire néerlandais): "De ce dernier point (le point A), le long de la Noël Bilomi jusqu'à Nunkalaï, de là traversant Tasona, Kin Napua, Humusu, jusqu'à la source de la Noël Boll Bass; puis le long de cette rivière jusqu'à l'embouchure." Aux Conférences de La Haye de 1902, ce tracé (D B) fut abandonné dès la séance du 26 juin par la Délégation portugaise et remplacé par la demande d'un tracé intermédiaire et diagonal A B qui prenait pour frontière au nord-est le cours de la Noël Boll Bass au lieu de la Noël Meto (voir la carte ci-jointe II). Le 28 juin, la délégation portugaise abandonnait cette ligne de retraite A B, reculait vers l'ouest de la Noël Boll Bass à la Noël Meto (voir carte ci-jointe II), et acceptait la ligne A C réclamée par les Pays-Bas. Cette ligne A C était aussitôt tracée sur une carte qui a été annexée officiellement au traité de 1904 (voir carte annexe III).

Sur cette carte, la frontière, partant du point A auquel aboutissait la frontière incontestée du cours inférieur de la Noël Bilomi remonte dans la direction du nord le cours d'un petit affluent appelé d'un commun accord Oè Sunan, puis continue vers le nord jusqu'à l'emplacement, alors inconnu, de la source de la Noël Meto. Ce tracé de la carte était défini et commenté comme suit dans le traité, art. 3, chiffre 10: "à partir de ce point (A), la limite suit le thalweg de l'Oè Sunan, traverse autant que possible Nipani et Kelali (Keli), gagne la source de la Noël Meto et suit le thalweg de cette rivière jusqu'à son embouchure." Or ce texte, devenu définitif dans le traité de 1904, *est la reproduction mot à mot du texte proposé par les commissaires néerlandais* à cette même séance de Kœpang, 21 février 1899, en opposition aux prétentions portugaise d'alors. La simple mise en regard de ces deux cartes et le fait qu'en 1902–1904, la proposition portugaise a été totalement écartée et la proposition néerlandaise insérée mot à mot, suffit à établir avec évidence l'intention des Parties contractantes: lorsqu'elles ont négocié et signé l'accord de 1904, elles ont adopté le tracé néerlandais et écarté le tracé désiré par le Portugal sur cette partie des frontières des deux États dans l'île de Timor. Les deux parties ont donc eu, dans la pensée de l'arbitre, *la volonté réelle et concordante d'adopter le tracé plus occidental,* non seulement sur le versant nord de l'île entre la Noël Boll Bass et la Noël Meto, mais aussi dans le centre de l'île, entre le cours de la Noël Bilomi et la source de la Noël Meto.

Il convient maintenant d'entrer dans les détails de l'examen de ce tracé le plus occidental :

4. Le Portugal fait observer aujourd'hui que le cours d'eau dénommé Oè Sunan sur les cartes officielles de 1899 et de 1904 et dans l'art. 3, chiffre 9, du traité de 1904, n'existe pas ; que ce cours d'eau porte en réalité le nom de Kabun chez les membres de la tribu des Tumbabas ou de Lèos chez les membres de la tribu des Ambenos, et que le véritable Oé Sunan se trouve à six ou sept kilomètres plus à l'est. Il est vrai, ajoute le Gouvernement portugais, que cet autre Oè Sunan n'est pas un affluent de la rivière Bilomi, qu'il prend sa source à une certaine distance de cette rivière, sur le versant nord du Mont Kinapua, mais cet autre Oè Sunan et le Mont Kinapua sont revendiqués par les Ambenos (portugais) comme formant d'ancienne date la frontière entre eux à l'ouest et les Amakonos néerlandais à l'est. C'est donc bien, dans la pensée du Gouvernement portugais, à cet autre Oé Sunan que les deux Gouvernements ont pensé lorsqu'ils ont, à l'art. 3, chiffre 10, du traité de 1904, stipulé que la frontière suivrait le cours de l'Oè Sunan.

Pour apprécier la portée de cette allégation, il y a lieu de se rappeler que, sur la carte dressée par les commissaires délimitateurs des deux Pays le 16 février 1899 à Kœpang (carte annexe IV), la frontière demandée alors par le Portugal est indiquée par un pointillé *en suivant à la montée le cours présumé de la Noël Bilomi* dans la direction de l'est à partir du point (A) auquel les dits commissaires avaient dû alor arrêters leurs travaux, c'est-à-dire à partir du confluent de la Noël Bilomi avec ce qu'on appelait alors d'un commun accord l'Oè Sunan ; on a eu soin, dans cette carte de 1899, de faire suivre le pointillé des mots "Noël Bilomi," pour bien indiquer le désir des commissaires portugais de continuer à suivre, en le remontant, le cours de la rivière.

D'autre part, lors de la signature du traité de 1904, on a, au contraire, sur la carte annexée au traité, supprimé tout ce pointillé à l'est du point auquel on s'était arrêté en 1899, pour bien montrer qu'il n'y avait plus lieu de continuer à remonter dans la direction de l'est le cours alors inexploré de la Noël Bilomi, et qu'au contraire, la frontière devait se diriger vers le nord (voir carte transparente annexe III). Cela implique, dans la pensée de l'arbitre, l'intention concordante d'attribuer, en amont du point A, les *deux rives* de la Noèl Bilomi aux Pays-Bas.

Un autre fait qui paraît à l'arbitre impliquer la même intention concordante des Parties lors de la signature de la Convention de 1904, est que, dans la description de la frontière proposée en 1899 par les commissaires portugais, ils ont suggéré de *l'ouest à l'est* le tracé suivant : "De ce dernier point (le confluent de la Noèl Bilomi avec l'affluent nommé alors l'Oè Sunan) le long de la Noèl Bilomi *jusqu'à Nunkalaï*, de là traversant Tasona, Kinapua . . ."; d'après cette description portugaise, Nunkalaï se trouve donc à l'est de la rivière d'Oè Sunan et à l'ouest de Kinapua. Or l'autre rivière Oé-Sunan, actuellement revendiquée comme frontière par le Portugal, se trouve située à plusieurs kilomètres *à l'est* et non à l'ouest de Nunkalaï, d'où résulte l'impossibilité que cette rivière ait été visée par les délégués portugais dans leurs propositions d'alors.

Ce qui confirme encore cette impression de l'arbitre, c'est le fait que le nouvel Oè Sunan, celui qui, six kilomètres plus à l'est, a sa source sur le versant septentrional du mont Kinapua, n'est pas un *affluent* de la Noèl Bilomi.

Enfin, cet autre Oè Sunan ne se dirige pas "vers Nipani et Kelali (Keli)" comme le prescrit le traité de 1904, mais se confond très vite avec d'autres rivières se dirigeant vers l'est pour aboutir finalement dans des régions incontestablement néerlandaises.

Tout cet ensemble de circonstances concordantes amène l'arbitre à la conviction qu'il n'y a pas lieu de s'arrêter à l'erreur de nom commise par les commissaires délimitateurs en 1899 et par les négociateurs des actes internationaux de 1902 et 1904 lorsqu'ils ont donné au Kabun ou Lèos le nom d'Oè Sunan, et qu'il y a lieu au contraire d'admettre que c'est bien le Kabun ou Lèos que les Parties ont eu l'intention de viser comme devant servir de frontière à partir du point A dans la direction du nord. Cette erreur commune aux commissaires des deux Pays s'explique d'ailleurs lorsqu'on constat que la plupart des cours d'eau de la région portent plusieurs noms ou portent le nom de la région qu'il traversent et qu'une région voisine du Kabun ou Lèos porte le nom de Sunan dont la consonnance se rapproche d'Oè Sunan.

Admettre une autre solution, accepter un tracé remontant le cours de la Noèl Bilomi jusqu'au mont Kinapua, puis passant dans le bassin d'un autre Oè Sunan que n'est pas un affluent de la Bilomi et qui ne se dirige pas vers Nipani et Kelali, serait contraire à tout l'esprit de la négociation de 1902–1904, et inconciliable avec la carte annexée à la convention de 1904. Le Portugal ne saurait équitablement revendiquer après coup, entre la Noèl Bilomi et la source de la Noèl Meto et à propos d'un bornage, presque exactement le territoire auquel il a expressément renoncé en 1902–1904 contre des compensations jugées par lui suffisantes ou parce qu'il a voulu éviter alors de la part des Pays-Bas un appel à l'arbitrage ou des revendications plus étendues dans la région d'Okussi (voir cartes annexes V et VI).

De ce qui précède, se dégage, en d'autres termes, la conviction que la volonté des Parties contractantes doit être interprétée en ce sens qu'à partir du point A situé sur la rivière Bilomi, la frontière suit, dans la direction du nord, le thalweg de la rivière Kabun ou Lèos jusqu'à la source de ce dernier cours d'eau dénommé à tort Oè Sunan en 1899, 1902 et 1904.

Le raisonnement exposé ci-dessus sous chiffre 4 serait superflu si, comme l'affirme le Gouvernement des Pays-Bas (Second mémoire, chiffre VII, page 6) les dernières reconnaissance faites sur place ont établi que ce nouvel Oè Sunan n'existe pas et que le cours d'eau auquel des portugais donnent ce nom s'appelle en réalité Noèl Polan ou Poeamesse.

5. Il ne reste plus à rechercher l'intention des Parties que pour la section comprise entre la source de la rivière Kabun ou Lèos (dénommée à tort Oè Sunan de 1899 à 1904) et la source de la Noèl Meto.

La Convention de 1904 s'exprime comme suit: "Le Thalweg de l'Oè Sunan [reconnu sous N° 4 ci-devant devoir être dénommé Kabun ou Lèos] traverse *autant que possible* Nipani et Kelali (Keli), [et] gagne la source de la Noèl Meto. . . ."

Les commissaires délimitateurs néerlandais et leur Gouvernement proposent de relier les sources des rivières Kabun et Noèl Meto en suivant presque exactement la ligne de partage des eaux, c'est-à-dire une suite de sommets dont les principaux porteraient, du sud au nord, les noms de Netton, Adjausene, Niseu ou Nisene, Wanat ou Vanate, Fatu Nipani ou Fatoe Nipani, Fatu Kabi (Fatoe Kabi) et Kelali (Keli).

Cette proposition est contestée par le Gouvernement portugais parce qu'elle serait contraire aux intentions des Parties dont le but aurait été, lors de la conclusion des traités entre les deux Gouvernements, de ne pas séparer les États indigènes; or cette ligne détacherait de l'Ambeno portugais toute la partie orientale; le Gouvernement portugais invoque, dans son premier et surtout dans les annexes de son second Mémoire, les dépositions de nombreux chefs indigènes pour établir, en substance, que tout l'espace qui serait attribué aux Pays-Bas fait partie de l'Ambeno et appartient aux Ambenos. Il invoque en outre une carte privée éditée à Batavia, sur laquelle les Ambenos sont indiqués comme occupant le territoire revendiqué par les Pays-Bas. Le Gouvernement portugais est d'avis que l'Ambenu-Oïkussi a incontestablement été attribué au Portugal par le traité de 1859 et que la tribu des Ambenos ne saurait être partagée entre deux souverainetés.

Une fois de plus, l'arbitre doit chercher à reconstituer la volonté des Parties. Or d'après le texte du traité de 1859, le Portugal a obtenu seulement la "partie" de l'État d'Ambeno qui "a arboré le pavillon portugais"; il n'y aurait donc rien d'anormal à ce que certaines parties de l'Ambeno eussent été considérées, dés 1859, comme restant sous la souveraineté des Pays-Bas. En outre, la carte privée éditée à Batavia ne saurait prévaloir contre les deux cartes officielles signés par les commissaires ou délégués des deux États en 1899 et en 1904 et ces deux cartes officielles (annexes III et IV) ne font pas figurer le nom d'Ambeno dans le territoire contesté; l'une et l'autre inscrivent ce nom à l'ouest et en dehors du territoire contesté. Il résulte, d'ailleurs, des documents fournis que, dès 1899, les commissaires néerlandais produisaient des déclarations des chefs indigènes tumbabas et amakonos assurant que ce territoire leur appartenait et ne faisait pas parties de l'Ambeno (annexe III au second Mémoire néerlandais, déclaration faite à la séance tenue à Kœpang le 21 février 1899). On se trouve donc en présence d'affirmations contradictoires des indigènes. Ceux-ci se battaient en 1899 depuis plus de vingt ans (premier Mémoire portugais, p. 22), lors de l'arrivée dans cette région des commissaires-délimitateurs, et le Gouvernement portugais reconnait (dans son premier Mémoire, p. 9) comme "certain que les peuples à l'Est de l'Oikussi Ambeno se disputent depuis longtemps les territoires contigus et que ces peuples se trouvent de telle sorte entremêlés, qu'il est difficile de distinguer ce qui leur appartient en réalité." Voir aussi dans le second Mémoire portugais, p. 10, la déposition du chef ambeno Béné Necat: "La partie orientale d'Oikussi et d'Ambeno a été habitée par le peuple Tumbaba qui en a été chassé il y a trois génération . . . par les Ambenos. . . . Depuis lors cette région est déserte, bien qu'elle soit parcourue par les Tumbabas et par les Ambenos."

L'intention des Parties lors de la négociation de 1902 se trouve documentée par le procès-verbal de la séance du 26 juin (procès-verbaux, page 7) au cours de laquelle le premier Délégué portugais a, lui-même, conseillé "de ne pas trop se laisser guider en cette matière par les préoccupations d'humanité envers les peuples dans l'île de Timor; pour des causes peu graves, ces tribus quittent leur sol natal pour s'établir ailleurs et ont plusieurs fois quitté le territoire néerlandais pour s'établir dans le territoire portugais et inversement." Le lendemain, procès-verbaux, page 11, le premier délégué néerlandais faisait observer que son Gouvernement faisait "une grande concession" en ne réclamant pas la totalité de l'Ambeno, "attendu qu'à son avis la convention de 1893 impliquait la disparition de l'enclave d'Oikussi"; il déclarait que, si les deux Gouvernements ne pouvaient en venir à un arrangement sur la base de la ligne A C proposée par les Pays-Bas, ceux-ci se verraient engagés à recourir à l'arbitrage pour établir si l'Ambeno n'était pas une "enclave" devant leur ètre attribuée toute entière, et c'est alors que, le 28 juin, la délégation portugaise accepta sans restriction ni réserve la ligne A C telle qu'elle était réclamée par la délégation néerlandaise.

De tout cet ensemble de faits résulte pour l'arbitre la conviction qu'en 1902–1904, l'accord s'est fait sans tenir compte du risque de détacher telle ou telle parcelle réclamée par les Ambenos, les Tumbabas ou les Amakonos et en constatant expressément qu'on ne se préoccuperait pas des prétentions, d'ailleurs contradictoires, des indigènes. Des procès-verbaux de 1902 résulte, en d'autres termes, pour l'arbitre, le conviction que le Portugal a accepté la ligne A C telle qu'elle était réclamée *par les Pays-Bas,* précisément parce que le Portugal préférait abandonner des prétentions d'ordre secondaire à l'est afin de conserver le gros morceau, c'est-à-dire afin de conserver ce que le traité de 1859 avait appelé l'"enclave" d'Ambeno-Okussi. C'est avec raison aussi, dans la pensée de l'arbitre, que le Gouvernement néerlandais soutient dans son second mémoire, page 2, que rien dans le traité de 1859 ne s'opposait à la division du royaume d'Ambeno et ajoute: "Même si le traité de 1859 n'avait pas sanctionné une telle division . . . le Gouvernement portugais ne pourrait légitimement s'opposer *à présent* à une pareille division. De telles objections viendraient trop tard et auraient dû être élevées *avant* la conclusion du traité de 1904."

L'arbitre fait observer en outre que, sur les deux cartes officielles de 1899 et de 1904 (annexes III et IV), le Nipani est indiqué comme se trouvant très près et légèrement à l'est de la ligne A C, à peu de distance de la source de l'Oè Sunan (aujourd'hui reconnu devoir être appelé Kabun ou Lèos) ; si l'on adoptait le tracé actuellement réclamé par le Portugal, ce tracé passerait fort loin à l'est et au nord du Nipani et par conséquent "traverserait" encore moins ce territoire que le tracé proposé par les Pays-Bas. Il est vrai que le Gouvernement portugais place le Nipani (voir la carte annexée sous chiffre VI au premier Mémoire néerlandais et mot *Nipani* inscrit *en bleu* sur la carte ci-jointe annexe IV) au nord-est du territoire contesté, mais cette carte unilatérale portugaise ne saurait être opposée aux deux cartes officielles de 1899 et de 1904 (annexes III et IV), signées des délégués des deux États; d'ailleurs, même sur cette carte exclusivement portugaise, la frontière desirée par le Portugal semble tracée au nord de Nipani et ne paraît pas "traverser" ce territoire.

6. Le Gouvernement de la République portugaise objecte enfin à ce tracé d'une ligne à peu près directe du sud au nord entre la source de la rivière Kabun ou Lèos et la source de la Noèl Meto, que c'est une frontière terrestre, devant nécessiter la pose de bornes tandis que la ligne orientale suggérée par le Portugal est essentiellement formée par une succession de rivières, ce qui est préférable pour éviter des conflits entre les indigènes. Dans la pensée de l'arbitre, cette objection ne repose sur aucune indication résultant des négociations de 1899 à 1904. Sur la frontière méridionale de l'Okussi-Ambeno, la frontière adoptée en 1904 est, sur un assez grand nombre de points, indépendante des cours d'eau et a dû ou pourra devoir être marquée sur le terrain par des bornes. Le tracé suggéré par le Portugal comporterait, lui aussi, des parties terrestres et la plantation de bornes, notamment à l'angle sud-est (aux environs du mont Kinapua, entre le cours de la rivière Bilomi et le cours de la rivière dénommée Oè Sunan par les Portugais), et à l'angle nord-ouest (entre la source de la rivière appelée par les Portugais Ni-Fullan et la source de la Noèl Meto).

Le tracé suggéré par les commissaires néerlandais paraît à l'arbitre constituer une frontière suffisamment naturelle pour être facilement délimitable sur le terrain. Il se compose d'une série continue de sommets assez élevés, portant, du sud au nord, les noms de Netton, Loamitoe, Adjausene, Niseu, Wanat, Fatoe-Nipani, Kelali ou Keli, dont l'altitude est indiquée entre 500 et 1,000 mètres. Cette chaîne sert de ligne de partage des eaux et les rivières à l'est de cette ligne coulent vers l'orient. Il ne semble donc pas qu'il soit techniquement difficile de procéder à la délimitation le long de cette chaîne de hauteurs, dont la direction générale répond entièrement à la ligne théorique A C adoptée d'un commun accord en 1904.

VII

CONCLUSIONS

Les considérations defait et de droit qui précèdent ont amené l'arbitre aux conclusions suivantes :

1. Le traité de 1859 avait attribué au Portugal, dans la partie occidentale de l'île de Timor, l'"enclave" d'Oikussi-Ambenu, et les Pays-Bas ont cédé alors au Portugal *"cette partie* d'Ambenu qui, depuis plusieurs années, a arboré le pavillon portugais."

2. La Convention de 1893 a eu pour but "d'établir d'une façon plus claire et plus exacte la démarcation" des possessions respectives à Timor et d'y "faire disparaître les enclaves actuellement existantes."

3. La Convention de 1904 a régularisé la frontière au centre de l'île en attribuant au Portugal l'enclave néerlandaise de Maukatar et d'autres territoires contestés, et aux Pays-Bas au sud-ouest de l'île, l'enclave portugaise de Noemuti. D'autre part, les Pays-Bas ont renoncé, au cours des négociations de 1902, à soulever la grosse question de savoir si l'Oikussi Ambenu n'était pas, comme l'indiquait le traité de 1859, une "enclave" devant leur revenir. Cet accord a eu lieu à la condition, expressément acceptée par le Portugal, d'adopter, pour la frontière orientale de ce royaume d'Oikussi (Ambenu), la ligne A C réclamée au cours des négociations de 1902 par les Pays-Bas. Cette ligne A C a été consacrée par le traité de 1904 (voir Cartes annexes I et II).

4. Le point C de cette ligne n'est pas contesté ; il est situé sur la côte nord de l'île de Timor, à l'embouchure dans la mer de la Noël Meto, dont le cours a été substitué en 1902–1904 au cours de la rivière Noël Boll Bass, située plus à l'est et qu'avait réclamé le Portugal.

Le cours de la Noël Meto, dont le thalweg doit servir de frontière jusqu'à sa source, a été reconnu, n'est pas contesté, et une borne a été plantée contradictoirement à sa source.

5. Le point A, à l'extrémité méridionale de la ligne convenue en 1904, est le point auquel les travaux de délimitation ont été interrompus en 1899. Cela n'est pas sérieusement contesté par le Portugal, qui, à deux reprises dans son premier Mémoire, se sert des mots: "On ne peut pas nier que la ligne part de point A, auquel se rapportent les procès-verbaux des négociations (p. 10) . . . On ne conteste pas que la frontière dont il s'agit ne parte du point où les arpenteurs de 1899 ont été empêchés d'aller plus loin" (p. 15). Contester l'emplacement du point A serait remettre en question la délimitation du cours inférieur de la Noël Bilomi en aval de ce point ; or cette partie de la frontière a été réglée définitivement par le chiffre 9 de l'article 3 du traité de 1904 ; le point A a été d'ailleurs repéré contradictoirement sur les cartes officielles de 1899 et de 1904 (voir annexes III et IV).

6. Les négociateurs de 1902–1904 se sont trouvés à partir de ce point A en présence de deux propositions. L'une, la proposition portugaise, consistait à faire remonter à la frontière la rivière Noèl Bilomi dans la direction de l'est jusqu'à Nunkalaï, puis à diriger la frontière vers le nord, par Humusu, afin d'atteindre la source de la rivière la Noèl Boll Bass se jetant dans la mer à l'orient de la Noèl Meto (ligne B D). L'autre, la proposition néerlandaise, dite ligne A C, consistait à se diriger vers le nord dès le point A jusqu'aux sources de la Noèl Meto. Les négociateurs ont nettement, catégoriquement, répudié le premier tracé portugais pour accepter la seconde ligne A C réclamée par les Pays-Bas ; ils ont, sur la carte annexée au traité de 1904, attribué aux Pays-Bas *les deux rives* de la Noèl Meto en amont du point A, auquel les délimitateurs avaient arrêté leurs travaux en 1899 (voir les cartes III et IV).

7. La description dans le traité de 1904, article 3, chiffre 10, de cette ligne A C, la carte contradictoirement dessinée en 1899 et sur laquelle les négociateurs de 1902 ont délibéré, comme enfin la carte officiellement annexée au traité de 1904, mentionnent au point A, comme devant former limite dans la direction du nord, un affluent auquel toutes les Parties ont donné de 1899 à 1909 le nom d'Oè Sunan. Les Parties sont aujourd'hui d'accord que cet affluent porte en réalité le nom de Kabun ou de Lèos. Une autre rivière, découverte postérieurement à environ six kilomètres plus à l'est, porte, d'après les Portugais, le nom d'Oè Sunan et prend sa source au nord du Kinapua, montagne située très près de la rive nord de la Bilomi. L'existence de cette rivière Oè Sunan est contestée par les Pays-Bas dans leur second Mémoire à la suite de deux reconnaissances récentes ; ce prétendu Oè Sunan s'appellerait en réalité Poeamesse ou Noèl Polan.

Il est, dans la pensée de l'arbitre, impossible que cette autre rivière Oè Sunan, si elle existe, ait été celle que les négociateurs de 1899 et de 1902–1904 avaient en vue, car

a) Elle n'est pas un affluent de la Noèl Bilomi ;

b) La frontière *proposée* à cette époque *par le Portugal* et *écartée* d'un commun accord en 1902–1904 devait, en partant du point A et en se dirigeant *vers l'est,* passer par *Nunkalaï* puis par Kinapua ; or Nunkalaï est situé plusieurs kilomètres à l'*ouest* du mont Kinapua et à l'*ouest* de la source de cette nouvelle rivière dénommée Oè Sunan par les Portugais ;

c) Les *deux* rives de la Noèl Bilomi en amont et à l'est du point A ayant été attribuées aux Pays-Bas en 1904, l'affluent devant servir de frontière dans la direction du nord ne peut être recherché en amont et à l'est du point A.

Les principes généraux sur l'interprétation des Conventions exigent qu'on tienne compte "de la réelle et commune intention des Parties sans s'arrêter aux expressions ou dénominations inexactes dont elles ont pu se servir par erreur." Les Parties ont, il est vrai, commis une erreur en donnant le nom d'Oè Sunan à l'affluent venant du nord au point A, mais c'est cet affluent seul (dénommé alors par erreur Oè Sunan) qui était nécessairement, dans la pensée concordante des Parties, le point auquel la frontière devait quitter la Noël Bilomi pour se diriger vers le nord,—et non une autre rivière à laquelle les Portugais donnent ce nom d'Oè Sunan et qui serait située six kilomètres plus à l'est.   En d'autres termes, c'est bien le thalweg de la rivière aujourd'hui dénommé Kabun ou Lèos qui doit servir de frontière à partir du point A dans la direction du nord.

8. A partir de la source de cette rivière Kabun ou Lèos (dénommée à tort Oè Sunan de 1899 à 1909) au sud, la frontière doit, à teneur de l'article 3, chiffre 10, du traité de 1904, "traverser autant que possible Nipani et Kelali (Keli)" pour gagner la source de la Noël Meto, au nord.

La délimitation proposée par le Portugal contournerait entièrement la région désignée sur la carte officielle de 1904 sous le nom de Nipani et située, d'après cette carte, près de la source du Kabun ou Lèos ; la frontière s'éloignerait de Nipani de plusieurs kilomètres dans la direction de l'est.   Même si, comme le fait une carte portugaise qui n'a pas de caractère contradictoirement reconnu, on donnait le nom de Nipani à une région située beaucoup plus au nord, à l'orient des sources de la Noël Meto, la frontière réclamée par le Portugal ne traverserait pas davantage Nipani, mais le contournerait par le nord.

Le traité de 1904 prescrit de traverser "autant que possible" le Nipani.   Le tracé suggéré par le Pays-Bas longe la partie occidentale du Nipani et s'en trouve plus près que le tracé proposé par le Portugal.

9. Le Portugal objecte que la ligne directe nord-sud entre les sources de la rivière Kabun et de la rivière Noël Meto morcellerait le territoire des Ambenos en l'attribuant partie aux Pays-Bas et partie au Portugal ; ce morcellement serait contraire au traité de 1859.

Dans la pensée de l'arbitre, cette objection n'est pas fondée en ce sens que, déjà en 1859, une "partie" de l'Ambeno était incontestablement placée sous la souveraineté des Pays-Bas.   En outre, au cours des négociations de 1899 à 1904, il a été produit des déclarations contradictoires des indigènes, les Amakonos et les Tumbabas néerlandais revendiquant le territoire contesté et les Ambenos portugais le revendiquant de leur côté.   Ce prétendu morcellement n'est donc pas démontré. De plus, il a été entendu aux Conférences de 1902, sur les observations du premier délégué portugais lui-même, qu'il n'y avait pas lieu de se préoccuper outre mesure des prétentions de tribus qui se déplacent fréquemment et passent successivement du territoire de l'un des États dans celui de l'autre.   L'objection que les territoires d'une même tribu ne doivent pas être morcelés, ne saurait ainsi être retenue par l'arbitre, car elle aurait dû être présentée au cours des négociations de 1902-1904 ; actuellement, elle est tardive, parce que le traité de 1904, le seul dont l'arbitre ait à interpréter l'article 3, chiffre 10, ne fait aucune mention d'une volonté des Parties de ne jamais séparer des populations indigènes ; ce traité a au contraire tracé la ligne de démarcation à la suite de Conférences au cours desquelles il a été entendu que les considérations de ce genre ne doivent pas être prépondérantes.

10. La lingne de faite proposée par le Gouvernement néerlandais entre la source de la rivière Kabun (Lèos), au sud, et la source

de la Noèl Meto, au nord, est suffisamment naturelle pour pouvoir être tracée sur le terrain sans grandes difficultés pratiques. Elle offre l'avantage que les cours d'eau descendent uniformé de cette ligne de faîte vers des territoires tous placés sous la souveraineté néerlandaise. Le tracé suggéré par le Gouvernement portugais attribuerait au contraire à des souverainetés différentes la partie supérieure et la partie inférieure de ces divers cours d'eau.

11. D'une façon générale, la demande du Portugal reproduit, en fait, complètement, pour tout le territoire entre la Noèl Bilomi au sud et le source de la Noèl Meto au nord, la ligne que cet État revendiquait en 1902 et qu'il a abandonnée tant à la fin de la Conférence de 1902 que par le traité de 1904. Si la demande portugaise actuelle était fondée, on ne s'expliquerait pas pourquoi les Pays-Bas ont fait, en 1902, du rejet de cette demande portugaise une condition *sine qua non*. Les Conventions entre États, comme celles entre particuliers, doivent être interprétées "plutôt dans le sens avec lequel elles peuvent avoir quelque effet que dans le sens avec lequel elles n'en pourraient produire aucun." La menace néerlandaise de rompre les négociations en 1902 n'aurait pas de sens si l'intention avait été alors d'attribuer au Portugal précisément le territoire réclamé par les Pays-Bas comme une condition de l'accord.

12. Enfin, si l'on se place au point de vue de l'équité, qu'il importe de ne pas perdre devue dans les relations internationales, la ligne de faîte suggérée par les Pays-Bas n'est pas contraire à l'équité, en ce sens que le Portugal recevra plus de territoires qu'il n'en devait espérer selon la ligne théorique A C, à laquelle il a consenti en 1904, avant qu'on pût aller reconnaître le terrain. La ligne A C est toute entière tracée à l'intérieur du territoire qui reviendra au Portugal ; la République portugaise sera de la sorte mieux partagée, en fait, qu'elle ne pouvait s'y attendre (voir carte annexée VII). Si, au contraire, le tracé oriental suggéré par le Gouvernement portugais était adopté, les Pays-Bas pourraient avec raison prétendre qu'on les prive de presque tout le territoire qui leur avait été attribué théoriquement en 1904 en contre-partie de l'abandon de l'enclave de Maukatar au centre de l'île de Timor et en contre-partie de l'abandon des revendications néerlandaises sur l'ensemble de l'"enclave" d'Ambeno.

En conséquence,

L'ARBITRE

vu les deux traités signés à Lisbonne les 20 avril 1859 et 10 juin 1893 et le traité signé à La Haye le 1ᵉʳ octobre 1904 entre les Pays-Bas et le Portugal pour la délimitation de leurs possessions respectives dans l'île de Timor ;

vu le compromis d'arbitrage signé à La Haye le 3 avril 1913, et notamment l'article 2 ainsi conçu : "L'arbitre, statuant sur les données fournies par les Parties, décidera en se basant sur les traités et les principes généraux du droit international, comment doit être fixée conformément à l'article 3, 10° de la Convention conclue à La Haye 1ᵉʳ octobre 1904, concernant la délimitation des possessions néerlandaises et portugaises dans l'île de Timor, la limite à partir de la Noèl Bilomi jusqu'à la source de la Noèl Meto";

vu les Notes diplomatiques faisant part au soussigné de sa désignation comme arbitre par application de l'article 1er du compromis;

vu les premiers et seconds Mémoires remis en temps utile par chacune des hautes Parties contestantes, ainsi que les cartes et documents annexés aux dits mémoires;

vu les considérations de fait et de droit formulées ci-dessus sous chiffres I à VII;

vu la Convention signée à La Haye le 18 octobre 1907 pour le règlement pacifique des conflits internationaux;

ARRÊTE

L'article 3, chiffre 10, de la Convention conclue à La Haye le 1er octobre 1904 concernant la délimitation des possessions néerlandaises et portugaises dans l'île de Timor doit être interprété conformément aux conclusions du Gouvernement royal des Pays-Bas, pour la limite à partir de la Noël Bilomi jusqu'à la source de la Noël Meto; en conséquence, il sera procédé à l'arpentage de cette partie de la frontière sur la base de la carte au 1/50,000 annexée sous N°. IV au premier Mémoire remis à l'arbitre par le Gouvernement néerlandais. Une reproduction de cette carte signée par l'arbitre est jointe comme annexe VII à la présente sentence dont elle fera partie intégrante.

Les frais, fixés à fr. 2,000, ont été prélevés sur la somme de 4,000 fr. consignée entre les mains de l'arbitre en exécution de l'art. 8 du compromis du 3 avril 1913; la différence, soit fr. 2,000, sera restituée aux deux parties par égales portions et contre quittance, au moment de la notification de la sentence.

Fait en trois exemplaires dont l'un sera remis contre récépissé par M. le secrétaire général du Bureau international de la Cour permanente d'arbitrage à La Haye, à Son Excellence le Ministre des Affaires Étrangères des Pays-Bas pour valoir notification au Gouvernement royal néerlandais, et dont le second sera remis le même jour et dans les mêmes formes à Son Excellence l'Envoyé extraordinaire et Ministre Plénipotentiaire de la République portugaise près S. M. la Reine des Pays-Bas pour valoir notification au Gouvernement de la République portugaise. Le troisième exemplaire sera déposé aux archives du Bureau international de la Cour permanente d'arbitrage.

Paris, le 25 juin 1914.

LARDY

Agreement for Arbitration, April 3, 1913[1]

Sa Majesté la Reine des Pays-Bas et le Président de la République Portugaise considérant que l'exécution de la Convention conclue entre les Pays-Bas et le Portugal à La Haye le 1er octobre 1904, concernant

---

[1] Official report, p. 41, annex D.

la délimitation des possessions néerlandaises et portugaises dans l'île de Timor, a fait naître un différend au sujet de l'arpentage de la partie de la limite visée à l'article 3, 10°. de cette Convention ;

désirant mettre fin à l'amiable à ce différend ;

vus l'article 14 de la dite Convention et l'article 38 de la Convention pour le règlement pacifique des conflits internationaux conclue à La Haye le 18 octobre 1907 ;

ont nommé pour Leurs plénipotentiaires, savoir :

lesquels, dûment autorisés à cet effet, sont convenus des articles suivants :

ARTICLE 1ᵉʳ

Le Gouvernement de Sa Majesté la Reine des Pays-Bas et le Gouvernement de la République Portugaise conviennent de soumettre le différend susmentionné à un arbitre unique à choisir parmi les membres de la Cour permanente d'Arbitrage.

Si les deux Gouvernements ne pouvaient tomber d'accord sur le choix de tel arbitre, ils adresseront au Président de la Confédération Suisse la requête de la désigner.

ART. 2

L'arbitre statuant sur les données fournies par les Parties, décidera en se basant sur les traités et les principes généraux du droit international, comment doit être fixée conformément à l'article 3, 10°. de la Convention conclue à La Haye le 1ᵉʳ octobre 1904, concernant la délimitation des possessions néerlandaises et portugaises dans l'île de Timor, la limite à partir de la Noël Bilomi jusqu'à la source de la Noël Meto.

ART. 3

Chacune des Parties remettra par l'intermédiaire du Bureau International de la Cour permanente d'Arbitrage à l'arbitre dans un délai de 3 mois après l'échange des ratifications de la présente Convention un mémoire contenant l'exposé de ses droits et les documents à l'appui et en fera parvenir immédiatement une copie certifiée conforme à l'autre Partie.

A l'expiration du délai susnommé chacune des Parties aura un nouveau délai de 3 mois pour remettre par l'intermédiaire susindiqué à l'arbitre, si elle le juge utile, un second mémoire dont elle fera parvenir une copie certifiée conforme à l'autre Partie.

L'arbitre est autorisé à accorder à chacune des Parties qui le demanderait une prorogation de 2 mois par rapport aux délais mentionnés dans cet article. Il donnera connaissance de chaque prorogation à la Partie adverse.[1]

---

[1]Une prorogation de deux mois a été accordée aux Parties par l'arbitre pour la remise de leurs *seconds* mémoires.

Art. 4

Après l'échange de ces mémoires aucune communication écrite ou verbale ne sera faite à l'arbitre, à moins que celui-ci ne s'adresse aux Parties pour obtenir d'elles ou de l'une d'elles des renseignements ultérieurs par écrit.

La Partie qui donnera ces renseignements en fera parvenir immédiatement une copie certifiée conforme à l'autre Partie et celle-ci pourra, si bon lui semble, dans un délai de 2 mois après la réception de cette copie, communiquer par écrit à l'arbitre les observations auxquelles ils lui donneront lieu. Ces observations seront également communiquées immédiatement en copie certifiée conforme à la Partie adverse.

Art. 5

L'arbitre siégera à un endroit à désigner par lui.

Art. 6

L'arbitre fera usage de la langue française tante dans la sentence que dans les communications qu'il aura à adresser aux Parties dans le cours de la procédure. Les mémoires et autres communications émanant des Parties seront dressés dans cette langue.

Art. 7

L'arbitre décidera de toutes les questions qui pourraient surgir relativement à la procédure dans le cours du litige.

Art. 8

Aussitôt après la ratification de la présente Convention chacune des Parties déposera entre les mains de l'arbitre une somme de deux mille francs à titre d'avance pour les frais de la procédure.

Art. 9

La sentence sera communiquée par écrit par l'arbitre aux Parties. Elle sera motivée.

L'arbitre fixera dans sa sentence le montant des frais de la procédure. Chaque Partie supportera ses propres frais et une part égale des dits frais de procédure.

Art. 10

Les Parties s'engagent à accepter comme jugement en dernier ressort la décision prononcée par l'arbitre dans les limites de la présente Convention et à l'exécuter sans aucune réserve.

Tous différends concernant l'exécution seront soumis à l'arbitre.

ART. 11

La Présente Convention sera ratifiée et entrera en vigueur immédiatement après l'échange des ratifications qui aura lieu à La Haye aussitôt que possible.

En foi de quoi, les plénipotentiaires respectifs ont signé la présente Convention qu'ils ont revêtue de leurs cachets.

Fait en double à La Haye, le 3 avril 1913.

(L.-S.) (Signé) R. DE MAREES VAN SWINDEREN
(L.-S.) " ANTONIO MARIA BARTHOLOMEU FERREIRA

Agreement of April 20, 1859, between the Netherlands and Portugal relative to Boundary Possessions[1]

Sa Majesté le Roi des Pays-Bas et Sa Majesté le Roi de Portugal et des Algarves, ayant jugé utile de mettre fin aux incertitudes existantes relativement aux limites des possessions Néerlandaises et Portugaises dans l'Archipel de Timor et Solor, et voulant prévenir à jamais tout malentendu que pourraient provoquer des limites mal définies et des enclaves trop multipliées, ont muni, afin de s'entendre à cet égard, de leurs pleins-pouvoirs, savoir :

.   .   .   .   .   .

Lesquels, après s'être communiqués les dits pleins-pouvoirs, trouvés en bonne et due forme, sont convenus de conclure un traité de démarcation et d'échange, contenant les articles suivants :

ARTICLE 1ᵉʳ

Les limites entre les possessions Néerlandaises et Portugaises sur l'île de Timor seront au nord, les frontières qui séparent Cova de Juanilo ; et au sud, celles qui séparent Sua de Lakecune.

Entre ces deux points, les limites des deux possessions sont les mêmes que celles des Etats limitrophes Néerlandais et Portugais.

Ces Etats sont les suivants :

Etats limitrophes sous la domination de la Néerlande :	*Etats limitrophes sous la domination du Portugal :*
Juanilo,	Cova,
Silawang,	Balibo,
Fialarang (Fialara),	Lamakitu,
Lamaksanulu,	Tafakaij ou Takaij
Lamakanée,	Tatumea,
Naitimu (Nartimu),	Lanken,
Manden,	Dacolo,
Dirma,	Tamiru Eulalang (Eulaleng), Suai.
Lakecune.	

[1] Official report, p. 31.

Art. 2

Le Néerlande reconnait la souveraineté du Portugal sur tous les Etats qui se trouvent à l'est des limites ainsi circonscrites, à l'exception d l'Etat Néerlandais de Maucatar ou Caluninène (Coluninène), qui se trouve enclavé dans les Etats Portugais de Lamakitu, de Tanterine, de Follafaix (Follefait) et du Suai.

Le Portugal reconnait la souveraineté de la Néerlande sur tous les Etats qui se trouvent à l'ouest de ces limites, à l'exception de l'enclave d'Oikoussi, qui demeure Portugaise.

Art. 3

L'enclave d'Oikoussi comprend l'Etat d'Ambenu partout où y est arboré le pavillon Portugais, l'Etat d'Oikoussi proprement dit, et celui de Noimuti.

Les limites de cette enclave sont les frontières entre Ambenu et Amfoang à l'ouest, d'Insana et Reboki (Beboki), y compris Cicale à l'est, et Sonnebait, y compris Amakono et Tunebaba (Timebaba) au sud.

Art. 4

Sur l'île de Timor, le Portugal reconnaît donc la souveraineté de la Néerlande sur les Etats d'Amarassi, de Bibico (Traijnico, Waijniko), de Buboque (Reboki), de Derima (Dirma), de Fialara (Fialarang), de Lamakanée, de Nira (Lidak), de Juanilo, de Mena et de Fulgarite ou Folgarita (dépendances de l'Etat de Harnenno).

Art. 5

La Néerlande cède au Portugal le royaume de Moubara (Maubara) et cette partie d'Ambenu ou d'Ambeno (Sutrana) qui, depuis plusieurs années, a arboré le pavillon Portugais.

Immédiatement après que l'échange des ratifications de ce traité par Leurs Majestés le Roi des Pays-Bas et le Roi de Portugal aura eu lieu, le Gouvernement des Pays-Bas donnera l'ordre à l'autorité supérieure des Indes Néerlandaises de remettre le royaume de Moubara (Maubara) à l'autorité supérieure Portugaise de Timor Dilly.

Art. 6

La Néerlande se désiste de toute prétention sur l'île de Kambing (Pulo Kambing), au nord de Dilly, et reconnait la souveraineté du Portugal sur cette île.

Art. 7

Le Portugal cède à la Néerlande les possessions suivantes :
sur l'île de Flores, les Etats de Larantuca, Sicca et Paga, avec leurs dépendances ;
sur l'île d'Adenara, l'Etat de Wouré ;
sur l'île de Solor, l'Etat de Pamangkaju.
Le Portugal se désiste de toutes les prétentions que peut-être, il

aurait pu faire valoir sur d'autres Etats ou endroits situés sur les îles ci-dessus nommées, ou sur celles de Lomblen, de Pantar et d'Ombaij, que ces Etats portent le pavillon Néerlandais ou Portugais.

ART. 8

En vertu des dispositions de l'article précédent, la Néerlande obtient la possession entière en non-partagée de toutes les îles situées au nord de Timor, savoir : celles de Flores, d'Adenara, de Solor, de Lomblen, de Pantar (Quantar) et d'Ombaij, avec les petites îles environnantes appartenant à l'Archipel de Solor.

ART. 9

En compensation de ce que le Portugal pourrait perdre à l'échange des possessions respectives ci-dessus mentionnées, le Gouvernement des Pays-Bas :

1°. donnera au Gouvernement Portugais quittance complète de la somme de 80,000 florins, empruntée en 1851 par le Gouvernement des possessions Portugaises dans l'Archipel de Timor au Gouvernement des Indes Néerlandaises ;

2°. remettra en outre au Gouvernement Portugais une somme de 120,000 florins des Pays-Bas.

Cette somme sera versée un mois après l'échange des ratifications du présent traité.

ART. 10

La liberté des cultes est garantie de part et d'autre aux habitants des territoires échangés par le présent traité.

ART. 11

Le présent traité, qui sera soumis à la sanction des pouvoirs législatifs en conformité des règles prescrites par les lois fondamentales en vigueur dans les Royaumes des Pays-Bas et du Portugal, sera ratifié et les ratifications seront échangées à Lisbonne, dans le délai de huit mois, à partir de sa signature, ou plus tôt, si faire se peut.

En foi de quoi les plénipotentiaires respectifs ont signé le présent traité, et y ont apposé le sceau de leurs armes.

Fait à Lisbonne, le vingt Avril mil huit cent cinquante-neuf.

(L. S.) (Signé) M. HELDEWIER
(L. S.) (Signé) A. M. DE FONTES PEREIRA DE MELLO

Convention of June 10, 1893, between the Netherlands and Portugal relative to Commerce, Navigation, Boundaries, etc.[1]

Sa Majesté la Reine des Pays-Bas et en Son Nom Sa Majesté la Reine-Régente du Royaume.

---

[1] Official report, p. 34.

et Sa Majesté le Roi de Portugal et des Algarves, reconnaissant la communauté d'intérêts qui existe entre Leurs possessions dans l'Archipel de Timor et Solor et voulant régler dans un esprit de bonne entente mutuelle les conditions les plus favorables au développement de la civilisation et du commerce dans Leurs dites possessions, ont résolu de conclure une convention spéciale et ont nommé à cet effet pour Leurs plénipotentiaires, savoir :

.   .   .   .

lesquels, après s'être communiqué leurs pleins pouvoirs respectifs, trouvés en bonne et due forme, sont convenus des articles suivants :

ARTICLE 1er

Afin de faciliter l'exercice de leurs droits de Souveraineté, les Hautes Parties contractantes estiment qu'il y a lieu d'établir d'une façon plus claire et plus exacte la démarcation de leurs possessions à l'île de Timor et de faire disparaître les enclaves actuellement existantes.

ART. 2

Les Hautes Parties contractantes nommeront à cet effet une commission d'experts qui sera chargée de formuler une proposition pouvant servir de base à la conclusion d'une convention ultérieure, déterminant la nouvelle ligne de démarcation dans la dite île.

Cette convention sera soumise à l'approbation de la législature des deux pays.

ART. 3

Il sera accordé à l'île de Timor aux bateaux pêcheurs appartenant aux sujets de chacune des Hautes Parties contractantes, ainsi qu'à leurs équipages, la même protection de la part des autorités respectives, que celles dont jouiront les sujets respectifs.

Le commerce, l'industrie et la navigation des deux pays y jouiront du traitement de la nation étrangère la plus favorisée, sauf le traitement spécial accordé respectivement par les Hautes Parties contractantes aux Etats indigènes.

ART. 4

Les Hautes Parties contractantes décident que l'importation et l'exportation de toutes armes à feu entières ou en pièces détachées, de leurs cartouches, des capsules ou d'autres munitions, destinées à les approvisionner, sont interdites dans leurs possessions de l'Archipel de Timor et Solor.

Indépendamment des mesures prises directement par les Gouvernements pour l'armement de la force publique et l'organisation de leur défense, des exceptions pourront être admises à titre individuel pour leurs sujets Européens, offrant une garantie suffisante que l'arme et les munitions qui leur seraient délivrées, ne seront pas cédées ou vendues à des tiers, et pour des voyageurs étrangers, munis d'une déclaration de leur Gouvernement constatant que l'arme et les munitions sont exclusivement destinées à leur défense personnelle.

Art. 5

Toutefois les autorités supérieures de la partie néerlandaise et de la partie portugaise de l'île de Timor seront autorisées à fixer annuellement, d'un commun accord, le nombre et la qualité des armes à feu non perfectionnées et la quantité de munitions qui pourront être introduites dans le courant de la même année, ainsi que les conditions dans lesquelles cette importation pourra être accordée.

Cette importation cependant ne pourra se faire que par l'intermédiaire de certaines personnes ou agents qui résident à l'île même et qui auront obtenu à cet égard un autorisation spéciale de l'administration supérieure respective.

En cas d'abus cette autorisation sera immédiatement retirée et ne pourra être renouvelée.

Art. 6

Le Gouvernement néerlandais, voulant donner une preuve de son désir de consolider ses rapports de bon voisinage, déclare renoncer à l'indemnité à laquelle il prétend avoir droit du chef de certains traitements que des pêcheurs Néerlando-Indiens ont subi de 1889 à 1892 de la part des autorités du Timor-portugais.

Art. 7

Dans le cas où quelque difficulté surgirait par rapport à leurs relations intercoloniales dans l'Archipel de Timor et Solor ou au sujet de l'interprétation de la présente convention, les Hautes Parties contractantes s'engagent à se soumettre à la décision d'une commission d'arbitres.

Cette commission sera composée d'un nombre égal d'arbitres choisis par les Hautes Parties contractantes et d'un arbitre désigné par ces arbitres.

Art. 8

La présente convention sera ratifiée et les ratifications en seront échangées à Lisbonne.

En foi de quoi, les plénipotentiaires l'ont signée et y ont apposé leurs chachets.

Fait à Lisbonne, en double expédition, le dix juin mil huit cent quatre-vingt-treize.

(L. S.) (Signé) CAREL VAN HEECKEREN
"   "   ERNESTO RODOLPHO HINTZE RIBEIRO

———

Declaration of July 1, 1893, regarding Cession of Territory[1]

Les soussignés plénipotentiaires des Gouvernements signataires de la convention du 10 juin 1893 sont convenus de la déclaration suivante.

Afin d'assurer le résultat de leur action commune qui tend surtout à

———
[1]Official report, p. 36.

encourager le commerce et l'industrie de leurs nationaux par des garanties de sécurité et de stabilité, les Hautes Parties contractantes déclarent qu'elles se reconnaissent réciproquement, en cas de cession soit en partie soit en totalité de leurs territoires ou de leurs droits de souveraineté dans l'Archipel de Timor et Solor, le droit de préférence à des conditions similaires ou équivalentes à celles qui auront été offertes. Les cas de désaccord sur ces conditions tombent également sous l'application de l'article septième de la convention précitée.

La présente déclaration qui sera ratifiée en même temps que la convention conclue à Lisbonne le 10 juin 1893, sera considerée comme faisant partie intégrante de cette convention et aura la même force et valeur.

En foi de quoi, les plénipotentiaires respectifs ont signé la présente déclaration et y ont apposé leurs cachets.

Fait à Lisbonne en double expédition, le 1er juillet 1893.

(L. S.) (Signé) Carel van Heeckeren
" " Ernesto Rodolpho Hintze Ribeiro

Convention of October 1, 1904, settling the Boundary of the Island of Timor[1]

Sa Majesté la Reine des Pays-Bas et Sa Majesté le Roi de Portugal et des Algarves, etc., etc.

reconnaissant la communauté d'intérêts qui existe entre Leurs possessions dans l'Archipel de Timor et de Solor, et désirant arriver à une démarcation claire et exacte de ces possessions dans l'Ile de Timor, après avoir pris connaissance du résultat des travaux de la Commission mixte pour la régularisation des frontières néerlandaises et portugaises dans l'Ile de Timor, instituée par les Gouvernements respectifs en vertu de l'article II de la Convention conclue entre les Hautes Parties à Lisbonne le 10 juin 1893, ont résolu de conclure une Convention à cet effet et ont nommé pour Leurs plénipotentiaires.

. . . .

Lesquels après s'être communiqué leurs pleins-pouvoirs, trouvés en bonne et due forme, sont convenus de ce qui suit:

Article 1er

Les Pays-Bas cèdent le Maucatar au Portugal.

Art. 2

Le Portugal cède aux Pays-Bas le Noimuti, le Tahakay et le Tamiru Ailala.

Art. 3

La limite entre O'Kussi-Ambenu, appartenant au Portugal, et les possessions néerlandaises dans l'île de Timor est formée par une ligne:

---

[1] Official report, p. 37.

1°. partant du point à l'embouchure de la Noèl (rivière) Besi d'où le point culminant de Pulu-(île) Batek se voit sous un azimut astronomique de trente degrés quarante-sept minutes Nord-Ouest, suivant le thalweg de la Noèl Besi, celui de la Noèl Niema et celui dé la Bidjael Sunan jusqu'à sa source;

2°. montant de là jusqu'au sommet Bidjael Sunan, et descendant par le thalweg de la Noèl Miu Mavo jusqu'au point situé au Sud-Ouest du village Oben;

3°. de là passant à l'ouest de ce village par les sommets Banat et Kita jusqu'au sommet Nivo Nun Po; de là suivant le thalweg des rivières la Nono Boni et la Noèl Pasab jusqu'à son affluent le Nono Susu, et montant le Nono Susu jusqu'à sa source;

4°. passant le Klus (Crus) jusqu'au point où la frontière entre Abani et Nai Bobbo croise la rivière la Fatu Basin, et de là au point nommé Subina;

5°. descendant ensuite par le thalweg de la Fatu Basin jusqu'à la Kè An; de là jusqu'au Nai Naö;

6°. passant le Nai Naö et descendant dans la Tut Nonie, par le thalweg de la Tut Nonie jusqu'à la Noèl Ekan;

7°. suivant le thalweg de la Noèl Ekan jusqu'à l'affluent le Sonau, par le thalweg de cet affluent jusqu'à sa source et de là à la rivière Nivo Nono;

8°. montant par le thalweg de cette rivière jusqu'à sa source, pour aboutir, en passant le point nommé Ohoè Baki, à la source de la Nono Balena;

9°. suivant le thalweg de cette rivière, celui de la Nono Nisè et celui de la Noèl Bilomi jusqu'à l'affluent de celle-ci le Oè Sunan;

10°. à partir de ce point la limite suit le thalweg de l'Oè Sunan, traverse autant que possible Nipani et Kelali (Keli), gagne la source de la Noèl Meto et suit le thalweg de cette rivière jusqu'à son embouchure.

Art. 4

La partie de la limite entre O'Kussi Ambenu et les possessions néerlandaises, visée à l'article 3 10°., sera arpentée et indiquée sur le terrain dans le plus court délai possible.

L'arpentage de cette partie et l'indication sur le terrain seront certifiés par un procès-verbal avec une carte à dresser en deux exemplaires qui seront soumis à l'approbation des Hautes Parties contractantes; après leur approbation, ces documents seront signés au nom des Gouvernements respectifs.

Ce n'est qu'après la signature de ces documents que les Hautes Parties contractantes acquèreront la souveraineté des régions mentionnées aux articles 1 et 2.

Art. 5

La limite entre les possessions des Pays-Bas dans la partie occidentale et du Portugal dans la partie orientale de l'île de Timor suivra du Nord au Sud une ligne:

1°. partant de l'embouchure de la Mota Biku (Silaba) par le thalweg de cette rivière jusqu'à son affluent le We Bedain, par le thalweg du We Bedain, jusqu'à la Mota Asudaät (Assudat), par le thalweg de cette rivière jusqu'à sa source, et suivant de là dans la direction du Nord au Sud les coteaux du Kleek Teruin (Klin Teruin) et du Berènis (Birènis) Kakótun;

2°. puis jusqu'à la rivière Muda Sorun, suivant le thalweg de cette rivière, et celui de la Tuah Naruk jusqu'à la rivière le Telau (Talau);

3°. suivant le thalweg de la Telau jusqu'à la rivière la Malibaka, par le thalweg de cette rivière, celui de la Mautilu, et celui de la Pepies jusqu'à la montagne Bulu Hulu (Bulu Bulu);

4°. de là jusqu'au Karawa Kotun, du Karawa Kotun par le thalweg de la rivière la Marees (Lolu) jusqu'à la rivière la Tafara, par le thalweg de cette rivière jusqu'à sa source appelée la Mota Tiborok (Tibor), et montant de là au sommet Dato Miet et descendant à la Mota Alun;

5°. par le thalweg de la Mota Alun, celui de la Mota Sukaër (Sukar), et celui de la Mota Baukama, jusqu'à l'affluent de celle-ci, appelé Kalan-Féhan;

6°. passant les montagnes Tahi Fehu, Fatu Suta, Fatu Rusa, le grand arbre nommé Halifea, le sommet Uas Lulik, puis traversant la rivière la We Merak où elle reçoit son affluent We Nu, puis passant la grande pierre nommée Fatu Rokon, les sommets Fitun Monu, Debu Kasabauk, Ainin Matan et Lak Fuin;

7°. du Lak Fuin jusqu'au point où la Hali Sobuk se jette dans la Mota Haliboï et par le thalweg de cette rivière jusqu'à sa source;

8°. de cette source jusqu'à celle de la Mota Bebulu, par le thalweg de cette rivière jusqu'à la We Diek, montant aux sommets Ai Kakar et Takis, descendant dans la Mota Masin et suivant le thalweg de la Mota Masin et de son embouchure nommée Mota Talas.

Art. 6

Sauf les dispositions de l'article 4, les limites décrites aux articles 3 et 5 sont tracées sur les cartes annexées à la présente Convention et signées par les plénipotentiaires respectifs.

Art. 7

Les territoires respectivement cédes seront évacuées et l'administration en sera remise aux autorités compétentes dans les six mois après l'approbation du procès-verbal visé à l'article 4.

Art. 8

Les archives, cartes et autres documents relatifs aux territoires cédés, seront remis aux nouvelles autorités en même temps que les territoires mêmes.

Art. 9

La navigation sur les rivières formant limite sera libre aux sujets des deux Hautes Parties contractantes à l'exception du transport d'armes et de munitions.

Art. 10

Lors de la remise des territoires cédés, des bornes en pierre indiquant l'année de la présente convention, d'une forme et d'une dimension convenables au but qu'elles sont destinées à remplir, seront plantées avec solennité à un endroit convenable de la côte près de l'embouchure des rivières nommées ci-après. Les bornes néerlandaises seront plantées sur les rives occidentales de la Mota Biku et de la Mota Masin et les bornes portugaises sur les rives orientales de ces rivières. Les quatre bornes en pierre seront fournies par le Gouvernement Néerlandais aux frais des deux gouvernements et le Gouvernement Néerlandais mettra un bâtiment de la marine royale à la disposition des autorités respectives pour la remise solennelle des territoires cédés et la plantation des bornes.

En outre la frontière, où elle n'est pas formée par des limites naturelles, sera d'un commun accord démarquée sur le terrain par les autorités locales.

Art. 11

Sauf les dispositions de l'article 4, il sera dressé procès-verbal en langue française constatant la cession des territoires et la plantation des bornes.

Les procès-verbaux seront dressés en doubles exemplaires et signés par les autorités respectives des deux pays.

Art. 12

La liberté des cultes est garantie de part et d'autre aux habitants des territoires échangés par la présente Convention.

Art. 13

Les Hautes Parties contractantes se reconnaissent réciproquement, en cas de cession soit en partie soit en totalité de leurs territoires ou de leurs droits de souveraineté dans l'Archipel de Timor et Solor, le droit de préférence à des conditions similaires ou équivalentes à celles qui auraient été offertes.

Art. 14

Toutes questions ou tous différends sur l'interprétation ou l'exécution de la présente Convention, s'ils ne peuvent être réglés à l'amiable, seront soumis à la Cour Permanente d'Arbitrage conformément aux dispositions prévues au chapitre II de la Convention internationale du 29 juillet 1899 pour la solution pacifique des conflits internationaux.

Art. 15

La présente Convention sera ratifiée et les ratifications en seront échangées aussitôt que possible après l'approbation de la législature des deux Pays.

En foi de quoi les plénipotentiaires respectifs ont signé la présente Convention et y ont apposé leurs cachets.

Fait, en double expédition, à La Haye le 1er Octobre 1904.

(L.-S.) (Signé) Bn Melvil de Lynden
(L.-S.)   "   Idenburg
(L.-S.)   "   Conde de Selir

THE NORTH SEA or DOGGER BANK CASE

Report of the Commission of Inquiry, February 26, 1905[1]

1ᵉʳ. Les Commissaires, après un examen minutieux et prolongé de l'ensemble des faits parvenus à leur connaissance sur l'incident soumis à leur enquête par la Déclaration de Saint-Pétersbourg du 12 (25) Novembre 1904, ont procédé dans ce Rapport à un exposé analytique de ces faits suivant leur enchainement rationnel.

En faisant connaître les appréciations dominantes de la Commission en chaque point important ou décisif de cet exposé sommaire, ils pensent avoir mis suffisament en lumière les causes et les conséquences de l'incident en question en même temps que les responsabilités qui s'en dégagent.

2. La seconde escadre Russe de la flotte du Pacifique, sous le commandement en chef du Vice-Amiral Aide-de-camp Général Rojdestvensky, mouillait le 7 (20) Octobre 1904, auprès du Cap Skagen avec l'intention de faire du charbon avant de continuer sa route pour l'Extrême-Orient.

Il paraît, d'après les dépositions acquises, que, dès le départ de l'escadre de la rade de Reval, l'Amiral Rojdestvensky avait fait prendre des précautions minutieuses par les bâtiments placés sous ses ordres afin de les mettre pleinement en état de repousser pendant la nuit une attaque de torpilleurs, soit à mer, soit au mouillage.

Ces précautions semblaient justifiées par les nombreuses informations des Agents du Gouvernement Impérial au sujet de tentatives hostiles à redouter, et qui, selon toutes vraisemblances, devaient se produire sous la forme d'attaques de torpilleurs.

En outre, pendant son séjour à Skagen l'Amiral Rojdestvensky avait été averti de la présence de bâtiments suspects sur la côte de Norvège. Il avait appris, de plus, par le Commandant du transport "Bakan," arrivant du nord, que celui-ci avait aperçu la nuit précédente quatre torpilleurs portant un seul feu et en tête de mât.

Ces nouvelles décidèrent l'Amiral à avancer son départ de vingt-quatre heures.

3. En conséquence, chacun des six echelons distincts de l'escadre appareilla séparément à son tour et gagna la Mer du Nord, indépendamment, dans l'ordre indiqué par le rapport de l'Amiral Rojdestvensky ; cet officier général commandant en personne le dernier échelon formé par les quatre nouveaux cuirassés "Prince Souvoroff," "Empereur Alexandre III," "Borodino," "Orel," et le transport "Anadyr."

Cet échelon quitta Skagen le 7 (20) Octobre à 10 heures du soir.

La vitesse de 12 noeuds fut prescrite aux deux premiers échelons, formés de torpilleurs, et celle de 10 noeuds aux échelons suivants.

[1]*British and Foreign State Papers*, vol. 99, p. 921.

4. Entre 1 heure 30 et 4 heures 15 de l'après-midi du lendemain, 8 (21) Octobre, tous les échelons de l'escadre furent croisés successivement par le vapeur Anglais, "Zéro," dont le Capitaine examina avec assez d'attention les différentes unités pour permettre de les reconnaître d'après la description qu'il en fit.

Les résultats de ses observations sont conformes d'ailleurs en général aux indications du rapport de l'Amiral Rojdestvensky.

5. Le dernier navire croisé par le "Zéro" était le "Kamchatka," d'après la description qu'il en donna.

Ce transport, qui formait primitivement groupe avec le "Dmitri Donskoi" et l' "Avrora," se trouvait donc alors attardé et isolé à une dizaine de milles environ en arrière de l'escadre; il avait été obligé de diminuer de vitesse à la suite d'une avarie de machine.

Ce retard accidentel fût peut-être la cause incidente des événements qui suivirent.

6. Vers 8 heures du soir, en effet, ce transport rencontra le bâtiment Suédois "Aldebaran" et d'autres navires inconnus, qu'il canonna sans doute par suite des préoccupations que lui causaient dans les circonstances du moment son isolement, ses avaries de machine et son peu de valeur militaire.

Quoiqu'il en soit, le Commandant du "Kamchatka" transmit à 8 heures 45 à son Commandant-en-chef par la télégraphie sans fil, au sujet de cette rencontre, l'information qu'il était "attaqué de tous côtés par des torpilleurs."

7. Pour se rendre compte de la part que cette nouvelle put prendre dans les déterminations ultérieures de l'Amiral Rojdestvensky, il faut considérer que dans ses prévisions les torpilleurs assaillants, dont la présence lui était ainsi signalée, a tort ou à raison, à une cinquantaine de milles en arrière de l'échelon des vaisseaux qu'il commandait, pouvaient le rejoindre pour l'attaquer a son tour vers 1 heure du matin.

Cette information décida l'Amiral Rojdestvensky à signaler à ses bâtiments vers 10 heures du soir de redoubler de vigilance et de s'attendre à une attaque de torpilleurs.

8. A bord du "Souvoroff" l'Amiral avait jugé indispensable que l'un des deux officiers supérieurs de son état-major fût de quart sur la passerelle de commandement pendant la nuit afin de surveiller, à sa place, la marche de l'escadre et de le prevenir immédiatement s'il se produisait quelque incident.

A bord de tous les bâtiments, d'ailleurs, les ordres permanents de l'Amiral prescrivaient que l'Officier chef de quart était autorisé à ouvrir le feu dans le cas d'une attaque évidente et imminente de torpilleurs.

Si l'attaque venait de l'avant il devait le faire de sa propre initiative, et, dans le cas contraire, beaucoup moins pressant, il devait en référer à son Commandant.

Au sujet de ces ordres la majorité des Commissaires estime qu'ils n'avaient rien d'excessif en temps de guerre, et particulierement dans les circonstances, que l'Amiral Rojdestvensky avait tout lieu de considérer comme très alarmantes, dans l'impossibilité où il se trouvait de contrôler l'exactitude des avertissements qu'il avait reçus des Agents de son Gouvernement.

9. Vers 1 heure du matin le 9 (22) Octobre, 1904, la nuit était à demi obscure, un peu voilée par une brume légère et basse. La lune ne se montrait que par intermittences entre les nuages. Le vent soufflait moderément du sud-est, en soulevant une longue houle qui imprimait aux vaisseaux des roulis de 5 degrés de chaque bord.

La route suivie par l'escadre vers le sud-ouest devait conduire les deux derniers échelons, ainsi que la suite des événements l'a prouvé, à passer à proximité du lieu de pêche habituel de la flottille des chalutiers de Hull, composée d'une trentaine de ces petits bâtiments à vapeur et couvrant une étendue de quelques milles.

Il résulte des dépositions concordantes des témoins Britanniques que tous ces bateaux portaient leurs feux réglementaires et chalutaient conformément à leurs règles usuelles, sous la conduite de leur maître de pêche, suivant les indications de fusées conventionnelles.

10. D'après les communications reçues par la télégraphie sans fil, rien d'anormal n'avait été signalé par les échelons qui précédaient celui de l'Amiral Rojdestvensky en franchissant ces parages.

On a su depuis, notamment, que l'Amiral Fölkersam, ayant été conduit à contourner la flotille dans le nord, éclaira de très près avec ses projecteurs électriques les chalutiers les plus voisins et, les ayant reconnus ainsi pour des bâtiments inoffensifs, continua tranquillement sa route.

11. C'est peu de temps après qu'arrivait à son tour, à proximité du lieu de pêche des chalutiers, le dernier échelon de l'escadre conduit par le "Souvoroff," battant pavillon de l'Amiral Rojdestvensky.

La route de cet échelon le conduisait à peu près sur le gros de la flottille des chalutiers, qu'il allait donc être obligé de contourner, mais dans le sud, quand l'attention des officiers de service sur les passerelles du "Souvoroff" fut attirée par une fusée verte qui les mit en défiance.

Cette fusée, lancée par le maître depêche, indiquait en réalité, suivant leurs conventions, que les chalutiers devaient draguer le côté tribord au vent.

Presque immédiatement après cette première alerte et en se rapportant aux dépositions, les observateurs, qui des passerelles du "Souvoroff" fouillaient l'horizon avec des jumelles de nuit, decouvrirent "sur la crête des lames dans la direction du bossoir de tribord et à une distance approximative de 18 à 20 encablures" un bâtiment qui leur parut suspect parce qu'ils ne lui voyaient aucun feu et que ce bâtiment leur semblait se diriger vers eux à contre-bord.

Lorsque le navire suspect fut éclairé par un projecteur, les observateurs crurent reconnaître un torpilleur à grande allure.

C'est d'après ces apparences que l'Amiral Rojdestvensky fit ouvrir le feu sur ce navire inconnu.

La majorité des Commissaires exprime à ces sujet l'opinion que la responsabilité de cet acte et les résultats de la cannonade essuyée par la flottille de pêche incombent a l'Amiral Rojdestvensky.

12. Presque aussitôt après l'ouverture du feu par tribord, le "Souvoroff" aperçut sur son avant un petit bateau lui barrant la route et fut obligé de lancer sur la gauche pour éviter de l'aborder. Mais ce bateau, éclairé par un projecteur, fut reconnu être un chalutier.

Pour empêcher que le tir des vaisseux fût dirigé sur ce bâtiment inoffensif, l'axe du projecteur fut aussitôt relevé à 45°. vers le ciel.

Ensuite, l'Amiral fit adresser par signal à l'escadre l'ordre "de ne pas tirer sur les chalutiers."

Mais en même temps que le projecteur avait éclairé ce bateau de pêche, d'après les dépositions des témoins, les observateurs du "Souvoroff" aperçurent à bâbord un autre bâtiment qui leur paru suspect, à cause de ses apparences de même nature que celles de l'objectif du tir par tribord.

Le feu fut aussitôt ouvert sur ce deuxième but et se trouva ainsi engagé des deux bords, la file des vaisseaux étant revenue par un mouvement de contre-marche à sa route primitive sans avoir changé de vitesse.

13. D'après les ordres permanents de l'escadre, l'Amiral indiquait les buts sur lesquels devait être dirigé le tir des vaisseaux en fixant sur eux ses projecteurs. Mais comme chaque vaisseau balayait l'horison en tout sens autour de lui avec ses propres projecteurs pour se garder d'une surprise, il était difficile qu'il ne se produisît pas de confusion.

Ce tir, d'une durée de dix à douze minutes, causa de graves dommages dans la flottille des chalutiers. C'est ainsi que deux hommes furent tués et six autres blessés; que le "Crane" sombra; que le "Snipe," le "Mino," le "Moulmein," le "Gull," et le "Majestic" reçurent des avaries plus ou moins importantes.

D'autre part le croiseur "Avrora" fut atteint par plusieurs projectiles.

La majorité des Commissaires constate qu'elle manque l'éléments précis pour reconnaître sur quel but ont tiré les vaisseaux; mais les Commissaires reconnaissent unanimement que les bateaux de la flottille de pêche n'ont commis aucun acte hostile; et la majorité des Commissaires étant d'opinion qu'il n'y avait, ni parmi les chalutiers, ni sur les lieux, aucun torpilleur, l'ouverture du feu par l'Amiral Rojdestvensky n'était pas justifiable.

Le Commissaire Russe, ne se croyant pas fondé a partager cette opinion, enonce la conviction que ce sont précisément les bâtiments suspects s'approchant de l'escadre dans un but hostile qui ont provoqué le feu.

14. Au sujet des but réels de ce tir nocturne, le fait que l'"Avrora" a reçu quelques projectiles de 47 millim. et de 75 millim. serait de nature à faire supposer que ce croiseur, et peut-être même quelque autre bâtiment Russe, attardé sur la route du "Souvoroff" à l'insu de ce vaisseau, ait pu provoquer et attirer les premiers feux.

Cette erreur pouvait être motivée par le fait que ce navire, vu de l'arrière, ne montrait aucune lumière apparente, et par une illusion d'optique nocturne dont les observateurs du vaisseau-amiral auraient été l'objet.

A ce propos les Commissaires constatent qu'il leur manque des renseignements importants leur permettant de connaître les raisons qui ont provoqué la continuation du tir à bâbord.

Dans cette conjecture certains chalutiers éloignés auraient pu être confondus ensuite avec les buts primitifs et ainsi canonnés directement. D'autres, au contraire, ont pu être atteints par un tir dirigé sur des buts plus éloignés.

Ces considérations ne sont pas d'ailleurs en contradiction avec les impressions de certains chalutiers qui, en se voyant atteints par des projectiles et restant éclairés dans le pinceau des projecteurs, pouvaient se croire l'objet d'un tir direct.

15. La durée du tir sur tribord, même en se plaçant au point de vue de la version Russe, a semblé à la majorité des Commissaires avoir été plus longue qu'elle ne paraissait nécessaire.

Mais cette majorité estime qu'elle n'est pas suffisamment renseignée ainsi qu'il vient d'être dit, au sujet de la continuation du tir par bâbord.

En tout cas, les Commissaires se plaisent à reconnaître a l'unanimité que l'Amiral Rojdestvensky a fait personnellement tout ce qu'il pouvait, du commencement à la fin, pour empêcher que les chalutiers, reconnus comme tels, fussent l'objet du tir de l'escadre.

16. Quoiqu'il en soit, le "Dmitri Donskoi" ayant fini par signaler son numéro, l'Amiral se decida à faire le signal général de "cesser le feu"; la file de ses vaisseaux continua alors sa route et disparut dans le sud-ouest sans avoir stoppé.

A cet égard, les Commissaires sont unanimes à reconnaître, qu'après les circonstances qui ont précédé l'incident et celles qui l'ont produit, il y avait à la fin du tir assez d'incertitudes au sujet du danger que courait l'échelon des vaisseaux pour décider l'Amiral à continuer sa route.

Toutefois, la majorité des Commissaires regrette que l'Amiral Rojdestvensky n'ait pas eu la préoccupation, en franchissant le Pas de Calais, d'informer les autorités des Puissances maritimes voisines qu'ayant été amené à ouvrir le feu près d'un groupe de chalutiers, ces bateaux, de nationalité inconnue, avaient besoin de secours.

17. Les Commissaires, en mettant fin à ce Rapport, déclarent que leurs appréciations, qui s'y trouvent formulées, ne sont dans leur esprit de nature à jeter aucune déconsidération sur la valuer militaire ni sur les sentiments d'humanité de l'Amiral Rojdestvensky et du personnel de son escadre.

SPAUN
FOURNIER
DOUBASSOFF
LEWIS BEAUMONT
CHARLES HENRY DAVIS

Agreement for Inquiry, November 12/25, 1904[1]

Le Gouvernement de Sa Majesté Britannique et le Gouvernement Impérial de Russie s'étant mis d'accord pour confier à une Commission Internationale d'Enquête, réunie conformément aux Articles IX–XIV de la Convention de La Haye du 29 (17) Juillet 1899, pour le réglement pacifique des conflits internationaux, le soin d'éclaircir par un examen impartial et consciencieux les questions de fait se rapportant à l'incident qui s'est produit durant la nuit du 21–22 (8–9) Octobre, 1904, dans la mer du Nord—au cours duquel le tir des pièces de canon de la flotte Russe occasionna la perte d'un bateau et la mort de deux personnes appartenant à une flotille de pêcheurs Britanniques, ainsi que des dommages à d'autres bateaux de la dite flotille et des blessures aux équipages de quelques-uns de ces bateaux—les Soussignés, dûment autorisés à cet effet, sont convenus des dispositions suivantes:

Art. I. La Commission Internationale d'Enquête sera composée de cinq membres (Commissaires), dont deux seront des officers de haut rang des marines Britannique et Impériale Russe respectivement. Les Gouvernements de France et des États-Unis d'Amérique seront priés de choisir, chacun, un de leurs officiers de marine de haut rang comme membre de la Commission. Le cinquième membre sera élu d'accord par les quatre membres susmentionnés.

Dans le cas où il ne se produirait pas d'entente entre les quatres Commissaires pour le choix du cinquième membre de la Commission, Sa Majesté l'Empereur d'Autriche, Roi de Hongrie, sera invité à le nommer.

Chacune des deux Hautes Parties Contractantes nommera également un jurisconsulte-assesseur avec voix consultative et un agent, chargés, à titre officiel, de prendre part aux travaux de la Commission.

II. La Commission devra faire une enquête et dresser un rapport sur toutes les circonstances relatives à l'incident de la mer du Nord, en particulier sur la question où gît la responsabilité et sur le degré de blâme concernant les ressortissants des deux Hautes Parties Contractantes ou d'autres pays, dans le cas où leur responsabilité se trouverait constatée par l'enquête.

III. La Commission fixera les détails de la procédure qui sera suivie par elle pour l'accomplissement de la tâche qui lui est dévolue.

IV. Les deux Hautes Parties Contractantes s'engagent à fournir à la Commission Internationale d'Enquête, dans la plus large mesure qu'elles jugeront possible, tous les moyens et les facilités nécessaires pour la connaissance complète et l'appréciation exacte des faits en question.

V. La Commission se réunira à Paris aussitôt que faire se pourra, après la signature de cet Arrangement.

VI. La Commission présentera aux deux Hautes Parties Contractantes son rapport signé par tous les membres de la Commission.

VII. La Commission prendra toutes ses décisions à la majorité des voix des cinq Commissaires.

----

[1] *British and Foreign State Papers*, vol. 97, p. 77.

VIII. Les deux Hautes Parties Contractantes s'engagent à garder chacune à sa charge, par réciprocité, les frais de l'enquête faite par elle préalablement à la réunion de la Commission. Quant aux dépenses qui incomberont à la Commission Internationale d'Enquête à partir du moment de sa réunion pour l'installation de ses services et les investigations nécessaires, elles seront faites en commun par les deux Gouvernements.

En foi de quoi les Soussignés ont signé la présente Déclaration et y ont apposé le sceau de leurs armes.

Fait en double à Saint-Pétersbourg, le 25 (12) Novembre, 1904.

(L. S.) CHARLES HARDINGE
(L. S.) COMTE LAMSDORFF

Supplementary Protocol of November 12/25, 1904, to the Agreement for Inquiry[1]

Les Soussignés se sont réunis aujourd'hui a l'Hôtel du Ministère Impérial des Affaires Étrangères pour procéder à la signature d'une Déclaration entre le Gouvernement de Sa Majesté Britannique et le Gouvernement Impérial de Russie concernant l'institution d'une Commission Internationale d'Enquête au sujet de l'incident de la mer du Nord.

Après lecture des instruments respectifs, lesquels ont été trouvés en bonne et due forme, la signature de la dite Déclaration a en lieu selon l'usage.

En foi de quoi les Soussignés ont dressé le présent Protocole et l'ont revêtu du sceau de leurs armes.

Fait en double à Saint-Pétersbourg, le 25 (12) Novembre, 1904.

(L. S.) CHARLES HARDINGE
(L. S.) COMTE LAMSDORFF

---

[1] *British and Foreign State Papers*, vol. 97, p. 79.

THE TAVIGNANO, CAMOUNA AND GAULOIS CASES

Report of the Commission of Inquiry, July 23, 1912[1]

Les Commissaires, après avoir examiné et rapproché les renseignements fournis, tant par les documents présentés par les deux parties que par les témoignages recueillis, après avoir fait la part d'importance qui peut revenir à chacun des renseignements recueillis et tenu compte du degré d'incertitude relative de chacun d'eux, a délibéré et conclu ainsi qu'il suit:

I

Les renseignements et les documents présentés ne sont pas de nature à permettre de déterminer des points géographiques précis pour les diverses circonstances soumises à l'enquête, mais simplement des zones dans lesquelles ces circonstances se seraient produites, sans qu'il soit possible de choisir un point particulier dans ces zones.

1°. Sur le point où a été arrêté la *Tavignano*.

Ce point est compris à l'intérieur d'un quadrilatère rectiligne déterminé par les quatre sommets suivants:

Sommet C ..... { Latitude	33°	29′	20″	Nord.
{ Longitude	8°	56′	40″	Est de Paris.
Sommet B ..... { Latitude	33°	29′	10″	Nord.
{ Longitude	8°	55′	10″	Est de Paris.
Sommet A ..... { Latitude	33°	26′	30″	Nord.
{ Longitude	8°	54′	40″	Est de Paris.
Sommet D ..... { Latitude	33°	26′	30″	Nord.
{ Longitude	8°	56′	40″	Est de Paris.

2°. En ce qui concerne la poursuite des mahonnes.

A. Par le *Fulmine*.

Le *Fulmine*, partant d'un point indéterminable de la zone ci-dessus définie, a poursuivi les mahonnes, peut-être en sortant de cette zone, dans une direction qui n'a pu être précisée, mais qui est comprise entre le Sud-Est et le Sud-Ouest par le Sud.

Les mahonnes poursuivies se trouvaient aux points suivants, qui sont le centre d'un cercle d'incertitude d'un demi-mille de rayon:

Camouna .... { Latitude	33°	24′	10″	Nord
{ Longitude	9°	00′	15″	Est de Paris
Gaulois .... { Latitude	33°	22′	40″	Nord
{ Longitude	8°	59′	55″	Est de Paris

---

[1] Official report, p. 177.

Après cette poursuite, le *Fulmine* est revenu mouiller près du *Tavignano*, en un point H que la Commission choisit comme centre d'un cercle d'incertitude d'un demi-mille de rayon.

B. Le *Canopo* a canonné la mahonne *Gaulois* alors que cette mahonne se trouvait au point indiqué ci-dessus et que lui *Canopo* provenait, avec le cap au Nord, du point indiqué dans son rapport de mer par

> Latitude   33° 20′ 45″ Nord
> Longitude   9° 00′ 50″ Est de Paris

et que la Commission adopte également comme centre d'un cercle d'incertitude d'un demi-mille de rayon.

La visite des deux mahonnes *Camouna* et *Gaulois* par le *Canopo* a eu lieu en un point déterminé par

> Latitude   33° 22′ 00″ Nord
> Longitude   9° 00′ 25″ Est de Paris

et qui est le centre d'un cercle d'incertitude d'un demi-mille de rayon.

La Commission, après sa visite sur les lieux, et à la suite de ses constatations dans les eaux de Zarzis, décide de s'en rapporter, pour l'hydrographie, la configuration et la nature de la côte et des bancs avoisinants, à la carte française du Service hydrographique N°. 4247. Elle rappelle que ses constatations ont fait l'objet de son procès-verbal en date du 15 juillet 1912 et classé sous la cote 68.

Le Président ayant donné lecture du présent rapport à MM. les Commissaires, ce rapport et ses conclusions ont été adoptés à l'unanimité.

Fait à Malte, en trois exemplaires, le 23 juillet 1912.

Les Commissaires: GIUSEPPE GENOESE ZERBI
SOMBORN
SEGRAVE

Agreement for Inquiry, May 20, 1912[1]

Le Gouvernement de la République française et le Gouvernement Royal italien, également désireux de pourvoir au règlement des difficultés auxquelles ont donné lieu la capture et la saisie momentané du vapeur postal français *Tavignano*, le 25 janvier 1912, par le bâtiment de la Marine

Il R. Governo italiano e il Governo della Repubblica Francese, mossi da egual desiderio di provvedere al regolamento delle difficoltà cui hanno dato luogo la cattura ed il sequestro temporaneo del piroscafo postale francese *Tavignano*, il 25 gennaio 1912, da parte della nave della R. Marina

---

[1] Official report, pp. 7, 9.

royale italienne *Fulmine*, ainsi que le tir effectué sur les mahonnes *Camouna* et *Gaulois*, le 25 janvier 1912, par le torpilleur italien *Canopo*,

Ont résolu, conformément au titre III de la Convention de La Haye, du 18 octobre 1907, pour le règlement pacifique des conflits internationaux, de confier à une Commission internationale d'enquête le soin d'élucider les circonstances de fait dans lesquelles lesdites capture et saisie et ledit tir ont été effectués.

Et sont, à cet effet, convenus des dispositions suivantes :

ARTICLE 1

Une Commission internationale d'enquête composée, comme il est dit ci-après, est chargée de :

I. Rechercher, relever et préciser le point géographique où ont été effectués : 1°. l'arrestation du vapeur postal français *Tavignano*, par le bâtiment de la Marine royale italienne *Fulmine*, le 25 janvier 1912 ; 2°. la poursuite des mahonnes *Camouna* et *Gaulois*, par le même bâtiment, puis par le bâtiment de la Marine royale italienne *Canopo* et le tir effectué par ce dernier sur lesdites mahonnes.

II. Préciser l'hydrographie, la configuration et la nature de la côte et des bancs avoisinants, la distance entre eux des différents points que l'un ou l'autre des Commissaires jugeront utiles de relever, et la distance de ces points à ceux où se sont passés les faits susvisés.

III. Consigner dans un rapport écrit le résultat de ses investigations.

italiana *Fulmine*, ed il tiro eseguito contro le maone *Camouna e Gaulois*, il 25 gennaio 1912, da parte della torpediniera italiana *Canopo*,

Hanno stabilito, in conformità del titolo III della Convenzione dell'Aja dell' 18 ottobre 1907 per il regolamento pacifico dei conflitti internazionali, di affidare ad una Commissione internazionale d'inchiesta il compito di chiarire le circostanze di fatto nelle quali la cattura, il sequestro ed il tiro predetti furono eseguiti ;

E sono, a questo fine, convenuti delle disposizioni seguenti :

ARTICOLO I

Una commissione internazionale d'inchiesta composta come serà detto in seguito, è incaricata di :

1) Cercare, rilevare e precisare il punto geografico in cui furono eseguiti : *a*) il fermo del piroscafo postale francese *Tavignano* da parte della nave della R. Marina italiana *Fulmine*, il 25 gennaio 1912 ; *b*) l'inseguimento delle maone *Camouna* e *Gaulois* da parte della medesima nave e poi della nave della R. Marina italiana *Canopo,* ed il tiro eseguito da quest'ultima contro le maone suddette ;

2) Precisare l'idrografia, la configurazione e la natura della costa e dei banchi adiacento, la distanza tra loro dei diversi punti che l'uno o l'altro dei commissari stimerà utile di rilevare, e la distanza tra questi punti e quelli in cui sono accaduti i fatti sopra ennuciati ;

3) Conseguare in un rapporto scritto il resultato delle sue indagini.

ARTICLE 2

La Commission internationale d'enquête sera composée de trois Commissaires, dont deux seront des officiers des Marines nationales française et italienne, d'un grade au moins égal à celui de Capitaine de frégate. Le Gouvernement de Sa Majesté britannique sera prié de choisir le troisième Commissaire parmi ses officiers de marine d'un grade supérieur ou plus anciens en grade. Celui-ci remplira les fonctions de président.

Deux secrétaires seront chargés de remplir les fonctions de greffiers de la Commission et d'assister celle-ci dans ses opérations, l'un étant désigné par le Gouvernement de la République française, et l'autre par le Gouvernement royal italien.

ARTICLE 3

La Commission internationale d'enquête aura qualité pour s'entourer de tous renseignements, interroger et entendre tous témoins, examiner tous papiers de bord de l'un ou de l'autre desdits navires, bâtiments et mahonnes, procéder, s'il y a lieu, aux sondages nécessaires, et en général recourir à tous moyens d'information propres à assurer la manifestation de la vérité.
Les deux Gouvernements s'engagent à cet égard à fournier à la Commission, dans la plus large mesure qu'ils jugeront possible, tous les moyens et facilités et notamment les moyens de transport lui permettant d'accomplir sa tâche.

ARTICOLO II

La commissione internazionale d'inchiesta sarà composta di tre commissari, due dei quali saranno ufficiali delle marine nazionali italiana e francese, di grado eguale almeno a quello di capitano di fregata. Il Governo di Sua Maestà Britannica sarà pregato di scegliere il terzo commissario tra i suoi ufficiali di Marina di grado superiore o più anziani in grado. Quest'ultimo adempirà le funzioni di presidente.

Due segretari, designati uno dal R. Governo Italiano, l'altro dal Governo della Repubblica francese, saranno incaricati di adempiere le funzioni di cancellieri della Commissione e di assisterla nei suoi atti.

ARTICOLO III

La Commissione internazionale d'inchiesta avrà veste per raccogliere qualsiasi informazione, interrogare ed ascoltare qualsiasi testimone, esaminare qualsiasi carta di bordo dell'una o dell'altra delle dette navi e maone, procedere occorrendo agli scandagli necessari, e, in generale, ricorrere a qualsiasi mezzo di indagine atto ad assicurare la manifestazione della verità.
I due Governi s'impegnano a questo riguardo di fornire alla Commissione, nella più larga misura che stimeranno possibile, tutti i mezzi e le facilitazioni, e particolarmente i mezzi di trasporto, che le permettano di adempiere il compito suo.

ARTICLE 4

La Commission internationale d'enquête se réunira à Malte aussitôt que faire se pourra et aura la faculté de se déplacer conformément à l'article 20 de la Convention de La Haye, du 18 octobre 1907, pour le règlement pacifique des conflits internationaux.

ARTICLE 5

La langue française est la langue de la Commission internationale d'enquête ; toutefois, dans leurs délibérations, les Commissaires pourront faire usage de leur propre langue.

ARTICLE 6

Dans un délai qui n'excédera pas quinze jours, à dater de sa première réunion, la Commission internationale d'enquête arrêtera les conclusions de son rapport et les communiquera à chacun des deux Gouvernements.

ARTICLE 7

Chaque Partie supportera ses propres frais et une part égale des frais de la Commission.

ARTICLE 8

Pour tout ce qui n'est pas prévu par la présente convention d'enquête, et notamment pour la procédure d'enquête, les dispositions de la Convention de La Haye, du 18 octobre 1907, pour le règlement pacifique des conflits internationaux, seront applicables à la présente Commission internationale d'enquête.

Fait en double exemplaire, à Rome, le 20 mai 1912.

ARTICOLO IV

La Commissione internazionale d'inchiesta si riunirà a Malta appena sarà possibile e avrà facoltà di spostarsi, conformemente all'articolo 20 della convenzione dell'Aja del 18 ottobre 1907 per il regolamento pacifico dei conflitti internazionali.

ARTICOLO V

La lingua francese è la lingua della Commissione internazionale d'inchiesta ; i commissari potranno tuttavia servirsi della propria nelle loro deliberazioni.

ARTICOLO VI

Entro un termine non maggiore di 15 giorni, a datare dalla sua prima riunione, la Commissione internazionale d'inchiesta determinerà le conclusioni del suo rapporto e le communicherà a ciascuno dei due governi.

ARTICOLO VII

Ciascuna parte sosterrà le proprie spese e una quota eguale di quelle della commissione.

ARTICOLO VIII

Per tutto ciò che non è preveduto dalla presente convenzione, saranno applicabili alla Commissione le disposizioni della Convenzione dell'Aja del 18 ottobre 1907 per il regolamento pacifico dei conflitti internazionali.

Fatto in doppio esemplare, a Roma, il 20 maggio 1912.

Signe: CAMILLE BARRÈRE
DI SAN GIULIANO

Agreement of April 15, 1912, relative to the Arbitration of the "Tavignano," "Camouna" and "Gaulois" Cases[1]

Les Gouvernements français et italien décident de soumettre à une Commission internationale d'enquête les questions de fait soulevées:

1°. Au sujet de la saisie du vapeur français *Tavignano* par le torpilleur italien *Fulmine*, le 25 janvier 1912 dans les parages de Ras-Zira;

2°. Au sujet des coups de canon tirés par le torpilleur *Canopo* le même jour et dans les mêmes parages sur les deux mahonnes tunisiennes *Kamouna* et *Gaulois*.

Après que ladite Commission internationale aura terminé son enquête, le résultat en sera transmis s'il y a lieu au même tribunal arbitral chargé de statuer sur les affaires du *Carthage* et du *Manouba*, afin qu'il se prononce sur les questions de droit, qu'il établisse les responsabilités et qu'il détermine les réparations morales et matérielles qu'elles comporteraient.

Rome, le 15 avril 1912.

Signé: CAMILLE BARRÈRE
DI SAN GIULIANO

Compromis of Arbitration, November 8, 1912[2]

Le Gouvernement de la République Française et le Gouvernement Royal Italien s'étant mis d'accord le 15 avril 1912,

1°. Pour soumettre à une Commission internationale d'enquête les questions de fait soulevées au sujet de la saisie du vapeur français *Tavignano* par le torpilleur italien *Fulmine*, le 25 janvier 1912, dans les parages de Ras-Zira et au sujet des coups de canon tirés par le torpilleur italien *Canopo*, le même jour et dans les mêmes parages, sur les deux mahonnes tunisiennes *Kamouna* et *Gaulois*;

2°. Pour transmettre, s'il y avait lieu, le résultat de l'enquête au Tribunal arbitral chargé de statuer sur les affaires du *Carthage* et du *Manouba*, afin qu'il se prononce sur les questions de droit, qu'il établisse les responsabilités et qu'il détermine les réparations morales et matérielles qu'elles comporteraient,

Ayant pris connaissance du rapport présenté le 23 juillet 1912 par ladite Commission Internationale d'enquête,

Les soussignés, dûment autorisés à cet effet, sont convenus du Compromis suivant:

ARTICLE 1er

Le Tribunal arbitral chargé de statuer sur les affaires du *Carthage* et du *Manouba* est aussi chargé de statuer sur les incidents concernant la saisie du vapeur français *Tavignano* et les coups de canon tirés sur les mahonnes tunisiennes, afin de se prononcer sur les questions de

[1] Official report, *Mémoire* of the French Republic, p. 5, note 1.
[2] *Ibid.*, p. 5.

droit, d'établir les responsabilités et de déterminer les réparations morales et matérielles qu'elles comporteraient.

ARTICLE 2

Pour ce qui concerne les questions de fait soulevées par les deux incidents, le Tribunal arbitral devra faire état du rapport présenté par la Commission internationale d'enquête le 23 juillet 1912, ainsi que des procès-verbaux de ladite Commission.

Ledit rapport et lesdits procès-verbaux seront imprimés à frais communs par les soins des Parties et dans le plus bref délai possible.

ARTICLE 3

A la date du 15 janvier 1913, chaque Partie déposera au Bureau de la Cour Permanente d'arbitrage quinze exemplaires de son mémoire, avec les copies certifiées conformes de tous les documents et pièces qu'elle compte invoquer dans la cause.

Le Bureau en assurera sans retard la transmission aux arbitres et aux Parties, savoir deux exemplaires pour chaque arbitre, trois exemplaires pour la Partie adverse; deux exemplaires resteront dans les archives du Bureau.

A la date du 1er mars 1913, chaque Partie déposera, dans les mêmes conditions que ci-dessus, son contre-mémoire avec les pièces à l'appui et ses conclusions finales.

Le Tribunal se réunira à La Haye dans la seconde quinzaine de mars sur la convocation de son Président.

ARTICLE 4

Pour tout ce qui n'est pas prévu par le présent Compromis, les dispositions des Compromis du 6 mars 1912 et de l'Accord du 4 avril 1912 seront applicables au présent litige.

Fait à Paris, le 8 novembre 1912.

Signé: L. RENAULT
Signé: G. FUSINATO

Agreement of May 2, 1913, Settling Definitively the "Tavignano," "Camouna" and "Gaulois" Controversy[1]

Les deux affaires du "Carthage" et du "Manouba" étant sur le point d'être réglées par jugement arbitral, le Gouvernement de la République française et le Gouvernement royal italien ont considéré qu'un arrangement direct de l'affaire concernant le "Tavignano" et les deux mahonnes tunisiennes serait, par la nature même de ce différend, particulièrement désirable. Les deux Gouvernements son d'autant plus disposés à entrer dans cette voie qu'elle leur offre une nouvelle occasion

---

[1]Copy furnished by the International Bureau of the Permanent Court of Arbitration.

de manifester l'esprit de cordiale amitié qui les anime mutuellement. A cet égard, ils sont tombés d'accord qu'il serait équitable d'indemniser les particuliers à raison des dommages qu'ils ont soufferts.   Le Gouvernement royal italien s'étant déclaré prêt à verser à cet effet la somme de cinq mille francs, le Gouvernement de la République française a déclaré qu'il l'accepte et qu'il considère cette affaire comme étant ainsi définitivement réglée.

Les soussignés ont constaté l'accord de leurs Gouvernements par le présent acte pour valoir ce que de droit.

Signé: L. RENAULT
Signé: G. FUSINATO

INDEX

INDEX

—

—